The Editor

EDWARD PECHTER's books include *Dryden's Classical Theory of Literature, What Was Shakespeare? "Othello" and Interpretive Traditions*, and, most recently, *Shakespeare Studies Today: Romanticism Lost*. He has taught at universities in the United States, England, and Canada and is Distinguished Professor Emeritus at Concordia University (Montreal) and Adjunct Professor of English at the University of Victoria, British Columbia.

NORTON CRITICAL EDITIONS
SHAKESPEARE

ANTONY AND CLEOPATRA
AS YOU LIKE IT
HAMLET
1 HENRY IV
JULIUS CAESAR
KING LEAR
MACBETH
MEASURE FOR MEASURE
THE MERCHANT OF VENICE
OTHELLO
RICHARD III
ROMEO AND JULIET
THE TAMING OF THE SHREW
THE TEMPEST

For a complete list of Norton Critical Editions, visit
wwnorton.com/nortoncriticals

A NORTON CRITICAL EDITION

William Shakespeare
OTHELLO

AUTHORITATIVE TEXT

TEXTUAL SOURCES AND
CULTURAL CONTEXTS

CRITICISM

SECOND EDITION

Edited by

EDWARD PECHTER
CONCORDIA UNIVERSITY
AND
UNIVERSITY OF VICTORIA

W · W · NORTON & COMPANY · *New York* · *London*

W. W. Norton & Company has been independent since its founding in 1923, when William Warder Norton and Mary D. Herter Norton first published lectures delivered at the People's Institute, the adult education division of New York City's Cooper Union. The firm soon expanded its program beyond the Institute, publishing books by celebrated academics from America and abroad. By midcentury, the two major pillars of Norton's publishing program—trade books and college texts—were firmly established. In the 1950s, the Norton family transferred control of the company to its employees, and today—with a staff of four hundred and a comparable number of trade, college, and professional titles published each year—W. W. Norton & Company stands as the largest and oldest publishing house owned wholly by its employees.

For Benjamin and Eli

Manufacturing by Maple Press
Book design by Antonina Krass
Production manager: Sean Mintus

Library of Congress Cataloging-in-Publication Data

Names: Shakespeare, William, 1564–1616, author. | Pechter, Edward, 1941– editor.
Title: Othello : authoritative text, textual sources and cultural contexts, criticism / William Shakespeare ; edited by Edward Pechter.
Description: Second edition. | New York : W. W. Norton & Company, 2016. | Series: Norton critical edition | Includes bibliographical references.
Identifiers: LCCN 2016031025 | ISBN 9780393264227 (pbk.)
Subjects: LCSH: Othello (Fictitious character)—Drama. | Interracial marriage—Drama. | Jealousy—Drama. | Muslims—Drama. | Shakespeare, William, 1564–1616. Othello. | Othello (Fictitious character) | GSAFD: Tragedies.
Classification: LCC PR2829.A2 P43 2016 | DDC 822.3/3—dc23 LC record available at https://lccn.loc.gov/2016031025

W. W. Norton & Company, Inc., 500 Fifth Avenue, New York, N.Y. 10110
www.wwnorton.com

W. W. Norton & Company Ltd., 15 Carlisle Street, London W1D 3BS

7 8 9 0

Contents

List of Illustrations   vii
Introduction   ix

The Text of *Othello*

THE TRAGEDY OF OTHELLO, THE MOOR OF VENICE   1
A NOTE ON THE TEXT   3
THE TEXT AND EDITORIAL PROCEDURES   125
TEXTUAL NOTES   133

Textual Sources and Cultural Contexts

OTHELLO IN ITS OWN TIME   139
Giraldi Cinthio • [The Moor of Venice]   174

Criticism

OTHELLO IN THEATRICAL AND CRITICAL HISTORY   187
Thomas Rymer • ["A Bloody Farce"]   227
Charles Gildon • [Comments on Rymer's *Othello*]   236
Samuel Johnson • [Shakespeare, the Rules, and
    Othello]   242
Charles Lamb • [Othello's Color: Theatrical versus
    Literary Representation]   247
William Hazlitt • [Iago, Heroic Tragedy, and Othello]   248
Samuel Taylor Coleridge • [Comments on *Othello*]   256
A. C. Bradley • ["The Most Painfully Exciting and the
    Most Terrible" of Shakespeare's Tragedies]   261
T. S. Eliot • ["The Last Great Speech of Othello"]   270
Kenneth Burke • *Othello*: An Essay to Illustrate
    a Method   271
G. K. Hunter • *Othello* and Colour Prejudice   275
Stanley Cavell • Epistemology and Tragedy:
    A Reading of *Othello*   289
James R. Siemon • "Nay, That's Not Next": *Othello*, V.ii
    in Performance, 1760–1900   297
Michael Neill • Unproper Beds: Race, Adultery, and the
    Hideous in *Othello*   314

Michael D. Bristol • Charivari and the Comedy of
   Abjection in *Othello*   338
Lois Potter • [Five Modern Productions]   354

Bibliography   365

Illustrations

Fig. 1 First page of *Othello* as it appeared in the First Folio   6
Fig. 2 Man without a head   141
Fig. 3 Moro Neri   146
Fig. 4 Moro de Barbaria   146
Fig. 5 Moro di conditione   146
Fig. 6 Moro nobile del Cairo   146
Fig. 7 Portrait of 'Abd al-Wahid bin Mass'oud bin
          Mohammad 'Annouri   148
Fig. 8 Act 1, Scene 3: "Here's my husband"   198
Fig. 9 Act 2, Scene 1: Othello and Desdemona   198
Fig. 10 Act 1, Scene 3: Othello relating his adventures   198
Fig. 11 Act 3, Scene 4: "Fetch me that handkerchief"   198
Fig. 12 Playbill promoting Ira Aldridge's first appearance at
          Covent Garden as Othello   202
Fig. 13 Illustration of Ira Aldridge as Othello   204
Fig. 14 Lithograph of Ira Aldridge as Othello   205
Fig. 15 Engraving of a Venetian courtesan   367

Introduction

"It is hard to imagine that any of Shakespeare's plays has a more obvious contemporary relevance." Andrew Hadfield's claim, made in 2003 in the first sentence of his Literary Sourcebook on *Othello*, was reiterated the next year by Lena Cowen Orlin, who introduces her New Casebook on *Othello* with the assertion that the play "registers all the concerns of the newly politicized readings of the last decades" (1). The claim was reiterated again the year after that by Julie Hankey, who declares, introducing a new edition of her study of the play's production history, that during "the last twenty years or so, *Othello* has leapt into focus as a play for our times" (1). And it was reiterated yet again by Michael Neill, whose 2006 Oxford edition begins by asserting (or quoting the assertion of a 1999 book on the play) that *Othello* "'has become the tragedy of choice for the present generation'" (1).

This is an extraordinary consensus, but it is not universally shared. In the introduction to the most recent Arden edition of the play, E. A. J. Honigmann begins his discussion under the rubric "The Greatest Tragedy?" and returns to the topic in his final section, "Again: The Greatest Tragedy?" (1, 102–11). The question evokes A. C. Bradley's misgivings about *Othello*—that its "comparatively narrow world" made for less of an impact than the "more solemn and serene" impressions left by *Hamlet*, *Lear*, and *Macbeth*, the other plays treated in his *Shakespearean Tragedy* (134, 135). Bradley is the first critic Honigmann mentions as "partly responsible" for the failure of *Othello*'s preeminence, as Honigmann sees it, to be "generally conceded" (104). The question "the greatest tragedy?" seems designed to be provocative, first simply by summoning up Bradley, who is not much cited these days as an authority, and then by giving such prominence to his work, suggesting with "greatest" that some idea of transhistorical aesthetic value, the framework for the discussion in Bradley's book, still provides the appropriate context within which to engage Shakespeare's plays. This idea has a long history, going back at least as early as to Ben Jonson's tribute to Shakespeare in the First Folio, "He was not of an age but for all time"; but it has for some time been absent from the discourse of most professional Shakespeareans, perhaps displaced by the idea with which we began, of a differential historical specificity—a play not for all time but for our time.

Honigmann notwithstanding, the consensus about *Othello*'s current relevance merits some reflection. If *Othello* has become our play, replacing *King Lear* in the way *Lear* had earlier replaced *Hamlet* as the play that speaks most directly to current interests, how should we account for this development? Robert Scholes suggests a way to begin. Designing a new capstone English course for twelfth-grade students, Scholes selects *Othello* as the one obligatory Shakespeare play because "the issues of cultural conflict are in the foreground" (136). Conflict is Mitchell Greenberg's emphasis as well; *Othello*'s special hold on us derives from its peculiar power "to haunt us as an uncanny projection, from the past, of our conflicted present" (1). Conflict, though, is not unique either to *Othello* or to our own time. If "conflict is the theatre's lifeblood" (Als, 74) and arguably central to all times, commentators seeking critical leverage need to be more specific; and here the critics quoted at the beginning help to fill in the details: "gender, sexuality, race and status" (Hadfield, 1); "gender and marriage" and "race and reception" (Orlin, 18); "racism and misogyny" (Hankey, 1); "the history of 'race'" (Neill, 1).

During the period of *Othello*'s ascendancy, literary and cultural analysis has been transformed by feminist, African American, and postcolonial critics, three groups to whose central concerns the play seems directly to appeal. *Othello* focuses on marriage as a domestic relationship where the most intimately private experiences are shaped by the pressures of society and political power. The play is preoccupied with questions of gender difference, the expectations of men and women for themselves and about each other, including those that underwrite and undermine marriage. It is preoccupied with racial difference as well. Its protagonist is an alien to white Christian Europe, what we would now call an immigrant, whose visible difference seems to be the defining aspect of his identity, the source of his charismatic power to excite interest and to generate horror. As a result, according to Thomas Cartelli, "*Othello* is well on the way to replacing *The Tempest* as a favored field of debate and contention both for scholars and critics of Shakespeare, and for the increasingly numerous workers in the field of postcolonial studies" (124). Or as Mythili Kaul puts it in introducing a collection of essays by black writers on the play, "all the contributors" see *Othello* as "of utmost relevance today in terms of" a variety of "pressing contemporary issues," including "politics, colonial exploitation, cultural relativism, and, above all, race" (xii). These concentrations on gender and racial difference coincide with appalling intensity in the play's final image: Othello and Desdemona, the "old black ram" and "white ewe" Iago summoned to Brabantio's imagination at the beginning, locked in a perverse embrace on the marriage bed revealed finally as the place of murder.

This Norton Critical Edition reflects the intense contemporary interest in Othello—in fact, enthusiastically adopts it—by including many critical commentaries that emphasize race, sex, and gender. But this edition also includes a generous selection of earlier responses to the play produced by readers and audiences and theatrical practitioners who do not share—and in some cases might not even understand—our interests in the play. Eighteenth-century audiences, for example, paid relatively little or no attention to race as an issue in Othello. Race no doubt "mattered" in the eighteenth century (Vaughan), but so tenuously and obliquely compared to the way that it matters to us as to seem very perplexing: Whatever were they thinking? The strangeness of early responses may be just what makes them useful. The relative inconsequence of race to eighteenth-century audiences is one of those astonishment-inducing revelations of reception history—like the insignificance of delay as a central issue in Hamlet or, closer to home, the general lack of interest in Iago, both dating from the same "preromantic" period—that make for critical self-consciousness: Whatever are we thinking? Sometimes a historicizing detachment from the familiarity of the present can help intensify imaginative engagement. "The past is a foreign country," according to the celebrated first sentence of L. P. Hartley's Go-Between; but travel, as everybody says, broadens the mind.

What makes this broadening possible is that, despite the continuation of Hartley's sentence about the past, "they" do not altogether "do things differently there." We naturally feel proprietary about the interests we bring to and take from Othello, and we have generated these interests in most cases without much conscious knowledge of critical or performance traditions. But these traditions matter, perhaps more than we think; they shape our desires and understanding in ways of which we may be imperfectly aware. The continuities inherent in this situation do not always reinforce progressive hopes, as when (to take an example we'll meet in the "Criticism" section of this book) the critique of Victorian gender ideology turns out to occupy a position substantially similar to the ideology it purports to critique. (As the cartoon character Pogo said in the 1970s, "We have met the enemy and he is us.") People are free to "make their own history," Marx says in The Eighteenth Brumaire, "but they do not make it under circumstances chosen by themselves, but under circumstances directly encountered, given, and transmitted from the past" (15). From this angle, our freedom to interpret Othello is constrained by the "tradition of all the dead generations," as Marx continues, which "weighs like a nightmare on the brain of the living." This gloomy claim may be especially relevant to *Othello*, which is largely about the dead weight of inherited prejudice.

But this burden is not the whole story. In *Marxism and Literature*, Raymond Williams reconfigures the structure of thought in *The Eighteenth Brumaire* in order, while still acknowledging the existential limits of the original, to emphasize the substantial possibilities for action that remain. "In most description and analysis, culture and society are expressed in an habitual past tense. The strongest barrier to the recognition of human cultural activity is this immediate and regular conversion of experience into finished products" (128). It's not over till it's over, in other words; and it's never over. From Williams's perspective, the continuing influence of tradition is potentially a good thing; it can enrich "human cultural activity" as well as impoverish it. *Othello*, though perhaps the most cheerless of Shakespeare's tragedies, furnishes glimmers of transcendence, and this edition includes historical material that registers not only as constraint but as "edification" in Richard Rorty's sense of the term (357–72): useful for building new ideas.

Such an edifying process seems even now underway. As literary and theatrical scholars are coming to concentrate on religious and cognitive topics, *Othello* has proven extraordinarily accommodating to these new (or newly intensified) interests. The result is not to ignore those topics that accounted for the play's earlier "contemporary relevance" (how can we approach *Othello* without considering race and gender and sex?), but the grip these topics held on the critical imagination around 2004 seems to be less tight.

Consider in this regard *"Othello": The State of Play*, a collection of essays edited by Lena Cowen Orlin, published in 2014, that in effect updates her Casebook of ten years earlier. Where the previous volume organized its contributions around "two clusters," one on "gender and marriage" and "one on race and reception" (18), Orlin now foregrounds affective impact. Beginning her introduction with instances of spectators so moved by the action on stage that they feel compelled to intervene, she asks, "What is it about *Othello* that provokes so intense a level of audience engagement?" The question carries over to the piece, on "audience cognition," that leads the new collection. This essay argues that, by disrupting the supposedly "ideal balance" between "audience involvement" and "emotional distance," *Othello* "under-distances" its spectators (1).

The new emphasis here is of a piece with the "cognitive turn" in current work, but even as *"Othello": The State of Play* breaks new ground, it occupies a territory more or less continuous with the traditional one from which it has departed. There's a striking resonance between Orlin's new book and Honigmann's old-fashioned version of the play in his Arden edition: "We may fairly call it the most exciting of the tragedies—even the most unbearably exciting—so why not the greatest?" (1). For Honigmann, too, *Othello* "under-distances" its spectators. We shouldn't make too much of this coincidence; other evidence suggests different conclusions. In 2016, the publisher reissued Honigmann's edition with rumpled bloody sheets instead of the floating white handkerchief on the original cover and a new introduction by Ayanna Thompson, which, the book's webpage tells us, "addresses such key issues as race, religion and gender." Nonetheless, Orlin's *State of Play* suggests that *Othello*'s critical future may exhibit elements of continuity with the aesthetic interests driving commentary and performance in the play's unfinished critical and theatrical past.

Works Cited

Als, Hilton. "The Theatre: I Remember Mama." *New Yorker* (May 25, 2015), 74–75.

Bradley, A. C. *Shakespearean Tragedy: Lectures on "Hamlet," "Othello," "King Lear," "Macbeth."* 1904. 4th ed. Houndmills, Basingstoke, Hampshire, Eng., and New York: Palgrave Macmillan, 2007.

Cartelli, Thomas. *Repositioning Shakespeare: National Formations, Postcolonial Appropriations*. London and New York: Routledge, 1999.

Greenberg, Mitchell. "Shakespeare's *Othello* and the 'Problem' of Anxiety." In *Canonical States, Canonical Stages: Oedipus, Othering, and Seventeenth-Century Drama*. Minneapolis and London: University of Minnesota Press, 1994, 1–32.

Hadfield, Andrew. Introduction. In Hadfield, ed. *William Shakespeare's "Othello."* A Routledge Literary Sourcebook. London and New York: Routledge, 2003, 1–3.

Hankey, Julie. Introduction. In Hankey, ed. *Othello*. Shakespeare in Production. 2nd ed. Cambridge, Eng.: Cambridge University Press, 2005, 1–111.

Hartley, L. P. *The Go-Between*. London: Hamilton, 1956.

Honigmann, E. A. J. Introduction. In Honigmann, ed. *Othello*. Walton-on-Thames, Eng.: Nelson, 1997, 1–111.

Kaul, Mythili. Preface. In Kaul, ed. *"Othello": New Essays by Black Writers*. Washington, D.C.: Howard University Press, 1997, ix–xii.

Marx, Karl. *The Eighteenth Brumaire of Louis Bonaparte*. New York: International Publishers, 1963.

Neill, Michael. Introduction. In Neill, ed. *Othello, the Moor of Venice*. Oxford: Oxford University Press, 2006, 1–179.

Orlin, Lena Cowen. Introduction. In Orlin, ed. *"Othello": The State of Play*. London: Bloomsbury, 2014, 1–16.

————. Introduction. In Orlin, ed. *"Othello": William Shakespeare*. New Casebooks. Houndmills, Basingstoke, Hampshire, Eng., and New York: Palgrave Macmillan, 2004, 1–21.

Rorty, Richard. *Philosophy and the Mirror of Nature*. Princeton: Princeton University Press, 1979.

Scholes, Robert. "Pacesetter English." In *The Rise and Fall of English: Reconstructing English as a Discipline*. New Haven: Yale University Press, 1998, 128–42.

Thompson, Ayanna, and E. A. J. Honigmann, eds. *Othello*. 2nd ed. London: Bloomsbury, 2016. <www.bloomsbury.com/US/Othello-9781472571786>

Vaughan, Virginia Mason. "Race Mattered: *Othello* in Late Eighteenth-Century England." *Shakespeare Survey 51*. Cambridge, Eng.: Cambridge University Press, 1998, 57–66.

Williams, Raymond. *Marxism and Literature*. Oxford: Oxford University Press, 1977.

In keeping with the Norton Critical Editions series style, the text of the play is here followed by the section "Textual Sources and Cultural Contexts." This section begins with my essay "Othello in Its Own Time," which introduces various topics—including religion, race, marriage, gender, and the production practices of Shakespeare's theater—as they likely shaped response to *Othello*'s first performances. This essay is followed by a translation of the sixteenth-century Italian narrative that was Shakespeare's primary textual source for the play. The next section, "Criticism," begins with my essay "*Othello* in Theatrical and Critical History," which sketches out the more significant changes in belief and taste that have punctuated *Othello*'s reception history, reflecting also on the qualities that have enabled the play to engage so many different spectators and readers over such a long time. This section then presents a selection of interpretive responses to *Othello* going back to its origins and continuing to the present. Finally, a 15-part bibliography guides readers looking to develop their critical interests in greater detail.

My thanks to Alan Galey, now at the University of Toronto, and Farouk Mitha, who teaches in the Education Faculty at the University of Victoria and the Institute of Ismaili Studies of Aga Khan University, London, whose work on an earlier edition is still contributing here. Farouk continues to be a source of information and ideas, not to say inspiration, especially in conjunction with the Islamic material emphasized in this edition. I am grateful to Sara Beam and Erin Kelly and my other colleagues in the Early Modern Discussion Collective at the University of Victoria, especially to the historians who tolerated and even encouraged my visits to their disciplinary territory.

An astounding number of people responded generously to my requests for advice about improving the first Norton Critical Edition of *Othello*—more than I can acknowledge here; but for their extraordinarily detailed suggestions, I am indebted to Penelope Anderson, Peter Erickson, John Gibson, Mollie Godfrey, Jerry Harp, James Hirsh, Dennis Huston, Suha Kudsieh, David Miller, Steven Mullaney, Rob Patterson, George Pigman, Lawrence Rhu, Mark Sanford, Cecilia Sidenbladh, Ayanna Thompson, Pauline Homsi Vinson, and Garry Walton.

At Norton, I owe a lot to Carol Bemis, who has been there for me since the beginning; to Thea Goodrich, whose good-natured intelligence made the work fun; and to Kurt Wildermuth, about whose scrupulous judgment (and patient forebearance) I can never say enough. A good editor is a writer's best friend.

The Text of
THE TRAGEDY OF
OTHELLO, THE MOOR
OF VENICE

A Note on the Text

This edition is based on the text printed in the First Folio, 1623, identified as F in the explanatory notes, with additions and emendations adopted from the First Quarto, 1622, identified as Q or sometimes Q1. Q readings are not highlighted in the text but specified in the textual notes (133–36 below). All other interpolated material is placed within square brackets. For more details about the differences between F and Q *Othello*, and my ways of dealing with them, see "The Text and Editorial Procedures" (125–32 below). Here I want only to acknowledge some of the many editors and commentators to whom I am indebted for the information and explanations in the footnotes accompanying the text. As the citations in these notes indicate, my greatest obligations are to E. A. J. Honigmann and Michael Neill, on whose richly informed and shrewdly intelligent editions I have especially relied. But I am indebted to the many other editors and commentators cited in the explanatory notes as well—and to still others whom I have not cited and of whom I am no doubt unaware. Working on Shakespeare entails obligations beyond practical acknowledgment and (standing on the shoulders of sometimes anonymous giants) beyond even conscious knowledge.

WORKS CITED IN THE FOOTNOTES TO THE TEXT

Austern, Linda Phyllis. "Appendix D: The Music in the Play." In Neill, ed., *Othello*, 445–54.

Bate, Jonathan. "Ovid and the Mature Tragedies: Metamorphosis in *Othello* and *King Lear*." *Shakespeare Survey 41*. Cambridge, Eng.: Cambridge University Press, 1989, 133–44.

Capell, Edward. *Mr. William Shakespeare: His Comedies, Histories, and Tragedies*. 10 vols. London, 1768.

———. *Notes and Various Readings to Shakespeare*. 3 vols. London, 1780. Rpt. New York: AMS Press, 1973.

Fineman, Joel. *The Subjectivity Effect in Western Literary Tradition: Essays Toward the Release of Shakespeare's Will*. Cambridge, Mass.: MIT Press, 1991.

Furness, Horace Howard, ed. *A New Variorum Edition of "Othello."* 7th ed. Philadelphia: Lippincott, 1886.

Geneva Bible. 1560. Rpt. Madison: University of Wisconsin Press, 1969 (all scriptural citations, unless quoted from another commentary, to this version).

Greenblatt, Stephen, et al., eds. *The Norton Shakespeare.* 3rd ed. New York: Norton, 2016 (all non-*Othello* Shakespearean references to this edition).

Hamlin, Hannibal. *The Bible in Shakespeare.* Oxford: Oxford University Press, 2013.

Hankey, Julie. *Othello.* Plays in Performance Series. Bristol: Bristol Classical Press, 1987.

Holland, Peter, ed. *Coriolanus.* London: Bloomsbury, 2013.

Honigmann, E. A. J., ed. *Othello.* Walton-on-Thames, Eng.: Thomas Nelson, 1997.

Hornbeck, Robert. "'Speak[ing] Parrot' and Ovidian Echoes in *Othello*: Recontextualizing Black Speech in the Global Renaissance." In Lena Cowen Orlin, ed. *"Othello": The State of Play.* London: Bloomsbury, 2014, 63–93.

Johnson, Samuel, ed. *The Plays of William Shakespeare.* 8 vols. London, 1765. Notes rpt. in Arthur Sherbo, ed. *The Works of Samuel Johnson.* Vols. 7 and 8, *Johnson on Shakespeare.* New Haven: Yale University Press, 1968.

Kahane, Henry, and Renée Kahane. "Desdemona: A Star-Crossed Name." *Names* 35 (1987): 232–35.

Kernan, Alvin, ed. *Othello.* 2nd ed. New York: Penguin, 1998.

Kittredge, George Lyman, ed. *Othello.* 1941. 2nd ed. Rev. Irving Ribner. Waltham, Mass.: Ginn, 1966.

Lupton, Julia Reinhard. *Citizen Saints: Shakespeare and Political Theology.* Chicago: University of Chicago Press, 2005.

Malone, Edmond. *The Plays and Poems of William Shakespeare.* 10 vols. London, 1790. Rpt. New York: AMS Press, 1966.

McDonald, Russ, ed. *Othello.* New York: Penguin, 2001.

Mowat, Barbara A., and Paul Werstine, eds. *Othello.* New York: Washington Square Press, 1993.

Neill, Michael, ed. *Othello, the Moor of Venice.* Oxford: Oxford University Press, 2006.

OED. *Oxford English Dictionary.* 2nd ed. 20 vols. Prep. J. A. Simpson and E. S. C. Weiner. Oxford: Clarendon, 1989.

Ovid. *Metamorphoses.* 1567. In John Frederick Nims, ed. *Ovid's Metamorphoses: The Arthur Golding Translation.* New York: Macmillan, 1965.

Pechter, Edward. *"Othello" and Interpretive Traditions.* Iowa City: University of Iowa Press, 1999.

Pope, Alexander. *The Works of William Shakespear.* 6 vols. London, 1723–25.

Raatzsch, Richard. *The Apologetics of Evil: The Case of Iago*. Trans. Ladislaus Löb. Princeton: Princeton University Press, 2009.

Ridley, M. R., ed. *Othello*. London: Methuen, 1958.

Ross, Lawrence J., ed. *The Tragedy of Othello, the Moor of Venice*. Indianapolis and New York: Bobbs-Merrill, 1974.

Rowe, Nicholas. *The Works of Mr. William Shakespear*. 6 vols. London, 1709. Rpt. London: Pickering & Chatto, 1999.

Sanders, Norman, ed. *Othello*. Cambridge, Eng.: Cambridge University Press, 1984.

Schmidt, Alexander. *Shakespeare Lexicon and Quotation Dictionary*. 2 vols. 3rd ed. Rev. Gregor Sarrazin. 1902. Rpt. New York: Dover, 1971.

Steevens, George. *The Plays of William Shakespeare, With the Corrections and Illustrations of Various Commentators, To Which Are Added Notes by Samuel Johnson and George Steevens*. London, 1813.

Theobald, Lewis. *The Works of Shakespeare*. 7 vols. London, 1733. Rpt. New York: AMS Press, 1968.

Tynan, Kenneth, ed. *"Othello": The National Theatre Production*. New York: Stein and Day, 1967.

Vitkus, Daniel, ed. *Othello*. New York: Barnes & Noble, 2007.

Warburton, William. *The Works of Shakespear*. 8 vols. London, 1747.

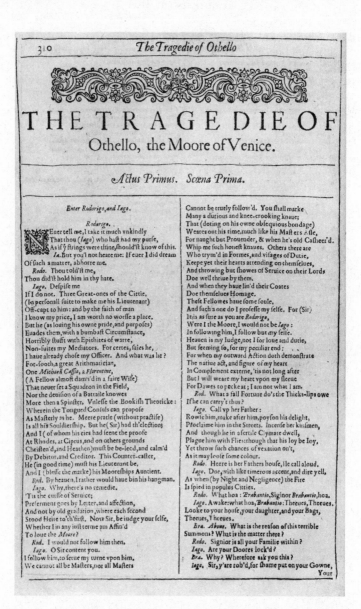

Figure 1. From *The Norton Facsimile: The First Folio of Shakespeare,* ed. Charlton Hinman (New York: Norton), 1968, p. 818. Copyright © 1996, 1968 by W. W. Norton & Company. Reprinted by permission of W. W. Norton & Company, Inc.

The Names of the Actors

Othello, the Moor [and General of the Venetian forces].
Brabantio, father to Desdemona [and a Venetian Senator].
Cassio, an honorable lieutenant [to Othello].
Iago, a villain [and Othello's standard bearer or ensign].
Roderigo, a gulled gentleman.   5
Duke of Venice.
Senators.
Montano, Governor of Cyprus.
Gentlemen of Cyprus.
Lodovico and Gratiano, two Noble Venetians [and kinsmen to
   Brabantio].   10
Sailors.
Clown.
Desdemona, wife to Othello.
Emilia, wife to Iago.
Bianca, a courtesan.   15

0. **The Names . . . Actors:** i.e., *Dramatis Personae* or, as we would say, "Characters"; reproduced in order from the list printed at the end of the folio text. Six other plays in the First Folio include similar lists; all have the same title, which, as here, identifies the roles rather than the actors playing them.
1. **Othello:** Called simply "a Moor" in the Italian narrative that served as the play's main source (see 174 below), "Othello" is Shakespeare's invention. The name suggests Thorello, the comically jealous husband in Ben Jonson's 1598 play *Every Man in His Humor* (which Shakespeare had acted in around this time) and/or Othoman, the founder of the Turkish Empire. Some commentators call attention to "hell" in the middle of the name, and Fineman suggests a derivation from "the Greek verb *ethelō*, which means 'wish,' 'want,' 'will,' 'desire.'"
4. **Iago:** Santiago Matamoros, Saint James the Moor Slayer, is the patron saint of Spain (see 152–53 below); a pun on "ego" (Raatzsch) was probably unavailable to Shakespeare's audience. **villain:** The play emphatically associates Iago with "villainy," a "richer word than now, ranging from boorishness to discourtesy to extreme wickedness" (Honigmann). Commentators frequently connect Iago with "the Vice," a stock type in the old morality plays still sometimes performed in Shakespeare's day, whose dramatic function, to seduce the protagonist into evil, was performed with boisterous comedy.
5. **gulled:** duped.
12. **Clown:** As with "villain," the play text provides authority for the designation (see the speech prefixes in 3.1 and 3.4). "*Clown*" could = peasant" or "ignorant or rude fellow," but as "comic servant" (Honigmann), it looks like a version of the conventional "witty servant" in Roman comedy (the plays written in the third and second centuries B.C.E. by Plautus and Terence, whose plot complications and character types were frequently imitated on the Renaissance stage).
13. **Desdemona:** the one character named in Shakespeare's source, where Cinthio notes the derivation of "Disdemona" from the Greek for "unfortunate." In a different Greek derivation, the name may mean "God-fearing" (Kahane and Kahane). Some commentators call attention to "demon" in the middle of the name.
15. **Bianca:** "white" in Italian. **courtesan:** something like "elegant lady of pleasure," this term also identifies a stock type of Roman comedy. Venetian courtesans were much commented on in the period (see 366–68 below), and Shakespeare uses the designation in other plays; but though the *Othello* text uses an extraordinary abundance of descriptive terminology for Bianca, this particular word is not included (see Pechter).

ACT 1 SCENE 1

Enter RODERIGO *and* IAGO.

RODERIGO   Tush, never tell me! I take it much unkindly
    That thou, Iago, who hast had my purse
    As if the strings were thine, shouldst know of this.
IAGO   'Sblood, but you'll not hear me! If ever I did dream
    Of such a matter, abhor me.
RODERIGO   Thou toldst me   5
    Thou didst hold him in thy hate.
IAGO   Despise me
    If I do not. Three great ones of the city,
    In personal suit to make me his lieutenant,
    Off-capped to him; and by the faith of man
    I know my price; I am worth no worse a place.   10
    But he, as loving his own pride and purposes,
    Evades them with a bombast circumstance,
    Horribly stuffed with epithets of war,
    Non-suits my mediators. For "Certes," says he,
    "I have already chose my officer." And what was he?   15
    Forsooth, a great arithmetician,
    One Michael Cassio, a Florentine,
    A fellow almost damned in a fair wife,
    That never set a squadron in the field,
    Nor the division of a battle knows   20
    More than a spinster; unless the bookish theorick,
    Wherein the tonguèd consuls can propose
    As masterly as he. Mere prattle without practice
    Is all his soldiership. But he, sir, had th' election;
    And I—of whom his eyes had seen the proof   25
    At Rhodes, at Cyprus, and on other grounds,
    Christened and heathen—must be beleed and calmed

---

1. **Tush:** expression of irritation.
3. **of this:** As with "such a matter" and "him" following, the referent is unclear; we have to guess pending clarification within the scene.
4. **'Sblood:** By God's blood.
7. **great ones of the city:** politically influential Venetians.
9. **Off-capped:** removed their hats respectfully.
12–13. **bombast . . . of war:** intimidatingly high-sounding military jargon.
14. **Non-suits:** rejects. **Certes:** Surely; the word may have sounded old-fashioned or bombastic to Shakespeare's audience.
16. **arithmetician:** theorist; six syllables: *-cian* and *-tion* normally pronounced "shee-UN."
18. **A fellow . . . wife:** Without explanation, the line plants an association between male desire in marriage and sin.
19–23. **That never . . . as he:** has no more experience in the deployment of troops than a woman does, except for the pedantic abstractions he shares with glib politicians.
24. **had th'election:** was chosen.
27. **beleed:** like a stalled ship; "Cassio had got to the wind of him" (Malone).

By debitor and creditor. This countercaster,
He in good time must his lieutenant be,
And I—God bless the mark!—his Moorship's ancient.   30
RODERIGO   By heaven, I rather would have been his hangman.
IAGO   Why, there's no remedy. 'Tis the curse of service;
Preferment goes by letter and affection,
And not by old gradation, where each second
Stood heir to th' first. Now, sir, be judge yourself   35
Whether I in any just term am affined
To love the Moor.
RODERIGO   I would not follow him then.
IAGO   O, sir, content you.
I follow him to serve my turn upon him.
We cannot all be masters, nor all masters   40
Cannot be truly followed. You shall mark
Many a duteous and knee-crooking knave
That, doting on his own obsequious bondage,
Wears out his time, much like his master's ass,
For naught but provender; and when he's old—cashiered.   45
Whip me such honest knaves! Others there are
Who, trimmed in forms and visages of duty,
Keep yet their hearts attending on themselves
And, throwing but shows of service on their lords,
Do well thrive by them; and when they have lined their coats,   50
Do themselves homage. These fellows have some soul,
And such a one do I profess myself. For, sir,
It is as sure as you are Roderigo,
Were I the Moor, I would not be Iago.
In following him, I follow but myself.   55

---

28. countercaster: bean counter.
29. in good time: appropriately (with a sneer).
30. God . . . mark: expresses disgust at an unjust situation. **ancient:** ensign or standard bearer, a lower rank than lieutenant (= "place-holder" or substitute, who occupies the authoritative position in the commander's absence). **his Moorship:** a pun on the conventionally respectful "his worship" (as in the quarto).
32. service: "military service; serving a master" (Neill).
33. letter and affection: influence and bias.
34. old gradation: traditional promotion through seniority.
36. affined: obliged.
39. serve my turn upon: get my own back from.
42. knee-crooking: bowing.
45. provender: animal fodder.
46. Whip me: i.e., they deserve what they get as far as I'm concerned.
47. trimmed . . . visages: putting on shows.
51. Do themselves homage: defer to their own needs.
53–54. It is . . . be Iago: This sounds like a self-evident truism, but isn't; Iago's meaning "may be, 'Were I in the Moor's place, I should be quite another man than I am.' Or, 'if I had the Moor's nature, if I were such an honest dunce as he is, I should be just a fit subject for men that "have some soul" to practise upon'" (Furness, quoting Hudson).

Heaven is my judge, not I for love and duty,
But seeming so, for my peculiar end;
For when my outward action doth demonstrate
The native act and figure of my heart
In complement extern, 'tis not long after   60
But I will wear my heart upon my sleeve
For daws to peck at. I am not what I am.

RODERIGO What a full fortune does the thick-lips owe
If he can carry't thus!

IAGO   Call up her father,
Rouse him, make after him, poison his delight.   65
Proclaim him in the streets, incense her kinsmen,
And though he in a fertile climate dwell,
Plague him with flies. Though that his joy be joy,
Yet throw such chances of vexation on't,
As it may lose some color.   70

RODERIGO Here is her father's house. I'll call aloud.

IAGO Do, with like timorous accent and dire yell
As when, by night and negligence, the fire
Is spied in populous cities.

RODERIGO What ho, Brabantio! Signior Brabantio, ho!   75

IAGO Awake! what ho, Brabantio! Thieves, thieves!
Look to your house, your daughter, and your bags!
Thieves, thieves!

[*Enter*] BRABANTIO *above at a window.*

BRABANTIO What is the reason of this terrible summons?
What is the matter there?   80

RODERIGO Signior, is all your family within?

IAGO Are your doors locked?

BRABANTIO   Why? Wherefore ask you this?

---

56. **not I:** I do not serve (elliptical).
57. **peculiar:** personal.
58–60. **outward . . . complement extern:** visible behavior corresponds to private intention.
62. **daws:** birds reputed for stupidity. **I am not what I am:** The second "am" must be taken
    to mean "seem." In Exodus 3:1, God declares, "I am that I am."
63. **owe:** possess.
64. **carry't:** pull it off.
65. **him:** The "first and second" pronouns seem "to relate to different persons" (Capell),
    slipping from "her father" to "the thick-lips."
69. **chances:** possibilities.
70. **lose some color:** diminish in intensity.
72. **timorous accent:** frightening noise.
73. **by night and negligence:** i.e., "*by night*, and *thro' negligence*. Otherwise the particle
    by would be made to signify *time* applied to one word, and *cause* applied to the other"
    (Warburton).
78. **STAGE DIRECTION** *above:* "on the small upper stage above and to the rear of the
    main platform stage, which resembled the projecting upper story of an Elizabethan
    house" (Kernan).

IAGO   Zounds, sir, you're robbed! For shame, put on your gown!
   Your heart is burst, you have lost half your soul.
   Even now, now, very now, an old black ram   85
   Is tupping your white ewe. Arise, arise!
   Awake the snorting citizens with the bell,
   Or else the devil will make a grandsire of you.
   Arise, I say!
BRABANTIO   What, have you lost your wits?
RODERIGO   Most reverend signior, do you know my voice?   90
BRABANTIO   Not I; what are you?
RODERIGO   My name is Roderigo.
BRABANTIO   The worser welcome!
   I have charged thee not to haunt about my doors;
   In honest plainness thou hast heard me say
   My daughter is not for thee. And now in madness,   95
   Being full of supper and distemp'ring draughts,
   Upon malicious knavery, dost thou come
   To start my quiet.
RODERIGO   Sir, sir, sir—
BRABANTIO   But thou must needs be sure,
   My spirits and my place have in their power   100
   To make this bitter to thee.
RODERIGO   Patience, good sir.
BRABANTIO   What tell'st thou me of robbing? This is Venice;
   My house is not a grange.
RODERIGO   Most grave Brabantio,
   In simple and pure soul, I come to you.
IAGO   Zounds, sir; you are one of those that will not serve God   105
   if the devil bid you. Because we come to do you service,
   and you think we are ruffians, you'll have your daughter
   covered with a Barbary horse; you'll have your nephews
   neigh to you; you'll have coursers for cousins and
   jennets for germans.   110

---

 83. **Zounds:** By God's wounds. **gown:** the "nightgown" specified in the stage direction at
    line 156; a casual garment for inside and outside—not the modern meaning.
 85. **very:** right or truly (emphatic).
 86. **tupping:** used to describe animal copulation.
 87. **snorting:** snoring; but the modern sense of animal noises is available. **bell:** alarm to
    warn of fire or insurrection.
 96. **distemp'ring draughts:** alcohol.
 98. **start:** startle.
100. **spirits and . . . place:** anger and influential position.
103. **grange:** isolated rural abode.
105–06. **not serve God if the devil bid you:** i.e., not do good if urged to by a bad person.
108–10. **covered . . . germans:** Iago shifts abruptly from one kind of horse to another (the
    Barbary steed having a particular association with the Moor) and from one example of
    human kinship to another, paying more attention to alliteration than to the

BRABANTIO   What profane wretch art thou?
IAGO   I am one, sir, that comes to tell you your daughter
  and the Moor are making the beast with two backs.
BRABANTIO   Thou art a villain.
IAGO   You are a senator.   115
BRABANTIO   This thou shalt answer. I know thee, Roderigo.
RODERIGO   Sir, I will answer anything. But I beseech you,
  If't be your pleasure, and most wise consent,
  As partly I find it is, that your fair daughter,
  At this odd-even and dull watch o'th' night,   120
  Transported with no worse nor better guard
  But with a knave of common hire, a gondolier,
  To the gross clasps of a lascivious Moor—
  If this be known to you, and your allowance,
  We then have done you bold and saucy wrongs.   125
  But if you know not this, my manners tell me
  We have your wrong rebuke. Do not believe
  That from the sense of all civility
  I thus would play and trifle with your reverence.
  Your daughter, if you have not given her leave,   130
  I say again, hath made a gross revolt,
  Tying her duty, beauty, wit and fortunes
  In an extravagant and wheeling stranger
  Of here and everywhere. Straight satisfy yourself.
  If she be in her chamber or your house,   135
  Let loose on me the justice of the state
  For thus deluding you.
BRABANTIO   Strike on the tinder, ho!
  Give me a taper, call up all my people!
  This accident is not unlike my dream;
  Belief of it oppresses me already.   140

---

  specific familial connections (all are "germans" or close relatives). The common
  ground is bestial contamination; like "tupping" earlier, "covered" was used to describe
  animal copulation.
113. **making the beast with two backs:** a proverbial image representing human sexual
  intercourse as bestial.
114–15. **Thou art . . . a senator:** Iago's exaggerated deference, in switching to the formal "you," slyly attributes snobbery to Brabantio.
120. **odd-even and dull watch:** neither night nor morning; indefinite.
122. **But:** than.
124. **your allowance:** done with your permission.
128. **from:** contrary to.
131. **gross:** great; also outrageous (as in Othello's "gross clasps," line 123).
132. **wit:** reason or understanding.
133. **extravagant and wheeling:** wandering without restraint outside established
  boundaries.
134. **Straight:** Immediately.
137. **Strike on the tinder:** Make flame for a torch.
139. **accident:** unanticipated happening.

Light, I say, light!   *Exit [above].*

IAGO   Farewell, for I must leave you.
   It seems not meet nor wholesome to my place
   To be producted—as, if I stay, I shall—
   Against the Moor. For I do know the state,
   However this may gall him with some check,   145
   Cannot with safety cast him; for he's embarked
   With such loud reason to the Cyprus wars,
   Which even now stands in act, that for their souls
   Another of his fathom they have none
   To lead their business. In which regard,   150
   Though I do hate him as I do hell pains,
   Yet for necessity of present life
   I must show out a flag and sign of love,
   Which is indeed but sign. That you shall surely find him,
   Lead to the Sagittary the raisèd search,   155
   And there will I be with him. So farewell.   *Exit.*

Enter BRABANTIO *[below] in his nightgown*
with Servants and Torches.

BRABANTIO   It is too true an evil. Gone she is,
   And what's to come of my despisèd time
   Is naught but bitterness. Now, Roderigo,
   Where didst thou see her?—O unhappy girl!—   160
   With the Moor, say'st thou?—Who would be a father?—
   How didst thou know 'twas she?—O, she deceives me
   Past thought!—what said she to you?—Get more tapers,
   Raise all my kindred! Are they married, think you?
RODERIGO   Truly I think they are.   165
BRABANTIO   O heaven! How got she out? O treason of the blood!
   Fathers, from hence trust not your daughters' minds
   By what you see them act. Is there not charms
   By which the property of youth and maidhood
   May be abused? Have you not read, Roderigo,   170

---

143. **producted:** summoned for testimony.
145. **gall him with some check:** irritate him with some restraint.
146. **cast:** dismiss.
147. **loud:** urgent.
148. **even now stands in act:** are being undertaken at this very moment (cf. "even now," line 85); "wars" can be taken as a singular subject.
149. **of his fathom:** with his abilities.
155. **Sagittary:** Centaur, a legendary creature with a man's head on a horse's body; its image would appear on the so-named inn, where Othello may be found.
158. **despisèd time:** miserable life, expressing grief at his loss and/or shame at the affront to his public image.
166. **treason of the blood:** rebellion against paternal authority and/or by passion against reason.
169. **property:** appropriate behavior.
170. **abused:** misled.

Of some such thing?
RODERIGO   Yes, sir, I have indeed.
BRABANTIO   Call up my brother.—O, would you had had her!—
    Some one way, some another.—Do you know
    Where we may apprehend her and the Moor?
RODERIGO   I think I can discover him, if you please   175
    To get good guard and go along with me.
BRABANTIO   Pray you lead on. At every house I'll call;
    I may command at most.—Get weapons, ho!
    And raise some special officers of night.—
    On, good Roderigo; I will deserve your pains.   *Exeunt.* 180

ACT 1 SCENE 2

Enter OTHELLO, IAGO [*and*] *Attendants, with Torches.*

IAGO   Though in the trade of war I have slain men,
    Yet do I hold it very stuff o'th' conscience
    To do no contrived murder. I lack iniquity
    Sometime to do me service. Nine or ten times
    I had thought t'have yerked him here under the ribs.   5
OTHELLO   'Tis better as it is.
IAGO   Nay, but he prated
    And spoke such scurvy and provoking terms
    Against your honor
    That with the little godliness I have
    I did full hard forbear him. But I pray you, sir,   10
    Are you fast married? Be assured of this,
    That the magnifico is much beloved,
    And hath in his effect a voice potential
    As double as the duke's. He will divorce you,
    Or put upon you what restraint or grievance   15
    The law, with all his might to enforce it on,

---

175. **discover:** uncover, reveal.
179. **special officers of night:** nocturnal patrols were a noted feature of the Venetian civic order (see 365–66 below).
180. **deserve your pains:** reward your efforts. **STAGE DIRECTION Exeunt:** "they leave the stage" (the Latin plural of *exit*—a distinction not subsequently maintained with rigor).
  2. **very stuff:** the essence.
  5. **yerked:** poked, stabbed.
 10. **did full hard forbear:** could scarcely resist attacking; alludes to Colossians 3:13: "Forbearing one another, if any man have a quarrel to another: even as Christ forgave, even so do ye" (Ross).
 11. **fast:** secure; perhaps an implicit question about sexual consummation, without which "the marriage can be annulled" (Vitkus).
 12. **magnifico:** important person (i.e., Brabantio).
 14. **double:** powerful.

Will give him cable.

OTHELLO   Let him do his spite;
My services, which I have done the signiory,
Shall out-tongue his complaints. 'Tis yet to know—
Which, when I know that boasting is an honor,   20
I shall promulgate—I fetch my life and being
From men of royal siege; and my demerits
May speak unbonneted to as proud a fortune
As this that I have reached. For know, Iago,
But that I love the gentle Desdemona,   25
I would not my unhousèd free condition
Put into circumscription and confine
For the sea's worth. But look, what lights come yond?

Enter CASSIO, *with Officers and Torches.*

IAGO   Those are the raisèd father and his friends.
You were best go in.

OTHELLO   Not I; I must be found.   30
My parts, my title, and my perfect soul
Shall manifest me rightly. Is it they?

IAGO   By Janus, I think no.

OTHELLO   The servants of the duke? And my lieutenant?
The goodness of the night upon you, friends.   35
What is the news?

CASSIO   The duke does greet you, general,
And he requires your haste-post-haste appearance
Even on the instant.

OTHELLO   What is the matter, think you?

CASSIO   Something from Cyprus, as I may divine.
It is a business of some heat. The galleys   40
Have sent a dozen sequent messengers

---

17. **cable:** latitude.
18. **the signiory:** the Venetian governors.
19. **to know:** to be made known.
22. **siege:** rank. **demerits:** merits; a secondary meaning even in Shakespeare's time.
23. **unbonneted:** having "off-capped" (cf. 1.1.9); Othello claims he has earned his suc-
    cess, so should not need to remove his cap.
26. **unhousèd free condition:** undomesticated independence.
28. **the sea's worth:** immeasurable value.
29. **raisèd:** aroused.
31. **parts:** natural gifts (?). **title:** status or claim (?). **perfect soul:** clear conscience or
    guiltless spirit (?). Ross quotes Hebrews 10:14: "For by one offering he hath perfected
    forever them that are sanctified," adding that "the Christian's 'perfection of soul'" is
    "an imputed one, posited on Christ's."
32. **manifest:** represent, reveal.
33. **Janus:** Roman deity with contradictory faces—one smiling, one frowning—on either
    side of his head.
39. **divine:** guess.
40. **heat:** urgency.
41. **sequent:** consecutive.

This very night at one another's heels,
And many of the consuls, raised and met,
Are at the duke's already. You have been hotly called for;
When, being not at your lodging to be found,   45
The Senate hath sent about three several quests
To search you out.
OTHELLO   'Tis well I am found by you.
I will but spend a word here in the house
And go with you.   [*Exit.*]
CASSIO   Ancient, what makes he here?
IAGO   Faith, he tonight hath boarded a land carrack.   50
If it prove lawful prize, he's made forever.
CASSIO   I do not understand.
IAGO   He's married.
CASSIO   To who?
IAGO   Marry, to—   [*Enter* OTHELLO.]
                    Come, captain, will you go?
OTHELLO   Have with you.
CASSIO   Here comes another troop to seek for you.

> *Enter* BRABANTIO [*and*] RODERIGO, *with Officers and*
> *Torches.*

IAGO   It is Brabantio; general, be advised,   55
He comes to bad intent.
OTHELLO   Holla, stand there!
RODERIGO   Signior, it is the Moor.
BRABANTIO   Down with him, thief!

                    [*They draw on both sides.*]

IAGO   You, Roderigo? Come, sir, I am for you.
OTHELLO   Keep up your bright swords, for the dew will rust
   them.
Good signior, you shall more command with years   60
Than with your weapons.
BRABANTIO   O thou foul thief, where hast thou stowed my
   daughter?
Damned as thou art, thou hast enchanted her;
For I'll refer me to all things of sense,
If she in chains of magic were not bound,   65

46. **sent about three several quests:** sent out three separate searches.
49. **makes he:** is he doing.
50. **boarded a land carrack:** got onto a treasure ship (sexual innuendo, with further insinuations of piracy and theft).
53. **Marry:** By the Virgin Mary. **Have with you:** I'm ready.
59. **Keep up your bright swords:** Put away your unused weapons (the ironically dismissive command of an experienced soldier); echoing "Put vp thy sworde into the sheath" (John 18:11).
64. **refer me . . . sense:** appeal to all reasonable evidence.

Whether a maid, so tender, fair, and happy,
So opposite to marriage that she shunned
The wealthy curlèd darlings of our nation,
Would ever have, t' incur a general mock,
Run from her guardage to the sooty bosom   70
Of such a thing as thou—to fear, not to delight.
Judge me the world if 'tis not gross in sense
That thou hast practiced on her with foul charms,
Abused her delicate youth with drugs or minerals
That weakens motion. I'll have't disputed on;   75
'Tis probable and palpable to thinking.
I therefore apprehend and do attach thee
For an abuser of the world, a practicer
Of arts inhibited and out of warrant.
Lay hold upon him; if he do resist   80
Subdue him at his peril!

OTHELLO   Hold your hands,
Both you of my inclining and the rest.
Were it my cue to fight, I should have known it
Without a prompter. Where will you that I go
To answer this your charge?

BRABANTIO   To prison, till fit time   85
Of law and course of direct session
Call thee to answer.

OTHELLO   What if I do obey?
How may the duke be therewith satisfied,
Whose messengers are here about my side
Upon some present business of the state   90
To bring me to him?

OFFICER   'Tis true, most worthy signior.
The duke's in council, and your noble self
I am sure is sent for.

BRABANTIO   How? The duke in council?
In this time of the night? Bring him away.
Mine's not an idle cause. The duke himself,   95

68. **curlèd**: fashionably coifed.
69. **general mock**: widespread scorn.
70. **guardage**: parental custody.
72. **Judge me the world**: Let the world judge. **gross in sense**: self-evident; see 1.1.131
    and note.
73. **practiced on**: plotted against.
75. **motion**: natural inclination. **disputed on**: decided in court.
77. **attach**: arrest.
78. **abuser**: deceiver.
79. **inhibited**: prohibited.
82. **of my inclining**: on my side.
85–86. **till fit time . . . session**: two technically distinct ways of saying "till the law runs
    its course."
95. **an idle cause**: an unimportant case.

Or any of my brothers of the state,
Cannot but feel this wrong as 'twere their own;
For if such actions may have passage free,
Bondslaves and pagans shall our statesmen be.   *Exeunt.*

ACT I SCENE 3

Enter DUKE *and Senators, set at a table with lights and Attendants*

DUKE   There's no composition in this news
That gives them credit.

FIRST SENATOR   Indeed, they are disproportioned;
My letters say a hundred and seven galleys.

DUKE   And mine a hundred forty.

SECOND SENATOR   And mine two hundred.
But though they jump not on a just account—   5
As in these cases where the aim reports
'Tis oft with difference—yet do they all confirm
A Turkish fleet, and bearing up to Cyprus.

DUKE   Nay, it is possible enough to judgment;
I do not so secure me in the error,   10
But the main article I do approve
In fearful sense.

SAILOR *within*.   What ho! what ho! what ho!
            Enter SAILOR.

OFFICER   A messenger from the galleys.

DUKE   Now, what's the business?

SAILOR   The Turkish preparation makes for Rhodes.
So was I bid report here to the state   15
By Signior Angelo.

DUKE   How say you by this change?

FIRST SENATOR   This cannot be
By no assay of reason. 'Tis a pageant
To keep us in false gaze. When we consider
Th' importancy of Cyprus to the Turk,   20
And let ourselves again but understand

98–99. **For if . . . statesmen be:** rebellion against paternal authority undermines the
social and religious hierarchy of the state as well.
 1. **composition:** coherence.
 2. **gives them credit:** makes them believable.
 5. **jump not on a just account:** don't agree on an exact number.
 6. **the aim reports:** estimates are given.
10–12. **so secure . . . fearful sense:** take advantage of the inconsistency to dismiss the
basic threat.
14. **preparation:** force.
18–19. **pageant . . . gaze:** show to divert us.
20. **the Turk:** the Turks—"he" for "they," here and following.

That, as it more concerns the Turk than Rhodes,
So may he with more facile question bear it,
For that it stands not in such warlike brace,
But altogether lacks th' abilities   25
That Rhodes is dressed in—if we make thought of this,
We must not think the Turk is so unskillful
To leave that latest which concerns him first,
Neglecting an attempt of ease and gain
To wake and wage a danger profitless.   30
DUKE   Nay, in all confidence, he's not for Rhodes.
OFFICER   Here is more news.

      Enter a MESSENGER.

MESSENGER   The Ottomites, reverend and gracious,
  Steering with due course toward the isle of Rhodes,
  Have there injointed them with an after fleet.   35
FIRST SENATOR   Ay, so I thought. How many, as you guess?
MESSENGER   Of thirty sail; and now they do re-stem
  Their backward course, bearing with frank appearance
  Their purposes toward Cyprus. Signior Montano,
  Your trusty and most valiant servitor,   40
  With his free duty recommends you thus,
  And prays you to believe him.
DUKE   'Tis certain then for Cyprus.
  Marcus Luccicos—is not he in town?
FIRST SENATOR   He's now in Florence.   45
DUKE   Write from us to him. Post-post-haste, dispatch!
FIRST SENATOR   Here comes Brabantio and the valiant Moor.

     Enter BRABANTIO, OTHELLO, CASSIO,
        IAGO, RODERIGO, *and Officers.*

DUKE   Valiant Othello, we must straight employ you
  Against the general enemy Ottoman.

                [*To* BRABANTIO.]

I did not see you; welcome, gentle signior.   50
We lacked your counsel and your help tonight.

---

23. **with more facile question bear:** more easily conquer.
24. **stands not in such warlike brace:** is not in such a state of military alert.
33. **Ottomites:** Ottomans, Turks. **reverend and gracious:** respectful address to the senators ("sirs" understood).
35. **injointed:** combined. **after:** following; perhaps punning on "more aft."
37. **re-stem:** redirect.
38–39. **bearing . . . purposes:** openly headed.
40–42. **Your trusty . . . believe him:** conventionally deferential diplomatic formulas.
48. **straight:** immediately.
49. **general enemy Ottoman:** the Turks, hostile "to all Christians" (Mowat and Werstine;
  Honigmann).
50. **gentle:** noble.

BRABANTIO   So did I yours. Good your grace, pardon me.
 Neither my place nor aught I heard of business
 Hath raised me from my bed; nor doth the general care
 Take hold on me. For my particular grief   55
 Is of so floodgate and o'erbearing nature,
 That it engluts and swallows other sorrows,
 And it is still itself.

DUKE   Why? What's the matter?

BRABANTIO   My daughter, O my daughter!

SENATOR   Dead?

BRABANTIO   Ay, to me.
 She is abused, stol'n from me and corrupted   60
 By spells and medicines bought of mountebanks;
 For nature so preposterously to err,
 Being not deficient, blind, or lame of sense,
 Sans witchcraft could not.

DUKE   Whoe'er he be that in this foul proceeding   65
 Hath thus beguiled your daughter of herself
 And you of her, the bloody book of law
 You shall yourself read in the bitter letter
 After your own sense; yea, though our proper son
 Stood in your action.

BRABANTIO   Humbly I thank your grace.   70
 Here is the man. This Moor, whom now it seems
 Your special mandate for the state affairs
 Hath hither brought.

ALL   We are very sorry for't.

DUKE [To OTHELLO.]   What in your own part can you say to
 this?

BRABANTIO   Nothing, but this is so.   75

OTHELLO   Most potent, grave, and reverend signiors,
 My very noble and approved good masters:
 That I have ta'en away this old man's daughter
 It is most true; true I have married her.

---

53. **place:** senatorial position.
56. **floodgate and o'erbearing:** restraint-breaching.
60. **abused:** misled.
61. **mountebanks:** con artists.
64. **sans:** without.
66. **beguiled . . . of her self:** tricked . . . from her true nature.
67–69. **the bloody book . . . own sense:** you can punish as severely as you think the law
  allows.
69. **proper:** own.
70. **Stood in your action:** was vulnerable to your accusation.
73. ALL: may mean that "one senator speaks, others indicate agreement" (Honigmann), or
  that words are "to be shared between two or more individuals or groups" (Holland).
77. **approved:** worthy.

The very head and front of my offending   80
Hath this extent, no more. Rude am I in my speech,
And little blessed with the soft phrase of peace;
For since these arms of mine had seven years' pith
Till now some nine moons wasted, they have used
Their dearest action in the tented field;   85
And little of this great world can I speak
More than pertains to feats of broils and battle,
And therefore little shall I grace my cause
In speaking for myself. Yet, by your gracious patience,
I will a round unvarnished tale deliver,   90
Of my whole course of love: what drugs, what charms,
What conjuration and what mighty magic—
For such proceeding I am charged withal—
I won his daughter.

BRABANTIO   A maiden never bold;
Of spirit so still and quiet that her motion   95
Blushed at herself; and she—in spite of nature,
Of years, of country, credit, everything—
To fall in love with what she feared to look on?
It is a judgment maimed and most imperfect
That will confess perfection so could err   100
Against all rules of nature, and must be driven
To find out practices of cunning hell
Why this should be. I therefore vouch again
That with some mixtures powerful o'er the blood,
Or with some dram, conjured to this effect,   105
He wrought upon her.

DUKE   To vouch this is no proof,
Without more wider and more overt test
Than these thin habits and poor likelihoods

---

80. **very head and front:** truly utmost extent (literally, true head and forehead).
81. **Rude:** Inexperienced, unsophisticated. Othello "seems to know that his statement, 'Rude am I in my speech,' alludes to 2 Corinthians 11:6, 'And thogh I am rude in speaking, yet I am not so in knowledge'" (Hamlin).
83. **pith:** strength.
84. **nine moons wasted:** nine months ago.
84–85. **used . . . action:** been chiefly exercised.
87. **broils:** skirmishes.
90. **round unvarnished:** direct unadorned.
95. **motion:** feeling or desire.
96. **Blushed at herself:** embarrassed even her.
97. **years . . . credit:** age, of Venetian convention, reputation.
101. **and must:** The phrase is elliptical, implying a new and contrasting subject: "and *un*maimed judgment must. . . ."
102. **practices:** "intrigues, treacheries" (Honigmann).
104. **the blood:** passion, desire.
106. **wrought:** worked.
107–09. **more wider . . . seeming:** The duke rejects the fashionably superficial conventions of "modern seeming" for something more readily apparent ("overt"): the reality

Of modern seeming do prefer against him.
SENATOR   But, Othello, speak;   110
Did you by indirect and forced courses
Subdue and poison this young maid's affections?
Or came it by request and such fair question
As soul to soul affordeth?
OTHELLO   I do beseech you
Send for the lady to the Sagittary,   115
And let her speak of me before her father.
If you do find me foul in her report,
The trust, the office I do hold of you,
Not only take away, but let your sentence
Even fall upon my life.
DUKE   Fetch Desdemona hither.   120
OTHELLO   Ancient, conduct them; you best know the place.

                    Exit [IAGO and] two or three [Attendants].

And till she come, as truly as to heaven
I do confess the vices of my blood,
So justly to your grave ears I'll present
How I did thrive in this fair lady's love   125
And she in mine.
DUKE   Say it, Othello.
OTHELLO   Her father loved me, oft invited me,
Still questioned me the story of my life
From year to year, the battles, sieges, fortunes
That I have past.   130
I ran it through, even from my boyish days
To th' very moment that he bade me tell it;
Wherein I spoke of most disastrous chances,
Of moving accidents by flood and field,
Of hair-breadth scapes i'th' imminent-deadly breach,   135
Of being taken by the insolent foe
And sold to slavery, of my redemption thence

---

under the appearance. "Is this an appeal against racial prejudice?" (Honigmann).
But the clothes metaphor in "thin habits and poor likelihoods" suggests (contradic-
torily) that richly adorned clothing is necessary to perceive the naked truth.
111. **indirect and forcèd courses:** devious manipulations.
113. **fair question:** open and uncoerced conversation.
117. **foul:** ugly; also "black," in implicit contrast to "fair" as white just earlier.
122–24. **as truly . . . I'll present:** at once acknowledges an inherent and existential guilt
("vices of my blood" = my sinful desires), and expresses faith in the power of a benevolent authority ("heaven," "your grave ears") to hear his confession and clear him of any
wrongdoing. Alternatively, "blood" carries "the suggestion of 'race' (i.e., 'the vices
peculiar to my nature as a Moor')" (Neill).
128. **still:** continually.
134. **moving accidents by flood and field:** affecting events on sea and land.
135. **imminent-deadly breach:** immediately life-threatening gap in fortification.
137. **redemption:** liberation, ransom.

And portance in my traveler's history;
Wherein of antars vast and deserts idle,
Rough quarries, rocks and hills whose heads touch heaven,   140
It was my hint to speak—such was my process—
And of the cannibals that each other eat,
The anthropophagi, and men whose heads
Do grow beneath their shoulders. These things to hear
Would Desdemona seriously incline,   145
But still the house affairs would draw her thence,
Which ever as she could with haste dispatch,
She'd come again and with a greedy ear
Devour up my discourse; which I, observing,
Took once a pliant hour and found good means   150
To draw from her a prayer of earnest heart
That I would all my pilgrimage dilate,
Whereof by parcels she had something heard,
But not intentively. I did consent
And often did beguile her of her tears   155
When I did speak of some distressful stroke
That my youth suffered. My story being done,
She gave me for my pains a world of kisses;
She swore in faith 'twas strange, 'twas passing strange,
'Twas pitiful, 'twas wondrous pitiful.   160
She wished she had not heard it, yet she wished
That heaven had made her such a man. She thanked me
And bade me, if I had a friend that loved her,
I should but teach him how to tell my story,
And that would woo her. Upon this hint I spake.   165
She loved me for the dangers I had past,
And I loved her that she did pity them.
This only is the witchcraft I have used.

---

138. **portance:** bearing, deportment.
139. **antars vast and deserts idle:** huge caves and empty wildernesses.
141. **It was my hint:** it was my opportunity or occasion; I was called upon. **process:** a
    term from formal rhetoric meaning "narrative development"; refers at once to his
    life and to his account of it.
143. **anthropophagi:** Latinate version of cannibals ("man eaters").
150. **pliant:** convenient, perhaps implying a time when she was compliant.
151. **prayer of earnest heart:** a strongly felt request.
152. **dilate:** expand or elaborate on.
153. **by parcels:** in bits and pieces.
154. **intentively:** carefully, with sustained attention.
155. **beguile:** Cf. 1.3.66.
158. **my pains:** "Equivocates between 'my sufferings' and 'my trouble' (in telling the story)"
    (Neill).
159. **passing:** surpassingly, beyond.
162. **made her:** made for her, made her into.
165. **hint:** opportunity or occasion; as in line 142, the modern sense of "suggestion"
    should not be altogether eliminated.

Here comes the lady; let her witness it.

Enter DESDEMONA, IAGO [*and*] *Attendants.*

DUKE   I think this tale would win my daughter too.   170
 Good Brabantio, take up this mangled matter at the best.
 Men do their broken weapons rather use,
 Than their bare hands.
BRABANTIO   I pray you hear her speak.
 If she confess that she was half the wooer,
 Destruction on my head if my bad blame   175
 Light on the man. Come hither, gentle mistress.
 Do you perceive in all this noble company
 Where most you owe obedience?
DESDEMONA   My noble father,
 I do perceive here a divided duty.
 To you I am bound for life and education;   180
 My life and education both do learn me
 How to respect you; you are the lord of duty;
 I am hitherto your daughter. But here's my husband;
 And so much duty as my mother showed
 To you, preferring you before her father,   185
 So much I challenge that I may profess
 Due to the Moor my lord.
BRABANTIO   God be with you; I have done.
 Please it your grace, on to the state affairs;
 I had rather to adopt a child than get it.
 Come hither, Moor.   190
 I here do give thee that with all my heart
 Which, but thou hast already, with all my heart
 I would keep from thee. For your sake, jewel,
 I am glad at soul I have no other child,
 For thy escape would teach me tyranny   195
 To hang clogs on them. I have done, my lord.
DUKE   Let me speak like yourself and lay a sentence

171–73. **take up . . . bare hands:** two versions of proverbial advice to make the best of a
  bad situation.
180. **education:** upbringing.
181. **learn:** teach.
183–87. **But here's . . . my lord:** Demanding the right that Scripture bestows on "a man"
  to "leaue father and mother" and "cleaue vnto his wife" (Matthew 19:5, and cf. Mark
  10:7), Desdemona claims to follow a traditionally sanctioned course; but did her
  mother elope with Brabantio?
186. **challenge:** claim.
189. **get:** beget.
193. **For your sake, jewel:** Because of you, my prized possession.
196. **hang clogs:** attach weights as on prisoners; impose stringent restraints.
197. **like yourself:** according to your own real interests or better nature. **lay a sentence:**
  put a proverb in place.

Which, as a grise or step, may help these lovers
Into your favor.
When remedies are past, the griefs are ended   200
By seeing the worst, which late on hopes depended.
To mourn a mischief that is past and gone
Is the next way to draw new mischief on.
What cannot be preserved, when fortune takes,
Patience her injury a mockery makes.   205
The robbed that smiles steals something from the thief;
He robs himself that spends a bootless grief.
BRABANTIO   So let the Turk of Cyprus us beguile:
We lose it not so long as we can smile.
He bears the sentence well that nothing bears,   210
But the free comfort which from thence he hears.
But he bears both the sentence and the sorrow
That, to pay grief, must of poor patience borrow.
These sentences, to sugar or to gall,
Being strong on both sides, are equivocal.   215
But words are words; I never yet did hear
That the bruisèd heart was piercèd through the ear.
I humbly beseech you proceed to th' affairs of state.
DUKE   The Turk with a most mighty preparation
makes for Cyprus. Othello, the fortitude of the place is   220
best known to you; and though we have there a substitute
of most allowed sufficiency, yet opinion, a more
sovereign mistress of effects, throws a more safer
voice on you. You must therefore be content to slubber
the gloss of your new fortunes with this more stubborn   225
and boisterous expedition.
OTHELLO   The tyrant custom, most grave senators,
Hath made the flinty and steel [couch] of war
My thrice-driven bed of down. I do agnize

198. **grise:** stair.
200–07. **When remedies . . . grief:** Four aphorisms reiterate the idea that the patient acceptance of loss eliminates suffering.
208–18. **So let . . . of state:** Responding aphoristically to the duke's aphorisms, Brabantio claims that proverbs are contradictory ("equivocal") and anyway powerless either to cause or cure real grief.
208. **beguile:** Cf. 1.3.66, 155.
217. **piercèd:** either "wounded" or "lanced (for medicinal purposes)."
220. **fortitude:** military strength.
221–22. **substitute . . . sufficiency:** a well-respected deputy.
222–24. **opinion . . . on you:** reputation, a better bet for results, makes you a more secure choice.
224. **slubber:** smear, sully.
225–26. **stubborn and boisterous:** unyielding and harsh.
229. **thrice-driven:** very soft (a fan drives away light feathers from heavy ones).
229–31. **agnize . . . hardness:** "acknowledge (that) I find a natural and ready eagerness (in myself) in (situations of) hardship" (Honigmann).

A natural and prompt alacrity   230
I find in hardness and do undertake
This present wars against the Ottomites.
Most humbly, therefore, bending to your state,
I crave fit disposition for my wife,
Due reference of place, and exhibition,   235
With such accommodation and besort
As levels with her breeding.
DUKE   Why, at her father's.
BRABANTIO   I will not have it so.
OTHELLO   Nor I.
DESDEMONA   Nor would I there reside
To put my father in impatient thoughts   240
By being in his eye. Most gracious duke,
To my unfolding lend your prosperous ear,
And let me find a charter in your voice
T' assist my simpleness.
DUKE   What would you, Desdemona?   245
DESDEMONA   That I love the Moor to live with him,
My downright violence and storm of fortunes
May trumpet to the world. My heart's subdued
Even to the very quality of my lord.
I saw Othello's visage in his mind,   250
And to his honors and his valiant parts
Did I my soul and fortunes consecrate,
So that, dear lords, if I be left behind,
A moth of peace, and he go to the war,
The rites for why I love him are bereft me,   255
And I a heavy interim shall support

---

233. **bending to your state:** deferring to your authority.
234. **crave fit disposition:** seek appropriate arrangements.
235. **Due . . . exhibition:** "proper respect for her place (as my wife) and maintenance" (Honigmann).
236. **accommodation and besort:** adjustment (and probably the modern "housing") and company.
237. **levels with:** befits.
242. **prosperous:** favorable.
243. **charter:** authority.
244. **simpleness:** inexperience.
247. **downright:** utter, absolute. **violence:** "rupture with conventional behaviour" (Honigmann).
249. **Even . . . very:** For these intensifiers, cf. 1.1.85 and note.
250. **saw Othello . . . mind:** subsumed his foul face in his fair mind; saw Othello as he sees himself.
251. **honors and valiant parts:** distinctions and heroic qualities.
254. **moth:** inactive creature (deprived of Othello's attracting light?).
255. **rites:** military rituals; also marital rights (acknowledging sexual interest).
256. **heavy . . . support:** In Desdemona's metaphor, Othello's absence registers as a bodily weight on her.

By his dear absence. Let me go with him.
OTHELLO   Let her have your voice.
Vouch with me, heaven, I therefore beg it not
To please the palate of my appetite,   260
Nor to comply with heat the young affects
In my defunct and proper satisfaction
But to be free and bounteous to her mind;
And heaven defend your good souls that you think
I will your serious and great business scant   265
When she is with me. No, when light-winged toys
Of feathered Cupid seel with wanton dullness
My speculative and officed instrument,
That my disports corrupt and taint my business,
Let housewives make a skillet of my helm,   270
And all indign and base adversities
Make head against my estimation.
DUKE   Be it as you shall privately determine,
Either for her stay or going. Th' affair cries haste,
And speed must answer it.   275
SENATOR   You must away tonight.
OTHELLO   With all my heart.
DUKE   At nine i'th' morning here we'll meet again.
Othello, leave some officer behind,
And he shall our commission bring to you,
And such things else of quality and respect   280
As doth import you.
OTHELLO   So please your grace, my ancient;
A man he is of honesty and trust.
To his conveyance I assign my wife,

261–62. **Nor to comply . . . satisfaction:** This passage has generated a huge amount of
    commentary and, despite the agreement of the two early editions of the text on the
    version printed here, many suggestions for emendation. Editors have, following
    Capell, substituted "me" for "my" (in conjunction with some assertive punctuation—
    see 126 below); or, following Theobald, substituted "distinct" for "defunct"; or (with
    much the same effect as Theobald's emendation) suggested that the primary sense
    of "defunct" as deceased might somehow be displaced by the secondary Latinate
    sense of "discharged." They have also pointed out that **proper** "often means little
    more than *own*" or "personal" (Ridley), though the modern sense of "legitimate" was
    current during the period. All of this activity tries to answer questions raised by the
    passage about the nature of Othello's sexual interest in Desdemona, and about the
    nature of his understanding of that interest; but the answers don't yield a general
    sense of satisfaction, and as Samuel Johnson said, "what made the difficulty, will
    continue to make it."
266–68. **light-winged . . . instrument:** trivial love games blind my judgment. **seel:** cover a
    hawk's face with a hood.
270. **make a skillet of my helm:** transform my helmet to a cooking utensil.
271. **indign:** ignoble.
272. **Make head . . . estimation:** attack my reputation.
280–81. **such . . . import you:** whatever else you require.
283. **conveyance:** escort.

With what else needful your good grace shall think
To be sent after me.
DUKE   Let it be so.   285
Good night to every one. And, noble signior,
If virtue no delighted beauty lack,
Your son-in-law is far more fair than black.

                                    [*Exit* DUKE.]
SENATOR   Adieu, brave Moor; use Desdemona well.
                         [*Exeunt Senators and Officers.*]
BRABANTIO   Look to her, Moor, if thou hast eyes to see: 290
She has deceived her father, and may thee. *Exit* [BRABANTIO].
OTHELLO   My life upon her faith!—Honest Iago,
My Desdemona must I leave to thee.
I prithee let thy wife attend on her,
And bring them after in the best advantage.   295
Come, Desdemona; I have but an hour
Of love, of worldly matter and direction
To spend with thee. We must obey the time.   *Exit Moor and*
                                            DESDEMONA.

RODERIGO   Iago?
IAGO   What say'st thou, noble heart?   300
RODERIGO   What will I do, think'st thou?
IAGO   Why, go to bed and sleep.
RODERIGO   I will incontinently drown my self.
IAGO   If thou dost, I shall never love thee after. Why,
   thou silly gentleman?   305
RODERIGO   It is silliness to live when to live is torment;
   and then have we a prescription to die when death is
   our physician.
IAGO   O villainous! I have looked upon the world
   for four times seven years, and since I could distinguish   310
   betwixt a benefit and an injury, I never found man that
   knew how to love himself. Ere I would say I would
   drown myself for the love of a guinea-hen, I would
   change my humanity with a baboon.
RODERIGO   What should I do? I confess it is my shame   315

---

287. **delighted**: an epithet transferred from "delightful" or "delighting"; "Shakspeare
   often uses the active and passive participles indiscriminately" (Malone).
288. **more fair than black**: i.e., Othello's inner beauty makes him outwardly handsome.
295. **in the best advantage**: at the most appropriate opportunity.
297. **worldly matter and direction**: practical business and advice.
303. **incontinently**: immediately, rashly.
307–08. **prescription . . . physician**: authorization for suicide when death is a cure.
310. **four times seven**: A twenty-eight-year-old Iago coincides with the young (and handsome) figure in Cinthio.
313. **guinea-hen**: woman (with contempt and sexual innuendo).
314. **change**: exchange.

to be so fond, but it is not in my virtue to amend it.
IAGO Virtue? a fig! 'Tis in ourselves that we are
   thus or thus. Our bodies are our gardens, to the which
   our wills are gardeners. So that if we will plant nettles
   or sow lettuce, set hyssop and weed up thyme,   320
   supply it with one gender of herbs or distract it with
   many—either to have it sterile with idleness or manured
   with industry—why, the power and corrigible authority
   of this lies in our wills. If the balance of our lives
   had not one scale of reason to poise another of sensuality,   325
   the blood and baseness of our natures would
   conduct us to most preposterous conclusions. But we
   have reason to cool our raging motions, our carnal
   stings or unbitted lusts; whereof I take this that you
   call love to be a sect or scion.   330
RODERIGO It cannot be.
IAGO It is merely a lust of the blood and a permission
   of the will. Come, be a man! Drown thyself? Drown
   cats and blind puppies. I have professed me thy friend,
   and I confess me knit to thy deserving with cables of   335
   perdurable toughness. I could never better stead thee
   than now. Put money in thy purse. Follow thou the
   wars; defeat thy favor with an usurped beard. I say,
   put money in thy purse. It cannot be long that Desdemona
   should continue her love to the Moor—put money in   340
   thy purse—nor he his to her. It was a violent commencement

316. **virtue:** either power or morality.
317. **Virtue? a fig!:** Iago presumably accompanies this contemptuous dismissal with an obscene gesture—either biting his thumb or thrusting it between two fingers.
319. **wills:** the modern "choice" or "volition," but associated with appetite or sexual drive.
319–20. **nettles . . . thyme:** plants with "complementary qualities of dryness and wetness and so believed to aid the growth of each other" (Sanders); Iago appears to advocate multi(horti)culturalism.
321–22. **supply . . . many:** sustain (our body) with one kind ("gender") or divide and confuse ("distract") it with variety; Iago now appears to advocate horticultural apartheid.
322–23. **either . . . industry:** If "manured" contrasts with "sterile," its primary meaning is "fertilized"; but Iago's rapid-fire speech makes unclear how the binaries in this phrase connect with the contradictory ones earlier.
323. **corrigible authority:** power to correct; perhaps also a power that may be corrected if we change our minds or wills.
325. **poise:** counterbalance.
326. **blood and baseness:** animal passion (literally, passion and animality).
328. **motions:** appetites.
329. **unbitted:** unreined, uncontrolled.
330. **sect or scion:** cutting or offshoot—i.e., subcategory.
332. **merely:** wholly.
335. **knit to thy deserving:** attached to your merit.
336. **perdurable:** everlasting. **stead thee:** serve your needs.
337. **Put money in thy purse:** proverbially, "it's a sure thing," "you can count on it"; also urging Roderigo to sell property for cash (to give Iago to help his cause).
338. **defeat . . . beard:** disguise your face with a false beard.

in her, and thou shalt see an answerable sequestration—
put but money in thy purse. These Moors
are changeable in their wills—fill thy purse with money.
The food that to him now is as luscious as locusts   345
shall be to him shortly as bitter as coloquintida. She
must change for youth: when she is sated with his body,
she will find the errors of her choice. Therefore, put money
in thy purse. If thou wilt needs damn thyself, do
it a more delicate way than drowning—make all the money   350
thou canst. If sanctimony and a frail vow betwixt
an erring barbarian and super-subtle Venetian be
not too hard for my wits and all the tribe of hell, thou
shalt enjoy her. Therefore make money. A pox of drowning
thyself; it is clean out of the way. Seek thou rather   355
to be hanged in compassing thy joy than to be
drowned and go without her.

RODERIGO   Wilt thou be fast to my hopes, if I depend on the
issue?

IAGO   Thou art sure of me—go make money. I have   360
told thee often, and I retell thee again and again, I
hate the Moor. My cause is hearted; thine hath no less
reason. Let us be conjunctive in our revenge against
him. If thou canst cuckold him, thou dost thyself a
pleasure, me a sport. There are many events in the   365
womb of time which will be delivered. Traverse, go,
provide thy money. We will have more of this tomorrow.
Adieu.

RODERIGO   Where shall we meet i'th' morning?

---

342. **answerable sequestration:** equally swift withdrawal of interest.
345. **locusts:** sweet carobs (fruits).
346. **coloquintida:** a sour apple.
347. **change for youth:** drop Othello for a younger lover.
349. **damn thyself:** suicide is a mortal sin.
350. **delicate:** pleasant.
351. **sanctimony . . . vow:** pretended righteousness and a weakly binding promise.
352. **erring barbarian . . . Venetian:** wandering foreigner—a "wheeling stranger / Of here and everywhere" (1.1.133–34)—more specifically, a Berber, someone from Barbary; "erring" also suggests straying, sinning, or just mistaking: as a naive outsider, Othello won't be able to cope with Desdemona's duplicity as a "super-subtle Venetian."
353. **tribe of hell:** society or family of devils; cf. *Merchant of Venice* 1.3.51; "may be an aside" (Honigmann).
354. **A pox of:** "i.e., 'a curse on,' 'to hell with' (*pox* = venereal disease)" (McDonald).
355. **clean out of the way:** totally misdirected.
355–56. **Seek . . . hanged:** Risk execution, but with innuendo: look for sexual satisfaction.
358. **fast:** securely allied, steadfast.
358–59. **depend . . . issue:** persevere in the outcome.
362. **hearted:** deeply motivated.
363. **be conjunctive:** join forces.
366. **Traverse:** Get going, carry on.

IAGO   At my lodging.   370
RODERIGO   I'll be with thee betimes.
IAGO   Go to, farewell. Do you hear, Roderigo?
RODERIGO   I'll sell all my land.   *Exit.*
IAGO   Thus do I ever make my fool my purse;
   For I mine own gained knowledge should profane   375
   If I would time expend with such a snipe
   But for my sport and profit. I hate the Moor,
   And it is thought abroad that 'twixt my sheets
   H'as done my office. I know not if't be true,
   But I for mere suspicion in that kind   380
   Will do as if for surety. He holds me well;
   The better shall my purpose work on him.
   Cassio's a proper man. Let me see now . . .
   To get his place and to plume up my will
   In double knavery—how? how? Let's see . . .   385
   After some time, to abuse Othello's ears
   That he is too familiar with his wife.
   He hath a person and a smooth dispose
   To be suspected, framed to make women false.
   The Moor is of a free and open nature   390
   That thinks men honest that but seem to be so,
   And will as tenderly be led by th' nose
   As asses are. . . .
   I have't! It is engendered! Hell and night
   Must bring this monstrous birth to the world's light.   *Exit.* 395

ACT 2 SCENE 1

Enter MONTANO *and two Gentlemen [one above].*

MONTANO   What from the cape can you discern at sea?
FIRST GENTLEMAN   Nothing at all; it is a high-wrought flood.

371. **betimes:** early.
372. **Go to:** colloquial agreement: "Okay."
374. **ever . . . purse:** always use fools for my advantage.
378. **thought abroad:** widely rumoured.
379. **done my office:** done my job, my business; had sex with Iago's wife.
380. **in that kind:** of that sort of thing.
381. **holds me well:** has a good opinion of me.
384. **plume up:** puff up my feathers, preen.
387–88. **he . . . his . . . He:** Many editors are at pains to identify these pronouns respectively as Cassio, Othello, and Cassio. Presumably, the references are uncertain. See 1.1.3 and 1.1.65 and notes.
388. **person . . . dispose:** Cassio is good-looking and charming.
390. **free and open:** generously trusting.
   1. **What . . . sea:** addressed to the lookout position—presumably the same projecting upper stage where Brabantio appeared at 1.1.78.
   2. **high-wrought flood:** stormy sea.

    I cannot 'twixt the heaven and the main
    Descry a sail.

MONTANO   Methinks the wind hath spoke aloud at land;   5
    A fuller blast ne'er shook our battlements;
    If it hath ruffianed so upon the sea,
    What ribs of oak, when mountains melt on them,
    Can hold the mortise? What shall we hear of this?

SECOND GENTLEMAN   A segregation of the Turkish fleet: 10
    For do but stand upon the foaming shore,
    The chidden billow seems to pelt the clouds;
    The wind-shaked surge, with high and monstrous mane,
    Seems to cast water on the burning Bear,
    And quench the guards of th' ever-fixèd pole.   15
    I never did like molestation view
    On the enchafèd flood.

MONTANO   If that the Turkish fleet
    Be not ensheltered and embayed, they are drowned;
    It is impossible to bear it out.

        Enter a Third Gentleman.

THIRD GENTLEMAN   News, lads! Our wars are done.   20
    The desperate tempest hath so banged the Turks
    That their designment halts. A noble ship of Venice
    Hath seen a grievous wrack and sufferance
    On most part of their fleet.

MONTANO   How? Is this true?

THIRD GENTLEMAN   The ship is here put in,   25
    A Veronnesa. Michael Cassio,
    Lieutenant to the warlike Moor, Othello,
    Is come on shore; the Moor himself at sea,
    And is in full commission here for Cyprus.

---

7. **ruffianed:** gusted fiercely (acted like a ruffian).
8–9. **What ribs . . . mortise?:** What hull's curved timbers can avoid splitting under such huge waves' pressure?
10. **segregation:** dispersal.
12. **chidden:** rebuked by the wind or repelled from the shore; also "chiding" or "raging" (see "delighted," note to 1.3.287).
13. **high and monstrous mane:** i.e., like a huge animal's neck; punning on "main" (ocean).
14–15. **Bear . . . pole:** two brightly shining ("burning") stars in Ursa Minor, represented as guarding the polestar.
16. **like molestation:** such turmoil.
17. **enchafèd flood:** raging sea.
19. **bear it out:** endure the storm (without protection).
21. **desperate:** dire, depriving of all hope.
22. **designment halts:** projects is crippled.
23. **grievous . . . sufferance:** experienced extensive damage.
26. **Veronnesa:** either a certain kind of vessel or a ship from Verona.
29. **is in . . . Cyprus:** "is (heading) for Cyprus with full delegated authority here" (Honigmann).

MONTANO I am glad on't—'tis a worthy governor.   30
THIRD GENTLEMAN But this same Cassio, though he speak of
    comfort
  Touching the Turkish loss, yet he looks sadly
  And prays the Moor be safe; for they were parted
  With foul and violent tempest.
MONTANO   Pray heavens he be,
  For I have served him, and the man commands   35
  Like a full soldier. Let's to the seaside—ho!—
  As well to see the vessel that's come in
  As to throw out our eyes for brave Othello,
  Even till we make the main and th' aerial blue,
  An indistinct regard.
THIRD GENTLEMAN   Come, let's do so;   40
  For every minute is expectancy
  Of more arrivancy.

        Enter CASSIO.

CASSIO Thanks, you the valiant of the warlike isle,
  That so approve the Moor. O, let the heavens
  Give him defence against the elements,   45
  For I have lost him on a dangerous sea.
MONTANO Is he well shipped?
CASSIO His bark is stoutly timbered, and his pilot
  Of very expert and approved allowance;
  Therefore my hopes, not surfeited to death,   50
  Stand in bold cure.
[VOICES] *within.*   A sail! a sail! a sail!
CASSIO What noise?
GENTLEMAN The town is empty; on the brow o' th' sea
  Stand ranks of people, and they cry "A sail!"
CASSIO My hopes do shape him for the governor.   *A shot.* 55
SECOND GENTLEMAN They do discharge their shot of courtesy:
  Our friends at least.
CASSIO   I pray you, sir, go forth
  And give us truth who 'tis that is arrived.

30. **I am...governor:** "ungrudging praise from the man replaced as governor" (Honigmann).
31–32. **speak...Touching:** brings comforting news regarding.
32. **sadly:** solemnly, worriedly.
39–40. **make...regard:** become unable to distinguish sea from sky.
43–44. **Thanks...Moor:** As Othello's lieutenant (= placeholder), Cassio is grateful for Montano's regard for Othello.
44. **approve:** esteem.
49. **of very expert...allowance:** acknowledged to be well experienced and competent.
50–51. **my hopes...cure:** Cassio is hopeful but not overly optimistic.
56. **shot of courtesy:** "cannon shot, in friendly salute (off stage)" (Honigmann).
57. **at least:** an allied ship, if not necessarily Othello's (as Cassio had hoped).

SECOND GENTLEMAN   I shall.   *Exit.*
MONTANO   But, good lieutenant, is your general wived?   60
CASSIO   Most fortunately: he hath achieved a maid
  That paragons description and wild fame,
  One that excels the quirks of blazoning pens,
  And in th' essential vesture of creation
  Does tire the ingener.

      Enter Second Gentleman.

                    How now? Who has put in?   65
SECOND GENTLEMAN   'Tis one Iago, ancient to the general.
CASSIO   He's had most favorable and happy speed:
  Tempests themselves, high seas and howling winds,
  The guttered rocks and congregated sands,
  Traitors ensteeped to enclog the guiltless keel,   70
  As having sense of beauty, do omit
  Their mortal natures, letting go safely by
  The divine Desdemona.
MONTANO   What is she?
CASSIO   She that I spake of, our great captain's captain,
  Left in the conduct of the bold Iago,   75
  Whose footing here anticipates our thoughts
  A se'night's speed. Great Jove, Othello guard,
  And swell his sail with thine own powerful breath,
  That he may bless this bay with his tall ship,
  Make love's quick pants in Desdemona's arms,   80
  Give renewed fire to our extincted spirits,
  And bring all Cyprus comfort!

      Enter DESDEMONA, IAGO, RODERIGO, *and* EMILIA.

               O, behold!

---

60. wived: "not quite the same as 'married'. Cf. 3.4.195 [191], 'womaned'." (Honigmann).
61. achieved: "won (chivalric term for accomplishing a quest)" (Neill). Cf. "my achievements mock me" in *Troilus and Cressida* (4.2a.69).
62. paragons . . . fame: surpasses description and extravagant rumor.
63. quirks of blazoning pens: ingenious poetic descriptions; *blasons* are conventional lyric poems that catalog the mistress's beautiful traits.
64–65. th' essential vesture . . . ingener: her own natural excellence exhausts (and adorns—"tire" = attire) anyone contriving praise—an elaborately courtly renunciation of elaborate courtliness.
69. guttered: furrowed, jagged. **congregated sands:** sandbanks.
70. ensteeped . . . keel: submerged to obstruct the innocent (unknowing) ship.
71. omit: renounce.
72. mortal: deadly, lethal; more courtliness: like Orpheus's music, Desdemona's divine beauty tames the natural world into suspending its threat to a higher (human) nature.
74. captain's captain: As Othello rules the army, so Desdemona rules Othello.
76–77. Whose . . . speed: whose arrival occurs a week earlier than we expected.
77–82. Great Jove . . . comfort: As Cassio imagines it, Othello and Desdemona's lovemaking revitalizes "all Cyprus." **79. tall:** tall-masted. **80. quick:** "rapid" but also "alive" and "imparting life." **81. extincted:** extinguished.

The riches of the ship is come on shore.
You men of Cyprus, let her have your knees.
Hail to thee, lady, and the grace of heaven,   85
Before, behind thee, and on every hand
Enwheel thee round.

DESDEMONA   I thank you, valiant Cassio.
What tidings can you tell me of my lord?

CASSIO   He is not yet arrived, nor know I aught
But that he's well and will be shortly here.   90

DESDEMONA   O, but I fear!—How lost you company?

CASSIO   The great contention of sea and skies
Parted our fellowship.

[VOICES] *within*.   A sail! a sail!   [*A shot*.]

CASSIO   But hark—a sail.

GENTLEMAN   They give this greeting to the citadel;
This likewise is a friend.

CASSIO   See for the news. [*Exit Gentleman*.] 95
Good ancient, you are welcome.
[*To* EMILIA.]   Welcome, mistress.
      [*Kisses* EMILIA.]
Let it not gall your patience, good Iago,
That I extend my manners. 'Tis my breeding
That gives me this bold show of courtesy.

IAGO   Sir, would she give you so much of her lips   100
As of her tongue she oft bestows on me,
You would have enough.

DESDEMONA   Alas, she has no speech.

IAGO   In faith, too much:
I find it still when I have leave to sleep.
Marry, before your ladyship, I grant,   105
She puts her tongue a little in her heart
And chides with thinking.

EMILIA   You have little cause to say so.

IAGO   Come on! come on! You are pictures out of door,

---

84. **let her have your knees:** bow to her.
85. **Hail . . . lady:** "An echo of 'Hail Mary', reinforced by kneeling and 'the grace of heaven'?" (Honigmann).
87. **enwheel:** encircle.
92. **contention:** four syllables (see note to 1.1.16).
97. **gall your patience:** vex your peace.
98. **extend . . . manners:** express or enlarge upon my greeting. **breeding:** upbringing, training, customary behavior.
100–01. **lips . . . tongue:** Iago's words slip glibly between the literal "kissing" and the metaphorical "speaking" and "scolding."
104. **leave:** permission (implicitly from her).
106–07. **She puts . . . thinking:** She berates me even when she is silent.
109. **You are pictures out of door:** You (women) are ideal images (pretty and silent) in public.

Bells in your parlors, wildcats in your kitchens,   110
Saints in your injuries, devils being offended,
Players in your huswifery, and huswives in your beds.

DESDEMONA   O, fie upon thee, slanderer!

IAGO   Nay, it is true, or else I am a Turk:
You rise to play and go to bed to work.   115

EMILIA   You shall not write my praise.

IAGO   No, let me not.

DESDEMONA   What wouldst write of me, if thou shouldst
praise me?

IAGO   O, gentle lady, do not put me to't,
For I am nothing if not critical.

DESDEMONA   Come on, assay. There's one gone to the harbor?   120

IAGO   Ay, madam.

DESDEMONA   I am not merry, but I do beguile
The thing I am by seeming otherwise.—
Come, how wouldst thou praise me?

IAGO   I am about it, but indeed my invention   125
Comes from my pate as birdlime does from frieze:
It plucks out brains and all. But my muse labors,
And thus she is delivered:
If she be fair and wise, fairness and wit,
The one's for use, the other useth it.   130

DESDEMONA   Well praised! How if she be black and witty?

IAGO   *If she be black, and thereto have a wit,*
She'll find a white that shall her blackness fit.

DESDEMONA   Worse and worse!

EMILIA   How if fair and foolish?   135

IAGO   *She never yet was foolish that was fair,*

---

110. **bells . . . kitchens:** noisy and enraged in your house.
111. **Saint . . . injuries:** looking innocent of the harms you inflict.
112. **Players . . . huswifery:** indifferent to (faking interest in) domestic responsibilities.
     huswives: pronounced "hussifs"; can slip from neutral ("housewives") to pejorative ("hussies").
114. **I am a Turk:** "I'm a monkey's uncle" but stronger: "turn Turk" (like "go native") evokes anxiety about reverting to the savagery of infidels.
115. **play:** "deceive" and "engage in sport" (sexual innuendo); with "players" a theatrical metaphor. **go . . . work:** i.e., sex is your real and serious interest.
120. **assay:** try.
122–23. **beguile . . . am:** distract myself from worrying about Othello (?); sometimes represented as an aside. Cf. 1.3.66, 155, and 208 note.
126. **pate:** head. **birdlime:** gummy stuff used to trap birds. **frieze:** coarse fabric.
129. **fair:** blonde and light-complexioned (conventional signs of female beauty at the time). **wit:** intelligence, cunning.
130. **The one . . . it:** attractiveness has value, cleverness cashes it in.
131. **black:** dark-complexioned or dark-haired—hence unattractive.
133. **white:** man (punning on "wight"), fair man (to complement her foul or black identity); center of a target or bull's eye (variously applicable sexual metaphors).

For even her folly helped her to an heir.

DESDEMONA   These are old fond paradoxes, to make fools
  laugh i' th' alehouse. What miserable praise hast thou
  for her that's foul and foolish?   140

IAGO   *There's none so foul and foolish thereunto,*
  But does foul pranks which fair and wise ones do.

DESDEMONA   O, heavy ignorance! Thou praisest the worst
  best. But what praise couldst thou bestow on a deserving
  woman indeed? One that in the authority of her   145
  merit did justly put on the vouch of very malice itself.

IAGO   *She that was ever fair, and never proud,*
  Had tongue at will, and yet was never loud,
  Never lacked gold, and yet went never gay,
  Fled from her wish, and yet said "now I may."   150
  She that, being angered, her revenge being nigh,
  Bade her wrong stay, and her displeasure fly.
  She that in wisdom never was so frail
  To change the cod's head for the salmon's tail.
  She that could think, and ne'er disclose her mind,   155
  See suitors following, and not look behind:
  She was a wight (if ever such wights were) . . .

DESDEMONA   To do what?

IAGO   *To suckle fools and chronicle small beer.*

DESDEMONA   O, most lame and impotent conclusion! Do   160
  not learn of him, Emilia, though he be thy husband.
  How say you, Cassio? Is he not a most profane and liberal
  counselor?

CASSIO   He speaks home, madam. You may relish
  him more in the soldier than in the scholar.   165

IAGO [*Aside.*]   He takes her by the palm. Ay, well said, whisper!
  With as little a web as this will I ensnare as great

---

137. *folly*: foolishness, sexual indiscretion.
138–39. *old . . . alehouse*: i.e., trite barroom humor. The italics for Iago's misogynist
  jokes, reproduced from the folio text, may signal a stylized delivery—as of familiar
  comic routines.
142. *pranks*: "sexual tricks" (Neill).
146. **justly put on the vouch**: truly deserve or encourage the approval.
149. *gay*: elegantly dressed.
150. *Fled . . . I may*: renounced desire, while knowing herself capable of acting on it.
152. *Bade . . . fly*: commanded her (sense of) injury to restrain itself and her irritation to
  disappear.
154. *cod's head . . . salmon's tail*: unclear, but presumably another example of the self-
  restraint exercised by "a deserving woman indeed" (lines 144–45).
159. *To suckle . . . beer*: for breeding and trivial domestic chores.
162. **profane and liberal**: nasty and unrestrained.
164. **home**: bluntly. **relish**: appreciate, take delight in.
165. **more . . . scholar**: i.e., more for his directness than for his courtliness.
166. **said**: done.

a fly as Cassio. Ay, smile upon her, do! I will gyve thee
in thine own courtship.—You say true, 'tis so indeed.
—If such tricks as these strip you out of your   170
lieutenantry, it had been better you had not kissed your three
fingers so oft, which now again you are most apt to play
the sir in. Very good! well kissed and excellent courtesy!
—'Tis so indeed.—Yet again, your fingers to your lips?
Would they were clyster pipes for your sake!   175
Trumpets within.   The Moor! I know his trumpet.

CASSIO   'Tis truly so.

DESDEMONA   Let's meet him and receive him.

CASSIO   Lo, where he comes.

     Enter OTHELLO *and Attendants.*

OTHELLO   O, my fair warrior!

DESDEMONA   My dear Othello!   180

OTHELLO   It gives me wonder great as my content
To see you here before me. O! my soul's joy,
If after every tempest come such calms,
May the winds blow till they have wakened death,
And let the laboring bark climb hills of seas,   185
Olympus-high, and duck again as low
As hell's from heaven! If it were now to die,
'Twere now to be most happy; for I fear
My soul hath her content so absolute
That not another comfort like to this   190
Succeeds in unknown fate.

DESDEMONA   The heavens forbid
But that our loves and comforts should increase
Even as our days do grow.

OTHELLO   Amen to that, sweet powers!

---

168. **gyve:** shackle.
170. **tricks:** ritualized gestures—i.e., the kisses Cassio blows to Desdemona.
172. **now again:** Either Cassio repeats his courtly gestures with Desdemona, or Iago is think-
      ing back to Cassio's earlier gentlemanly behavior ("play the sir") in kissing Emilia
      (line 98).
173. **courtesy:** along with "courtship" (line 169), may echo the "manners" and "breeding"
      by which Cassio earlier justified kissing Emilia (98).
175. **clyster pipes:** used to administer rectal enemas or vaginal douches.
176. **his trumpet:** the "recognizable call" or "tucket" associated with "distinguished people"
      (Ridley); also punning on "his strumpet" ("his whore").
180. **warrior:** remembering her desire to share in "the rites" (1.3.255) of his military
      occupation.
187. **If it were now to die:** If death came to me now; "die" is a common pun for "have sex."
191. **succeeds:** follows.
192. **comforts:** pluralizes Othello's term (line 190), variously glossed as "satisfaction,"
      "delight," "gladness," and "relief (after distress)"; a word loaded with reiterated reso-
      nance (cf. 31, 82, and 205).

I cannot speak enough of this content;
It stops me here; it is too much of joy.   195
And this, and this—

> *They kiss.—*

            the greatest discords be
That e'er our hearts shall make!
IAGO [*Aside.*]   O, you are well tuned now;
But I'll set down the pegs that make this music,
As honest as I am.
OTHELLO   Come, let us to the castle.
News, friends; our wars are done. The Turks are drowned.   200
How does my old acquaintance of this isle?—
Honey, you shall be well desired in Cyprus;
I have found great love amongst them. O, my sweet,
I prattle out of fashion, and I dote
In mine own comforts. I prithee, good Iago,   205
Go to the bay and disembark my coffers.
Bring thou the master to the citadel;
He is a good one, and his worthiness
Does challenge much respect. Come, Desdemona;
Once more well met at Cyprus.   210

> *Exit* OTHELLO *and* DESDEMONA
> [*and all but* IAGO *and* RODERIGO].

IAGO   Do thou meet me presently at the harbor.
Come thither. If thou be'st valiant—as they say base men,
being in love, have then a nobility in their natures
more than is native to them—list me. The lieutenant
tonight watches on the court of guard. First I must tell   215
thee this: Desdemona is directly in love with him.
RODERIGO   With him? Why, 'tis not possible.
IAGO   Lay thy finger thus, and let thy soul be instructed.
Mark me with what violence she first loved
the Moor, but for bragging and telling her fantastical   220

194. **content:** another loaded and reiterated word (cf. lines 181, 189, and 292), with an
    erotic charge hard to identify exactly.
198. **set down the pegs:** "slacken (the strings or pegs of a musical instrument)" (Honig-
    mann); hence "untune" and perhaps implying "debase."
199. **As honest as I am:** for all his supposed "honesty."
201. **my old acquaintance:** addressed to Montano (cf. line 35), or acknowledging a more
    generally communal acquaintanceship.
202. **well desired:** sought after with much pleasure.
204. **out of fashion:** in an inappropriate manner.
206. **disembark my coffers:** unload my trunks.
207. **master:** captain.
209. **challenge:** command, merit.
214. **list:** listen to.
215. **watches on the court of guard:** "is on duty with the corps de garde, the patrol
    assigned to headquarters" (McDonald).
218. **thus:** on your lips; i.e., be quiet.
219. **violence:** intensity, compare Desdemona's "downright violence" (1.3.247).
220. **but:** only, wholly.

lies. To love him still for prating, let not thy discreet
heart think it. Her eye must be fed. And what delight
shall she have to look on the devil? When the blood
is made dull with the act of sport, there should be—
again to enflame it, and to give satiety a fresh appetite—   225
loveliness in favor, sympathy in years, manners
and beauties, all which the Moor is defective in. Now
for want of these required conveniences, her delicate
tenderness will find itself abused, begin to heave the
gorge, disrelish and abhor the Moor. Very nature will   230
instruct her in it and compel her to some second choice.
Now, sir, this granted—as it is a most pregnant and unforced
position—who stands so eminent in the degree of
this fortune as Cassio does? a knave very voluble, no
further conscionable than in putting on the mere form   235
of civil and humane seeming for the better compass
of his salt and most hidden loose affection. Why none!
why none! A slipper and subtle knave, a finder of occasion,
that has an eye can stamp and counterfeit advantages,
though true advantage never present itself.   240
A devilish knave! Besides, the knave is handsome, young
and hath all those requisites in him that folly and green
minds look after. A pestilent complete knave! And the
woman hath found him already.

RODERIGO   I cannot believe that in her; she's full of most   245
blessed condition.

IAGO   Blessed fig's-end! The wine she drinks is
made of grapes. If she had been blessed, she would

221. **discreet:** judicious.
223. **the devil:** conventionally represented as foul and black.
223–24. **When . . . sport:** When (repeated or habitual) sexual activity jades desire.
226. **loveliness in favor:** good looks. **sympathy:** similarity.
228. **conveniences:** similarities.
228–29. **delicate tenderness:** exquisite sensibility, refined appetite.
229. **abused:** deceived; disappointed.
229–30. **heave the gorge:** vomit.
230. **Very nature:** Nature itself, basic instinct.
232–33. **pregnant and unforced position:** self-evident and plausible claim.
233–34. **stands . . . as:** is better positioned to receive the benefits of this situation than.
234. **voluble:** glib, smooth-talking.
234–36. **no . . . seeming:** whose conscience extends only to outward appearances—the
    manners, not the morals.
236–37. **for . . . affection:** to improve the odds of satisfying his covert lust.
238. **slipper:** slippery. **finder of occasion:** opportunist.
239–40. **has . . . present itself:** can fraudulently manufacture advantages where no real
    or honest ones exist.
242. **green:** inexperienced.
243. **look after:** covet.
245–46. **full . . . condition:** most divinely virtuous.
247. **Blessed fig's-end:** See 1.3.317 and note.
247–48. **wine . . . grapes:** Continuing to disclaim ideas of religious transcendence, Iago
    insists that the wine is never transformed into the blood of Christ, as in the sacra-
    ment: Desdemona is only human—that is, libidinous.

never have loved the Moor. Blessed pudding! Didst thou
not see her paddle with the palm of his hand? Didst not   250
mark that?

RODERIGO   Yes, that I did, but that was but courtesy.

IAGO   Lechery, by this hand! an index and obscure
prologue to the history of lust and foul thoughts.
They met so near with their lips that their breaths   255
embraced together. Villainous thoughts, Roderigo: when
these mutualities so marshal the way, hard at hand
comes the master and main exercise, th' incorporate
conclusion. Pish! But, sir, be you ruled by me. I have
brought you from Venice. Watch you tonight. For   260
the command, I'll lay't upon you. Cassio knows you
not. I'll not be far from you. Do you find some occasion
to anger Cassio, either by speaking too loud or
tainting his discipline, or from what other course
you please, which the time shall more favorably minister.   265

RODERIGO   Well.

IAGO   Sir, he's rash and very sudden in choler and
haply may strike at you. Provoke him that he may; for
even out of that will I cause these of Cyprus to mutiny;
whose qualification shall come into no true taste again   270
but by the displanting of Cassio. So shall you
have a shorter journey to your desires by the means I
shall then have to prefer them, and the impediment
most profitably removed without the which there were
no expectation of our prosperity.   275

RODERIGO   I will do this if you can bring it to any opportunity.

---

249. **pudding:** sausage, blood pudding—continuing to sexualize the spiritual.
250. **paddle with:** caress. **his hand:** "i.e., Cassio's" (Mowat and Werstine). See 1.3.387–88 and note.
253. **index:** table of contents. **obscure:** concealed.
254. **history:** story, narrative.
257–59. **mutualities . . . conclusion:** reciprocally flirtatious gestures inaugurate a sequence leading irresistibly to full sexual intercourse. **incorporate:** bodily.
259. **Pish:** an expression of revulsion.
260. **Watch you:** Join the security patrol.
260–61. **For . . . you:** I'll arrange for you to have authority.
264. **tainting his discipline:** impugning his military professionalism; sullying his self-control.
266. **Well:** Okay.
267. **sudden in choler:** short-tempered.
268. **haply:** perhaps.
270–71. **whose . . . Cassio:** i.e., the only way to restore the populace to sober obedience is by eliminating ("displanting") Cassio. **qualification:** pacification or moderation (with "taste," a drinking metaphor: dilution).
273. **prefer:** advance.

IAGO   I warrant thee. Meet me by and by at the citadel.
    I must fetch his necessaries ashore. Farewell.
RODERIGO   Adieu.   *Exit.*
IAGO   That Cassio loves her, I do well believ't;   280
    That she loves him, 'tis apt and of great credit.
    The Moor, howbeit that I endure him not,
    Is of a constant, loving, noble nature,
    And I dare think he'll prove to Desdemona
    A most dear husband. Now I do love her too,   285
    Not out of absolute lust (though peradventure
    I stand accountant for as great a sin),
    But partly led to diet my revenge,
    For that I do suspect the lusty Moor
    Hath leaped into my seat—the thought whereof   290
    Doth, like a poisonous mineral, gnaw my inwards,
    And nothing can or shall content my soul
    Till I am evened with him, wife for wife;
    Or failing so, yet that I put the Moor
    At least into a jealousy so strong   295
    That judgment cannot cure; which thing to do,
    If this poor trash of Venice, whom I trace
    For his quick hunting, stand the putting on,
    I'll have our Michael Cassio on the hip,
    Abuse him to the Moor in the right garb   300
    (For I fear Cassio with my nightcap too),
    Make the Moor thank me, love me and reward me
    For making him egregiously an ass,
    And practicing upon his peace and quiet
    Even to madness. 'Tis here, but yet confused;   305
    Knavery's plain face is never seen till used.   *Exit.*

277. **I warrant thee:** You have my word.
278. **his:** "i.e., Othello's" (Mowat and Werstine). See 1.3.387–88 and note.
281. **apt . . . credit:** likely and very plausible.
282. **howbeit that:** although.
287. **stand accountant for:** may be accused of.
288. **diet:** feed.
290. **leaped . . . seat:** i.e., "jumped" my wife.
291. **gnaw my inwards:** eat my guts.
297–98. **trace . . . hunting:** pursue in order to goad to an even faster (sexual) chase.
298. **stand the putting on:** is up to my incitement.
299. **on the hip:** in my power (a wrestling term).
300. **Abuse . . . garb:** slander him in an appropriate (effective) fashion.
301. **with my nightcap:** "wearing my pajamas"—i.e., doing my bedroom job.
303. **egregiously an ass:** extremely foolish.
304. **practicing upon:** plotting against.
305. **Even to madness:** i.e., not stopping until Othello is mad (elliptical; the literal sense may suggest that the madness belongs to Iago's intention rather than effect).
305–06. **'Tis here . . . till used:** i.e., I'm not sure how this will work, but villains never know what they're doing until they're actually doing it.

ACT 2 SCENE 2

Enter OTHELLO's HERALD *with a proclamation.*

HERALD [*Reads.*]   "It is Othello's pleasure, our noble and valiant
   general, that upon certain tidings now arrived
   importing the mere perdition of the Turkish fleet,
   every man put himself into triumph—some to dance,
   some to make bonfires, each man to what sport and   5
   revels his addition leads him. For besides these beneficial
   news, it is the celebration of his nuptial." So
   much was his pleasure should be proclaimed. All offices
   are open, and there is full liberty of feasting from this
   present hour of five till the bell have told eleven. Heaven   10
   bless the isle of Cyprus and our noble general Othello!   *Exit.*

[ACT 2 SCENE 3]

Enter OTHELLO, DESDEMONA, CASSIO, *and Attendants.*

OTHELLO   Good Michael, look you to the guard tonight.
   Let's teach ourselves that honorable stop,
   Not to outsport discretion.
CASSIO   Iago hath direction what to do;
   But notwithstanding, with my personal eye   5
   Will I look to't.
OTHELLO   Iago is most honest.
   Michael, goodnight. Tomorrow with your earliest
   Let me have speech with you.—Come, my dear love.
   The purchase made, the fruits are to ensue,
   That profit's yet to come 'tween me and you.   10
   Goodnight.   *Exit* [OTHELLO, DESDEMONA *and Attendants*].
          Enter IAGO.
CASSIO   Welcome, Iago; we must to the watch.
IAGO   Not this hour, lieutenant; 'tis not yet ten o'th' clock.
   Our general cast us thus early for the love of his Desdemona,

3. **mere perdition:** complete loss.
4. **put . . . triumph:** celebrate.
6. **his addition leads him:** is appropriate to his status.
8. **offices:** kitchens.
10. **told:** tolled.
1. **look you to:** supervise.
2. **honorable stop:** commendable restraint.
3. **outsport discretion:** celebrate beyond self-possession.
7. **with your earliest:** as early as possible.
9–10. **The purchase . . . and you:** Othello's statement raises the question of whether
   the marriage has been consummated.
13. **cast:** got rid of, dismissed.
14–15. **thus early and not yet:** Iago's phrases put a different spin on Othello's "earliest"
   (line 7) and "yet to come" (10).

who let us not therefore blame: he hath not yet made wanton   15
the night with her, and she is sport for Jove.

CASSIO   She's a most exquisite lady.

IAGO   And, I'll warrant her, full of game.

CASSIO   Indeed, she's a most fresh and delicate creature.

IAGO   What an eye she has! Methinks it sounds a parley to
provocation.   20

CASSIO   An inviting eye; and yet, methinks, right modest.

IAGO   And when she speaks, is it not an alarum to love?

CASSIO   She is indeed perfection.

IAGO   Well, happiness to their sheets! Come, lieutenant,
I have a stoup of wine, and here without are a   25
brace of Cyprus gallants that would fain have a measure
to the health of black Othello.

CASSIO   Not tonight, good Iago. I have very poor
and unhappy brains for drinking. I could well wish
courtesy would invent some other custom of entertainment.   30

IAGO   O, they are our friends; but one cup; I'll
drink for you.

CASSIO   I have drunk but one cup tonight, and that
was craftily qualified too; and behold what innovation
it makes here. I am unfortunate in the infirmity and   35
dare not task my weakness with any more.

IAGO   What, man! 'Tis a night of revels—the gallants
desire it.

CASSIO   Where are they?

IAGO   Here at the door; I pray you call them in.   40

CASSIO   I'll do't, but it dislikes me.   *Exit.*

IAGO   If I can fasten but one cup upon him
With that which he hath drunk tonight already,
He'll be as full of quarrel and offense
As my young mistress' dog. Now my sick fool, Roderigo,   45
Whom love hath turned almost the wrong side out,

18–19. **game:** can mean "spirit" but carries a nasty sexual innuendo, which Cassio's
agreement ("Indeed") suggests he does not (or pretends not to) understand.
20–22. **parley and alarum:** military signals; i.e., Desdemona solicits sexual advances.
25. **stoup:** "tankard (of varying sizes)" (Honigmann); "large drinking vessel" (Mowat and
Werstine). **without:** outside.
26. **brace:** couple. **have a measure:** drink.
29. **unhappy:** unfortunate.
30. **courtesy . . . entertainment:** social convention determined some other form of
celebration.
34. **craftily qualified:** carefully diluted.
34–35. **behold . . . here:** Cassio points to some sign of transformation ("innovation"),
perhaps his unsteady legs.
41. **it dislikes me:** I'd prefer not.
45. **my young mistress':** referring generically (= "milady's") to a girl's untrained dog.

To Desdemona hath tonight caroused
Potations pottle-deep; and he's to watch.
Three else of Cyprus (noble swelling spirits,
That hold their honors in a wary distance,   50
The very elements of this warlike isle)
Have I tonight flustered with flowing cups,
And they watch too. Now, 'mongst this flock of drunkards
Am I to put our Cassio in some action
That may offend the isle. But here they come.   55

    Enter CASSIO, MONTANO *and Gentlemen* [*with wine*].

If consequence do but approve my dream,
My boat sails freely, both with wind and stream.
CASSIO   'Fore God, they have given me a rouse already.
MONTANO   Good faith, a little one; not past a pint, as I am a
   soldier.   60
IAGO   Some wine, ho!

    [*Sings.*]

        And let me the cannikin clink, clink,
        And let me the cannikin clink.
        A soldier's a man,
        O man's life's but a span,
        Why then, let a soldier drink.   65

Some wine, boys!
CASSIO   'Fore God, an excellent song!
IAGO   I learned it in England, where indeed they are
   most potent in potting. Your Dane, your Germans,   70
   and your swag-bellied Hollander—drink, ho!—are
   nothing to your English.
CASSIO   Is your Englishman so exquisite in his drinking?

---

48. **Potations pottle-deep:** drafts "to the bottom of a half-gallon tankard"
    (Honigmann).
49. **else:** others. **swelling:** puffed up, ambitious.
50. **hold . . . distance:** i.e., are careful to protect—and thus aggressive in countering any
    threat to—reputation.
51. **very elements . . . isle:** i.e., they capture the essential edginess of the embattled
    Cypriot situation.
56. **consequence . . . dream:** matters proceed as I hope.
58. **rouse:** drink.
62–66. **And let . . . drink:** "a popular drinking song" (Neill). 62. **cannikin:** "small drink-
    ing can; *-kin* is diminutive" (Honigmann).
65. **but a span:** short.
70. **most potent in potting:** big drinkers.
71. **swag-bellied:** fat-gutted, beer-bellied.
70–71. **Your . . . your . . . your:** i.e., the typical Dane et al. Wine, song, and soldierly
    camaraderie channel thought into national stereotypes.
73. **exquisite:** refined. Cassio sees drinking as a courtly accomplishment.

IAGO   Why, he drinks you with facility your Dane
    dead drunk. He sweats not to overthrow your Almaine.   75
    He gives your Hollander a vomit ere the next
    pottle can be filled.
CASSIO   To the health of our general!
MONTANO   I am for it, lieutenant, and I'll do you justice.
IAGO   O sweet England!   80

        [*Sings.*]

            King Stephen was and-a worthy peer,
                His breeches cost him but a crown;
            He held them sixpence all too dear,
                With that he called the tailor lown.
            He was a wight of high renown,   85
                And thou art but of low degree;
            'Tis pride that pulls the country down,
                And take thy auld cloak about thee.
    Some wine, ho!
CASSIO   'Fore God, this is a more exquisite song than the other.   90
IAGO   Will you hear't again?
CASSIO   No, for I hold him to be unworthy of his place
    that does those things. Well, God's above all, and
    there be souls must be saved, and there be souls must
    not be saved.   95
IAGO   It's true, good lieutenant.
CASSIO   For mine own part—no offense to the general,
    nor any man of quality—I hope to be saved.
IAGO   And so do I too, lieutenant.
CASSIO   Ay; but by your leave, not before me. The   100
    lieutenant is to be saved before the ancient. Let's have
    no more of this. Let's to our affairs. God forgive us our
    sins. Gentlemen, let's look to our business. Do not
    think, gentlemen, I am drunk. This is my ancient, this
    is my right hand, and this is my left. I am not drunk   105
    now. I can stand well enough, and I speak well enough.
GENTLEMAN   Excellent well.

---

75. **your Almaine:** i.e., the typical German.
79. **I am . . . justice:** I'll drink to that, and I'll match you glass for glass.
81–88. Adapted from an early ballad, "retaining the character of the original"—its "impatience with privilege" and "'class' feeling. We may assume that Shakespeare's audience was familiar with the ballad" (Honigmann).
84. **lown:** rogue.
88. **auld:** old.
92–93. **unworthy . . . things:** The referent for "those things" is unclear. Cassio's indefinite anxiety about self-betrayal resonates in allusions, just following, to sin, forgiveness, and salvation.
101. **ancient:** Cf. 1.1.30.

CASSIO   Why, very well then. You must not think, then,
   that I am drunk.   *Exit.*
MONTANO   To th' platform, masters; come, let's set the   110
   watch.

                         [Exeunt some Gentlemen.]

IAGO [*Detains* MONTANO.]   You see this fellow that is gone before:
   He's a soldier fit to stand by Caesar
   And give direction. And do but see his vice:
   'Tis to his virtue a just equinox,   115
   The one as long as th' other. 'Tis pity of him;
   I fear the trust Othello puts him in
   On some odd time of his infirmity
   Will shake this island.
MONTANO   But is he often thus?
IAGO   'Tis evermore his prologue to his sleep.   120
   He'll watch the horologe a double set
   If drink rock not his cradle.
MONTANO   It were well
   The general were put in mind of it.
   Perhaps he sees it not, or his good nature
   Prizes the virtue that appears in Cassio   125
   And looks not on his evils. Is not this true?

      Enter RODERIGO.

IAGO [*Aside.*]   How now, Roderigo?
   I pray you, after the lieutenant—go!   *Exit* RODERIGO.
MONTANO   And 'tis great pity that the noble Moor
   Should hazard such a place as his own second   130
   With one of an ingraft infirmity.
   It were an honest action to say so
   To the Moor.
IAGO   Not I, for this fair island.
   I do love Cassio well and would do much
   To cure him of this evil. But hark, what noise?   135

      Enter CASSIO *pursuing* RODERIGO.

---

115. **just equinox:** exact counterpart (like day and night at the equinox).
117. **I fear . . . him in:** "The construction makes the pronoun *him* ambiguous in refer-
     ence": if to Cassio, "trust" = position of authority; if to Othello, "trust" = "the state of
     confidence Othello puts himself in" (Ross). See 1.3.387–88 and note.
118. **On some . . . infirmity:** when he happens to be drunk.
119. **shake this island:** produce general mayhem.
121. **watch . . . double set:** stay up for two rounds of the clock—24 hours.
130. **second:** deputy, lieutenant.
131. **ingraft:** "grown to be part of him" as "a shoot becomes part of the plant to which it
     is grafted" (Mowat and Werstine).

CASSIO   Zounds, you rogue! you rascal!

MONTANO   What's the matter, lieutenant?

CASSIO   A knave teach me my duty? I'll beat the knave into a
twiggen bottle.

RODERIGO   Beat me?   140

CASSIO   Dost thou prate, rogue?   [*Attacks* RODERIGO.]

MONTANO   Nay, good lieutenant! I pray you, sir, hold your
hand.

CASSIO   Let me go, sir, or I'll knock you o'er the mazzard.

MONTANO   Come, come; you're drunk!

CASSIO   Drunk?   [CASSIO *and* MONTANO *fight.*]   145

IAGO [*Aside to* RODERIGO.]   Away, I say! Go out and cry a
mutiny.   [*Exit* RODERIGO.]

Nay, good lieutenant! God's will, gentlemen!
Help ho! Lieutenant! Sir Montano!
Help, masters! Here's a goodly watch indeed!   *A bell rung.*
Who's that which rings the bell? Diablo, ho!   150
The town will rise. God's will, lieutenant, hold!
You'll be ashamed forever.

          Enter OTHELLO *and Attendants.*

OTHELLO   What is the matter here?

MONTANO   Zounds, I bleed still; I am hurt to th' death. [*Attacks*
                                                          CASSIO.]

He dies.

OTHELLO   Hold, for your lives!   155

IAGO   Hold, ho! Lieutenant—sir—Montano—gentlemen!
Have you forgot all place of sense and duty?
Hold! The general speaks to you. Hold, for shame!

OTHELLO   Why, how now, ho? From whence ariseth this?
Are we turned Turks? and to ourselves do that   160
Which heaven hath forbid the Ottomites?
For Christian shame, put by this barbarous brawl!
He that stirs next, to carve for his own rage,

---

138. **beat the knave:** "Social inferiors were beaten, equals had to be challenged" (Honigmann). Cf. "rascal" and "rogue" two lines earlier.
139. **twiggen:** wicker-covered; Cassio will leave a grid of welts on Roderigo.
143. **mazzard:** head.
150. **the bell:** Roderigo has sounded the alarm, as Iago commanded. **Diablo:** devil.
160. **turned Turks:** the proverbial anxiety of reverting to the savagery of infidels (see
2.1.114 and note); Othello has presumably reversed the trajectory in converting from
Islam to Christianity—though see 151 below.
160–61. **do . . . Ottomites?:** Perhaps (1) defeat ourselves (which God prevented the
Turks from doing by sending storms at sea); (2) squabble with ourselves (alluding to
the widespread self-criticism of the time that Muslims were better unified than
Christians); or (3) get drunk (Muslims are enjoined not to drink alcohol).
163. **carve for his own rage:** feed his own anger.

Holds his soul light; he dies upon his motion.
Silence that dreadful bell—it frights the isle   165
From her propriety. What is the matter, masters?
Honest Iago, that looks dead with grieving,
Speak. Who began this? On thy love, I charge thee.

IAGO   I do not know. Friends all, but now, even now.
In quarter and in terms like bride and groom   170
Divesting them for bed; and then, but now,
As if some planet had unwitted men,
Swords out and tilting one at other's breasts
In opposition bloody. I cannot speak
Any beginning to this peevish odds,   175
And would in action glorious I had lost
Those legs that brought me to a part of it.

OTHELLO   How comes it, Michael, you are thus forgot?

CASSIO   I pray you pardon me; I cannot speak.

OTHELLO   Worthy Montano, you were wont to be civil;   180
The gravity and stillness of your youth
The world hath noted, and your name is great
In mouths of wisest censure. What's the matter
That you unlace your reputation thus
And spend your rich opinion for the name   185
Of a night brawler? Give me answer to it.

MONTANO   Worthy Othello, I am hurt to danger.
Your officer, Iago, can inform you—
While I spare speech, which something now offends me—
Of all that I do know; nor know I aught   190
By me that's said or done amiss this night,
Unless self-charity be sometimes a vice,
And to defend ourselves it be a sin
When violence assails us.

OTHELLO   Now, by heaven,

---

164. **Holds . . . light:** is indifferent to the prospect of damnation.
166. **propriety:** true or appropriately peaceful condition.
169. **Friends . . . even now:** Honigmann detects a "cheeky" innuendo about what Othello
     and Desdemona were presumably doing "now, even now"; cf. "Even now, now, very
     now" (1.1.85).
170. **In quarter and in terms:** i.e., acting and speaking.
172. **some planet . . . men:** subject to some maddening supernatural force.
173. **tilting . . . other's:** charging or thrusting at one another's; a (sexualized) metaphor
     from knightly combat.
174–75. **I cannot . . . odds:** I don't know how this senseless quarrel began.
182–83. **your name . . . censure:** your reputation is high among the most judicious.
184–85. **unlace . . . opinion:** loosen the strings of (the purse containing the money of)
     your good name.
187. **to danger:** seriously, critically.
189. **something now offends:** i.e., is somewhat difficult.
192. **self-charity:** looking to one's own needs.

My blood begins my safer guides to rule,   195
And passion, having my best judgment collied,
Assays to lead the way. Zounds, if I stir
Or do but lift this arm, the best of you
Shall sink in my rebuke. Give me to know
How this foul rout began, who set it on;   200
And he that is approved in this offense,
Though he had twinned with me, both at a birth,
Shall lose me. What! in a town of war,
Yet wild, the people's hearts brimful of fear,
To manage private and domestic quarrel?   205
In night, and on the court and guard of safety?
'Tis monstrous. Iago, who began't?
MONTANO   If partially affined, or league[d] in office,
Thou dost deliver more or less than truth,
Thou art no soldier.
IAGO   Touch me not so near.   210
I had rather have this tongue cut from my mouth
Than it should do offense to Michael Cassio;
Yet I persuade myself to speak the truth
Shall nothing wrong him. This it is, general:
Montano and myself being in speech,   215
There comes a fellow crying out for help,
And Cassio following him with determined sword
To execute upon him. Sir, this gentleman
Steps in to Cassio and entreats his pause;
Myself the crying fellow did pursue,   220
Lest by his clamor—as it so fell out—
The town might fall in fright. He, swift of foot,
Outran my purpose; and I returned then rather
For that I heard the clink and fall of swords

---

195. **blood:** anger. **safer guides:** more reliable (rational) faculties.
196. **collied:** blackened (with coal); thus eclipsed or diminished.
199. **sink in my rebuke:** fall in my chastisement.
200. **rout:** brawl. **set it on:** instigated it.
201. **approved:** proven to be guilty.
203. **lose me:** be deprived of my favor or regard. **of war:** in a state of military alert—cf. "this warlike isle" (line 51).
205. **manage:** engage in.
206. **night:** i.e., the most dangerous time. **court . . . safety:** the area where security is most necessary (see note to 2.1.215).
208. **partially . . . office:** biased as a result of personal or military connection (to Cassio).
210. **Touch . . . near:** Don't impugn my military discipline.
217. **determined:** "transferred epithet: Cassio was determined" (Honigmann; see note on "delighted," 1.3.287).
218. **execute upon:** act (perhaps lethally) against.
221. **so fell out:** in fact happened.
224. **fall:** downward stroke.

And Cassio high in oath, which till tonight   225
I ne'er might say before. When I came back—
For this was brief—I found them close together
At blow and thrust, even as again they were
When you yourself did part them.
More of this matter cannot I report.   230
But men are men: the best sometimes forget.
Though Cassio did some little wrong to him,
As men in rage strike those that wish them best,
Yet surely Cassio, I believe, received
From him that fled some strange indignity   235
Which patience could not pass.
OTHELLO   I know, Iago,
Thy honesty and love doth mince this matter,
Making it light to Cassio. Cassio, I love thee,
But never more be officer of mine.—

            Enter DESDEMONA *attended.*

Look if my gentle love be not raised up!—   240
I'll make thee an example.
DESDEMONA   What is the matter, dear?
OTHELLO   All's well, sweeting;
Come away to bed. [*To* MONTANO.]   Sir, for your hurts
Myself will be your surgeon. Lead him off.   [MONTANO *is led*
                                                        off.]

Iago, look with care about the town,   245
And silence those whom this vile brawl distracted.
Come, Desdemona; 'tis the soldier's life
To have their balmy slumbers waked with strife.

            Exit MOOR, DESDEMONA *and Attendants.*

IAGO   What, are you hurt, lieutenant?
CASSIO   Ay, past all surgery.   250
IAGO   Marry, God forbid!
CASSIO   Reputation, reputation, reputation! O, I have
lost my reputation! I have lost the immortal part of
myself, and what remains is bestial. My reputation,
Iago, my reputation!   255

---

225. **high in oath:** raging profanely.
235. **strange indignity:** outlandish insult.
236. **pass:** ignore.
242. **sweeting:** sweetheart.
244. **Myself . . . surgeon:** I will personally make sure you get medical attention. **sur-
    geon** = medical practitioner generally.
246. **distracted:** alarmed.
250. **past all surgery:** i.e., beyond medical help.
253–54. **immortal part . . . bestial:** "The *immortal part* would normally refer to the
    soul," taken "to distinguish human beings from beasts" (Neill).

IAGO   As I am an honest man, I had thought you had
    received some bodily wound; there is more sense in that
    than in reputation. Reputation is an idle and most false
    imposition, oft got without merit and lost without deserving.
    You have lost no reputation at all, unless you   260
    repute yourself such a loser. What, man! there are
    more ways to recover the general again. You are
    but now cast in his mood, a punishment more in policy
    than in malice, even so as one would beat his offenseless
    dog to affright an imperious lion. Sue to   265
    him again, and he's yours.

CASSIO   I will rather sue to be despised than to deceive
    so good a commander with so slight, so drunken and so
    indiscreet an officer. Drunk? And speak parrot? And
    squabble? Swagger? Swear? And discourse fustian   270
    with one's own shadow? O, thou invisible spirit of
    wine! if thou hast no name to be known by, let us call
    thee devil.

IAGO   What was he that you followed with your
    sword? What had he done to you?   275

CASSIO   I know not.

IAGO   Is't possible?

CASSIO   I remember a mass of things, but nothing distinctly;
    a quarrel, but nothing wherefore. O God! that
    men should put an enemy in their mouths to steal away   280
    their brains! that we should with joy, pleasance,
    revel and applause transform ourselves into beasts!

IAGO   Why, but you are now well enough. How
    came you thus recovered?

CASSIO   It hath pleased the devil drunkenness to give   285
    place to the devil wrath; one unperfectness shows me
    another, to make me frankly despise myself.

---

257. **sense:** "(1) feeling; (2) reason (for being concerned)" (Mowat and Werstine).
258. **idle:** useless, inconsequential.
259. **imposition:** extraneous addition.
262. **recover the general:** get back into Othello's good graces.
263. **but now . . . mood:** dismissed in a mere fit of pique.
263–64. **more . . . malice:** motivated more by strategy than ill will.
264–65. **beat . . . lion:** i.e., making an example to establish authority (proverbial); "the 'lion' is either the Venetian army or the Cypriots" (Honigmann).
265. **Sue:** Appeal.
269–70. **And speak . . . fustian:** Cassio twice charges himself with talking nonsense ("speak parrot" and "discourse fustian") and twice with picking fights ("squabble" and "swagger").
279. **wherefore:** about why it started.
281–82. **joy . . . applause:** presumably, the conventional social sanctions he worried about earlier (line 30).
286. **unperfectness:** imperfection.
287. **frankly:** unreservedly.

IAGO   Come, you are too severe a moraler. As the
    time, the place and the condition of this country stands,
    I could heartily wish this had not befallen; but since it is as   290
    it is, mend it for your own good.

CASSIO   I will ask him for my place again, he shall tell
    me I am a drunkard. Had I as many mouths as Hydra,
    such an answer would stop them all. To be now a sensible
    man, by and by a fool, and presently a beast!—O,   295
    strange! Every inordinate cup is unblessed, and the ingredient
    is a devil.

IAGO   Come, come; good wine is a good familiar
    creature if it be well used. Exclaim no more against it.
    And, good lieutenant, I think you think I love you.   300

CASSIO   I have well approved it, sir: I drunk!

IAGO   You or any man living may be drunk at a
    time, man. I tell you what you shall do. Our general's
    wife is now the general. I may say so in this respect,
    for that he hath devoted and given up himself to the   305
    contemplation, mark and devotement of her parts
    and graces. Confess yourself freely to her; importune
    her help to put you in your place again. She is
    of so free, so kind, so apt, so blessed a disposition,
    she holds it a vice in her goodness not to do more   310
    than she is requested. This broken joint between
    you and her husband entreat her to splinter, and my
    fortunes against any lay worth naming, this crack of
    your love shall grow stronger than it was before.

CASSIO   You advise me well.   315

IAGO   I protest, in the sincerity of love and honest
    kindness.

---

288. **severe a moraler:** self-critical.
292. **I will ask:** if I were to ask.
293. **Hydra:** many-headed beast of ancient mythology.
294. **stop:** put a plug (or stopper) on; silence.
295. **presently:** soon.
296. **inordinate:** excessive. **unblessed:** damned.
298. **familiar:** friendly or natural (disagreeing with Cassio's "strange"); also punning on a "familiar" as an evil spirit.
301. **approved . . . drunk:** experienced it by (taking your advice and) drinking.
302–03. **at a time:** on a given occasion.
303–04. **Our . . . general:** Desdemona commands Othello.
306. **contemplation . . . devotement:** three ways of describing rapt attention, suggesting that Othello has surrendered ("given up himself") to uxorious obsession. **parts:** natural gifts or qualities (cf. 1.2.31 and 1.3.251), but the sexual meaning is irresistible.
307. **graces:** charms, virtues.
309. **apt:** fit; likely to respond favorably (to your request).
312. **splinter:** set with a splint.
313. **lay:** bet. **crack of:** fracture in.
314. **shall grow . . . before:** based on proverbial lore about healed fractures; literally, Iago's words claim that the break will grow stronger.
316. **protest:** declare.

CASSIO   I think it freely; and betimes in the morning
  I will beseech the virtuous Desdemona to undertake
  for me. I am desperate of my fortunes if they check me.   320
IAGO   You are in the right. Good night, lieutenant; I
  must to the watch.
CASSIO   Good night, honest Iago.   *Exit* CASSIO.
IAGO   And what's he then that says I play the villain,
  When this advice is free I give and honest,   325
  Probal to thinking, and indeed the course
  To win the Moor again? For 'tis most easy
  Th' inclining Desdemona to subdue
  In any honest suit: she's framed as fruitful
  As the free elements; and then for her   330
  To win the Moor, were't to renounce his baptism,
  All seals and symbols of redeemèd sin,
  His soul is so enfettered to her love
  That she may make, unmake, do what she list,
  Even as her appetite shall play the god   335
  With his weak function. How am I then a villain
  To counsel Cassio to this parallel course
  Directly to his good? Divinity of hell!
  When devils will the blackest sins put on,
  They do suggest at first with heavenly shows,   340
  As I do now. For whiles this honest fool
  Plies Desdemona to repair his fortune,
  And she for him pleads strongly to the Moor,
  I'll pour this pestilence into his ear:
  That she repeals him for her body's lust,   345
  And by how much she strives to do him good,
  She shall undo her credit with the Moor.

318. **freely:** without qualification. **betimes:** early.
319–20. **undertake for me:** take up my cause.
320. **desperate of:** in despair about. **check:** block.
321. **in the right:** correct; justified in your appeal.
324. **And what's he:** addressing the spectators? **play the villain:** act the villain's part.
326. **probal to thinking:** plausible when scrutinized.
328. **Th' inclining . . . subdue:** to get the compliant Desdemona to yield.
329–30. **framed . . . elements:** as generously disposed "as the unrestrained elements . . . to be used" (Honigmann).
331. **win:** convince.
332. **seals . . . sin:** guarantees and outward manifestations (like baptism and the other sacraments) of redemption from sin; another transferred epithet (see line 217 and note).
333. **enfettered . . . love:** chained to his love for her or hers for him (or both).
334. **list:** pleases.
335–36. **her appetite . . . function:** either his desire for her or her lust for power (or both) will enjoy absolute control over his diminished judgment.
337. **parallel:** "*level* and *even with his design*" (Johnson).
338. **Divinity of hell!:** infernal theology—i.e., wicked goodness; Iago abruptly abandons his (now clearly hypocritical) denial of villainous designs.
342. **Plies:** repeatedly solicits.
344. **pestilence:** poison.
345. **repeals him:** seeks his reinstatement.

So will I turn her virtue into pitch,
And out of her own goodness make the net,
That shall enmesh them all.

   Enter RODERIGO. How now, Roderigo?   350

RODERIGO I do follow here in the chase, not
like a hound that hunts, but one that fills up the
cry. My money is almost spent; I have been tonight
exceedingly well cudgelled; and I think the issue
will be I shall have so much experience for my pains, 355
and so, with no money at all, and a little more wit, return
again to Venice.

IAGO How poor are they that have not patience!
What wound did ever heal but by degrees?
Thou know'st we work by wit and not by witchcraft, 360
And wit depends on dilatory time.
Does't not go well? Cassio hath beaten thee,
And thou by that small hurt hath cashiered Cassio.
Though other things grow fair against the sun,
Yet fruits that blossom first will first be ripe. 365
Content thyself awhile. By the mass, 'tis morning!
Pleasure and action make the hours seem short.
Retire thee; go where thou art billeted.
Away! I say; thou shalt know more hereafter.
Nay, get thee gone!   *Exit* RODERIGO.

    Two things are to be done: 370
My wife must move for Cassio to her mistress—
I'll set her on—
Myself a while to draw the Moor apart
And bring him jump when he may Cassio find
Soliciting his wife. Ay, that's the way!   375
Dull not device by coldness and delay.   *Exit.*

---

348. pitch: "black, malodorous, and extremely sticky" and "thus the perfect substance" to
 "'enmesh' his victims" (Mowat and Werstine).
353. cry: trailing pack.
354. exceedingly well cudgelled: very badly beaten. **issue:** result.
355. so much: (only) this much. **pains:** efforts (with a pun).
361. dilatory: gradually unfolding; like his denial of witchcraft, an intriguing echo of
 Othello's speech to the senate (see 1.3.152 and 168).
363. cashiered: got dismissed.
364–65. Though . . . ripe: "sound like proverbs that ought to persuade Roderigo . . . but
 the lines themselves are obscure" (Mowat and Werstine).
367. Pleasure and action: can evoke sexual and/or military affairs, devising and/or
 implementing plots. **make . . . short:** i.e., "time flies when you're having fun."
368. billeted: lodged.
371. move: petition, plead.
373. a while: meanwhile.
374. jump: right at the very moment.
376. Dull not . . . delay: i.e., let's keep it quick and hot. **device:** "plot, stratagem; pleasure, desire" (Honigmann).

ACT 3 SCENE 1

Enter CASSIO, *Musicians and* CLOWN.

CASSIO   Masters, play here—I will content your pains—
Something that's brief; and bid, "Good morrow, general."

CLOWN   Why, masters, have your instruments been in Naples,
that they speak i'th' nose thus?

MUSICIAN   How, sir? how?   5

CLOWN   Are these, I pray you, wind instruments?

MUSICIAN   Ay, marry, are they, sir.

CLOWN   O, thereby hangs a tale!

MUSICIAN   Whereby hangs a tale, sir?

CLOWN   Marry, sir, by many a wind instrument that I   10
know. But, masters, here's money for you; and the general
so likes your music that he desires you for love's
sake to make no more noise with it.

MUSICIAN   Well, sir, we will not.

CLOWN   If you have any music that may not be heard,   15
to't again. But, as they say, to hear music the general
does not greatly care.

MUSICIAN   We have none such, sir.

CLOWN   Then put up your pipes in your bag, for I'll
away. Go! Vanish into air, away!   *Exit Musicians.*   20

CASSIO   Dost thou hear, mine honest friend?

CLOWN   No, I hear not your honest friend:
I hear you.

CASSIO   Prithee keep up thy quillets. There's a poor
piece of gold for thee. If the gentlewoman that attends   25
the general be stirring, tell her there's one Cassio
entreats her a little favor of speech. Wilt thou do this?

CLOWN   She is stirring, sir. If she will stir hither, I shall
seem to notify unto her.

---

1. **content your pains:** reward your efforts.
2. **Good morrow, general:** "the traditional *aubade:* to wake bride and groom after the wedding night" (Honigmann); and see Bristol, 338–54 below.
3. **SPEECH PREFIX** CLOWN: See note 12 to the Names of the Actors at the beginning of the play.
3–10. **your instruments . . . wind instrument:** an explosion of sexual and scatological puns. Men whose (sexual) instruments visit Naples contract syphilis, usually designated a French or Italian disease ("the Neapolitan bone-ache," *Troilus and Cressida* 2.3, Quarto text), and wind up losing their noses. "Wind" as flatulence introduces jokes about anality, sodomy, and bestiality; "tale" puns on "tail," which suggests "penis."
24. **Prithee . . . quillets:** i.e., please, no more puns.
25–26. **the gentlewoman . . . general:** Emilia, who in serving Desdemona serves Othello as well (see 4.2.103).
26. **stirring:** awake.
28. **stirring:** sexually appealing.
29. **seem to notify unto her:** inform her (mocking Cassio's elaborate courtliness).

CASSIO   Do, good my friend.   *Exit* CLOWN.
   Enter IAGO.   In happy time, Iago. 30
IAGO   You have not been abed then?
CASSIO   Why, no; the day had broke before we parted.
 I have made bold, Iago, to send in to your wife.
 My suit to her is that she will to virtuous Desdemona
 Procure me some access.
IAGO   I'll send her to you presently; 35
 And I'll devise a mean to draw the Moor
 Out of the way, that your converse and business
 May be more free.
CASSIO   I humbly thank you for't.   *Exit* [IAGO].
        I never knew
 A Florentine more kind and honest. 40

  Enter EMILIA.

EMILIA   Good morrow, good lieutenant. I am sorry
 For your displeasure, but all will sure be well.
 The general and his wife are talking of it,
 And she speaks for you stoutly. The Moor replies
 That he you hurt is of great fame in Cyprus 45
 And great affinity, and that in wholesome wisdom
 He might not but refuse you; but he protests he loves you
 And needs no other suitor but his likings
 To bring you in again.
CASSIO   Yet I beseech you,
 If you think fit, or that it may be done, 50
 Give me advantage of some brief discourse
 With Desdemon alone.
EMILIA   Pray you come in.
 I will bestow you where you shall have time
 To speak your bosom freely.
CASSIO   I am much bound to you. *Exit.*

---

30. In happy time: i.e., "just the man I want to see."
35. presently: right away.
36. a mean: an occasion.
40. A Florentine: "even in one of my own countrymen" (Malone).
44. stoutly: "vigorously (stronger than today)" (Honigmann).
45–46. of great . . . affinity: well respected and well connected.
46. wholesome wisdom: healthy judgment; i.e., common sense or solicitude for the general good.
47. might not but: has to.
48. And needs . . . likings: "i.e., his own inclination would be sufficient by itself" (McDonald).
49. bring you in again: reinstate you.
54. bosom: inmost thoughts.

ACT 3 SCENE 2

Enter OTHELLO, IAGO, *and Gentlemen.*

OTHELLO These letters give, Iago, to the pilot,
  And by him do my duties to the Senate.
  That done, I will be walking on the works;
  Repair there to me.
IAGO   Well, my good lord; I'll do't.
OTHELLO This fortification, gentlemen, shall we see't?   5
GENTLEMAN We'll wait upon your lordship.   *Exeunt.*

ACT 3 SCENE 3

Enter DESDEMONA, CASSIO, *and* EMILIA.

DESDEMONA Be thou assured, good Cassio, I will do
  All my abilities in thy behalf.
EMILIA Good madam, do. I warrant it grieves my husband
  As if the cause were his.
DESDEMONA O, that's an honest fellow. Do not doubt, Cassio,   5
  But I will have my lord and you again
  As friendly as you were.
CASSIO   Bounteous madam,
  Whatever shall become of Michael Cassio,
  He's never anything but your true servant.
DESDEMONA I know't; I thank you. You do love my lord;   10
  You have known him long; and be you well assured
  He shall in strangeness stand no farther off
  Than in a politic distance.
CASSIO   Ay, but, lady,
  That policy may either last so long,
  Or feed upon such nice and waterish diet,   15
  Or breed itself so out of circumstances,
  That—I being absent, and my place supplied—
  My general will forget my love and service.
DESDEMONA Do not doubt that. Before Emilia here,
  I give thee warrant of thy place. Assure thee,   20

  2. **by him . . . duties:** through him pay my respects.
  3. **works:** fortifications.
  4. **Repair:** come.
  12–13. **shall . . . politic distance:** will keep only a strategic aloofness.
  14. **policy:** i.e., tactical delay, aimed at the eventual restoration of Cassio.
  15. **nice and waterish:** finicky and thin.
  16. **breed:** reproduce. **circumstances:** trivialities.
  17. **place supplied:** position occupied.
  19. **doubt:** fear.
  20. **give thee warrant of:** guarantee.

If I do vow a friendship, I'll perform it
To the last article. My lord shall never rest:
I'll watch him tame and talk him out of patience;
His bed shall seem a school, his board a shrift;
I'll intermingle everything he does   25
With Cassio's suit. Therefore be merry, Cassio,
For thy solicitor shall rather die
Than give thy cause away.

> *Enter* OTHELLO *and* IAGO.

EMILIA   Madam, here comes my lord.
CASSIO   Madam, I'll take my leave.   30
DESDEMONA   Why, stay and hear me speak.
CASSIO   Madam, not now: I am very ill at ease,
    Unfit for mine own purposes.
DESDEMONA   Well, do your discretion.   *Exit Cassio.*
IAGO   Ha? I like not that.
OTHELLO   What dost thou say?   35
IAGO   Nothing, my lord; or if . . . I know not what.
OTHELLO   Was not that Cassio parted from my wife?
IAGO   Cassio, my lord? No, sure, I cannot think it
    That he would steal away so guilty-like,
    Seeing your coming.
OTHELLO   I do believe 'twas he.   40
DESDEMONA   How now, my lord?
    I have been talking with a suitor here,
    A man that languishes in your displeasure.
OTHELLO   Who is't you mean?
DESDEMONA   Why, your lieutenant, Cassio. Good my lord,   45
    If I have any grace or power to move you,
    His present reconciliation take;
    For if he be not one that truly loves you,
    That errs in ignorance and not in cunning,
    I have no judgment in an honest face.   50
    I prithee call him back.
OTHELLO   Went he hence now?
DESDEMONA   Yes, faith; so humbled

---

23. **watch him tame:** "Hawks and other birds are tamed by keeping them from sleep"
    (Steevens). **talk . . . patience:** keep talking to him about it until he loses patience.
24. **school:** i.e., a place of rigorous instruction. **board a shrift:** dining table a confes-
    sional (where penance is prescribed).
28. **give . . . away:** abandon, renounce.
34. **your discretion:** what you judge appropriate.
42. **suitor:** supplicant; but including the sense of romantic pursuit.
47. **His present . . . take:** effect an immediate reconciliation.
49. **in ignorance:** unintentionally.

That he hath left part of his grief with me
To suffer with him. Good love, call him back.

OTHELLO   Not now, sweet Desdemon; some other time.   55

DESDEMONA   But shall't be shortly?

OTHELLO   The sooner, sweet, for you.

DESDEMONA   Shall't be tonight, at supper?

OTHELLO   No, not tonight.

DESDEMONA   Tomorrow dinner then?

OTHELLO   I shall not dine at home;
I meet the captains at the citadel.

DESDEMONA   Why then, tomorrow night, on Tuesday morn,   60
On Tuesday noon or night, on Wednesday morn.
I prithee name the time, but let it not
Exceed three days. In faith, he's penitent;
And yet his trespass, in our common reason—
Save that they say the wars must make example   65
Out of her best—is not almost a fault
T' incur a private check. When shall he come?
Tell me, Othello. I wonder in my soul
What you would ask me that I should deny,
Or stand so mamm'ring on? What? Michael Cassio,   70
That came a-wooing with you? and so many a time,
When I have spoke of you dispraisingly,
Hath ta'en your part—to have so much to do
To bring him in? By'r Lady, I could do much—

OTHELLO   Prithee no more. Let him come when he will: 75
I will deny thee nothing.

DESDEMONA   Why, this is not a boon;
'Tis as I should entreat you wear your gloves,
Or feed on nourishing dishes, or keep you warm,
Or sue to you to do a peculiar profit
To your own person. Nay, when I have a suit   80
Wherein I mean to touch your love indeed,
It shall be full of poise and difficult weight
And fearful to be granted.

---

64. **in our common reason:** "i.e., looked at by ordinary standards" (McDonald).
65. **the wars:** the military profession (perhaps also alluding to the current warlike alert).
66–67. **is not . . . check:** hardly merits even a personal rebuke.
70. **so mamm'ring on:** in such hesitant uncertainty about; possibly, stammering so.
73. **ta'en your part:** argued on your behalf.
74. **bring him in:** reinstate him, as in 3.1.49; an unintended sexual suggestion—as earlier with "came a-wooing with you" and "ta'en your part."
76. **boon:** favor for herself.
79. **sue to:** beg. **peculiar:** particular.
81. **touch:** test.
82–83. **full of . . . granted:** serious and hard to decide and with risky consequences.

OTHELLO   I will deny thee nothing.
Whereon I do beseech thee grant me this,
To leave me but a little to myself.   85
DESDEMONA   Shall I deny you? No. Farewell, my lord.
OTHELLO   Farewell, my Desdemona; I'll come to thee straight.
DESDEMONA   Emilia, come.—Be as your fancies teach you.
Whate'er you be, I am obedient. *Exit* DESDEMONA *and* EMILIA.
OTHELLO   Excellent wretch! Perdition catch my soul   90
But I do love thee! and when I love thee not,
Chaos is come again.
IAGO   My noble lord . . .
OTHELLO   What dost thou say, Iago?
IAGO   Did Michael Cassio, when you wooed my lady,
Know of your love?
OTHELLO   He did, from first to last.   95
Why dost thou ask?
IAGO   But for a satisfaction of my thought,
No further harm.
OTHELLO   Why of thy thought, Iago?
IAGO   I did not think he had been acquainted with her.
OTHELLO   O yes, and went between us very oft.   100
IAGO   Indeed!
OTHELLO   Indeed? Ay, indeed. Discern'st thou aught in that?
Is he not honest?
IAGO   Honest, my lord?
OTHELLO   Honest? Ay, honest.   105
IAGO   My lord, for aught I know.
OTHELLO   What dost thou think?
IAGO   Think, my lord?
OTHELLO   "Think, my lord?" By heaven, thou echo'st me
As if there were some monster in thy thought   110
Too hideous to be shown. Thou dost mean something:
I heard thee say even now thou lik'st not that,
When Cassio left my wife. What didst not like?
And when I told thee he was of my counsel,
Of my whole course of wooing, thou cried'st, "Indeed!"   115

---

90. **wretch:** can express endearment as well as distaste. **Perdition catch my soul:** can be taken literally or figuratively for "I'll be damned."
91. **when:** can mean "before" ("ere," according to Malone) or "if," as well as "as soon as."
92. Alludes "to the classical legend that Love was the first of the gods to spring out of original chaos" (Honigmann), though it may also refer to Othello's earlier life.
100–01. **went between . . . Indeed:** i.e., carried messages between; but Iago's innuendo reinforces the subtextual impropriety of a "go-between."
112. **even now:** See 2.3.169 and note.
114–15. **of my . . . wooing:** my confidant throughout the courtship.

And didst contract and purse thy brow together
As if thou then hadst shut up in thy brain
Some horrible conceit. If thou dost love me,
Show me thy thought.

IAGO   My lord, you know I love you.

OTHELLO   I think thou dost;   120
And for I know thou'rt full of love and honesty,
And weigh'st thy words before thou giv'st them breath,
Therefore these stops of thine fright me the more:
For such things in a false disloyal knave
Are tricks of custom; but in a man that's just   125
They're close dilations, working from the heart
That passion cannot rule.

IAGO   For Michael Cassio,
I dare be sworn I think that he is honest.

OTHELLO   I think so too.

IAGO   Men should be what they seem,
Or those that be not, would they might seem none.   130

OTHELLO   Certain, men should be what they seem.

IAGO   Why then, I think Cassio's an honest man.

OTHELLO   Nay, yet there's more in this.
I prithee speak to me as to thy thinkings,
As thou dost ruminate, and give thy worst of thoughts   135
The worst of words.

IAGO   Good my lord, pardon me.
Though I am bound to every act of duty,
I am not bound to that all slaves are free to:
Utter my thoughts? Why, say they are vile and false—
As where's that palace whereinto foul things   140
Sometimes intrude not? Who has that breast so pure
But some uncleanly apprehensions
Keep leets and law-days, and in sessions sit
With meditations lawful?

OTHELLO   Thou dost conspire against thy friend, Iago,   145

118. **conceit:** idea.
121. **for:** for that, because.
123. **stops:** hesitations, pauses.
125. **of custom:** characteristic, habitual, to be expected.
126. **close:** secret, mysterious. **dilations:** effusions; delays; unfoldings, as of narratives
    (see Iago's "dilatory time," 2.3.361, and note).
126–27. **working . . . rule:** i.e., proceeding from a reliably dispassionate source.
130. **Or those . . . none:** i.e., men who aren't (honest) shouldn't seem to be so.
134–36. **Speak . . . words:** say whatever comes into your mind, no matter how tentative
    or vile.
138. **that . . . free to:** "that which even slaves are free to do [or not to do]" (Neill).
142. **uncleanly apprehensions:** dirty thoughts.
143. **Keep . . . sit:** appear in court together with. **leets, law-days,** and **sessions:** all refer
    to legal proceedings.

If thou but think'st him wronged and mak'st his ear
  A stranger to thy thoughts.
IAGO   I do beseech you—
  Though I perchance am vicious in my guess
  (As I confess it is my nature's plague
  To spy into abuses, and oft my jealousy   150
  Shapes faults that are not)—that your wisdom
  From one that so imperfectly conceits
  Would take no notice, nor build yourself a trouble
  Out of his scattering and unsure observance.
  It were not for your quiet, nor your good,   155
  Nor for my manhood, honesty and wisdom,
  To let you know my thoughts.
OTHELLO   What dost thou mean?
IAGO   Good name in man and woman, dear my lord,
  Is the immediate jewel of their souls;
  Who steals my purse steals trash: 'tis something, nothing; 160
  'Twas mine, 'tis his, and has been slave to thousands.
  But he that filches from me my good name
  Robs me of that which not enriches him
  And makes me poor indeed.
OTHELLO   By heaven, I'll know thy thoughts!
IAGO   You cannot, if my heart were in your hand,   165
  Nor shall not, whilst 'tis in my custody.
OTHELLO   Ha?
IAGO   O, beware, my lord, of jealousy!
  It is the green-eyed monster, which doth mock
  The meat it feeds on. That cuckold lives in bliss
  Who, certain of his fate, loves not his wronger;   170
  But O, what damnèd minutes tells he o'er
  Who dotes yet doubts, suspects yet strongly loves!
OTHELLO   O misery!
IAGO   Poor and content is rich, and rich enough,

---

146. **but think'st him wronged:** merely guess him harmed.
150. **jealousy:** vigilance, suspicion, envy.
151. **Shapes:** constructs.
151–53. **your wisdom . . . notice:** your discretion would ignore someone given to such mistaken or inappropriate thoughts.
154. **scattering . . . observance:** "random and unfounded observations" (McDonald).
155. **were not for:** would not serve the interests of.
158–64. **Good name . . . indeed:** Cf. Cassio's lament for lost "reputation" (2.3.252–55).
159. **immediate jewel:** most valuable possession or quality.
168–69. **mock . . . feeds on:** toys with its prey (the jealous lover); or (*as* the jealous lover) is repelled by his beloved or his own suspicions.
169–72. **That cuckold . . . strongly loves:** i.e., better to know and hate your betrayer than hang suspended in uncertainty about the fidelity of your beloved. **tells he o'er:** counts over and over again.
172. **dotes:** adores; with a hint of foolish infatuation or dotage.

But riches fineless is as poor as winter   175
To him that ever fears he shall be poor.
Good God, the souls of all my tribe defend
From jealousy!
OTHELLO   Why, why is this?
Think'st thou I'd make a life of jealousy,
To follow still the changes of the moon   180
With fresh suspicions? No! To be once in doubt
Is once to be resolved. Exchange me for a goat
When I shall turn the business of my soul
To such exsufflicate and blowed surmises,
Matching thy inference. 'Tis not to make me jealous   185
To say my wife is fair, feeds well, loves company,
Is free of speech, sings, plays and dances:
Where virtue is, these are more virtuous.
Nor from mine own weak merits will I draw
The smallest fear or doubt of her revolt,   190
For she had eyes and chose me. No, Iago,
I'll see before I doubt; when I doubt, prove;
And on the proof there is no more but this:
Away at once with love or jealousy!
IAGO   I am glad of this; for now I shall have reason   195
To show the love and duty that I bear you
With franker spirit. Therefore, as I am bound,
Receive it from me. I speak not yet of proof.
Look to your wife; observe her well with Cassio;
Wear your eyes thus: not jealous nor secure.   200
I would not have your free and noble nature
Out of self-bounty be abused. Look to't.
I know our country disposition well:
In Venice they do let God see the pranks

175. **riches fineless:** infinite wealth.
177. **Good God . . . defend:** may the good Lord . . . protect. **tribe:** Cf. 1.3.353.
180. **follow . . . moon:** i.e., always ("still") wax and wane (like a lunatic).
182. **once:** at once; once and for all.
184. **exsufflicate and blowed surmises:** "(1) spat out and flyblown (i.e., disgusting) spec-
     ulations, (2) inflated and blown abroad (rumored) notions" (McDonald).
185. **matching thy inference:** to correspond with your suggestion.
186. **feeds well:** enjoys eating.
190. **revolt:** turning away (revulsion); infidelity.
192. **when:** See line 91 and note.
197. **bound:** in dutiful service.
200. **Wear your eyes:** either "observe" or "put on the appearance."
201. **free:** open-hearted, trusting.
202. **self-bounty:** your own generosity; your inherent good nature.
203. **our country disposition:** how Venetian women act; with an obscene sexual pun (cf.
     "country matters," *Hamlet* 3.2.104).
204. **they:** i.e., Venetian wives. **pranks:** See 2.1.142.

They dare not show their husbands; their best conscience 205
Is not to leave't undone, but [keep't] unknown.

OTHELLO   Dost thou say so?

IAGO   She did deceive her father, marrying you,
And when she seemed to shake, and fear your looks,
She loved them most.

OTHELLO   And so she did.

IAGO   Why, go to then. 210
She that, so young, could give out such a seeming
To seel her father's eyes up close as oak
He thought 'twas witchcraft . . . ; but I am much to blame.
I humbly do beseech you of your pardon
For too much loving you.

OTHELLO   I am bound to thee forever. 215

IAGO   I see this hath a little dashed your spirits.

OTHELLO   Not a jot, not a jot.

IAGO   I' faith, I fear it has.
I hope you will consider what is spoke
Comes from your love. But I do see you're moved.
I am to pray you not to strain my speech 220
To grosser issues nor to larger reach
Than to suspicion.

OTHELLO   I will not.

IAGO   Should you do so, my lord,
My speech should fall into such vile success
Which my thoughts aimed not. Cassio's my worthy friend— 225
My lord, I see you're moved.

OTHELLO   No, not much moved;
I do not think but Desdemona's honest.

IAGO   Long live she so! and long live you to think so!

OTHELLO   And yet how nature, erring from itself—

IAGO   Ay, there's the point! as to be bold with you, 230

---

205. **best conscience:** utmost care; highest scruple.
211. **give out . . . seeming:** be so deceptive.
212. **seel:** See 1.3.267 and note. **close as oak:** i.e., the cloth hoodwinking Brabantio was tight as (the grain of) oak.
215. **bound:** indebted, but cf. line 197.
219. **your love:** "my love of you" (Neill)?; your love for Desdemona?
220–22. **strain . . . suspicion:** push my words beyond misgiving into explicit imaginings ("grosser" and "larger" have sexual resonances; see 1.2.72 and note).
224–25. **vile success . . . aimed not:** nasty consequence I didn't intend; "*success* = outcome (good or bad)" (Honigmann).
229. **erring from itself:** straying from propriety; Othello echoes Brabantio's "nature so preposterously to err" (1.3.62). Iago had been echoing Brabantio earlier: with "Look to your wife" (line 199), cf. 1.3.290; with "She did deceive her father, marrying you" (208), cf. 1.3.291; with "fear your looks" (209), cf. 1.3.98.
230. **bold:** can refer to Iago's presumption here or to the headstrong pursuit of Othello earlier by Desdemona, "a maiden never bold" (1.3.94) until that point.

Not to affect many proposèd matches
Of her own clime, complexion and degree,
Whereto we see in all things nature tends—
Foh! one may smell in such a will most rank,
Foul disproportions, thoughts unnatural.   235
But, pardon me, I do not in position
Distinctly speak of her, though I may fear
Her will, recoiling to her better judgment,
May fall to match you with her country forms,
And happily repent.

OTHELLO   Farewell, farewell.   240
If more thou dost perceive, let me know more.
Set on thy wife to observe. Leave me, Iago.

IAGO [*Begins to depart.*]   My lord, I take my leave.

OTHELLO   Why did I marry? This honest creature, doubtless,
Sees and knows more, much more, than he unfolds.   245

IAGO [*Returning.*]   My lord, I would I might entreat your honor
To scan this thing no farther; leave it to time.
Although 'tis fit that Cassio have his place
(For sure he fills it up with great ability),
Yet if you please to hold him off awhile,   250
You shall by that perceive him and his means.
Note if your lady strain his entertainment
With any strong or vehement importunity;
Much will be seen in that. In the meantime
Let me be thought too busy in my fears   255
(As worthy cause I have to fear I am),
And hold her free, I do beseech your honor.

OTHELLO   Fear not my government.

IAGO   I once more take my leave.   *Exit.*

OTHELLO   This fellow's of exceeding honesty,   260
And knows all qualities with a learned spirit
Of human dealings. If I do prove her haggard,

231. affect: like.
232. clime, complexion and degree: country, temperament, and social position.
234. Foh: calls upon the actor to express nausea. such: perverse behavior like that. will: sexual appetite. rank: extreme, "(after smell) rancid, foul-smelling" (Honigmann).
236–37. in position . . . her: i.e., my claim is not about her in particular.
238. recoiling: reverting (with instinctive disgust).
239. fall: happen or descend. match: compare. country forms: typical Venetian appearances; but cf. line 203 and note.
240. happily: perhaps.
248. place: military position.
249. fills it up: furnishes a sexual suggestion for "place."
251. means: procedures; also agents or go-betweens (i.e., Desdemona).
252. strain his entertainment: push for his reinstatement.
257. free: i.e., from any wrongdoing.
258. Fear not my government: Don't worry about my conduct.
262. haggard: untamed; "lit. a wild female hawk" (Honigmann).

Though that her jesses were my dear heartstrings,
I'd whistle her off and let her down the wind
To prey at fortune. Haply for I am black,   265
And have not those soft parts of conversation
That chamberers have, or for I am declined
Into the vale of years—yet that's not much—
She's gone, I am abused, and my relief
Must be to loathe her. O curse of marriage!   270
That we can call these delicate creatures ours
And not their appetites! I had rather be a toad
And live upon the vapor of a dungeon
Than keep a corner in the thing I love
For others' uses. Yet 'tis the plague to great ones: 275
Prerogatived are they less than the base;
'Tis destiny unshunnable, like death;
Even then this forkèd plague is fated to us
When we do quicken.

      Enter DESDEMONA *and* EMILIA.

                  Look where she comes!
If she be false, heaven mocked itself;   280
I'll not believe't.

DESDEMONA   How now, my dear Othello?
Your dinner, and the generous islanders
By you invited, do attend your presence.

OTHELLO   I am to blame.

DESDEMONA   Why do you speak so faintly?
Are you not well?   285

---

263. Though . . . heartstrings: no matter how fondly I am attached to her. **jesses:** the straps tying the hawk to the falconer's wrist.

264–65. whistle . . . fortune: more hawking metaphors—"let her go to take her own chances."

265. Haply for: perhaps because.

266–67. soft . . . have: refined social skills of experienced courtiers.

268. yet that's not much: either "I'm not very old" or "age isn't very important."

269. abused: deceived.

271–72. we: men, husbands. **delicate creatures . . . appetites:** women, wives, who are legal possessions ("ours") while remaining sexually autonomous ("not their appetites").

274–75. keep . . . for others' uses: another distinction between custody and possession. **corner:** "small place . . . here with secondary sexual sense" (Honigmann). **thing:** Desdemona or her "corner" (cf. "scan this thing no farther," line 247).

275–76. Yet . . . the base: Othello claims it as a general rule (though without identifiable authority) that men of high status ("great ones") are less well protected ("prerogatived") against infidelity.

278. this forkèd plague: alluding to the cuckold's horns but also to the anatomical "corner" (cf. "poor, bare, forked animal," *King Lear* 3.4.97–98).

279. do quicken: are born; become sexually aroused (picking up on "death" as orgasm in line 277; see 2.1.80 and note).

280. mocked itself: counterfeited its own transcendent beauty (?).

282. generous: noble.

OTHELLO I have a pain upon my forehead, here.
DESDEMONA   Faith, that's with watching; 'twill away again.
  Let me but bind it hard, within this hour
  It will be well.
OTHELLO   Your napkin is too little;

                      [*The handkerchief is dropped.*]

  Let it alone. Come, I'll go in with you.   290
DESDEMONA   I am very sorry that you are not well.

                      Exit OTHELLO *and* DESDEMONA.

EMILIA   I am glad I have found this napkin;
  This was her first remembrance from the Moor.
  My wayward husband hath a hundred times
  Wooed me to steal it. But she so loves the token   295
  (For he conjured her she should ever keep it)
  That she reserves it evermore about her
  To kiss and talk to. I'll have the work ta'en out,
  And giv't Iago; what he will do with it
  Heaven knows, not I: 300
  I nothing but to please his fantasy.

            Enter Iago.

IAGO   How now? What do you here alone?
EMILIA   Do not you chide; I have a thing for you.
IAGO   You have a thing for me? It is a common thing—
EMILIA   Ha?   305
IAGO   To have a foolish wife.
EMILIA   O, is that all? What will you give me now
  For that same handkerchief?
IAGO   What handkerchief?
EMILIA   What handkerchief?
  Why, that the Moor first gave to Desdemona,   310
  That which so often you did bid me steal.
IAGO   Hast stolen it from her?
EMILIA   No, faith; she let it drop by negligence,
  And to th' advantage I, being here, took't up.

286. **a pain upon my forehead:** i.e., from a cuckold's horns.
287. **watching:** sleeplessness; being on watch.
289. **napkin:** handkerchief.
290. **it:** either the handkerchief or the headache.
294. **wayward:** willful, perverse.
296. **conjured:** "made her swear. The accent falls on the second syllable" (Neill).
298. **work ta'en out:** design copied.
301. **I nothing:** elliptical—an implicit "do" or "know" or "am."
303–04. **thing . . . thing . . . common thing:** emphatically repeats Othello's "thing . . . for others' uses" (see lines 274–75 and note).
314. **to th'advantage:** fortunately, opportunely.

Look, here 'tis.

IAGO   A good wench, give it me.   315

EMILIA   What will you do with't, that you have been so earnest
To have me filch it?

IAGO [*Taking it.*]   Why, what is that to you?

EMILIA   If it be not for some purpose of import,
Giv't me again. Poor lady, she'll run mad
When she shall lack it.

IAGO   Be not acknown on't;   320
I have use for it. Go—leave me!   *Exit* EMILIA.
I will in Cassio's lodging lose this napkin
And let him find it. Trifles light as air
Are to the jealous confirmations strong
As proofs of holy writ. This may do something.   325
The Moor already changes with my poison:
Dangerous conceits are in their natures poisons,
Which at the first are scarce found to distaste,
But with a little act upon the blood
Burn like the mines of sulphur.
           Enter OTHELLO   I did say so—   330
Look where he comes! Not poppy nor mandragora
Nor all the drowsy syrups of the world
Shall ever medicine thee to that sweet sleep
Which thou owedst yesterday.

OTHELLO   Ha! ha! false to me?

IAGO   Why, how now, general? No more of that!   335

OTHELLO   Avaunt! be gone! Thou hast set me on the rack.
I swear 'tis better to be much abused
Than but to know't a little.

IAGO   How now, my lord?

---

320. **lack:** miss. **Be . . . on't:** "in effect, don't acknowledge . . . a part in it, keep out of it"
     (Honigmann).
325. **holy writ:** the Bible.
327. **conceits:** ideas, thoughts.
328. **are scarce found to distaste:** hardly seem to repel appetite.
329. **act . . . blood:** effect on passion.
330. **mines of sulphur:** are hot and virtually inextinguishable.
330–31. **I did . . . comes:** See, I told you so (to the audience).
331. **mandragora:** narcotic derived from the fork- or groin-shaped mandrake root;
     cf. Donne, "Song," line 2: "Get with child a mandrake root."
332. **drowsy syrups:** sleep-inducing potions.
333. **medicine:** "restore by physic, cure" (Schmidt).
334. **owedst:** possessed. **Ha! ha!:** "a signal to the actor to make the appropriate noise"
     (Honigmann).
336. **Avaunt:** exclamation used to banish evil spirits. **the rack:** device that gradually
     stretched the limbs till they were pulled out of their sockets.
337. **abused:** deceived.

OTHELLO   What sense had I of her stol'n hours of lust?
  I saw't not, thought it not; it harmed not me;   340
  I slept the next night well, fed well, was free and merry;
  I found not Cassio's kisses on her lips.
  He that is robbed, not wanting what is stol'n,
  Let him not know't, and he's not robbed at all.

IAGO   I am sorry to hear this.   345

OTHELLO   I had been happy if the general camp,
  Pioneers and all, had tasted her sweet body,
  So I had nothing known. O now, forever
  Farewell the tranquil mind! farewell content!
  Farewell the plumèd troops and the big wars   350
  That makes ambition virtue! O, farewell!
  Farewell the neighing steed and the shrill trump,
  The spirit-stirring drum, th' ear-piercing fife,
  The royal banner and all quality,
  Pride, pomp and circumstance of glorious war!   355
  And O you mortal engines whose rude throats
  Th' immortal Jove's dread clamors counterfeit,
  Farewell! Othello's occupation's gone!

IAGO   Is't possible, my lord?

OTHELLO   [grabs IAGO by the throat.]   Villain, be sure thou prove
  my love a whore!   360
  Be sure of it, give me the ocular proof,
  Or by the worth of mine eternal soul,
  Thou hadst been better have been born a dog
  Than answer my waked wrath.

IAGO   Is't come to this?

341. **fed:** ate.
343. **wanting:** missing.
346–47. **the general . . . and all:** the whole army, including even the most menial trench-diggers ("pioneers").
349. **content:** Cf. 2.1.194 and note.
350. **plumèd:** splendidly uniformed (literally, feathered; cf. 1.3.384 and note). **big:** great, fierce.
351. **makes ambition virtue:** endows personal motivation with a higher sanction (the public good?); for the singular verb after "wars," see 1.1.148 and note.
352. **trump:** trumpet.
354. **royal:** "magnificent, splendid" (Neill); though cf. "royal siege" in 1.2.22. **quality:** nature; cf. "very quality" in 1.3.249.
355. **Pride . . . circumstance:** elaborate pageantry.
356. **mortal engines:** deadly artillery. **rude throats:** harsh sounds.
357. **Th' immortal . . . clamors:** i.e., the thunderbolts hurled down by the chief Roman deity. **counterfeit:** reproduce, imitate (perhaps a hint of the modern "fake").
358. **occupation:** profession, (legitimating) position; "*occupy* could = cohabit with" (Honigmann).
360. *grabs* IAGO *by the throat*: Starting with Rowe's "Catching hold of him" in 1709, editors have inserted stage directions here to indicate that Othello puts a stranglehold on Iago—the "collaring scene," as it has been designated, in a venerable theatrical tradition.
361. **ocular:** visible.

OTHELLO   Make me to see't, or at the least so prove it   365
    That the probation bear no hinge nor loop
    To hang a doubt on, or woe upon thy life!
IAGO   My noble lord—
OTHELLO   If thou dost slander her and torture me,
    Never pray more; abandon all remorse;   370
    On horror's head horrors accumulate;
    Do deeds to make heaven weep, all earth amazed;
    For nothing canst thou to damnation add
    Greater than that.
IAGO   O grace! O heaven forgive me!
    Are you a man? Have you a soul? or sense?   375
    God buy you; take mine office. O wretched fool,
    That lov'st to make thine honesty a vice!
    O monstrous world! Take note, take note, O world:
    To be direct and honest is not safe.
    I thank you for this profit, and from hence   380
    I'll love no friend, sith love breeds such offence.
OTHELLO   Nay, stay; thou shouldst be honest.
IAGO   I should be wise; for honesty's a fool
    And loses that it works for.
OTHELLO   By the world,
    I think my wife be honest, and think she is not;   385
    I think that thou art just, and think thou art not.
    I'll have some proof. My name, that was as fresh
    As Dian's visage, is now begrimed and black
    As mine own face. If there be cords or knives,
    Poison, or fire, or suffocating streams,   390
    I'll not endure it. Would I were satisfied!
IAGO   I see you are eaten up with passion;

---

366. **probation:** proof.
366–67. **bear . . . doubt on:** i.e., be absolutely certain (though the metaphors are obscure).
370. **remorse:** (futile attempts at) repentance.
371. **head:** "perhaps = summit" (Honigmann).
376. **God buy you:** "abbreviation for 'God be with you'—i.e., 'good-bye'" (McDonald).
377. **honesty a vice:** Iago claims to be "honest to a fault."
380. **profit:** useful lesson. **from hence:** henceforth.
381. **sith:** since.
384. **that it works for:** "i.e. trust, and the rewards trust deserves" (Ross).
385. **honest:** chaste.
386. **just:** upright; right (i.e., accurate in your suggestion).
387. **My name:** Despite the agreement in F and Q, editors regularly emend to "Her name," as printed in the second quarto (1630); but see note to 3.3.158–64 and 128 below. **fresh:** undefiled, clean.
388. **Dian:** Diana (Roman goddess of chastity).
389–90. **cords . . . streams:** means to commit suicide or murder.
391. **satisfied:** released from uncertainty.

I do repent me that I put it to you.
You would be satisfied?

OTHELLO   Would? Nay, and I will.

IAGO   And may . . . but how? how satisfied, my lord?   395
Would you, the supervisor, grossly gape on?
Behold her topped?

OTHELLO   Death and damnation! O!

IAGO   It were a tedious difficulty, I think,
To bring them to that prospect. Damn them then,
If ever mortal eyes do see them bolster   400
More than their own. What then? How then?
What shall I say? Where's satisfaction?
It is impossible you should see this,
Were they as prime as goats, as hot as monkeys,
As salt as wolves in pride, and fools as gross   405
As ignorance made drunk. But yet, I say,
If imputation and strong circumstances
Which lead directly to the door of truth
Will give you satisfaction, you might have't.

OTHELLO   Give me a living reason she's disloyal.   410

IAGO   I do not like the office.
But sith I am entered in this cause so far,
Pricked to't by foolish honesty and love,
I will go on. I lay with Cassio lately,
And being troubled with a raging tooth,   415
I could not sleep. There are a kind of men
So loose of soul that in their sleeps will mutter
Their affairs; one of this kind is Cassio.
In sleep I heard him say, "Sweet Desdemona,

---

393. put it: suggested Desdemona's possible infidelity; imparted this rage (?).
396. supervisor: observer (literally, someone who looks on from above); director. **grossly:** blatantly, lewdly (see lines 220–22 and note).
397. topped: Cf. "tupping" (1.1.86 and note).
400. bolster: a pillow or support (hence as a verb, metaphorically: to have sex).
401. more . . . own: illegitimately.
404. Were they: (even if) they were.
404–06. as prime . . . made drunk: three instances of animal lust, capped by drunkenness as bestial stupidity.
407. imputation: accusation; designation, assumption. **strong circumstances:** likely evidence.
408. lead . . . truth: "Othello is led in imagination to stand outside the closed bedroom door" (Ridley).
410. living: sustainable, valid.
411. office: task, duty.
412. sith: since. **cause:** matter, legal case.
413. Pricked: incited.
414. I lay . . . lately: That soldiers might share a bed is not by itself a noteworthy peculiarity.
415. raging tooth: toothache.
417. loose of soul: "careless about their inmost secrets" with an "additional suggestion of 'dissolute'" (Neill).

Let us be wary, let us hide our loves!"   420
And then, sir, would he gripe and wring my hand,
Cry, "O sweet creature!" then kiss me hard,
As if he plucked up kisses by the roots
That grew upon my lips, laid his leg o'er my thigh,
And sigh, and kiss, and then cry "Cursèd fate   425
That gave thee to the Moor!"

OTHELLO   O monstrous! monstrous!

IAGO   Nay, this was but his
    dream.

OTHELLO   But this denoted a foregone conclusion;
    'Tis a shrewd doubt, though it be but a dream.

IAGO   And this may help to thicken other proofs   430
    That do demonstrate thinly.

OTHELLO   I'll tear her all to pieces!

IAGO   Nay, yet be wise; yet we see nothing done;
    She may be honest yet. Tell me but this:
    Have you not sometimes seen a handkerchief
    Spotted with strawberries in your wife's hand?   435

OTHELLO   I gave her such a one; 'twas my first gift.

IAGO   I know not that; but such a handkerchief—
    I am sure it was your wife's—did I today
    See Cassio wipe his beard with.

OTHELLO   If it be that—

IAGO   If it be that, or any, it was hers.   440
    It speaks against her with the other proofs.

OTHELLO   O that the slave had forty thousand lives!
    One is too poor, too weak for my revenge.
    Now do I see 'tis true. Look here, Iago:
    All my fond love thus do I blow to heaven.   445
    'Tis gone.
    Arise, black vengeance, from the hollow hell!
    Yield up, O love, thy crown and hearted throne
    To tyrannous hate! Swell, bosom, with thy fraught,
    For 'tis of aspics' tongues!

IAGO   Yet be content.   450

---

421. **gripe:** grip.
428. **denoted . . . conclusion:** indicated an already consummated experience.
429. **shrewd doubt:** acute fear.
431. **do demonstrate thinly:** i.e., are inadequately conclusive in themselves (cf. "thin
    habits," 1.3.108, and note).
432. **yet be wise:** continue to exercise self-control.
435. **Spotted:** decorated; stained. **strawberries:** "might suggest a hidden evil, or the
    purity of the Virgin" or "drops of blood" (Honigmann); and see 175 below.
440. **or any . . . hers:** wildly illogical (hence Malone's emendation—see Textual Notes).
448. **hearted:** ensconced in the heart.
449. **fraught:** load.
450. **of aspics' tongues:** i.e., venomous.

OTHELLO   O, blood! blood! blood!

IAGO   Patience, I say; your mind may change.

OTHELLO   Never, Iago. Like to the Pontic Sea,
Whose icy current and compulsive course
Ne'er keeps retiring ebb but keeps due on   455
To the Propontic and the Hellespont,
Even so my bloody thoughts with violent pace
Shall ne'er look back, ne'er ebb to humble love,
Till that a capable and wide revenge
Swallow them up.   *OTHELLO kneels.*
                    Now, by yond marble heaven,   460
In the due reverence of a sacred vow,
I here engage my words.

IAGO   Do not rise yet.   *IAGO kneels.*
Witness, you ever-burning lights above,
You elements that clip us round about,
Witness that here Iago doth give up   465
The execution of his wit, hands, heart,
To wronged Othello's service. Let him command,
And to obey shall be in me remorse,
What bloody business ever.   [*They rise.*]

OTHELLO   I greet thy love,
Not with vain thanks but with acceptance bounteous,   470
And will upon the instant put thee to't.
Within these three days let me hear thee say
That Cassio's not alive.

IAGO   My friend is dead;
'Tis done at your request. But let her live.

OTHELLO   Damn her, lewd minx! O, damn her! damn her!   475
Come, go with me apart; I will withdraw
To furnish me with some swift means of death
For the fair devil. Now art thou my lieutenant.

IAGO   I am your own forever.   *Exeunt.*

---

453. **Pontic:** Black.
454. **compulsive:** "compelled; or, compelling" (Honigmann); "irresistible and headlong" (Ross).
459. **capable and wide:** all-embracing and broad-ranging.
460. **marble:** obdurate; dispensing rigorous judgment.
461. **a sacred vow:** With the kneeling, a kind of marriage ceremony.
463. **ever-burning lights:** stars; cf. the "ever-fixèd pole" of 2.1.15.
464. **elements:** either the heavenly bodies invoked again or the constituents of mutable nature. **clip:** embrace.
466. **execution . . . heart:** implementation of all his faculties.
468–69. **to obey . . . ever:** See Johnson's gloss, 244 below. **remorse:** compassion (cf. line 370).
471. **to't:** to the proof.
479. **your own forever:** consummates the marital ritual (see note to line 460) and "the Mephistophelian bargain" that "has ensnared Othello's soul" for all eternity (Neill).

ACT 3 SCENE 4

Enter DESDEMONA, EMILIA *and* CLOWN.

DESDEMONA   Do you know, sirrah, where lieutenant Cassio
lies?

CLOWN   I dare not say he lies anywhere.

DESDEMONA   Why, man?

CLOWN   He's a soldier, and for me to say a soldier lies,   5
'tis stabbing.

DESDEMONA   Go to; where lodges he?

CLOWN   To tell you where he lodges is to tell you where
I lie.

DESDEMONA   Can anything be made of this?   10

CLOWN   I know not where he lodges, and for me to devise
a lodging and say he lies here or he lies there were
to lie in mine own throat.

DESDEMONA   Can you inquire him out and be edified by report?

CLOWN   I will catechize the world for him—that is, make   15
questions and by them answer.

DESDEMONA   Seek him, bid him come hither. Tell him I
have moved my lord on his behalf and hope all will
be well.

CLOWN   To do this is within the compass of man's wit,   20
and therefore I will attempt the doing it.   *Exit* CLOWN.

DESDEMONA   Where should I lose the handkerchief, Emilia?

EMILIA   I know not, madam.

DESDEMONA   Believe me, I had rather have lost my purse
Full of crusadoes; and but my noble Moor   25
Is true of mind and made of no such baseness
As jealous creatures are, it were enough
To put him to ill-thinking.

EMILIA   Is he not jealous?

DESDEMONA   Who, he? I think the sun where he was born
Drew all such humors from him.

---

1. **sirrah:** fellow, boy; used to address a servant.
2. **lies:** resides.
5–6. **to say . . . stabbing:** a soldier accused of untruth would aggressively defend his honor.
7. **Go to:** expresses (perhaps amused) impatience: "no, really . . ."
11. **devise:** invent.
13. **in mine own throat:** i.e., blatantly, outrageously.
14. **edified:** instructed.
15. **catechize:** give religious instruction to.
16. **by:** by means of (as in the catechism, the questions predetermine the answers).
18. **moved:** urged.
22. **should:** might.
25. **crusadoes:** gold coins (stamped with a cross). **but:** although, except for the fact that.
27. **were:** would be.

Enter OTHELLO.

EMILIA   Look where he comes.   30

DESDEMONA [*Aside.*]   I will not leave him now till Cassio be
   Called to him.—How is't with you, my lord?

OTHELLO   Well, my good lady. [*Aside.*] O, hardness to
   dissemble!—
   How do you, Desdemona?

DESDEMONA   Well, my good lord.

OTHELLO   Give me your hand. This hand is moist, my lady.   35

DESDEMONA   It hath felt no age nor known no sorrow.

OTHELLO   This argues fruitfulness and liberal heart.
   Hot, hot, and moist. This hand of yours requires
   A sequester from liberty: fasting and prayer,
   Much castigation, exercise devout;   40
   For here's a young and sweating devil here
   That commonly rebels. 'Tis a good hand,
   A frank one.

DESDEMONA   You may indeed say so,
   For 'twas that hand that gave away my heart.

OTHELLO   A liberal hand. The hearts of old gave hands,   45
   But our new heraldry is hands, not hearts.

DESDEMONA   I cannot speak of this. Come now, your promise.

OTHELLO   What promise, chuck?

DESDEMONA   I have sent to bid Cassio come speak with you.

OTHELLO   I have a salt and sorry rheum offends me;   50
   Lend me thy handkerchief.

DESDEMONA   Here, my lord.

OTHELLO   That which I gave you.

DESDEMONA   I have it not about me.

OTHELLO   Not?

DESDEMONA   No, faith, my lord.

OTHELLO   That's a fault. That
   handkerchief

---

30. **Drew . . . him:** as though African heat evaporated those bodily fluids ("humors") that
   determined psychological states (such as jealousy). Desdemona's belief coexisted
   unpeacefully during the Renaissance with claims for African hot-bloodedness. **Look
   where he comes:** Cf. 3.3.279 and 331.
31. **Cassio:** may be a disyllable (Cass-YO).
37. **argues:** suggests; a moist palm conventionally signified an abundantly affectionate
   and possibly lubricious nature. **liberal heart:** could imply virtue (cf. 3.3.188) or las-
   civiousness (cf. 2.1.162).
39. **sequester:** quarantine.
40. **castigation:** moral correction, discipline.
42. **commonly rebels:** frequently (promiscuously, lasciviously) disobeys.
45–46. **The hearts . . . not hearts:** Unlike formerly, the current fashion is for marriage
   without sincere affection.
47. **I . . . this:** I don't know what you mean.
48. **chuck:** term of affection.
50. **salt . . . me:** irritating cold.

Did an Egyptian to my mother give.
She was a charmer and could almost read   55
The thoughts of people. She told her, while she kept it,
'T would make her amiable and subdue my father
Entirely to her love; but if she lost it
Or made a gift of it, my father's eye
Should hold her loathèd, and his spirits should hunt   60
After new fancies. She, dying, gave it me,
And bid me, when my fate would have me wived,
To give it her. I did so; and—take heed on't!—
Make it a darling like your precious eye.
To lose't or give't away were such perdition   65
As nothing else could match.
DESDEMONA   Is't possible?
OTHELLO   'Tis true. There's magic in the web of it:
A sibyl that had numbered in the world
The sun to course two hundred compasses,
In her prophetic fury sewed the work;   70
The worms were hallowed that did breed the silk,
And it was dyed in mummy, which the skillful
Conserved of maidens' hearts.
DESDEMONA   I'faith? Is't true?
OTHELLO   Most veritable; therefore look to't well.
DESDEMONA   Then would to God that I had never seen't!   75
OTHELLO   Ha? wherefore?
DESDEMONA   Why do you speak so startingly and rash?
OTHELLO   Is't lost? Is't gone? Speak, is't out o'th' way?
DESDEMONA   Heaven bless us!
OTHELLO   Say you?   80
DESDEMONA   It is not lost; but what an if it were?
OTHELLO   How?
DESDEMONA   I say it is not lost.
OTHELLO   Fetch't, let me see't!
DESDEMONA   Why, so I can; but I will not now.   85
   This is a trick to put me from my suit.

---

55. **charmer:** sorceress.
57. **amiable:** loveable, desirable.
61. **fancies:** objects of desire, sources of satisfaction.
64. **darling:** highly prized possession. **eye:** proverbially valuable body part, with sexual
   associations (the female "nether eye").
65. **perdition:** loss, catastrophe; cf. 3.3.90.
68–69. **A sybil . . . compasses:** "a 200-year-old prophetess" (Mowat and Werstine).
70. **fury:** rapture. **work:** design or pattern.
72. **mummy:** medicine derived from dead bodies. **the skillful:** those adept in magic.
73. **Conserved of maidens':** distilled from virgins'.
77. **so startingly and rash:** with such fitful urgency.
78. **out o'th' way:** missing.
81. **an if:** if.
86. **put:** divert. **suit:** petition.

Pray you let Cassio be received again.

OTHELLO Fetch me the handkerchief, my mind misgives—

DESDEMONA Come, come!

You'll never meet a more sufficient man—   90

OTHELLO The handkerchief!—

DESDEMONA   A man that all his time

Hath founded his good fortunes on your love,

Shared dangers with you—

OTHELLO   The handkerchief!

DESDEMONA I'faith, you are to blame.

OTHELLO Zounds!   *Exit* OTHELLO. 95

EMILIA Is not this man jealous?

DESDEMONA I ne'er saw this before.

Sure, there's some wonder in this handkerchief;

I am most unhappy in the loss of it.

EMILIA 'Tis not a year or two shows us a man.   100

They are all but stomachs, and we all but food;

They eat us hungerly, and when they are full

They belch us.

       Enter IAGO *and* CASSIO.

       Look you, Cassio and my husband.

IAGO There is no other way; 'tis she must do't;

And lo the happiness! go and importune her.   105

DESDEMONA How now, good Cassio, what's the news with you?

CASSIO Madam, my former suit. I do beseech you

That by your virtuous means I may again

Exist and be a member of his love,

Whom I, with all the office of my heart,   110

Entirely honor. I would not be delayed.

If my offense be of such mortal kind

That nor my service past nor present sorrows

---

88. **misgives:** worries.
90. **sufficient:** capable (the word can have a sexual resonance).
100. **shows us a man:** "reveal[s] to us (women) what (a monster) a man is" (Honigmann).
101. **all but:** nothing but.
102. **hungerly:** hungrily, voraciously.
103. **belch:** puke.
105. **lo the happiness:** what good luck; "look, here she is." **importune:** plead with.
109. **member:** the "bodies" of all Christians "are the members of Christ," which, when alienated through sin, become "the members of an harlot" (1 Corinthians 6:15).
110. **office:** duty, loyal service.
112. **mortal:** Roman Catholic theology distinguishes between venial and mortal sins. The former are easily pardonable, but the latter cut the sinner off from God and, if not forgiven by a sacramental act of confession, result in damnation.
113–15. **That . . . me:** In conjunction with the venial/mortal allusion, the appeal to a feminine "virtuous means" (like the interceding Virgin Mary) evokes Roman Catholic feeling. However, that neither good works ("service") nor repentance ("sorrows")

Nor purposed merit in futurity
Can ransom me into his love again,   115
But to know so must be my benefit;
So shall I clothe me in a forced content
And shut myself up in some other course
To fortune's alms.
DESDEMONA   Alas, thrice-gentle Cassio,
My advocation is not now in tune.   120
My lord is not my lord, nor should I know him,
Were he in favor as in humor altered.
So help me every spirit sanctified
As I have spoken for you all my best
And stood within the blank of his displeasure   125
For my free speech. You must awhile be patient.
What I can do I will, and more I will
Than for myself I dare. Let that suffice you.
IAGO   Is my lord angry?
EMILIA   He went hence but now,
And certainly in strange unquietness.   130
IAGO   Can he be angry? I have seen the cannon
When it hath blown his ranks into the air
And, like the devil, from his very arm
Puffed his own brother—and is he angry?
Something of moment then. I will go meet him;   135
There's matter in't indeed if he be angry.
DESDEMONA   I prithee do so.   *Exit* [IAGO].
                    Something sure of state—
Either from Venice, or some unhatched practice
Made demonstrable here in Cyprus to him—
Hath puddled his clear spirit; and in such cases   140
Men's natures wrangle with inferior things,
Though great ones are their object. 'Tis even so.

---

can earn ("merit") salvation ("ransom" = redeem from sin) is emphasized in "Protestant doctrine" (Ross).
116. **to know . . . benefit:** Cassio would find satisfaction in at least being freed from doubt.
117. **clothe . . . content:** perforce take whatever protective advantage is available.
119. **fortune's alms:** as distinct from the charitable gifts of his lord.
120. **advocation:** advocacy. **in tune:** appropriate.
122. **favor:** appearance. **humor:** mood.
124. **As I have:** if I have not.
125. **blank:** center of a target (see "white," 2.1.133, and note).
133. **his very arm:** right next to him
134. **Puffed:** blown away, blasted.
135. **of moment:** important.
137. **Something . . . of state:** Some political matter.
138–39. **unhatched . . . demonstrable:** covert plot coming to his attention.
140. **puddled:** muddied, agitated (a humors reference).
141–42. **wrangle . . . object:** project their irritation onto trivialities.
142. **'Tis even so:** "Yes, that must be it."

For let our finger ache, and it endues
Our other healthful members even to a sense
Of pain. Nay, we must think men are not gods,   145
Nor of them look for such observancy
As fits the bridal.—Beshrew me much, Emilia.
I was, unhandsome warrior as I am,
Arraigning his unkindness with my soul;
But now I find I had suborned the witness,   150
And he's indicted falsely.

EMILIA   Pray heaven it be
State matters, as you think, and no conception
Nor no jealous toy concerning you.

DESDEMONA   Alas the day! I never gave him cause.

EMILIA   But jealous souls will not be answered so;   155
They are not ever jealous for the cause,
But jealous for they're jealous. It is a monster
Begot upon itself, born on itself.

DESDEMONA   Heaven keep the monster from Othello's mind!

EMILIA   Lady, amen!   160

DESDEMONA   I will go seek him; Cassio, walk here about.
If I do find him fit, I'll move your suit
And seek to effect it to my uttermost.

CASSIO   I humbly thank your ladyship.

                                    Exeunt DESDEMONA *and* EMILIA.

        Enter BIANCA.

BIANCA   Save you, friend Cassio!

CASSIO   What make you from home?   165
How is't with you, my most fair Bianca?
I'faith, sweet love, I was coming to your house.

BIANCA   And I was going to your lodging, Cassio.

---

144. **members:** bodily parts (see line 109). **even to a:** to a similar or same.
146. **observancy:** attentiveness.
147. **As fits the bridal:** "expected on the wedding day" (McDonald); a temporarily unillusioned version of Emilia's permanently disillusioned disgust in lines 100–03. **Beshrew me:** mild oath—"shame on me."
148. **unhandsome warrior:** remembering Othello's "fair warrior" (2.1.180).
149. **Arraigning his unkindness:** accusing him of unnaturally cruel behavior.
150. **suborned:** corrupted. **the witness:** presumably "my soul," from whose earlier accusations she now experiences detachment ("I find").
152. **conception:** idea, invention.
153. **toy:** fantasy.
157. **for:** because of.
158. **begot:** conceived (sexually). **on:** from out of.
162. **fit:** in a receptive mood.
165. **Save you:** God save you. **make you:** are you doing away. Bianca is "out of door" (cf. 2.1.109) and "here alone" (cf. 3.3.302)—both conventionally improper.
167. **your house:** Bianca is apparently a property owner—another unconventionality.

What? keep a week away? seven days and nights?
Eight score eight hours? And lovers' absent hours   170
More tedious than the dial eight score times!
O weary reckoning!
CASSIO   Pardon me, Bianca;
  I have this while with leaden thoughts been pressed,
  But I shall in a more continuate time
  Strike off this score of absence. Sweet Bianca,   175
                    [*Gives her* DESDEMONA's *handkerchief.*]
  Take me this work out.
BIANCA   O, Cassio! whence came this?
  This is some token from a newer friend;
  To the felt absence now I feel a cause.
  Is't come to this? Well, well.
CASSIO   Go to, woman!
  Throw your vile guesses in the devil's teeth,   180
  From whence you have them. You are jealous now
  That this is from some mistress some remembrance;
  No, by my faith, Bianca.
BIANCA   Why, whose is it?
CASSIO   I know not neither; I found it in my chamber.
  I like the work well; ere it be demanded,   185
  As like enough it will, I would have it copied.
  Take it and do't, and leave me for this time.
BIANCA   Leave you? Wherefore?
CASSIO   I do attend here on the general
  And think it no addition, nor my wish,   190
  To have him see me womaned.
BIANCA   Why, I pray you?
CASSIO   Not that I love you not.
BIANCA   But that you do not love me.
  I pray you bring me on the way a little,
  And say if I shall see you soon at night.

---

170. **eight score eight:** 168 (7 times 24).
170–72. **And lovers' . . . reckoning:** Bianca comically exaggerates a proverbial distinction between the clock ("dial") and the slow time of separated lovers, then pretends
  dismay at the computational complexity (160 times 168).
173. **I have . . . been pressed:** "alluding to the torture known as 'pressing with weights'"
  (Ross).
174. **continuate:** uninterrupted.
175. **Strike . . . score:** cancel this obligation, pay this bill (punning on Bianca's "score").
176. **Take . . . out:** copy this design for me (see 3.3.298).
177. **friend:** Cf. "friend Cassio," line 165; variously glossed: "mistress" (Honigmann, Mowat
  and Werstine), "polite for 'paramour'" (Ross). See Names of the Actors, line 15 and note.
  Bianca's costume might have helped clarify her identity on the Renaissance stage.
178. **To . . . cause:** i.e., now I understand why I haven't seen you.
190. **addition:** "mark of distinction" (Schmidt); a heraldic term.
191. **womaned:** in female company.

CASSIO   'Tis but a little way that I can bring you,   195
  For I attend here; but I'll see you soon.
BIANCA   'Tis very good—I must be circumstanced.

Exeunt omnes.

ACT 4 SCENE 1

  Enter IAGO *and* OTHELLO.
IAGO   Will you think so?
OTHELLO   Think so, Iago?
IAGO   What,
  To kiss in private?
OTHELLO   An unauthorized kiss!
IAGO   Or to be naked with her friend in bed
  An hour or more, not meaning any harm?
OTHELLO   Naked in bed, Iago, and not mean harm?   5
  It is hypocrisy against the devil.
  They that mean virtuously, and yet do so,
  The devil their virtue tempts, and they tempt heaven.
IAGO   If they do nothing, 'tis a venial slip;
  But if I give my wife a handkerchief—   10
OTHELLO   What then?
IAGO   Why then, 'tis hers, my lord; and being hers,
  She may, I think, bestow't on any man.
OTHELLO   She is protectress of her honor too;
  May she give that?   15
IAGO   Her honor is an essence that's not seen;
  They have it very oft that have it not.
  But for the handkerchief—
OTHELLO   By heaven, I would most gladly have forgot it!
  Thou said'st—O, it comes o'er my memory   20
  As doth the raven o'er the infectious house,
  Boding to all!—he had my handkerchief.

---

197. be circumstanced: accept your conditions; accept my conditions, i.e., things as they
  are; be put off with excuses.
SD. *Enter* IAGO *and* OTHELLO: The Quarto reverses "the normal order of social prece-
  dence" in the Folio stage direction (Neill): The servant has become the master. **1.
  think so . . . Think so:** "Othello now echoes Iago, reversing their roles" in 3.3.107 ff
  (Honigmann).
  6. hypocrisy . . . devil: appearing to act sinfully while actually being good.
  7. do so: i.e., be naked . . . in bed.
  8. tempts: entices. **tempt:** dare or challenge to protect. "Thou shalt not tempt the Lord
  thy God" (Matthew 4:7).
  9. venial: minor, easily pardoned; see note to 3.4.112.
  17. They have . . . have it not: One of these "haves" = "seems to have."
  21–22. the raven . . . all: a universally bad omen, here associated with spreading
  plague or sexual disease.

IAGO   Ay, what of that?

OTHELLO   That's not so good now.

IAGO   What if I had said I had seen him do you wrong?
Or heard him say—as knaves be such abroad   25
Who (having by their own importunate suit
Or voluntary dotage of some mistress
Convincèd or supplied them) cannot choose
But they must blab—

OTHELLO   Hath he said anything?

IAGO   He hath, my lord, but be you well assured,   30
No more then he'll unswear.

OTHELLO   What hath he said?

IAGO   Faith, that he did . . . I know not what he did.

OTHELLO   What? What?

IAGO   Lie . . .

OTHELLO   With her?

IAGO   With her, on her; what you will.

OTHELLO   Lie with her? lie on her? We say lie on her   35
when they belie her. Lie with her? Zounds, that's fulsome.—
Handkerchief! confessions! handkerchief!—To confess,
and be hanged for his labor. First to be hanged,
and then to confess: I tremble at it. Nature would not
invest herself in such shadowing passion without some   40
instruction. It is not words that shakes me thus. Pish!
Noses, ears and lips! is't possible? Confess? Handkerchief?

25. **knaves . . . abroad:** scoundrels are around.
26. **importunate suit:** perseverant wooing.
27. **voluntary dotage:** willing infatuation.
28. **convincèd or supplied:** seduced or sexually "serviced."
34. **With her, on her:** Iago shifts emphasis from Othello's "her" to "with" and to a sequence of sexual positions, recapitulating the action of Cassio's dream ("lay with Cassio. . . . And then . . . laid his leg o'er my thigh," 3.3.414–24). **what you will:** "a conventional phrase—'as you like it'—ending with the sexually charged *will*" (McDonald); a "poisonous phrase: it implies 'anything you like to think (or do with her)'" (Honigmann).
35–36. **We say . . . belie her:** For the plural pronouns ("we" and "they"), cf. 3.3.271 ff.; "belie" can=lie about or lie on top of (cf. the Clown's puns about Cassio's lodgings in 3.1.1 ff.).
36. **fulsome:** disgusting; used of "rank" or in-heat sheep ("the fulsome ewes," *Merchant of Venice* 1.3.80).
39–41. **I tremble . . . shakes me thus:** Othello may be referring to his own fit: "(my) nature would not have been provoked to this paroxysm unless it had some motivation more substantial than (mere) words"; but he may rather (or also) be referring to Desdemona. "Nature" is conventionally gendered female, and Iago repeatedly associates it with Desdemona's sexual appetite: "very nature will instruct her" to "heave the gorge, disrelish and abhor" Othello (2.1.229–31). Othello's word to describe his spastic fit, "shakes," reiterates Iago's word to describe Desdemona's attraction to Othello: "when she seemed to shake, and fear your looks, / She loved them most" (3.3.209–10).
40. **shadowing:** darkening, but also "imaging a reality," as an actor would dress up ("invest") to shadow a substance: Othello or Desdemona has been instructed to perform a passionate part—their behavior is scripted by cultural norms.

O devil!   *Falls in a trance.*

IAGO   Work on,
My medicine, work! Thus credulous fools are caught,   45
And many worthy and chaste dames even thus,
All guiltless, meet reproach.—What ho! my lord!
My lord, I say! Othello?

Enter CASSIO.

How now, Cassio?

CASSIO   What's the matter?

IAGO   My lord is fallen into an epilepsy.   50
This is his second fit; he had one yesterday.

CASSIO   Rub him about the temples.

IAGO   No, forbear.
The lethargy must have his quiet course;
If not, he foams at mouth and by and by
Breaks out to savage madness. Look, he stirs.   55
Do you withdraw yourself a little while;
He will recover straight. When he is gone,
I would on great occasion speak with you.

[*Exit* CASSIO.]

How is it, general? Have you not hurt your head?

OTHELLO   Dost thou mock me?

IAGO   I mock you not, by heaven.   60
Would you would bear your fortune like a man!

OTHELLO   A hornèd man's a monster and a beast.

IAGO   There's many a beast then in a populous city,
And many a civil monster.

OTHELLO   Did he confess it?

IAGO   Good sir, be a man: 65
Think every bearded fellow that's but yoked
May draw with you. There's millions now alive
That nightly lie in those unproper beds
Which they dare swear peculiar. Your case is better.

---

45. **My medicine:** Cf. "my poison," 3.3.326.
53. **lethargy:** loss of consciousness. **his:** its. **quiet:** undisturbed.
58. **great occasion:** a matter of real importance.
60. **mock me:** i.e., by referring to the head-hurting cuckolds' horns.
64. **civil monster:** civilized beast.
65. **be a man:** bear it patiently, keep your wits about you (but with more play on the natural man and the monstrous beast).
66. **bearded fellow:** mature man. **yoked:** joined in matrimony (like oxen or beasts of burden).
67. **draw:** compare; drag (as a cart).
68. **unproper:** indecent; "not (solely) his own" (Ridley).
69. **peculiar:** exclusively their own.

O, 'tis the spite of hell, the fiend's arch-mock,   70
To lip a wanton in a secure couch,
And to suppose her chaste. No, let me know;
And knowing what I am, I know what she shall be.

OTHELLO   O, thou art wise, 'tis certain.

IAGO   Stand you a while
      apart,
Confine yourself but in a patient list.   75
Whilst you were here, o'er-whelmèd with your grief—
A passion most unsuiting such a man—
Cassio came hither. I shifted him away
And laid good 'scuses upon your ecstasy,
Bade him anon return and here speak with me,   80
The which he promised. Do but encave yourself,
And mark the fleers, the gibes and notable scorns
That dwell in every region of his face;
For I will make him tell the tale anew:
Where, how, how oft, how long ago and when   85
He hath and is again to cope your wife.
I say, but mark his gesture. Marry, patience!
Or I shall say you're all in all in spleen,
And nothing of a man.

OTHELLO   Dost thou hear, Iago?
I will be found most cunning in my patience;   90
But—dost thou hear?—most bloody.

IAGO   That's not amiss,
But yet keep time in all. Will you withdraw?

           [OTHELLO *withdraws*.]

Now will I question Cassio of Bianca,
A huswife that by selling her desires
Buys herself bread and cloth. It is a creature   95

71. **lip . . . couch:** "kiss a whore in an apparently untainted bed" (McDonald).
73. **I am:** a cuckold (?); a real man (?). **shall be:** a whore (?); punished (?); dead (?).
75. **Confine . . . list:** i.e., keep your self-control.
79. **ecstasy:** fit (ex-stasis: the spirit stands outside the body, leaving it comatose).
80. **anon:** soon.
81. **encave:** conceal.
82. **fleers:** mockeries. **notable:** overt.
86. **cope:** encounter with (sexually).
88. **all in all in spleen:** totally given over to bestial passion.
92. **keep time:** maintain harmonious behavior; perhaps suggests "don't be premature in revenge."
94. **huswife:** "could mean 'prostitute', and clearly this is the sense in which Iago is using it here. But Bianca appears not to be a professional courtesan exactly" (Sanders and see note to 2.1.112). **desires:** "appetites" (Ross), or perhaps desirability, as in "others' desire of her" (Neill).

That dotes on Cassio—as 'tis the strumpet's plague
To beguile many and be beguiled by one.
He, when he hears of her, cannot restrain
From the excess of laughter. Here he comes.

    Enter CASSIO.

As he shall smile, Othello shall go mad;   100
And his unbookish jealousy must conster
Poor Cassio's smiles, gestures and light behaviors
Quite in the wrong. How do you, lieutenant?
CASSIO   The worser that you give me the addition
   Whose want even kills me.   105
IAGO   Ply Desdemona well, and you are sure on't.
   Now if this suit lay in Bianca's power,
   How quickly should you speed!
CASSIO   Alas, poor caitiff!
OTHELLO   Look how he laughs already!
IAGO   I never knew woman love man so.   110
CASSIO   Alas, poor rogue! I think, i'faith, she loves me.
OTHELLO   Now he denies it faintly and laughs it out.
IAGO   Do you hear, Cassio?
OTHELLO   Now he importunes him
   To tell it o'er. Go to! well said, well said!
IAGO   She gives it out that you shall marry her.   115
   Do you intend it?
CASSIO   Ha, ha, ha!
OTHELLO   Do ye triumph, Roman? do you triumph?
CASSIO   I marry? What! a customer? Prithee bear some
   charity to my wit; do not think it so unwholesome.
   Ha, ha, ha!   120
OTHELLO   So, so, so, so! they laugh that wins.
IAGO   Faith, the cry goes that you marry her.

96–97. **as 'tis . . . by one:** The "beguiler beguiled" was proverbial, but no authority is
   available for Iago's application specifically to whores. For "beguile," see 2.1.122.
101. **unbookish:** inexperienced. **conster:** construe.
104. **addition:** title, and see 3.4.190.
105. **want:** lack.
108. **speed:** prosper. **caitiff:** scoundrel.
111. **rogue:** rascal; like "caitiff," available as a term of endearment.
112. **denies it faintly:** pretends to protest.
114. **Go to . . . well said:** Carry on, well done.
118. **triumph, Roman:** referring to the ceremonial celebrations of military conquest in
   ancient Rome.
119. **customer:** means prostitute in *All's Well That Ends Well* 5.3.280, but Shakespeare
   more often uses "customer" in its modern sense, "consumer of goods," the primary
   meaning in the Renaissance. Cf. Honigmann's gloss, "one who purchases (sexual
   services) (= Cassio); or, a prostitute (= Bianca)"; and see note to "desires" in line 94.
119–20. **bear . . . wit:** give me credit for more sense.
120. **unwholesome:** diseased.
122. **cry:** noise; rumor.

CASSIO   Prithee say true.

IAGO   I am a very villain else.

OTHELLO   Have you scored me? Well.   125

CASSIO   This is the monkey's own giving out. She is persuaded I
will marry her out of her own love and flattery, not out of my
promise.

OTHELLO   Iago beckons me; now he begins the story.

CASSIO   She was here even now; she haunts me in every
place. I was the other day talking on the sea bank   130
with certain Venetians, and thither comes the
bauble and, by this hand, falls me thus about my neck—

OTHELLO   Crying "O dear Cassio!" as it were: his gesture
imports it.

CASSIO   So hangs and lolls and weeps upon me, so shakes   135
and pulls me. Ha, ha, ha!

OTHELLO   Now he tells how she plucked him to my chamber.
O! I see that nose of yours, but not that dog I
shall throw it to.

CASSIO   Well, I must leave her company.   140

IAGO   Before me! look where she comes!

   Enter BIANCA.

CASSIO   'Tis such another fitchew! marry, a perfumed
one! What do you mean by this haunting of me?

BIANCA   Let the devil and his dam haunt you! what
did you mean by that same handkerchief you gave   145
me even now? I was a fine fool to take it. I must take
out the work? A likely piece of work, that you should
find it in your chamber and know not who left it there!
This is some minx's token, and I must take out the work?
There, give it your hobby-horse! Wheresoever you had   150
it, I'll take out no work on't.

CASSIO   How now, my sweet Bianca?
How now? how now?

OTHELLO   By heaven, that should be my handkerchief!

---

125. **scored:** designated; branded; insulted (?).
126. **monkey:** associated with lust, though could suggest affection (cf. note to line 111).
128. **beckons me:** signals me to approach or pay closer heed.
132. **bauble:** toy (dismissive contempt). **thus:** Cassio acts out a gesture, perhaps on Iago's body (cf. 3.3.414 ff.).
135. **So and so:** like "thus" (line 132), requires gestures. **shakes:** See lines 39–41 and note.
141. **look where she comes:** see note to 3.4.30.
142. **such another:** "like all the rest of them" (Ridley). **fitchew:** polecat, emblem of lust, noted for its stench (hence "perfumed"); cf. Iago's "smell in such," 3.3.234.
147. **piece of work:** "a set phrase"; here = "a likely story!" (Honigmann).
149. **minx:** whore, as in Othello's description of Desdemona (3.3.475).
150. **hobby-horse:** a "mock-horse's body strapped round" the waist of a morris dancer in May Day celebrations (note to *Hamlet* 3.2.122); a "mountable wench" (Ross).
154. **should:** must.

BIANCA   If you'll come to supper tonight, you may; if   155
  you will not, come when you are next prepared for.   *Exit.*

IAGO   After her, after her!

CASSIO   Faith, I must; she'll rail in the streets else.

IAGO   Will you sup there?

CASSIO   Faith, I intend so.   160

IAGO   Well, I may chance to see you, for I would very
  fain speak with you.

CASSIO   Prithee come, will you?

IAGO   Go to; say no more.   *Exit* CASSIO.

OTHELLO [*Comes forward.*]   How shall I murder him, Iago?   165

IAGO   Did you perceive how he laughed at his vice?

OTHELLO   O Iago!

IAGO   And did you see the handkerchief?

OTHELLO   Was that mine?

IAGO   Yours, by this hand! and to see how he prizes   170
  the foolish woman, your wife! She gave it him, and he
  hath given it his whore.

OTHELLO   I would have him nine years a killing!—A
  fine woman, a fair woman, a sweet woman!

IAGO   Nay, you must forget that.   175

OTHELLO   Ay, let her rot and perish and be damned tonight,
  for she shall not live! No, my heart is turned to
  stone; I strike it, and it hurts my hand.—O, the world
  hath not a sweeter creature! She might lie by an emperor's
  side and command him tasks.   180

IAGO   Nay, that's not your way.

OTHELLO   Hang her!—I do but say what she is: so delicate
  with her needle; an admirable musician (O, she will
  sing the savageness out of a bear!); of so high and plenteous
  wit and invention!   185

IAGO   She's the worse for all this.

OTHELLO   O, a thousand, a thousand times!—
  And then of so gentle a condition!

---

156. **you . . . prepared for:** I'm ready (and not before).
162. **fain:** much like to.
170. **by this hand:** I swear by my own hand. **prizes:** cherishes.
173. **nine . . . killing:** suffer prolonged torture.
173–91. **A fine woman . . . pity of it, Iago:** With the "sudden flipover" of these mechanical repetitions, "from hate to love" and back again, Othello is turned into an autom-
   aton and "tragedy comes close to farce" (Honigmann).
180. **command him tasks:** like the lady in medieval romance, assigning quests to her
   knight.
184. **sing . . . bear:** like Orpheus's music in Greek mythology, taming wild nature.
184–85. **so high . . . invention:** such accomplished intelligence and abundant imagination.
188. **gentle a condition:** sweet disposition; noble birth.

IAGO   Ay, too gentle.

OTHELLO   Nay, that's certain.—But yet the pity of it, Iago! O   190
Iago, the pity of it, Iago!

IAGO   If you are so fond over her iniquity, give her patent
to offend, for if it touch not you it comes near nobody.

OTHELLO   I will chop her into messes! Cuckold me!

IAGO   O, 'tis foul in her.   195

OTHELLO   With mine officer!

IAGO   That's fouler.

OTHELLO   Get me some poison, Iago, this night. I'll not
expostulate with her, lest her body and beauty unprovide
my mind again. This night, Iago.   200

IAGO   Do it not with poison. Strangle her in her bed,
even the bed she hath contaminated.

OTHELLO   Good, good! The justice of it pleases. Very good!

IAGO   And for Cassio, let me be his undertaker.
You shall hear more by midnight.   205

OTHELLO   Excellent good!

A trumpet [*within*].   What trumpet is that same?

IAGO   I warrant something from Venice.

Enter LODOVICO, DESDEMONA, *and Attendants.*

'Tis Lodovico; this comes from the duke.
See, your wife's with him.

LODOVICO   God save you, worthy general.   210

OTHELLO   With all my heart, sir.

LODOVICO   The duke and the senators of Venice greet you.

[*Gives him a letter.*]

OTHELLO   I kiss the instrument of their pleasures.

[*Opens the letter and reads.*]

DESDEMONA   And what's the news, good cousin Lodovico?

IAGO   I am very glad to see you, signior.   215

---

189. **gentle:** Iago takes the word as meaning "pliant."
192. **fond . . . iniquity:** dote upon her wickedness. **patent:** licence, authority.
193. **touch:** concern; move.
194. **messes:** meal-sized gobbets; "bits" or "mincemeat."
199. **expostulate:** reason, argue, discourse. **body and beauty:** "bodily beauty—hendiadys" (Ross).
199–200. **unprovide my mind:** change my mind; disarm my rational faculties.
200. **again:** refers perhaps to the way her mere image has been repeatedly sapping his resolution throughout this exchange with Iago; perhaps to the actual experience of her bodily beauty at some unspecified earlier time (perhaps last night as distinct from "this night"?).
204. **be his undertaker:** undertake (take care of, dispose of) him.
213. **kiss:** i.e., defer to, though perhaps a literal action is called for. **instrument . . . pleasures:** means by which they convey their desires (with "kiss," possible sexual resonance).

Welcome to Cyprus.

LODOVICO   I thank you. How does Lieutenant Cassio?

IAGO   Lives, sir.

DESDEMONA   Cousin, there's fallen between him and my lord
An unkind breach; but you shall make all well.   220

OTHELLO   Are you sure of that?

DESDEMONA   My lord?

OTHELLO [*Reads.*]   "This fail you not to do, as you will . . ."

LODOVICO   He did not call: he's busy in the paper.
Is there division 'twixt my lord and Cassio?   225

DESDEMONA   A most unhappy one; I would do much
T' atone them, for the love I bear to Cassio.

OTHELLO   Fire and brimstone!

DESDEMONA   My lord?

OTHELLO   Are you wise?

DESDEMONA   What, is he angry?

LODOVICO   Maybe the letter moved him;
For, as I think, they do command him home,   230
Deputing Cassio in his government.

DESDEMONA   By my troth, I am glad on't.

OTHELLO   Indeed!

DESDEMONA   My lord?

OTHELLO   I am glad to see you mad.

DESDEMONA   Why, sweet Othello?

OTHELLO   Devil!   [*Strikes her.*]

DESDEMONA   I have not deserved this.   235

LODOVICO   My lord, this would not be believed in Venice,
Though I should swear I saw't. 'Tis very much;
Make her amends—she weeps.

OTHELLO   O devil, devil!
If that the earth could teem with woman's tears,
Each drop she falls would prove a crocodile.   240
Out of my sight!

DESDEMONA   I will not stay to offend you.

LODOVICO   Truly obedient lady!
I do beseech your lordship call her back.

OTHELLO   Mistress!

DESDEMONA   My lord?   245

---

227. **atone:** reconcile (make one). **love I bear:** i.e., affection I owe (carry as obligation or duty).
228. **wise:** discreet; sane.
231. **government:** position as governor.
233. **glad to see you mad:** happy ("satisfied") to see you have abandoned discretion and sanity (?).
237. **very much:** excessive, outrageous.
240. **falls:** lets fall. **prove a crocodile:** the proverbially misleading "crocodile tears."

OTHELLO   What would you with her, sir?
LODOVICO   Who I, my lord?
OTHELLO   Ay, you did wish that I would make her turn.
    Sir, she can turn, and turn, and yet go on
    And turn again. And she can weep, sir, weep.
    And she's obedient; as you say, obedient,   250
    Very obedient.—Proceed you in your tears.—
    Concerning this, sir—O well-painted passion!—
    I am commanded home.—Get you away!
    I'll send for you anon.—Sir, I obey the mandate
    And will return to Venice.—Hence, avaunt!   255

                              [*Exit* DESDEMONA.]

    Cassio shall have my place. And, sir, tonight
    I do entreat that we may sup together.
    You are welcome, sir, to Cyprus.—Goats and monkeys!   *Exit*.
LODOVICO   Is this the noble Moor whom our full Senate
    Call all in all sufficient? Is this the nature   260
    Whom passion could not shake? whose solid virtue
    The shot of accident nor dart of chance
    Could neither graze nor pierce?
IAGO   He is much changed.
LODOVICO   Are his wits safe? Is he not light of brain?
IAGO   He's that he is; I may not breathe my censure.   265
    What he might be—if what he might he is not—
    I would to heaven he were.
LODOVICO   What! Strike his wife?
IAGO   'Faith, that was not so well; yet would I knew
    That stroke would prove the worst.
LODOVICO   Is it his use?
    Or did the letters work upon his blood   270
    And new create his fault?
IAGO   Alas, alas!

---

247. **turn:** return; but also change faith, as in "turn Turk" (2.3.160).
248–49. **can turn . . . turn again:** is indefatigable in her capacity to shift allegiance; has an insatiable sexual appetite.
250–51. **obedient . . . Very obedient:** The word comes to mean "compliant" in the sexual sense.
255. **avaunt:** See 3.3.336 and note.
256. **my place:** military command; sexual position.
258. **Goats and monkeys:** Cf. 3.3.404.
260. **all in all sufficient:** totally self-contained.
260–61. **nature . . . shake:** Cf. lines 39–41.
261–63. **solid virtue . . . pierce:** i.e., his inner strength was impervious to external assaults. **shot . . . chance:** Cf. "The slings and arrows of outrageous fortune," *Hamlet* 3.1.57. **accident:** unanticipated happening.
265–67. **I may . . . he were:** Iago claims that his duty prevents him from criticism, then speaks obscurely in a way designed to reinforce suspicion about Othello's sanity.
269. **use:** regular habit.

It is not honesty in me to speak
What I have seen and known. You shall observe him,
And his own courses will denote him so
That I may save my speech. Do but go after   275
And mark how he continues.

LODOVICO   I am sorry that I am deceived in him.   *Exeunt.*

ACT 4 SCENE 2

Enter OTHELLO *and* EMILIA.

OTHELLO   You have seen nothing then?
EMILIA   Nor ever heard, nor ever did suspect.
OTHELLO   Yes, you have seen Cassio and she together.
EMILIA   But then I saw no harm, and then I heard
   Each syllable that breath made up between them.   5
OTHELLO   What, did they never whisper?
EMILIA   Never, my lord.
OTHELLO   Nor send you out o'th' way?
EMILIA   Never.
OTHELLO   To fetch her fan, her gloves, her mask, nor nothing?
EMILIA   Never, my lord.   10
OTHELLO   That's strange.
EMILIA   I durst, my lord, to wager she is honest,
   Lay down my soul at stake. If you think other,
   Remove your thought; it doth abuse your bosom.
   If any wretch have put this in your head,   15
   Let heaven requite it with the serpent's curse,
   For if she be not honest, chaste and true,
   There's no man happy. The purest of their wives
   Is foul as slander.
OTHELLO   Bid her come hither—go.   *Exit* EMILIA.
   She says enough; yet she's a simple bawd   20
   That cannot say as much. This is a subtle whore:
   A closet lock and key of villainous secrets;

---

274. **courses:** behavior.
  9. **mask:** "conventional public attire for women of the time" (Mowat and Werstine).
 12. **durst:** would dare.
 13. **at stake:** "at hazard (after *wager*); at the stake (like a martyr dying for his faith)" (Honigmann). **other:** otherwise.
 14. **abuse your bosom:** mislead your feelings.
 16. **the serpent's curse:** "vpon thy belly shalt thou go, and dust shalt thou eat all the dayes of thy life" (Genesis 3:14).
 20–21. **she's . . . say:** i.e., any foolish procurer ("simple bawd") would maintain.
 21. **This:** i.e., Emilia, but then slipping into Desdemona at some point in the speech.
 22. **closet lock and key:** at once the space ("closet" = small private enclosure), the means to protect the space, and the tool to penetrate the space; cf. the thing in the thing, 3.3.274–75, and note.

And yet she'll kneel and pray; I have seen her do't.

Enter DESDEMONA *and* EMILIA.

DESDEMONA   My lord, what is your will?

OTHELLO   Pray you, chuck, come
  hither.

DESDEMONA   What is your pleasure?

OTHELLO   Let me see your eyes.   25
  Look in my face.

DESDEMONA   What horrible fancy's this?

OTHELLO [*To* EMILIA.]   Some of your function, mistress:
  Leave procreants alone and shut the door;
  Cough or cry "hem" if anybody come.
  Your mystery, your mystery! Nay, dispatch!   *Exit* EMILIA. 30

DESDEMONA   Upon my knee, what doth your speech import?
  I understand a fury in your words,
  But not the words.

OTHELLO   Why? What art thou?

DESDEMONA   Your wife, my lord, your true and loyal wife.

OTHELLO   Come, swear it! damn thyself!   35
  Lest, being like one of heaven, the devils themselves
  Should fear to seize thee. Therefore be double-damned:
  Swear thou art honest!

DESDEMONA   Heaven doth truly know it.

OTHELLO   Heaven truly knows that thou art false as hell.

DESDEMONA   To whom, my lord? With whom? How am I false?   40

OTHELLO   Ah, Desdemon! away, away, away!

DESDEMONA   Alas the heavy day! Why do you weep?
  Am I the motive of these tears, my lord?
  If haply you my father do suspect
  An instrument of this your calling back,   45
  Lay not your blame on me. If you have lost him,
  I have lost him too.

OTHELLO   Had it pleased heaven
  To try me with affliction, had they rained
  All kind of sores and shames on my bare head,
  Steeped me in poverty to the very lips,   50

---

27. **function:** office (as bawd).
28. **procreants:** breeders.
30. **mystery:** trade.
31. **Upon my knee:** "Kneeling in submission was not unusual" (Honigmann); in the absence of stage directions, actors/readers have to determine when she will rise.
36. **one of heaven:** i.e., beautifully angelic.
37. **double-damned:** adding perjury to adultery.
45. **An instrument of:** instrumental in.
50. **Steeped:** immersed.

Given to captivity me and my utmost hopes,
I should have found in some place of my soul
A drop of patience. But, alas, to make me
The fixèd figure for the time of scorn
To point his slow and moving finger at!   55
Yet could I bear that too—well, very well;
But there where I have garnered up my heart,
Where either I must live or bear no life,
The fountain from the which my current runs
Or else dries up; to be discarded thence,   60
Or keep it as a cistern for foul toads
To knot and gender in!—Turn thy complexion there,
Patience, thou young and rose-lipped cherubin;
I here look grim as hell!

DESDEMONA   I hope my noble lord esteems me honest.   65

OTHELLO   O, ay, as summer flies are in the shambles,
That quicken even with blowing. O thou weed,
Who art so lovely fair and smell'st so sweet
That the sense aches at thee,
Would thou hadst never been born!   70

DESDEMONA   Alas, what ignorant sin have I committed?

OTHELLO   Was this fair paper, this most goodly book,
Made to write "whore" upon? What committed?

---

51. utmost: uttermost (i.e., fondest).

54–55. The stationery number at which the clock hand points accusatorily; i.e., the public mockery of the cuckold as an unbearably sustained embarrassment. **slow and moving:** slowly moving.

57. garnered . . . heart: stored my deepest feelings (most vital sustenance).

59–62. The fountain . . . gender in!: "The use of fountain and cistern as metaphors for marriage derives from Proverbs 5:15" (Hamlin, 10, and see notes in Neill, Honigmann, and Sanders). Cf. "a toad" and "keep a corner" in 3.3.272–74. **cistern:** can = cesspit. **knot and gender:** fuck and breed.

62. Turn thy complexion there: (1) direct your attention to that view; (2) transform your disposition—or (3) facial color (from white to black "as hell")—at that prospect.

63. rose-lipped: "a coinage (with sexual overtones?)" (Honigmann).

64. As printed here, Othello is describing his own appearance as black. Many editors emend the "I" found in Q and F to "Ay" (which is regularly represented as "I" in Renaissance texts), often adding a comma: "Ay, here look grim." With this emendation, Othello is addressing a command to the angelic boy (the personified "Patience"), rather than describing his own appearance. In the theater, "I" and "Ay" would be indistinguishable.

66. flies . . . shambles: the "flesh-flies" that breed in excrement or rotting meat ("shambles" = slaughterhouse); cf. "exsufflicate," 3.3.184, and note.

67. quicken: are born; become aroused; cf. 3.3.279 and note. **even with blowing:** at the very moment—even now—when the eggs are deposited. For the association of flies, fertility, and contamination, cf. 1.1.67–68. **weed:** perhaps suggested by "blowing" as "blooming."

71. ignorant: epithet transferred from Desdemona, who does not know what she is supposed to have done.

72. this fair paper: her white flesh.

73. made to write "whore" upon: Cf. Revelation 17:5: "And in her forhead *was* a name written, A mysterie, great Babylon, the mother of whoredomes, and abominations of the earth."

Committed? O, thou public commoner!
I should make very forges of my cheeks   75
That would to cinders burn up modesty
Did I but speak thy deeds. What committed?
Heaven stops the nose at it, and the moon winks;
The bawdy wind that kisses all it meets
Is hushed within the hollow mine of earth   80
And will not hear't. What committed?

DESDEMONA   By heaven, you do me wrong!

OTHELLO   Are not you a strumpet?

DESDEMONA   No, as I am a Christian!
If to preserve this vessel for my lord
From any other foul unlawful touch   85
Be not to be a strumpet, I am none.

OTHELLO   What, not a whore?

DESDEMONA   No, as I shall be saved!

OTHELLO   Is't possible?

DESDEMONA   O, heaven forgive us!

OTHELLO   I cry you mercy then.
I took you for that cunning whore of Venice   90
That married with Othello.—You! Mistress!
That have the office opposite to Saint Peter
And keeps the gate of hell. You, you!

        Enter EMILIA.

                              Ay, you.
We have done our course; there's money for your pains;
I pray you turn the key and keep our counsel.   *Exit.* 95

EMILIA   Alas, what does this gentleman conceive?

73–74. **committed? / Committed?:** Othello's enraged repetitions here and in lines 77
and 81 depend on the word's Elizabethan application "particularly to unlawful acts of
love" (Malone, who cites *King Lear* 3.4.75–76: "commit not with man's sworn spouse").
74. **public commoner:** "common whore" (Honigmann).
75–76. **forges . . . modesty:** "an image of blushing" (McDonald).
79. **The bawdy wind:** Even (understood) the promiscuous wind is embarrassed.
84. **this vessel:** my body; "euerie one of you shulde know, how to possesse his vessel in
holiness & honour, *And* not in the lust of concupiscence" (1 Thessalonians 4:4).
88. **Is't possible:** "This question echoes through the play" (Honigmann, citing 2.3.277,
3.3.359, 3.4.66, and 4.1.42). In Sam Mendes's 1997 production, "the line provided the
cue for a despairingly tender and lingering embrace, broken violently on 'I cry you
mercy then'" (Neill).
89. **cry you mercy:** beg your pardon.
92–93. **the office . . . hell:** Christ gave St. Peter "the keyes of the kingdome of heauen,"
declaring that "vpon this rocke I wil buylde my Church: and the gates of hel shal not
ouercome it" (Matthew 16:18–19). **gate of hell:** "term for the female genitals"
(McDonald).
94. **course:** business. **pains:** efforts.
96. **conceive:** think, imagine.

How do you, madam? how do you, my good lady?
DESDEMONA   Faith, half asleep.
EMILIA   Good madam,
  What's the matter with my lord?   100
DESDEMONA   With who?
EMILIA   Why, with my lord, madam.
DESDEMONA   Who is thy lord?
EMILIA   He that is yours, sweet lady.
DESDEMONA   I have none. Do not talk to me, Emilia;
  I cannot weep, nor answers have I none   105
  But what should go by water. Prithee tonight
  Lay on my bed my wedding sheets; remember,
  And call thy husband hither.
EMILIA   Here's a change indeed!   *Exit.*
DESDEMONA   'Tis meet I should be used so, very meet.
  How have I been behaved that he might stick   110
  The small'st opinion on my least misuse?

        Enter IAGO *and* EMILIA.

IAGO   What is your pleasure, madam? How is't with you?
DESDEMONA   I cannot tell. Those that do teach young babes
  Do it with gentle means and easy tasks.
  He might have chid me so; for in good faith   115
  I am a child to chiding.
IAGO   What is the matter, lady?
EMILIA   Alas, Iago, my lord hath so bewhored her,
  Thrown such despite and heavy terms upon her,
  That true hearts cannot bear it.
DESDEMONA   Am I that name, Iago?
IAGO   What name, fair lady?   120
DESDEMONA   Such as she said my lord did say I was.
EMILIA   He called her whore. A beggar in his drink
  Could not have laid such terms upon his callet.

---

106. **go by water:** be communicated through tears.
107. **my wedding sheets:** "to remind Othello of their former love. . . . Also ominous, as
  wives were sometimes buried in their wedding sheets" (Honigmann).
109. **meet . . . used:** appropriate . . . treated (presumably a sarcastic reference to Othello's cruelty).
110–11. **stick . . . misuse:** even casually reprimand any inconsequential lapse on my part.
114. **tasks:** "perhaps = reproofs" (Honigmann).
116. **a child:** responsive (because eager to please); inexperienced, unused.
117. **bewhored:** (1) treated her like a whore; (2) called her a whore (cf. "belie," 4.1.36);
  imposed whoredom on.
118. **Thrown . . . her:** abused and berated her so, representing Othello's words as a painfully burdensome weight; cf. 1.3.256.
123. **callet:** "used by all our old writers for a strumpet of the basest kind" (cited in Furness); "like 'hussy,' 'strumpet,' 'minx,' 'harlot,' 'harlotry,' and 'whore,' . . . a term of
  abuse attached to women accused of having sex outside of marriage" (Mowat and
  Werstine); see note to "friend" in 3.4.177.

IAGO   Why did he so?

DESDEMONA   I do not know; I am sure I am none such.   125

IAGO   Do not weep, do not weep. Alas the day!

EMILIA   Hath she forsook so many noble matches,
  Her father and her country and her friends,
  To be called whore? Would it not make one weep?

DESDEMONA   It is my wretched fortune.

IAGO   Beshrew him for't!   130
  How comes this trick upon him?

DESDEMONA   Nay, heaven doth know.

EMILIA   I will be hanged if some eternal villain,
  Some busy and insinuating rogue,
  Some cogging, cozening slave, to get some office,
  Have not devised this slander. I will be hanged else.   135

IAGO   Fie! there is no such man; it is impossible.

DESDEMONA   If any such there be, heaven pardon him.

EMILIA   A halter pardon him, and hell gnaw his bones!
  Why should he call her whore? who keeps her company?
  What place? what time? what form? what likelihood?   140
  The Moor's abused by some most villainous knave,
  Some base notorious knave, some scurvy fellow.
  O heaven, that such companions thou'dst unfold,
  And put in every honest hand a whip
  To lash the rascals naked through the world   145
  Even from the east to th' west!

IAGO   Speak within door.

EMILIA   O, fie upon them! Some such squire he was
  That turned your wit the seamy side without
  And made you to suspect me with the Moor.

IAGO   You are a fool; go to.

DESDEMONA   O God, Iago,   150

---

127. **forsook:** turned down; abandoned. **matches:** husbands, marriages.
130. **Beshrew:** Shame on.
131. **trick:** fantasy.
132. **eternal:** metaphorically, "incorrigible, never-changing" (McDonald); literally, "almost = a devil" (Honigmann).
134. **cogging, cozening:** cheating, deceptive.
138. **halter:** hangman's noose; like the "mercy" Graziano would "render" Shylock in *Merchant of Venice*: "A halter gratis—nothing else, for God's sake!" (4.1.374).
140. **form:** means, method.
141. **abused:** deceived.
142. **notorious:** outrageous (not "blatantly disreputable" because the villainy is hidden). **scurvy:** disgusting (metaphorically, from the skin disease).
143. **companions:** "fellow[s] in a bad sense" (Schmidt). **unfold:** reveal.
146. **within door:** i.e., more quietly; transfers one measure of female propriety (enclosure within domestic space) to another (silence). Cf. 3.4.165 and 2.1.109.
147. **squire:** "gentleman" (with ironic contempt).
148. **the seamy side without:** inside out.

What shall I do to win my lord again?
Good friend, go to him; for by this light of heaven,
I know not how I lost him. Here I kneel:
If e'er my will did trespass 'gainst his love,
Either in discourse of thought or actual deed,   155
Or that mine eyes, mine ears, or any sense
Delighted them [in] any other form,
Or that I do not yet, and ever did,
And ever will (though he do shake me off
To beggarly divorcement) love him dearly—   160
Comfort forswear me! Unkindness may do much,
And his unkindness may defeat my life,
But never taint my love. I cannot say "whore."
It does abhor me now I speak the word.
To do the act that might the addition earn   165
Not the world's mass of vanity could make me.

IAGO   I pray you be content; 'tis but his humor;
The business of the state does him offence.

DESDEMONA   If 'twere no other—

IAGO   It is but so, I warrant.

            [*Trumpets within.*]

Hark how these instruments summon to supper.   170
The messengers of Venice stays the meat;
Go in, and weep not; all things shall be well.

                              Exeunt DESDEMONA *and* EMILIA.

        Enter RODERIGO.

How now, Roderigo?

RODERIGO   I do not find that thou deal'st justly with me.

IAGO   What in the contrary?   175

RODERIGO   Every day thou doff'st me with some device,
    Iago, and rather, as it seems to me now, keep'st from
    me all conveniency than suppliest me with the least
        advantage

---

153. **Here I kneel:** Cf. line 31 and note.
154. **will:** desire. **did trespass 'gainst:** performed an action that strayed from.
155. **discourse:** (verbal) process.
157. **form:** appearance (but his).
161. **forswear:** abandon.
162. **defeat:** destroy.
164. **abhor:** disgust; turn into a whore. Cf. "bewhored" (line 117) and "made to write 'whore' upon" (73).
165. **addition:** title, reputation.
166. **the world's mass of vanity:** all earthly riches.
171. **stays the meat:** wait for their meal.
176. **doff'st me:** turn me away. **device:** subterfuge.
178. **conveniency:** fit circumstances (for wooing Desdemona?).

of hope. I will indeed no longer endure it. Nor
am I yet persuaded to put up in peace what already I   180
have foolishly suffered.

IAGO   Will you hear me, Roderigo?

RODERIGO   Faith, I have heard too much; and your words and
performances are no kin together.

IAGO   You charge me most unjustly.   185

RODERIGO   With naught but truth. I have wasted myself
out of my means. The jewels you have had from
me to deliver Desdemona would half have corrupted a
votarist. You have told me she hath received them,
and returned me expectations and comforts of sudden   190
respect and acquaintance, but I find none.

IAGO   Well, go to; very well.

RODERIGO   Very well! go to! I cannot go to, man, nor
'tis not very well. Nay, I think it is scurvy, and begin to
find myself fopped in it.   195

IAGO   Very well.

RODERIGO   I tell you 'tis not very well. I will make myself
known to Desdemona. If she will return me my
jewels, I will give over my suit and repent my unlawful
solicitation. If not, assure yourself I will seek   200
satisfaction of you.

IAGO   You have said now.

RODERIGO   Ay, and said nothing but what I protest
intendment of doing.

IAGO   Why, now I see there's mettle in thee, and   205
even from this instant do build on thee a better opinion
than ever before. Give me thy hand, Roderigo.
Thou hast taken against me a most just exception,
but yet I protest I have dealt most directly in thy
affair.   210

RODERIGO   It hath not appeared.

IAGO   I grant indeed it hath not appeared, and
your suspicion is not without wit and judgment.

---

180. **persuaded to put up in peace:** convinced to accept without a fight.
182. **Will you hear me:** Cf. "but you'll not hear me!" (1.1.4).
183–84. **your words . . . together:** you say one thing and do another.
186–87. **wasted . . . means:** pissed away my wealth.
189. **votarist:** nun.
190. **expectations and comforts:** comforting expectations.
190–91. **sudden respect:** prompt consideration.
195. **fopped:** duped.
201. **satisfaction:** the restoration of his money or of his honor (threatening a duel).
203–04. **but what . . . doing:** that I swear I won't act on.
208. **just exception:** legitimate complaint.
209. **directly:** forthrightly, honestly.

But, Roderigo, if thou hast that in thee indeed which
I have greater reason to believe now than ever—I   215
mean purpose, courage and valor—this night
show it. If thou the next night following enjoy not
Desdemona, take me from this world with treachery
and devise engines for my life.

RODERIGO   Well, what is it? Is it within reason and compass?   220

IAGO   Sir, there is especial commission come from
Venice to depute Cassio in Othello's place.

RODERIGO   Is that true? Why, then Othello and Desdemona
return again to Venice.

IAGO   O no; he goes into Mauritania and taketh   225
away with him the fair Desdemona, unless his abode
be lingered here by some accident; wherein
none can be so determinate as the removing
of Cassio.

RODERIGO   How do you mean removing him?   230

IAGO   Why, by making him uncapable of Othello's
place—knocking out his brains.

RODERIGO   And that you would have me to do.

IAGO   Ay, if you dare do yourself a profit and a
right. He sups tonight with a harlotry, and thither   235
will I go to him. He knows not yet of his honorable
fortune. If you will watch his going thence, which
I will fashion to fall out between twelve and one,
you may take him at your pleasure. I will be near
to second your attempt, and he shall fall between   240
us. Come, stand not amazed at it, but go along with
me. I will show you such a necessity in his death that
you shall think yourself bound to put it on him. It
is now high suppertime, and the night grows to waste.
About it!   245

RODERIGO   I will hear further reason for this.

IAGO   And you shall be satisfied.   *Exeunt.*

---

219. **engines:** instruments (of torture); plots.
220. **within reason and compass:** likely to succeed and practical to implement.
225. **Mauritania:** the North African home of Moors, here a site of erotic fantasy.
227. **lingered:** protracted.
228. **determinate:** decisive.
234–35. **a profit and a right:** something both beneficial and legitimate.
235. **a harlotry:** Bianca (see line 123 and note).
238. **fashion to fall out:** arrange to occur.
240–41. **between us:** as a result of our joint effort; perhaps suggesting the logistics of
the assault.
244. **suppertime:** usually "at five or six o-clock" (Schmidt). **grows to waste:** i.e., time is
passing, hurry up.

ACT 4 SCENE 3

Enter OTHELLO, LODOVICO, DESDEMONA, EMILIA *and Attendants.*

LODOVICO   I do beseech you, sir, trouble yourself no further.

OTHELLO   O, pardon me; 'twill do me good to walk.

LODOVICO   Madam, good night. I humbly thank your ladyship.

DESDEMONA   Your honor is most welcome.

OTHELLO   Will you walk, sir?
O, Desdemona—   5

DESDEMONA   My lord?

OTHELLO   Get you to bed on th' instant. I will be returned
   forthwith. Dismiss your attendant there. Look't
   be done.

DESDEMONA   I will, my lord.   10

Exit [OTHELLO *with* LODOVICO *and Attendants.*]

EMILIA   How goes it now? He looks gentler than he did.

DESDEMONA   He says he will return incontinent,
   And hath commanded me to go to bed,
   And bid me to dismiss you.

EMILIA   Dismiss me?

DESDEMONA   It was his bidding; therefore, good Emilia,   15
   Give me my nightly wearing, and adieu.
   We must not now displease him.

EMILIA   I would you had never seen him.

DESDEMONA   So would not I: my love doth so approve him
   That even his stubbornness, his checks, his frowns—   20
   Prithee unpin me—have grace and favor.

EMILIA   I have laid those sheets you bade me on the bed.

DESDEMONA   All's one. Good faith, how foolish are our minds!
   If I do die before thee, prithee shroud me
   In one of these same sheets.

EMILIA   Come, come—you talk   25

DESDEMONA   My mother had a maid called Barbary;

7–8. **returned forthwith**: back immediately.
12. **incontinent**: right away; but see 1.3.303 and note—the modern meaning, "without control," is available.
16. **nightly wearing**: sleep garments.
20. **stubbornness**: harshness. **checks**: reprimands.
21. **unpin me**: "presumably the fastenings of her dress or hair" (Sanders).
23. **All's one**: No matter.
25. **Come . . . talk**: i.e., stop talking nonsense, don't be silly.
26. **Barbary**: Barbara; "suggests the Barbary coast, home of the Moors" (Honigmann). "Black body-servants were becoming fashionable in this period, and perhaps we should think of Barbary as a black maid" (Neill).

She was in love, and he she loved proved mad
And did forsake her. She had a Song of "Willow"—
An old thing 'twas, but it expressed her fortune—
And she died singing it. That song tonight   30
Will not go from my mind; I have much to do
But to go hang my head all at one side
And sing it like poor Barbary. Prithee dispatch.
EMILIA   Shall I go fetch your nightgown?
DESDEMONA   No, unpin me here.
   This Lodovico is a proper man.   35
EMILIA   A very handsome man.
DESDEMONA   He speaks well.
EMILIA   I know a lady in Venice would have walked
   barefoot to Palestine for a touch of his nether lip.
DESDEMONA [Sings.]

The poor soul sat singing by a sycamore tree,   40
   Sing all a green willow.
Her hand on her bosom, her head on her knee,
   Sing willow, willow, willow.
The fresh streams ran by her and murmured her moans,
   Sing willow, willow, willow;   45
Her salt tears fell from her and softened the stones,
   Sing willow, willow, willow.

[To EMILIA.] Lay by these.
   [Sings.]
      Willow, willow.

[To EMILIA.] Prithee hie thee—he'll come anon.   50
   [Sings.]
         Sing all a green willow must be my garland.
         Let nobody blame him, his scorn I approve.

Nay, that's not next. [To EMILIA.] Hark, who is't that knocks?

31–32. **I have much . . . But to:** "it is all I can do not to" (Ridley).
35. **proper:** true, good; Desdemona's apparently gratuitous comment has provoked much
critical speculation.
39. **Palestine:** i.e., as a crusading lover; with Mauritania and Barbary, sustains the play's
symbolic geography. **nether:** lower. **touch . . . lip:** a graphically sexual way of saying
"kiss."
40–57. Like Iago's "King Stephen" (see note to 2.3.81–88), Desdemona's "Willow" is
based on "a very old song" (Capell). Of the "many English laments for lost love with
refrains evoking the willow," Shakespeare's "is the only known example in which the
lamenting lover is a woman" (Austern).
48. **Lay by these:** Put these (sheets?) aside.
53. **Nay, that's not next:** i.e., no, that's wrong. In what is probably the most popular version, the line is "Let nobody blame me, her scornes I do prove."

EMILIA   It's the wind.

DESDEMONA [*Sings*.]

> I called my love false love, but what said he then?   55
>   Sing willow, willow, willow;
> If I court more women, you'll couch with more men.

[*To* EMILIA.] So, get thee gone, good night. Mine eyes do itch—
Doth that bode weeping?

EMILIA   'Tis neither here nor there.

DESDEMONA   I have heard it said so. O, these men, these men!   60
Dost thou in conscience think—tell me, Emilia—
That there be women do abuse their husbands
In such gross kind?

EMILIA   There be some such, no question.

DESDEMONA   Wouldst thou do such a deed for all the world?

EMILIA   Why, would not you?

DESDEMONA   No, by this heavenly light!   65

EMILIA   Nor I, neither, by this heavenly light:
I might do't as well i'th' dark.

DESDEMONA   Wouldst thou do such a deed for all the world?

EMILIA   The world's a huge thing:
It is a great price for a small vice.   70

DESDEMONA   In troth, I think thou wouldst not.

EMILIA   In troth, I think I should—and undo't when
I had done. Marry, I would not do such a thing for a
joint ring, nor for measures of lawn, nor for gowns,
petticoats, nor caps, nor any petty exhibition. But for   75
all the whole world—'Uds pity! who would not make her
    husband
a cuckold to make him a monarch? I should venture
purgatory for't.

DESDEMONA   Beshrew me if I would do such a wrong

---

62. **abuse:** deceive.
63. **gross kind:** vile way.
68. **all the world:** Neill hears echoes of Matthew 16:26 and Luke 4:5–6.
70. **price:** prize, reward.
71–72. **In truth:** By my truth; a mild oath, presumably repeated by Emilia in affectionate mockery.
74. **joint ring:** made of two or more pieces fitting together; a love or marriage token. **measures of lawn:** "quantities of fine linen" (Honigmann).
75. **petty exhibition:** inconsequential offering.
76. **Ud's pity:** by the grace of God.
77. **venture:** risk.
78. **purgatory:** the realm in Roman Catholic (but not Protestant) depictions of the afterlife where sins were expiated before souls entered heaven. For Emilia, adultery is only "a small vice" (see "venial," 4.1.9, and note).
79. **Beshrew:** Shame on.

For the whole world!   80

EMILIA   Why, the wrong is but a wrong i'th' world;
and having the world for your labor, 'tis a wrong in
your own world, and you might quickly make it right.

DESDEMONA   I do not think there is any such woman.

EMILIA   Yes, a dozen; and as many to'th' vantage as   85
would store the world they played for.
But I do think it is their husbands' faults
If wives do fall. Say that they slack their duties
And pour our treasures into foreign laps;
Or else break out in peevish jealousies,   90
Throwing restraint upon us; or say they strike us,
Or scant our former having in despite.
Why, we have galls; and though we have some grace,
Yet have we some revenge. Let husbands know
Their wives have sense like them. They see, and smell,   95
And have their palates both for sweet and sour,
As husbands have. What is it that they do
When they change us for others? Is it sport?
I think it is. And doth affection breed it?
I think it doth. Is't frailty that thus errs?   100
It is so too. And have not we affections,
Desires for sport, and frailty, as men have?
Then let them use us well; else let them know,
The ills we do, their ills instruct us so.

DESDEMONA   Good night, good night. God me such uses send,   105
Not to pick bad from bad, but by bad, mend!   *Exeunt.*

82. **for your labor:** (as a reward) for your (sexual) exertions.
82–83. **'tis a wrong . . . your own world:** i.e., you have the power to determine right and wrong.
85. **a dozen:** "facetious understatement" (Honigmann). **as many . . . vantage:** another dozen.
86. **store:** "stock with people" (Schmidt), the products of their "labor." **played:** "gambled (with sexual undertone)" (McDonald).
88. **fall:** sin generally and, in particular, sexually (Neill). **duties:** obligations generally and, in particular, the sexual obligations enjoined upon husbands and wives in order that they might "auoide fornication" (1 Corinthians 7:2).
88–89. **they . . . our:** The pronouns signal a shift from general to personal.
89. **foreign:** outside the domain of marriage.
91. **Throwing restraint:** imposing restriction(s).
92. **scant:** diminish. **having:** allowance.
93. **galls . . . grace:** "capacities for resentment . . . goodness, forgiveness" (Mowat and Werstine).
99. **affection:** desire.
104. **instruct us so:** Cf. Shylock's "better the instruction" and the rest of his "Hath not a Jew" speech in *Merchant of Venice* (3.1.44–60). "Such protests against 'double standards' were not uncommon" (Honigmann, citing *Comedy of Errors* 2.1.10 ff.).
105. **uses:** practices.
106. **Not . . . mend:** perplexing in the details, but clearly refusing Emilia's earthy and pragmatic relativism.

ACT 5 SCENE 1

Enter IAGO *and* RODERIGO.

IAGO   Here, stand behind this bulk; straight will he come.
   Wear thy good rapier bare, and put it home.
   Quick, quick, fear nothing! I'll be at thy elbow.
   It makes us or it mars us; think on that
   And fix most firm thy resolution.   5

RODERIGO   Be near at hand; I may miscarry in't.

IAGO   Here, at thy hand. Be bold, and take thy stand. *[Stands
aside.]*

RODERIGO   I have no great devotion to the deed,
   And yet he hath given me satisfying reasons;
   'Tis but a man gone. Forth my sword: he dies!   10

IAGO   I have rubbed this young quat almost to the sense,
   And he grows angry. Now, whether he kill Cassio
   Or Cassio him, or each do kill the other,
   Every way makes my gain. Live Roderigo,
   He calls me to a restitution large   15
   Of gold and jewels that I bobbed from him
   As gifts to Desdemona.
   It must not be. If Cassio do remain,
   He hath a daily beauty in his life
   That makes me ugly; and besides, the Moor   20
   May unfold me to him; there stand I in much peril.
   No, he must die. But so—

Enter CASSIO.

                  I heard him coming.

RODERIGO   I know his gate; 'tis he. Villain, thou diest! *[Thrusts
at* CASSIO.*]*

CASSIO   That thrust had been mine enemy indeed,
   But that my coat is better than thou know'st.   25
   I will make proof of thine.   *[Wounds* RODERIGO.*]*

5.1: "one of three scenes" in which "an exhilarated Iago orchestrates an explosion of public violence," culminating in his "apparently complete success" (Neill).
  1. bulk: small enclosure jutting out from the wall of the "tiring house" (where the actors
   attired themselves) at the rear of the stage.
  2. bare: drawn from the scabbard, ready.
11. quat: pimple. **sense:** quick.
14. Live Roderigo: Should Roderigo live.
16. bobbed from him: tricked him out of.
21. unfold: reveal (cf. 4.2.143).
25. coat: "hidden armor protecting the upper half of the body (like a bullet-proof vest)"
   (Ross).
26. make proof of: test.

105

RODERIGO   O, I am slain!

[IAGO *wounds* CASSIO *in the leg and exits.*]

CASSIO   I am maimed forever! Help, ho! murder! murder!

Enter OTHELLO.

OTHELLO   The voice of Cassio. Iago keeps his word.
RODERIGO   O, villain that I am!
OTHELLO   It is even so.
CASSIO   O, help ho! light! a surgeon!   30
OTHELLO   'Tis he. O brave Iago, honest and just,
  That hast such noble sense of thy friend's wrong!
  Thou teachest me. Minion, your dear lies dead,
  And your unblest fate hies. Strumpet, I come.
  Forth of my heart those charms, thine eyes, are blotted.   35
  Thy bed, lust-stained, shall with lust's blood be spotted.

                                          Exit OTHELLO.

Enter LODOVICO *and* GRATIANO.

CASSIO   What ho! no watch? no passage? Murder, murder!
GRATIANO   'Tis some mischance; the voice is very direful.
CASSIO   O help!
LODOVICO   Hark!   40
RODERIGO   O, wretched villain!
LODOVICO   Two or three groan. 'Tis heavy night;
  These may be counterfeits; let's think't unsafe
  To come into the cry without more help.
RODERIGO   Nobody come? Then shall I bleed to death.   45
LODOVICO   Hark.

Enter IAGO *with a light.*

GRATIANO   Here's one comes in his shirt, with light and
     weapons.
IAGO   Who's there? Whose noise is this that cries on murder?

---

26. **STAGE DIRECTION** IAGO . . . *and exits:* Most editors, following eighteenth-century traditions, specify that Iago stabs Cassio from behind.
28. **STAGE DIRECTION** *Enter* OTHELLO: "usually enters 'above'" (Honigmann); cf. note to 2.1.1.
33. **Minion:** Sweetheart (referring ironically to Desdemona).
34. **unblest:** unholy, damned. **hies:** hastens.
35. **of:** from. **blotted:** to blot is "to obliterate with ink; and hence to efface" (Schmidt; cf. 4.2.72–73).
36. **spotted:** stained; cf. the handkerchief, "spotted with strawberries" (3.3.435).
37. **watch:** night patrol. **passage:** passersby.
38. **direful:** dreadful, dismal.
42. **heavy:** bleak, dark.
44. **come into the cry:** approach or enter the scene of clamor.
47. **shirt:** nightdress (as though roused from sleep).
48. **cries on:** shouts of.

LODOVICO   We do not know.

IAGO   Do not you hear a cry?

CASSIO   Here, here! for heaven sake, help me!

IAGO   What's the matter?   50

GRATIANO   This is Othello's ancient, as I take it.

LODOVICO   The same indeed, a very valiant fellow.

IAGO   What are you here that cry so grievously?

CASSIO   Iago? O, I am spoiled, undone by villains!
   Give me some help.   55

IAGO   O me, lieutenant! What villains have done this?

CASSIO   I think that one of them is hereabout
   And cannot make away.

IAGO   O treacherous villains!
   What are you there? Come in, and give some help.

RODERIGO   O, help me there!   60

CASSIO   That's one of them.

IAGO   O murd'rous slave! O villain!
      [*Stabs* RODERIGO.]

RODERIGO   O damned Iago! O inhuman dog!

IAGO   Kill men i'th' dark?—Where be these bloody thieves?—
   How silent is this town!—Ho, murder, murder!—
   What may you be? Are you of good or evil?   65

LODOVICO   As you shall prove us, praise us.

IAGO   Signior Lodovico?

LODOVICO   He, sir.

IAGO   I cry you mercy. Here's Cassio hurt by villains.

GRATIANO   Cassio?   70

IAGO   How is't, brother?

CASSIO   My leg is cut in two.

IAGO   Marry, heaven forbid!
   Light, gentlemen. I'll bind it with my shirt.

      Enter BIANCA.

BIANCA   What is the matter, ho? Who is't that cried?

IAGO   Who is't that cried?

BIANCA   O, my dear Cassio!   75
   My sweet Cassio! O Cassio, Cassio, Cassio!

IAGO   O notable strumpet! Cassio, may you suspect

---

52. **fellow:** "They do not remember his name (he is a social inferior), but he remembers
   theirs" (Honigmann).
54. **spoiled:** destroyed.
58. **make:** get.
66. **As you . . . praise us:** i.e., judge us by our actions.
69. **I cry you mercy:** "I beg your pardon," a "'genteel' phrase" (Honigmann); = excuse me
   for not recognizing you.
77. **notable:** flagrant.

Who they should be that have thus mangled you?
CASSIO   No.
GRATIANO   I am sorry to find you thus; I have been to seek you.   80
IAGO   Lend me a garter. So . . . O for a chair
   To bear him easily hence!
BIANCA   Alas, he faints! O Cassio, Cassio, Cassio!
IAGO   Gentlemen all, I do suspect this trash
   To be a party in this injury.—   85
   Patience awhile, good Cassio.—Come, come!
   Lend me a light. Know we this face or no?
   Alas! my friend and my dear countryman,
   Roderigo! No—yes, sure! O heaven, Roderigo!
GRATIANO   What, of Venice?
IAGO   Even he, sir. Did you know him?   90
GRATIANO   Know him? Ay.
IAGO—Signior Gratiano? I cry your gentle pardon.
   These bloody accidents must excuse my manners
   That so neglected you.
GRATIANO   I am glad to see you.
IAGO   How do you, Cassio? O, a chair, a chair!   95
GRATIANO   Roderigo?
IAGO   He, he, 'tis he.   [*A litter is brought in.*]
               O, that's well said, the chair.
   Some good man bear him carefully from hence;
   I'll fetch the general's surgeon.—For you, mistress,
   Save you your labor.—He that lies slain here, Cassio,   100
   Was my dear friend. What malice was between you?
CASSIO   None in the world, nor do I know the man.
IAGO [*To* BIANCA.]   What, look you pale?—O, bear him out o'th'
   air.
   Stay you, good gentlemen.—Look you pale, mistress?—
   Do you perceive the gastness of her eye?—   105
   Nay, if you stare, we shall hear more anon.
   Behold her well; I pray you look upon her.
   Do you see, gentlemen? Nay, guiltiness will speak
   Though tongues were out of use.

---

81. **garter:** "band, worn as a sash or belt" (Honigmann), to use as tourniquet. **chair:** "framework couch for carrying the wounded" (McDonald).
92. **I cry . . . pardon:** I.e., excuse me for not recognizing you.
97. **said:** done.
100. **Save . . . labor:** don't trouble yourself.
103. **out o'th' air:** inside to a more secure and (it was assumed) less infectious environment.
105. **gastness:** terror.
106. **stare . . . anon:** you will soon confess the guilt betrayed by your appearance.
108–09: **speak . . . use:** be visible without verbal confirmation.

Enter EMILIA.

EMILIA   Alas, what is the matter? what is the matter, husband? 110
IAGO   Cassio hath here been set on in the dark
  By Roderigo and fellows that are scaped.
  He's almost slain, and Roderigo quite dead.
EMILIA   Alas, good gentleman! alas, good Cassio!
IAGO   This is the fruits of whoring. Prithee, Emilia,   115
  Go know of Cassio where he supped tonight.—
  What, do you shake at that?
BIANCA   He supped at my house, but I therefore shake not.
IAGO   O did he so? I charge you go with me.
EMILIA   O fie upon thee, strumpet!   120
BIANCA   I am no strumpet, but of life as honest
  As you that thus abuse me.
EMILIA   As I? Fie upon thee!
IAGO   Kind gentlemen, let's go see poor Cassio dressed.—
  Come, mistress, you must tell's another tale.
  Emilia, run you to the citadel,   125
  And tell my lord and lady what hath happed.   [*Exit* EMILIA.]
  Will you go on afore?   *Exeunt* [*all but* IAGO].
              This is the night
That either makes me or foredoes me quite.   [*Exit.*]

ACT 5 SCENE 2

Enter OTHELLO *with a light,* DESDEMONA *in her bed* [*asleep*].

OTHELLO   It is the cause, it is the cause, my soul.
  Let me not name it to you, you chaste stars.
  It is the cause. Yet I'll not shed her blood,
  Nor scar that whiter skin of hers than snow,
  And smooth as monumental alabaster.   5

117–18. **shake . . . shake:** Cf. 4.1.135 and note.
120. **fie:** shame.
122. **As I?:** can suggest outrage or a genuine uncertainty.
128. **fordoes me quite:** totally breaks me.
  0. **STAGE DIRECTION** *her bed:* maybe thrust out from the tiring-house facade, or
    may be a stationary enclosure like the "bulk" located in front of it (see note to 5.1.1);
    in either case, curtained and uncurtained as required.
1–3. **the cause . . . the cause:** The phrase can mean "legal matter" and "principle . . . not
    merely a personal grievance" (McDonald). Both senses fit Othello's claim to be repre-
    senting a disinterested and impersonal justice (hence his addresses to "the chaste
    stars" and "my soul"), but the "abruptness of this soliloquy makes it obscure" (John-
    son; see 245 below).
  3. **not shed her blood:** Cf. 4.1.201–02, but contrast the "oddly inconsistent" (Sanders)
    intention of 5.1.36: "Thy bed, lust-stained, shall with lust's blood be spotted." "Is it
    Shakespeare or Othello who cannot decide how she should be killed?" (Honigmann).
  5. **monumental alabaster:** the white marble of funeral monuments.

Yet she must die, else she'll betray more men.
Put out the light, and then put out the light.
If I quench thee, thou flaming minister,
I can again thy former light restore,
Should I repent me. But once put out thy light,   10
Thou cunning'st pattern of excelling nature,
I know not where is that Promethean heat
That can thy light relume. When I have plucked thy rose,
I cannot give it vital growth again;
It needs must wither. I'll smell thee on the tree.   15

    [He smells, then kisses her.]

O balmy breath, that dost almost persuade
Justice to break her sword! One more; one more.

    [He kisses her.]

Be thus when thou art dead, and I will kill thee
And love thee after. One more, and that's the last.

    He kisses her.

So sweet was ne'er so fatal. I must weep,   20
But they are cruel tears. This sorrow's heavenly:
It strikes where it doth love. She wakes.
DESDEMONA   Who's there? Othello?
OTHELLO   Ay, Desdemona.
DESDEMONA   Will you come to bed, my lord?
OTHELLO   Have you prayed tonight, Desdemon?
DESDEMONA   Ay, my lord.   25
OTHELLO   If you bethink yourself of any crime

---

  7. **the light:** The second "light" must be metaphorical for her life.

  8. **flaming minister:** the candle or torch, which ministers to his needs. Cf. Psalms 104:4 ("maketh the spirits his messengers, & a flaming fyre his ministers") and Hebrews 1:7 ("maketh the Spirits his messengers, and his ministers a flame of fyre").

11. **cunning'st pattern . . . nature:** supreme achievement of natural excellence; perverse surpassing of the natural.

12. **Promethean heat:** "divine spark" (McDonald); "Prometheus stole fire from heaven with which he animated an image he had made of clay and was punished by Jupiter," the supreme god (Ross).

13. **relume:** rekindle.

15. **I'll smell thee on the tree:** "Thee" compresses Desdemona's identity into what was, two lines earlier, only a part of that identity ("thy rose"); cf. 4.2.22 and note.

15. **STAGE DIRECTION** *smells, then kisses:* Othello's "smell thee" may be metaphorical for "kiss thee," but because "the sense of smell is so important" throughout the play (Honigmann), this stage direction takes Othello's words literally.

17. **Justice:** conventionally represented as a woman with a sword in one hand, scales in the other. **One more; one more:** Cf. "And this, and this," 2.1.196.

20. **fatal:** lethal, inescapable.

22. **strikes . . . love:** Cf. Hebrews 12:6: "For whome the Lord loueth, he chasteneth: and he scourgeth euerie sonne that he receiueth." Neill compares Psalms 94:12, Proverbs 3:12, and Revelation 3:19.

Unreconciled as yet to heaven and grace,
Solicit for it straight.
DESDEMONA   Alack, my lord, what may you mean by that?
OTHELLO   Well, do it, and be brief; I will walk by.   30
I would not kill thy unpreparèd spirit.
No, heavens forfend! I would not kill thy soul.
DESDEMONA   Talk you of killing?
OTHELLO   Ay, I do.
DESDEMONA   Then heaven
Have mercy on me!
OTHELLO   Amen, with all my heart!
DESDEMONA   If you say so, I hope you will not kill me.   35
OTHELLO   Humh.
DESDEMONA   And yet I fear you, for you're fatal then
When your eyes roll so. Why I should fear, I know not,
Since guiltiness I know not; but yet I feel I fear.
OTHELLO   Think on thy sins.
DESDEMONA   They are loves I bear to you.   40
OTHELLO   Ay, and for that thou diest.
DESDEMONA   That death's unnatural that kills for loving.
Alas, why gnaw you so your nether lip?
Some bloody passion shakes your very frame.
These are portents; but yet I hope, I hope,   45
They do not point on me.
OTHELLO   Peace, and be still.
DESDEMONA   I will so. What's the matter?
OTHELLO   That handkerchief,
Which I so loved and gave thee, thou gav'st to Cassio.
DESDEMONA   No, by my life and soul! Send for the man
And ask him.   50
OTHELLO   Sweet soul, take heed; take heed of perjury;
Thou art on thy deathbed.
DESDEMONA   Ay, but not yet to die.
OTHELLO   Presently.

28. **solicit:** seek forgiveness. **straight:** right now.
32. **forfend:** forbid. **kill thy soul:** Dying in a state of mortal sin without confessing and
    asking forgiveness, she would be damned; see 3.4.112 and note.
40. **loves I bear to you:** i.e., the pure wifely affections that are no sins at all (?); she has
    just declared feeling guiltless.
41. **that:** i.e., revealing your lust, with "bear" heard as "bare"=reveal (?); perhaps Othello
    hears an echo of "the love I bear to Cassio" (4.1.227).
42. **That death . . . loving:** If "death" means "killing" (what he administers), she
    declares Othello's admixture of feelings—killing and loving after—to be perverse
    ("unnatural").
44. **passion shakes:** Cf. 4.1.135 and 4.1.260–61 and notes.
46. **Peace . . . still:** "And he rose vp, and rebuked the winde, and said vnto the sea, Peace,
    and be stil" (Mark 4:39).
52. **thy deathbed:** See note to 4.2.107.

Therefore confess thee freely of thy sin;
For to deny each article with oath   55
Cannot remove nor choke the strong conception
That I do groan withal. Thou art to die.

DESDEMONA   Then Lord have mercy on me!

OTHELLO   I say amen.

DESDEMONA   And have you mercy too! I never did
Offend you in my life; never loved Cassio   60
But with such general warranty of heaven
As I might love. I never gave him token.

OTHELLO   By heaven, I saw my handkerchief in's hand!
O perjured woman! thou dost stone my heart,
And makes me call what I intend to do   65
A murder, which I thought a sacrifice.
I saw the handkerchief.

DESDEMONA   He found it then.
I never gave it him. Send for him hither.
Let him confess a truth.

OTHELLO   He hath confessed.

DESDEMONA   What, my lord?   70

OTHELLO   That he hath used thee.

DESDEMONA   How? unlawfully?

OTHELLO   Ay.

DESDEMONA   He will not say so.

OTHELLO   No, his mouth is stopped.
Honest Iago hath ta'en order for't.

DESDEMONA   O, my fear interprets. What, is he dead?

OTHELLO   Had all his hairs been lives, my great revenge   75
Had stomach for them all.

DESDEMONA   Alas, he is betrayed and I undone!

OTHELLO   Out, strumpet! Weep'st thou for him to my face?

DESDEMONA   O banish me, my lord, but kill me not!

OTHELLO   Down, strumpet!   80

DESDEMONA   Kill me tomorrow, let me live tonight!

56–57. nor choke . . . withal: given "conception" and "groan" (as with labor pains), suggests that Othello thinks of himself as unabortably pregnant; cf. Iago's "monstrous birth" (1.3.395).
60. offend: wrong.
66. murder . . . sacrifice: See Johnson's note, 245 below.
73. ta'en order: arranged.
74. interprets: guesses the worst.
75. had all his hairs been lives: Honigmann compares Psalms 40:12: "my sinnes . . . are mo in nomber than the heeres of mine head." Neill compares Luke 12:7: "all the heeres of your head are nombred: feare not therefore."
76. Had stomach for: would have been able to swallow.
80. Down: an embedded stage direction, with "strive" (= resist) two lines later: the assault has turned physical.

OTHELLO   Nay, if you strive—
DESDEMONA   But half an hour!
OTHELLO   Being done, there is no pause.
DESDEMONA   But while I say one prayer!
OTHELLO   It is too late.

      Smothers her.

DESDEMONA   O Lord, Lord, Lord!   85
EMILIA *Calls within.*   My lord, my lord! What ho! My lord, my
  lord!
OTHELLO   What noise is this? Not dead? not yet quite dead?
  I that am cruel am yet merciful;
  I would not have thee linger in thy pain.
  So, so.   90
EMILIA *Within.*   What ho? my lord, my lord?
OTHELLO   Who's there?
EMILIA [*Within.*]   O good my lord, I would speak a word with
  you.
OTHELLO   Yes.—'Tis Emilia.—By and by.—She's dead.
  'Tis like she comes to speak of Cassio's death.
  The noise was high. Ha, no more moving?   95
  Still as the grave. Shall she come in? Were't good?
  I think she stirs again. No. What's best to do?
  If she come in, she'll sure speak to my wife.
  My wife, my wife! what wife? I have no wife.
  O insupportable! O heavy hour!   100
  Methinks it should be now a huge eclipse
  Of sun and moon, and that th' affrighted globe
  Did yawn at alteration.
EMILIA [*Within.*]   I do beseech you
  That I may speak with you. O good my lord!
OTHELLO   I had forgot thee. O, come in Emilia.   105
  Soft, by and by; let me the curtains draw.

---

83. **Being done . . . pause:** Othello's relentlessness has been variously and unsatisfac-
    torily explained.
90. **So, so:** "In the eighteenth century it became the custom to finish Desdemona off"
    here with a dagger. "Modern Othellos have tended to respect Othello's intention of
    not scarring her, and have strangled her at 'So, so'" (Hankey); cf. 5.2.3 and note.
93. **By and by:** (I'll be there) in a moment.
94. **like:** likely.
95. **high:** loud.
101–03. **eclipse . . . alteration:** According to Matthew 27:51–52 and Luke 23:44–45,
    earthquakes (producing yawning chasms) and eclipses accompanied the fall into
    original sin and Christ's crucifixion; Othello feels Desdemona's death as a cosmic
    transformation ("alteration").
102. **th'affrighted globe:** The play was written for performance at the Globe theater;
    cf. "memory holds a seat / In this distracted globe" in *Hamlet* (1.5.96–97).

[*He closes the bed curtains.*]

Where art thou? What's the matter with thee now?

[*He unlocks the door.*] *Enter* EMILIA.

EMILIA   O my good lord, yonder's foul murders done!
OTHELLO   What? now?
EMILIA   But now, my lord.   110
OTHELLO   It is the very error of the moon;
    She comes more nearer earth than she was wont
    And makes men mad.
EMILIA   Cassio, my lord, hath killed
    A young Venetian called Roderigo.
OTHELLO   Roderigo killed? and Cassio killed?   115
EMILIA   No, Cassio is not killed.
OTHELLO   Not Cassio killed? Then murder's out of tune,
    And sweet revenge grows harsh.
DESDEMONA   O falsely, falsely murdered!
EMILIA   O Lord! what cry is that?   120
OTHELLO   That? What?
EMILIA   Out and alas! that was my lady's voice.   [*She opens the
                                                    bed curtains.*]
    Help, help ho, help! O, lady, speak again!
    Sweet Desdemona, O sweet mistress, speak!
DESDEMONA   A guiltless death I die.   125
EMILIA   O, who hath done this deed?
DESDEMONA   Nobody. I myself. Farewell.
    Commend me to my kind lord. O, farewell!   [*She dies.*]
OTHELLO   Why, how should she be murdered?
EMILIA   Alas, who knows?
OTHELLO   You heard her say herself it was not I.   130
EMILIA   She said so; I must needs report the truth.
OTHELLO   She's like a liar gone to burning hell!
    'Twas I that killed her!
EMILIA   O, the more angel she,
    And you the blacker devil!
OTHELLO   She turned to folly, and she was a whore.   135

---

110. **But now:** Even now; cf. 2.3.169 ff. and note.
111. **very:** authentic, essential (emphatic; see "very now," 1.1.85, and note). **error:** lapse, delusion; in the root sense, straying or wandering (see "erring barbarian," 1.3.352, and note).
112. **She:** the moon (Luna). **she was wont:** she was accustomed; normally.
113. **mad:** An association between lunacy and the moon was taken seriously at the time. Cf. 3.3.180 and note.
127. **Nobody. I myself:** "can sound to modern ears painfully like self-cancellation" (Neill).
129. **should she be:** does it come about that she is.

EMILIA   Thou dost belie her, and thou art a devil.

OTHELLO   She was false as water.

EMILIA   Thou art rash as fire to say
That she was false. O, she was heavenly true!

OTHELLO   Cassio did top her. Ask thy husband else.
O, I were damned beneath all depth in hell   140
But that I did proceed upon just grounds
To this extremity. Thy husband knew it all.

EMILIA   My husband?

OTHELLO   Thy husband.

EMILIA   That she was false to wedlock?   145

OTHELLO   Ay, with Cassio. Had she been true,
If heaven would make me such another world
Of one entire and perfect chrysolite,
I'd not have sold her for it.

EMILIA   My husband?

OTHELLO   Ay, 'twas he that told me on her first.   150
An honest man he is, and hates the slime
That sticks on filthy deeds.

EMILIA   My husband?

OTHELLO   What needs this iterance, woman?
I say, thy husband.

EMILIA   O mistress, villainy hath made mocks with love!   155
My husband say she was false?

OTHELLO   He, woman;
I say, thy husband; dost understand the word?
My friend, thy husband; honest, honest Iago.

EMILIA   If he say so, may his pernicious soul
Rot half a grain a day! he lies to th' heart.   160
She was too fond of her most filthy bargain.

OTHELLO   Ha!

EMILIA   Do thy worst.

---

136. **Thou:** The shift from "you" is "defiant and insulting" (Neill); her "indignation" increasingly "carries her away" (Honigmann). On the modern stage, her fury—"'like a bellow from the mouth of Melpomene [the ancient Greek Muse of tragedy] herself,'" as Edith Evans's portrayal was described—can "dominate the play" (Hankey).
139. **top:** See note to "tupping," 1.1.86. **else:** "if you doubt me" (Mowat and Werstine).
140. **were:** would be.
141. **But:** except.
147. **me such another world:** for me a world like this one.
148. **chrysolite:** precious stone, perhaps jasper, perhaps green or translucent white; in Pliny, the material used by an Egyptian king for a statue of his wife; in Revelation (21:20), the seventh foundation of the New Jerusalem.
151–52. **the slime . . . deeds:** "moral pollution; semen or vaginal fluid" (Neill). Cf. the "lust-stained" bed (5.1.36) and "cistern for foul toads" (4.2.61).
153. **iterance:** repetition.
155. **made mocks with:** made a mockery of.
160. **to th' heart:** flagrantly, outrageously.
161. **filthy bargain:** disgusting marriage.

This deed of thine is no more worthy heaven
Than thou wast worthy her.

OTHELLO   Peace, you were best!   165

    [*Moves threateningly toward her.*]

EMILIA   Thou hast not half that power to do me harm
As I have to be hurt. O gull, O dolt!
As ignorant as dirt! thou hast done a deed—

    [*He draws his sword.*]

I care not for thy sword; I'll make thee known,
Though I lost twenty lives. Help, help, ho, help!   170
The Moor hath killed my mistress! Murder, murder!

    Enter MONTANO, GRATIANO, IAGO *and others.*

MONTANO   What is the matter? How now, general?
EMILIA   O, are you come, Iago? You have done well,
That men must lay their murders on your neck.
GRATIANO   What is the matter?   175
EMILIA   Disprove this villain, if thou be'st a man.
He says thou told'st him that his wife was false.
I know thou didst not; thou'rt not such a villain.
Speak, for my heart is full.
IAGO   I told him what I thought, and told no more   180
Than what he found himself was apt and true.
EMILIA   But did you ever tell him she was false?
IAGO   I did.
EMILIA   You told a lie, an odious damnèd lie!
Upon my soul, a lie! a wicked lie!   185
She false with Cassio? Did you say with Cassio?
IAGO   With Cassio, mistress! Go to, charm your tongue!
EMILIA   I will not charm my tongue; I am bound to speak:
My mistress here lies murdered in her bed—
ALL   O heavens forfend!—   190
EMILIA   And your reports have set the murder on.
OTHELLO   Nay, stare not, masters; it is true indeed.
GRATIANO   'Tis a strange truth.
MONTANO   O monstrous act!

---

165. **Peace . . . best:** Best shut up.
168. **dirt:** excrement.
174. **lay . . . neck:** burden you with the responsibility for.
179. **full:** replete with such anxiety that she (1) can no longer speak or (2) requires reassurance (?).
187. **charm:** "cast a spell on (i.e., silence)" (McDonald).
188. **bound:** obliged (by ties of duty and affection to Desdemona).
190. ALL: See note to 1.3.73.

EMILIA   Villainy, villainy, villainy!   195
　I think upon't, I think I smell't. O villainy!
　I thought so then.—I'll kill myself for grief!
　O villainy! villainy!

IAGO   What, are you mad? I charge you get you home!

EMILIA   Good gentlemen, let me have leave to speak.   200
　'Tis proper I obey him, but not now.
　Perchance, Iago, I will ne'er go home.

OTHELLO   O! O! O!   *Falls on the bed.*

EMILIA   Nay, lay thee down and roar,
　For thou hast killed the sweetest innocent   205
　That e'er did lift up eye.

OTHELLO   O, she was foul!   [*Rises.*]
　I scarce did know you, uncle. There lies your niece,
　Whose breath, indeed, these hands have newly stopped.
　I know this act shows horrible and grim.

GRATIANO   Poor Desdemon, I am glad thy father's dead;   210
　Thy match was mortal to him, and pure grief
　Shore his old thread in twain. Did he live now,
　This sight would make him do a desperate turn;
　Yea, curse his better angel from his side
　And fall to reprobance.   215

OTHELLO   'Tis pitiful; but yet Iago knows
　That she with Cassio hath the act of shame
　A thousand times committed. Cassio confessed it,
　And she did gratify his amorous works
　With that recognizance and pledge of love   220

196: **think upon't:** am reflecting on it; "it's coming to me." **smell:** "suspect, detect" (Honigmann), and cf. 5.2.15, 4.1.142–43, 3.3.234.
197. **then:** compels us to think back on the action (presumably to 4.2.132 ff.), without giving us the leisure or the details to be precise.
200. **Good gentleman . . . leave to speak:** Cf. Desdemona's "let me find a charter in your voice" (1.3.243).
201. **'Tis proper . . . not now:** Cf. Desdemona's "Whate'er you be, I am obedient" (3.3.89).
202. **Perchance . . . home:** "an absolute repudiation of her social 'place'" in the marital household (Neill); but "perchance" and her direct address to Iago suggest residual loyalties to obligations of obedience.
206. **lift up eye:** suggests deference.
207. **uncle:** Gratiano is "presumably Brabantio's brother" (Honigmann).
209. **shows:** looks.
211. **mortal:** lethal.
212. **Shore . . . twain:** severed the cord of his old life (like the Fate Atropos in ancient mythology).
213. **desperate turn:** act of despair, suicide.
214–15. Gratiano imagines a morality play (a residually vital tradition at the time), in which good and bad angels contend whether the protagonist's soul should receive salvation or "fall to reprobance"—that is, be consigned to damnation, "for which *reprobation* was the technical theological term" (Ridley); cf. note 4 to the Names of Actors at the beginning of the play.
219. **gratify his amorous works:** requite his erotic labors.
220. **recognizance:** token.

Which I first gave her. I saw it in his hand;
It was a handkerchief, an antique token
My father gave my mother.

EMILIA   O God! O heavenly God!

IAGO   Zounds, hold your peace!

EMILIA   'Twill out, 'twill out! I peace?   225
No, I will speak as liberal as the north;
Let heaven and men and devils, let them all,
All, all cry shame against me, yet I'll speak!

IAGO   Be wise, and get you home.

> [IAGO *threatens* EMILIA *with his sword.*]

EMILIA   I will not!

GRATIANO   Fie! Your sword upon a woman?   230

EMILIA   O thou dull Moor, that handkerchief thou speak'st of
I found by fortune and did give my husband;
For often with a solemn earnestness—
More than indeed belonged to such a trifle—
He begged of me to steal't.

IAGO   Villainous whore!   235

EMILIA   She give it Cassio? No, alas, I found it,
And I did giv't my husband.

IAGO   Filth, thou liest!

EMILIA   By heaven, I do not! I do not, gentlemen.—
O murderous coxcomb! what should such a fool
Do with so good a wife?

OTHELLO   Are there no stones in heaven   240
But what serves for the thunder? Precious villain!

> *The Moor runs at* IAGO. IAGO *stabs his wife.*

GRATIANO   The woman falls; sure he hath killed his wife.

> *Exit* IAGO.

---

222. **antique:** old; but the word often implies "grotesque" or perhaps "uncanny."
223. **My father . . . mother:** in 3.4.53 ff., Othello describes a different origin for the handkerchief; maybe a rich ambivalence, a theatrically inconsequential oversight, or both.
226. **liberal as the north:** "freely (and bitingly) as the north wind blows" (Kernan).
231. **dull:** dense.
232. **fortune:** chance.
239. **coxcomb:** cap worn by the court jester; she is calling Othello (or Iago) a fool.
240. **stones in heaven:** thunderbolts (sometimes called thunderstones), associated with godlike power.
241. **But . . . thunder:** i.e., none left to administer heavenly justice; cf. "immortal Jove's dread clamors," 3.3.357, and note. **Precious:** "out and out (a sarcastic intensifier)" (Neill).
241. **STAGE DIRECTION** IAGO . . . *wife:* That Frank Finlay, playing Iago opposite Laurence Olivier's Othello, dispatched his Emilia with "a brisk and business-like stab in the back" (Tynan) may owe something to eighteenth-century traditions (see 5.1.26 and note).

EMILIA   Ay, ay. O lay me by my mistress' side.   [*They do so.*]
GRATIANO   He's gone, but his wife's killed.
MONTANO   'Tis a notorious villain. Take you this weapon,   245
  Which I have here recovered from the Moor.
  Come, guard the door without; let him not pass,
  But kill him rather. I'll after that same villain,
  For 'tis a damnèd slave.

> *Exit* MONTANO, GRATIANO [*and all but*
> OTHELLO *and* EMILIA].

OTHELLO   I am not valiant neither,
  But every puny whipster gets my sword.   250
  But why should honor outlive honesty?
  Let it go all.
EMILIA   What did thy song bode, lady?
  Hark, canst thou hear me? I will play the swan,
  And die in music. [*Sings*] "Willow, willow, willow."
  Moor, she was chaste. She loved thee, cruel Moor.   255
  So come my soul to bliss as I speak true!
  So speaking as I think, alas, I die.   [*She dies.*]
OTHELLO   I have another weapon in this chamber;
  It was a sword of Spain, the ice-brook's temper.
  O, here it is.—Uncle, I must come forth.   260
GRATIANO   [*Within.*] If thou attempt it, it will cost thee dear;
  Thou hast no weapon and perforce must suffer.
OTHELLO   Look in upon me then and speak with me,
  Or, naked as I am, I will assault thee.

> [*Enter* GRATIANO.]

GRATIANO   What is the matter?
OTHELLO   Behold, I have a weapon;   265
  A better never did itself sustain
  Upon a soldier's thigh. I have seen the day
  That with this little arm and this good sword
  I have made my way through more impediments

---

245. **notorious:** flagrant (see 4.2.142 and note).
247. **without:** on the outside.
250. **puny whipster:** "foolish, insignificant person (cf. whippersnapper)" (McDonald).
251. **honor outlive honesty:** an obscure distinction: perhaps "why should military reputation survive authentic inner virtue?"; perhaps "why should I survive the chaste
Desdemona?"
253–54. **swan . . . music:** "Proverbially, swans were said to sing at their deaths" (Mowat
and Werstine).
259. **of Spain . . . temper:** origin and manufacturing process testifying to quality.
264. **naked:** unarmed; a "typically Shakespearean device: to follow the tragic moment of
Emilia's death by this semi-comic trick" (Granville-Barker, quoted in Ridley).
268. **this little arm:** i.e., merely this arm.

Than twenty times your stop. But O, vain boast!   270
Who can control his fate? 'Tis not so now.
Be not afraid, though you do see me weaponed.
Here is my journey's end, here is my butt
And very seamark of my utmost sail.
Do you go back dismayed? 'Tis a lost fear.   275
Man but a rush against Othello's breast
And he retires. Where should Othello go?

[He looks toward the bed.]

Now, how dost thou look now? O ill-starred wench,
Pale as thy smock. When we shall meet at compt,
This look of thine will hurl my soul from heaven,   280
And fiends will snatch at it.

[He touches her.]

                              Cold, cold, my girl?
Even like thy chastity. O cursèd, cursèd slave!
Whip me, ye devils,
From the possession of this heavenly sight!
Blow me about in winds, roast me in sulphur,   285
Wash me in steep-down gulfs of liquid fire!
O Desdemon! dead Desdemon; dead. O, O!

Enter LODOVICO, CASSIO *in a chair,* MONTANO, *and* IAGO
with Officers.

LODOVICO   Where is this rash and most unfortunate man?
OTHELLO   That's he that was Othello; here I am.
LODOVICO   Where is that viper? Bring the villain forth.   290
OTHELLO   I look down towards his feet; but that's a fable;
    If that thou be'st a devil, I cannot kill thee.   [Wounds IAGO.]
LODOVICO   Wrench his sword from him.
IAGO   I bleed, sir, but not killed.
OTHELLO   I am not sorry neither; I'd have thee live,

---

270. **stop:** obstacle
273. **butt:** destination.
274. **very seamark . . . utmost sail:** absolute boundary of my farthest voyage.
275. **a lost:** an unnecessary.
276. **Man but a rush against:** Attack with only a reed.
277. **retires:** withdraws, retreats (a military term).
278. **ill-starred:** ill-fated; see 1.1.13 and note.
279. **compt:** the Last Judgment. The details following conform to biblical descriptions
    and pictorial representations familiar at the time.
286. **steep-down:** precipitous.
287. **STAGE DIRECTION** *chair:* litter; cf. 5.1.81 and note.
291. **that's a fable:** i.e., that cloven feet reveal the devil.
293. **but not killed:** Cf. 4.2.132 and note.

For in my sense 'tis happiness to die.   295
LODOVICO   O thou Othello, that was once so good,
　　Fallen in the practice of a cursèd slave,
　　What shall be said to thee?
OTHELLO   Why, anything:
　　An honorable murderer, if you will;
　　For naught I did in hate, but all in honor.   300
LODOVICO   This wretch hath part confessed his villainy.
　　Did you and he consent in Cassio's death?
OTHELLO   Ay.
CASSIO   Dear general, I never gave you cause.
OTHELLO   I do believe it, and I ask your pardon.   305
　　Will you, I pray, demand that demi-devil
　　Why he hath thus ensnared my soul and body?
IAGO   Demand me nothing. What you know, you know.
　　From this time forth I never will speak word.
LODOVICO   What, not to pray?
GRATIANO   Torments will ope your lips. 310
OTHELLO   Well, thou dost best.
LODOVICO   Sir, you shall understand what hath befall'n,
　　Which, as I think, you know not. Here is a letter
　　Found in the pocket of the slain Roderigo,
　　And here another. The one of them imports   315
　　The death of Cassio, to be undertook
　　By Roderigo.
OTHELLO   O villain!
CASSIO   Most heathenish and most gross!
LODOVICO   Now here's another discontented paper
　　Found in his pocket too; and this, it seems,   320
　　Roderigo meant t'have sent this damnèd villain,
　　But that, belike, Iago in the interim
　　Came in and satisfied him.
OTHELLO   O thou pernicious caitiff!—

295. **in my sense:** feeling as I do. **'tis happiness to die:** Cf. "If it were now to die, / 'Twere now to be most happy" (2.1.187–8).
297. **Fallen in the practice:** With the theological burden of "fallen," "in" can mean "into" or "as a result of" Iago's plot ("practice").
299. **an honorable murderer:** Othello seems to take Lodovico's "to thee" (i.e., "what encouragement can we offer?") as "of thee" (i.e., "how should we tell your story?").
302. **consent:** collaborate.
308. **What . . . you know:** Cf. Pontius Pilate after the crucifixion: "What I haue written, I haue written" (John 19:22).
310. **What, not to pray:** i.e., not even to avoid eternal damnation. **Torments:** Torture.
318. **heathenish and . . . gross:** godless (immoral) and disgusting.
319. **discontented:** "filled with grievances" (Honigmann).
322. **belike:** presumably.
323. **caitiff:** villain.

How came you, Cassio, by that handkerchief
That was my wife's?

CASSIO   I found it in my chamber;   325
And he himself confessed it but even now
That there he dropped it for a special purpose
Which wrought to his desire.

OTHELLO   O fool, fool, fool!

CASSIO   There is besides in Roderigo's letter
How he upbraids Iago that he made him   330
Brave me upon the watch, whereon it came
That I was cast; and even but now he spake,
After long seeming dead, Iago hurt him,
Iago set him on.

LODOVICO [To OTHELLO.]   You must forsake this room and go
    with us.   335
Your power and your command is taken off,
And Cassio rules in Cyprus. For this slave,
If there be any cunning cruelty
That can torment him much and hold him long,
It shall be his. You shall close prisoner rest   340
Till that the nature of your fault be known
To the Venetian state. Come, bring away.

OTHELLO   Soft you; a word or two before you go.
I have done the state some service, and they know't;
No more of that. I pray you in your letters,   345
When you shall these unlucky deeds relate,
Speak of me as I am. Nothing extenuate,
Nor set down aught in malice. Then must you speak
Of one that loved not wisely but too well;
Of one not easily jealous but, being wrought,   350
Perplexed in the extreme; of one whose hand,
Like the base Judean, threw a pearl away

---

328. **wrought to his desire:** worked as he wanted.
331. **Brave:** challenge, provoke.
332. **cast:** dismissed. **even but now:** Cf. "but even now" (line 326) and notes to 110 and 111.
335. **forsake:** "leave; i.e. he is under arrest" (Honigmann).
339. **hold him long:** keep him alive for sustained torture.
340. **close prisoner rest:** "remain a closely guarded prisoner" (Mowat and Werstine).
343. **Soft you:** Wait a moment.
344. **some service:** "returns to the theme of Iago's opening diatribe" (Neill).
346. **unlucky:** unfortunate.
347. **extenuate:** alleviate, mitigate.
350. **wrought:** worked up or on by passion (or by Iago?).
352. **the base Judean:** "perhaps Judas Iscariot, betrayer of Christ, or Herod, who impul-
    sively killed his wife" (McDonald); "base Indian" in the Quarto suggests lowly igno-
    rance, rather than willful evil. **threw a pearl away:** may echo Matthew 13.45–46:
    "the kingdome of heauen is like to a marchant man, that seketh good perles, Who
    hauing founde a perle of great price, went and solde all that he had, and boght it."

Richer than all his tribe; of one whose subdued eyes,
Albeit unusèd to the melting mood,
Drops tears as fast as the Arabian trees   355
Their medicinable gum. Set you down this;
And say besides that in Aleppo once,
Where a malignant and a turbanned Turk
Beat a Venetian and traduced the state,
I took by th' throat the circumcisèd dog,   360
And smote him—thus!   *He stabs himself.*

LODOVICO   O bloody period!
GRATIANO   All that is spoke is marred.
OTHELLO   I kissed thee ere I killed thee. No way but this,
Killing myself, to die upon a kiss.   *He* [*kisses* DESDEMONA *and*]
                                                            dies.

CASSIO   This did I fear, but thought he had no weapon,   365
For he was great of heart.
LODOVICO   O Spartan dog,
More fell than anguish, hunger, or the sea,
Look on the tragic loading of this bed:
This is thy work. The object poisons sight;
Let it be hid. Gratiano, keep the house   370
And seize upon the fortunes of the Moor,
For they succeed on you. To you, lord governor,
Remains the censure of this hellish villain;
The time, the place, the torture—O, enforce it!
Myself will straight aboard, and to the state   375
This heavy act with heavy heart relate.   *Exeunt.*

---

353   tribe: "could be the tribes of Israel or an Indian 'tribe'" (Honigmann); but cf. "tribe of hell," 1.3.353 and note. subdued: Cf. 1.3.248.
355. Drops tears: the present tense; he is weeping.
356. medicinable gum: "myrrh, the resinous perfume brought by the Magi to Christ's manger" in Matthew 2:11 (Lupton), deemed curative (as were repentant tears).
357. Aleppo: cosmopolitan "city in Turkey [modern Syria] where Venetians were allowed special trading privileges but where it was death for a Christian to strike a Turk" (Kittredge).
360. circumcisèd: "a term of opprobrium and abuse" (Ross). Bodily circumcision is enjoined on Muslims (and Jews), but Christians claim "circumcision made without hands . . . through the circumcision of Christ" (Colossians 2:11).
362. period: conclusion (a term from formal rhetoric).
366. Spartan dog: In Ovid's *Metamorphoses*, the first of Actaeon's dogs to turn on his "Lorde and Mayster" was "of Spart" (III.277 and 247); see Bate and Hornbeck, and cf. *Othello* 3.3.363 and *A Midsummer Night's Dream* 4.1.111.
367. fell: relentlessly destructive.
370. hid: a cue to draw the bed curtains. keep: guard.
371. seize upon the fortunes: take possession of the estate.
372. they succeed on you: you inherit them.
373. censure: judgment, punishment.

The Text and Editorial Procedures

The two earliest editions of *Othello* are the First Quarto, of 1622 (Q), and the First Folio, of 1623 (F). They differ first of all in their size as objects. For a folio, "the printer folded the sheet once, making two leaves, or four pages front and back; the book was thus about 9 by 14 inches." For a quarto, "the printer folded the sheet twice, making four leaves (hence the name *quarto*), or eight pages front and back; this book was thus about 7 by 9 inches" (McDonald, 199). In addition, these editions diverge in some of their contents: F includes some substantial passages—about 160 lines—missing from Q, possibly added on or (more probably) cut for performance (or perhaps for a particular performance); Q offers more-detailed stage directions; Q includes oaths absent from F, probably deleted as a result of a statute passed in 1606 requiring the suppression of profanity in theatrical performance. In addition, the two texts differ in thousands of specific readings, probably for a variety of reasons—some resulting from the practice of the compositors and printers responsible for the editions, some from theatrical cutting and the practice of "the actors themselves" (McMillin, *First Quarto*, i), some perhaps from Shakespeare's own revisions.

Textual scholars have developed many more or less plausible stories (some of them suggested just above) to account for the features of each of these texts on its own and in relation to the other. Given the present state of knowledge (which is unlikely to change substantially), these stories are inevitably speculative explanations, and none has succeeded in gaining anything close to universal acceptance. Meanwhile, editors have to make judgments based not only on the textual variables but on the interests, themselves various and difficult to determine, of their readers. This edition is based on F, primarily because of the quality of its additional material. As McMillin remarks, "no one doubts" that the F-only lines "are Shakespearian," but this is not just because they "are rich in metaphor and verbal energy" (McMillin, *First Quarto*, 2); these F-only lines, which include Desdemona's Willow Song and Emilia's speech on the double standard (to focus on just one scene), contribute powerfully to the play's theatrical impact. From Q, I have included the oaths (these too are generally accepted as Shakespearean and reflect the emotional intensity of the play) and some more-detailed stage directions (whether Shakespeare himself was responsible for them or not, they seem to reflect theatrical practice and offer interesting possibilities for performance). Finally, I have added a few Q-only lines, and Q variants, that seemed to me to add to the play's power. (Many other variants I resisted, without firm conviction, and I have included a representative sampling of these unadopted possibilities in the Textual Notes (133–36 below).

These procedures may sound commonsensical, and in fact they coincide more or less closely with the choices of most modern *Othello* editions. However, textual scholars and critics have moved beyond the effective consensus that sustained previous practice and now disagree about not only the details of their work but its basic values and goals. Some of them doubt that it is desirable (even if it were possible) to get underneath the surviving texts to an original authorial intention and would question the legitimacy of an even modestly conflated text like the one printed here. This skepticism is connected to a transfer of interest away from the literary or aesthetic effects of engaging with the text and over to the social and cultural factors influencing textual transmission and theatrical history.

Readers interested in these questions are invited to look at the works listed below. McDonald's chapter provides a clear and helpful introduction to the general problem of editing Shakespeare; Honigmann's *Stability*, Marcus, Jowett, Kastan, Egan, Werstine's "Narratives," and Lesser focus more specifically on current controversies; other items are, as indicated in their titles, addressed to the problems of *Othello* in particular. Even those readers who prefer not to bother with such matters should know that the text they read of *Othello*—the one printed here or any other—has been perforce shaped in significant ways by editorial assumptions and values that are (to put it mildly) subject to dispute. Editors change the spelling and punctuation of almost every line of Shakespeare they transmit, and with reason. Neither practice had been regularized in Shakespeare's time, and the hodgepodge of idiosyncratic habits motivating the various individuals who contributed to the production of the texts (authors, actors, scribes, compositors) makes it impossible to rely on the spelling and punctuation that have come down to us. But however necessary, editorial intervention has an unavoidably significant impact. Capell's "me" for "my," for instance (see 1.3.260–62 and note), has won widespread acceptance in explaining a passage that arguably affects our view of the play as a whole. The emendation depends for its revisionary clarification not just on "the single change of a letter," as Capell suggests, but also, as he has to acknowledge, on "the putting in parenthesis what the oldest copy puts between comma's": "Nor to comply with heat (the young affects / In [me] defunct) and proper satisfaction." And although editors often highlight changed letters or words in the play text, they rarely if ever signal emended punctuation, even in their textual notes. No one would know, but for my confession here, that "In my defunct and proper satisfaction," as printed in this edition, has been bereft of the comma after "defunct" in F and Q. And even the most scrupulous editors proceed in the same quiet way (e.g., "No sources are given for emendations of punctuation," Mowat and Werstine, 267).

Punctuation rarely assumes the major consequence it has in the case of this emendation by Capell (though see 4.2.64 and 4.3.18 for other examples). Nonetheless, even when individual editorial decisions about punctuation are trivial, they cannot help, multiplied by thousands of times, but affect the meaning and impact. (Compare the first page of F, reproduced page 6 above, with the text printed on 8–11 to see how many changes get made to even a relatively clean early text by a relatively unintrusive editor.) Facsimile reproductions of original texts might seem to represent an alternative to editorial intervention; but they would not be intelligible to most readers and would entail the dissemination of what in many cases we believe to be errors. And in any case, facsimiles are, no less than conflated or emended texts, the product of editorial value judgments—in this case, the judgment to do nothing. "Unediting," as Leah Marcus and Randall McLeod call it, is just another kind of editing. Editorial practice is interpretive through and through, as much so as critical practice. Editorial decisions are as much subject to dispute as are the discussions and arguments on display in the "Criticism" section of this book.

I have called my editorial procedure "unintrusive," but less flattering characterizations are available. In "The Rationale of Copy-Text," Walter W. Greg, the great bibliographer and textual critic of the last century, inveighs against the practice of editors who, having chosen what they judge to be the best text on which to base their edition, then abandon subsequent judgment, mindlessly reproducing the details of their copy-text as though these details had been automatically validated—grandfathered, as it were—by the original choice. From Greg's perspective, my reluctance to depart from F in favor either of Q variants or of emendations suggested by subsequent editors, might look like acquiescence to "the tyranny of the copy-text" (26).

Acquiescence, however, is not always a bad thing. Occasionally, F obscurity is not clarified by Q or by any emendation editors have come up with. The passage that provoked Capell's "my" for "me" is a good example of a situation where, as Samuel Johnson shrewdly remarked, "what made the difficulty, will continue to make it," and in such cases it is arguably better not to intervene, or to intervene minimally. More frequently, my decisions to stay with F derive from the conviction that the alternatives do not constitute any substantial improvement or, to put it the other way around, that the F readings make better sense than usually acknowledged. In 3.3.387, most editors substitute "Her name" for "My name" in F. The immediate context makes "Her" a plausible choice. It evidently seemed so to the anonymous editor of the 1630 Quarto, who originated the emendation and is regularly cited as the authority for "Her" in subsequent editions. But as suggested by several earlier *Othello* passages cited in my note to the line, "My name" is a plausible (and compelling) reading; and given its presence in both the earliest texts, Q as well as F, I was not persuaded to make the change.

The most striking example of my retaining F occurs in Desdemona's affirmation "That I love the Moor to live with him" (1.3.46). Almost all editors adopt the Q reading, "That I did love the Moor to live with him," usually without comment, but presumably because the inclusion of "did" produces a metrically more regular line and because it seems more likely that printers or compositors would miss the word ("eye-skip") than add it. But regularity is not the be-all and end-all of poetic value ("And ten low words oft creep in one dull line," as Pope says in "An Essay on Criticism" [347]), and *Othello* has many lines as irregular as the F text here. Moreover, if Q is a theatrical text, as editors generally believe, then histrionic tamping is no less probable than compositorial "eye-skip"; according to Neill, commenting on a comparable variant only three lines later, "The greater iambic regularity of the Q version suggests a possible actor's substitution."

In the absence of conclusive evidence, theatrically expressive power becomes decisive. The shorter F line puts a stress on the internal near-rhyme, "love"/"live," reinforcing the sense of the totality of Desdemona's commitment to Othello. Without "did," F is not restricted to the description of a past action; it expresses Desdemona's feeling in the present, and by trumpeting her conjugal interest aloud in the senate, she reproduces the "downright violence and storm of fortunes" (line 247) of her prior action. (She does what Othello's great speech to the senate did earlier in the scene—at once report on and reenact an earlier experience.) All this might work to intensify either admiration or anxiety among the spectators, or perhaps both (as Potter argues, both early texts equivocate about this matter); but the intensification of affect by itself, whether we are attracted or repelled, seems appropriate to the dramatic situation. This edition prints F because I think it's the better line. No one has to agree with this judgment (most editors apparently don't), but it's not the abandonment of judgment that worried Greg.

I should also explain my procedures for handling stage directions and scene locations. In many cases where an action seems to be called for, the early texts include either no stage directions or imprecise generalities located somewhere near what appears to be the appropriate line. Beginning with Nicholas Rowe in 1709, editors have expanded upon these perfunctory practices, systematically repositioning, elaborating, and inventing stage directions to serve the needs of readers for whom the ability to think in terms of theatrical performance could not be taken for granted. I have continued with this practice of editorial intervention, reproducing (and sometimes relocating) the stage directions added by earlier editors and inventing some of my own, as well as calling attention occasionally in the explanatory and textual notes to stage actions that might seem to be suggested by the text. "Suggested" is the key word: "Here is something that might be done on stage at this point, among many other things—including nothing." To read Shakespeare theatrically means acknowledging a long and continuing stage history in which performers have shaped the texts to the exigencies of their particular dramatic, occasional, and cultural situations.

Scene locators also begin with Rowe, again to accommodate readers; but the situation here is more complicated because—as Peter Holland argues in a piece to which I am much indebted—Rowe was trying to accommodate his playgoing contemporaries as well. Theatrical performance had come to differ significantly from the kind audiences at the Globe theater experienced when *Othello* was new, and scene location was one of the most significant of the changes. By Rowe's time, the stage had developed a fairly sophisticated set of scenic properties and conventions to localize the action, distinguishing between inside and outside and between various external environments. Shakespeare's stage, by contrast, lacked scenery almost altogether. The action took place in an unspecified place that could be inferred from the circumstances and that would (when required) be specified in the dialogue. The resulting flexibility allowed for "split scenes," where the action could shift back and forth between different places. In 3.4, for example, the "place is nowhere specified, only implied by character and action. Thus although much of the dialogue seems to assume an 'interior' and private setting, there is no discrepancy created when Cassio is told to 'walk here about' [line 161] . . . and Bianca enters 'going to [Cassio's] lodging'" (Ross, 143). In 4.2, similarly, the "scene starts indoors (cf. 28), and in some productions in Desdemona's bedroom. Later, Roderigo wanders in [172], and it seems to be outdoors: one of the advantages of unlocalized staging" (Honigmann, 272). "The truth is," as Malone puts it, after describing in detail the "great difficulties in ascertain-ing the place" of 4.2, that "our poet and his audience, in this instance as in many other, were content, from want of scenery, to consider the very same spot, at one and at the same time, as the outside and inside of a house" (9.595–96).

Malone, a devoted and accomplished historian, understood that scene locators are misleading. Nonetheless, following the practice of all his predecessors going back to Rowe, he included them in his 1790 edition (4.2 is said to take place in "A Room in the Castle"), as have most subsequent editors to this day (though sometimes hedged about with square brackets or apologetic explanations, or relegated to the notes). This practice may be driven by inertia, but inertia can be good as well as bad; and the reassuring familiarity provided by scene locators, especially in a text designed for a nonspecialist audi-ence, has clear benefits.

But it has disadvantages as well. If we locate the action of 3.4 in "A Room in the Castle" or some comparably specific interior space, Desdemona's "walk about here" produces a distracting discrepancy. Without any sense of a fixed or definite location, the effect is less intrusive, but Ross's "no discrepancy" is too absolute. The exterior location still comes as a surprising discovery, and the surprise is functional. It makes us emphatically aware that Bianca (like Desde-mona at the beginning) abruptly inserts herself into the public arena, defying gender norms, which are a topic of paramount impor-tance in *Othello*. The play does more than just allow itself a conve-nient flexibility—it exploits the flexibility to achieve a significant dramatic effect.

There are many other instances in which Shakespeare takes advantage of the unlocalized (perhaps better called variously local-ized) stage; two representative examples occur early in the action. *One*: At the beginning of Act 2 (as it is designated in the Folio and subsequent texts), the absence of any decisive break between the simultaneously exiting Iago and the entering figures suggests that the action is still located in Venice. Before determining that the scene now takes place at (say) "A Stormy Seaport in Cyprus," specta-tors might well surmise that the violent sounds of the storm cued by the opening lines of the scene are produced by Iago's last words just earlier: "I have't! It is engendered! Hell and night / Must bring this monstrous birth to the world's light" (1.3.394–95). *Two*: Having failed (apparently) to tempt Cassio into salacious thoughts about Desdemona, Iago tries a new tactic: "Come, lieutenant, I have a stoup of wine, and here without are a brace of Cyprus gallants that would fain have a measure to the health of black Othello" (2.3.24–27). "Here without" must come as a surprise. There has been no reason to assume a change from the Herald's speech just earlier in

2.2, with its strong suggestion of exterior location. (In fact, 2.3 is, in all editions of the play prior to Theobald's in 1733, printed as a continuation of 2.2 rather than a new scene.) The shift goes by too quickly to have great significance, but Cassio's "Where are they?" asked about the same gallants only a moment later (39), reinforces the effect. He can hardly have forgotten; apparently he is trying (desperately) to buy time before agreeing against his better judgment to what we know to be Iago's plot to destroy him. And now, in Iago's response, the play reminds us with renewed emphasis of the interior location: "Here at the door; I pray you call them in" (40). Again, though not a contradiction, the abrupt revelation and then confirmation of an interior location constitutes a discrepancy and (my main point) a functional one. Making us suddenly aware of Cassio's physical enclosure, it reinforces the sense that he is metaphorically enclosed as well—enmeshed willy-nilly inside the plot Iago is spinning to destroy him.

In these cases, we are dealing with impressions central to the play—about gender norms, entrapment, guilt, an irresistible and seemingly omnipotent Iago; and scene locators would diminish consequential theatrical and thematic effects. The point need not be exaggerated; the meanings reinforced by these effects are amply available without them. Nonetheless, having come in the course of producing this edition to conclude that scene locators, no matter how qualified or inconspicuous, do more harm than good, I have not included them in the text.

Works Cited

Egan, Gabriel. *The Struggle for Shakespeare's Text: Twentieth-Century Editorial Theory and Practice*. Cambridge, Eng.: Cambridge University Press, 2010.

Foakes, R. A. "Shakespeare Editing and Textual Theory: A Rough Guide." *Huntington Library Quarterly* 60 (1999): 425–42.

Greg, W. W. "The Rationale of Copy-Text." *Studies in Bibliography* 3 (1950–51): 19–36.

Hill, W. Speed. "Editing *Othello*: The Indefatigable in Pursuit of the Intractable." *Shakespeare Newsletter* 246:50 (2000): 67 ff.

Honigmann, E. A. J. Letter to the Editor. *Shakespeare Newsletter* 246:50 (2000): 66.

———. Letter to the Editor. *Shakespeare Newsletter* 248–49:51 (2001): 10.

———. *The Stability of Shakespeare's Text*. London: Edward Arnold, 1965.

———. *The Texts of "Othello" and Shakespearian Revision*. London and New York: Routledge, 1996.

Holland, Peter. Introduction. In Nicholas Rowe, ed. *The Works of Mr. William Shakespear*. 6 vols. London, 1709. Rpt. London: Pickering & Chatto, 1999, 1.vii–xxx.

Jackson, MacDonald P. Review of Honigmann's *Texts of "Othello."* *Shakespeare Studies* 26. Madison, N.J.: Associated University Presses, 1998, 364–72.

Jowett, John. "After Oxford: Recent Developments in Textual Studies." In *The Shakespearean International Yearbook 1: Where Are We Now in Shakespeare Studies?* Aldershot and Brookfield, Vt.: Ashgate, 1999, 65–86.

Kastan, David Scott. "The Mechanics of Culture: Editing Shakespeare Today." In *Shakespeare After Theory*. London and New York: Routledge, 1999, 59–70.

Lesser, Zachary. *"Hamlet" after Q1: An Uncanny History of the Shakespearean Text*. Philadelphia: University of Pennsylvania Press, 2015.

Marcus, Leah S. *Unediting the Renaissance: Shakespeare, Marlowe, Milton*. London and New York: Routledge, 1996.

Malone, Edmond. *The Plays and Poems of William Shakespeare*. 10 vols. London, 1790. Rpt. New York: AMS Press, 1966.

McDonald, Russ. "What Is Your Text?" In *The Bedford Companion to Shakespeare: An Introduction with Documents*. 2nd ed. Boston and New York: Bedford/St. Martin's, 2001, 194–218.

McLeod, Randall. "UN *Editing* Shak-speare." *Sub-Stance* 33–34 (1982): 26–55.

McMillin, Scott, ed. *The First Quarto of "Othello."* Cambridge, Eng.: Cambridge University Press, 2001.

———. "The *Othello* Quarto and the 'Foul-Paper' Hypothesis." *Shakespeare Quarterly* 51 (2000): 67–85.

Mowat, Barbara A., and Paul Werstine, eds. *Othello*. New York: Washington Square Press, 1993.

Neill, Michael, ed. *Othello, the Moor of Venice*. Oxford: Oxford University Press, 2006.

Potter, Lois. "Editing Desdemona." In Ann Thompson and Gordon McMullan, eds. *In Arden: Editing Shakespeare: Essays in Honour of Richard Proudfoot*. London: Thomson, 2003, 81–94.

Ross, Lawrence J., ed. *The Tragedy of Othello, the Moor of Venice*. Indianapolis and New York: Bobbs-Merrill, 1974.

Werstine, Paul. Letter to the Editor. *Shakespeare Newsletter* 247:50 (2000): 94.

———. "Narratives about Printed Shakespeare Texts: 'Foul Papers' and 'Bad' Quartos." *Shakespeare Quarterly* 41 (1990): 65–86.

———. Review of Honigmann's *Texts of "Othello."* *Shakespeare Quarterly* 51 (2000): 240–44.

Textual Notes

The most common category of note below identifies some of the very many Q variants not adopted in this edition. These notes take the form: *present reading] unadopted reading.* If no alternative sources are specified, the present reading derives from F and the unadopted variant from Q. The next most common category identifies those non-F readings I have adopted from Q or, in a few specified cases, from other texts. This category typically takes the form: *present reading] Q (or some other text); rejected F reading.*

The names cited in the notes refer to the editions listed on pages 3–5 above. Q2 refers to the Second Quarto, published in 1630 by an anonymous editor who evidently had access to F and Q. Where stage directions added to the Norton text derive from a long editorial tradition, usually going back to the eighteenth century, I have not always specified the origins. Where I have adopted stage directions specific to recent editions, the source is identified in the notes below. Abbreviations used as follows: *abs*=absent; NS=new scene; SD=stage direction; SP=speech prefix.

1.1: 1. Tush] Q; *abs.* 4. 'Sblood] Q; *abs.* 13–14. of war, / Non-suits] of war, / And in conclusion / Non-suits. 22. tonguèd] togèd. 27. Christened] Christian. 30. God] Q; *abs.* 30. Moorship's] worship's. 78 SD. *at a window*] Q; *abs.* 105. Zounds] Q; *abs.* 118–34. If't be . . . satisfy yourself] *abs.* 143. producted] produced. 156 SD. *in his night-gown*] Q; *abs.* 179. night] Q; might.

1.2: 28 SD. *Officers and*] Q; *abs.* 34 duke] Q; dukes. 68. darlings] Q; darling. 84. Where] Q; Whether. 87. I] Q; *abs.*

1.3: 0 SD. *Enter* DUKE *and Senators, set at a table with lights and Attendants*] Q; *Enter* DUKE, *Senators and Officers.* 59 SP. SENATOR] ALL; FIRST SENATOR (Mowat and Werstine); SENATORS (Kernan). 106 SP. DUKE] Q; *abs.* 121 SD. *Exit two or three*] Q; *abs.* 129. battles] Q; battle. 129. fortunes] Q; fortune. 140. rocks and hills whose heads] Q; rocks, hills whose head. 142. other] Q; others. 143. anthrophagi] Q; antropophague. 144. Do grow] grew. 146. thence] Q; hence. 154. intentively] Q; instinctively. 158. kisses] sighs. 199. Into your favor] Q; *abs.* 217. ear] Q; ears. 228. couch] Pope; coach, F; cooch, Q.

239. Nor would I there reside] Nor I. I would not there reside. 246. That I love the Moor] That I did love the Moor. 247. storm] scorn. 249. very quality] utmost pleasure. 262. my] F and Q; me, Capell. 262. defunct] F and Q; distinct, Theobald. 275–76. And speed . . . tonight] And speed must answer; you must hence tonight. / DESDEMONA Tonight, my lord? / DUKE This night. 291 SD. Exit] Exeunt. 297. worldly] Q; wordly. 324. balance] brain. 352. super-subtle] a super-subtle. 376. a snipe] Q; snpe. 379. H'as] Q; She h'as. 395 SD. Exit] Q; abs.

2.1: 12. chidden] chiding. 19 SD. Third] Q; abs. 33. prays] Q; pray. 40 SP. THIRD] Q; abs. 42. arrivancy] arrivance. 51 SP. within] MESSENGER. 55 SD. A shot] Q; abs. 56 SP. SECOND] Q; abs. 59 SP. SECOND] Q; abs. 65 SD. Second] Q; abs. 66 SP. SECOND] Q; abs. 82. And bring all Cyprus comfort!] Q; abs. 88. me] Q; abs. 176 SD. Trumpets within] Q; abs. 196 SD. They kiss] Q; abs. 212. thither] hither. 225. again] Q; a game. 238. finder of] finder out of. 239. has] Q; he's. 257. mutualities] Q; mutabilities. 297. trace] crush. 300. right] rank.

2.2: 10. Heaven] Q; abs.

2.3: 0 NS. ACT 2 SCENE 3] Theobald, Capell, et seq. 35. unfortunate] Q; infortunate. 49. else] lads. 58. God] Q; Heaven. 68. God] Q; Heaven. 73. Englishman] Q; Englishmen. 88. And] Then. 90. 'Fore God] Q; Why. 93. God's] Q; Heaven's. 102. God] abs. 128 SD. Exit RODERIGO] Q; abs. 136. Zounds] Q; abs. 147. God's will] Q; Alas. 149 SD. A bell rung] Q; abs. 151. God's will, lieutenant] Q; Fie fie, lieutenant. 154. Zounds] Q; abs. 197. Zounds, if I] Q; If I once. 208. leagued] Pope; league, F and Q. 223. then rather] the rather. 248 SD. MOOR, DESDEMONA and Attendants] Q; abs. 251. God] Q; Heaven. 269–71. Drunk . . . shadow] abs. 279. God] Q; abs. 306. devotement] denotement. 331. were't] Q; were. 366. By the mass] Q; In troth. 372–73. I'll set her on—/ Myself a while to draw the Moor apart] Q; I'll set her on myself a while to draw the Moor apart.

3.1: 21. Dost thou hear] Q; Dost thou hear me. 26. general] general's wife. 30. CASSIO Do, good my friend] Q; abs. 48–49. his likings / To bring] his likings / To take the safest occasion by the front / To bring. 54 SD Exit] Q; abs.

3.3: 52. Yes, faith] Q; I sooth. 61. on] or. 74. By'r Lady] Q; Trust me. 89 SD. DESDEMONA and EMILIA] Q; abs. 94. you] Q; he. 109. By heaven] Q; Alas. 114. of] in. 138. that all slaves are free to] Q; that: All slaves are free. 142. But some] Q; Wherein. 150. oft] Q; of. 157. What dost thou mean?] Zounds. 164. By heaven] Q; abs. 177. Good God] Q; Good Heaven. 181. once] Q; abs. 187. dances] dances well. 204. God] Q; Heaven. 206. leave't] leave. 206. keep't] Q2; kept F; keep Q. 217. I'faith] Q; Trust me. 219. your] my. 225. Which my

thoughts aimed not] As my thoughts aim not at. 250. hold] Q; *abs.*
261. qualities] Q; quantities. 275. to] of. 280. heaven mocked] O
then heaven mocks. 287. Faith] Q; Why. 291 SD. OTHELLO *and* DES-
DEMONA] Q; *abs.* 313. No, faith] Q; No, but. 326. The Moor . . .
poison] *abs.* 329. act] art. 339. of] Q; in. 362. mine] man's. 384–91.
By the world . . . satisfied] *abs.* 387. My] F and Q; Her, Q2. 395.
and] *abs.* 396. supervisor] Q; supervision. 412. in] into. 420. wary]
merry. 424. laid] then laid. 424. laid] lay (Rowe and many subsequent editors). 425. sigh . . . kiss . . . cry] sighed . . . kissed . . .
cried. 429. 'Tis] IAGO 'Tis. 440. it] any, it (Q); any that (Malone and
many subsequent editors). 447. the hollow hell] thy hollow cell.
453–60. Iago . . . heaven] *abs.* 455. Ne'er keeps] Ne'er feels, Q2.
460 SD. OTHELLO *kneels*] Q; *abs.* 462 SD. IAGO *kneels*] Q; *abs.*

3.4: 22. the] that. 31. now till] now; let. 53. faith] Q; indeed. 73.
I'faith] Q; Indeed. 75. God] Q; Heaven. 79. Heaven] Q; *abs.* 85.
can] can, sir. 94. I'faith] Q; In sooth. 95. Zounds] Q; Away. 144. a]
that. 159. the] that. 164 SD. *Exeunt* DESDEMONA *and* EMILIA] Q;
Exit. 167. I'faith] Q; Indeed. 174. continuate] convenient. 183. by
my faith] Q; in good troth.

4.1: 0. SD *Enter* IAGO *and* OTHELLO] Q; *Enter* OTHELLO *and* IAGO.
21. infectious] infected. 32. Faith] Q; Why. 36. Zounds] Q; *abs.* 45.
work] Q; works. 52. No, forbear] Q; *abs.* 77. unsuiting] Q; resulting.
101. conster] Q; conserve. 107. power] Q; dower. 110. woman] a
woman. 111. i'faith] Q; indeed. 122. Faith] Q; Why. 128. beckons]
Q; becomes. 132. by this hand] Q; *abs.* 158. Faith] Q; *abs.* 160. Faith]
Q; Yes. 164 SD. CASSIO] Q; *abs.* 206 SD. *A trumpet*] Q; *abs.* 232. By
my troth] Q; Trust me. 242 Truly obedient] Truly, an obedient.

4.2: 18. their wives] her sex. 30. Nay] Q; May. 31. knee] knees.
33. But not the words] Q; *abs.* 55. and moving finger at] unmoving
fingers at—O O. 74–77. Committed . . . committed] *abs.* 81. committed?] committed? Impudent strumpet! 103. Who . . . lady] *abs.* 111.
least misuse] greatest abuse. 116. to] at. 143. heaven] Q; heavens.
150. O God] Honigmann and Neill; Alas, F; O Good, Q. 153–66.
Here . . . me] *abs.* 157. them in] Q2; them; or. 168. offence.] offence, /
And he does chide with you. 183. Faith] Q; *abs.* 191. acquaintance]
acquittance. 230. removing] removing of. 235. harlotry] harlot.

4.3: 18. I would] Q; I, would; Ay—would, Honigmann and
McDonald. 23. Good faith] Q; Good Father. 24. thee] Q; *abs.* 32–53.
I have . . . not next] *abs.* 40. singing] sighing, Q2. 55–57. I called . . .
more men] *abs.* 60–63. I have . . . question] *abs.* 71. In troth] Good
troth. 72. In troth] By my troth. 76. 'Ud's pity] Q; Why. 87–104. But
I . . . us so] *abs.* 105. God] Q; Heaven. 105. uses] usage.

5.1: 1. bulk] Q; bark. 22. But] Be't. 22. heard] hear. 26 SD. IAGO
wounds CASSIO *in the leg and exits*] *abs.* F and Q; *Iago cuts Cassio*

behind in the Leg, and Exit (Theobald); Iago *rushes from his post, cuts* Cassio *behind in the Leg, and exit* (Malone). 35. Forth] Q; For. 46 SD. *with a light*] Q; *abs.* 89. O heaven] Q; Yes, 'tis. 103. out] Q; *abs.* 104. gentlemen] gentlewoman. 109 SD. *Enter* EMILIA] Q; *abs.* 122. Fie] Fough! Fie.

   5.2: 0 SD. *with a light*] Q; *abs.* 13. thy] the. 15. thee] it. 19 SD. *He kisses her*] *He smells, then kisses her* (Honigmann). 35. so] Q; *abs.* 58. Then Lord] Q; O Heaven. 64. my] thy. 71. Hath used thee] hath— 'ud's death. 83. Being . . . pause] *abs.* 84 SD. *Smothers her*] *He stifles her.* 85. O Lord, Lord, Lord] Q; *abs.* 85 SD *Calls within*] Q; *At the door.* 87. noise] voice. 103. did] should. 120. O Lord] Q; Alas. 155–58. O mistress . . . honest Iago] *abs.* 171 SD. *and others*] Q; *abs.* 189–98. My mistress . . . villainy] *abs.* 203 SD. *Falls on the bed*] Q; *abs.* 224. O God! O heavenly God] Q; O Heaven, o heavenly powers. 224. Zounds] Q; Come. 225–26. 'Twill out . . . the north] 'Twill out, 'twill; I hold my peace, sir? no! / I'll be in speaking liberal as the air. 241 SD. *The Moor runs at* IAGO. IAGO *stabs his wife*] Q; *abs.* 242 SD. *Exit* IAGO] Q; *abs.* 243 SD. *They do so*] (Ross); *abs.* F and Q. 246 here] Q; *abs.* 249 SD. MONTANO, GRATIANO] Q; *abs.* 272–77. Be not . . . Othello go] *abs.* 277 SD. *He looks toward the bed*] Mowat and Werstine; *abs.* F and Q. 281 SD. *He touches her*] Ross; *abs.* F and Q. 287 SD. *in a chair*] Q; *abs.* 297. cursèd] damnèd. 352. Judean] Indian. 361 SD. *He stabs himself*] Q; *abs.* 364 SD. *kisses* DESDEMONA *and*] Ross; Honigmann; *abs.* F and Q. 364 SD. *dies*] Q; *abs.* 368. loading] lodging.

TEXTUAL SOURCES AND
CULTURAL CONTEXTS

Othello in Its Own Time

The main textual source for *Othello*, a sixteenth-century tale by Giraldi Cinthio from which Shakespeare took his basic plot and most of the characters, is printed just after this essay; details from various other texts find their way into *Othello* as well (see 365 below). Recent commentators have sought to "expand [the] definition of *source*" beyond any such "obviously influential" material (McDonald, 146) to include the "deep sources" (Miola, 16) that seem to be nourishing *Othello* even without identifiable echoes—the ensemble of often contradictory beliefs and unconscious assumptions, along with the institutional arrangements that helped produce them, that might have shaped the first spectators' responses to the play. This essay sketches out some of these "discursive formations" (Vaughan, 4), including Moors, Turks, Muslims, black Africans, and Spanish Catholics in the first section; wives, daughters, domesticity, patriarchal authority, and the shape (or shapelessness) of sexual desire in the second. A final section situates these formations in terms of theatrical experience—the performance practices specific to Shakespeare's Globe, where the play was first performed around 1602, within which the original audiences would have registered their impressions.

I. Strangers

"I think this tale would win my daughter too" (1.3.170): The Duke's response to Othello's account of his marvelous adventures seems designed to reinforce a sense of delight in the protagonist's exotic charisma. A. C. Bradley was generously receptive to this charisma. Othello, he writes, is "by far the most romantic figure among Shakespeare's heroes; and he is so partly from the strange life of war and adventure which he has lived from childhood. He does not belong to our world, and he seems to enter it we know not whence—almost as if from wonderland," a figure "dark and grand, with a light upon him from the sun where he was born" (265 below). According to Mark Rose, "romantic aspects" suffuse the play as a whole. "Not just

Othello's imagination" but "Shakespeare's own is informed by the patterns of chivalric romance" (295). In one such pattern, the "fondness" for "converting Muslim characters to Christianity" serves to "incorporate non-European characters" into a "restorative" familiarity (Britton, 28). Chivalric romances were widely read in the Renaissance, and their influence was not limited to books; romance materials were assimilated into the ceremonial pageants performed across "a diverse range of cultural environments," extending from the court to "countryfolk and ordinary townspeople" (Alex Davis, 28 and 37).

Like romance, travel writing must have contributed significantly to the experience of Othello's first audiences. The kinds of collections put together by Richard Hakluyt and Samuel Purchas were often reprinted and expanded at the time, and their extravagantly elaborate titles (see 372 below) give an idea of the appetite to which they were catering: a fascination with strange and wonderful creatures, human and otherwise, and the mysterious and exotic places they inhabited. In Mandeville's Travels, for instance, a hugely popular collection compiled in the fourteenth century and still widely read long after Shakespeare's time, readers are invited to abandon "the dream of a sacred center" in the Holy Land, the destination toward which the fictional narrator's pilgrimage is ostensibly directed, in favor of the "diversity, difference," and "bewildering variety of 'marvelous things'" encountered along the way (Greenblatt, Marvelous Possessions, 29). Among the most frequently circulated of these are the "men that haue no heads & theyr eyen are in theyr shoulders" (Figure 2), as they are described in Richard Pynson's late-fifteenth-century edition of Mandeville. The same chapter includes a discussion of cannibalism (Ashton, 149–53). That both men without heads and cannibals appear in Othello's speech to the senate (1.3.142–44) is a striking coincidence noted by Anthony Bale: "Othello's reading of a text like Mandeville to Desdemona" suggests "the currency of such books in the Age of Discovery" and "the powerful pull of otherworldly romance" (xxvii).

Material considerations help account for the popularity of travel literature in Shakespeare's time. Advances in navigational skill and mapmaking made exploratory travel less difficult, and "the popularity of adventure drama" must have been "tied to England's commercial expansion during this period" (Howard, 94). But travel writing was generating great interest long before the technological, commercial, and conceptual breakthroughs of Shakespeare's day. Mary B. Campbell traces "exotic European travel writing" back to 400 C.E., and its appeal is evident as early as Pliny the Elder's popular Natural History (ca. 75 C.E.), an encyclopedic compendium of established facts and imaginary wonders translated from the Latin by Philemon Holland and published in 1601 as The Histories of the World. Pliny sometimes acknowledges the line between reality and fiction but rarely respects

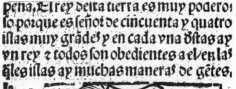

Figure 2. Man without a head. By permission of the
Houghton Library, Harvard University.

it. Renaissance travel writers lived in an age of increased respect for
scientific knowledge, and they had more actual experience with which
to verify their stories; but although these advances had a significant
"cross-fertilizing" impact on their work (Hayden), the distinction
between what's really out there and what's imagined to be out there
does not greatly matter to them—or to Shakespeare, who seems to
borrow freely from Holland's Pliny for the exotic material in *Othello*.

The interests accommodated by romance and travel writing
belonged not just to readers; they extended to those illiterate or
marginally literate spectators standing in the pits of outdoor amphitheaters such as the Globe. Renaissance playwrights mock the
"groundlings" for their gullibility. In Shakespeare's *Tempest*, Trin-
culo imagines the riches he will amass showing off monster Caliban
to the London crowds: "When they will not give a doit to relieve a
lame beggar, they will lay out ten to see a dead Indian" (2.2.30–31).
In Ben Jonson's *Volpone*, Peregrine ridicules Sir Politic Would-Be's

susceptibility to rumor (lions in the Tower, whales on the Thames, and the like): "Oh, this knight . . . would be a precious thing / To fit our English stage" [2.1.56–58]). But practitioners of commercial theater would think twice before biting the hands that helped feed them. They exploited an undiscriminating interest in strange creatures and exotic places even as they made fun of it (and of themselves, occasionally, for exploiting it).

As Samuel Johnson saw it, Desdemona's impulse, reaching out beyond the "wealthy curlèd darlings" of her own nation (1.2.68) to embrace a stranger from a strange land, is not specific to "any age or . . . any nation" (243 below). That the exotic details in Othello's life story seem to derive from Pliny as well as from medieval and Renaissance travel literature reinforces Johnson's claim: Exogamous desire is universal, transcending time and place. But then so, too, is its contrary feeling, an intense loathing of and repulsion from the alien. According to John Gillies, "The need to constitute an identity by excluding the other is not just primal, but perennial" (6). And *Othello* seems to cater equally to the need Gillies describes as it does to its opposite, generating repulsion and anxiety in conjunction with attraction and delight.

When it comes to the darker side of *Othello*'s effects, the most prominent candidate for Threatening Other is the Turk. The period around *Othello*'s composition "marks a high point in the production of texts of all kinds relating to the Ottoman Empire" (Dimmock, *New Turkes*, 6). Richard Knolles's *General History of the Turks* (the full title is listed in the Works Cited below) was published in 1603, probably too late for Shakespeare to have used it as a source for *Othello*. But Knolles's discussion draws on material already widely available in other Renaissance texts, including lyric and narrative poems (Jacobson) and, above all, works for the stage. If some Renaissance plays transport audiences to the romance of brave new worlds across the Atlantic, many more focus on the intimidating old worlds in the Mediterranean east. In various tallies, there were "dozens of plays about Turks and Moors" (Matar, 4), at least 17 "Turk Plays," in which "Turkish cruelty" and "Turkish villains" are "center stage" (Vitkus, *Three Turk Plays*, 2), and as many as 62 plays produced between 1579 and 1624 featuring "Islamic characters, themes, or settings" (Burton, 257–58).

If *Othello* may be grouped among these plays, it is also an outlier. The Turkish menace is not "center stage" in *Othello*—only "threatened," as Vitkus adds, "then displaced." The implied equivalence in Matar's "Turks and Moors" can be questioned. Othello's own references—"turned Turks" in the brawl scene (2.3.160), "turbanned Turk" at the end (5.2.368)—vehemently dissociate himself from Turkish villainy; and there is evidence to suggest that readers in

Shakespeare's England made a sharp "distinction" between the barbarous cruelty of the Turks and the civilized nobility of "other Islamic people" (Clegg, 7). But Othello's claims are hardly disinterested (many commentators take his dismissals to suggest the reverse of what he intends), and even if the play's better-read spectators distinguished between Moors and Turks, the play seems rather to collapse the distinction than to fortify it. In the opening scene, when Iago refers to "the Cyprus wars, / Which even now stands in act" (147–48), the echo of his startling image just earlier, "Even now, now, very now, an old black ram / Is tupping your white ewe" (85–86), suggests a structural analogy: As Othello takes violent possession of Brabantio's patriarchal property, so the Turks threaten an outpost of Venetian order. The suggestion is reinforced when the same word, "beguile," is used to describe both Othello's effect on Desdemona (1.3.66) and the Turks' assault on Cyprus (1.3.208). The Duke's acknowledgment that he takes the Turkish menace "in fearful sense" (1.3.12) resonates with Brabantio's description of Othello as "a thing . . . to fear" (1.2.71). The Turkish peril seems to prey on primal anxieties as well—the age-old specter of barbarians assaulting Europe from the margins. Brabantio evokes the idea to dismiss it. "What tell'st thou me of robbing? This is Venice: / My house is not a grange" (1.1.102–03). By the next scene, however, his confidence has been shattered: "For if such actions may have passage free / Bond-slaves and pagans shall our statesmen be" (1.2.98–99).

Othello may not be a prototypical Turk Play, but Turk Plays must have figured prominently in the expectations of *Othello*'s first audiences, adding anxiety to the range of responses to the protagonist. We may recoil from Brabantio's racist description of Othello's "sooty bosom" (1.2.70), but Renaissance audiences probably didn't. Iago, the origin and chief spokesman for such sentiments in the play, is evidently cast as "The Malcontent," a conventional type in the drama of the period, whose malign resentment constitutes the perspective from which audiences are invited to view the corrupt and stressful world he inhabits. Iago's prejudice coincides with Shakespearean assumptions elsewhere, as in the mostly villainous Moor Aaron in *Titus Andronicus*, and the mostly endearing Portia in *The Merchant of Venice*, who dismisses her unsuccessful suitor, the Prince of Morocco, with "Let all of his complexion choose me so" (2.7.79). In "*Othello* and Colour Prejudice," G. K. Hunter describes the "traditional view of what Moors are like" in Shakespeare's time—"gross , disgusting, inferior, carrying the symbol of their damnation on their skin" (281 below). This view seems to coincide with government policy, as promulgated in a Privy Council order of 1596 concerned with "the great numbers of Negroes and blackamoors" in the realm (McDonald, 302), reinforced in a royal proclamation of 1601 authorizing that "those kind of people" should be "sent out of the land" (Hughes and Larkin, 221–22).

The matter is not straightforward. Hunter's "traditional view" does not monopolize the Renaissance imagination; other, more favorable views of Moors circulated at the time. The racist sentiment we detect in the Privy Council order may have been a pretext to divert attention from the potentially embarrassing implications of negotiating a prisoner exchange with a hostile Catholic Spain (Bartels, 100–17). But these qualifications do not dislodge the basic point. Renaissance audiences could be counted on (initially, at any rate) to respond antipathetically to "Negroes and blackamoors." Maybe Othello understands his blackness as "the color of a romantic hero," of "one of enchanted powers and of magical protection," and, "above all," of "purity, of a perfect soul" (see Cavell, 290 below), but this is not how the play's early spectators would have understood it—or not the only and perhaps not the principal way.

If creaturely and geographic differences have provoked intensely ambivalent feelings throughout recorded history, significant local variations still need to be explained. When the irresistible appeal of Bradley's "romantic" Othello, "dark and grand," collides with "the aversion of our blood" at the prospect of Desdemona's sexual interest in a "coal-black" Othello (247 and 269 below), his contradictory feelings are expressed from within the conviction of distinct and biologically determined identities. Given the scientifically authorized facts (as then construed), Bradley and his nineteenth-century predecessors sought to manage their conflicted response by imagining Othello as a tawny Moor rather than a black African. But since "'race' as we comprehend it now simply did not exist until the nineteenth century" (Gilroy, 57), their efforts to impose a "racialist" interpretation back onto the product of a "pre-racial" culture were bound to run into problems (Appiah, 278). Far from distinguishing between Othello's black and Moorish characteristics, the play lumps them together. Lumping is a regular practice in the period, as in George Best's reference, written originally in 1578 and subsequently incorporated into Hakluyt's 1600 compendium, to "all these black Moores which are in Africa" (quoted in Newman, 147). Best conflates North African and sub-Saharan racial types within the then-standard term to describe "those kind of people": "blackamoors." In this context, the Privy Council's "Negroes and blackamoors" registers as intensifying an apposition rather than fine tuning a distinction. Richard Burbage, the original Othello, apparently performed the part in blackface and Moorish costume—as a "blackamoor"; but Renaissance audiences probably wouldn't have registered the suggestions as contradictory, perhaps partly as a result of the period's histrionic conventions, which did not coincide totally with realistic representation as we now understand it, but chiefly because the spectators weren't used to thinking in terms of the scientific (or pseudoscientific) category of race that was being contradicted.

The figures on page 146 suggest how audiences might have made sense of what they saw in Burbage's performance at the Globe. Taken from Cesare Vecellio's late-sixteenth-century collection of more than 500 woodcuts illustrating "ancient and modern attire from all over the world," these are the only four (except for a "Vergine Mora," or Moorish girl) identified as Moors.[1] Taken together, these representations of—to translate the captions in the woodcuts—"Black Moors" (Figure 3), a "Barbary Moor" (Figure 4), a "Wealthy Moor" (Figure 5), and a "Noble Moor of Cairo" (Figure 6) make it clear that Renaissance Italians, like "the early modern English," did in fact "differentiate North Africa from the rest of the continent" (Bak, 200) and recognized that "Africans south of the Sahara were not at all the same people as the much more familiar Moors" (Matar, 7). Vecellio's images display tangible differences—in deportment and garb as well as in what we tend now to understand as racial attributes—in ways vividly present even at a glance. Vecellio's commentary, moreover, reinforces the visual details with textually specific references to a black or tawny complexion ("*colore oliuastro*"), frizzy hair ("*crespica peli*"), blunt, flat, and wide noses ("*i loro nasi fraccati, & sechiacciati larghi*"), and white teeth ("*i denti bianchi*"). But these details, subsumed within the capacious designation of "Moor" and scattered higgledy-piggledy over the map, seem to float inconsequentially in an indeterminate space. Vecellio identifies black skins with the "*Morineri*" in the sub-Saharan south but then, unaccountably to a modern observer, locates the "*Moro de Barbaria*," despite his evidently Negroid features, in the Caucasoid north. Removing his hood, he would presumably reveal the "*crespica peli*" Vecellio later specifies for the "Morineri." But since the hunter in Figure 3 is designed to illustrate the blackamoors of Zanzibar ("*i mori negri di Zanguebar*"), how, we might wonder, has his kinky hair migrated so far to the north? And why does Vecellio declare that the dignified Moor in Figure 5 has the "*colore oliuastro*" more properly attributed to someone like the "*Moro nobile del Cairo*," despite clearly contrary evidence in the accompanying image?

In *Othello*, similarly, racial attributes are specified, but they lack the coherent stability required for us to see them as such—to register them *as* racial attributes. This instability is not much of a problem in performance. Having swallowed a camel (taking Laurence

---

1. The Works Cited below includes bibliographical information for Vecellio's first edition in 1590 and the expanded second version of 1598. The images reproduced here, supplemented with translations of Vecellio's text, are conveniently accessible in Jones and Rosenthal's sumptuously informative modern edition (pp. 533, 539, 540, and 550).

Figure 3. Moro Neri. From Cesare Vecellio, *Habiti antichi et moderni di diverse parti del mondo* (Venice, 1590), 497v. Used by permission of the Folger Shakespeare Library. Shelfmark GT509.V4 1590a Cage.

Figure 5. Moro di conditione. From Cesare Vecellio, *Habiti antichi et moderni di diverse parti del mondo* (Venice, 1590), 486v. Used by permission of the Folger Shakespeare Library. Shelfmark GT509 .V4 1590a Cage.

Figure 4. Moro de Barbaria. From Cesare Vecellio, *Habiti antichi et moderni di diverse parti del mondo* (Venice, 1598). Used by permission of the Library of Congress. Call number GT509.V43 1598, Batchelder Collection.

Figure 6. Moro nobile del Cairo. From Cesare Vecellio, *Habiti antichi et moderni di diverse parti del mondo* (Venice, 1598). Used by permission of the Library of Congress. Call number GT509 .V43 1598, Batchelder Collection.

Olivier for Othello, say), we won't strain at a gnat (he's not really "the thick-lips" specified in 1.1.63). Readers have more of a problem, especially if they are trying to figure out what Othello and *Othello* looked like in their own time, and here G. K. Hunter, who brought the issue into focus for modern criticism, greatly helps. "The word 'Moor' had no clear racial status," he explains in the piece excerpted below (278), adding in a later version that it was used indiscriminately to describe any people "in that outer circuit of non-Christian lands where the saving grace of Jerusalem is weakest in its whitening power" ("*Othello*," 41). By transferring skin color from the (for us) normal context of biological identity to a framework defined by sin and redemption, Hunter represents Renaissance belief as grounded in a religious understanding. In this respect, he anticipates a "religious turn" that has profoundly influenced current literary study—as in Daniel Vitkus, who sees Othello at the beginning of the play as "neither 'white' nor 'black,' in the sense that his spiritual 'blackness' has been 'whitened' by conversion to Christianity" (*Turning Turk*, 23); or in Julia Reinhard Lupton, who declares that "in *Othello* religious difference is more powerfully felt, or at least more deeply theorized, than racial difference" (106).

In burrowing underneath nineteenth-century and later "racialism" to questions of "spiritual" and "religious differences," Vitkus and Lupton are trying to see what *Othello* might have looked like in its own time. But the religious turn, through its powerful potential to enrich the affective impact of Shakespeare's play, has far-reaching consequences in the aesthetic as well as the historicist domain. As long as we approach *Othello* in racial terms, we are likely to hear an "effort of defensive self-representation" in Othello's speech, the "'compensatory . . . counterstrategy'" of someone condemned by the "'loss of his own origins'" to the "'perpetual reiteration of the norms of another culture'" (Berger, 107, quoting Katharine Maus and Stephen Greenblatt). As represented here, Othello is an abject victim of prejudicial norms, pitiable for the "humiliating" effects of his situation. It is hard to imagine any response to Othello that does not give prominence to pity, but by itself, pity seems like a simplification of what Globe audiences might have thought and felt. Pity, moreover, is strikingly inadequate to account for the intolerable weight of guilt and pain *Othello* has for centuries loaded upon its spectators and readers—"not to be endured," as Samuel Johnson puts it (245 below). Darker feelings are evidently at work in the intensity of the play's tragic effects, and this is where the religious turn, with its shift of focus to a Moorish and a Muslim Othello, can help.

Consider the "Portrait of a Moor" in Figure 7, a representation of 'Abd al-Wahid bin Mas'oud bin Mohammad 'Annouri (Matar's

1600

ABDVLGVAHID.

LEGATVS REGIS BARBARIÆ
IN ANGLIAM.

ÆTATIS:42.

Figure 7. Portrait of ʿAbd al-Wahid bin Massʿoud bin Mohammad ʿAnnouri. © The University of Birmingham Research and Cultural Collections.

transliteration, 33), who, along with an embassy of sixteen Muslims, arrived in London in August 1600, representing the king of Morocco to the English court. On and off for six months, partly under the pretext of discussing trade, 'Abd al-Wahid explored with Queen Elizabeth I the possibility of a military alliance against Spain. According to Matar, the "stern face and fierce look" in the portrait suggests that the anonymous "English painter, like the populace, may have found the Moors not just alienating but intimidating too" (34). In Bernard Harris's detailed description, 'Abd al-Wahid's sojourn in London brought him into contact, sometimes direct and personal, with people and places (Lewis Lewkenor, John Pory, Aleppo) that figure in the composition of *Othello*, and it is easy to understand why E. A. J. Honigmann extends Matar's speculation "to suppose that this very face haunted Shakespeare's imagination and inspired the writing of his tragedy" (4). Maybe it haunted the spectators' imaginations as well. There wouldn't have been much resemblance between this "intense and aristocratic face" (Honigmann, 3) and the blacked-up Richard Burbage audiences saw on the Globe stage; but it's rather what the audience might have sensed in and around Burbage's personation of Shakespeare's noble Moor, the impact on their mind's eye, that is at issue. In its compelling gaze—sinister if not threatening, canny and sophisticated, directed unflinchingly at the observer's eye—there is nothing like abjection and everything like power: an object of sympathetic interest, perhaps, but more immediately, to recall Brabantio's words, "a thing . . . to fear."

Whatever the early audiences saw (or sensed) on stage, the experience probably left them with the same overall problem with which we began—how to negotiate the violent swings between radically contradictory impressions of the protagonist. Given the "antithetical uses made of blackness in the Christian tradition," a black Othello must have been "perceived in diametrically opposite ways" (Moran, 25–26): on the one hand, as a symbol of unregenerate and diabolical evil; on the other, of "pagan virtue" and the redemptive power of baptism.[2] The same kind of ambivalence, moreover, probably characterized the response of Shakespeare's spectators to a tawny Moor, owing in large part to the similarly contradictory representations of Islam in Renaissance thought and feeling.

One place in which to situate these representations is John Leo Africanus's *History and Geography of Africa*, the most authoritative

---

2. The latter developed from the account of the black-skinned Ethiopian whose soul is washed white in Acts 8:27–40, prefigured in Isaiah 1:16 and Psalms 51:7. See the discussions in Neill, 188, and Hornbeck, "'Speaking Parrot,'" 72–75. The idea was still current in the middle of the seventeenth century, in Richard Crashaw's "On the Baptized Ethiopian" (Martin, 85). For "pagan virtue," see Grady and Decosimo.

source for things African in the Renaissance (and beyond), which Shakespeare almost certainly made use of in *Othello* (see 368–69 below). The book differentiates sharply between "Barbaria" in the north, "the most noble and worthie region of all Africa," whose "browne or tawnie" inhabitants are "greatly addicted vnto the studie of good artes and sciences," with "religion . . . esteemed by them in the first place"; and "the land of Negros" in the south, whose denizens, "neither Mahumetans, Iewes, nor Christians," have "no churches at all, nor any kinde of prayers" and who, thus "vtterly estranged from all godly devotion," are reduced to "a sauage and beastly life" (Robert Brown, 123, 182, 129, 186). John Leo registers differences in location and skin color, but just coincidentally; his underlying distinction is between godly and ungodly lives. If tawny Moors are more "noble and worthie" than black Africans, this is not because they are tawny but because they are Moors—Muslims, that is, who, whatever their location or appearance, share with Christians and Jews their faith in one God.

Twenty-first-century audiences, inundated with stories about "Islamist terrorism," may find John Leo's inclusiveness startling, but it would not have seemed peculiar in Shakespeare's world. For "Christian writers in early modern Europe," the commonality of beliefs derived from monotheism (the authority of the Hebrew Bible, for instance, and the enduring promise of God's covenant with Abraham) constituted a "common ground" for "the three religions, or peoples, of the book" (Dimmock and Hadfield, 1). But John Leo, though technically "a Christian writer in early modern Europe" when he wrote his *History*, was born a Muslim. I emphasize the point because the idea of a common core of faith among the "peoples of the book" originates in Islamic thought (the phrase *Ahl al-Kitāb* is prominently reiterated in the Qur'an, where it associates Jews and Christians with Muslims against the *kuffār*, or "unbelievers"), and John Leo's systematic clarity on the matter probably derives from his Muslim origins. Although the idea was taken up into European Christendom, as Dimmock and Hadfield claim, it was never fully assimilated, because the imagination of Christian Europe was already occupied by an intensely hostile view of Islam. In recognizing Jesus as a prophet, Muslims established a bond with Christians, but Islamic claims for Muhammad as a later and final prophet were regularly taken by Christians to constitute a denial of the sufficiency of Christian revelation, and thus a repudiation of Christ equivalent to the Jews'. As a consequence, Muslims were regularly depicted as demonic infidels, as in Hunter's "traditional view," defined not by their proximity to the true faith but by their remoteness from it. Bernard Lewis, remarking on the proliferation of "ethnic names" for Muslims in early modern Europe ("Saracens, Moors, Turks, or Tatars"), interprets this "curious reluctance to

call the Muslims by any name with a religious connotation" as a way
to empty Islam of religious content, reducing it to "a false doctrine,
founded by" an "impostor" (7). "'Mahomet-lore,'" the folklore version
of Islamic origins that circulated with a "monotonous . . . uniformity"
from the Middle Ages to Shakespeare's day, worked to the same purpose, embellishing a story in which heretical monks conspired with
disaffected Jews to lure "the pagan 'Mahomet' into representing a
'New Law' by masquerading as a divinely appointed Prophet" (Dimmock, "A Human Head," 72 and 73; and see his *Mythologies of the
Prophet Muhammad*, 101–48).

Julia Reinhard Lupton unpacks the implications of this configuration for the play's first audiences, developing the two different scenarios with which *Othello*, as she sees it, encouraged them to imagine
the protagonist's prior religious identification. In the first scenario,
Othello "would appear" as a "darker-skinned" immigrant from somewhere "far to the south" in "pagan Africa," whose "religious innocence" renders him especially "open to a transformative Christian
reinscription"—perhaps (I am extrapolating from her description)
like the "base Indian" in the Quarto version of Othello's last speech.
In the second scenario, "[l]ooking east, toward Arabia and Turkey,"
we would see a "lighter-skinned" Muslim, whose "monotheistic"
inheritance and "frequent contacts with Christian Europe" make
him "more likely to go renegade" (105–06)—perhaps (extrapolating
again) like the "base Judean" in the Folio (see 5.2.352 and note).

In Lupton's view, Shakespeare's Moor, like the Moors in Vecellio,
manages to be both a tawny North African or Middle Eastern Muslim and a black sub-Saharan "Pagan" at the same time, or as part of
the same experience. Not everyone respects the play's slippages
on this matter. "Moors are Muslims," Daniel Boyarin declares with
definitive confidence in "Othello's Penis" (257), but as Graham
Bradshaw remarks, there is "no textual evidence" for "the assumption" that "Othello must have been a Muslim before he became a
Christian" (21). By making suggestions but withholding conclusive
details, *Othello* leaves it up to spectators to imagine what it is they
think they see. (In this respect, the play works on its audience like
Iago on the protagonist: "With her, on her," as Iago says in the words
that precipitate Othello's spastic fit; "what you will" [4.1.34]).

Even Lupton's generous open-mindedness has its limits. Within
the "Renaissance scene," she argues, reversing the values by which
nineteenth-century commentators demanded a tawny protagonist,
an "Othello more closely resembling the Turk," when compared with
"a black Othello," might "actually challenge more deeply" the "integrity of the Christian paradigms set up in the play as the measure of
humanity" (106). But this configuration is no more firmly conclusive
than the one it has turned upside down. For Shakespeare's

audiences, the reversal could itself be reversed, restoring "browne or tawnie" Muslims to the position John Leo accords them of superiority to black African unbelievers. The "Renaissance scene" seems rather to be a kaleidoscope of shifting scenes, and its volatility is intensified by the fact the "Christian paradigms set up by the play" may lack the "integrity" Lupton attributes to them.

Here we need to expand the picture to include the Protestant Reformation, the consequences of which would be hard to overestimate at the time of *Othello*'s first production. When Martin Luther attempted early in the sixteenth century to reform the abuses of the Roman Catholic Church, he precipitated schisms between Protestantism and Catholicism (or among variously nuanced kinds of Protestants and Catholics) throughout Christian Europe. In breaking with Rome, England avoided the carnage of the religious wars on the Continent, but the threat of an assault from Catholic forces in France or Spain was felt as immediate long after the defeat of the Spanish Armada in 1588. When Pope Pius V promulgated *Regnans in Excelsis* (1570), excommunicating Queen Elizabeth and exempting English Catholics from any obligation of loyalty to her, he reinforced anxieties about a foreign invasion with the specter of a secret conspiracy operating inside the country, and these anxieties survived undiminished well into the seventeenth century.[3]

The divisions within Christianity are nowhere mentioned in *Othello*, but they don't have to be. What Dimmock and Hadfield say about the Christian/Jewish differences in *The Merchant of Venice* is true also of the Christian/Muslim differences in *Othello*: "no Christian audience could have failed to realise" that "Christians themselves were irrevocably divided over exactly the same sort of issues" (5). As Vitkus puts it, "the interest in Christian-Muslim conversion clearly related to contemporaneous polemical writings about Protestants and Roman Catholics who renounced one brand of Christianity for the other" (*Turning Turk*, 83). *Othello* allows us glimpses of these divisions, as in Iago's name. When Shakespeare invented a name for Cinthio's "wicked Ensign," why did he choose a Spanish name, especially when the character is a Venetian insider ("I know our country disposition well," 3.3.203), and why specifically the name of the patron saint of Spain, Santiago Matamoros, Saint James the Moor Slayer, if not to reinforce the specter of Spanish Catholicism already threatening the minds (or infiltrating

---

3. Some commentators, noting that the papal bull was subsequently suspended and that English Catholics ignored it, attribute a "paranoid atmosphere" and "paranoia" to the anti-Catholic politics of late-Tudor England (Parker, 62; Smith); but the Ridolfi Plot of the not-too-distant past (1571) and the Gunpowder Plot of the immediate future (1605) suggest that even the paranoid spectators included among *Othello*'s first audiences had real enemies.

the unconscious) of the play's first spectators (Everett, Griffin)? Robert Watson's claims that *Othello* is a "Reformation tragedy" or "Protestant propaganda" sound exaggerated, but they are not created out of nothing.

Living amid the immediate consequences of the Reformation, the first audiences of *Othello* must have been not only at odds with one another but divided within themselves in the substance and intensity of the convictions they carried into the Globe. They shared Christian paradigms, but these failed to coalesce into systematic coherence, remaining multiple and flexibly capacious. From this angle, the religious differences percolating in *Othello*—Protestant and Catholic, Muslim and "pagan," etc.—supplement rather than displace one another, like the associated feelings of racial difference pressed on us by the play, for which, as Robert J. C. Young describes them, "however many new meanings may be constructed," the "old meanings refuse to die" but "rather accumulate in clusters of ever-increasing power, resonance and persuasion" (83).

Shift focus from religious feeling to material conditions—the economic and political pressures obtaining at the time of *Othello*'s first production—and the effect of anxious contradiction does not appreciably change. On one side, Turkish power represented a real threat that might easily have reinforced primal fears. Between 1453, when they captured Constantinople, and 1571, when they seized Cyprus from the Venetians, the Ottoman Turks either conquered or laid siege to Athens, Otranto, Rhodes, Budapest, and Vienna. The victory of a Christian navy at the Battle of Lepanto (1571) was significant, but the Turks regrouped and continued to dominate the eastern Mediterranean well into the seventeenth century, forcing the English to invest in the roundabout project of a western passage to the riches of the East. King James's 1595 poem about Lepanto was republished on his accession in 1603, around the time of *Othello*'s earliest performance; but by this time, the poem's celebration of a turning point must have rung hollow, and audiences may have detected something of Lepanto's fragility in the victory that falls into the Venetians' laps at the beginning of Act 2.

If economics and politics reinforced the fear of a demonic other, they accounted for friendlier and more familiar images as well. Queen Elizabeth I was "the first English monarch to cooperate openly with the Muslims, and to allow her subjects to trade and interact with them without being liable to prosecution for dealing with 'infidels' " (Matar, 19). The English became partners with the Turks in the highly profitable Levant trade, even beginning to supplant the Venetians as the chief Western beneficiary of this enterprise. The Moors were sometimes political partners with the English as well. Jack D'Amico details negotiations undertaken during Elizabeth's reign to enlist Moorish support against the threats represented by Catholic France and Spain. 'Abd al-Wahid's embassy of 1600–1601 is part of this story, as is Tom Stukley, the Englishman whose heroic exploits fighting for Ahmad bin Abdallah against Spanish Catholic interests were celebrated in George Peele's *Battle of Alcazar* (c. 1589) and in a host of other dramatic and non-dramatic renditions well into the seventeenth century (Edelman). "Relations between England and Morocco were extremely complex" around this time, "and the opinions" about Moors generated by those relations" varied "from the dangerously inscrutable alien to the exotically attractive ally" (D'Amico, 39).

Faced with all this, we should not expect to recapture the original experience of *Othello* in the form of a clear and stable image. *Othello* is a moving target, like the sometimes alluring and sometimes intimidating protagonist that served as the starting point of the discussion. Maybe movement itself is what deserves emphasis. If so, an early spectator of *Othello*, careening restlessly from one position to another, might look like the play's protagonist in Roderigo's description, "an extravagant and wheeling stranger / Of here and everywhere" (1.1.133–34); maybe even like Desdemona as she appears to Othello's crazed imagination—a creature who "can turn, and turn, and yet go on / And turn again" (4.1.248–49).

II. Women

Unlike Othello, whose representation assumes beliefs and feelings clearly different from those that twenty-first-century audiences bring to the play, Desdemona may seem not to need historical contextualization. We have become used to stories about the satisfactions and tribulations of domestic life; the subject and genre of *Othello* are likely to seem familiar: A married couple whose feelings for one another, though largely without consequence for the public domain, produce a tragedy for themselves. To *Othello*'s first audiences, however, the play must have looked strange, an early instance of the not-yet-recognizable transformation Richard Helgerson describes, in which "the nonaristocratic home . . . emerges not simply as an adjunct of state power but as an alternative to it, a space that by the late eighteenth century would be making its own claim to both representation and political value as the affective base for a new revolutionary order" (4). Moreover, even as these new values were emerging into consciousness at the time, they both coexisted with and displaced more traditional ideas about women and the social order; and these residual values must also have contributed significantly to the complex responses of *Othello*'s first audiences, especially to Desdemona's powerful presence in the play.

To start with marriage: With the decline of the monastic ideal of celibacy inherited from the Catholic middle ages, marriage came out from under the shadow of a necessary compromise into prominence as a justified and indeed sanctified condition. Saint Paul advises "widowes" and "the vnmaried" to "abide" in chastity "euen as I *do*," but to those who "can not absteine," he counsels marriage, "for it is better to marie then to burne" (1 Corinthians 7:8–9). The Protestant Reformers of the sixteenth century accepted the traditional utilitarian justifications for marriage (containing the fires of lust, propagating and reinforcing the values of Christian community), but went far beyond them in celebrating the affective bond between husband and wife as a positive value in itself. They put forth an ideal of "companionate marriage," developed in a rich tradition of homiletic literature—sermons and practical manuals offering guidance about the choice of husband or wife (itself now less a matter of parental imposition) and the behavior likely to sustain affection through the complications of a long shared life. This ideal achieves its most resonant expression in *Paradise Lost* (1667), where Milton's panegyric "Hail wedded Love" (4.750) celebrates Adam and Eve's marriage as the affectionate and spiritual center of individual and social experience.

According to Mary Beth Rose, the new "prestige and centrality" of marriage and the domestic domain were first incorporated into drama on the Jacobean stage. Where tradition dictated a "heroism of public action," manifested in "political and military struggles" that relegate "women, eros, and sexuality to the periphery," a new kind of drama appears giving "prominence" to nonaristocratic female protagonists who exemplify "a heroism of personal endurance" in their "private life" (95–96). In this line, pride of position might be given to *Patient Grissill* (Bowers)—a collaboration among three playwrights, first performed in 1600—which celebrates the protagonist's unswerving loyalty in the face of her husband's unaccountably cruel trials. *Patient Grissill* initiated a fad: "over twenty extant plays in the period c. 1600–1612" devoted to "the 'patient wife'" (Clark, 2:247). The titles of three of these—Thomas Heywood's *How a Man May Choose a Good Wife from a Bad* (1602) and *A Woman Killed with Kindness* (1603) and George Wilkins's *The Miseries of Enforced Marriage* (1607)—give a sense of what they are about.

Rose, concentrating on the new "heroics of marriage" (93–177) in a more elevated social milieu, takes *Othello* and John Webster's *Duchess of Malfi* as her prime exhibits, and from its opening, *Othello* offers abundant evidence to support her claims. Nearly the whole first act is unnecessary for the plot; it's not in Cinthio, and Boito eliminates it from the libretto of Verdi's opera. But the play goes out of its way to focus on the feelings that lead Othello and Desdemona to choose each other. Desdemona's account may be the more powerful. "That I love the Moor to live with him" (1.3.246) avows her desire for Othello before the full senate. Sex is not all she means in asserting her rights to the pleasure of Othello's company: "To live with him" entails sharing his exotic past, as well as the romance of military affairs to come; and it extends to the inner beauty she has intuited, "Othello's visage in his mind" (1.3.250), the bond between his "perfect soul" (1.2.31) and her own as she did "consecrate" it to him (1.3.252). Desdemona refuses the traditional distinctions between body and spirit, and private and public; and in doing so she rejects the traditional supremacy of male values and masculine identity that stands behind them. Equality inheres in her conception of holy matrimony as a mutually elective affinity derived from the most profound depths of Protestant feeling, the equality of all souls before God—"nether male nor female," as Paul affirms it, "all one in Christ Iesus" (Galatians 3:28). Othello's "my fair warrior" in 2.1.180 delightedly recognizes her claim to equal status. Later on, her own "unhandsome warrior" (3.4.148) acknowledges a struggle to maintain the integrity of her original affection in the face of betrayal—an endeavor, moreover, in which she is more successful than anyone else in the play. If *Othello* is centered in "the heroics of marriage," Desdemona may be its true protagonist.

But this is only part of a complex and contradictory story. The "dramatic change" represented by companionate marriage does not displace the strong elements of "unbroken continuity" with traditional views of women and their place in the world (Dolan, *Marriage*, 27). Whatever its investment in equality, the homiletic literature is sustained with incessant reminders about male dominance, regularly reiterating Paul's injunctions to wives to "submit your selues vnto your housbands, as vnto the Lord" (Ephesians 5:21 and see Colossians 3:18). Despite Paul Badiou's efforts (103–06), there seems to be no way to square Pauline patriarchalism with the egalitarian universalism of "nether male nor female . . . all one in Christ Iesus." A sharp sense of incongruity must have informed the experience of early audiences of *Othello*; as Valerie Wayne puts it, when Desdemona's "advocacy of marriage" collides with "an anti-matrimonial misogyny," the "heroics of marriage breaks down" through "its own unresolved contradictions" (168, 177).

The most striking expressions of misogyny in *Othello* take the form of a violent aversion to the female body. Iago punningly refers to Desdemona's "country disposition" and "country forms" in terms of a disgusting odor: "Foh! one may smell in such a will most rank" (3.3.203, 239, 234); and Othello becomes infected with the same revulsion. He associates the "corner in the thing I love" with the "vapor of a dungeon," "a cistern for foul toads / To knot and gender in," learning to share "honest" Iago's repugnance to "the slime / That sticks on filthy deeds" (3.3.273–74 , 4.2.61–62, 5.2.51–52). We might wish to quarantine these images within a compartment of deviant psychology (an evil character, a sex-nauseated author); but the anxieties about women expressed in *Othello* are situated generally within the "networks of terms that shaped politics, institutions, and laws, as well as discourses of the body" (Parker, 86); as Gail Paster represents it, an aversion to the female body is neither aberrant nor pathological in the Renaissance but generally dispersed and normative. According to the theory of bodily humors, accepted for centuries and still authoritative at the time of *Othello*, the female body is inherently leakier than the male—more "effluent, overproductive, out of control"; and "it is precisely woman's literal saturation by the cold clamminess of the female complexion that philosophically undergirds the most virulent, most conservative forms of Renaissance misogyny" (*Body Embarrassed*, 21; "Unbearable Coldness," 430).

Renaissance misogyny was legitimated by religious as well as scientific authority (a distinction less real for *Othello*'s audience than for us). Othello's "cause" at the end, his claim to administer punitive justice against female sexual transgression, does not derive from some "alien" code attributable to "uncivilized notions of barbarian blackness" but "lies, rather, at the root of Western religious law" going back to the Hebrew Bible (Boose, 372). Christianity thus inherits an anxiety about sex that even the Pauline compromise referred to earlier ("better to marie then to burne") fails to relieve. Stephen Greenblatt, citing Catholic commentators for whom "an adulterer is he who is too ardent a lover of his wife," argues that "the dark essence of Iago's whole enterprise" is "to play upon Othello's buried perception of his own sexual relations with Desdemona as adulterous" ("Improvisation of Power," 248, 233; Iago's much-discussed "fellow almost damned in a fair wife" [1.1.18] seems to prey on such anxieties). Misogyny and sexual anxiety were never the totality of sanctioned Catholic belief, and the Protestant Reformers vigorously contested such views in their own claims for holy matrimony. But given the depth of this tradition, "an underlying guilt and disgust about sexuality itself" (Snow, 388) must have been strongly enough present in Renaissance audiences for the expressions of misogyny in *Othello* to receive at least a general, conditional assent.

These expressions informed "the woman question," the literary debate—begun around 1540 and sustained in various texts for a century or more—about such matters as the virtues inherent in or absent from female nature, the relation between nature and culture in defining female identity, the training appropriately given to or withheld from women, and the behavior legitimately expected or feared from them. The durability of this debate might suggest that it reflected deeply felt concerns, but according to Linda Woodbridge, the "Formal Controversy" about women was such a highly stylized and self-enclosed rhetorical game that its connections to social reality are hard to determine (11–136).

In the popular culture of the period, however—and this includes the public theaters for which *Othello* was written—the obsessive focus on shrews, scolding wives, and other insubordinate women may be more immediately revealing. In *Arden of Faversham* and *A Warning for Fair Women*, two domestic tragedies that held the stage during the 1590s, wives betray and then conspire with their lovers to kill their husbands. According to Frances E. Dolan, "husband-murder . . . captured the popular imagination and generated extensive representations" in pamphlets and ballads as well as plays, "despite the fact that it was never very common" (*Dangerous Familiars*, 13). Along with master-slaying, moreover, husband-murder was legally designated as petty treason—that is, as "a crime against civil authority," even though "legal records suggest that women and servants were more often the victims than the perpetrators of domestic violence" (4). In the face of such evidence, "Many social historians agree that early modern England witnessed a crisis of order, focusing on gender relations" and situated in the domestic domain (17).

The phenomenon of "women on top," in Natalie Zemon Davis's at once politically and sexually charged phrase, must have contributed to this crisis, especially in England, where for so long Queen Elizabeth was the "one vital exception" to a social order in which "all forms of public and domestic authority . . . were vested in men" (Montrose, 64). Even here there are complications, however; queenship could be the basis for protofeminism as well as misogynist anxiety (Eggert), even (as Amanda Shephard demonstrates) among conservative Catholic aristocrats, who might seem a less hospitable constituency for progressive ideas. Modern grids don't fit neatly over the Renaissance terrain, and the proliferation of variables— gender, social status, religious affiliation, and so on—make interpretive clarity hard to achieve. The "woman question" was probably many different questions, clustered around a symbolic core that allowed for and encouraged multiple and contradictory sorts of engagement.

"If this be not barbarous," says the speaker/author of *Hic Mulier; or, The Man-Woman*, a 1620 contribution to the Formal Controversy about women, referring to the female arrogation of male clothing and prerogatives, then "make the rude Scythians, the untamed Moor, the naked Indian, or the wild Irish, Lords and Rulers of well-governed Cities" (Henderson and McManus, 269). The words sound uncannily like Brabantio's outburst "For if such actions may have passage free / Bond slaves and pagans shall our statesmen be," and the echo suggests an analogy: These unspecified "actions" can refer equally to an assault on Brabantio's status as a senator, launched from outside by an "extravagant and wheeling stranger" (1.1.133), and on his authority as a father, mounted from within his own family by a "maiden [heretofore] never bold" (1.3.94). The play's language reinforces the analogy. In describing Desdemona's "revolt" as "gross" (1.1.131), Roderigo echoes "the gross clasps of a lascivious Moor" (123), thereby situating Othello and Desdemona in an unconfined space of erotic wandering, outside the constraints of stabilizing order. The functional vagueness of "thing" supports the analogy as well, associating Othello's terrifyingly indefinite presence ("such a thing as thou," 1.2.71) with Desdemona's "thing" (her "country disposition," the "appetite" that belongs to her), which Othello can never securely own, merely "keep" (3.3.272 and 274).

In the earliest recorded comment on *Othello* (discussed 188 below), Henry Jackson describes an audience "moved . . . to tears" by "the celebrated Desdemona"; and since similar expressions have been reiterated in an almost uninterrupted reception history to our own day, we may assume that Jackson's reaction represents the norm for early response. But if an affectionate sympathy drew the play's first audiences to Desdemona, this was not all they felt. Grief and admiration coexisted unpeacefully with equally strong but contradictory sentiments, including anxiety and dread. Like the alluring and threatening protagonist of the play, Desdemona must have struck the first spectators of the play as at once a focus of desire and "a thing to fear."

III. Theater

Since any attempt to read people's minds from four centuries ago is bound to rely on speculation, it should come as no surprise that the position developed in the two preceding sections of this essay, of an audience beset with irresolvably contradictory desires, is not universally shared. In this section, I'll reflect on some of the more influential alternative views in recent commentary, and as part of this reflection I'll expand the focus to include another dimension. *Othello* was not available as a reading text until 1622, and the vast majority of the people from four centuries ago whose minds we wish to read were watching a play. The responses of theatrical audiences do not map exactly onto the beliefs they hold outside the theater and, in an additional complication, *Othello's* first audiences saw the play in a theater whose physical environment and production practices differed considerably from what we're used to. Speculating about *Othello* in its own time thus requires speculation about *Othello* in its own place as well.

This prospect is daunting, but it includes an encouraging element. The theatrical dimension can, even as it complicates the problem, also clarify—if not resolve—it. Theater historians have determined a lot about the architecture of the Globe and its production methods, as well as about its audience's playgoing practices—enough to draw reasonable inferences about their effects; and these inferences offer guidance for choosing among the various suggestions put forth about what *Othello* might have looked like in its own time. We'll never get to a position of certainty (this approach is right, the others are wrong), but since *Othello* originated as a Globe performance, any critical approach will gain in plausibility to the extent that it is consistent with the effects likely produced by the original theatrical practices, or will lose in plausibility to the extent that it isn't.

With that in mind, we can turn to alternative descriptions of the play's first impressions, beginning with an approach that might be called strategic pragmatism. According to Nabil Matar, the extent of "*actual* interaction" among the "numerous Britons" who regularly "worked and lived" with Muslims must have moderated whatever hostile preconceptions they inherited from Hunter's "traditional view" (6–7). Revisionist claims along Matar's lines have proliferated of late, among scholars for whom the systematic "East-West binary" set up in Edward Said's *Orientalism* has come to seem "anachronistic and reductive" (Andrea and McJannet, 6).[4] If the Christian and Muslim merchants rubbing shoulders in the Levant trade focused on immediately material realities (what they could exchange with one another, and for how much), they might well have let received ideas about each other's religious (or sacrilegious) convictions recede into the background.

The differences within Christianity present an even more plausible case. Many more English Protestants lived and worked with Catholics than did "numerous Britons" with Muslims; and quite apart from the likelihood that many of these English Protestants harbored residual affection for the old faith, there is good reason to believe that they downplayed their anti-Catholic feelings and beliefs.

---

4. See Burton, 11; Dimmock and Hadfield, 15; Brummett, 111–13 and 133; and, for the most fully worked out version of the current consensus, Bartels, 1–20.

A neighbor may be a Catholic (or a Protestant) but is, nonetheless, a neighbor on whom one must sometime depend, and may even esteem, regardless of confessional loyalty. And even for a committed Protestant, the near certainty that one's grandparents, anyhow, would have been Catholics must have occasionally unsettled the confidence that justification always came by faith alone. (Kastan, 29)

As with religious differences, so with gender. Though empirical evidence is hard to come by, we may assume that many early modern couples turned a blind eye to the ideological contradictions that constituted a "crisis" in their gender relations in order to find elements of the contentment in which, according to the first words of Tolstoy's *Anna Karenina*, "All happy families are alike."

But whatever really happened in the markets of London or the eastern Mediterranean, or in the churches and streets of London, or in the kitchens and bedrooms of domestic households, how does it relate to what was happening on stage? The revisionist view emphasizes *"actual* interaction" at the expense of "fantasy or fiction" (Matar, 6), but if theater *is* fantasy or fiction, the emphasis might be reversed: less on strategic pragmatism than on the darkly symbolic representations of Islamophobic anxiety. A terrified reaction to strangers was probably only a minor element in the day-to-day experience of *Othello*'s first audiences, no more significant than the happily-ever-after elation generated by the multiple marriages at the end of Shakespeare's *A Midsummer Night's Dream*. Theatrical fictions condense and intensify reality; they do not reproduce it.

What we know about the Renaissance playgoing suggests that the spectators understood what was required of them by this situation, and that their understanding was shaped, as I have implied, by a sense of generic distinction. Some spectators had some specific foreknowledge of what awaited them (from word of mouth or from the bills some of them could read posted in public places), but most knew only that the flag was up on the theater and they were going to see a play. To help these spectators narrow down the unaccommodatingly broad category of "a play," theatrical companies "regularly used black hangings to signal to the audience that they should expect a tragedy" (Gurr, 76). Sophisticated genre theory existed in Shakespeare's time, but as Gurr interprets them, the black hangings signaled "the play's conclusion" rather "than any generic name" (74). Look for deaths, they told the audience, not the marriages of conventional comic closure.

In this rough-and-ready way, expectations were established differentially—tragedy is *not-comedy*. When the young Desdemona's marital desires triumph over old Brabantio's patriarchal authority, the play not only celebrates the heroics of companionate marriage; it enacts the structure of dramatic comedy with almost mechanical precision; as Cavell puts it, "this play opens exactly as a normal comedy closes" (see 292 below). But it does so as a way to write comedy out of the audience's expectations: this is *what's-not-going-to-happen-here*. (*A Midsummer Night's Dream* does the same thing in reverse, as Theseus's first words specify tragic elements precisely to exclude them.) The black curtains served as reminders that tragic performances entailed stylization and condensation, and that spectators thus needed to exclude elements of their amorphously varied real experience if they wanted to get the most from the distinctly theatrical experience in store for them. Emily Bartels may be right to suggest that within the "open, evolving, and heterogeneous world picture" of the newly globalized Renaissance, Moors would not provoke a sense of "anxiety-provoking strangeness" (16); but the black curtains visible from the beginning of Globe performances of *Othello, the Moor of Venice* made for a different picture.

Some recent commentators, while acknowledging the likelihood of "anxiety-provoking" cognitive dissonance, nonetheless argue that *Othello* makes a concerted effort to move its first audiences to a sense of resolution. As Hunter describes it below, *Othello* "manipulates our sympathies" in its opening movements, "supposing that we will have brought to the theatre a set of careless assumptions about 'Moors,'" but then introduces "new valuations" of Othello, diametrically opposed to the fear and loathing first generated by Iago (282 below). In "The Design of Desdemona: Doubt Raised and Resolved," Ann Jennalie Cook makes the same case for Desdemona: The play "seems deliberately to be setting up doubts about Desdemona" at the beginning but then, gradually shifting perspective to accommodate the sorts of values emerging in companionate marriage, it finally "permit[s] the playgoer to trust fully" in her with "the concluding act" (189, 193).

Versions of Hunter's and Cook's argument—"disconfirmation," as I have called it elsewhere—are a regular presence in recent commentary;[5] but there are reasons to treat it with some caution. For one thing, disconfirmation does not coincide with the processes dramatized on stage, where from the beginning, characters are shown to arrive at their conclusions according to a very different route. "This accident is not unlike my dream; / Belief of it oppresses me already" (1.1.139–40). Brabantio has every reason to distrust Iago and Roderigo, and everything he knows about Desdemona from years of experience would seem to make her elopement unlikely, but he becomes convinced that she has betrayed his trust

---

5. See Ridley, xlviii–l; Eldred Jones, 87–93; Pechter; Hornbeck, "Emblems," 89; and Lupton, 110.

even in the absence of any "ocular proof." Conviction here has nothing to do with reason, probability, or evidence. Brabantio does not reach his conclusion—he is made to jump to it. Belief happens to him—oppressively, against his will. Some malignant force infiltrates his consciousness and sensibility. The evidence derived from "*actual* interaction" (to recall Matar's language) is overwhelmed by "fantasy or fiction"; his "dream," the nightmarish premonition of betrayal at the most intimate level, determines his belief.

Brabantio's fate clearly foreshadows Othello's (and Cassio's) in the play, and according to some of the most compelling recent critics (including Burke, Cavell, Bristol, and Neill below), it is the spectators' fate as well. The play as they see it, working through Iago as its surrogate, intrudes images and ideas, erotic ones especially, into the foundation of the audience's cognitive faculties, and these images and ideas lead to convictions that, however blatantly improbable— the "double-time scheme" (Bradley and countless followers) or repellent ("an old black ram / Is tupping your white ewe," 1.1.85–6)—the spectators are unable to resist. Shakespeare does in *Othello* what Plato's sophists do in the *Gorgias*—"make his listeners take his fantastic images, presented to their inner eye by verbal accounts of heightened emotional power, as eicastically true" (Altman, 204). Though the play's deceptions are openly acknowledged, its "dangerous conceits" (3.3.327) prove irresistible. *Othello* "thinks abomination into being and then taunts the audience with the knowledge that it can never be *un*thought" (Neill, 323 below).

This version of *Othello*—insinuation, it might be called, as distinct from disconfirmation—gains in plausibility when the play is situated within the production practices specific to the Globe. Years ago, John Russell Brown distinguished between the director's theater we are used to these days, in which a single person has the authority to choreograph the various elements of the production, and the actors' theater of Shakespeare's day, when— without a director (or an author whose text exercised dominating control)—an array of different persons cooperated and competed with one another on a more or less equal footing to produce the performance. Recent theater historians have reinforced Brown's position, arguing that there was no group rehearsal in Shakespeare's theater (Stern), and that the actors, although they would have known the basic plot of the play, learned only their own parts and a few words from other parts meant to cue their speech (Palfrey and Stern). The effect of all this must have been to increase the variability or "freedom" Brown emphasizes in the original productions. Reviewers and directors of modern productions routinely claim to identify *the* idea of *the* production, but in an actors' theater like Shakespeare's, the dispersal of authority into an assortment of different performative energies would seem to make any such endeavor misguided.

And this is the problem with disconfirmation: Its impulse to organize different effects into a hierarchy is contradicted by what we know about the practices of Shakespeare's company—that Globe productions did not (to recall Bottom's words in *A Midsummer Night's Dream*) "grow to a point" (1.2.8). *Othello*'s first audiences may have wished to repudiate their first impressions but felt at the same time (or at different moments within the same performance) trapped in what they had come to recognize as the malignant bias of their initial response.

Perhaps, then, the spectators took it upon themselves to produce the effects the performance couldn't or wouldn't provide—if not resolving their contradictory impressions, at least reducing them to a manageable coherence. This response is what René Girard suggests in his compelling work on scapegoating, which he understands as central to all cultural expression. According to Girard, scapegoating works in two contradictory ways. In structural scapegoating, the "crowd that condemns the victim is presented as rational by the writer, who really belongs to that crowd," whereas in thematic scapegoating, "the crowd is presented as irrational by the writer," who expects us to see through its high-sounding justifications to the self-serving hypocrisy really driving mob violence. Girard is thinking about the Jew and the Venetian Christians in *The Merchant of Venice*, but his distinction works for the Moor and the Venetian Christians in *Othello* equally well, with audiences drawn either to Iago's vicious aspersions or to the exotic glamor of the dark stranger Iago would destroy. As Girard sees it, the availability of both scenarios demonstrates Shakespeare's canny responsiveness to "the various demands placed upon him by the cultural diversity of his audience." Shakespeare "can stage a scapegoating" that is "entirely convincing to those who want to be convinced, and simultaneously undermine that process with ironic touches that will reach only those who can be reached." A Shakespeare play, Girard concludes, "would always present itself to each viewer under aspects best suited to his own perspective" (248–49).

That Shakespeare catered to the diverse interests of a big room has long been taken as a major factor in his initial popularity and subsequent durability; but Girard's argument diverges fundamentally from critical tradition. When Shakespeareans use terms such as "ambiguity," "multi-consciousness," "dialectics," and "complementarity" (Empson, Bethell, Rossiter, Rabkin), they allow for the possibility of negotiating the irreconcilable positions generated by and brought into the performance. In Girard's construction, however, Shakespeare's spectators come into the theater locked wholly into their own convictions, whether xenophobic or cosmopolitan, and they go out of the theater locked wholly into the same convictions. As isolated individuals, protected from any potentially transformative effects emanating either from the actions on stage or the reactions of other spectators, they are, like Charles Whitney's spectators in *Early Responses to Renaissance Drama*, never "addressed collectively" (67), because the plays "disseminate meaning pluralistically" among "diverse constituents" (147). "Self-made and self-centered," as Whitney describes the protagonist of his account, Simon Forman "was drawn to plays featuring specialties of his own, prognostication, magic, and medicine" (149); and if a Shakespeare play is an aggregation of such separate effects, each targeting its own distinct spectatorial niche, Forman must have found what he was looking for. Nothing unpredictable (let alone untoward) could happen to him, or to any spectator viewing a play "under aspects best suited to his own perspective"; the only effect would be to reinforce entrenched positions. In this version of Shakespearean theatrical experience—compartmentalization, it might be called—what you see is what you've got.

Reinforcement may or may not be a good thing, but to judge from what we know about the spatial configuration of the Globe theater, it was not the effect that *Othello*'s first performances were likely to produce. Unlike modern audiences, who sit silently in darkness watching plays illuminated by the machinery of a lighting designer, audiences at outdoor amphitheaters shared the same natural light with the actors performing on stage. The stage was not contained behind a curtain, the "fourth wall" of the proscenium arch, but thrust out into spectators surrounding it on three sides. This situation, with only porous boundaries separating the audience from the actors and individual spectators from one another, squares with the many surviving reports of spectators actively engaging with each other during performances, and of actors directly addressing spectators and spectators talking back, sometimes even interrupting the action. We can't be sure how often such transgressions actually occurred during Renaissance productions, but the proliferation of reports suggests that border-crossing was an ever-present possibility for everyone performing a part at the Globe, whether on one side of the nonexistent curtain or the other.

If no one looking for reinforcement was likely to find it at *Othello* performances at the Globe, why would anyone submit to the anxiety produced by *Othello*'s abrupt dislocations, let alone seek them out? To be sure, theatrical anxiety is not as threatening as real anxiety. It's just theater; in the theater, no one really dies. But diminished anxiety is still anxiety, and it remains unclear why crowds flocked to see *Othello* at the Globe, as they evidently did.

It helps here to reflect a bit on the meaning of "anyone." According to Edwin Hutchins's *Cognition in the Wild*, "human cognition," rather than existing "somewhere 'inside' the individual," is "always situated in a complex sociocultural world" the variety of which extends beyond the "abstract properties of individual minds" (xiii, 354). From within this situation of "distributed cognition," differences might not be fended off as contaminating threats to a besieged individuality, but welcomed as the constitutive elements of an enriched way of knowing and being in the world.

Shakespeareans have been quick to appropriate distributed cognition for their own purposes (Johnson, Tribble), probably because of the effect William Empson described long before the term became available to critical analysis: "so far as an audience is an inter-conscious unit," he wrote in his essay on the double-plot, "they all work on [the performance] together" and thereby constitute a "small 'public opinion'; the mutual influence of its members' judgments, even though expressed by the most obscure means or only imagined from their presence, is so strong as to produce a sort of sensibility held in common, and from their variety it may be wider, more sensible, than of any of its members" (67). From this perspective, "it's just theater" is not so much an apologetic qualification as the assertion of value in its own right. In the protected space of theater, spectators can afford to venture forth from the compartmentalized beliefs and feelings that secure their quotidian selves to engage with the contradictory beliefs and feelings emanating from the stage and from other spectators. As a result of these engagements, the spectators, however fractured along religious, political, social, and gender lines, might find themselves emerging from the theater more of a community and less of the mere crowd they were when they went in.

The idea of community is subject to sentimentality—"the communal, the seamless, the harmonious, or the otherwise utopian," as Steven Mullaney puts it (15). In the same way, the transformative effects of theatrical experience are subject to exaggeration. Maybe spectators are all members in the body of the same audience, but their "sensibility in common" does not extend beyond an aesthetic dimension ("interconsciousness" is likely to produce a more exciting play), and it disintegrates with the end of the performance. Even the most moving performance of *Othello* would have nothing like the consequence of Saint Paul's experience of conversion on the road to Damascus. The compartmentalizers are right: Spectators must have exited the Globe with basically the same ideological and affective investments they brought in with them at the beginning. But experience, though terminated, can never be annihilated; something happened at the Globe, and it was in some measure still happening after the show was over. Perhaps Globe *Othello*s helped to produce the sense of "a collective self" (to borrow from Mullaney again)—"a matrix held together by affective and ideational and ideological bonds of all kinds," which nonetheless, since many of these bonds subsisted "in contradiction with one another," was "composed at least in part by its flaws and fractures" (14–15). Though less grand than community, a collective self, as Mullaney sees it, is nonetheless "a much-needed if not necessary means to engage unsettling ruptures in the social imaginary and fundamental structures of feeling" (173). If intimations of collective selfhood are what the play's first spectators were getting from performances of *Othello*, the experience must have felt—given the multiple polarizations of their newly globalized environment, and given the irresolvable contradictions generated by this environment—like a good thing.

Works Cited

Altman, Joel B. *The Improbability of "Othello": Rhetorical Anthropology and Shakespearean Selfhood*. Chicago: University of Chicago Press, 2010.

Andrea, Bernadette, and Linda McJannet. "Introduction: Islamic Worlds in Early Modern English Literature." In Andrea and McJannet, eds. *Early Modern England and Islamic Worlds*. Houndmills, Basingstoke, Hampshire, Eng., and New York: Palgrave Macmillan, 2011, 1–20.

Appiah, Kwame Anthony. "Race." In Frank Lentricchia and Thomas McLaughlin, eds. *Critical Terms for Literary Study*. Chicago: University of Chicago Press, 1990, 274–87.

Ashton, John, ed. *The Voiage and Travayle of Sir John Maundeville, Knight, Which Treateth of the Way Toward Hierusalem and of Marvayles of Inde with Other Islands and Countreys*. London: Pickering & Chatto, 1887.

Badiou, Alain. *Saint Paul: The Foundation of Universalism*. Trans. Ray Brassier. Stanford: Stanford University Press, 2003.

Bak, Greg. "Different Differences: Locating Moorishness in Early Modern Culture." *Dalhousie Review* 76 (1996): 197–217.

Bale, Anthony. Introduction. In Bale, ed. and trans. *Sir John Mandeville: The Book of Marvels and Travels*. Oxford: Oxford University Press, 2012, vii–xxviii.

Bartels, Emily C. *Speaking of the Moor: From "Alcazar" to "Othello."* Philadelphia: University of Pennsylvania Press, 2008.

Berger, Jr., Harry. *A Fury in the Words: Love and Embarrassment in Shakespeare's Venice*. New York: Fordham University Press, 2013.

Bethell, S. L. *Shakespeare and the Popular Dramatic Tradition*. Durham: Duke University Press, 1944.

Boose, Lynda E. "Othello's Handkerchief: 'The Recognizance and Pledge of Love.'" *English Literary Renaissance* 5 (1975): 360–74.

Bowers, Fredson, ed. *The Pleasant Comodie of Patient Grissill.* In *The Dramatic Works of Thomas Dekker.* 4 vols. Cambridge, Eng.: Cambridge University Press, 1953, 1.207–98.

Boyarin, Daniel. "Othello's Penis: Or Islam in the Closet." In Madhavi Menon, ed. *Shakesqueer.* Durham: Duke University Press, 2011, 254–62.

Bradley, A. C. "Note I: The Duration of the Action in *Othello.*" In Bradley, *Shakespearean Tragedy,* 329–35.

———. *Oxford Lectures on Poetry.* Bloomington: Indiana University Press, 1961.

———. "Poetry for Poetry's Sake." In Bradley, *Oxford Lectures,* 3–34.

———. *Shakespearean Tragedy: Lectures on "Hamlet," "Othello," "King Lear," "Macbeth."* 1904. 4th ed. Houndmills, Basingstoke, Hampshire, Eng., and New York: Palgrave Macmillan, 2007.

———. "Shakespeare's Theatre and Audience." In Bradley, *Oxford Lectures,* 361–93.

Bradshaw, Graham. *The Connell Guide to Shakespeare's "Othello."* London: Connell Guides, 2012.

Britton, Dennis Austin. "Re-'Turning' *Othello*: Transformative and Restorative Romance." *ELH* 78 (2011): 27–50.

Brown, John Russell. *Free Shakespeare.* London: Heinemann, 1974.

Brown, Robert, ed. *The History and Description of Africa and of the Notable Things Therein Contained, written by Al-Hassan Ibn-Mohammed Al-Wezaz Al-Fasi, a Moor, Baptised as Giovannie Leone, But better Known as Leo Africanus. Done into English in the year 1600, by John Pory.* London, 1600. Rpt. London: Hakluyt Society, 1896.

Brummett, Palmira. "'Turks' and 'Christians': The Iconography of Possession in the Depiction of the Ottoman-Venetian-Hapsburg Frontiers, 1550–1689." In Dimmock and Hadfield, eds. *The Religions of the Book,* 110–39.

Burton, Jonathan. *Traffic and Turning: Islam and English Drama, 1579–1624.* Newark: University of Delaware Press, 2005.

Campbell, Mary B. *The Witness and the Other World: Exotic European Travel Writing, 400–1600.* Ithaca and London: Cornell University Press, 1988.

Clark, Andrew. *Domestic Drama: A Survey of the Origins, Antecedents and Nature of the Domestic Play in England, 1500–1640.* 2 vols. Salzburg Studies in English Literature. Jacobean Drama Studies 49. Salzburg: Institut für Englische Sprache und Literatur, Universität Salzburg, 1975.

Clegg, Cyndia Susan. "English Renaissance Books on Islam and Shakespeare's *Othello*." *Pacific Coast Philology* 41 (2006): 1–12.

Cook, Ann Jennalie. "The Design of Desdemona: Doubt Raised and Resolved." *Shakespeare Studies* 13 (1980): 187–96.

D'Amico, Jack. *The Moor in English Renaissance Drama*. Tampa: University of South Florida Press, 1991.

Davis, Alex. *Chivalry and Romance in the English Renaissance*. Cambridge, Eng.: D. S. Brewer, 2003.

Davis, Natalie Zemon. "Women on Top." In *Society and Culture in Early Modern France*. Stanford: Stanford University Press, 1975, 124–51.

Decosimo, David. *Ethics as a Work of Charity: Thomas Aquinas and Pagan Virtue*. Stanford: Stanford University Press, 2014.

Dimmock, Matthew. "'A Human Head to the Neck of a Horse': Hybridity, Monstrosity and Early Christian Conceptions of Muhammad and Islam." In Dimmock and Andrew Hadfield, eds. *The Religions of the Book: Christian Perceptions, 1400–1660*. Houndmills, Basingstoke, Hampshire, Eng., and New York: Palgrave Macmillan, 2008, 66–88.

———. *Mythologies of the Prophet Muhammad in Early Modern English Culture*. Cambridge, Eng: Cambridge University Press, 2013.

———. *New Turkes: Dramatizing Islam and the Ottomans in Early Modern England*. Aldershot and Burlington, Vt.: Ashgate, 2005.

———, and Andrew Hadfield. "Introduction: The Devil Citing Scripture: Christian Perceptions of the Religions of the Book." In Dimmock and Hadfield, eds. *The Religions of the Book: Christian Perceptions, 1400–1660*. Houndmills, Basingstoke, Hampshire, Eng., and New York: Palgrave Macmillan, 2008, 1–22.

Dolan, Frances E. *Dangerous Familiars: Representations of Domestic Crime in England, 1550–1700*. Ithaca and London: Cornell University Press, 1994.

———. *Marriage and Violence: The Early Modern Legacy*. Philadelphia: University of Pennsylvania Press, 2008.

Edelman, Charles. *The Stukeley Plays: "The Battle of Alcazar" by George Peele; "The Famous History of the Life and Death of Captain Thomas Stukeley."* Manchester: Manchester University Press, 2005.

Eggert, Katherine. *Showing Like a Queen: Female Authority and Literary Experiment in Spenser, Shakespeare, and Milton*. Philadelphia: University of Pennsylvania Press, 2000.

Empson, William. "Double Plots: Heroic and Pastoral in the Main Plot and Sub-Plot." In Empson, *Some Versions of Pastoral*. 1935. Rpt. New York: New Directions, 1960, 25–84.

Everett, Barbara. "'Spanish' Othello: The Making of Shakespeare's Moor." *Shakespeare Survey* 35. Cambridge, Eng.: Cambridge University Press, 1982, 101–12.

Geneva Bible. 1560. Rpt. Madison: University of Wisconsin Press, 1969.

Gillies, John. *Shakespeare and the Geography of Difference.* Cambridge Studies in Renaissance Literature and Culture 4. Cambridge, Eng.: Cambridge University Press, 1994.

Gilroy, Paul. *Against Race: Imagining Political Culture behind the Color Line.* Cambridge, Mass.: Harvard University Press, 2000.

Girard, René. *A Theater of Envy: William Shakespeare.* New York: Oxford University Press, 1991.

Grady, Frank. *Representing Righteous Heathens in Late Medieval England.* Houndmills, Basingstoke, Hampshire, Eng., and New York: Palgrave Macmillan, 2005.

Greenblatt, Stephen. "The Improvisation of Power." In *Renaissance Self-Fashioning: From More to Shakespeare.* Chicago: University of Chicago Press, 1980, 222–54.

———. *Marvelous Possessions: The Wonder of the New World.* Chicago: University of Chicago Press, 1991.

———, General Editor. *The Norton Shakespeare.* 3rd ed. New York: Norton, 2016.

Griffin, Eric. "*Othello*'s Spanish Spirits: Or, Un-sainting James." In Griffin, *English Renaissance Drama and the Specter of Spain: Ethnopoetics and Empire.* Philadelphia: University of Pennsylvania Press, 2009, 168–206.

Gurr, Andrew. "'The stage is hung with black': Genre and the Trappings of Stagecraft in Shakespearean Tragedy." In Anthony R. Guneratne, ed. *Shakespeare and Genre: From Early Modern Inheritances to Postmodern Legacies.* Houndmills, Basingstoke, Hampshire, Eng., and New York: Palgrave Macmillan, 2011, 67–82.

Hadfield, Andrew. *Literature, Travel, and Colonial Writing in the English Renaissance, 1545–1625.* Oxford: Clarendon, 1998.

———, ed. *Amazons, Savages, and Machiavels: Travel and Colonial Writing in English, 1550–1630: An Anthology.* Oxford: Oxford University Press, 2001.

Harris, Bernard. "A Portrait of a Moor." *Shakespeare Survey 11.* Cambridge, Eng.: Cambridge University Press, 1958, 89–97.

Hayden, Judy A. "Intersections and Cross-Fertilization." In Hayden, ed. *Travel Narratives, the New Science, and Literary Discourse, 1569–1750.* Farnham and Burlington, Vt.: Ashgate, 2012, 1–24.

Helgerson, Richard. *Adulterous Alliances: Home, State, and History in Early Modern European Drama and Painting.* Chicago and London: University of Chicago Press, 2000.

Henderson, Katherine Usher, and Barbara F. McManus. *Half Humankind: Contexts and Texts of the Controversy about Women in England, 1540–1640*. Urbana and Chicago: University of Illinois Press, 1985.

Honigmann, E. A. J. Introduction. In Honigmann, ed. *Othello*. Walton-on-Thames, Eng.: Nelson, 1997, 1–111.

Hornbeck, Robert. "Emblems of Folly in the first *Othello*: Renaissance Blackface, Moor's Coat, and 'Muckender.'" *Comparative Drama* 35:1 (2001): 69–99.

———. "'Speaking Parrot' and Ovidian Echoes in *Othello*: Recontextualizing Black Speech in the Global Renaissance." In Lena Cowen Orlin, ed. *"Othello": The State of Play*. London and New York: Bloomsbury, 2014, 63–93.

Howard, Jean E. "*Othello* as an Adventure Play." In Peter Erickson and Maurice Hunt, eds. *Approaches to Teaching Shakespeare's "Othello."* New York: Modern Language Association of America, 2005, 90–99.

Hughes, Paul L., and James F. Larkin, eds. *Tudor Royal Proclamations. Vol III: The Later Tudors (1588–1603)*. New Haven and London: Yale University Press, 1969.

Hunter, G. K. "*Othello* and Colour Prejudice." In Hunter, *Dramatic Identities and Cultural Tradition: Studies in Shakespeare and His Contemporaries*. Liverpool: Liverpool University Press, 1978, 31–59.

Hutchins, Edwin. *Cognition in the Wild*. Cambridge, Mass., and London: MIT Press, 1995.

Jacobson, Miriam. *Barbarous Antiquity: Reorienting the Past in the Poetry of Early Modern England*. Philadelphia: University of Pennsylvania Press, 2014.

Johnson, Laurie. "Cogito Ergo Theatrum: Redistributing Cognition on the Early Modern Stage." In Johnson, John Sutton, and Evelyn Tribble, eds. *Embodied Cognition and Shakespeare's Theatre: The Early Modern Body-Mind*. Abingdon, Oxon, Eng., and New York: Routledge, 2014, 216–33.

———. "The Distributed Consciousness of Shakespeare's Theatre." In Paul Budra and Clifford Werier, eds. *Shakespeare and Consciousness*. Houndmills, Basingstoke, Hampshire, Eng., and New York: Palgrave Macmillan, 2016, 119–38.

Jones, Ann Rosalind, and Margaret Rosenthal, eds. and trans. *The Clothing of the Renaissance World: Europe, Asia, Africa, the Americas: Cesare Vecellio's Habiti Antichi et Moderni*. London and New York: Thames & Hudson, 2008.

Jones, Eldred. *Othello's Countrymen: The African in English Renaissance Drama*. London: Oxford University Press, 1965.

Jordan, Winthrop. *White over Black: American Attitudes Toward the Negro, 1550–1812*. Chapel Hill: University of North Carolina Press, 1968.

Kastan, David Scott. *A Will to Believe: Shakespeare and Religion*. Oxford: Oxford University Press, 2014.

Knolles, Richard. *The generall historie of the Turkes, from the first beginning of that nation to the rising of the Othoman familie: with all the notable expeditions of the Christian princes against them. Together with the liues and conquests of the Othoman kings and emperours faithfullie collected out of the best histories, both auntient and moderne, and digested into one continuat historie vntill this present yeare 1603*. London, 1603.

Lewis, Bernard. *Islam and the West*. New York: Oxford University Press, 1993.

Lupton, Julia Reinhard. *Citizen-Saints: Shakespeare and Political Theology*. Chicago: University of Chicago Press, 2005.

Martin, L. C., ed. *The Poems of Richard Crashaw*. Oxford: Clarendon, 1927.

Matar, Nabil. *Turks, Moors, and Englishmen in the Age of Discovery*. New York: Columbia University Press, 1999.

McDonald, Russ. *The Bedford Companion to Shakespeare: An Introduction with Documents*. 2nd ed. Boston: Bedford/St. Martins, 2001.

Miola, Robert S. *Shakespeare's Rome*. Cambridge, Eng.: Cambridge University Press, 1983.

Montrose, Louis Adrian. "'Shaping Fantasies': Figurations of Gender and Power in Elizabethan Culture." *Representations* 2 (1983): 61–94.

Moran, Andrew. "From Maurice to Muhammad: Othello, Islam, and Baptism." In Andrea and McJannet, *Early Modern England and Islamic Worlds*.

Mullaney, Steven. *The Reformation of Emotions in the Age of Shakespeare*. Chicago: University of Chicago Press, 2015.

Neill, Michael. "The Look of Othello." *Shakespeare Survey* 62. Cambridge, Eng.: Cambridge University Press, 2009, 104–22.

Newman, Karen. "'And Wash the Ethiop White': Femininity and the Monstrous in *Othello*." In Jean E. Howard and Marion F. O'Connor, eds. *Shakespeare Reproduced: The Text in History and Ideology*. London: Methuen, 1987, 140–62.

Palfrey, Simon, and Tiffany Stern. *Shakespeare in Parts*. New York: Oxford University Press, 2007.

Parker, Patricia. "*Othello* and *Hamlet*: Dilation, Spying, and the 'Secret Place' of Woman." *Representations* 44 (1993): 60–95.

Paster, Gail Kern. *The Body Embarrassed: Drama and the Disci-*

plines of Shame in Early Modern England. Ithaca: Cornell University Press, 1993.

———. "The Unbearable Coldness of Female Being: Women's Imperfection and the Humoral Economy." *English Literary Renaissance* 28 (1998): 416–40.

Pechter, Edward. "Disconfirmation." In Pechter, *"Othello" and Interpretive Traditions.* Iowa City: University of Iowa Press, 30–52.

Peele, George. *The Battle of Alcazar, 1594.* W. W. Greg, ed. Malone Society Reprints. London: Charles Whittingham & Co., 1907.

Pliny the Elder. *The Histories of the World: Commonly called, the Naturall Historie of C. Plinius Secundus.* Translated into English by Philemon Holland Doctor in Physicke. London, 1601.

Pliny the Elder. *Pliny's Natural History: A Selection from Philemon Holland's Translation.* J. Newsome, ed. Oxford: Clarendon Press, 1964.

Rabkin, Norman. *Shakespeare and the Common Understanding.* Chicago: University of Chicago Press, 1967.

Ridley, M. R. ed. *Othello.* London: Methuen, 1958.

Rose, Mark. "Othello's Occupation: Shakespeare and the Romance of Chivalry." *English Literary Renaissance* 15 (1985): 293–311.

Rose, Mary Beth. *The Expense of Spirit: Love and Sexuality in English Renaissance Drama.* Ithaca and London: Cornell University Press, 1988.

Rossiter, A. P. *Angel with Horns and Other Shakespeare Lectures.* Graham Storey, ed. London: Longman, 1961.

Shephard, Amanda. *Gender and Authority in Sixteenth-Century England: The Knox Debate.* Keele: Ryburn Publishing, 1994.

Smith, Lacey Baldwin. *Treason in Tudor England: Politics and Paranoia.* Princeton: Princeton University Press, 1986.

Stern, Tiffany. *Rehearsal from Shakespeare to Sheridan.* Oxford: Clarendon, 2000.

Snow, Edward. "Sexual Anxiety and the Male Order of Things in *Othello.*" *English Literary Renaissance* 10 (1980): 384–412.

Tribble, Evelyn B. *Cognition in the Globe: Attention and Memory in Shakespeare's Theatre.* Houndmills, Basingstoke, Hampshire, Eng., and New York: Palgrave Macmillan, 2011.

Vaughan, Virginia Mason. *"Othello": A Contextual History.* Cambridge, Eng.: Cambridge University Press, 1994.

Vecellio, Cesare. *De gli Habiti Antichi e Moderni di Diuerse parti del Mondo.* Venice, 1590.

———. *De gli Habiti Antichi et Moderni di tutto il Mondo.* Venice, 1598.

Vitkus, Daniel J. "Early Modern Orientalism." In David R. Blanks and Michael Frassetto, eds. *Western Views of Islam in Medieval and Early Modern Europe: Perception of the Other*. New York: St. Martin's Press, 1999, 207–30.

———. *Turning Turk: English Theater and the Multicultural Mediterranean, 1570–1630*. Houndmills, Basingstoke, Hampshire, Eng., and New York: Palgrave Macmillan, 2003.

———, ed. *Three Turk Plays from Early Modern England*. New York: Columbia University Press, 2000.

Watson, Robert N. "*Othello* as Protestant Propaganda." In Claire McEachern and Debora Shuger, eds. *Religion and Culture in Renaisssance England*. Cambridge, Eng., and New York: Cambridge University Press, 1997, 234–57.

———. "*Othello* as Reformation Tragedy." In Thomas Moisan and Douglas Bruster, eds. *In the Company of Shakespeare: Essays on English Renaissance Literature in Honor of G. Blakemore Evans*. Cranbury, N.J.: Associated University Presses, 2002, 65–96.

Wayne, Valerie. "Historical Differences: Misogyny and *Othello*." In Wayne, ed. *The Matter of Difference: Materialist Feminist Criticism of Shakespeare*. Ithaca: Cornell University Press, 1991, 153–80.

Whitney, Charles. *Early Responses to Renaissance Drama*. Cambridge, Eng.: Cambridge University Press, 2006.

Woodbridge, Linda. *Women and the English Renaissance: Literature and the Nature of Womankind, 1540–1620*. Urbana and Chicago: University of Illinois Press, 1984.

Young, Robert J. C. *Colonial Desire: Hybridity in Theory, Culture and Race*. London and New York: Routledge, 1995.

GIRALDI CINTHIO (1504–1573)

[The Moor of Venice]†

The main textual source for *Othello* is Giraldi Cinthio's *Gli Hecatommithi* ("A Hundred Tales"), from which the play's basic plot, most of the characters, and many of its details derive. Shakespeare read Cinthio in the original Italian (1565), a French translation (1584), or both. *Gli Hecatommithi* is divided into ten "decades" of interlinked narratives, the third of which concentrates on marital infidelity. The seventh story of the third decade presents a contrast to the tale of a faithless wife just ended. In Geoffrey Bullough's translation, the narrator focuses on "a faithful and loving lady" who, "through the insidious plots (*tesele*) of

† From John Edward Taylor, trans., *The Moor of Venice: Cinthio's Tale and Shakspere's Tragedy* (London: Chapman and Hall, 1855). Taylor's notes are not included. For information about this and other translations of Cinthio, and about other texts that may have influenced the composition of *Othello*, see 365–71 below.

a villainous mind, and the frailty of one who believes more than he need, is murdered by her faithful husband."[1]

In modifying and expanding Cinthio's material, the play transforms the rhythm, feeling, and meaning of the action. One example: Out of almost nothing—two disconnected sentences in which Cinthio refers to two apparently distinct women, neither of whom is named or speaks or contributes to the action, one designated as Cassio's wife, the other as a prostitute—Shakespeare creates the fascinating Bianca. Lynda Boose's influential piece on Othello's handkerchief provides another example. Cinthio's vague "embroidered in the Moorish fashion" becomes the play's specific "spotted with strawberries," a description that, in conjunction with Othello's emotionally fraught and contradictory accounts of how the handkerchief came to him, generates intensely powerful images and contradictory feelings about sexual purity and the loss of innocence.[2] Even unchanged details (wavering between poison and dagger as ways to kill Desdemona, for example) illustrate the imaginative power by which the play transforms inert inconsequence into resonant significance.

There once lived in Venice a Moor, who was very valiant, and of a handsome person; and having given proofs in war of great skill and prudence, he was highly esteemed by the Signoria of the Republic, who in rewarding deeds of valour advanced the interests of the State.

It happened that a virtuous lady, of marvellous beauty, named Disdemona, fell in love with the Moor, moved thereto by his valour; and he, vanquished by the beauty and the noble character of Disdemona, returned her love; and their affection was so mutual, that, although the parents of the lady strove all they could to induce her to take another husband, she consented to marry the Moor; and they lived in such harmony and peace in Venice, that no word ever passed between them that was not affectionate and kind.

Now it happened at this time that the Signoria of Venice made a change in the troops whom they used to maintain in Cyprus, and they appointed the Moor commander of the soldiers whom they despatched thither. Joyful as was the Moor at the honour proffered him,—such dignity being only conferred on men of noble rank and well-tried faith, and who had displayed bravery in arms,—yet his pleasure was lessened when he reflected on the length and dangers of the voyage, fearing that Disdemona would be pained at his absence. But Disdemona, who had no other happiness in the world than the Moor, and who rejoiced to witness the testimony

1. Geoffrey Bullough, *Narrative and Dramatic Sources of Shakespeare*. London and New York: Routledge and Columbia University Press, 1973, 7.242.
2. Lynda E. Boose. "Othello's Handkerchief: 'The Recognizance and Pledge of Love.'" *English Literary Renaissance* 5 (1975): 360–74. Ian Smith registers an equally stirring though entirely different set of suggestions in "Othello's Black Handkerchief." *Shakespeare Quarterly* 64 (2013): 1–25.

of his valour her husband had received from so powerful and noble a Republic, was all impatient that he should embark with his troops, and longed to accompany him to so honourable a post. And all the more it vexed her to see the Moor so troubled; and not knowing what could be the reason, one day, when they were at dinner, she said to him, "How is it, O Moor, that when so honourable a post has been conferred on you by the Signoria, you are thus melancholy?"

The Moor answered Disdemona, "My pleasure at the honour I have received is disturbed by the love I bear you; for I see that of necessity one of two things must happen; either that I take you with me, to encounter the perils of the sea, or, to save you from this danger, I must leave you here in Venice. The first could not be otherwise than serious to me, for all the toil you would have to bear, and every danger that might befall you, would cause me extreme anxiety and pain. Yet, were I to leave you behind me, I should be hateful to myself, since in parting from you I should part from my own life."

Disdemona, on hearing this, replied, "My husband, what thoughts are these that wander through your mind? Why let such things disturb you? I will accompany you whithersoe'er you go, were it to pass through fire, as now to cross the water in a safe and well-provided ship: if indeed there are toils and perils to encounter, I will share them with you. And in truth I should think you loved me little, were you to leave me here in Venice, denying me to bear you company, or could believe that I would liefer bide in safety here, than share the dangers that await you. Prepare then for the voyage, with all the readiness which the dignity of the post you hold deserves."

The Moor, in the fulness of his joy, threw his arms around his wife's neck, and with an affectionate and tender kiss exclaimed, "God keep you long in such love, dear wife!" Then speedily donning his armour, and having prepared everything for his expedition, he embarked on board the galley, with his wife and all his troops; and setting sail, they pursued their voyage, and with a perfectly tranquil sea arrived safely at Cyprus.

Now amongst the soldiery there was an Ensign, a man of handsome figure, but of the most depraved nature in the world. This man was in great favour with the Moor, who had not the slightest idea of his wickedness; for despite the malice lurking in his heart, he cloaked with proud and valorous speech, and with a specious presence, the villainy of his soul, with such art, that he was to all outward show another Hector or Achilles.[1] This man had likewise taken with him his wife to Cyprus, a young, and fair, and virtuous lady; and being of Italian birth, she was much loved by Disdemona, who spent the greater part of every day with her.

1. In Homer's *Iliad*, Hector and Achilles are the leaders of the Trojan and Greek forces during the Trojan War, noted for their military valor or skill.

In the same Company there was a certain Captain of a troop, to whom the Moor was much affectioned. And Disdemona, for this cause, knowing how much her husband valued him, showed him proofs of the greatest kindness, which was all very grateful to the Moor. Now the wicked Ensign, regardless of the faith that he had pledged his wife, no less than of the friendship, fidelity, and obligation which he owed the Moor, fell passionately in love with Disdemona, and bent all his thoughts to achieve his conquest; yet he dared not to declare his passion openly, fearing that, should the Moor perceive it, he would at once kill him. He therefore sought in various ways, and with secret guile, to betray his passion to the lady. But she, whose every wish was centred in the Moor, had no thought for this Ensign more than for any other man; and all the means he tried to gain her love, had no more effect than if he had not tried them. But the Ensign imagined that the cause of his ill success was that Disdemona loved the Captain of the troop; and he pondered how to remove him from her sight. The love which he had borne the lady now changed into the bitterest hate; and, having failed in his purposes, he devoted all his thoughts to plot the death of the Captain of the troop, and to divert the affection of the Moor from Disdemona. After revolving in his mind various schemes, all alike wicked, he at length resolved to accuse her of unfaithfulness to her husband, and to represent the Captain as her paramour. But knowing the singular love the Moor bore to Disdemona, and the friendship which he had for the Captain, he was well aware that, unless he practised an artful fraud upon the Moor, it were impossible to make him give ear to either accusation: wherefore he resolved to wait, until time and circumstance should open a path for him to engage in his foul project.

Not long afterwards, it happened that the Captain, having drawn his sword upon a soldier of the guard, and struck him, the Moor deprived him of his rank; whereat Disdemona was deeply grieved, and endeavoured again and again to reconcile her husband to the man. This the Moor told to the wicked Ensign, and how his wife importuned him so much about the Captain, that he feared he should be forced at last to receive him back to service. Upon this hint the Ensign resolved to act, and began to work his web of intrigue; "Perchance," said he, "the lady Disdemona may have good reason to look kindly on him."

"And wherefore?" said the Moor.

"Nay, I would not step 'twixt man and wife," replied the Ensign; "but let your eyes be witness to themselves."

In vain the Moor went on to question the officer,—he would proceed no further; nevertheless his words left a sharp stinging thorn in the Moor's heart, who could think of nothing else, trying to guess their meaning, and lost in melancholy. And one day, when his wife had been endeavouring to pacify his anger toward the Captain, and praying him not to be unmindful of ancient services and friendship, for one small fault, especially since peace had been made between the Captain and the soldier he had struck, the Moor was angered, and exclaimed, "Great cause have you, Disdemona, to care so anxiously about this man! Is he a brother, or your kinsman, that he should be so near your heart?"

The lady, with all gentleness and humility, replied, "Be not angered, my dear lord; I have no other cause to bid me speak, than sorrow that I see you lose so dear a friend as, by your own words, this Captain has been to you: nor has he done so grave a fault, that you should bear him so much enmity. Nay, but you Moors are of so hot a nature, that every little trifle moves you to anger and revenge."

Still more enraged at these words, the Moor replied, "I could bring proofs—by heaven it mocks belief! but for the wrongs I have endured, revenge must satisfy my wrath."

Disdemona, in astonishment and fright, seeing her husband's anger kindled against her, so contrary to his wont, said humbly and with timidness, "None save a good intent has led me thus to speak with you, my lord; but to give cause no longer for offence, I'll never speak a word more on the subject."

The Moor, observing the earnestness with which his wife again pleaded for the Captain, began to guess the meaning of the Ensign's words; and in deep melancholy he went to seek that villain, and induce him to speak more openly of what he knew. Then the Ensign, who was bent upon injuring the unhappy lady, after feigning at first great reluctance to say aught that might displease the Moor, at length pretended to yield to his entreaties, and said, "I can't deny, it pains me to the soul to be thus forced to say what needs must be more hard to hear than any other grief; but since you will it so, and that the regard I owe your honour compels me to confess the truth, I will no longer refuse to satisfy your questions and my duty. Know then, that for no other reason is your lady vext to see the Captain in disfavour, than for the pleasure that she has in his company whenever he comes to your house, and all the more since she has taken an aversion to your blackness."

These words went straight to the Moor's heart; but in order to hear more (now that he believed true all that the Ensign had told him), he replied, with a fierce glance, "By heavens, I scarce can hold this hand from plucking out that tongue of thine, so bold, which dares to speak such slander of my wife!"

"Captain," replied the Ensign, "I looked for such reward, for these my faithful offices,—none else; but since my duty, and the jealous care I bear your honour, have carried me thus far, I do repeat, so stands the truth, as you have heard it from these lips: and if the lady

Disdemona hath, with a false show of love for you, blinded your eyes to what you should have seen, this is no argument but that I speak the truth. Nay, this same Captain told it me himself, like one whose happiness is incomplete until he can declare it to another: and, but that I feared your anger, I should have given him, when he told it me, his merited reward, and slain him. But since informing you, of what concerns more you than any other man, brings me so undeserved a recompense, would I had held my peace, since silence might have spared me your displeasure."

Then the Moor, burning with indignation and anguish, said, "Make thou these eyes self-witnesses of what thou tell'st, or on thy life I'll make thee wish thou hadst been born without a tongue."

"An easy task it would have been," replied the villain, "when he was used to visit at your house; but now, that you have banished him, not for just cause, but for more frivolous pretext, it will be hard to prove the truth. Still I do not forgo the hope, to make you witness of that which you will not credit from my lips."

Thus they parted. The wretched Moor, struck to the heart as by a barbed dart, returned to his home, and awaited the day when the Ensign should disclose to him the truth which was to make him miserable to the end of his days. But the evil-minded Ensign was, on his part, not less troubled by the chastity which he knew the lady Disdemona observed inviolate; and it seemed to him impossible to discover a means of making the Moor believe what he had falsely told him; and turning the matter over in his thoughts, in various ways, the villain resolved on a new deed of guilt.

Disdemona often used to go, as I have already said, to visit the Ensign's wife, and remained with her a good part of the day. Now the Ensign observed, that she carried about with her a handkerchief, which he knew the Moor had given her, finely embroidered in the Moorish fashion, and which was precious to Disdemona, nor less so to the Moor. Then he conceived the plan, of taking this kerchief from her secretly, and thus laying the snare for her final ruin. The Ensign had a little daughter, a child three years of age, who was much loved by Disdemona; and one day, when the unhappy lady had gone to pay a visit at the house of this vile man, he took the little child up in his arms, and carried her to Disdemona, who took her, and pressed her to her bosom; whilst at the same instant this traitor, who had extreme dexterity of hand, drew the kerchief from her sash so cunningly, that she did not notice him, and overjoyed he took his leave of her.

Disdemona, ignorant of what had happened, returned home, and, busied with other thoughts, forgot the handkerchief. But a few days afterwards looking for it, and not finding it, she was in alarm, lest the Moor should ask her for it, as he oft was wont to do. Meanwhile the wicked Ensign, seizing a fit opportunity, went to the Captain of the troop, and with crafty malice left the handkerchief at the head of his bed, without his discovering the trick; until the following morning, when, on his getting out of bed, the handkerchief fell upon the floor, and he set his foot upon it. And not being able to imagine how it had come into his house, knowing that it belonged to Disdemona, he resolved to give it her; and waiting until the Moor had gone from home, he went to the back door, and knocked. It seemed as if fate conspired with the Ensign to work the death of the unhappy Disdemona. Just at that time the Moor returned home, and hearing a knocking at the back door, he went to the window, and in a rage exclaimed, "Who knocks there?" The Captain, hearing the Moor's voice, and fearing lest he should come downstairs and attack him, took to flight without answering a word. The Moor went down, and opening the door, hastened into the street, and looked about, but in vain. Then returning into the house, in great anger, he demanded of his wife who it was that had knocked at the door. Disdemona replied, as was true, that she did not know: but the Moor said, "It seemed to me the Captain."

"I know not," answered Disdemona, "whether it was he, or another person."

The Moor restrained his fury, great as it was, wishing to do nothing before consulting the Ensign, to whom he hastened instantly, and told him all that had passed, praying him to gather from the Captain all he could respecting the affair. The Ensign, overjoyed at the occurrence, promised the Moor to do as he requested; and one day he took occasion to speak with the Captain, when the Moor was so placed that he could see and hear them as they conversed. And whilst talking to him of every other subject than of Disdemona, he kept laughing all the time aloud; and feigning astonishment, he made various movements with his head and hands, as if listening to some tale of marvel. As soon as the Moor saw the Captain depart, he went up to the Ensign, to hear what he had said to him. And the Ensign, after long entreaty, at length said, "He has hidden from me nothing, and has told me that he has been used to visit your wife whenever you went from home, and that on the last occasion she gave him this handkerchief, which you presented to her when you married her."

The Moor thanked the Ensign, and it seemed now clear to him that, should he find Disdemona not to have the handkerchief, it was all true that the Ensign had told to him. One day, therefore, after dinner, in conversation with his wife on various subjects, he asked her for the kerchief. The unhappy lady, who had been in great fear of this, grew red as fire at this demand; and to hide the scarlet of her cheeks, which was closely noted by the Moor, she ran to a chest, and pretended to seek the handkerchief: and after hunting for it a long time, she said, "I know not how it is—I cannot find it—can you perchance have taken it?"

"If I had taken it," said the Moor, "why should I ask it of you? but you will look better another time."

On leaving the room, the Moor fell to meditating how he should put his wife to death, and likewise the Captain of the troop, so that their death should not be laid to his charge. And as he ruminated over this day and night, he could not prevent his wife's observing that he was not the same toward her as he had been wont; and she said to him again and again, "What is the matter? what troubles you? how comes it that you, who were the most light-hearted man in the world, are now so melancholy?"

The Moor feigned various reasons in reply to his wife's questioning, but she was not satisfied; and, although conscious that she had given the Moor no cause, by act or deed, to be so troubled, yet she feared that he might have grown wearied of her; and she would say to the Ensign's wife, "I know not what to say of the Moor; he used to be all love toward me; but within these few days he has become another man; and much I fear, that I shall prove a warning to young girls not to marry against the wishes of their parents, and that the Italian ladies may learn from me not to wed a man whom nature and habitude of life estrange from us. But as I know the Moor is on such terms of friendship with your husband, and communicates to him all his affairs, I pray you, if you have heard from him aught that you may tell me of, fail not to befriend me." And as she said this, she wept bitterly.

The Ensign's wife, who knew the whole truth (her husband wishing to make use of her to compass the death of Disdemona), but could never consent to such a project, dared not, from fear of her husband, disclose a single circumstance: all she said was, "Beware lest you give any cause of suspicion to your husband, and show to him by every means your fidelity and love."

"Indeed I do so," replied Disdemona; "but it is all of no avail."

Meanwhile the Moor sought in every way to convince himself of what he fain would have found untrue; and he prayed the Ensign to contrive that he might see the handkerchief in the possession of the Captain. This was a difficult matter to the wicked Ensign, nevertheless he promised to use every means to satisfy the Moor of the truth of what he said.

Now the Captain had a wife at home, who worked the most marvellous embroidery upon lawn; and seeing the handkerchief, which belonged to the Moor's wife, she resolved, before it was returned to her, to work one like it. As she was engaged in this task, the Ensign observed her standing at a window, where she could be seen by all passers-by in the street; and he pointed her out to the Moor, who was now perfectly convinced of his wife's guilt. Then he arranged with the Ensign to slay Disdemona, and the Captain of the troop, treating them as it seemed they both deserved. And the Moor prayed the Ensign that he would kill the Captain, promising eternal gratitude to him. But the Ensign at first refused to undertake so dangerous a task, the Captain being a man of equal skill and courage; until at length, after much entreating, and being richly paid, the Moor prevailed on him to promise to attempt the deed.

Having formed this resolution, the Ensign, going out one dark night, sword in hand, met the Captain, on his way to visit a courtesan, and struck him a blow on his right thigh, which cut off his leg, and felled him to the earth. Then the Ensign was on the point of putting an end to his life, when the Captain, who was a courageous man, and used to the sight of blood and death, drew his sword, and, wounded as he was, kept on his defence, exclaiming with a loud voice, "I'm murdered!" Thereupon the Ensign, hearing the people come running up, with some of the soldiers who were lodged thereabouts, took to his heels, to escape being caught; then turning about again, he joined the crowd, pretending to have been attracted by the noise. And when he saw the Captain's leg cut off, he judged that, if not already dead, the blow must at all events end his life; and whilst in his heart he was rejoiced at this, he yet feigned to compassionate the Captain as he had been his brother.

The next morning the tidings of this affair spread through the whole city, and reached the ears of Disdemona; whereat she, who was kind-hearted and little dreamed that any ill would betide her, evinced the greatest grief at the calamity. This served but to confirm the Moor's suspicions, and he went to seek for the Ensign, and said to him, "Do you know, that ass my wife is in such grief at the Captain's accident, that she is well-nigh gone mad."

"And what could you expect, seeing he is her very soul?" replied the Ensign.

"Ay, soul forsooth!" exclaimed the Moor; "I'll draw the soul from out her body: call me no man, if that I fail to shut the world upon this wretch."

Then they consulted of one means and another—poison and daggers—to kill poor Disdemona, but could resolve on nothing. At length the Ensign said, "A plan comes to my mind, which will give you satisfaction, and raise cause for no suspicion,—it is this: the house in which you live is very old, and the ceiling of your chamber has many cracks; I propose we take a stocking, filled with sand, and beat Disdemona with it till she dies; thus will her body bear no signs of violence. When she is dead, we can pull down a portion of the ceiling, and thus make it seem as if a rafter falling on her head had killed the lady. Suspicion can not rest on you, since all men will impute her death to accident."

This cruel counsel pleased the Moor, and he only waited for a fitting time to execute the plot. One night, when he and Disdemona had retired to bed, the Ensign, whom the Moor had concealed in a closet which opened into the chamber, raised a noise in the closet, according to a concerted plan; whereat the Moor said to his wife, "Did you not hear that noise?"

"Indeed I heard it," she replied.

"Rise," said the Moor, "and see what 'tis."

The unhappy Disdemona rose from bed, and the instant she approached the closet, out rushed the Ensign, and being strong and of stout nerve, he beat her cruelly with the bag of sand across her back; upon which Disdemona fell to the ground, scarce able to draw her breath: but with the little voice she had left, she called upon the Moor for aid. But the Moor, leaping from bed, exclaimed, "Thou wickedest of women, thus has thy falseness found its just reward,— the recompense to wives, who counterfeiting love, place horns upon their husbands' brows."

The wretched lady, hearing these words, and feeling that she was near her end (for the Ensign had given her another blow), appealed to the justice of Heaven, since justice here had failed her, in proof of her fidelity and truth; and as she was thus calling Heaven to witness, the wicked Ensign inflicted a third blow, under which she sank lifeless on the floor.

Then the Ensign and the Moor, laying Disdemona on the bed, and wounding her head, pulled down part of the ceiling of the chamber, as they had arranged; whereupon the Moor began to call aloud for help, exclaiming that the house was falling. Hearing this uproar, the neighbours all came running up, and there found Disdemona lying dead beneath a rafter,—a sight which, from the good life of that poor lady, did fill all hearts with sorrow.

On the following day Disdemona was buried, followed to the grave by the universal grief of the people. But Heaven, the just regarder of all hearts, willed not that so wicked a deed should go unpunished. Ere long the Moor, whom Disdemona had loved more than her own life, began to feel such sorrow at her loss, that he went wandering about, as one bereft of reason, searching in every part of the house. And reflecting in his thoughts that the Ensign had been the cause that he had lost, with Disdemona, all joy in life, he conceived so deep a hatred to that wicked man, he could not bear to set eyes on him; and had it not been for his fear of the inviolable justice of the Signoria of Venice, he would have slain him openly. But being unable to do this with safety, he deprived him of his rank, and would not allow him to remain in his Company; whereat such an enmity arose between the two, that no greater or more deadly can be imagined.

The Ensign, that wickedest of all bad men, now turned his thoughts to injuring the Moor; and seeking out the Captain, whose wound was by this time healed, and who went about with a wooden leg, in place of the one that had been cut off, he said to him, " 'Tis time you should be avenged for your lost limb; and if you will come with me to Venice, I'll tell you who the malefactor is, whom I dare not mention to you here, for many reasons, and I will bring you proofs."

The Captain of the troop, whose anger returned fiercely, but without knowing why, thanked the Ensign, and went with him to Venice. On arriving there, the Ensign told him that it was the Moor who had cut off his leg, on account of the suspicion he had formed of Disdemona's conduct with him; and for that reason he had slain her, and then spread the report that the ceiling had fallen and killed her. Upon hearing which, the Captain accused the Moor to the Signoria, both of having cut off his leg and killed his wife, and called the Ensign to witness the truth of what he said. The Ensign declared both charges to be true, for that the Moor had disclosed to him the whole plot, and had tried to persuade him to perpetrate both crimes; and that having afterwards killed his wife, out of jealousy he had conceived, he had narrated to him the manner in which he had perpetrated her death.

The Signori of Venice, when they heard of the cruelty inflicted by a barbarian upon a lady of their city, commanded that the Moor's arms should be pinioned in Cyprus, and he be brought to Venice, where with many tortures they sought to draw from him the truth. But the Moor, bearing with unyielding courage all the torment, denied the whole charge so resolutely, that no confession could be drawn from him. But although, by his constancy and firmness, he escaped death, he was, after being confined for several days in prison, condemned to perpetual banishment, in which he was eventually slain by the kinsfolk of Disdemona, as he merited. The Ensign returned to his own country, and following up his wonted villainy, he accused one of his companions of having sought to persuade him to kill an enemy of his, who was a man of noble rank; whereupon this person was arrested, and put to the torture; but when he denied the truth of what his accuser had declared, the Ensign himself was likewise tortured, to make him prove the truth of his accusation; and he was tortured so that his body ruptured, upon which he was removed from prison and taken home, where he died a miserable death. Thus did Heaven avenge the innocence of Disdemona, and all these events were narrated by the Ensign's wife, who was privy to the whole, after his death, as I have told them here.

THE END

CRITICISM

Othello in Theatrical and Critical History

Othello was probably first performed at the Globe Theater, on London's South Bank, around 1601–03; the first recorded production
occurred November 1, 1604, at the Banqueting House, Whitehall,
London. The play seems to have been well received, with regular
revivals up to the closing of the theaters, by Puritan ordinances, in
1642. When the theaters reopened, in 1660, *Othello* achieved a
popularity "second, perhaps, only to that of *Hamlet*, among Shakespeare's plays," and it "has never been long from the stage in later
times" (Sprague, *Shakespeare and the Actors*, 185). The result is a
long and diverse stage history, the collective work of a multitude of
talented theatrical practitioners, whose interpretive efforts have
been complemented—and regularly nourished—by a comparably
various company of smart and knowledgeable critics. The selections
beginning on page 227 below display some highlights from this
four-century embarrassment of riches. This essay sketches out the
more significant changes in theatrical and critical taste that have
punctuated *Othello*'s reception history, reflecting also on the qualities that have enabled the play to engage so many different spectators and readers over such a long time.

I. Early Days

Early response is scanty for all of Shakespeare's plays, but hindsight can disclose strong suggestions of the more fully documented
interpretive history to follow. In a diary entry of around 1637, Abraham Wright commends Othello and Iago as "two parts well penned"
(Munro, 1.411), and Leonard Digges's commemorative poem about
Shakespeare, published in 1640, cites "Honest *Iago*" and "the jealous
Moore" as examples of Shakespeare's memorable characters (quoted
in Chambers, 2.233). Wright and Digges assign equal importance to
the protagonist/hero and the antagonist/villain of the tragedy, and

this equivalence, a striking deviation from Shakespeare's normal practice, has both energized and problematized theatrical and critical production since at least the eighteenth century. For Digges, Shakespeare's characterization is most notable for its impact on spectators—"oh how the Audience, / Were ravish'd, with what wonder they went thence" (*ibid*.); and this emphasis on affective power anticipates what would become another recurring element, arguably the dominant one, in response to *Othello* through to our own day. The stage history of *Othello* is "full of stories about audiences so disturbed" that, unable to "contain themselves within the bounds of conventional response," they are driven "to assert their presence and even intervene in the dramatic action" (Pechter, "*Othello*," 11 and 4).

Digges's anticipation was itself anticipated. In the first recorded response to the play, the scholar Henry Jackson describes the overwhelming emotional effects of a performance he witnessed at Oxford in 1610:

> They also had tragedies, which they acted with propriety and fitness. In which (tragedies), not only through speaking but also through acting certain things, they moved (the audience) to tears. But truly the celebrated Desdemona, slain in our presence by her husband, although she pleaded her case very effectively throughout, yet moved (us) more after she was dead, when, lying on her bed, she entreated the pity of the spectators by her very countenance. (Quoted in Evans, 1978)

That Jackson's Desdemona upstages Othello is a sign of things to come; a comparable interest in the female lead does not materialize until much later. But it's not just the protagonist who is absent from Jackson's account. Emilia (lying on the same bed with the dead couple) and Iago and everyone else on stage have effectively disappeared as well. Overwhelmed with anguished pity, Jackson loses sight even of what actually occupies the intensified focus of his attention—not "the celebrated Desdemona . . . after she was dead" but a boy acting as if he were the dead Desdemona. The histrionic "propriety and fitness" registered in Jackson's first words have been usurped by the power of the performance; he becomes so absorbed in the theatrical fiction that he ceases to experience it *as* a fiction. The phrase "slain in our presence," as Allison Deutermann remarks, "collapses the distance between audience and actors, between bedchamber and Oxford hall" (62). Such self-abandonment is not Jackson's usual mode of response. Reflecting on Ben Jonson's *Alchemist*, performed by the King's Men as part of the same Oxford run, he is notably detached, including "himself among the 'pious and learned men' who took umbrage at the lampoon of Puritans" in the play (Sutton).

That his response to *Othello* exceeds normal limits says more about *Othello* than about him.

If Jackson's border-shattering grief sets the tone for the play's reception, it's not just audiences who are displaced. The same stage history that proliferates accounts of disturbed spectators catalogs an abundance of stories about actors for whom the "boundaries" have "gone wrong" (Maguire, 19). Two nineteenth-century examples: Junius Brutus Booth would on one occasion "have smothered Desdemona in earnest if the other actors had not rushed in from the wings and pulled him off his victim" (Shattuck, 46); Edwin Forrest played the role against the background of a divorce case in which his wife's (and his own) infidelities were fodder for tabloid trash over a period of years, prompting a contemporary to declare that "in place of interpreting Othello, he interpreted himself, enacting Forrest under a borrowed name" (quoted Rosenberg, 98). This confusion may help explain the stories of more-recent Othellos, such as Paul Robeson and Orson Welles, becoming the offstage lovers of their Desdemonas. It underlies *A Double Life*, the 1947 film in which Ronald Colman, playing a modern actor performing Othello to his wife's Desdemona, becomes obsessively jealous with murderous consequences in "real life."

With Thomas Rymer's *Short View of Tragedy* (1693), we move beyond testimony about the play's shattering impact into analysis based on systematic principles. Rymer's chapter on *Othello* submits Shakespeare's play to the neoclassical standards that dominated taste pretty much for the next century. The two quotations from Horace in the excerpt below give a sense of the effects produced by "the rules"—a mixture of prescription and advice derived most immediately from seventeenth-century French critics and going back from there through sixteenth-century Italian commentary to Horace and Aristotle in Roman and Greek antiquity. In the first quotation, Rymer cites the main idea of Horace's general introduction: Make sure the parts fit together naturally so the work will seem unified and not display any shocking discrepancy. In the second, Horace adds external to internal consistency, recommending that the poem correspond to conventional expectation and established tradition, again as a way to avoid jarring effects.

As Rymer sees it, *Othello* fails miserably to fulfill these requirements; instead of smoothly integrating its parts, the play violently conjoins contradictory material. Rymer makes his point with the oxymoron of his title, "The Tragedy of the Handkerchief." Handkerchiefs belong to the trivial world of domestic comedy, not to the noble and public dignity of tragedy. Crossing generic boundaries, *Othello* breaks down social and professional distinctions as well, shocking expectations by presenting characters against type.

Supreme military command is conferred on a "blackamoor," who indulges in detailed expressions of affection for his new bride at times when the curt discourse of the barracks seems in order. His wife prattles on about love—fair enough; but she is a senator's daughter talking about a lover beneath her station and in circumstances above it, a formal public deliberation about the threat of war. A senator is treated with a blatant disrespect for his position. For the subaltern's part, instead of the honest soldier called for by tradition, we get a diabolical villain. In Rymer's summary judgment, *Othello* is "a bloody farce without salt or savor" (236 below).

If Rymer looks like a narrow-minded pedant to us, he looked that way to his contemporaries as well. In *The Impartial Critick* (1693), John Dennis argued that Rymer's position, "instead of reforming" the stage, as it claimed, "would ruine the English Drama" (quoted in Vickers, 2.60). A year later, Charles Gildon offered the vindication of *Othello* excerpted below. The play's popularity, acknowledged grudgingly by Rymer, continued throughout the period when neo-classicism determined the critical agenda. Given the self-evident "beauties" Samuel Johnson describes in his summary assessment below—characters immediately engaging our deepest interest, an intensely thrilling plot—*Othello* proved as invulnerable to critical assault as it was (in Johnson's view) unneedful of "aid from critical illustration" (246 below). Neoclassical critics recognized the prerogative of "genius" to snatch a grace beyond the rules of art, and when Johnson's Preface to his edition of Shakespeare (1765) boldly rejects the unities of time and place, *Othello* is the example that comes naturally to mind. Addressing the more serious impropriety of Shakespeare's failure to maintain generic distinction, Johnson does not mention "The Tragedy of the Handkerchief," but he might have done. Acknowledging that "contrary to the rules of criticism" Shakespeare's plays "are not in the rigorous and critical sense either tragedies or comedies," he nonetheless insists that "there is always an appeal open from criticism to nature." The rules are just the means to an end, "to instruct by pleasing," and Shakespeare's "mingled drama" captivates our concern more deeply than the technically "regular" drama championed by people such as Rymer (Bronson, 15).

By this time, critics no longer felt obliged to engage with Rymer, and nineteenth-century commentators treated him as an amusing curiosity. If we take Rymer seriously these days, a lot of the impetus derives from the casual remarks T. S. Eliot dropped into two "tantalizing brief footnotes" (Zimansky, 260), one declaring that Rymer "makes out a very good case" against *Othello*, the other that the case has never been submitted to "a cogent refutation" ("Four Elizabethan Dramatists," 97; "*Hamlet*," 121). For Rymer's immediate successors, Eliot's claim about nonrefutation seems justified.

Eighteenth-century commentators dissented vigorously from Rymer's conclusions about *Othello*, but they were unwilling or unable to reject the standards from which these conclusions were generated.

Lewis Theobald, for example, in his 1733 edition of Shakespeare, defends Shakespeare against "Snarler and Buffoon-Criticks" such as Rymer, yet quotes 130 words from Rymer's invective and then refuses to pass judgment on it: "Whether this be from the Spirit of a *true Critic*, or from the License of a *Railer*, I may be too much preju-diced to determine." Theobald wants to distance himself from "the coarse Pleasantries of Mr. *Rymer*" (7.468), but his equivocations reveal "how close he was to being Rymer's follower" despite himself (Zimansky, 264). The Gildon excerpts reprinted below betray a simi-lar ambivalence. In his *Miscellaneous Letters* (1694), Gildon responds to Rymer's complaints about Iago's scurrility by claiming that the bit about "the clown and the valet jesting with their betters" was forced on Shakespeare by the debased taste of his audience. Gildon evi-dently accepts Rymer's principles, and only cultural nationalism (Rymer should show more respect for the "hero . . . of his own coun-try") keeps Gildon on Shakespeare's side (237 below). Given this insecure foundation, it is no surprise when, revisiting *Othello* in his *Remarks on the Plays of Shakespeare* (1710), Gildon has to concede Rymer's points—Othello's military command and the transgressive marriage are "shocking" violations of propriety after all.

Reversals and contradictions are not limited to relative light-weights such as Theobald and Gildon. Dr. Johnson thunders that "Whoever ridicules" the process of Desdemona's falling in love "shows his ignorance not only of history but of nature and manners" (243 below). But in warning against the "irregularity" and "impru-dent generosity of disproportionate marriages" (244 below) Johnson sounds a lot like Rymer and, in describing the play's moral points in the more spontaneously jocular context of conversation, even more so: "In the first place, Sir, we learn from *Othello* this very useful moral, not to make an unequal match; in the second place, we learn not to yield too readily to suspicion. . . . No, Sir, I think *Othello* has more moral than almost any play" (Chapman, 745, and cf. Rymer 227–28 below).

If Rymer's views are detectable behind Johnson's language, the figure in Rymer's own background is Iago. *Othello*'s villain is the chief irritant for Rymer, the embodiment of what is "most intolera-ble" in the play's "Characters or Manners" and the object of "by far the most famous of Rymer's accusations" against the play (Ziman-sky, xxviii.). Repeatedly Rymer complains that Iago's malignity vio-lates the norms of both literary convention (soldiers shouldn't be represented in such a way) and life (soldiers aren't really like that).

The point seems thick-headed even for Rymer, but later commentators seem unable to dispose of it once and for all. In his 1747 edition of Shakespeare, William Warburton, despite dismissing Rymer as "one continued heap of ignorance and insolence," quotes at length from Rymer's complaint that Iago doesn't square with the "*open-hearted, frank, plain-dealing-soldier*" of tradition, then reluctantly admits that the complaint is justified, managing finally to defend Shakespeare against "this impertinent criticism" only with the lame comment that at least the other soldiers in the play are in line with what we expect (8.404–05). As Zimansky remarks, such "cumbersome attempts" to rescue Shakespeare from Rymer's animadversions are a regular feature of criticism during this time (xxviii). We might say of eighteenth-century commentary what Desdemona says to Othello in his crazed jealousy: "I understand a fury in your words, / But not the words" (4.2.32–33).

What was really bothering them? Gildon, in one of his apparently shrewd responses that came to nothing, helps clarify the matter. Justifying the violence that offended Rymer in Iago's "Even now, now, very now, an old black ram / Is tupping your white ewe" (1.1.85–86), Gildon observes that the brutal image succeeds as an attempt "to transport" Brabantio "from consideration to a violent passion" (237 below). In other words, Iago's motivation overrides the decorum of rank because it is necessary to the play's design; the aesthetic trumps the social. This claim may seem plausible to us, but in Gildon's time the assumption of an aesthetic domain with its own distinct properties had nothing like the fully formed stability it has come to achieve. Eighteenth-century critics were more likely to see the social as trumping the aesthetic or to ignore the distinction altogether. In this context, Gildon has no solid position from which to transform his insight into a stable principle. Referring the question of "Characters or Manners" to "the same [René] Rapin" invoked by Rymer, he defers willy-nilly to the seventeenth-century French writer who epitomized neoclassical authority. "Manners" here signifies within *les bienséances externes* or "extrinsic proprieties" (Bray, 224–30): Characters should use speech and behavior in a way that coincides with social decorum, because social decorum determines theatrical taste. As Pierre Martino puts it, "If the subject does not conform to the spectators' feelings, it will never succeed" (72, my translation). In this environment, Rymer's complaint is justified equally by social norms and theatrical effects; just as Iago offends Brabantio so the play offends us.

And here Rymer seems right, at least in his conclusion, not just for his contemporaries, but for subsequent audiences as well. Later critics—Furness in the nineteenth century (167), Kirsch in the twentieth (11–15)—reenact Theobald's ambivalent performance, throwing up their hands in dismay at Rymer even as they cite him at length and thus disseminate his opinions. As Joel B. Altman remarks, Rymer's catalog of improbabilities and improprieties "turns out," by "setting the crucial question," to "have been the most influential" of *Othello*'s commentaries "after all" (131). Rymer's foundational influence, moreover, derives not just from setting the crucial question; he sets the tone of uncontrolled rage with which the question is asked. Commenting on the "surprising . . . *personal* acrimony" in recent *Othello* criticism," Peter Davison suggests that "the peculiar viciousness that animates some critics" may "stem from what in *Othello* subconsciously disturbs them" (10, 53). Like the play's audiences and actors, *Othello*'s critics cannot secure their experience within the conventional boundaries of detached and evenhanded analysis. Kenneth Burke's influential piece is a case in point: "Iago has done this play some service," he claims, by propelling "the plot forward step by step, for the audience's villainous entertainment and filthy purgation" (272 and 275 below). Burke's disgusted fascination is of a piece with the perplexed irritation pulsating in Rymer's assault. In complaining that *Othello* flouts "extrinsic proprieties," Rymer seems to have stumbled onto the play's intrinsic property—its power to produce an overheated mixture of anxiety, grief, affection, anger, guilty resistance, and malign aversion; and we have found ourselves compelled to deal with this diverse assortment of responses ever since.

II. The Nineteenth Century

If Iago troubled Rymer and eighteenth-century audiences, the disturbance was better contained than it was to become. Substantial cuts in eighteenth-century performance texts suggest that Iago was not generally considered compelling. Gildon's "very good" authority for a clownish Iago (236 below) reinforces Rymer's description of a mugging buffoon, performed with stereotypically villainous makeup and costume, as the norm for productions of the time. In the early nineteenth century, however, "a new Iago emerged—an Iago with a light touch, a light step, a sprightly wit, who reveled in his own ingenuity and sometimes charmed the audience into reveling with him" (Carlisle, 225).

The "new Iago" on stage was substantially created by Edmund Kean, the premier actor of the time, who inspired William Hazlitt's pieces excerpted below; but Kean's theatrical innovations found a receptive audience because they participated in a fundamental and wide-ranging shift away from the values and assumptions that had underwritten eighteenth-century response. To be sure, early nineteenth-century commentary starts from a position derived (however unconsciously) from Rymer—the sense of Iago as a jarring mixture of qualities and effects. They echo (perhaps deliberately) the phrase, "wickedness conjoined with abilities," by which Johnson identifies this mixture: Hazlitt sees "great intellectual activity, accompanied with a total want of moral principle"; Coleridge, "what is admirable . . . in the mind and what is most detestable in the heart"; and Bradley, "absolute evil united with supreme intellectual power." But these continuities do not extend to Johnson's confidence that audiences will not be charmed into any complicity with Iago's villainy. The risk of "scandal" for Coleridge and "of untruth or . . . a desperate pessimism" for Bradley is much more real now. Hazlitt claims that "the genius of Shakespeare" protected Desdemona's image against Iago's assault, but his subsequent discussion puts this claim in doubt. (For this material, see 246, 248, 256, 270, 257, 270, and 250 below.)

So what was the new taste? It helps to contrast the Romantics' developing ideas with "the rules," especially as defined in Johnson's reflections on genre. Although Johnson made room for the exceptional genius with which Shakespeare "mingled" tragic and comic effects, "the exception," he argues in the Preface to his edition of Shakespeare, "only confirms the rule." Generic separation, a principle sustained over the centuries, retained its normative force for Johnson. Even as Shakespeare violates a particular prohibition, he obeys the spirit of the law, deferring to the authority of a universal moral order, according to which "it is always a writer's duty to make the world better" (Sherbo, 85 and 71). Against the continuity of Johnson's "always," Coleridge asserts historical contingency and cultural relativism. Where the "very essence" of Greek tragedy "consists in the sternest separation of the diverse in kind and the disparate in the degree," Shakespeare "delights" rather "in interlacing by a rainbow-like transfusion of hues the one with the other." From this angle, the principle of generic separation is incommensurable with a dramatic practice that succeeds not despite but because of its "mingled" kinds. Applying the rules flexibly, as Johnson does, is not enough; we have to jettison them altogether. As Coleridge saw it, Shakespeare's "different genus" transports us into an undiscovered country where we need "a new word"—a whole new vocabulary—to tell us where we are (Foakes, 1.466–67).

Whatever the Romantics lost relinquishing the stability of moral norms, they compensated for with a more fully developed capacity for affective response. This is Coleridge's "cardinal point" about poetry in the *Biographia* (1817): Its "power of exciting the sympathy of the reader" produces "that willing suspension of disbelief for the moment, which constitutes poetic faith" (Engell and Bate, 2:5–6).

Hazlitt picks up on the idea at the beginning of his lecture "On Poetry in General" (1818), identifying the value of poetry with its effects of "exciting an involuntary movement of imagination and passion, and producing, by sympathy, a certain modulation of the voice, or sounds, expressing it" (Howe, 5:1). In "Poetry for Poetry's Sake" (1901), Bradley defines poetry as "imaginative experience," the "succession of experiences—sounds, images, thoughts, emotions—through which we pass when we are reading as poetically as we can" (4).

An intensely affective imaginative engagement in conjunction with a disengagement from moral norms—this admixture of aesthetic delight and ethical detachment underlies the new interest in Iago. It generates Keats's celebrated description "of the poetical Character itself" in his letter to Richard Woodhouse of October 27, 1818:

> it has no self—it is every thing and nothing—It has no character—it enjoys light and shade; it lives in gusto, be it foul or fair, high or low, rich or poor, mean or elevated—It has as much delight in conceiving an Iago or an Imogen [the heroine in Shakespeare's *Cymbeline*]. What shocks the virtuous philosopher, delights the camelion Poet. (Grant Scott, 195).

In Hazlitt's description, Kean's performance of Iago works on audiences when "the interest it excites, the sharper edge which it sets on their curiosity and imagination," resonates with "a natural tendency in the mind to strong excitement, a desire to have its faculties roused and stimulated to the utmost" (248–49 below). Coleridge's Iago exemplifies the same intensity: "Let the Reader *feel*" the "disappointed Passion & Envy" in Iago's mind, because the effect, like "music on an inattentive auditor, *swelling* the thoughts which prevented him from listening to it," allows entry into an area of sensibility that ethical standards render off-limits (Foakes, 2.313–14). As Bradley puts it, writing at the end of the Romantic line, Iago's "evil" nature may be more than we "can bear to contemplate," but "if we really imagine him, we feel admiration and some kind of sympathy" (270 below).

Such responsiveness was not limited to the malignity of Iago. According to Coleridge, we should "feel Cassio's religious love of Desdemona's purity" (260 below), and above all "we must perseveringly place ourselves in [Othello's] situation and under his circumstances" so that "we shall immediately feel the fundamental difference between the solemn agony of the noble Moor and the wretched fishing jealousies of Leontes [in Shakespeare's *The Winter's Tale*]" (258 below). Coleridge never tired of emphasizing the point (that there is "No jealousy, properly speaking in Othello," he acknowledged in conversation, is something "I have often told you" [Woodring, 1:74]); and the idea became an obligatory premise in nineteenth-century American and Russian commentary no less than the British (Hudson, "Introduction," 397; Dostoyevsky, 2:447). It survived as late as Bradley, who disparages "the ridiculous notion that Othello was jealous by temperament" like Leontes (264 below) and insists that "*any* man situated as Othello was would have been disturbed by Iago's communications" (266 below)—and even later (though one has to go outside of professional literary study to find it), in the twentieth-century philosopher Stanley Cavell's remark that "if such a man as Othello" succumbs as he does, "then no human being is free of this possibility" (296 below). These assertions seek to guarantee that the new Iago does not displace affectionate admiration for the protagonist, but at times their reiterated insistence verges on protesting too much. The terms with which Bradley registers feelings of jealousy and sexual anxiety indicate what is at stake in his denial: "ignoble . . . despicable . . . shrinking . . . ashamed . . . turn our eyes away . . . repulsive . . . repulsion . . . repulsiveness" (261–68 below). Admit this range of feeling and the "romantic figure" who "stirs . . . in most readers a passion of mingled love and pity which they feel for no other hero in Shakespeare" (265–66 below) might seem an unsustainable illusion.

Race generates similar feelings of aversion and motivates similarly reiterated denials of Othello's blackness. For Charles Lamb, writing in 1811, "the courtship and wedded caresses" between "a young Venetian lady of the highest extraction" and "a *coal-black Moor*" would be "extremely revolting" (247 below), especially in the theater. Lamb's point was not original. Gildon, in 1710, registers "shock" at the prospect of "admitting a Negro to a commerce" with "a woman of virtue" (241 below), and William Kenrick, in 1774, argues that Othello was "at worst only of a *tawny* colour," because a "Lady of Desdemona's delicacy of sentiment could never have fallen in love with a Negro" (Vickers, 6.116). But Lamb reached a large and influential audience, and his remark—coinciding with Kean's switch from the conventional blackface to a tawny makeup and with the claim attributed to Coleridge that a Moorish Othello avoided the "monstrous" prospect of "this beautiful Venetian girl falling in love with a veritable negro" (258 below)—helped such anxieties achieve a critical mass.

As with jealousy, denials of Othello's blackness became a standard feature of nineteenth-century commentary, notably in the United States. Henry Hudson parades Coleridge's "veritable negro" paragraph (399–400) to support the idea that Shakespeare's Othello is not "a full-blooded Negro" (*Shakespeare*, 2.448). In a notorious instance, Mary Preston, writing in Maryland four years after the end of the Civil War, acknowledges that "I have always *imagined* [Othello] as a white man" and then simply changes the facts to correspond with her desire. "Othello," she peremptorily declares, "*was* a *white* man!" (quoted in Furness, 395). Once again, the topic achieves summary discussion in Bradley, who, though trying to distance himself from Coleridge and from the "very amusing . . . horror" of "most American critics," winds up pretty much on their side of the issue, admitting that "the aversion of our blood" makes a black Othello an intolerable prospect (268 and 269, n. 4 below).

Nineteenth-century discussions of Othello's color oscillate uneasily between contradictory sentiments. Lamb expresses overtly racist feelings, declaring Moors "to be by many shades less unworthy of a white woman" than are blacks, but also claims that Desdemona's love for Othello registers on "the nobler parts of our nature" as "the perfect triumph of virtue over accidents" (247 below). Bradley acknowledges his share in a collective racism ("aversion of *our* blood") on the one hand and on the other dismisses racism as "filthy-minded cynic[ism]" (268 below). Coleridge wavers as well. The remark attributed to him about "monstrous" miscegenation is hedged about with the qualifying phrase "as we are constituted" (257 below), and complicated by other texts, such as the poem "Fears in Solitude," which expresses horror at the racist environment in which he finds himself guiltily immersed.

These slippages make it hard to determine actual conviction, but nineteenth-century commentators were motivated as much by rhetorical or aesthetic considerations as by their racial beliefs. They sought to encourage the richest possible responses to Shakespeare, which they identified in the engagements of readers with texts rather than of spectators with performances. Lamb's piece excerpted below, the foundational statement of Romantic antitheatricalism, takes *Othello* as a prime example of the "Fitness"—or unfitness—of Shakespearean tragedy "for Stage Representation." Desdemona's generous imagination "sees Othello's color in his mind," but "the imagination is no longer the ruling faculty" for theatrical audiences, who see rather with their "bodily eye" and thus tend to "sink Othello's mind in his color" (247 below). Bradley, asking whether Othello "should be represented as a black in our theatres now," reaches the same conclusion: "I dare say not. We do not like the real Shakespeare" (269, n. 4 below). Bradley's "real Shakespeare" is more like an ideal Shakespeare: not a psychological or historical person whose opinions (about black Africans or tawny Moors or anything else) we are supposed to infer, but an interpretive assumption. Like Coleridge's "poet for all ages" (257 below), the "real Shakespeare" figures forth an idea of creative agency capable of producing effects such as those Hazlitt attributes to *Othello*: "it substitutes imaginary sympathy for

Figure 8. Act 1, Scene 3: "Here's my husband." Engraving by Richard Cook (1784–1857), published 1821. Used by permission of the Folger Shakespeare Library. Shelfmark ART File S528ol no. 13.

Figure 10. Act 1, Scene 3: Othello relating his adventures. Engraving by Charles West Cope, R.A. (1811–1890), nineteenth century. Used by permission of the Folger Shakespeare Library. Shelf mark ART File S528ol no. 11.

Figure 9. Act 2, Scene 1: Othello and Desdemona. Mezzotint by Henry Liverseege (1803–1832), early- to mid-nineteenth century. Used by permission of the Folger Shakespeare Library. Shelfmark ART File S528ol no. 14.

Figure 11. Act 3, Scene 4: "Fetch me that handkerchief." Engraving by Joseph Kenny Meadows (1790–1874), published 1845. Used by permission of the Folger Shakespeare Library. Shelfmark ART File S528ol no. 29 copy 1.

mere selfishness. It gives us a high and permanent interest, beyond ourselves, in humanity as such" (252 below). That nineteenth-century audiences were unable to muster such a response to a black Othello on the stage may strike us as deplorable, and it may have struck Lamb and the others as deplorable as well. But given the practical realities as constituted by the beliefs of the time, a black Othello on the stage simply would not do.

What, then, would do? Figures 8–11, dating from 1821 to the middle of the century, give some sense of what the "real Shakespearean" Othello might look like. Though keyed to particular scenes, they do not depict actual performances; setting the action in stylized landscapes (even the palazzo- and Campanile-like structures visible through the windows in Figures 9–11 add to this effect), they represent Othello not as he appeared to the "bodily eye" of John Philip Kemble's or Edmund Kean's or William Macready's spectators, but to a reader's imagination or mind's eye. The images are diverse—in costume (Elizabethan armor, Moorish and Asian finery), physical posture, skin color and other racial markers (more or less woolly hair and thick lips). But even as they "glamorize Othello's cultural background" (Lois Potter, 187), they reduce the character to a pretty object. In this respect, they differ notably from the "Portrait of a Moor" (Figure 7, 148 above), whose exotic attire signifies alterity without idealizing the subject. On the contrary, 'Abd al-Wahid's name, age (42) and title (ambassador to the English court from the king of Barbary), all specified by the painter, combine with the meet-your-eyes gaze to give the figure an immediate material presence—if not necessarily as "a thing . . . to fear" (to recall Brabantio's words in (1.2.71), at least a person to respect.

Of the nineteenth-century representations shown here, only Figure 11 approximates any threatening effect, but this Othello, though sternly censorious, is hardly enraged; the upraised finger of his upraised hand signals only that he is making a point. Desdemona, leaning adoringly into her husband, and Emilia, serenely observing in the background, diminish any premonition of the slap a few scenes later, let alone the murder at the end. Historical circumstances help explain the reduced menace of these nineteenth-century representations. By this time, militant Islam had dwindled to inconsequence, and institutionalized slavery in British colonial dependencies, though abolished in 1834, had turned black Africans into chattel. The exoticizing of the nineteenth-century images may be understood as an attempt at aesthetic idealization—a way to preserve some of the admiration appropriate to the protagonist of heroic tragedy as Hazlitt describes it.

According to James Siemon's analysis reprinted below, nineteenth-century theater companies staged the last scene of

Othello to produce similarly idealizing effects. After strangling Desdemona, Othello looks for cosmic reverberations—"a huge eclipse
/ Of sun and moon," earthquakes in "th'affrighted globe" (5.2.101–
02)—to confirm his role as an impersonal agent of transcendent
justice. Nothing comes in the play text, but nineteenth-century
productions incorporated peals of thunder and flashes of lightning:
The spectators seem to have wanted such "sublime effects" as much
as the protagonist. "A titanic, Byronic Othello sundering the universal order was perhaps more acceptable as a subject of high tragedy
than the strangler of a defenseless wife" (303 below). Even as some
stage effects were added to enhance Othello's nobility, others were
eliminated that might diminish it. Desdemona's spirited resistance
makes Othello "call what I intend to do / A murder, which I thought
a sacrifice" (5.2.65–66), but nineteenth-century Desdemonas enact
a compliant passivity. The image "of 'prone womanhood' has a special attraction for the nineteenth century," Siemon remarks (305
below); the heroine's acquiescence reduces the intensity and duration of the violence. To the same end, productions typically hid the
murder behind curtains, and they equipped Othello with a "'stifling pillow'" (307 below) to avoid any suggestion that he uses his
bare hands on Desdemona's flesh. Given the intensity with which
Othello registers the smell and feel of Desdemona's flesh ("I'll smell
thee on the tree. / O balmy breath . . . One more; one more . . . One
more," 5.2.15–19), the pillow seems evasive. But given the morbidity
with which Othello invests his desire ("Be thus when thou art dead,
and I will kill thee / And love thee after," 5.2.18–19), the desire
not to see what is happening on stage may be a part of any full
engagement.

Evasion was not totally successful in the nineteenth-century theater, but it wasn't meant to be. Concealment is a felt need only if
there is some interest in what has to be concealed. As Siemon puts
it, nineteenth-century practice reflects the ambivalence of "a culture trying to control a text that it desires to experience in the
theater but that it also strongly disapproves" (299 below). Some
productions played more to the desire than to the disapproval,
moving away from suppression or idealization in favor of revelation.
The black American actor Ira Aldridge "used to take Desdemona
out of the bed by her hair and drag her around the stage before
he smothered her" (quoted Siemon, 303 below). Later in his
career, when Aldridge moved his performances to German and
East European stages, audiences "were thrilled" (or, in a minority
of cases, put off) by his "extreme emotionalism," the "rage" and
"unbridled irrationalism" of his "'loud howls and wild cries,'" which,
in conjunction with his "'African gestures,'" made for a "'wilder,

more untamable'" performance "'than that of a European'" (Lind-fors, *Performing Shakespeare*, 224 and 228). As a black actor, Aldridge was a special case, but his violence was not unique. "A few mavericks—notably Italians like [Tommaso] Salvini and [Ernesto] Rossi—use[d] bare hands" and played for similarly savage effects (307 below). Nineteenth-century audiences may have found Othel-lo's murderous jealousy easier to take when it was enacted in a for-eign language (as Salvini and Rossi did in England and the United States), or by an "indelibly African" actor, as Lindfors characterizes Aldridge (*Performing Shakespeare*, 229). If the spectators wanted an English gentleman, Sir Henry Irving could take care of business. Aldridge and the Italians accommodated a different clientele—or a different need in the same conflicted clientele; and in Aldridge's case, the accommodation appears to be part of a consciously self-promoting strategy. Though he was born in New York, he is identi-fied in the playbill reproduced in Figure 12 as "a native of Senegal." Aldridge regularly disseminated the fiction of his origins; the *Memoir* he authorized and likely authored claims that his Senegalese "fore-fathers were princes of the Fulah tribe." An even more "flagrant enhancement of his résumé," Bernth Lindfors declares (*Early Years*, 242), but perhaps Aldridge came half to believe the story—another instance of an Othello actor who has crossed the boundary between the performance and the role performed. In any case, as Herbert Marshall and Mildred Stock remark, recalling Othello's "fetch my life and being / From men of royal siege"(1.2.21–22), "the parallel" was "evidently too good to be missed by an actor with imagination" (15, 17).

Aldridge, who left New York in 1807 for England in the 1820s and achieved considerable distinction in eastern Europe and Rus-sia, has, thanks to the pioneering work of Marshall and Stock, Errol Hill (17–27), and Lindfors, emerged into prominence for theater historians. And for theatrical practitioners: Two current plays have put him on center stage. Cecilia Sidenbladh's *Black Othello* (2008, not currently in print) focuses on Aldridge's love affair in the 1850s with actress Amanda von Brandt, whom he married after the death of his first wife. In *Red Velvet*, a success on the London stage, where it was first produced in 2012, and in subsequent reviv-als on both sides of the Atlantic, Lolita Chakrabarti focuses on Aldridge's brief tenure replacing Kean as Othello at Covent Garden in 1833.

The action in *Red Velvet* hinges on Pierre Laporte, the stage manager who brings Aldridge to Covent Garden but then cancels the run on its third night. While the scurrilously racist reviews con-tribute to Laporte's decision, the main issue is the violent intensity

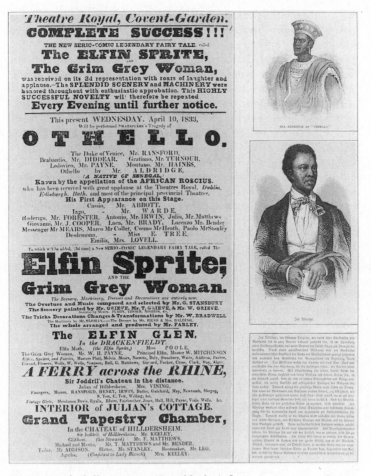

Figure 12. Playbill promoting Ira Aldridge's first appearance at Covent Garden as Othello (1833). Used by permission of the Folger Shakespeare Library. Shelfmark ART File A365.5 no. 5.

of Aldridge's performance. "I told you to play it . . . gently," he tells Aldridge; the spectators "need time to adjust," but "you played harder and fiercer than I have ever seen you" (86). *Red Velvet* contrasts Aldridge's expressive passion to "the 'teapot' school of acting" associated with John Philip Kemble (40), in which the actor assumes a statuesque pose, one hand on the hip, the other outstretched like the spout of a teapot and (as Lamb described it at the time) "play[s] the orator," adopting "theatrical airs and gestures" and speaking lines as though "*spouted* by declamatory boys" (97–100). *Red Velvet* gives us a comic example in the rendition of some lines in rehearsal by Charles Kean, Edmund's son. "Is that how you're going to do it?" an incredulous Aldridge asks (44), and "*a connection*" is "*made*" with Ellen Tree, Aldridge's Desdemona, who has also seen "Mr. Kemble perform" in the "teapot" mode, and who "need say no more" (40).

Although irrelevant to *Red Velvet*'s dramatic impact, the actual theatrical situation is more complicated than the one represented in the play. By 1833, Edmund Kean had already rendered the "tea-pot" style old-fashioned. Despite *Red Velvet*'s account, Aldridge's acting style, in the consensus of the time, was "essentially melo-dramatic" (Lindfors, *Early Years*, 265). To judge from the poses in Figures 13 and 14 (the first based on a sketch attributed to William Makepeace Thackeray of Aldridge's Covent Garden Othello witnessed the night before [see Lindfors, *Vagabond Years*, 7–13], the second on a photograph of an unidentified performance of Othello), Aldridge could play within "the 'teapot' school" of acting as well as against it.

Not only did Aldridge play Othello differently; he played a variety of different roles. His "composite image" included the "pathetic ignorance of Mungo" (Lois Potter, 117–18), the uppity slave in Isaac Bickerstaff's comically song-filled melodrama *The Padlock* (1768). Aldridge's Mungo seems intolerably racist now, as does the depiction of the "cunning nigger" who outsmarts the possum and the raccoon in "Opossum Up a Gum Tree," the song Aldridge regularly per-formed, accompanying himself on guitar or banjo after acting Othello or other more dignified parts. Yet Aldridge added both of these to Othello as his signature roles, and the *Memoir* highlights his ability to move between such radically different histrionic tonal-ities as a matter of professional pride. "The ecstasy of his long, shrill note in 'Opossum Up a Gum Tree' can only be equalled by the agony of his cry of despair over the body of Desdemona" (quoted Marshall and Stock, 44).

Aldridge's extraordinary range and flexibility could ravish audi-ences. According to a mid-century German reviewer, "everyone was astonished to see this wildness [of Mungo] next to the lofty earnestness in *Othello*" (quoted Lindfors, *Performing Shakespeare*, 204). It's not easy to see how the spectators negotiated Aldridge's abrupt transformations, but compartmentalization, keeping con-tradictory effects separate from one another, seems like a reason-able hypothesis, not least because it coincides with the institutional arrangements of the time. Prior to the Theatres Act of 1843, only Drury Lane and Covent Garden had patents to present serious

Mr ALDRIDGE
of the Theatre Royal Covent Garden,
[commonly known as the African Roscius,]
in the character of
OTHELLO.

"O blood! Iago, blood!"

Figure 13. Ira Aldridge as Othello, preserved in R. Percival's scrapbook of the Sadler's Wells Theatre. Shelfmark Crach. 1.Tab.4.b.4/5(86). © The British Library Board. Courtesy of the British Library.

"spoken drama." If other theaters wanted to do Shakespeare or other items from the elite repertoire, they had to include song-and-dance numbers—in effect reducing the performance into a kind of burlesque. In the early 1830s, when Maurice Dowling's *Othello Travestie, An Operatic Burlesque Burletta* opened in London, it

Figure 14. Ira Aldridge as Othello in a lithograph by S. Bühler, 1854. Used by permission of the Folger Library. Shelfmark ART File A365.5 no.4.

initiated a vogue for American minstrel shows, which typically "translated Othello's proud, florid gesturing, his stagy exoticism, into more comic antics[,] parodying the more typically remote and noble Othello" (Gross, 102 and 103; and see MacDonald). With the proliferation of such antics, the London theater scene was divided into two parts. In one, tragic actors, playing at Covent Garden or Drury Lane, delivered elevated renditions of Shakespeare and other classics, while in the second, minstrel performers transported spectators into a realm of coarse comedy that might seem inaccessibly remote from the experience available on "legitimate" stages down the street.

According to Richard Schoch, there was actually a good deal of crossover between the different theatrical venues. Spectators negotiated the space between the "real Shakespeare" and (as Schoch designates the burlesques) the "not Shakespeare." The law separating theatrical sites was not always rigorously enforced. As the playbill in Figure 12 suggests, tragic nobility and coarse comedy could coexist in the sequence of a single performance. Perhaps an analogy exists with the Renaissance public theater, where the actors performed a "jig," or brief dance, at the end of their tragic performances. But by the nineteenth century, a systematic distinction between the categories of "highbrow" and "lowbrow" (as we now call them) had been written into the prevailing discourse and established institutions of the culture (see Levine), and the tonal or conceptual boundaries must have been more carefully guarded on the Victorian stage.

They were guarded in commentary as well. The new Iago failed to displace the old Othello in nineteenth-century affections because the character's infectious scurrility was quarantined—confined, like the minstrel burlesque with which it has clear affinities, to its proper (or improper) place. When Iago's "dire yell" (1.1.72) thrusts bestial lust and miscegenation onto the stage—"Even now, now, very now, an old black ram / Is tupping your white ewe" (1.1.85–86)—Coleridge and his followers, like Roderigo at the beginning of the play, will "not hear" him (1.1.4). Nor will they acknowledge Desdemona's strongly sexual nature. Coleridge's emphatic denial of the "monstrous" idea that Desdemona might be attracted to a "veritable negro" (258 below) is clarified by his assurance elsewhere that the "sweet yet dignified" Desdemona is "characterless" (259 below); and this comment initiates a long nineteenth-century line of self-abnegating and domestically enclosed Desdemonas, whose self-assertive sexuality is, when acknowledged at all, scrupulously confined to a subordinate position. "Bating the commencement of her passion," according to Hazlitt, "her whole character consists in having no will of her own, no prompter but her obedience" (255 below). Despite a "transient energy arising from the power of affection," Anna B. Jameson tells us, the "prevailing tone to the character" of Desdemona is "gentleness verging on passiveness—gentleness, which not only cannot resent—but cannot resist" (175). Bradley's Desdemona begins with "the active assertion of her own soul and will" but becomes "helplessly passive," unable to "retaliate even in speech; no, not even in silent and feeling"; and it is this "later impression"—"the 'eternal womanly' in its most lovely and adorable form, simple and innocent as a child"—that "must be carried back and united with the earlier before we can see what Shakespeare imagined" (268–69 below).

For Bradley, just as the nobility of the Moor requires us to "turn our eyes away" from the visible signs of his jealousy (262 below), so an authentically tragic response ("reconciliation" is Bradley's term— see *Shakespearean Tragedy*, 25–26) requires us to ignore the material signifiers on stage (the rolling of Othello's eyes, the gnawing of his lip, the "bloody passion" that "shakes [his] very frame," 5.2.38–44) in favor of the spiritual realities they are said to signify: "if we fully imagine the inward tragedy in the souls of the persons as we read, the more obvious and almost physical sensations of pain or horror do not appear in their own likeness, and only serve to intensify the tragic feelings in which they are absorbed" (264 below).

The idealizing tendency of nineteenth-century response has not aged well, most notably in the case of Desdemona, where it has been dismissed as an example of Victorian gender ideology—as in the English poet Coventry Patmore's celebration of "the angel in the house." What Bradley and his predecessors celebrate as prostrate speechlessness we now repudiate as a "most disturbing" and "peculiar passivity"; the "terrible silence" when Desdemona's unwillingness "to resist" Othello's attack at the end "or even to cry out for help" is "hardest to bear" (Adamson, 200 and 257). According to Ania Loomba, "Desdemona's silence in the face of her husband's brutality" constitutes "a betrayal" of her self-assertiveness earlier in the play (39). The reversal of judgment is striking, but even more so is the continuity of the descriptions on which the judgments are exercised. Whether venerating or deploring, response "has been remarkably consistent for two centuries in representing Desdemona as silent, submissive and in a sense even complicit in her own murder" (Pechter, "Too Much Violence," 232). Between "characterless" and "no will of her own" in Coleridge and Hazlitt and "no character of her own" in Alan Sinfield's uncanny (and presumably unconscious) echo of both (54), the values have been reversed but the supposed facts are constant.

No less than Bradley and his predecessors, many modern commentators have turned blind eyes and deaf ears to Desdemona's active resistance and self-assertiveness. In the monologue *Desdemona—if only you had spoken!*, Christine Brückner's protagonist berates herself for a supposed recessiveness ("I was never taught how to speak of my feelings . . . A woman should keep herself in check and be reticent. How silly that is! And how deadly the consequences!"—117), as if the avowal of Desdemona's desire for Othello "trumpeted" to the senate in 1.3 had never occurred. In *Othello*, according to Peter

Sellars—commenting on *Desdemona*, his 2011 collaboration with Toni Morrison and Rokia Traoré—"Desdemona barely says anything all across the whole night." When Bradley and the others will not hear Desdemona's resistance, they are at least consistent with their commitments to sacrifice, transcendence, and "reconciliation." Ignoring Desdemona's voice in the name of giving voice to the voiceless is harder to understand.

In one notable exception to the idealizing and compartmentalizing strategies of nineteenth-century critical and theatrical production, Hazlitt allows himself to "feel" the manic excitement of Iago without sequestering it in the space of a reader's imagination. The brilliance of Kean's performance excites him, and the gusto with which he abandons himself to Iago's malicious ingenuity propels him "into the wildness and impetuosity of real enthusiasm" (250 below). When it concerns Desdemona's character, Hazlitt goes to alarming lengths in acceding to the power of Iago's point of view. In the long footnote reprinted on page 251 below, Hazlitt's contempt for the idealization of sexual desire is pure "honest Iago": virtue, a fig! Even more striking is his outrageous reading of Desdemona's sexuality; the "gross impropriety" of her "personal connection" to an older black man reinforces the "monstrous" prospect that Lamb, Coleridge, and Bradley labored hard to deny. The note shocked readers. The *Examiner* editor, Leigh Hunt, wrote a detailed response dissociating the journal from Hazlitt's position. Even twentieth-century readers explain the note away as the quirky self-indulgence of some "private torment" (Maclean, 315–17) or the result an "unhappy love-affair" (Jones, 152–53). Hazlitt himself omitted the note in reprints of this material, perhaps thinking he'd gone too far.

Even with all the risky pleasure he takes in channeling Iago's murderous aggression, Hazlitt never abandons his critical intelligence. He acknowledges Iago's perversity and never undervalues the radiant beauty Iago wishes to destroy. His Othello, whose "frankness and generosity" demand "our sympathy" without reserve (255 below), is of a piece with the nineteenth-century tradition of the noble Moor, and his *Othello* "purifies the affections" (252 below) in ways equal to anything claimed for it by Bradley's "reconciliation." In his generous openness to a variety of different impressions, Hazlitt produces a version of *Othello* that is more fully responsive to the play's contradictory voices than the idealized and Othello-dominated versions of his contemporaries—and, arguably, than the antiheroic and Iagocentric versions of modern times.

III. Modern Times

If Edmund's Kean's Iago challenged Othello as the play's star turn, Kean's Othello helped make the challenge at least temporarily unsuccessful. "Kean's *Othello* smothered *Desdemona* and my Iago too," Junius Brutus Booth said of an 1817 performance, refusing to repeat the experience as scheduled (quoted in Sprague, *Players*, 77). In 1833, on the verge of the career-ending collapse that brought Ira Aldridge on as his replacement, Kean repeated his triumph, this time over William Macready's Iago. As George Henry Lewes remembered the temptation scene (3.3), Kean's Othello "seemed to swell into a stature which made Macready appear small" (quoted in Hankey, 60). Kean was convinced "that however engagingly he played Iago, he could never win the sympathies of his audience" (Hankey, 54); "'Othello holds all the interest'" (quoted in Carlisle, 218). Kean's conviction reflected a theatrical consensus; the protagonist's role dominated performance up to the late middle of the nineteenth century. But by the time Henry Irving and Edwin Booth traded roles in 1881, in performances that "revealed two masterly Iagos and two unsatisfactory Othellos" (Odell, 2.376), it was "quite clear that Iago had emerged as the most interesting role" (Hankey, 91).

Iago's increased stature on the modern stage was accompanied by Othello's reduced stature in critical commentary, although the reduction does not become visible until later. The Othello of modern criticism can be dated with some precision to 1927, with T. S. Eliot's suggestion that Othello's last speech represents a self-deluding "*bovarysme*" (271 below). Eliot's personal authority at this time is hard to overestimate, but "*bovarysme*" stuck because it coincided with contemporary feeling and belief. The opulent spectacles that framed *Othello* on the nineteenth-century stage had become unsustainable aesthetically and economically. The moderns had no use for the idealized sentiments of their eminent Victorian forebears, and after the slaughter of World War I they were frankly hostile to "the pride, pomp, and circumstance of glorious war" with which Bradley's Othello "comes before us" (265 below). Ten years after Eliot demoted the noble Moor to a feminized and bourgeois banality, F. R. Leavis, himself a critic of considerable influence, projected this image of Othello's last speech backward to reveal a protagonist who is self-deluding "from the beginning" of the play (139). Seven years after that, Leo Kirschbaum assured readers that "Eliot could have gone much further" in exposing the "self-deluded" and "romantic idealism" by which Othello refuses "to face the reality of his own nature" (287–95). By 1956, when Robert Heilman's *Magic in the Web* appeared, the "romantic figure" eulogized in Bradley's

Shakespearean Tragedy (265 below) had been abandoned in favor of a protagonist characterized by his "deficiency in adult self-awareness," "self-protectiveness," "pompousness," and "unredeemed egotism" (171–74).

There's a lot more along this line (see Mark Scott, 457 ff.), but not every critic marched in step. A year after Heilman's book appeared, the British Academy published "The Noble Moor," Helen Gardner's moving tribute to the values of heroic tragedy in which her world had apparently lost interest. A decade later, G. K. Hunter, writing appreciatively of Othello's "romanticism and epic grandeur," is nonetheless forced to acknowledge then-current academic taste: "One has to be trained as a literary critic to find [Othello] unadmirable" (288 below). A half-century later, we are left trying to understand what the remarkable consensus around Othello's inadequacy was all about. Part of the explanation must derive from the social context for Shakespearean commentary, which has expanded and diversified since Eliot's (or Heilman's) time. When we look back from today's more inclusive institution, even a self-proclaimed outsider such as Leavis comes across as the member of an elite club, excluding Othello on the basis of criteria that seem narrowly censorious—ethical, psychological, social, and maybe even racial (see Neill, 320 note 9 below).

Dated as it seems, the early-twentieth-century *Othello* exhibits some remarkable continuities with more recent commentary. Mark Rose's disenchanted view—"the time came when the Elizabethan romances . . . no longer carry conviction" (297)—is basically of a piece with the antiheroic disillusion of Eliot and his followers. "Even without Iago's machinations," Rose claims, "the romantic image of the absolute worthiness of the lady is at best unstable" (294). Rose cites Stephen Greenblatt's 1980 account of the play as an example of other critics who have developed "this aspect of Othello's vulnerability to Iago" (294), but he could as well have cited Leavis's claim that, with Othello's initial appearance, "the essential traitor" of narcissism is already "within the gates" (139). The idea that Iago represents something inherent in Othello seems to originate in the early twentieth century (see Mark Scott's examples, 468–70 and 500–503), and it is still a significant presence in more recent commentary thanks in large part to Burke's influential analysis excerpted below.

Yet there are important differences as well. Where the moderns emphasized some particular and presumably corrigible failure on the protagonist's part, Rose focuses not on Othello but on the outmoded system of chivalric values he is said to embody. Edward Snow identifies Othello's state of mind not with a personal pathology but with the normative system of belief operating in the play. "What erupts in Othello's jealousy is not primitive barbaric man but the voice of the father, not 'those elements in man that oppose civilized order' but the outraged voice *of* that order" (410). This focus on the cultural system rather than on the individual subject helps generate many of the strongest current interpretations of the play (for examples, see 157 above). It is central to Michael Bristol's powerful reading of *Othello* as a "comedy of abjection" in which the "play's structure" is "interpreted schematically as a carnivalesque derangement of marriage as a social institution and as an illustration of the contradictory role of heterosexual desire within that institution" (339 below). Bristol does not deny Othello and Desdemona's charismatic presence, but he argues that any transcendence we might infer from their appeal as individualized dramatic characters is contained within (and crushed by) the regulative (and punitive) force of systemic norms.

In late-twentieth-century criticism, these inescapable norms have been represented across a spectrum of interpretive contexts. In perhaps the dominant version, Othello's existential vulnerability is analyzed in sociopolitical terms: the "self-doubt of this displaced stranger," which "opens him so fatally to Iago's attack" (Neill, "Changing Places," 127); the "precarious entry into the white world" of "a colonised subject existing on the terms of white Venetian society and trying to internalise its ideology" (Loomba, 48). From a psychosexual angle, Othello's vulnerability inheres in "the impossible condition of male desire, the condition always already lost," that "inevitably soils that object" in which it invests itself and therefore "threatens to 'corrupt and taint' [Othello's] business from the start" (Adelman, 69, 63 and 65). In the linguistically oriented terminology of post-Freudian psychoanalysis, Othello's fate is determined by desire itself, "which invests the self in another" and "necessarily precipitates a division in the subject. . . . This must be so" (Belsey, 95 and 86). According to Stephen Greenblatt, Othello's transformation is simply the "clearest and most important" example of textual construction as a general condition: Othello has "always already experienced submission to narrativity" (273). Finally (though examples could be multiplied pretty much indefinitely), James Calderwood develops Burke's analysis of an anxiety in the ownership of property into a claim that, since "even to *be* at all, is to possess," individual identity is inherently insecure: "the barbarian has always been inside the gate of Venice, not in the person of Othello, but latent in the civil unconscious" (10 and 8).

The play's name for this latent unconscious, Burke's "voice at Othello's ear" (272 below), is Iago, and this identification helps clarify the continuities between theatrical and critical practice. Just as Iago emerges as the dominant role in performance, so critical commentary, disparaging the heroics of "an extravagant and wheeling stranger" (1.1.133), invests in the sly sophistication of the canny insider, who can claim to "know our country disposition well" (3.3.204). Eliot only started this transformative process. His disengagement from Othello's heroism found compensation not in Iago, in whom he expresses no interest, but in the more private and theological virtue of humility. But when Leavis asserts the values of "a tough-minded realist assessment" against "Bradley's 'idealizing' approach" to *Othello*, he "becomes oddly intertwined with the drama played out between Othello and Iago" (Norris, 59). In appropriating (or being appropriated by) Iago's voice, Leavis establishes a disenchanted tone that has dominated *Othello* criticism ever since. This connection in outlook, frequently noted (see Bayley, 129–30; Kirsch, 31; and Wine, 36), is amply illustrated in the passages quoted in the paragraph just above: "always," "inevitably," "necessarily," "this must be so." In other words, Iago's words, "there's no remedy" (1.1.32). These critics know their culture disposition well—too well to entertain any illusions about transcending social norms. For critics writing after modernity, Leavis's "essential traitor" is now (to use a phrase that appears twice in the preceding paragraph) *always already* "within the gates."

The disenchanted tone of this commentary antedates critical modernism; it derives, along with so much else in *Othello* commentary, from the formative influence of Thomas Rymer. "The Ghost of Rymer" serves Nicholas Potter "as a reminder" of the "new sternness" that "entered criticism with the emergence of the 'modern'" (4). But Rymer had his own source: Rymer is just "a kind of critical Iago" (Newman, 152); Rymer "becomes as subject to Iago's inversions as Othello does" (Kirsch, 17); "Rymer's appropriation of Iago's language" illustrates an "odd ventriloquy," as though "the ensign's colonization of the hero's mind were at work in the critic" (Neill, 328–29 below). The only true begetter of Iago-centrism is Iago himself.

The moderns, then, didn't invent something out of nothing, and the position they reinforced has become even more dominant. A focus on Iago is now a regular feature of *Othello* commentary.[1] As Richard Raatzsch sums up the situation, "the play *should* have been called *Iago* rather than *Othello*. After all, it is probably Iago who leaves the sharpest, strongest, most lasting impressions of all the characters" (3). Even when not the object of attention, Iago constructs the perspective from which the action is registered and

---

1. In various (though sometimes overlapping) versions, Iago is said to be sodomitical (Matz), addictive (Kezar), charmingly gay (Orgel), anal (Saunders), self-loathing (Wood), masochistic (Cefalu), a con artist (Hedrick), and vindictive (Deutermann).

understood. As Hugh Grady remarks about a recent piece, "Iago is oddly underrepresented," but "the focus on 'emptiness' in effect gives Iago the determining vision of the play" (459).

Harry Berger's *Othello* commentary strikingly illustrates the effect Grady describes. In Berger's view, Desdemona, waiting for news of Othello's fate at sea, "warms to the spirit" of Iago's "misogynist witticisms." They serve as a "counterpoint" to "Cassio's gynephilic arias" and Othello's romanticizing, and "the contrast, as I see it, is all on [Iago's] side" (114–15). In the "tough-minded realist assessment" with which this position dismisses any vestiges of an "'idealizing' approach" to Desdemona (Norris, 59) Berger reproduces the unillusioned insouciance of Iago's assurances to Roderigo: "The wine she drinks is made of grapes" (2.1.247–48). Othello is similarly brought down to earth. Commenting on "the lilt" of Othello's "exit jingle" after the brawl scene ("Come, Desdemona; 'tis the soldiers life / To have their balmy slumbers waked with strife," 2.3.247–48), Berger declares that "it resembles nothing so much as the theme song of some heroic Disneyland dodo: 'Hi diddledy dee, it's the soldier's life for me!' Othello marches offstage with an air of Mission Accomplished" (127–28).

As Stanley Cavell remarks, contempt for the protagonist has become "conventional" in *Othello* commentary—"making Othello some kind of exotic, gorgeous, superstitious lunkhead; which is about what Iago thinks" (293 below). From this angle, Berger's Iago-centric commentary coincides with current norms but at the edge of the spectrum. Though expressing himself in Iago's voice and (as in Grady) adopting his perspective, Berger nonetheless insists that Iago's voice and perspective lack dramatic authority. Since Othello and Iago's other targets always already "deeply and darkly desire" their own destruction, Iago is only "the tool of his victims" and thus "all but dispensable relatively early in the play" (201); his inconsequentiality, Berger claims, "needs to be affirmed against the tendency to insist one-sidedly that the action takes place in 'Iago's world'" (126). It's hard to credit the claim that Iago does not own *Othello* when he evidently owns the discourse of the claimant, but whatever Berger's argument lacks in persuasive power it more than makes up for in exemplarity. It tells us something about *Othello* commentary that one of its most eminent practitioners echoes Iago even as he contemns him. And it tells us something about the play.

As in the commentary, so on the stage. Iago's emergent preeminence in the late nineteenth century was secured in subsequent theatrical practice. According to Martin Wine, the Othellos in four of five mid-twentieth-century productions "were no match for the vividly realised Iagos," who "developed their parts with such high spirits that they threw the emotional balance . . . out of kilter" (62). In Wine's account, only John Dexter's 1964 *Othello* at London's Old Vic avoided this imbalance, but the exceptional status claimed for this production is dubious. Dexter's Othello, Sir Laurence Olivier, was probably the strongest stage presence of the time, but even he was reluctant to take on the role. Perhaps remembering the "unrepentant scene-stealing spirit" with which his Iago had upstaged Ralph Richardson's Othello in 1938 (Hankey, 339), Olivier worried that the play "belonged to Iago, who could always make the Moor look a credulous idiot." He agreed only on condition that he didn't play opposite "a witty Machiavellian Iago. I want a solid, honest-to-God N. C. O." (Tynan, 2). Frank Finlay's Iago gave him the effect he wanted but didn't restore Othello to admiring interest. Olivier spent hours blackening and polishing himself before each performance, affected a pseudo–West Indian accent, and adopted stylized and racially stereotypical movements, all in the service of a self-absorbed narcissism derived consciously from Leavis. The performance was much celebrated, but as David Harewood suggests and the Stuart Burge film version confirms (see 355 and 388 below), it now makes sense mostly as archival data, the record of a theatrical tour de force from a world well lost. While Dexter's *Othello* did not belong to Iago, it did not belong to Othello either, but rather to the performer who played Othello—an Oliviercentric production; and given the foundation in Leavis, no real exception to the Iagocentrism dominating the modern stage.

There are better candidates. The productions directed by Tony Taccone at Ashland, Oregon, and by Michael Attenborough at Stratford-upon-Avon, both in 1999, offered "a return to the romantic and tragic *Othello*," based on the "view that a heroic role is one of great emotional range, while the villain is essentially a limited character" (Lois Potter, 208, 215). Nicholas Hytner's 2013 National Theatre production abjured romantic heroism, setting its action in a realistic modern world of London pubs and military barracks, and Adrian Lester, whose picture adorns the cover of this Norton Critical Edition, deliberately toned down the "histrionic declamatory style" of his Ira Aldridge in *Red Velvet* the year before (Moss). Nonetheless, Lester's nuanced and heartbreaking performance commands the center of attention, thanks in part to the generous Rory Kinnear, whose Iago, while powerfully interesting, avoids the easy triumphs of the "witty Machiavel" Olivier complained about, and never upstages the protagonist.

However noteworthy, these exceptions do not add up to much next to the sheer number of modern and later productions in which Iago displaces the protagonist from the central position he occupied on the nineteenth-century stage.[2] The shift is evident in the different strategies for representing the ending of the play. In the "predominant mode" on the nineteenth-century stage, the "audience gaze is first and last directed toward Othello" (Siemon, 313 below). "In Bell's acting edition," for example, Iago "exits '*guarded*,' a little before the beginning of Othello's apologia, the words 'Away with him' being interpolated" as a way "to get him off" before the protagonist's suicide (Sprague, *Shakespeare and the Actors*, 222). When, as a result, Lodovico's "O Spartan dog, . . . / This is thy work" (5.2.366–69) had no one on stage to be addressed, the whole last speech was cut. "From Macready onwards, up to the early twentieth century, it was usual to bring the curtain down" after Othello's "And smote him—thus!" (Hankey, 335). With the elimination of Othello's dying couplet, "I kissed thee ere I killed thee. No way but this, / Killing myself, to die upon a kiss" (5.2.363–64), productions avoided displaying the body-strewn bed in favor a silent terminal tableau focused on the protagonist.

More-recent productions, in contrast, tend to highlight Iago at the end. Jonathan Miller's 1981 BBC production "let the story end with the sound of Iago's laughter ringing down the now-empty corridors" (Potter, 358 below). Richard McCabe, Attenborough's Iago, describes a final "tableau" with "the three dead bodies in the foreground and myself at the rear of the stage, heavily guarded and with my back to the audience. As the lights went down, I would turn slowly and regard the bodies in profile, with a deliberately neutral expression on my face" (210). According to Antony Sher, who played the part in Greg Doran's (2004) production, "Iago was left in a sitting position after Othello wounded him; hand-cuffed, head bowed. Then after Lodovico's closing couplet, and just before a snap-blackout, we had Iago suddenly look up, confronting the audience with his eyes" (69).

The play text, arguably, calls for these Iagocentric endings. "Let it be hid," six lines from the end, is a cue to draw the bed curtains, hide the dead bodies, and substitute "this hellish villain" (5.2.370, 373) as the object of our final regard. G. M. Matthews claims that "Othello's final speech" represents "the complete recovery of his integrity as a human being," and that "All that Iago's poison has achieved is an object that 'poisons sight': a bed on which a black man and a white girl, although they are dead, are embracing.

2. Some recent examples: Christopher Plummer's portrayal in New York, 1982; Ian McKellen's in Stratford, 1989; Simon Russell Beale's at the National, 1997; and Antony Sher's in Stratford, 2004. To judge from response to the 1995 Oliver Parker film (see 361–62 and 389 below), in which Laurence "Fishburne looks lost" as Othello, and Kenneth Branagh's Iago "walks off with the movie" (Rafferty, 126), and the 1996 New York Shakespeare Festival production, in which no one "comes close to matching [Liev] Schreiber's playful interpretive intelligence" (Brantley), the imbalance Martin Wine described in mid-century productions has by now become routine.

Human dignity, the play says, is indivisible" (43). If the redirection of our gaze seems to discourage any such claim for transcendence, Matthews is not simply wrong. Endings do not erase the experiences that lead up to them, which may generate convictions about an indivisible human dignity, and they do not preclude the experiences that might follow from them: thinking, discussing, maybe even writing. But taken in this inclusive sense, *Othello* has produced so many different convictions over the centuries that a single statement of what "the play says" might not be what we should be looking for. Better to ask why Matthews's Marxist-humanist inflection of Bradley's "reconciliation" is so thinly represented in recent and current criticism or, to put it the other way around, why Iagocentrism remains the dominant mode of engaging *Othello*.

The short and perhaps circular answer to this question is that we are getting a lot out of it. An increased willingness to listen to Iago's voice, even respect its "tough-minded" resistance to any "'idealizing' approach," has added immeasurably to the intense and often intimate investments with which we engage the play. This willingness coincides with the eagerness in current work to share in the explicitly erotic feelings that the play's images produce. Around the time that Lynda E. Boose identified Othello's handkerchief with pictures in the mind's eye of virgin-blood-stained sheets, Stanley Cavell argued that *Othello* makes us think "not merely generally of marriage but specifically of the wedding night" (291 below), and by now *Othello* commentary includes a thriving cottage industry devoted to identifying "a hidden scene of desire" as the "focus of compulsive fascination for the audiences and characters alike" (Neill, "Hidden Malady," 98).[3]

Boose nods to Rymer in her piece, citing his "infamous title," "The Tragedy of the Handkerchief," as an "unwittingly . . . ironic perception" ("Othello's Handkerchief," 374); but although Rymer did not understand the play's sexual images as a subject for reflection, he was conscious of them. He associates the handkerchief with Desdemona's garter and with sexual smells, imagining it as "rumpled up with [her] wedding sheets" and "start[ing] up to disarm" Othello "whilst [he] was stifling her . . . to stop his ungracious mouth." Rymer picks up on the importance of the wedding night as well. In his litany of descriptions—"the first night no sooner warm in bed together," "no sooner in bed together," "bridegroom and bride in the first night of their coming together," "the very night she beds him," "the very night of their marriage" "go the first time to bed" (229–32 below)—Rymer fully registers (even if he does

---

3. For more along this line, see (in alphabetical order): Adelman, Boose ("'Let it be hid'"); Calderwood, 125 and 154; Greenberg, 27; Little; Maus ("Horns of Dilemma" and "Proof and Consequences"); Neill ("Changing Places"); Parker ("Fantasies" and "Shakespeare and Rhetoric"); Pechter ("Have"); and Rudnytsky.

not care to think about) the centrality of Othello and Desdemona's lovemaking to any account of the dramatic action.

That Rymer anticipates the erotic focus of modern approaches to *Othello* is not totally surprising. As the first Iagocentrist after Iago, Rymer might be expected to express himself in a voice that coincides, however differently inflected, with current interest. His voice resonates on a formalist register as well. In his complaint about the inappropriate combination of elements in *Othello*, Rymer foreshadows the heightened sensitivity to generic mixture in so much recent work on the play. Mark Rose sees *Othello* more as domestic than heroic tragedy, Hunter the other way around, but both recognize the risks *Othello* takes conjoining tonal effects usually kept distinct. For Rose, the different kinds of emotions associated with the romantic and satiric modes embodied in Othello and Iago tend to "cancel each other out" (311). Bristol's emphasis on the play's coarse and brutal charivari pushes the play to the edge of farce, a treatment anticipated by Peter Zadek's 1976 Hamburg production, in which a demented Othello, having flung the dead Desdemona "over the curtain guide-line with her bottom towards the audience . . . like a 'slaughtered steer,'" threw "a kiss at her naked posterior" and then engaged in a shouting match with the laughing spectators (Engle, 101). The play is now wholly a "comedy of abjection": Othello has become his own Iago, with Rymer as dramaturge, presiding over a production that is "none other than a bloody farce" (236 below).

Whatever the continuities between Rymer's Iagocentrism and our own, there are differences as well. For Rymer, *Othello* is a botch. Its generic slippage violates his sense of normative clarity, and the play's sexual explicitness is offensive for the same reason. Rymer is no prude, but for him sex belonged to the domestic and private domains, not the public and political realms within which tragic actions are supposed to unfold. In addition, his focus on the married couple's first night called attention to the play's temporal inconsistencies, which force "the audience [to] suppose" a sustained extension of time "to make the plot operate" plausibly (232 below).

The issue of temporal inconsistency provides a good way to highlight the differences between Rymer's taste and our own. Rymer dwells on every instance he can find where the play's extended time frame obtrudes on the main impression of a brief action. He admits that "absurdities of this kind break no bones" (230 below) just as Gildon, even in his most Rymeresque, is forgiving: "Those little forgetfulnesses are not worth minding" (242 below). But eighteenth-century commentators minded them nonetheless. Johnson, for whom *Othello*'s failure to observe the unity of time is inconsequential, still feels it necessary to point out that only minor adjustments are required to bring the play into "scrupulous regularity" (246 below). Whether admiring or disparaging, eighteenth-century commentators tend to treat *Othello*'s temporal contradictions as a stopgap improvisation meant to disguise a problem inherited from Cinthio. By the middle of the nineteenth century, however, so many analysts have invested so much interpretive sensibility on the matter that it begins to assume the shape of Shakespearean invention—something "contrived," to be "worked out, with meticulous care" (Hutson, 118). At the beginning of his 15 closely-printed pages on the "duration of the action," the New Variorum editor describes his topic as "this art, or even trick (be it respectfully termed)" (Furness, 358). Even this perfunctory equivocation has disappeared by 1958, when M.R. Ridley devotes the last section of his Introduction to "the 'double-time' scheme" (lxvii–lxx). *Scheme*—the "absurdities" of earlier have turned into a strategy to be celebrated for its brilliant effects: *Othello* "refuses linear temporality," according to Jonathan Gil Harris; "rather than a singular progression that can be geometrically plotted, time in *Othello* is a dynamic field whose contours keep shifting, bringing into startling and anachronistic proximity supposedly distant and disparate moments" (169).

If double time is not a defect but a virtue, to what end does it work? It's the same question as earlier: What values have made an Iagocentric *Othello* dominant in modern and more recent times? The early critics had trouble identifying the value of their own versions of the play. Gildon makes fun of Rymer's attempts to specify the moral but is no more successful. Johnson may not have been altogether serious telling Boswell that "*Othello* has more moral than almost any play," but he winds up more or less reiterating Rymer's silly points as confirmation. Rymer mocks any attempt to find a moral in *Othello*, but the anger and frustration he expresses about the ending seem to derive from its absence:

> We meet with nothing but blood and butchery, described much-what to the style of the last speeches and confessions of the persons executed [publicly] at [London's] Tyburn, with this difference—that there we have the fact and due course of justice, whereas our poet, against all justice and reason, against all law, humanity and nature, in a barbarous arbitrary way, executes and makes havoc of his subjects, hab-nab as they come to hand. (235 below).

Rymer's response anticipates Johnson's "I am glad that I have ended my revisal of this dreadful scene. It is not to be endured" (245 below); and Johnson's lament is echoed throughout nineteenth-century commentary. Furness quotes J. O. Halliwell-Phillipps's "Many readers will probably sympathize with Dr Johnson's concluding observation" that "a study of the drama of *Othello*" is "rather a painful duty than one of pleasure" and then adds his own voice to the chorus: Given "the unutterable agony of [its] closing Scene," he tells us, "I do not shrink from saying that I wish this Tragedy had never been written" (300). Rymer's Tyburn comparison has a rich afterlife as well. Hazlitt links Iago's appeal to the motives driving "so many [to] frequent executions" (248 below). The American theater critic William Winter, describing the "heartrending and terrible" qualities that make *Othello* an experience the "mind cannot dwell upon," concludes that "you feel as if you had seen a murder or attended an execution" (192–93).

The moralizing tone of earlier criticism survives into the mid-twentieth century, in Lionel Trilling's claim that "whenever the characters of a story suffer, they do so at the behest of their author—the author is responsible for their suffering and must justify his cruelty by the seriousness of his moral intention" (32). The same tone is detectable, at least by implication, as recently as Colleen Ruth Rosenfeld's comment in 2014 that, "according to Rymer, the playwright enters into the diegesis of the play as the murderer of his character" (271). There are important differences between Hazlitt's claim that the interpretation of *Othello* allows us to reach "a high and permanent interest, beyond ourselves, in humanity as such" (252 below) and Karen Newman's that the play enables us "to expose or demystify the ideological discourses which organize texts" (157); but both are committed to the idea that engaging with literary or theatrical fiction has consequences in the world and thus requires the exercise of value judgments. Such judgments are discernibly at work in the Ruth Cowhig's view, "I only want to see black actors in the part" of Othello (125), as they are in the contradictory view that Othello should be "played by a white man in blackface," as affirmed by Sheila Rose Bland (31) and others.[4] None of these commentators would, I suspect, feel comfortable declaring that "it is always a writer's duty to make the world better," but they all write as if they believed Johnson's pronouncement to be true.

That there is still no consensus about identifying the value of *Othello* may seem unfortunate, but we should not exaggerate the problem. *Othello* has managed for centuries to engage the most intense theatrical excitement and critical interest among audiences and readers at a loss to explain why this should be so, and the play is accommodating those new interests—the materialist turn, the religious turn, the cognitive turn—that readers and audiences are bringing to it even now. This long and continuing history suggests that

---

4. The others include Hugh Quarshie (5), Virginia Vaughan (105), and Hugh Richmond (94–95). Quarshie, a Ghanaian-born black English actor, has apparently changed his mind on this matter, since he played Othello for the RSC in a 2015 production.

Othello will sustain its power into the future—if not "for all time," as in Ben Jonson's tribute to Shakespeare in 1623 (Evans, 98), for at least as far as the eye can see.

Works Cited

Adamson, Jane. *"Othello" as Tragedy: Some Problems of Judgment and Feeling*. Cambridge, Eng.: Cambridge University Press, 1980.

Adelman, Janet. *Suffocating Mothers: Fantasies of Maternal Origin in Shakespeare's Plays, "Hamlet" to "The Tempest."* New York and London: Routledge, 1992.

Altman, Joel B. "'Preposterous Conclusions': Eros, *Enargeia*, and the Composition of *Othello*." *Representations* 18 (1987): 129–57.

Bayley, John. *The Characters of Love: A Study in the Literature of Personality*. London: Constable, 1960.

Belsey, Catherine. "Desire's Excess and the English Renaissance Theatre: *Edward II, Troilus and Cressida*, and *Othello*." In Susan Zimmerman, ed. *Erotic Politics: Desire on the Renaissance Stage*. London and New York: Routledge, 1992, 84–102.

Berger, Jr., Harry. *A Fury in the Words: Love and Embarrassment in Shakespeare's Venice*. New York: Fordham University Press, 2013.

Bland, Sheila Rose. "How I Would Direct *Othello*." In Mythili Kaul, ed. *"Othello": New Essays by Black Writers*. Washington, D.C.: Howard University Press, 1996, 29–41.

Boose, Lynda E. "'Let it be hid': Renaissance Pornography, Iago, and Audience Response." In Richard Marienstras and Dominique Guy-Blanquet, eds. *Autour d' "Othello."* Paris: C. E. R. L. A, à l'Institut Charles V, 1987, 135–43.

———. "Othello's Handkerchief: 'The Recognizance and Pledge of Love.'" *English Literary Renaissance* 5 (1975): 360–74.

Bradley, A. C. "Poetry for Poetry's Sake." In *Oxford Lectures on Poetry*. Bloomington: Indiana University Press, 1961, 3–34.

———. *Shakespearean Tragedy: Lectures on "Hamlet," "Othello," "King Lear," "Macbeth."* 1904. 4th ed. Houndmills, Basingstoke, Hampshire, Eng., and New York: Palgrave Macmillan, 2007.

Brantley, Ben. "A Revolt Against God With No Apology." *New York Times* (December 10, 2001). <www.nytimes.com/2001/12/1-/arts/theater10OTHE.html>

Bray, René. *La Formation de la Doctrine Classique en France*. Paris: Nizet, 1957.

Bronson, Bertrand H., ed. *Selections from Johnson on Shakespeare*. New Haven and London: Yale University Press, 1986.

Brückner, Christine. *Desdemona—if only you had spoken!: Eleven Uncensored Speeches of Eleven Uncensored Women*. Trans. Eleanor Bron. London: Virago Press, 1992.

Calderwood, James. *The Properties of "Othello."* Amherst: University of Massachusetts Press, 1989.

Carlisle, Carol Jones. *Shakespeare from the Greenroom: Actors' Criticisms of Four Major Tragedies.* Chapel Hill: University of North Carolina Press, 1969.

Cefalu, Paul. "The Burdens of Mind Reading in Shakespeare's *Othello*: A Cognitive and Psychoanalytic Approach to Iago's Theory of Mind." *Shakespeare Quarterly* 64 (2013): 265–94.

Chakrabarti, Lolita. *Red Velvet.* London: Samuel French, 2014

Chambers, E. K. *William Shakespeare: A Study of Facts and Problems.* 2 vols. Oxford: Clarendon, 1930.

Chapman, R. W., ed. *Boswell's Life of Johnson.* London: Oxford University Press, 1953.

Cowhig, Ruth. "Blacks in English Renaissance Drama and the Role of Shakespeare's *Othello*." In David Dabydeen, ed. *The Black Presence in English Literature.* Manchester: Manchester University Press, 1985, 1–25.

Davison, Peter. *Othello.* The Critics Debate Series. Atlantic Highlands, N.J.: Humanities Press International, 1988.

Deutermann, Allison K. "Hearing Iago's Withheld Confession." In Katharine A. Craik and Tanya Pollard, eds. *Shakespearean Sensations: Experiencing Literature in Early Modern England.* Cambridge, Eng.: Cambridge University Press, 2013, 47–63.

Dostoyevsky, Fyodor. *The Brothers Karamazov.* Trans. David Magarshack. 2 vols. Harmondsworth, Middlesex, Eng.: Penguin, 1958.

Eliot, T. S. "Four Elizabethan Dramatists." In *Selected Essays.* New Edition, 1927. Rpt. New York: Harcourt Brace, 1950, 91–97.

———. "Hamlet." In *Selected Essays.* New Edition, 1927. Rpt. New York: Harcourt Brace, 1950, 121–26.

Engell, James, and W. Jackson Bate, eds. *Biographia Literaria or Biographical Sketches of My Literary Life and Opinions.* In *The Collected Works of Samuel Taylor Coleridge.* Vol. 7, 2 parts. London and Princeton: Routledge and Princeton University Press, 1980.

Engle, Ron. "Audience, Style, and Language in the Shakespeare of Peter Zadek." In Dennis Kennedy, ed. *Foreign Shakespeare: Contemporary Performance.* Cambridge, Eng.: Cambridge University Press, 1993, 93–105.

Evans, G. B., et al, eds. *The Riverside Shakespeare.* Boston: Houghton Mifflin, 1997.

Foakes, R. A, ed. *Lectures, 1808–1819: On Literature. Collected Works of Samuel Taylor Coleridge.* Vol. 5, 2 parts. Princeton: Princeton University Press, 1988.

Furness, Horace Howard, ed. *A New Variorum Edition of "Othello."* 7th ed. Philadelphia: Lippincott, 1886.

Gardner, Helen. "The Noble Moor." *Proceedings of the British Academy* 41 (1955): 189–205.

Grady, Hugh. "Theory 'After Theory': Christopher Pye's Reading of *Othello*." *Shakespeare Quarterly* 60 (2009): 453–59.

Greenberg, Mitchell. "Shakespeare's *Othello* and the 'Problem' of Anxiety." In *Canonical States, Canonical Stages: Oedipus, Othering, and Seventeenth-Century Drama*. Minneapolis and London: University of Minnesota Press, 1994, 1–32.

Greenblatt, Stephen. "The Improvisation of Power." In *Renaissance Self-Fashioning: From More to Shakespeare*. Chicago: University of Chicago Press, 1980, 222–54.

Gross, Kenneth. *Shakespeare's Noise*. Chicago: University of Chicago Press, 2001.

Hankey, Julie, ed. *Othello*. Plays in Performance Series. Bristol: Bristol Classical Press, 1987.

Harewood, David. *Shakespeare Uncovered: Othello*. <www.video.pbs.org/video/2365412922> Accessible only in the U.S.

Harris, Jonathan Gil. *Untimely Matter in the Time of Shakespeare*. Philadelphia: University of Pennsylvania Press, 2009.

Hedrick, Donald. "Distracting Othello: Tragedy and the Rise of Magic." *PMLA* 129:4 (2014): 649–71.

Heilman, Robert. *Magic in the Web: Action and Language in "Othello."* Lexington: University of Kentucky Press, 1956.

Hill, Errol. *Shakespeare in Sable: A History of Black Shakespearean Actors*. Amherst: University of Massachusetts Press, 1984.

Howe, P. P., ed. *The Complete Works of William Hazlitt*. 21 vols. London: Dent, 1930–34.

Hudson, Henry N. "Introduction to the Tragedy of 'Othello.'" In *The Works of Shakespeare: The Text Carefully Restored According to the First Editions; with Introductions, Notes Original and Selected, and A Life of the Poet*. 11 vols. Boston and Cambridge, Mass.: James Munroe and Co., 1856, 10:381–407.

———. *Shakespeare: His Life, Art, and Characters*. 2 vols. Boston: Ginn, 1872.

Hunt, Leigh. "Note upon Note, Or a Word or Two on the Passion of Love, in Answer to Some Observations in our Last Week's *Examiner*." *Examiner* (August 14, 1814): 525–26.

Hutson, Lorna. *The Invention of Suspicion: Law and Mimesis in Shakespeare and Renaissance Drama*. Oxford and New York: Oxford University Press, 2007.

Jameson, Anna B. *Characteristics of Women—Moral, Poetical, and Historical*. 1832. Rpt. *Shakespeare's Heroines*. London: George Bell & Sons, 1905.

Jones, Stanley. *Hazlitt: A Life: From Winterslow to Frith Street*. Oxford: Clarendon, 1989.

Kezar, Dennis. "Shakespeare's Addictions." *Critical Inquiry* 30 (2003): 31–62.

Kirsch, Arthur. *Shakespeare and the Experience of Love*. Cambridge, Eng.: Cambridge University Press, 1981.

Kirschbaum, Leo. "The Modern Othello." *English Literary History* 11 (1944): 283–96.

Lamb, Charles. "On the Tragedies of Shakespeare, Considered with Reference to Their Fitness for Stage Representation." 1811. Rpt. E. V. Lucas, ed. *The Works of Charles and Mary Lamb*. London: Methuen, 1903, vol. 1, 97–111.

Leavis, F. R. "Diabolic Intellect and the Noble Hero." 1937. In *The Common Pursuit*. 1952. Rpt. Harmondsworth, Middlesex, Eng.: Penguin, 1969, 136–59.

Levine, Lawrence W. *Highbrow/Lowbrow: The Emergence of Cultural Hierarchy in America*. Cambridge, Mass.: Harvard University Press, 1988.

Lindfors, Bernth. *Ira Aldridge: The Early Years, 1807–1833*. Rochester: University of Rochester Press, 2011.

———. *Ira Aldridge: Performing Shakespeare in Europe, 1852–1855*. Rochester: University of Rochester Press, 2013.

———. *Ira Aldridge: The Vagabond Years, 1833–1852*. Rochester: University of Rochester Press, 2011.

———, ed. *Ira Aldridge: The African Roscius*. Rochester: University of Rochester Press, 2007.

Little, Jr., Arthur. "'An essence that's not seen': The Primal Scene of Racism in *Othello*." *Shakespeare Quarterly* 44 (1993): 304–24.

Loomba, Ania. *Gender, Race, Renaissance Drama*. Manchester: Manchester University Press, 1989.

MacDonald, Joyce Green. "Acting Black: *Othello*, *Othello* Burlesques, and the Performance of Blackness." *Theatre Journal* 46 (1994): 231–49.

Maclean, Catherine Macdonald. *Born under Saturn: A Biography of William Hazlitt*. London: Collins, 1943.

Maguire, Laurie. "*Othello*, Theatre Boundaries, and Audience Cognition." In Lena Cowen Orlin, ed. *"Othello": The State of Play*. London and New York: Bloomsbury, 2014, 17–43.

Marshall, Herbert, and Mildred Stock. *Ira Aldridge: The Negro Tragedian*. Carbondale and Edwardsville: Southern Illinois University Press, 1958.

Martino, Pierre, ed. *La Pratique du Théâtre* by François Hédelin, l'Abbé d'Aubignac. Algiers: Carbonel, 1927.

Matthews, G. M. "*Othello* and the Dignity of Man." In Arnold Kettle, ed. *Shakespeare in a Changing World: Essays*. New York: International, 1964, 123–45.

Matz, Robert. "Slander, Renaissance Discourses of Sodomy, and *Othello*." *English Literary History* 66 (1999): 261–76.

Maus, Katharine Eisaman. "Horns of Dilemma: Jealousy, Gender, and Spectatorship in English Renaissance Drama." *English Literary History* 54 (1987): 561–83.

———. "Proof and Consequences: Inwardness and Its Exposure in the English Renaissance." *Representations* 34 (1991): 29–52.

McCabe, Richard. "Iago in *Othello*." In Robert Smallwood, ed. *Players of Shakespeare* 5. Cambridge, Eng.: Cambridge University Press, 2003, 192–211.

Moss, Stern. "Adrian Lester and Rory Kinnear: 'Othello and Iago are a bit cracked.'" *Guardian* (April 10, 2013). <www.theguardian.com/stage/2013/apr/10/adrian-lester-rory-kinnear-othello>

Munro, John, ed. *The Shakspere Allusion-Book: A Collection of Allusions to Shakspere from 1591 to 1700.* 2 vols. London: Oxford University Press, 1932.

Neill, Michael. "Changing Places in *Othello*." *Shakespeare Survey* 37. Cambridge, Eng.: Cambridge University Press, 1984, 115–31.

———. "'Hidden Malady': Death, Discovery, and Indistinction in *The Changeling*." *Renaissance Drama* 22 (1991): 95–121.

Newman, Karen. "'And Wash the Ethiop White': Femininity and the Monstrous in *Othello*." In Jean E. Howard and Marion F. O'Connor, eds. *Shakespeare Reproduced: The Text in History and Ideology*. London: Methuen, 1987, 140–62.

Norris, Christopher. "Post-Structuralist Shakespeare: Text and Ideology." In John Drakakis, ed. *Alternative Shakespeares*. London: Methuen, 1985, 47–66.

Odell, George C. D. *Shakespeare from Betterton to Irving*. 2 vols. New York: Scribners, 1920.

Orgel, Stephen. "*Othello* and the End of Comedy." *Shakespeare Survey* 56. Cambridge, Eng.: Cambridge University Press, 2003, 105–16.

Parker, Patricia. "Fantasies of 'Race' and 'Gender': Africa, *Othello*, and Bringing to Light." In Margo Hendricks and Parker, eds. *Women, "Race," and Writing in the Early Modern Period*. New York and London: Routledge, 1993, 84–100.

———. "Shakespeare and Rhetoric: 'Dilation' and 'Delation.'" In Parker and Geoffrey Hartman, eds. *Shakespeare and the Question of Theory*. London: Methuen, 1985, 57–74.

Pechter, Edward. "'Have you not read of some such thing?': Sex and Sexual Stories in *Othello*." *Shakespeare Survey* 49. Cambridge, Eng.: Cambridge University Press, 1996, 201–16.

———. *"Othello" and Interpretive Traditions*. Iowa City: University of Iowa Press, 1999.

————. "'Too Much Violence': Murdering Wives in *Othello*." In Linda Woodbridge and Sharon Beehler, eds. *Women, Violence and English Renaissance Literature: Essays Honoring Paul Jorgensen*. Tempe: Arizona Center for Medieval and Renaissance Studies, 2003, 217–42.

Potter, Lois. *"Othello": Shakespeare in Performance*. Manchester: Manchester University Press, 2002.

Potter, Nicholas. *William Shakespeare: "Othello."* Columbia Critical Guides. New York: Columbia University Press, 2000.

Quarshie, Hugh. "Second Thoughts about *Othello*." Chipping Camden, Glouestershire, Eng.: International Shakespeare Association, 1999. ISA Occasional Paper No. 7.

Raatzsch, Richard. *The Apologetics of Evil: The Case of Iago*. Trans. Ladislaus Löb. Princeton: Princeton University Press, 2009.

Rafferty, Terence. "Fidelity and Infidelity." *New Yorker* (December 18, 1995): 124–27.

Richmond, Hugh Macrea. "The Audience's Role in *Othello*." In Philip C. Kolin, ed. *"Othello": New Critical Essays*. New York and London: Routledge, 2002, 89–101.

Ridley, M. R., ed. *Othello*. London: Methuen, 1958.

Rose, Mark. "Othello's Occupation: Shakespeare and the Romance of Chivalry." *English Literary Renaissance* 15 (1985): 293–311.

Rosenberg, Marvin. *The Masks of "Othello": The Search for the Identity of Othello, Iago, and Desdemona by Three Centuries of Actors and Critics*. Berkeley, Los Angeles, and London: University of California Press, 1961.

Rosenfeld, Colleen Ruth. "Shakespeare's Nobody." In Lena Cowen Orlin, ed. *"Othello": The State of Play*. London and New York: Bloomsbury, 2014, 257–79.

Rudnytsky, Peter L. "The Purloined Handkerchief in *Othello*." In Joseph Reppen and Maurice Charney, eds. *The Psychoanalytic Study of Literature*. Hillsdale, N.J.: The Analytic Press, 1985, 57–74.

Saunders, Ben. "Iago's Clyster: Purgation, Anality, and the Civilizing Process." *Shakespeare Quarterly* 55:2 (Summer 2004): 148–76.

Schoch, Richard W. *Not Shakespeare: Bardolatry and Burlesque in the Nineteenth Century*. Cambridge, Eng., and New York: Cambridge University Press, 2002.

Scott, Grant F. *Selected Letters of John Keats*. Cambridge, Mass., and London: Harvard University Press, 2002.

Scott, Mark W., ed. *Shakespearean Criticism: Excerpts from the Criticism of William Shakespeare's Plays and Poetry, from the First Published Appraisals to Current Evaluations*. Vol. 4. Detroit: Gale, 1987.

Sellars, Peter. "Desdemona Takes the Microphone: Toni Morrison and Shakespeare's Hidden Women." Townsend Center for the Humanities, Berkeley, October 27, 2011. <townsendcenter .berkeley.edu/media/peter-sellars-director-desdemona>

Shattuck, Charles H. *Shakespeare on the American Stage: From the Hallams to Edwin Booth*. Washington, D.C.: Folger Shakespeare Library, 1976.

Sher, Antony. "Iago." In Michael Dobson, ed. *Performing Shakespeare's Tragedies Today: The Actor's Perspective*. Cambridge, Eng.: Cambridge University Press, 2006, 57–69.

Sherbo, Arthur, ed. *Johnson on Shakespeare. The Yale Edition of the Works of Samuel Johnson*. Vol. 7. New Haven: Yale University Press, 1968.

Sinfield, Alan. *Faultlines: Cultural Materialism and the Politics of Dissident Reading*. Berkeley: University of California Press, 1992.

Sprague, Arthur Colby. *Shakespeare and the Actors: The Stage Business in His Plays (1660–1905)*. Cambridge, Mass.: Harvard University Press, 1948.

———. *Shakespearian Players and Performances*. Cambridge, Mass.: Harvard University Press, 1953.

Snow, Edward. "Sexual Anxiety and the Male Order of Things in *Othello*." *English Literary Renaissance* 10 (1980): 384–412.

Sutton, Dana. "Henry Jackson, Letter of September 1610." <www .philological.bham.ac.uk/jackson>

Theobald, Lewis. *The Works of Shakespeare*. 7 vols. London, 1733. Rpt. New York: AMS Press, 1968.

Trilling, Lionel. *A Gathering of Fugitives*. Boston: Beacon Press, 1956.

Tynan, Kenneth, ed. *"Othello": The National Theatre Production*. New York: Stein and Day, 1967.

Vaughan, Virginia Mason. *Performing Blackness on English Stages, 1500–1800*. Cambridge, Eng.: Cambridge University Press, 2005.

Vickers, Brian, ed. *Shakespeare: The Critical Heritage*. 6 vols. London and Boston: Routledge & Kegan Paul, 1974.

Warburton, William, ed. *The Works of Shakespeare*. 8 vols. London, 1747. Rpt. New York: AMS Press, 1968.

Wine, Martin. *"Othello": Text and Performance*. London: Macmillan, 1984.

Winter, William. *Life and Art of Edwin Booth*. New York: Macmillan, 1893.

Wood, Sam. "Where Iago Lies: Home, Honesty and the Turk in *Othello*." *Early Modern Literary Studies* 14:3 (2009). <extra.shu.ac .uk/emls/143/Woodiago.html>

Woodring, Carl, ed. *Table Talk*. In *The Collected Works of Samuel Taylor Coleridge*. Vol. 14, 2 parts. London and Princeton: Routledge and Princeton University Press, 1990.

Zimansky, Curt A., ed. *The Critical Works of Thomas Rymer*. New Haven: Yale University Press, 1956.

THOMAS RYMER (1643?–1713)

["A Bloody Farce"]†

From all the tragedies acted on our English stage, *Othello* is said to bear the bell away. The subject is more of a piece, and there is indeed something like—there is, as it were, some phantom of—a fable. The fable is always accounted the soul of tragedy.[1] * * *

* * *

Shakespeare alters [the fable] from the original [Cinthio narrative] in several particulars but always, unfortunately, for the worse. He bestows a name on his Moor and styles him the Moor of Venice—a note of preeminence which neither history nor heraldry can allow him. Cinthio, who knew him best and whose creature he was, calls him simply a Moor * * * [and] we see no such cause for the Moor's preferment to that dignity. * * *

Then [there] is the Moor's wife, from a simple citizen in Cinthio dressed up with her top knots[2] and raised to be Desdemona, a senator's daughter. All this is very strange and therefore pleases such as reflect not on the improbability. This match might well be without the parents' consent. Old Horace long ago forbade the banns:

> Sed non ut placidis Coeant immitia, non ut
> Serpentes avibus geminentur, tigribus agni.[3]

* * *

* * *[T]he moral, sure, of this fable is very instructive.

---

† From *A Short View of Tragedy* (London, 1693). Spelling and punctuation have been modernized, and all quotations from *Othello* modified to conform with this Norton Critical Edition. All notes are the editor's. For information about Rymer, his criticism, and its textual sources, see 380 below.

1. The fable (sometimes "argument") is roughly the action or plot. The term has technical suggestions deriving ultimately from Aristotle's *Poetics* and its many commentators.

2. Knots or bows of ribbon worn on the tops of their heads by fashionable women of Rymer's time.

3. Rymer quotes lines 12–13 of Horace's popular *Ars Poetica* (*Art of Poetry*), written about 19 B.C.E. After acknowledging that poets are allowed license to invent "extravagant conceits and unusual mixtures, Horace urges (in an 18th-century translation by George Colman), "But not the soft and savage to combine, / Serpents to doves, to tigers lambkins join."

1. First, this may be a caution to all maidens of quality how, without their parents' consent, they run away with blackamoors.

* * *

2. Secondly, this may be a warning to all good wives that they look well to their linen.

3. Thirdly, this may be a lesson to husbands that before their jealousy be tragical the proofs be mathematical.

Cinthio affirms that "she [Desdemona] was not overcome by a womanish appetite, but by the virtue of the Moor." It must be a good-natured reader that takes Cinthio's word in this case, though in a novel. Shakespeare, who is accountable both to the eyes and to the ears, and to convince the very heart of an audience, shows that Desdemona was won by hearing Othello talk [quotes 1.3.133–44: "I spoke of most disastrous chances. . . . Do grow beneath their shoulders"].

This was the charm, this was the philter, the love powder that took the daughter of this noble Venetian. This was sufficient to make the blackamoor white and reconcile all, though there had been a cloven foot into the bargain.

A meaner woman might be as soon taken. * * *

* * * But it seems the noble Venetians have another sense of things. The duke himself tells us "I think this tale would win my daughter too" [1.3.170].

* * *

* * * [T]here is nothing in the noble Desdemona that is not below any country chambermaid with us.

* * *

The character of that state is to employ strangers in their wars; but shall a poet thence fancy that they will set a Negro to be their general, or trust a Moor to defend them against the Turk? With us a blackamoor might rise to be a trumpeter, but Shakespeare would not have less than a lieutenant-general. With us a Moor might marry some little drab or small-coal wench; Shakespeare would provide him the daughter and heir of some great lord or privy councillor, and all the town should reckon it a very suitable match. Yet the English are not bred up with that hatred and aversion to the Moors as are the Venetians, who suffer by a perpetual hostility from them. * * *

* * *

The characters or manners, which are the second part in a tragedy, are not less unnatural and improper than the fable was improbable and absurd.[4] Othello is made a Venetian general. We see nothing done by him nor related concerning him that comports with the condition of a general or, indeed, of a man, unless the killing himself to avoid a death the law was about to inflict upon him. When his jealousy had wrought him up to the resolution of his taking revenge for the supposed injury, he sets Iago to the fighting part to kill Cassio and chooses himself to murder the silly woman his wife, that was like to make no resistance.

His love and his jealousy are no part of a soldier's character, unless for comedy.

But what is most intolerable is Iago. He is no blackamoor soldier, so we may be sure he should be like other soldiers of our acquaintance; yet never in tragedy nor in comedy nor in nature was a soldier with his character. Take it in the author's own words: "some eternal villain / Some busy and insinuating rogue, / Some cogging, cozening slave, to get some office" [4.2.132–34]. Horace describes a soldier otherwise: *"Impiger, iracundus, inexorabilis, acer."*[5] Shakespeare knew his character of Iago was inconsistent. In this very play he pronounces, "If . . . / Thou dost deliver more or less than truth, / Thou art no soldier" [2.3.208–10].

This he knew, but to entertain the audience with something new and surprising, against common sense and nature, he would pass upon us a close, dissembling, false, insinuating rascal instead of an open-hearted, frank, plain-dealing soldier, a character constantly worn by them for some thousands of years in the world.

* * *

Nor is our poet more discreet in his Desdemona. He had chosen a soldier for his knave and a Venetian lady to be the fool.

This senator's daughter runs away to a carrier's inn, the Sagittary, with a blackamoor; is no sooner wedded to him, but the very night she beds him is importuning and teasing him for a young smock-faced Lieutenant Cassio. And though she perceives the Moor jealous of Cassio, yet she will not forbear, but still rings "Cassio, Cassio" in both his ears.

* * *

The first [characters] we see are Iago and Roderigo, by night in the streets of Venice. After growling a long time together, they

---

4. "Characters" and "manners" are (like "fable") technical terms—see 191–93 above.
5. "Impatient, hot-tempered, ruthless, fierce" (*Ars Poetica*, 121). Horace's point is that if "you introduce yet again the 'far-famed [Greek hero] Achilles,'" you should comply with the associations of the conventional epithets: "stick to tradition or see that your inventions be consistent" (in Edward Blakeney's 1928 translation).

resolve to tell Brabantio that his daughter is run away with the black-amoor. Iago and Roderigo were not of quality to be familiar with Brabantio, nor had any provocation from him to deserve a rude thing at their hands. Brabantio was a noble Venetian, one of the sovereign lords and principal persons in the government, peer to the most serene duke, one attended with more state, ceremony and punctilio than any English duke or nobleman in the government will pretend to. This misfortune in his daughter is so prodigious, so tender a point, as might puzzle the finest wit of the most "supersubtle" Venetian to touch upon it, or break the discovery to her father. See then how delicately Shakespeare minces the matter: [quotes 1.1.75–89: "what ho, Brabantio! . . . Arise, I say!"].

*   *   *

For the second act, our poet, having dispatched his affairs at Venice, shows the action next I know not how many leagues off in the island of Cyprus. The audience must be there too, and yet our Bays[6] had it never in his head to make any provision of transport ships for them.

In the days that the Old Testament was acted in Clerkenwell by the parish clerks of London, the Israelites might pass through the Red Sea.[7] But alas, at this time we have no Moses to bid the waters make way and to usher us along. Well, the absurdities of this kind break no bones. They may make fools of us; but do not hurt our morals.

*   *   *

But pass we to something of a more serious air and complexion. Othello and his bride are the first night no sooner warm in bed together, but a drunken quarrel happening in the garrison, two soldiers fight, and the general rises to part the fray. He swears: [quotes 2.3.194–207: "Now, by heaven . . . who began't?"].

In the days of yore, soldiers did not swear in this fashion. What should a soldier say farther when he swears, unless he blaspheme? Action should speak the rest. What follows must be *ex ore gladii*;[8] he is to rap out an oath, not wire draw and spin it out. By the style one might judge that Shakespeare's soldiers were never bred in a camp, but rather had belonged to some affidavit office. Consider also throughout this whole scene how the Moorish general proceeds in

6. Shakespeare, the Bard. In antiquity, the bay, or laurel wreath, was bestowed as a reward for poetic and other forms of achievement. Rymer is also alluding to Bays, the name of the playwright character in a popular contemporary spoof, Buckingham's *Rehearsal*.
7. Earlier in *A Short View*, Rymer had dismissed such "improbabilities" in the medieval dramatizations of biblical history.
8. That is, "from the mouth of the sword"—barracks talk or, again, action rather than speech.

examining into this rout; no Justice Clod-pate[9] could go on with more phlegm and deliberation. The very first night that he lies with the "Divine Desdemona" to be thus interrupted might provoke a man's Christian patience to swear in another style. But a Negro general is a man of strange mettle. Only his Venetian bride is a match for him. She understands that the soldiers in the garrison are by the ears together, and presently she at midnight is in amongst them.

> DESDEMONA   What is the matter, dear?
> OTHELLO   All's well now,
>   sweeting;
>   Come away to bed. [2.3.242–43]

In the beginning of this second act, before they had lain together, Desdemona was said to be "our Captain's Captain"; now they are no sooner in bed together but Iago is advising Cassio in these words: [quotes 2.3.303–12: "Our general's wife . . . her to splinter"; and 327–36: "'tis most easy . . . With his weak function"]. * * *
This kind of discourse implies an experience and long conversation, the honeymoon over, and a marriage of some standing. Would any man in his wits talk thus of a bridegroom and bride in the first night of their coming together?

Yet this is necessary for our poet; it would not otherwise serve his turn. This is the source, the foundation of his plot; hence is the spring and occasion for all the jealousy and bluster that ensues.

                                *   *   *

[Quotes Desdemona's supplication for Cassio, 3.3.54–61: "Good love, call him back. . . . on Wednesday morn."] After forty lines more at this rate, they part, and then comes the wonderful scene where Iago by shrugs, half words, and ambiguous reflections works Othello up to be jealous. One might think, after what we have seen, that there needs no great cunning, no great poetry and address, to make the Moor jealous. Such impatience, such a rout for a handsome young fellow the very morning after her marriage, must make him either to be jealous, or to take her for a changeling, below his jealousy. After this scene, it might strain the poet's skill to reconcile the couple and allay the jealousy. Iago can now only *actum agere* [play the part] and vex the audience with a nauseous repetition.

Whence comes it, then, that this is the top scene, the scene that raises *Othello* above all other tragedies in our theaters? It is purely from the action—from the mops and the mows, the grimace, the grins and gesticulation. Such scenes as this have made all the world run after Harlequin and Scaramuccio.[1]

9. That is, blockhead.
1. Stock types of mime shows, derived from the Italian commedia dell'arte.

*   *   *

"I have a pain upon my forehead, here" [3.3.286].

Michael Cassio came not from Venice in the ship with Desdemona, nor till this morning could be suspected of an opportunity with her. And 'tis now but dinner time, yet the Moor complains of his forehead. He might have set a guard on Cassio, or have locked up Desdemona, or have observed their carriage a day or two longer. He is on other occasions phlegmatic enough. This is very hasty. But after dinner we have a wonderful flight: [quotes 3.3.339–42: "What sense had I . . . on her lips"].

A little after this, says he: [quotes 3.3.410–26: "Give me a living reason . . . gave thee to the Moor!'"].

By the rapture of Othello, one might think that he raves, is not of sound memory, forgets that he has not yet been two nights in the matrimonial bed with Desdemona. But we find Iago, who should have a better memory, forging his lies after the very same mode. The very night of their marriage at Venice, the Moor and also Cassio were sent away to Cyprus. In the second act, Othello and his bride go the first time to bed. The third act opens the next morning. The parties have been in view to this moment. We saw the opportunity which was given for Cassio to speak his bosom to her; once, indeed, might go a great way with a Venetian. But once will not do the poet's business. The audience must suppose a great many bouts to make the plot operate. They must deny their senses, to reconcile it to common sense or make it any way consistent and hang together.

*   *   *

[Quotes 3.4.17–30: "Seek him . . . Drew all such humors from him."] By this manner of speech one would gather the couple had been yoked together a competent while. What might she say more had they cohabited and been man and wife seven years?

*   *   *

" 'Tis not a year or two shows us a man" [3.4.100].

As if for the first year or two Othello had not been jealous? This third act begins in the morning, at noon she drops the handkerchief, after dinner she misses it, and then follows all this outrage and horrible clutter about it. If we believe a small damsel in the last scene of this act, this day is effectually seven days. [Quotes 3.4.169–72: "What? keep a week away? . . . O weary reckoning!"]

Our poet is at this plunge, that whether this act contains the compass of one day, of seven days, or of seven years, or of all together, the repugnance and absurdity would be the same. *   *   *

* * *

Iago had some pretence to be discontent with Othello and Cassio, and what passed hitherto was the operation of revenge. Desdemona had never done him harm, always kind to him and to his wife, was his countrywoman, a dame of quality. For him to abet her murder shows nothing of a soldier, nothing of a man, nothing of nature in it. The ordinary of Newgate[2] never had the like monster to pass under his examination. Can it be any diversion to see a rogue beyond what the Devil ever finished? Or would it be any instruction to an audience? Iago could desire no better than to set Cassio and Othello, his two enemies, by the ears together, so he might have been revenged on them both at once; and choosing his own share the murder of Desdemona, he had the opportunity to play booty and save the poor harmless wretch.[3] But the poet must do everything by contraries to surprise the audience still with something horrible and prodigious beyond any human imagination. At this rate he must out-do the Devil to be a poet in the rank with Shakespeare.

* * *

"Alas, Iago, / What shall I do to win my lord again?" [4.2.150–51].

No woman bred out of a pigsty could talk so meanly. After this she is called to supper with Othello, Lodovico, etc. After that comes a filthy sort of pastoral scene, where the "wedding sheets" and song of "willow" and her mother's maid, poor Barbary, are not the least moving things in this entertainment. * * *

* * *

* * * A noble Venetian lady is to be murdered by our poet in sober sadness, purely for being a fool. No pagan poet but would have found some machine for her deliverance. Pegasus would have strained hard to have brought old Perseus on his back, time enough, to rescue this Andromeda from so foul a monster. Has our Christian poetry no generosity, nor bowels? Ha, Sir Lancelot! ha, St. George! will no ghost leave the shades for us in extremity, to save a distressed damsel?[4]

But for our comfort, however felonious is the heart, hear with what soft language he does approach her, with a candle in his hand:

---

2. The chaplain of Newgate prison, whose duty it was to prepare prisoners for death.
3. "Play booty . . . wretch": i.e., revenge himself on Cassio and Othello while sparing Desdemona.
4. Rymer refers to heroic rescues in Greek mythology (Perseus) and medieval romance (Sir Lancelot and St. George). His point is that Desdemona's undeserved death violates poetic justice—the complaint he returns to and sustains at the end.

"Put out the light, and then put out the light. / If I quench thee thou flaming minister, / I can again thy former light restore" [5.2.7–9].

Who would call him a barbarian, monster, savage? Is this a blackamoor? *Soles occidere & redire possunt*: the very soul and quintessence of Sir George Etherege.[5]

One might think the general should not glory much in this action, but make a hasty work on it and have turned his eyes away from so unsoldierly an execution. Yet is he all pause and deliberation, handles her as calmly and is as careful of her soul's health as it had been her father confessor. "Have you prayed to night, Desdemon?" [5.2.25]. But the suspense is necessary, that he might have a convenient while so to "roll his eyes" [5.2.39] and so to "gnaw his nether lip" [5.2.43] to the spectators. Besides the greater cruelty—*sub tam lentis maxillis*.[6]

But hark, a most tragical thing laid to her charge [quotes from 5.2.47–67: "That handkerchief . . . I saw the handkerchief"].

So much ado, so much stress, so much passion and repetition about a handkerchief. Why was not this called "The Tragedy of the Handkerchief"? What can be more absurd * * * ? * * * Had it been Desdemona's garter, the sagacious Moor might have smelled a rat; but the handkerchief is so remote a trifle no booby on this side Mauritania could make any consequence from it.

We may learn here that a woman never loses her tongue, even though after she is stifled. [Quotes 5.2.119–28: "O falsely, falsely murdered! . . . Commend me to my kind lord. O, farewell!"]

* * *

[M]ay we ask here what unnatural crime Desdemona or her parents had committed to bring this judgment down upon her, to wed a blackamoor and, innocent, to be thus cruelly murdered by him? What instruction can we make out of this catastrophe? Or whither must our reflection lead us? Is not this to envenom and sour our spirits, to make us repine and grumble at Providence and the government of the world? If this be our end, what boots it to be virtuous?

Desdemona dropped the handkerchief and missed it that very day after her marriage. It might have been rumpled up with her wedding sheets, and this night that she lay in her wedding sheets

5. Poet and playwright (1636?–1662?) much admired for his wittily satiric but affectionate treatment of love; sometimes referred to as "gentle George" or "easy Etherege." Rymer quotes a well-known line, "Suns can set and rise again," from a love lyric by Catullus that continues, "For us, once our brief light has set; / There's one unending night for sleeping' (Trans. Guy Lee, *The Poems of Catullus*. Oxford: Clarendon, 1990, 7).
6. "To be ground by jaws that crunch so slowly." Reportedly said by the Emperor Augustus anticipating the fate of Rome under Tiberius's rule (Suetonius, *Tiberius* 21.2).

the fairy napkin (whilst Othello was stifling her) might have started up to disarm his fury and stop his ungracious mouth. Then might she (in a trance for fear) have lain as dead. Then might he, believing her dead, touched with remorse, have honestly cut his own throat by the good leave and with the applause of all the spectators, who might thereupon have gone home with a quiet mind, admiring the beauty of Providence, fairly and truly represented in the theater.

* * *

[At] the end of the play we meet with nothing but blood and butchery, described much-what to the style of the last speeches and confessions of the persons executed at Tyburn,[7] with this difference—that there we have the fact and the due course of justice, whereas our poet, against all justice and reason, against all law, humanity and nature, in a barbarous arbitrary way, executes and makes havoc of his subjects, hab-nab [at random] as they come to hand. Desdemona dropped her handkerchief; therefore she must be stifled. Othello, by law to be broken on the wheel, by the foe's cunning escapes with cutting his own throat. Cassio, for I know not what, comes off with a broken shin. Iago is not yet killed, because there never yet was such a villain alive. The Devil, if once he brings a man to be dipped in a deadly sin, lets him alone to take his course, and now when the "Foul Fiend" has done with him, our wise authors take the sinner into their poetical service, there to accomplish him and do the Devil's drudgery.

Philosophy tells us it is a principle in the nature of man to be grateful.

History may tell us that John an Oaks, John a Stile,[8] or Iago were ungrateful. Poetry is to follow nature. Philosophy must be his guide. History and fact in particular cases of John an Oaks or John of Styles are of no warrant or direction for a poet. Therefore Aristotle is always telling us that poetry is * * * more general and abstracted, is led more by the philosophy, the reason and nature of things, than history, which only records things, higgledy-piggledy, right or wrong as they happen. History might without any preamble or difficulty say that Iago was ungrateful. Philosophy then calls him unnatural, but the poet is, not without huge labor and preparation, to expose the monster and after show the divine vengeance executed upon him. The poet is not to add willful murder to his ingratitude: he has not

7. Tyburn Tree, site of public executions in London from the llth through the 18th centuries.
8. "John an Oaks" and "John a Stile" (or "John of Styles") are conventional designations of insignificant individuals: Mr. Smith, Mr. Jones, Joe Blow.

antidote enough for the poison. His Hell and Furies are not punishment sufficient for one single crime of that bulk and aggravation.[9]

*   *   *

What can remain with the audience to carry home with them from this sort of poetry for their use and edification? How can it work unless (instead of settling the mind and purging our passions) to delude our sense, disorder our thoughts, addle our brain, pervert our affections, hair our imaginations, corrupt our appetite, and fill our head with vanity, confusion, tintamarra,[1] and jingle-jangle beyond what all the parish clerks of London, with their Old Testament farces and interludes in Richard II's time, could ever pretend to? Our only hopes for the good of their souls can be that these people go to the playhouse as they do to church—to sit still, look on one another, make no reflection, nor mind the play more than they would a sermon.

There is in this play some burlesque, some humor and ramble of comical wit, some show and some mimicry to divert the spectators, but the tragical part is plainly none other than a bloody farce without salt or savor.

CHARLES GILDON (1665–1724)

[Comments on Rymer's *Othello*][†]

From the Preface

In the hurry of writing, I forgot one very good defense of a passage in the *Othello* of Shakespeare, which Mr. Rymer has loudly exclaimed against, and which a very good friend of mine advised me to insert in the preface; 'tis this: "Awake! what ho, Brabantio! . . . an old black ram / Is tupping your white ewe" [1.1.76 and 85–86].

Mr. Rymer will have it that a rap at the door would better express Iago's meaning than all that noise; but if Mr. Rymer would consult

---

9. Rymer's insistence that tragedy transform historical fact into ethical or philosophical precept was commonplace; the material elided from this passage includes a misquotation of Aristotle's *Poetics*, the effective origin of the claim.
1. Once again, Rymer returns to the medieval mystery plays ("Richard II's time" was the end of the 14th century) in objecting to *Othello*'s failure to achieve neoclassical clarity and control. *Hair*: to line with fur; presumably meant to suggest that the play is too provocative. *Tintamarra*: uproar.
† The first two passages are from the preface and the chapter "Some Reflections on Mr. Rymer's *Short View*" in Gildon's *Miscellaneous Letters and Essays* (1694); the third is from his *Remarks on the Plays of Shakespeare* (1710). Spelling and punctuation have been modernized, and all quotations from *Othello* modified to conform with this Norton Critical Edition. All notes are the editor's. For information about Gildon, his criticism, and its textual sources, see 380 below.

the reason of the thing, he'll find that the noise Roderigo and Iago made contributed very much to their design of surprising and alarming Brabantio, by that to transport him from consideration to a violent passion.

* * *

From "Some Reflections"

As soon as Mr. Rymer's book came to my hands, I resolved to make some reflections upon it, though more to show my will than my abilities. But finding Mr. Dennis had almost promised the world a vindication of the incomparable Shakespeare, I quitted the design.[1]

* * *

But expecting thus long without hearing any farther of it, * * * [and] since I find some build an assurance on this general silence of all the friends of Shakespeare that Mr. Rymer's objections are unanswerable, I resolved to bestow two or three days on an essay to prove the contrary. * * *

* * *

Had our critic entertained but common justice for the heroes of his own country, he would have set Shakespeare's faults in their true light and distinguished betwixt his and the vices of the age. * * * This is the reason that most of his tragedies have a mixture of something comical: the Delilah of the age must be brought in, the clown and the valet jesting with their betters, if he resolved not to disoblige the auditors.[2] And I'm assured from very good hands that the person that acted Iago was in much esteem for a comedian, which made Shakespeare put several words and expressions into his part (perhaps not so agreeable to his character) to make the audience laugh, who had not yet learnt to endure to be serious a whole play. This was the occasion of that particular place so much hooted at by our historiographer royal: "Awake! what ho, Brabantio! . . . an old black ram / Is tupping your white ewe" [1.1.76–86]. * * *

* * *

1. John Dennis (1657–1734), probably the "very good friend" mentioned in Gildon's preface, published his *Impartial Critick* in 1693, taking on Rymer's *Short View* in general terms, but not dealing with the detailed attack on *Othello*.
2. The appeal of low comedy is associated with female temptation, like Delilah's of Samson (in Judges 16). Samuel Johnson, commenting on Shakespeare's inability to resist punning, said that a "quibble was to him the fatal Cleopatra for which [like the Roman general Marc Antony] he lost the world and was content to lose it."

To begin with the fable (as our critic has done), I must tell him he has as falsely, as ridiculously represented it, which I shall endeavor to put in a juster light.

                              *   *   *

The fable to be perfect must be admirable and probable. * * *
I suppose none will deny that it is admirable—that is, composed of incidents that happen not every day. Its antagonist concedes as much. There is therefore nothing but the probability of it attacked by him. * * *

                              *   *   *

All the reason he gives, or rather implies, for the first improbability is that 'tis not likely the state of Venice would employ a "Moor" (taking him for a Mohammedan) against the Turk, because of the mutual bond of religion. He indeed says not so, but takes it for granted that Othello must be rather for the Turkish interest than the Venetian, because a Moor. But I think (nor does he oppose it with any reason) the character of the Venetian state being to employ strangers in their wars, it gives sufficient ground to our poet to suppose a Moor employed by them as well as a German[3]—that is, a Christian Moor, as Othello is represented by our poet—for from such a Moor there could be no just fear of treachery in favor of the Mohammedans. * * * Why therefore an African Christian may not by the Venetians be supposed to be as zealous against the Turks as a European Christian I cannot imagine. * * *

                              *   *   *

'Tis granted a Negro here does seldom rise above a trumpeter, nor often perhaps higher at Venice. But then that proceeds from the vice of mankind, which is the poet's duty as he informs us to correct, and to represent things as they should be, not as they are. Now 'tis certain there is no reason in the nature of things why a Negro of equal birth and merit should not be on an equal bottom with a German, Hollander, Frenchman, etc. The poet, therefore, ought to do justice to nations as well as persons and set to rights, which the common course of things confounds. The same reason stands in force for this, as for punishing the wicked and making the virtuous fortunate, which as Rapin[4] and all critics agree the poet ought to do, though it

---

3. A close relative, as in Iago's "jennets for germans" (1.1.110). Gildon's point is that Othello, though a Moor, is related by religious kinship and thus not altogether a "stranger" or foreigner.
4. René Rapin, an influential neoclassical critic of the 17th century, whose *Reflexions sur la poétique* (1674) Rymer had translated. Gildon is turning Rymer's authorities and ideas about "poetical justice" back against him.

generally happens otherways. The poet has therefore well chosen a polite people to call off this customary barbarity of confining nations, without regard to their virtue and merits, to slavery and contempt for the mere accident of their complexion.

* * * I shall proceed to the probability of Desdemona's love for the Moor, which I think is something more evident against him. Whatever he aims at in his inconsistent ramble against this may be reduced to the person and the manner. Against the person he quotes you two verses out of Horace that have no * * * reference to this * * * unless he can prove that the color of a man alters his species and turns him into a beast or a devil. 'Tis such a vulgar error, so criminal a fondness of ourselves, to allow nothing of humanity to any but our own acquaintance of the fairer hew. * * * Any man that has conversed with the best travels or read anything of the history of those parts on the continent of Africa discovered by the Portuguese must be so far from robbing the Negroes of some countries there of humanity, that they must grant them not only greater heroes, nicer observers of honor, and all the moral virtues that distinguished the old Romans, but also much better Christians (where Christianity is professed) than we of Europe generally are. They move by a noble principle, more open, free, and generous, and not such slaves to sordid interest.

After all this, Othello being of "royal blood" and a Christian, where is the disparity of the match? If either side is advanced, 'tis Desdemona. And why must this Prince, though a Christian and of known and experienced virtue, courage, and conduct, be made such a monster that the Venetian lady can't love him without perverting nature? Experience tells us that there's nothing more common than matches of this kind, where the whites and blacks cohabit, as in both the Indies; and even here at home, ladies that have not wanted white adorers have indulged their amorous dalliances with their sable lovers without any of Othello's qualifications, which is proof enough that nature and custom have not put any such unpassable bar betwixt creatures of the same kind because of different colors, which I hope will remove the improbability of the person, especially when the powerful auxiliaries of extraordinary merit and virtues come to plead with a generous mind.

The probability of the person being thus confirmed, I shall now consider that of the manner of his obtaining her love. * * * [W]e may easily suppose the story of his fortunes and dangers would make an impression of pity and admiration at least on the bosom of a woman of a noble and generous nature. No man of any generous principle but must be touched at suffering virtue and value the noble sufferer, whose courage and bravery bear him through uncommon trials and extraordinary dangers. Nor would it have less force on a woman of any principle of honor and tenderness; she must be moved and pleased with the narration, she must admire his constant virtue, and admiration is the first step to love, which will easily gain upon those who have entertained it.

* * *

[S]hould all I have said fail of clearing the probability of the fable from Mr. Rymer's objections, yet ought not that to rob Shakespeare of his due character of being a poet and a great genius, unless he will for the same reason deny those prerogatives to Homer and Sophocles. * * * [T]he latter, as Rapin justly observes, has not kept to probability even in his best performance, I mean in his *Oedipus Tyrannus*;[5] for as Rapin has it, Oedipus "ought not to have been ignorant of the assassination of Laius. The ignorance he's in of the murder, which makes all the beauty of the intrigue, is not probable." And if a man would play the droll with this fable of *Oedipus*, it would furnish full as ridiculous a comment as witty Mr. Rymer has done from this of *Othello*; and sure, I can't err in imitating so great a critic.

First then, let all men before they defend themselves on the highway think well of what they do, lest not being mathematically sure he's at home he kill his own father. * * *

Next, let every younger brother that ventures to ride in another man's boots be very circumspect, lest he marries his own mother.

* * *

These are much more the consequence of this fable of *Oedipus* than those wondrous truths he draws from that of *Othello*. Nay, the moral Sophocles concludes his *Oedipus* with will serve as justly for *Othello,* viz. "That no man can be called happy before his death." But the whole fable of *Oedipus,* though much admired, is so very singular and improbable that 'tis scarce possible it ever could have happened; on the other hand, the fatal jealousy of Othello and the revenge of Iago are the natural consequences of our ungoverned passions, which by a prospect of such tragical effects of their being indulged may be the better regulated and governed by us. So that though *Othello* ends not so formally with a moral sentence, as *Oedipus* does, yet it sets out one of much greater value. * * *

* * *

But I have dwelled so long on the fable that I have not time enough to discuss the other parts, as the characters. * * * Nor can

---

5. *Oedipus the King* (Latin): ancient Greek play by Sophocles in which Oedipus unknowingly kills Laius, his father, and marries Jocasta, his mother.

I proceed to a particular consideration of all the characters of the play at this time. Desdemona, I think, is the most faulty; but since our antagonist will have Iago the most "intolerable," I shall confine myself to that.

* * *

* * * The characters or manners, as the same Rapin observes, are to be drawn from experience, and that tells us that they differ in soldiers according to their nature and discipline; that also tells us that the camp is not free from designs, supplantings, and all the effects of the most criminal of passions. * * *

* * * But granting that Iago's character is defective something in the manners, * * * [and] though Mr. Rymer is so severe to deny that the character of Iago is that of a soldier, because so different from his military acquaintance, yet I'm confident he would take it extremely amiss if I should deny him to be a critic because so contrary to all the critics that I have met with, playing the merry droll instead of giving serious and solid reasons for what he advances.

From Remarks on the Plays of Shakespeare

* * *

I have drawn the fable with as much favor to the author as I possibly could, yet I must own that the faults found in it by Mr. Rymer are but too visible for the most part. That of making a Negro of the hero or chief character of the play would shock anyone; for it is not the rationale of the thing and the deductions that may thence be brought to diminish the opposition betwixt the different colors of mankind that would be sufficient to take away that which is shocking in this story, since this entirely depends on custom which makes it so. And on common women's admitting a Negro to a commerce with her everyone almost starts at the choice; much more in a woman of virtue; and indeed Iago, Brabantio, &c., have shown such reasons as make it monstrous. I wonder Shakespeare saw this in the persons of his play and not in his own judgment. If Othello had been made deformed and not over young but no black it had removed most of the absurdities, but now it pleases only by prescription. 'Tis possible that an innocent tender young woman who knew little of the world might be won by the brave actions of a gallant man not to regard his age or deformities; but nature, or (what is all one in this case) custom, having put such a bar as so opposite a color, it takes away our pity from her and only raises our indignation against him. * * *

Whether the motives of Othello's jealousy be strong enough to free him from the imputation of levity and folly I will not determine, since jealousy is born often of very slight occasions, especially in the breasts of men of those warmer climates. Yet this must be said: Shakespeare has managed the scene [3.3] so well that it is that alone which supports his play and imposes on the audience so very successfully that, till a reformation of the stage comes, I believe it will always be kindly received.

Iago is a Character that can hardly be admitted into the tragic scene—though it is qualified by his being pushed on by revenge, ambition, and jealousy—because he seems to declare himself a settled villain. * * *

* * *

The Moor has not bedded his lady till he come to Cyprus, nay it was not done [cites "That profit's yet to come," 2.3.10], and yet it is before and after urged that she was or might be sated with him. But those little forgetfulnesses are not worth minding.

* * *

SAMUEL JOHNSON (1709–1784)

[Shakespeare, the Rules, and *Othello*]†

From the Preface

* * *

Whether Shakespeare knew the unities and rejected them by design or deviated from them by happy ignorance, it is, I think, impossible to decide, and useless to inquire. We may reasonably suppose that, when he rose to notice, he did not want [lack] the counsels and admonitions of scholars and critics, and that he at last deliberately persisted in a practice which he might have begun by chance. As nothing is essential to the fable, but unity of action, and as the unities of time and place arise evidently from false assumptions and, by circumscribing the extent of the drama, lessen its variety, I cannot think it much to be lamented that they were not known by him or not observed. Nor if such another poet could arise should I very vehemently reproach him that his first act passed at Venice and his next in Cyprus. Such violations of rules merely positive[1] become

---

† From Johnson's edition of Shakespeare (London, 1765). Spelling and punctuation have been modernized, and all quotations from *Othello* modified to conform with this Norton Critical Edition. All notes are the editor's. For information about Johnson, his criticism, and its textual sources, see 380 below.

1. *Merely positive:* conventional; "settled by arbitrary appointment" in Johnson's *Dictionary.*

the comprehensive genius of Shakespeare, and such censures are suitable to the minute and slender criticism of Voltaire.[2]

* * *

Voltaire expresses his wonder that our author's extravagances are endured by a nation which has seen the tragedy of *Cato*. Let him be answered that Addison speaks the language of poets and Shakespeare of men.[3] We find in *Cato* innumerable beauties which enamor us of its author, but we see nothing that acquaints us with human sentiments or human actions; we place it with the fairest and the noblest progeny which judgment propagates by conjunction with learning, but *Othello* is the vigorous and vivacious offspring of observation impregnated by genius.

* * *

From Notes on *Othello*

Wherein of antres vast and deserts idle, / Rough quarries, rocks and hills whose heads touch heaven [1.3.139–40; Johnson quotes approvingly and expands on William Warburton, whose 1747 edition dismisses Rymer's ridicule of this passage as based on ignorance of "history"—that is, of the "fashion" in Shakespeare's time for exotic details about newly discovered lands].

Whoever ridicules this account of the progress of love shows his ignorance not only of history but of nature and manners. It is no wonder that in any age or in any nation a lady—recluse, timorous and delicate—should desire to hear of events and scenes which she could never see and should admire the man who had endured dangers and performed actions which, however great, were yet magnified by her timidity.

They're close dilations, working from the heart / That passion cannot rule [3.3.126–27].

The old copies give "dilations," except that the earlier quarto has "denotements," which was the author's first expression, afterwards changed by him, not to "dilations," but to "delations"; to *occult* and *secret accusations*, "working" involuntarily "from the heart," which, though resolved to conceal the fault, "cannot rule" its "passion" of resentment.

---

2. Voltaire is the pen name of François-Marie Arouet (1694–1778), the eminent French philosopher who admired Shakespeare but believed him lacking in the classical artistry of the great French tragedians of the 17th century.
3. Joseph Addison (1672–1719) was a great influence on early-18th-century taste through his periodical *The Spectator*. *Cato*, his admired classical drama, was written for production in 1713.

She did deceive her father, marrying you, / And when she seemed to shake, and fear your looks, / She loved them most [3.3.208–10].

This and the following argument of Iago ought to be deeply impressed on every reader. Deceit and falsehood, whatever conveniences they may for a time promise or produce, are in the sum of life obstacles to happiness. Those who profit by the cheat distrust the deceiver, and the act by which kindness is sought puts an end to confidence.

The same objection may be made with a lower degree of strength against the imprudent generosity of disproportionate marriages. When the first heat of passion is over, it is easily succeeded by suspicion that the same violence of inclination which caused one irregularity may stimulate to another; and those who have shown that their passions are too powerful for their prudence will, with very slight appearances against them, be censured as not very likely to restrain them by virtue.

Let him command / And to obey shall be in me remorse, / What bloody business ever [3.3.468–70].

Iago devotes himself to "wrong'd Othello," and says, "Let him command whatever bloody business," and in me it shall be an act not of cruelty but "of tenderness to obey him"; not of malice to others, but of "tenderness" for him. If this sense be thought too violent, I see nothing better than to follow Mr. Pope's reading ["*Not* to obey"] as it is improved by Mr. Theobald ["*Nor* to obey"].[4]

'Tis not a year or two shows us a man [3.4.100].

From this line it may be conjectured that the author intended the action of this play to be considered as longer than is marked by any note of time. Since their arrival at Cyprus, to which they were hurried on their wedding night, the fable seems to have been in one continual progress, nor can I see any vacuity into which a "year or two," or even a month or two, could be put. On the night of Othello's arrival a feast was proclaimed; at that feast Cassio was degraded and immediately applies to Desdemona to get him restored. Iago indeed advises Othello to hold him off a while, but there is no reason to think that he had been held off long. A little longer interval would increase the probability of the story, though it might violate the rules of the drama.

Nature would not / invest herself in such shadowing passion / without some instruction [4.1.39–41].

4. For details about Pope's and Theobald's early-18th-century editions of Shakespeare, see 4 and 5 above.

There has always prevailed in the world an opinion that when any great calamity happens at a distance notice is given of it to the sufferer by some dejection or perturbation of mind, of which he discovers no external cause. This is ascribed to that general communication of one part of the universe with another which is called sympathy and antipathy; or to the secret monition, "instruction," and influence of a Superior Being, which superintends the order of nature and of life. Othello says, "Nature could not invest herself in such shadowing passion, without *instruction*. It is not words that shake me thus." This passion, which spreads its clouds over me, is the effect of some agency more than the operation of words; it is one of those notices which men have of unseen calamities.

It is the cause, it is the cause, my soul. / Let me not name it to you, you chaste stars. / It is the cause [5.2.1–3].

The abruptness of this soliloquy makes it obscure. The meaning, I think, is this. "I am here," says Othello in his mind, "overwhelmed with horror. What is the reason of this perturbation? Is it want of resolution to do justice? Is it the dread of shedding blood? No; it is not the action that shocks me, but it is the cause, *it is the cause, my soul; let me not name it to you, ye chaste stars! it is the cause*."

This sorrow's heavenly: / It strikes where it doth love [5.2.21–22].

This tenderness, with which I lament the punishment which justice compels me to inflict, is a holy passion.

I wish these two lines could be honestly ejected. It is the fate of Shakespeare to counteract his own pathos.

O perjured woman! thou dost stone my heart, / And makes me call what I intend to do / A murder, which I thought a sacrifice [5.2.64–66].

This line is difficult. "Thou hast hardened my heart and makest me" kill thee with the rage of a "murderer," when "I thought to have sacrificed thee" to justice with the calmness of a priest striking a victim.

It must not be omitted that one of the elder quartos reads, "thou dost stone *thy* heart," which I suspect to be genuine. The meaning then will be, "thou forcest me" to dismiss thee from the world in the state of the "murdered" without preparation for death, "when I intended" that thy punishment should have been "a sacrifice" atoning for thy crime.

I am glad that I have ended my revisal of this dreadful scene. It is not to be endured.

That she with Cassio hath the act of shame / A thousand times committed [5.2.217–18].

This is another passage which seems to suppose a longer space comprised in the action of this play than the scenes include.

Final summary comment:

The beauties of this play impress themselves so strongly upon the attention of the reader that they can draw no aid from critical illustration. The fiery openness of Othello, magnanimous, artless, and credulous, boundless in his confidence, ardent in his affection, inflexible in his resolution, and obdurate in his revenge; the cool malignity of Iago, silent in his resentment, subtle in his designs, and studious at once of his interest and his vengeance; the soft simplicity of Desdemona, confident of merit and conscious of innocence, her artless perseverance in her suit, and her slowness to suspect that she can be suspected are such proofs of Shakespeare's skill in human nature as, I suppose, it is vain to seek in any modern writer. The gradual progress which Iago makes in the Moor's conviction and the circumstances which he employs to inflame him are so artfully natural that, though it will perhaps not be said of him as he says of himself that he is "a man not easily jealous," yet we cannot but pity him when at last we find him "perplexed in the extreme."

There is always danger lest wickedness conjoined with abilities should steal upon esteem, though it misses of approbation; but the character of Iago is so conducted that he is from the first scene to the last hated and despised.

Even the inferior characters of this play would be very conspicuous in any other piece, not only for their justness but their strength. Cassio is brave, benevolent, and honest, ruined only by his want of stubbornness to resist an insidious invitation. Roderigo's suspicious credulity and impatient submission to the cheats which he sees practiced upon him and which by persuasion he suffers to be repeated exhibit a strong picture of a weak mind betrayed by unlawful desires to a false friend; and the virtue of Emilia is such as we often find worn loosely but not cast off, easy to commit small crimes but quickened and alarmed at atrocious villainies.

The scenes from the beginning to the end are busy, varied by happy interchanges, and regularly promoting the progression of the story; and the narrative in the end, though it tells but what is known already, yet is necessary to produce the death of Othello.

Had the scene opened in Cyprus and the preceding incidents been occasionally related, there had been little wanting to a drama of the most exact and scrupulous regularity.

CHARLES LAMB (1775–1834)

[Othello's Color: Theatrical versus Literary Representation]†

* * *

Lear is essentially impossible to be represented on a stage. But how many dramatic personages are there in Shakespeare which, though more tractable and feasible (if I may so speak) than Lear, yet from some circumstance, some adjunct to their character, are improper to be shown to our bodily eye. Othello, for instance. Nothing can be more soothing, more flattering to the nobler parts of our nature, than to read of a young Venetian lady of highest extraction, through the force of love and from a sense of merit in him whom she loved, laying aside every consideration of kindred and country and color, and wedding with a *coal-black Moor* (for such he is represented, in the imperfect state of knowledge respecting foreign countries in those days, compared with our own, or in compliance with popular notions, though the Moors are now well enough known to be by many shades less unworthy of a white woman's fancy). It is the perfect triumph of virtue over accidents, of the imagination over the senses. She sees Othello's color in his mind. But upon the stage, when the imagination is no longer the ruling faculty, but we are left to our poor unassisted senses, I appeal to everyone that has seen Othello played whether he did not, on the contrary, sink Othello's mind in his color; and whether he did not find something extremely revolting in the courtship and wedded caresses of Othello and Desdemona; and whether the actual sight of the thing did not over-weigh all that beautiful compromise which we make in reading. And the reason it should do so is obvious, because there is just so much reality presented to our senses as to give a perception of disagreement, with not enough of belief in the internal motives—all that which is unseen—to overpower and reconcile the first and obvious prejudices.[1] What we see upon a stage is body and bodily action; what we

---

† From "On the Tragedies of Shakespeare, Considered with Reference to Their Fitness for Stage Representation" (*The Reflecter*, 1811). Spelling and punctuation have been modernized. For information about Lamb, his criticism, and its textual sources, see 381 below.

1. The error of supposing that because Othello's color does not offend us in the reading it should also not offend us in the seeing is just such a fallacy as supposing that an Adam and Eve in a picture shall affect us just as they do in the poem. But in the poem we for a while have paradisiacal senses given us, which vanish when we see a man and his wife without clothes in the picture. The painters themselves feel this, as is apparent by the awkward shifts they have recourse to, to make them look not quite naked; by a sort of prophetic anachronism antedating the invention of fig leaves. So in the reading of the play, we see with Desdemona's eyes; in the seeing of it, we are forced to look with our own.

are conscious of in reading is almost exclusively the mind and its movements; and this I think may sufficiently account for the very different sort of delight with which the same play so often affects us in the reading and the seeing.

* * *

WILLIAM HAZLITT (1778–1830)

[Iago, Heroic Tragedy, and Othello][†]

From "On Mr. Kean's Iago" and
"On Mr. Kean's Iago (Concluded)"

* * * The character of Iago, in fact, belongs to a class of characters common to Shakespeare, and at the same time peculiar to him, namely, that of great intellectual activity, accompanied with a total want of moral principle, and therefore displaying itself at the constant expense of others, making use of reason as a pander to will—employing its ingenuity and its resources to palliate its own crimes, and aggravate the faults of others, and seeking to confound the practical distinctions of right and wrong, by referring them to some overstrained standard of speculative refinement. Some persons, more nice than wise, have thought the whole of the character of Iago unnatural. Shakespeare, who was quite as good a philosopher as he was a poet, thought otherwise. He knew that the love of power, which is another name for the love of mischief, was natural to man. He would know this as well or better than if it had been demonstrated to him by a logical diagram, merely from seeing children paddle in the dirt, or kill flies for sport.[1] We might ask those who think the character of Iago not natural why they go to see it performed, but from the interest it excites, the sharper edge which it sets on their curiosity and imagination. Why do we go to see tragedies in general? Why do we always read the accounts in the newspapers of dreadful fires and shocking murders, but for the same reason? Why do so many frequent executions and trials, or why do the lower classes almost

---

† The first excerpt is taken from two theatrical reviews published in 1814, the second from a book published in 1817 (details on 385 below). Spelling and punctuation have been modernized. Most of the quotations from *Othello* have been modified to conform with this Norton Critical Edition. Some of Hazlitt's quotations from memory are left uncorrected, but they include a reference to the act, scene, and line numbers of this edition. All notes are the editor's, unless otherwise specified. For information about Hazlitt, his criticism, and its textual sources, see 381 below.

1. An echo of Gloucester in *King Lear* 4.1.37–38: "As flies to wanton boys are we to the gods; / They kill us for their sport."

universally take delight in barbarous sports and cruelty to animals, but because there is a natural tendency in the mind to strong excitement, a desire to have its faculties roused and stimulated to the utmost? Whenever this principle is not under the restraint of humanity or the sense of moral obligation, there are no excesses to which it will not of itself give rise, without the assistance of any other motive, either of passion or self-interest. Iago is only an extreme instance of the kind; that is, of diseased intellectual activity, with an almost perfect indifference to moral good or evil, or rather with a preference of the latter, because it falls more in with his favorite propensity, gives greater zest to his thoughts and scope to his actions. Be it observed, too (for the sake of those who are for squaring all human actions by the maxims of Rochefoucault[2]), that he is quite or nearly as indifferent to his own fate as to that of others; that he runs all risks for a trifling and doubtful advantage, and is himself the dupe and victim of his ruling passion—an incorrigible love of mischief, an insatiable craving after action of the most difficult and dangerous kind. Our ancient is a philosopher, who fancies that a lie that kills has more point in it than an alliteration or an antithesis; who thinks a fatal experiment on the peace of a family a better thing than watching the palpitations in the heart of a flea in an air-pump; who plots the ruin of his friends as an exercise for his understanding, and stabs men in the dark to prevent *ennui*. * * *

*   *   *

The general groundwork of the character of Iago as it appears to us is not absolute malignity but a want of moral principle, or an indifference to the real consequences of the actions which the meddling perversity of his disposition and love of immediate excitement lead him to commit. He is an amateur of tragedy in real life, and instead of exercising his ingenuity on imaginary characters or forgotten incidents, he takes the bolder and more desperate course of getting up his plot at home, casts the principal parts among his nearest friends and connections, and rehearses it in downright earnest, with steady nerves and unabated resolution. The character is a complete abstraction of the intellectual from the moral being; or, in other words, consists in an absorption of every common feeling

2. La Rochefoucauld (1613–1680), the French writer and moralist, was known for his *Maximes et Réflexions Morales*, the unillusioned tone of which is fairly represented by the maxim Jonathan Swift used as the starting point for his "Verses on the Death of Dr. Swift": "In the misfortunes of our best friends, we find something not altogether displeasing." Hazlitt believed that the maxims "contain a good deal of truth" in acknowledging "the *mixed* nature of motives," but then falsely "argue as if they were *simple*, that is, had but one principle, and that principle the worst"; and that Shakespeare's "The web of our life is of a mingled yarn" offers a "better account of the matter." See "On Rochefoucault's Maxims" in Howe, 20: 36–41, 36–37.

in the virulence of his understanding, the deliberate willfulness of his purposes, and in his restless untamable love of mischievous contrivance. * * *

* * *

* * * One of his most characteristic speeches is that immediately after the marriage of Othello: [quotes 1.1.63–70: "What a full fortune . . . lose some color"].

The pertinacious logical following up of his favorite principle in this passage is admirable. In the next, his imagination runs riot in the mischief he is plotting and breaks out into the wildness and impetuosity of real enthusiasm: [quotes 1.1.71–74: "Here is her father's house. . . . populous cities"].

* * * One of his most frequent topics, on which he is rich indeed and in descanting on which his spleen serves him for a muse, is the disproportionate match between Desdemona and the Moor. This is brought forward in the first scene and is never lost sight of afterwards [quotes 1.1.79–89: "What is the reason . . . Arise, I say!" and adds "And so on to the end of the passage"].

Now all this goes on springs well oiled. Mr. Kean's mode of giving the passage had the tightness of a drumhead and was muffled (perhaps purposely so) into the bargain.

This is a clue to the character of the lady which Iago is not at all ready to part with. He recurs to it again in the second act when, in answer to his insinuations against Desdemona, Roderigo says, "I cannot believe that in her; she's full of most blessed condition." Iago: "Blessed fig's-end! The wine she drinks is made of grapes. If she had been blessed, she would never have loved the Moor" [2.1.245–49].

And again with still more effect and spirit afterwards, when he takes advantage of this very suggestion arising in Othello's own breast: [quotes 3.3.229–35: "And yet how nature . . . thoughts unnatural"]. This is probing to the quick. "Our Ancient" here turns the character of poor Desdemona, as it were, inside out. It is certain that nothing but the genius of Shakespeare could have preserved the entire interest and delicacy of the part and have even drawn an additional elegance and dignity from the peculiar circumstances in which she is placed. The character has always had the greatest charm for minds of the finest sensibility.

For our own part, we are a little of Iago's council in this matter; and all circumstances considered and Platonics out of the question, if we were to cast the complexion of Desdemona physiognomically, we should say that she had a very fair skin and very light auburn hair, inclining to yellow! We at the same time give her infinite credit for purity and delicacy of sentiment; but it so happens that purity and grossness "nearly are allied / And thin partitions do their bounds divide."[3] Yet the reverse does not hold; so uncertain and undefinable a thing is morality. It is no wonder that Iago had some contempt for it, "who knew all qualities of human dealings with a learned spirit" [cf. 3.3.261].[4] There is considerable gaiety and ease in his dialogue with Emilia and Desdemona on their landing. It is then holiday time with him, but yet the general satire will be acknowledged (at least by one half of our readers) to be biting enough, and his idea of his own character is finely expressed in what he says to Desdemona when she asks him how he would praise her—'O, gentle lady, do not put me to't, / For I am nothing if not critical" [2.1.118–19]. * * *

The habitual licentiousness of Iago's conversation is not to be traced to the pleasure he takes in gross or lascivious images, but to a desire of finding out the worst side of everything and of proving himself an overmatch for appearances. He has none of "the milk of human kindness" in his composition. His imagination refuses everything that has not a strong infusion of the most unpalatable ingredients, and his moral constitution digests only poisons. Virtue or goodness or whatever has the least "relish of salvation in it"[5] is, to his depraved appetite, sickly and insipid, and he even resents the good opinion entertained of his own integrity, as if it were an affront cast on the masculine sense and spirit of his character. Thus at the meeting between Othello and Desdemona he exclaims, "O, you are well tuned now; but I'll set down the pegs that make this music, / As honest as I am" [2.1.197–99]—deriving an indirect triumph over the want of penetration in others from the consciousness of his own villainy.

---

3. Hazlitt echoes John Dryden's *Absalom and Achitophel* (1681): "Great wits are sure to madness near allied, / And thin partitions do their bounds divide" (163–64).
4. If Desdemona really "saw her husband's visage in his mind," or fell in love with the abstract idea of "his virtues and his valiant parts" [cf. 1.3.250–51], she was the only woman on record, either before or since, who ever did so. Shakespeare's want of penetration in supposing that those are the sort of things that gain the affections might perhaps have drawn a smile from the ladies, if honest Iago had not checked it by suggesting a different explanation. It should seem by this as if the rankness and gross impropriety of the personal connection, the difference in age, features, color, constitution, instead of being the obstacle, had been the motive of the refinement of her choice and had, by beginning at the wrong end, subdued her to the amiable qualities of her lord. Iago is indeed a most learned and irrefragable doctor on the subject of love, which he defines to be "merely a lust of the blood and a permission of the will" [1.3.332–33]. The idea that love has its source in moral or intellectual excellence, in good nature or good sense, or has any connection with sentiment or refinement of any kind, is one of those preposterous and willful errors which ought to be extirpated for the sake of those few persons who alone are likely to suffer by it, whose romantic generosity and delicacy ought not to be sacrificed to the baseness of their nature, but who, treading secure in the flowery path marked out for them by poets and moralists, the licensed artificers of fraud and lies, are dashed in pieces down the precipice and perish without help. [Hazlitt's note]
5. Hamlet, discovering Claudius at prayer, decides to defer murdering him until a time when he is "about some act / That has no relish of salvation in't" (*Hamlet* 3.3.91–92).

* * *

If he is bad enough when he has business on his hands, he is still worse when his purposes are suspended, and he has only to reflect on the misery he has occasioned. His indifference when Othello falls in a trance is perfectly diabolical but perfectly in character.

> IAGO: How is it, general? Have you not hurt your head?
> OTHELLO: Dost thou mock me?
> IAGO: I mock you not, by heaven.
>   [4.1.59–60]

The callous levity which Mr. Kean seems to consider as belonging to the character in general is proper here, because Iago has no feelings connected with humanity; but he has other feelings and other passions of his own which are not to be trifled with.

We do not, however, approve of Mr. Kean's pointing to the dead bodies after the catastrophe. It is not in the character of the part, which consists in the love of mischief, not as an end but as a means, and when that end is attained, though he may feel no remorse, he would feel no triumph. Besides, it is not the text of Shakespeare. Iago does not point to the bed, but Lodovico bids him look at it: "Look on the tragic loading of this bed" &c [5.2.368].

From *The Characters of Shakespeare's Plays*

It has been said that tragedy purifies the affections by terror and pity. That is, it substitutes imaginary sympathy for mere selfishness. It gives us a high and permanent interest, beyond ourselves, in humanity as such. It raises the great, the remote, and the possible to an equality with the real, the little, and the near. It makes man a partaker with his kind. It subdues and softens the stubbornness of his will. It teaches him that there are and have been others like himself, by showing him as in a glass what they have felt, thought, and done. It opens the chambers of the human heart. It leaves nothing indifferent to us that can affect our common nature. It excites our sensibility by exhibiting the passions wound up to the utmost pitch by the power of imagination or the temptation of circumstances, and corrects their fatal excesses in ourselves by pointing to the greater extent of sufferings and of crimes to which they have led others. Tragedy creates a balance of the affections. It makes us thoughtful spectators in the lists of life. It is the refiner of the species, a discipline of humanity. * * * *Othello* furnishes an illustration of these remarks. It excites our sympathy in an extraordinary degree. The moral it conveys has a closer application to the concerns of human life than that of almost any other of Shakespeare's plays. "It comes directly home to the bosoms and business of men."6 * * *

The picturesque contrasts of character in this play are almost as remarkable as the depth of the passion. The Moor Othello, the gentle Desdemona, the villain Iago, the good-natured Cassio, the fool Roderigo, present a range and variety of character as striking and palpable as that produced by the opposition of costume in a picture. Their distinguishing qualities stand out to the mind's eye, so that even when we are not thinking of their actions or sentiments, the idea of their persons is still as present to us as ever. These characters and the images they stamp upon the mind are the farthest asunder possible—the distance between them is immense; yet the compass of knowledge and invention which the poet has shown in embodying these extreme creations of his genius is only greater than the truth and felicity with which he has identified each character with itself, or blended their different qualities together in the same story. What a contrast the character of Othello forms to that of Iago! At the same time, the force of conception with which these two figures are opposed to each other is rendered still more intense by the complete consistency with which the traits of each character are brought out in a state of the highest finishing. The making one black and the other white, the one unprincipled, the other unfortunate in the extreme, would have answered the common purposes of effect and satisfied the ambition of an ordinary painter of character. Shakespeare has labored the finer shades of difference in both with as much care and skill as if he had to depend on the execution alone for the success of his design. * * *

* * * [I]n Othello, the doubtful conflict between contrary passions, though dreadful, continues only for a short time, and the chief interest is excited by the alternate ascendancy of different passions, by the entire and unforeseen change from the fondest love and most unbounded confidence to the tortures of jealousy and the madness of hatred. The revenge of Othello, after it has once taken thorough possession of his mind, never quits it, but grows stronger and stronger at every moment of its delay. The nature of the Moor is noble, confiding, tender, and generous; but his blood is of the most inflammable kind; and being once roused by a sense of his wrongs, he is stopped by no considerations of remorse or pity till he has given a loose to all the dictates of his rage and his despair. It is in working his noble nature up to this extremity through rapid but gradual

6. An echo of Sir Francis Bacon, who, dedicating his *Essays* to the Duke of Buckingham in 1625, reflects on their popularity in earlier editions: "it seems they came near to men's business and bosoms."

transitions, in raising passion to its height from the smallest begin-
nings and in spite of all obstacles, in painting the expiring conflict
between love and hatred, tenderness and resentment, jealousy and
remorse, in unfolding the strength and the weakness of our nature,
in uniting sublimity of thought with the anguish of the keenest
woe, in putting in motion the various impulses that agitate this our
mortal being, and at last blending them in that noble tide of deep
and sustained passion, impetuous but majestic, that "flows on to
the Propontic and knows no ebb" [cf. 3.3.453–56], that Shakespeare has shown the mastery of his genius and of his power over
the human heart. The third act of *Othello* is his finest display, not
of knowledge or passion separately, but of the two combined, of the
knowledge of character with the expression of passion, of consum-
mate art in the keeping up of appearances with the profound work-
ings of nature and the convulsive movements of uncontrollable
agony, of the power of inflicting torture and of suffering it. Not only
is the tumult of passion in Othello's mind heaved up from the very
bottom of the soul, but every the slightest undulation of feeling is
seen on the surface as it arises from the impulses of imagination or
the malicious suggestions of Iago. The progressive preparation for
the catastrophe is wonderfully managed from the Moor's first gallant recital of the story of his love, of "the spells and witchcraft he
has used" [cf. 1.3.61, 64, and 168], from his unlooked-for and
romantic success, the fond satisfaction with which he dotes on his
own happiness, the unreserved tenderness of Desdemona and her
innocent importunities in favor of Cassio, irritating the suspicions
instilled into her husband's mind by the perfidy of Iago and ran-
kling there to poison, till he loses all command of himself, and his
rage can only be appeased by blood. * * *

* * * In his conversations with Desdemona, the persuasion of her
guilt and the immediate proofs of her duplicity seem to irritate his
resentment and aversion to her; but in the scene immediately preceding her death, the recollection of his love returns upon him in all
its tenderness and force; and after her death, he all at once forgets
his wrongs in the sudden and irreparable sense of his loss: "My wife,
my wife! what wife? I have no wife. / O insupportable! O heavy
hour!" [5.2.99–100].

This happens before he is assured of her innocence; but afterwards his remorse is as dreadful as his revenge had been, and
yields only to fixed and death-like despair. His farewell speech
before he kills himself, in which he conveys his reasons to the senate for the murder of his wife, is equal to the first speech in which
he gave them an account of his courtship of her and "his whole
course of love" [cf. 1.3.91]. Such an ending was alone worthy of
such a commencement.

If anything could add to the force of our sympathy with Othello or compassion for his fate, it would be the frankness and generosity of his nature, which so little deserve it. * * *

* * *

The character of Desdemona is inimitable both in itself and as it appears in contrast with Othello's groundless jealousy and with the foul conspiracy of which she is the innocent victim. Her beauty and external graces are only indirectly glanced at: we see "her visage in her mind" [cf. 1.3.250]; her character everywhere predominates over her person: "A maiden never bold; / Of spirit so still and quiet that her motion / Blushed at herself" [1.3.94–96]. * * *

In general, as is the case with most of Shakespeare's females, we lose sight of her personal charms in her attachment and devotedness to her husband.

> My heart's subdued
> Even to the very quality of my lord. . . .
> And to his honors and his valiant parts
> Did I my soul and fortunes consecrate. [1.3.248–49 and 251–52]

The lady protests so much herself, and she is as good as her word. The truth of conception, with which timidity and boldness are united in the same character, is marvelous. The extravagance of her resolutions, the pertinacity of her affections, may be said to arise out of the gentleness of her nature. They imply an unreserved reliance on the purity of her own intentions, an entire surrender of her fears to her love, a knitting of herself (heart and soul) to the fate of another. Bating the commencement of her passion, which is a little fantastical and headstrong (though even that may perhaps be consistently accounted for from her inability to resist a rising inclination[7]), her whole character consists in having no will of her own, no prompter but her obedience. Her romantic turn is only a consequence of the domestic and practical part of her disposition; and instead of following Othello to the wars, she would gladly have "remained at home a moth of peace" [cf. 1.3.253–54], if her husband could have stayed with her. Her resignation and angelic sweetness of temper do not desert her at the last. * * *

* * *

The character of Iago is one of the supererogations of Shakespeare's genius. * * * The part indeed would hardly be tolerated, even as a foil to the virtue and generosity of the other characters in the play, but for its indefatigable industry and inexhaustible resources,

---

7. Iago. "Ay, too gentle." Othello. "Nay, that's certain." [4.1.189–90; Hazlitt's note]

which divert the attention of the spectator (as well as his own) from the end he has in view to the means by which it must be accomplished. Edmund the bastard in *Lear* is something of the same character placed in less prominent circumstances. Zanga is a vulgar caricature of it.[8]

SAMUEL TAYLOR COLERIDGE (1772–1834)

[Comments on *Othello*][†]

On Iago

* * * [Shakespeare] had read nature too heedfully not to know that courage, intellect, and strength of character are the most impressive forms of power, and that to power in itself, without reference to any moral end, an inevitable admiration and complacency appertains * * *. But in the exhibition of such a character it was of the highest importance to prevent the guilt from passing into utter monstrosity * * *. For such are the appointed relations of intellectual power to truth and of truth to goodness that it becomes both morally and poetically unsafe to present what is admirable—what our nature compels us to admire—in the mind and what is most detestable in the heart as coexisting in the same individual without any apparent connection or any modification of the one by the other. That Shakespeare has in one instance, that of Iago, approached to this, and that he has done it successfully, is perhaps the most astonishing proof of his genius and the opulence of its resources. * * *

* * *

* * * In what follows [after Iago's description of Cassio as "A fellow almost damned in a fair wife" (1.1.18)], let the reader feel how—by and through the glass of two passions, disappointed vanity and envy—the very vices of which he is complaining are made to act upon him as if they were so many excellencies, and the more appropriately because cunning is always admired and wished for by minds

---

8. Zanga is the villain in *The Revenge,* a tragedy by Edward Young (1683–1765), first performed in 1721 and still popular in the early 19th century. Hazlitt describes it as "an obvious transposition of *Othello:* the two principal characters are the same, only their colors are reversed. The giving the dark, treacherous, fierce, and remorseless character to the Moor is an alteration which is more in conformity to our prejudices as well as to historical truth" (Howe, 5: 227).

† Most of the passages here come from the notes of a lecture Coleridge gave on *Othello* in 1819, regrouped under topics invented for this Norton Critical Edition. Spelling and punctuation have been modernized, and the quotations from *Othello* modified to conform with this edition. All notes are the editor's. For information about Coleridge, his criticism, and its textual sources, see 383 below.

conscious of inward weakness. But they act only by half, like music on an inattentive auditor, swelling the thoughts which prevent him from listening to it.

* * *

This speech ["Virtue? a fig!" etc. (1.3.317 ff.)] comprises the passionless character of Iago. It is all will in intellect, and therefore he is here a bold partisan of a truth, but yet of a truth converted into a falsehood by the absence of all the necessary modifications caused by the frail nature of man. * * * Iago's soliloquy [at the end of act 1]—the motive-hunting of a motiveless malignity—how awful it is! Yea, whilst he is still allowed to bear the divine image, it is too fiendish for his own steady view—for the lonely gaze of a being next to devil—and only not quite devil—and yet a character which Shakespeare has attempted and executed without disgust and without scandal!

On Othello

Roderigo turns off to Othello, and here [in 1.1.63–64: "What a full fortune does the thick-lips owe / If he can carry't thus!"] comes one, if not the only, seeming justification of our blackamoor or negro Othello. Even if we suppose this an uninterrupted tradition of the theater, and that Shakespeare himself—from want of scenes and the experience that nothing could be made too marked for the senses of his audience—had sanctioned it, would this prove aught concerning his intention as a poet for all ages?[1] Can we imagine him so utterly ignorant as to make a barbarous negro plead royal birth—at a time, too, when negroes were not known except as slaves? As for Iago's language to Brabantio, it implies merely that Othello was a Moor—that is, black. Though I think the rivalry of Roderigo sufficient to account for his willful confusion of Moor and Negro, yet even if compelled to give this up, I should think it only adapted for the acting of the day and should complain of an enormity built on a single word in direct contradiction to Iago's "Barbary horse" [1.1.108]. Besides if we could in good earnest believe Shakespeare ignorant of the distinction, still why should we adopt one disagreeable possibility instead of a ten times greater and more pleasing probability? It is a common error to mistake the epithets applied by the *dramatis personae* to each other as truly descriptive of what the audiences ought to see or know. No doubt Desdemona saw Othello's visage in his mind, yet as we are constituted, and most surely as an

1. Coleridge is echoing Ben Jonson's commendatory verses at the beginning of the First Folio: "He was not of an age, but for all time!"

English audience was disposed in the beginning of the seventeenth century, it would be something monstrous to conceive this beautiful Venetian girl falling in love with a veritable negro. It would argue a disproportionateness, a want of balance, in Desdemona, which Shakespeare does not appear to have in the least contemplated.

* * *

Observe in how many ways Othello is made first our acquaintance, then our friend, then the object of our anxiety [awaiting news during the storm in 2.1], before the deeper interest is to be approached.

* * *

Othello must not be conceived as a negro but a high and chivalrous Moorish chief. Shakespeare learned the spirit of the character from the Spanish poetry, which was prevalent in England in his time. Jealousy does not strike me as the point in his passion; I take it to be rather an agony that the creature, whom he had believed angelic, with whom he had garnered up his heart and whom he could not help still loving, should be proved impure and worthless. It was the struggle *not* to love her. It was a moral indignation and regret that virtue should so fall: "But yet the pity of it, Iago! O Iago, the pity of it, Iago!" [4.1.190–91]. In addition to this, his honor was concerned: Iago would not have succeeded but by hinting that his honor was compromised. There is no ferocity in Othello; his mind is majestic and composed. He deliberately determines to die, and speaks his last speech with a view of showing his attachment to the Venetian state, though it had superseded him.

* * *

Finally, let me repeat that Othello does not kill Desdemona in jealousy but in a conviction forced upon him by the almost superhuman art of Iago—such a conviction as any man would and must have entertained who had believed Iago's honesty as Othello did. We, the audience, know that Iago is a villain from the beginning; but in considering the essence of the Shakespearean Othello, we must perseveringly place ourselves in his situation and under his circumstances. Then we shall immediately feel the fundamental difference between the solemn agony of the noble Moor and the wretched fishing jealousies of Leontes and the morbid suspiciousness of Leonatus, who is in other respects a fine character.[2] Othello had no life but in Desdemona; the belief that she, his angel, had

2. Leontes is the jealous husband in *The Winter's Tale* and Leonatus the jealous lover in *Cymbeline*.

fallen from the heaven of her native innocence wrought a civil war in his heart. She is his counterpart, and like him is almost sanctified in our eyes by her absolute unsuspiciousness and holy entireness of love. As the curtain drops, which do we pity the most?

On Desdemona

In Shakespeare's females the sweet yet dignified feeling of all that *continuates* society, as sense of ancestry, of sex, etc.—a purity unassailable by sophistry, because it does not rest on the analytic processes, but in feeling? Desdemona may be misinterpreted to the worst purposes—but in that same equipoise of the faculties during which the feelings *are* representative of all the past experience, not of the individual, but of all those by whom she has been educated, and of their predecessors *usque ad Evam* [as far back as Eve].

"Most women have no character at all," said Pope,[3] and meant it for satire. Shakespeare, who knew man and woman much better, saw that it, in fact, was the perfection of woman to be characterless. Everyone wishes a Desdemona or Ophelia for a wife—creatures who, though they may not always understand you, do always feel you, and feel with you.

On Textual Echoes and Interpretive Pleasure

[Quotes 1.3.290–92: "Look to her, Moor . . . My life upon / her faith!"] In real life, how do we look back to little speeches as presentimental of, or contrasted with, an affecting event! Even so Shakespeare, as secure of being read over and over, of becoming a family friend, provides this passage for his readers and leaves it to them.

On the Unities, Dr. Johnson, and Aesthetic Interest

Dr. Johnson has remarked that little or nothing is wanting to render *Othello* a regular tragedy but to have opened the play with the arrival of Othello in Cyprus and to have thrown the preceding act into the form of narration. Here then is the place to determine whether such a change would or would not be an improvement— nay (to throw down the gloves with a full challenge) whether the tragedy would or would not by such an arrangement become more

---

3. Alexander Pope's "Epistle II. To a Lady," published 1734, begins: "Nothing so true as what you once let fall, / 'Most Women have no Characters at all.' / Matter too soft a lasting stick to bear, / And best distinguish'd by black, brown, or fair."

regular—that is, more consonant with the rules dictated by universal reason on the true commonsense of mankind, in its application to the particular case. For in all acts of judgment it can never be too often recollected, and scarcely too often repeated, that rules are means to ends and, consequently, that the end must be determined and understood before it can be known what the rules are or ought to be. Now from a certain species of drama, proposing to itself the accomplishment of certain ends, * * * three rules have been abstracted. In other words, the means most conducive to the attainment of the proposed ends have been generalized and prescribed under the names of the three unities—the unity of time, the unity of place, and the unity of action—which last would, perhaps, have been as appropriately, as well as more intelligibly, entitled the unity of interest. With this last the present question has no immediate concern: in fact, its conjunction with the former two is a mere delusion of words. It is not properly a rule but in itself the great end not only of the drama but of the epic poem, the lyric ode, of all poetry—down to the candle-flame cone of an epigram—nay of poesy in general, as the proper generic term inclusive of all the fine arts as its species. But of the unities of time and place, which alone are entitled to the name of rules, the history of their origin will be their best criterion.

On Cassio, Unpossessive Affection, and Iago

[Quotes 2.1.60–65: "But, good lieutenant . . . tire the ingener."] Here is Cassio's warm-hearted yet perfectly disengaged praise of Desdemona and sympathy with the "most fortunately" wived Othello; and yet Cassio is an enthusiastic admirer, almost a worshipper, of Desdemona. O, that detestable code that excellence cannot be loved in any form that is female but it must needs be selfish! Observe Othello's "honest" and Cassio's "bold" Iago, and Cassio's full guileless-hearted wishes for the safety and love-raptures of Othello and "the divine Desdemona." And also note the exquisite circumstances of Cassio's kissing Iago's wife, as if it ought to be impossible that the dullest auditor should not feel Cassio's religious love of Desdemona's purity. Iago's answers are the sneers which a proud bad intellect feels towards woman and expresses to a wife. Surely it ought to be considered a very exalted compliment to women that all the sarcasms on them in Shakespeare are put in the mouths of villains.

A. C. BRADLEY (1851–1935)

["The Most Painfully Exciting and the Most Terrible" of Shakespeare's Tragedies][†]

From *Lecture V*

I

* * * Of all Shakespeare's tragedies * * * *Othello* is the most painfully exciting and the most terrible. From the moment when the temptation of the hero begins, the reader's heart and mind are held in a vice, experiencing the extremes of pity and fear, sympathy and repulsion, sickening hope and dreadful expectation. Evil is displayed before him, not indeed with the profusion found in *King Lear*, but forming, as it were, the soul of a single character, and united with an intellectual superiority so great that he watches its advance fascinated and appalled. He sees it, in itself almost irresistible, aided at every step by fortunate accidents and the innocent mistakes of its victims. He seems to breathe an atmosphere as fateful as that of *King Lear*, but more confined and oppressive, the darkness not of night but of a close-shut murderous room. His imagination is excited to intense activity, but it is the activity of concentration rather than dilation.

* * *

[Bradley offers five additional "distinguishing characteristics" to account for *Othello*'s uniquely "painful tension," the first of which is that the play's "conflict begins late, and advances without appreciable pause and with accelerating speed to the catastrophe."] (2) In the second place, there is no subject more exciting than sexual jealousy rising to the pitch of passion; and there can hardly be any spectacle at once so engrossing and so painful as that of a great nature suffering the torment of this passion, and driven by it to a crime which is also a hideous blunder. Such a passion as ambition, however terrible its results, is not itself ignoble; if we separate it in thought from the conditions which make it guilty, it does not appear despicable; it is not a kind of suffering, its nature is active; and therefore we can watch its course without shrinking. But jealousy, and especially sexual jealousy, brings with it a sense of shame and

---

[†] From *Shakespearean Tragedy: Lectures on "Hamlet," "Othello," "King Lear," "Macbeth"* (London: Macmillan, 1904; 2nd Ed., 1905; 13th Impression, 1919), 176–233. Bradley's quotations from *Othello* have been left unchanged but references to act, scene, and line numbers have been provided or altered to conform with this Norton Critical Edition. For information about Bradley and his criticism, see 384 below.

humiliation. For this reason it is generally hidden; if we perceive it we ourselves are ashamed and turn our eyes away; and when it is not hidden it commonly stirs contempt as well as pity. Nor is this all. Such jealousy as Othello's converts human nature into chaos, and liberates the beast in man; and it does this in relation to one of the most intense and also the most ideal of human feelings. What spectacle can be more painful than that of this feeling turned into a tortured mixture of longing and loathing, the 'golden purity' of passion split by poison into fragments, the animal in man forcing itself into his consciousness in naked grossness, and he writhing before it but powerless to deny it entrance, gasping inarticulate images of pollution, and finding relief only in a bestial thirst for blood? This is what we have to witness in one who was indeed 'great of heart' and no less pure and tender than he was great. And this, with what it leads to, the blow to Desdemona, and the scene where she is treated as the inmate of a brothel, a scene far more painful than the murder scene, is another cause of the special effect of this tragedy.[1]

(3) The mere mention of these scenes will remind us painfully of a third cause; and perhaps it is the most potent of all. I mean the suffering of Desdemona. This is, unless I mistake, the most nearly intolerable spectacle that Shakespeare offers us. For one thing, it is *mere* suffering; and, *ceteris paribus* [everything else being equal], that is much worse to witness than suffering that issues in action. Desdemona is helplessly passive. She can do nothing whatever. She cannot retaliate even in speech; no, not even in silent feeling. And the chief reason of her helplessness only makes the sight of her suffering more exquisitely painful. She is helpless because her nature is infinitely sweet and her love absolute. I would not challenge Mr. Swinburne's statement that we *pity* Othello even more than Desdemona; but we watch Desdemona with more unmitigated distress.[2] We are never wholly uninfluenced by the feeling that Othello is a man contending with another man; but Desdemona's suffering is like that of the most loving of dumb creatures tortured without cause by the being he adores.

(4) Turning from the hero and heroine to the third principal character, we observe (what has often been pointed out) that the action and catastrophe of *Othello* depend largely on intrigue. * * *

1. The whole force of the passages referred to can be felt only by a reader. The Othello of our stage can never be Shakespeare's Othello, any more than the Cleopatra of our stage can be his Cleopatra.
2. Algernon Charles Swinburne (1837–1901) wrote poetry, drama, and three books of Shakespeare criticism. Bradley cites him frequently, in this case from *A Study of Shakespeare* (London: Chatto and Windus, 1880), 182: "when Coleridge asks 'which do we pity the most' at the fall of the curtain, we can surely answer, Othello." [Editor's note]

Iago's intrigue occupies a position in the drama for which no parallel can be found in the other tragedies. * * * Now in any novel or play, even if the persons rouse little interest and are never in serious danger, a skilfully-worked intrigue will excite eager attention and suspense. And where, as in *Othello*, the persons inspire the keenest sympathy and antipathy, and life and death depend on the intrigue, it becomes the source of a tension in which pain almost overpowers pleasure. Nowhere else in Shakespeare do we hold our breath in such anxiety and for so long a time as in the later Acts of *Othello*.

(5) One result of the prominence of the element of intrigue is that *Othello* is less unlike a story of private life than any other of the great tragedies. And this impression is strengthened in further ways. In the other great tragedies the action is placed in a distant period, so that its general significance is perceived through a thin veil which separates the persons from ourselves and our own world. But *Othello* is a drama of modern life; when it first appeared it was a drama almost of contemporary life, for the date of the Turkish attack on Cyprus is 1570. The characters come close to us, and the application of the drama to ourselves (if the phrase may be pardoned) is more immediate than it can be in *Hamlet* or *Lear*.

* * *

* * * [S]ome readers, while acknowledging, of course, the immense power of *Othello*, and even admitting that it is dramatically perhaps Shakespeare's greatest triumph, still regard it with a certain distaste * * * due chiefly to two causes. First, to many readers in our time, men as well as women, the subject of sexual jealousy, treated with Elizabethan fulness and frankness, is not merely painful but so repulsive that not even the intense tragic emotions which the story generates can overcome this repulsion. * * *

To some readers, again, parts of *Othello* appear shocking or even horrible. They think—if I may formulate their objection—that in these parts Shakespeare has sinned against the canons of art, by representing on the stage a violence or brutality the effect of which is unnecessarily painful and rather sensational than tragic. The passages which thus give offence are probably those already referred to,—that where Othello strikes Desdemona (4.1.234), that where he affects to treat her as an inmate of a house of ill-fame (4.2), and finally the scene of her death.

* * * The first, and least important, of the three passages—that of the blow—seems to me the most doubtful. I confess that, do what I will, I cannot reconcile myself with it. It seems certain that the blow is by no means a tap on the shoulder with a roll of paper, as some actors, feeling the repulsiveness of the passage, have made it. It must occur, too, on the open stage. And there is not, I think, a

sufficiently overwhelming tragic feeling in the passage to make it
bearable. But in the other two scenes the case is different. There, it
seems to me, if we fully imagine the inward tragedy in the souls of
the persons as we read, the more obvious and almost physical sensations of pain or horror do not appear in their own likeness, and
only serve to intensify the tragic feelings in which they are absorbed.
Whether this would be so in the murder-scene if Desdemona had to
be imagined as dragged about the open stage (as in some modern
performances) may be doubtful; but there is absolutely no warrant
in the text for imagining this, and it is also quite clear that the bed
where she is stifled was within the curtains,[3] and so, presumably, in
part concealed.

2

* * *

* * * Othello's description of himself as

> one not easily jealous, but, being wrought,
> Perplexed in the extreme, [5.2.350–51]

is perfectly just. His tragedy lies in this—that his whole nature was
indisposed to jealousy, and yet was such that he was unusually
open to deception, and, if once wrought to passion, likely to act
with little reflection, with no delay, and in the most decisive manner conceivable.

Let me first set aside a mistaken view. I do not mean the ridiculous notion that Othello was jealous by temperament, but the idea,
which has some little plausibility, that the play is primarily a study
of a noble barbarian, who has become a Christian and has imbibed
some of the civilisation of his employers, but who retains beneath
the surface the savage passions of his Moorish blood and also the
suspiciousness regarding female chastity common among Oriental
peoples, and that the last three Acts depict the outburst of these
original feelings through the thin crust of Venetian culture. It would
take too long to discuss this idea,[4] and it would perhaps be useless to
do so, for all arguments against it must end in an appeal to the reader's
understanding of Shakespeare. If he thinks it is like Shakespeare
to look at things in this manner; that he had a historical mind and
occupied himself with problems of 'Culturgeschichte' [cultural

---

3. The dead bodies are not carried out at the end, as they must have been if the bed had
   been on the main stage (for this had no front curtain). The curtains within which the
   bed stood were drawn together at the words, 'Let it be hid' (5.2.370).
4. The reader who is tempted by it should, however, first ask himself whether Othello does
   act like a barbarian, or like a man who, though wrought almost to madness, does 'all in
   honour' [5.2.300].

history, anthropology]; that he laboured to make his Romans perfectly Roman, to give a correct view of the Britons in the days of Lear or Cymbeline, to portray in Hamlet a stage of the moral consciousness not yet reached by the people around him, the reader will also think this interpretation of *Othello* probable. To me it appears hopelessly un-Shakespearean. I could as easily believe that Chaucer meant the Wife of Bath for a study of the peculiarities of Somersetshire.[5] I do not mean that Othello's race is a matter of no account. It has, as we shall presently see, its importance in the play. It makes a difference to our idea of him; it makes a difference to the action and catastrophe. But in regard to the essentials of his character it is not important; and if anyone had told Shakespeare that no Englishman would have acted like the Moor, and had congratulated him on the accuracy of his racial psychology, I am sure he would have laughed.

Othello is, in one sense of the word, by far the most romantic figure among Shakespeare's heroes; and he is so partly from the strange life of war and adventure which he has lived from childhood. He does not belong to our world, and he seems to enter it we know not whence—almost as if from wonderland. There is something mysterious in his descent from men of royal siege; in his wanderings in vast deserts and among marvellous peoples; in his tales of magic handkerchiefs and prophetic Sibyls; in the sudden vague glimpses we get of numberless battles and sieges in which he has played the hero and has borne a charmed life; even in chance references to his baptism, his being sold to slavery, his sojourn in Aleppo.

And he is not merely a romantic figure; his own nature is romantic. * * * [Compared to Shakespeare's other tragic protagonists,] Othello is the greatest poet of them all. * * * And this imagination, we feel, has accompanied his whole life. He has watched with a poet's eye the Arabian trees dropping their med'cinable gum, and the Indian throwing away his chance-found pearl; and has gazed in a fascinated dream at the Pontic sea rushing, never to return, to the Propontic and the Hellespont; and has felt as no other man ever felt (for he speaks of it as none other ever did) the poetry of the pride, pomp, and circumstance of glorious war.

So he comes before us, dark and grand, with a light upon him from the sun where he was born. * * *

* * *

---

5. In the English poet Geoffrey Chaucer's *Canterbury Tales* (late 14th century), the Wife of Bath is memorable for her feisty protofeminism. That her abode is "biside Bathe" in Somerset ("General Prologue," 447) is, Bradley claims, inconsequential. [Editor's note]

   This character is so noble, Othello's feelings and actions follow so inevitably from it and from the forces brought to bear on it, and his sufferings are so heart-rending, that he stirs, I believe, in most readers a passion of mingled love and pity which they feel for no other hero in Shakespeare, and to which not even Mr. Swinburne can do more than justice. Yet there are some critics and not a few readers who cherish a grudge against him. * * * [E]ven when they admit that he was not of a jealous temper, they consider that he *was* 'easily jealous' * * * [—a "misconstruction of the text" derived from a "failure to realize certain essential facts," namely] that he is not an Italian, not even a European; that he is totally ignorant of the thoughts and the customary morality of Venetian women;[6] that he had himself seen in Desdemona's deception of her father how perfect an actress she could be. As he listens in horror, for a moment at least the past is revealed to him in a new and dreadful light, and the ground seems to sink under his feet. These suggestions are followed by a tentative but hideous and humiliating insinuation of what his honest and much-experienced friend fears may be the true explanation of Desdemona's rejection of acceptable suitors, and of her strange, and naturally temporary, preference for a black man. Here Iago goes too far. He sees something in Othello's face that frightens him, and he breaks off. Nor does this idea take any hold of Othello's mind. But it is not surprising that his utter powerlessness to repel it on the ground of knowledge of his wife, or even of that instinctive interpretation of character which is possible between persons of the same race,[7] should complete his misery, so that he feels he can bear no more, and abruptly dismisses his friend (3.3.242).

   Now I repeat that *any* man situated as Othello was would have been disturbed by Iago's communications. * * *

   The Othello of the Fourth Act is Othello in his fall. His fall is never complete, but he is much changed. * * *

   But before the end there is again a change. The supposed death of Cassio (5.1) satiates the thirst for vengeance. The Othello who enters the bed-chamber with the words,

   It is the cause, it is the cause, my soul, [5.2.1]

---

6. To represent that Venetian women do not regard adultery so seriously as Othello does, and again that Othello would be wise to accept the situation like an Italian husband, is one of Iago's most artful and most maddening devices.

7. If the reader has ever chanced to see an African violently excited, he may have been startled to observe how completely at a loss he was to interpret those bodily expressions of passion which in a fellow-countryman he understands at once, and in a European foreigner with somewhat less certainty. The effect of difference in blood in increasing Othello's bewilderment regarding his wife is not sufficiently realised. The same effect has to be remembered in regard to Desdemona's mistakes in dealing with Othello in his anger.

is not the man of the Fourth Act. The deed he is bound to do is no murder, but a sacrifice. He is to save Desdemona from herself, not in hate but in honour; in honour, and also in love. His anger has passed; a boundless sorrow has taken its place; and

> this sorrow's heavenly:
> It strikes where it doth love. [5.2.21–22]

Even when, at the sight of her apparent obduracy, and at the hearing of words which by a crowning fatality can only reconvince him of her guilt, these feelings give way to others, it is to righteous indignation they give way, not to rage; and, terribly painful as this scene is, there is almost nothing here to diminish the admiration and love which heighten pity.[8] And pity itself vanishes, and love and admiration alone remain, in the majestic dignity and sovereign ascendancy of the close. Chaos has come and gone; and the Othello of the Council-chamber and the quay of Cyprus has returned, or a greater and nobler Othello still. As he speaks those final words in which all the glory and agony of his life—long ago in India and Arabia and Aleppo, and afterwards in Venice, and now in Cyprus— seem to pass before us, like the pictures that flash before the eyes of a drowning man, a triumphant scorn for the fetters of the flesh and the littleness of all the lives that must survive him sweeps our grief away, and when he dies upon a kiss the most painful of all tragedies leaves us for the moment free from pain, and exulting in the power of 'love and man's unconquerable mind.'

3

The words just quoted come from Wordsworth's sonnet to Toussaint l'Ouverture.[9] Toussaint was a Negro; and there is a question, which, though of little consequence, is not without dramatic interest, whether Shakespeare imagined Othello as a Negro or as a Moor. Now I will not say that Shakespeare imagined him as a Negro and not as a Moor, for that might imply that he distinguished Negroes and Moors precisely as we do; but what appears to me nearly certain is that he imagined Othello as a black man, and not as a light-brown one.

* * *

8. See Note O. [In this note (402–03), Bradley accounts for his qualifying "almost," acknowledging that he is "shocked by the moral blindness of obliquity by which" Othello, in his response to Desdemona's dying words, "takes them only as a further sign of her worthlessness." Bradley's argument to explain the effect away is, he admits, "un-Shakespearean." His final comment on the matter, in the last edition of *Shakespearean Tragedy*, is that "I wish to withdraw the whole Note."]
9. François Dominique Toussaint L'Ouverture (1744?–1803), a self-educated freed slave who organized Haitians to fight against European colonial power. [Editor's note]

The horror of most American critics (Mr. Furness[1] is a bright exception) at the idea of a black Othello is very amusing, and their arguments are highly instructive. But they were anticipated, I regret to say, by Coleridge, and we will hear him. 'No doubt Desdemona saw Othello's visage in his mind; yet, as we are constituted, and most surely as an English audience was disposed in the beginning of the seventeenth century, it would be something monstrous to conceive this beautiful Venetian girl falling in love with a veritable negro. It would argue a disproportionateness, a want of balance, in Desdemona, which Shakespeare does not appear to have in the least contemplated.'[2] Could any argument be more self-destructive? It actually *did* appear to Brabantio 'something monstrous to conceive' his daughter falling in love with Othello,—so monstrous that he could account for her love only by drugs and foul charms. And the suggestion that such love would argue 'disproportionateness' is precisely the suggestion that Iago *did* make in Desdemona's case:

> Foh! one may smell in such a will most rank,
> Foul *disproportion*, thoughts unnatural. [3.3.234–35]

In fact he spoke of the marriage exactly as a filthy-minded cynic now might speak of the marriage of an English lady to a negro like Toussaint. Thus the argument of Coleridge and others points straight to the conclusion against which they argue.

But this is not all. The question whether to Shakespeare Othello was black or brown is not a mere question of isolated fact or historical curiosity; it concerns the character of Desdemona. Coleridge, and still more the American writers, regard her love, in effect, as Brabantio regarded it, and not as Shakespeare conceived it. They are simply blurring this glorious conception when they try to lessen the distance between her and Othello, and to smooth away the obstacle which his 'visage' offered to her romantic passion for a hero. Desdemona, the 'eternal womanly' in its most lovely and adorable form, simple and innocent as a child, ardent with the courage and idealism of a saint, radiant with that heavenly purity of heart which men worship the more because nature so rarely permits it to themselves, had no theories about universal brotherhood, and no phrases about 'one blood in all the nations of the earth' or 'barbarian, Scythian, bond and free'; but when her soul came in sight of the noblest soul on earth, she made nothing of the shrinking of her senses, but followed her soul until her senses took part with it, and

---

1. H.H. Furness, whose New Variorum edition of *Othello* (1886) included a discussion of Othello's color (389–96). [Editor's note]
2. See 257–58 above. [Editor's note]

'loved him with the love which was her doom.'[3] It was not prudent. It even turned out tragically. She met in life with the reward of those who rise too far above our common level; and we continue to allot her the same reward when we consent to forgive her for loving a brown man, but find it monstrous that she should love a black one.[4]

There is perhaps a certain excuse for our failure to rise to Shakespeare's meaning, and to realise how extraordinary and splendid a thing it was in a gentle Venetian girl to love Othello, and to assail fortune with such a 'downright violence and storm' [1.3.247] as is expected only in a hero. It is that when first we hear of her marriage we have not yet seen the Desdemona of the later Acts; and therefore we do not perceive how astonishing this love and boldness must have been in a maiden so quiet and submissive. And when we watch her in her suffering and death we are so penetrated by the sense of her heavenly sweetness and self-surrender that we almost forget that she had shown herself quite as exceptional in the active assertion of her own soul and will. She tends to become to us predominantly pathetic, the sweetest and most pathetic of Shakespeare's women, as innocent as Miranda and as loving as Viola, yet suffering more deeply than Cordelia or Imogen.[5] And she seems to lack that independence and strength of spirit which Cordelia and Imogen possess, and which in a manner raises them above suffering. She appears passive and defenceless, and can oppose to wrong nothing but the infinite endurance and forgiveness of a love that knows not how to resist or resent. * * *

Of course this later impression of Desdemona is perfectly right, but it must be carried back and united with the earlier before we can see what Shakespeare imagined. * * *

---

3. The description of Elaine's love for Launcelot in Tennyson's *Idylls of the King* (1859–1885). [Editor's note]
4. I will not discuss the further question whether, granted that to Shakespeare Othello was a black, he should be represented as a black in our theatres now. I dare say not. We do not like the real Shakespeare. We like to have his language pruned and his conceptions flattened into something that suits our mouths and minds. And even if we were prepared to make an effort, still, as Lamb observes, to imagine is one thing and to see is another. Perhaps if we saw Othello coal-black with the bodily eye, the aversion of our blood, an aversion which comes as near to being merely physical as anything human can, would overpower our imagination and sink us below not Shakespeare only but the audiences of the seventeenth and eighteenth centuries.
   As I have mentioned Lamb, I may observe that he differed from Coleridge as to Othello's colour, but, I am sorry to add, thought Desdemona to stand in need of excuse. 'This noble lady, with a singularity rather to be wondered at than imitated, had chosen for the object of her affections a Moor, a black. . . . Neither is Desdemona to be altogether condemned for the unsuitableness of the person whom she selected for her lover' (*Tales from Shakespeare*). Others, of course, have gone much further and have treated all the calamities of the tragedy as a sort of judgment on Desdemona's rashness, wilfulness and undutifulness. There is no arguing with opinions like this; but I cannot believe that even Lamb is true to Shakespeare in implying that Desdemona is in some degree to be condemned. What is there in the play to show that Shakespeare regarded her marriage differently from Imogen's [in *Cymbeline*]?
5. Heroines in *The Tempest, Twelfth Night, King Lear*, and *Cymbeline*.[Editor's note]

From *Lecture VI*

* * *

5

Iago stands supreme among Shakespeare's evil characters because the greatest intensity and subtlety of imagination have gone to his making, and because he illustrates in the most perfect combination the two facts concerning evil which seem to have impressed Shakespeare most. The first of these is the fact that perfectly sane people exist in whom fellow-feeling of any kind is so weak that an almost absolute egoism becomes possible to them, and with it those hard vices—such as ingratitude and cruelty—which to Shakespeare were far the worst. The second is that such evil is compatible, and even appears to ally itself easily, with exceptional powers of will and intellect. * * * How is it then that we can bear to contemplate him; nay, that, if we really imagine him, we feel admiration and some kind of sympathy? * * * [W]e are shown a thing absolutely evil, and—what is more dreadful still—this absolute evil is united with supreme intellectual power. Why is the representation tolerable, and why do we not accuse its author either of untruth or of a desperate pessimism?

T. S. ELIOT

["The Last Great Speech of Othello"]†

* * *

* * * I have always felt that I have never read a more terrible exposure of human weakness—of universal human weakness—than the last great speech of Othello. I am ignorant whether any one else has ever adopted this view, and it may appear subjective and fantastic in the extreme. It is usually taken on its face value, as expressing the greatness in defeat of a noble but erring nature. [Quotes 5.2.343–61: "Soft you . . . smote him—thus!"] What Othello seems to me to be doing in making this speech is *cheering himself up*. He is endeavouring to escape reality, he has ceased to think about Desdemona, and is thinking about himself. Humility is the most difficult of all virtues to achieve; nothing dies harder than the desire to think well of oneself. Othello succeeds in turning himself into a pathetic

† From "Shakespeare and the Stoicism of Seneca" (1927) in *Selected Essays*, Third Edition (New York: Harcourt, Brace and Co., 1950, pp. 110–11; London: Faber and Faber, 1951, pp. 130–31). Copyright © 1950 by Houghton Mifflin Harcourt Publishing Company. Copyright © renewed 1978 by Esme Valerie Eliot. Reprinted by permission of Houghton Mifflin Harcourt Publishing Company and by Faber and Faber Ltd. All rights reserved.

figure, by adopting an *aesthetic* rather than a moral attitude, drama-
tising himself against his environment. He takes in the spectator, but
the human motive is primarily to take in himself. I do not believe that
any writer has ever exposed this *bovarysme*,[1] the human will to see
things as they are not, more clearly than Shakespeare.

KENNETH BURKE

Othello: An Essay to Illustrate a Method[†]

OTHELLO.   Will you, I pray, demand that demi-devil
    Why he hath thus ensnared my soul and body?
IAGO.   Demand me nothing: what you know, you know:
    From this time forth I never will speak word.
LODOVICO.   What! not to pray?
GRATIANO.   Torments will ope your lips.
                                            [5.2.306–10]

I
Iago as Katharma

Othello: act v, scene ii. Desdemona, fated creature, marked for a
tragic end by her very name (Desdemona: "moan-death") lies smothered. Othello, just after the words cited as our motto, has stabbed
himself and fallen across her body. * * * Iago, "Spartan dog, /
More fell than anguish, hunger, or the sea", is invited by Lodovico to "look
on the tragic loading of this bed" [5.2.366–68]. *Exeunt omnes*, with
Iago as prisoner, we being assured that they will see to "the censure
of this hellish villain, / The time, the place, the torture" [5.2.373–74].
Thus like the tragic bed, himself bending beneath a load, he is universally hated for his ministrations. And in all fairness, as *advocatus
diaboli* [devil's advocates] we would speak for him, in considering the
cathartic nature of his role.

Reviewing, first, the definition of some Greek words central to
the ritual of cure:

Katharma: that which is thrown away in cleansing; the off-
scourings, refuse, of a sacrifice; hence, worthless fellow. "It was the
custom at Athens," lexicographers inform us, "to reserve certain
worthless persons, who in case of plague, famine, or other visitations

---

1. Emma Bovary is the self-absorbed and self-deluding title character of Gustave Flau-
bert's novel *Madame Bovary* (1856). [Editor's note]
† From *The Hudson Review* 4 (1951): 165–203. Reprinted with the permission of *The
Hudson Review*. The author's quotations from *Othello* have been retained, but bracketed references are to this Norton Critical Edition. A footnote has been omitted.

from heaven, were thrown into the sea," with an appropriate formula, "in the belief that they would cleanse away or wipe off the
guilt of the nation." And these were *Katharmata*. Of the same root, of
course, are our words *cathartic* and *catharsis*, terms originally related
to both physical and ritual purgation.

A synonym for *katharma* was *pharmakos*: poisoner, sorcerer,
magician; one who is sacrificed or executed as an atonement or
purification for others; a scapegoat. It is related to *pharmakon*:
drug, remedy, medicine, enchanted potion, philtre, charm, spell,
incantation, enchantment, poison.

Hence, with these terms in mind, we note that Iago has done this
play some service. Othello's suspicions, we shall aim to show, arise
from within, in the sense that they are integral to the motive he
stands for; but the playwright cuts through that tangle at one stroke,
by making Iago a voice at Othello's ear.

What arises within, if it wells up strongly and presses for long, will
seem imposed from without. One into whose mind melodies spontaneously pop, must eventually "hear voices". "Makers" become but
"instruments", their acts a sufferance. Hence, "inspiration", "affla-
tus", "angels", and "the devil". Thus, the very extremity of inwardness in the motives of Iago can make it seem an outwardness. Hence
we are readily disposed to accept the dramatist's dissociation. Yet
villain and hero here are but essentially inseparable parts of the one
fascination.

Add Desdemona to the inseparable integer. That is: add the privacy of Desdemona's treasure, as vicariously owned by Othello in
manly miserliness (Iago represents the threat implicit in such
cherishing), and you have a tragic trinity of ownership in the profoundest sense of ownership, the property in human affections, as
fetishistically localized in the object of possession, while the possessor is himself possessed by his very engrossment (Iago being the
result, the apprehension that attains its dramatic culmination in
the thought of an agent acting to provoke the apprehension). The
single mine-ownness is thus dramatically split into the three
principles of possession, possessor, and estrangement (threat of
loss). Hence, trust and distrust, though *living in* each other, can be
shown *wrestling with* each other. *La propriété, c'est le vol*. Property
fears theft because it is theft.

Sweet thievery, but thievery nonetheless. Appropriately, the first
outcry in this play was of "Thieves, thieves, thieves!" when Iago
stirred up Desdemona's father by shouting: "Look to your house,
your daughter, and your bags! / Thieves! thieves!" [1.1.77–78]—first
things in a play being as telltale as last things. Next the robbery was
spiritualized: "You have lost your soul" [1.1.84]. And finally it was
reduced to imagery both lewd and invidious: "An old black ram

is tupping your white ewe" [1.1.85–86], invidious because of the
social discrimination involved in the Moor's blackness. So we have
the necessary ingredients, beginning from what Desdemona's father,
Brabantio, called "the property of youth and maidenhood" [1.1.169].
(Nor are the connotations of *pharmakon*, as evil-working drug,
absent from the total recipe, since Brabantio keeps circling about
this theme, to explain how the lover robbed the father of his property in the daughter. So it is there, in the offing, as imagery, even
though rationalistically disclaimed; and at one point, Othello does
think of poisoning Desdemona.)

Desdemona's role, as one of the persons in this triune tension (or
"psychosis"), might also be illuminated by antithesis. In the article
on the Fine Arts (in the eleventh edition of the *Encyclopaedia Bri-
tannica*), the elements of pleasure "which are not disinterested" are
said to be:

> the elements of personal exultation and self-congratulation, the
> pride of exclusive possession or acceptance, all these emotions,
> in short, which are summed up in the lover's triumphant mono-
> syllable, "Mine."

Hence it follows that, for Othello, the beautiful Desdemona was
not an aesthetic object. The thought gives us a radical glimpse into
the complexity of her relation to the audience (her nature as a rhetorical "topic"). First, we note how, with the increased cultural and
economic importance of private property, an aesthetic might arise
antithetically to such norms, exemplifying them in reverse, by an
idea of artistic enjoyment that would wholly transcend "mine-own-
ness". The sharper the stress upon the *meum* [mine] in the practical
realm, the greater the invitation to its denial in an aesthetic *nostrum*
[ours].

We are here considering the primary paradox of dialectic, stated as
a maxim in the formula beloved by dialectician Coleridge: "Extremes
meet." Note how, in this instance, such meeting of the extremes adds
to our engrossment in the drama. For us, Desdemona is an aesthetic
object: we never forget that we have no legal rights in her, and we
never forget that she is but an "imitation". But *what* is she imitating?
She is "imitating" her third of the total tension (the disequilibrium
of monogamistic love, considered as a topic). She is imitating a
major perturbation of property, as so conceived. In this sense, however aloof from her the audience may be in discounting her nature
as a mere playwright's invention, her role can have a full effect upon
them only insofar as it draws upon firm beliefs and dark apprehensions that not only move the audience *within* the conditions of the
play, but prevail as an unstable and disturbing cluster of motives *outside* the play, or "prior to" it. Here the "aesthetic," even in negating or

transcending "mine-own-ness," would draw upon it for purposes of poetic persuasion. We have such appeal in mind when speaking of the "topical" element. You can get the point by asking yourself: "So far as catharsis and wonder are concerned, what is gained by the fact that the play imitates *this particular tension* rather than some other?"

In sum, Desdemona, Othello, and Iago are all partners of a single conspiracy. There were the enclosure acts, whereby the common lands were made private; here is the analogue, in the realm of human affinity, an act of spiritual enclosure. And might the final choking be also the ritually displaced effort to close a thoroughfare, as our hero fears lest this virgin soil that he had opened up become a settlement? Love, universal love, having been made private, must henceforth be shared vicariously, as all weep for Othello's loss, which is, round-about, their own. And Iago is a function of the following embarrassment: Once such privacy has been made the norm, its denial can be but promiscuity. Hence his ruttish imagery, in which he signalizes one aspect of a total fascination.

So there is a whispering. There is something vaguely feared and hated. In itself it is hard to locate, being woven into the very nature of "consciousness"; but by the artifice of Iago it is made local. The tinge of malice vaguely diffused through the texture of events and relationships can here be condensed into a single principle, a devil, giving the audience as it were flesh to sink their claw-thoughts in. Where there is a gloom hanging over, a destiny, each man would conceive of the obstacle in terms of the instruments he already has for removing obstacles, so that a soldier would shoot the danger, a butcher thinks it could be chopped, and a merchant hopes to get rid of it by trading. But in Iago the menace is generalized. (As were you to see man-made law as destiny, and see destiny as a hag, cackling over a brew, causing you by a spell to wither.)

In sum, we have noted two major cathartic functions in Iago: (1) as regards the tension centering particularly in sexual love as property and ennoblement (monogamistic love), since in reviling Iago the audience can forget that his transgressions are theirs; (2) as regards the need of finding a viable localization for uneasiness (*Angst*) in general, whether shaped by superhuman forces or by human forces interpreted as super-human (the scapegoat here being but a highly generalized form of the overinvestment that men may make in specialization). Ideally, in childhood, hating and tearing-at are one; in a directness and simplicity of hatred there may be a ritual cure for the bewilderments of complexity; and Iago may thus serve to give a feeling of integrity.

These functions merge into another, purely technical. For had Iago been one bit less rotten and unsleeping in his proddings, how

could this play have been kept going, and at such a pitch? Until very
near the end, when things can seem to move "of themselves" as the
author need but actualize the potentialities already massed, Iago has
goaded (tortured) the plot forward step by step, for the audience's
villainous entertainment and filthy purgation. * * *

* * *

G. K. HUNTER

Othello and Colour Prejudice[†]

It is generally admitted today that Shakespeare was a practical man
of the theatre: however careless he may have been about maintain-
ing consistency for the exact *reader* of his plays, he was not likely to
introduce a theatrical novelty which would only puzzle his audience; it does not seem wise, therefore, to dismiss his theatrical
innovations as if they were unintentional. The blackness of Othello
is a case in point. Shakespeare largely modified the story he took
over from Cinthio: he made a tragic hero out of Cinthio's passionate and bloody lover; he gave him a royal origin, a Christian baptism, a romantic *bravura* of manner and, most important of all, an
orotund magnificence of diction. Yet, changing all this, he did not
change his colour, and so produced a daring theatrical novelty—a
black hero for a white community—a novelty which remains too
daring for many recent theatrical audiences. Shakespeare cannot
merely have carried over the colour of Othello by being too lazy or
too uninterested to meddle with it; for no actor, spending the time
in 'blacking-up', and hence no producer, could be indifferent to
such an innovation, especially in that age, devoted to 'imitation'
and hostile to 'originality'. In fact, the repeated references to Othello's colour in the play and the wider net of images of dark and light
spread across the diction, show that Shakespeare was not only not
unaware of the implication of his hero's colour, but was indeed
intensely aware of it as one of the primary factors in his play.[1] I am
therefore assuming in this lecture that the blackness of Othello has

† From *Proceedings of the British Academy* 53 (1967): 139–63. © British Academy 1968.
  Reprinted by permission of the publisher. The author's quotations from *Othello* have
  been retained, but bracketed references are to this Norton Critical Edition. For stun-
  ning visual and textual illustrations, as well as some footnote references omitted from
  this excerpt, consult the original or the reprint in Hunter's *Dramatic Identities and
  Cultural Tradition: Studies in Shakespeare and His Contemporaries* (Liverpool: Liverpool University Press, 1978), 31–59.
1. See R. B. Heilman, 'More Fair than Black; Light and Dark in *Othello*', *Essays in Criticism*, i (1951), 313–35.

a theatrical purpose, and I intend to try to suggest what it was possible for that purpose to have been.

Shakespeare intended his hero to be a black man—that much I
take for granted;[2] what is unknown is what the idea of a black man
suggested to Shakespeare, and what reaction the appearance of a
black man on the stage was calculated to produce. It is fairly certain, however, that some modern reactions are not likely to have
been shared by the Elizabethans. The modern theatre-going European intellectual, with a background of cultivated superiority to
'colour problems' in other continents, would often choose to regard
Othello as a fellow man and to watch the story—which could so easily be reduced to its headline level: 'sheltered white girl errs: said,
"Colour does not matter"'—with a sense of freedom from such prejudices. But this lofty fair-mindedness may be too lofty for Shakespeare's play, and not take the European any nearer the Othello of
Shakespeare than the lady from Maryland quoted in the Furness
New Variorum edition: 'In studying the play of *Othello*, I have always
imagined its hero a white man.' Both views, that the colour of Othello
does not matter, and that it matters too much to be tolerable, err, I
suggest, by over-simplifying. Shakespeare was clearly deliberate in
keeping Othello's colour; and it is obvious that he counted on some
positive audience reaction to this colour; but it is equally obvious
that he did not wish the audience to dismiss Othello as a stereotype
nigger.

Modern rationalizations about 'colour' tend to be different from
those of the Middle Ages and Renaissance. We are powerfully aware
of the relativism of viewpoints; we distinguish easily between different racial cultures; and explicit arguments about the mingling of the
races usually begin at the economic and social level and only move
to questions of God's providence at the lunatic fringe.

The Elizabethans also had a powerful sense of the economic
threat posed by the foreign groups they had daily contact with—
Flemings or Frenchmen—but they had little or no continuous contact with 'Moors', and no sense of economic threat from them.[3]
This did not mean, however, that they had no racial or colour prejudice. They had, to start with, the basic common man's attitude that
all foreigners are curious and inferior—the more curious the more
inferior, in the sense of the proverb quoted by Purchas: 'Three
Moors to a Portuguese; three Portuguese to an Englishman.'[4] They

---

2. I ignore the many treatises devoted to proving that he was of tawny or sunburnt colour.
   These are, however, very worthy of study, as documents of prejudice.
3. See G. K. Hunter, 'Elizabethans and Foreigners', *Shakespeare Survey*, xvii ('Shakespeare in His Own Age') (1964), 37–52. [Rpt. in Hunter's *Dramatic Identities* (see the
   daggered source note to this essay), 3–30.]
4. See M. P. Tilley, *A Dictionary of Proverbs* (1950), M. 1132.

had also the basic and ancient sense that black is the colour of sin and death, 'the badge of hell, The hue of dungeons, and the Schoole of night' (as Shakespeare himself says).[5] This supposition is found all over the world (even in darkest Africa)[6] from the earliest to the latest times; and in the West there is a continuous and documented tradition of it. It may be worth while giving some account of this. In Greece and Rome black was the colour of ill luck, death, condemnation, malevolence. * * *

The coming of Christianity made no break in the tradition. Indeed, Christian eschatology seems to have taken over the black man from the underworld with great speed and enthusiasm. * * *

The linguistic change from Greek or Latin to English did not free the word *black* from the[se] associations. * * * This is a tradition that Shakespeare picks up in his description of Thomas Mowbray as a Crusader,

> Streaming the ensign of the Christian cross
> Against black pagans. Turks and Saracens.[7]

There was then, it appears, a powerful, widespread, and ancient tradition associating black-faced men with wickedness, and this tradition came right up to Shakespeare's own day. The habit of representing evil men as black-faced or negroid had also established itself in a pictorial tradition that persists from the Middle Ages through and beyond the sixteenth century. This appears especially in works showing the tormentors of Christ, in scenes of the Flagellation and the Mocking, though the tormentors of other saints are liable to have the same external characteristics used to show their evil natures. * * *

* * *

It is suggested by several of the authorities cited here that the pictorial tradition was associated with theatrical usage. Certainly the drama of the Middle Ages seems to have used black figures to represent the evil of this world and the next. Creizenach[8] describes the European diffusion of the black faces. The surviving accounts of the Coventry cycle[9] (which some think Shakespeare may have seen— and which he *could* have seen) retain the distinction between 'white

---

5. *Love's Labour's Lost*, IV. iii. 254 f.
6. See V. W. Turner, 'Colour Classification in Ndembu Ritual', *Anthropological Approaches to the Study of Religion*, ed. M. Banton (1966); Arthur Leib, 'The Mystical Significance of Colours in . . . Madagascar', *Folk-lore*, lvii (1946), 128–33; Joan Westcott, 'The Sculpture and Myths of Eshu-Elegba, the Yoruba Trickster', *Africa*, xxxii (1962).
7. *Richard II*, IV. i. 94 f.
8. *Geschichte des neuren Dramas*, i (1911), 201. * * *
9. Medieval townspeople performed plays representing events in biblical history, ranging from the fall into original sin to the resurrection of Christ. The cycle performed in Coventry (near where Shakespeare grew up) is one of the better known. [Editor's note]

(or saved) souls' and 'black (or damned) souls' * * * Even in a proverbial title like 'Like will to like quoth the Devil to the Collier' the widespread and universally accepted point is exposed as part of the air that
Englishmen of Shakespeare's age breathed. Indeed, as late as Wycherley's *The Plain Dealer* (1676) stray reference to the Devil's blackness
was supposed to be intelligible to a theatrical audience ('like a devil in
a play . . . this darkness . . . conceals her angel's face').[1]

How mindlessly and how totally accepted in this period was the
image of the black man as the devil may be seen from the use of
'Moors' or 'Morians' in civic pageants. 'Moors' were an accepted
part of the world of pageantry.[2] There were Moors in London Lord
Mayor's Pageants in 1519, 1521, 1524, 1536, 1541, 1551, 1589,
1609, 1611, 1624,[3] who seem to have acted as bogey-man figures to
clear the way before the main procession. They were sometimes
supplied with fireworks for this purpose, and in this function seem
to have been fairly indifferent alternatives to green-men, wode-
woses,[4] devils. As Withington has remarked,[5] 'it seems obvious that
all these figures are connected'; they are connected as frightening
marginal comments on the human state—as inhabitants of those
peripheral regions in the *mappae mundi* [world maps] where Moors,
together with

> Anthropophagi and men whose heads
> Do grow beneath their shoulders, [1.3.144–45]

rubbed shoulders (such as these were) with Satyrs, Hermaphrodites,
salvage [i.e., savage] men, and others of the species *semihoma*.* * *

Renaissance scepticism and the voyages of discovery might seem,
at first sight, to have destroyed the ignorance on which such thought-
less equations of black men and devils depended. But this does not
prove to have been so. The voyagers brought back some accurate
reports of black and heathen; but they often saw, or said they saw,
what they expected to see—the marvels of the East. In any case the
vocabulary at their disposal frustrated any attempt at scientific discrimination. The world was still seen largely, in terms of vocabulary,
as a network of religious names. The word 'Moor' had no clear racial
status. The first meaning in the *O.E.D.* (with examples up to 1629)
is 'Mahomedan'. And very often this means no more than 'infidel',
'non-Christian'. Like *Barbarian* and *Gentile* (or *Wog*) it was a word

---

1. *The Plain Dealer,* IV. ii.
2. Moors (like dwarfs and fools) were found also in the human menageries that the courts
   of the Renaissance liked to possess. The Moors at the court of James IV of Scotland
   appear often in the Treasurer's Accounts. * * *
3. See Malone Society Collections, iii (1945).
4. A wodewose, or woodwose, is "a wild man of the woods; a savage; a satyr, faun"
   (*O.E.D.*). [Editor's note]
5. R. Withington, *English Pageantry,* i (1918), 74.

for 'people not like us', so signalled by colour. The word *Gentile* itself
had still the religious sense of *Pagan*, and the combined phrase
'Moors and Gentiles' is used regularly to represent the religious
gamut of non-Christian possibilities (see *O.E.D.* for examples). Similarly, *Barbary* was not simply a place in Africa, but also the unclearly
located home of Barbarism, as in Chaucer['s *Canterbury Tales*]
(Franklin's Tale, 1451, Man of Law's Tale, 183).

I have suggested elsewhere that the discoveries of the voyagers
had little opportunity of scientific or non-theological development.[6] And this was particularly true of the problems raised by the
black-skinned races. No scientific explanation of black skins had
ever been achieved, though doctors had long disputed it. * * * The
theological explanation was left in possession of the field. Adam
and Eve, it must be assumed, were white; it follows that the creation of the black races can only be ascribed to some subsequent
fiat. The two favourite possibilities were the cursing of Cain and
the cursing of Ham or Cham and his posterity[7]—and sometimes
these two were assumed to be different expressions of the same
event; at least one might allege, with Sir Walter Ralegh, that 'the
sonnes of Cham did possesse the vices of the sonnes of Cain'.[8] The
Cham explanation had the great advantage that 'the threefold
world' of tradition could be described in terms of the three sons of
Noah—Japhet having produced the Europeans, Shem the Asiatics,
while the posterity of Ham occupied Africa, or, in a more sophisticated version, 'the Meridionall or southern partes of the world
both in Asia and Africa'—sophisticated, we should notice, without
altering the basic theological assumption that Cham's posterity
were banished to the most uncomfortable part of the globe, and a
foretaste of the Hell to come. * * * When this is linked to the other
point made in relation to the Cham story—that his posterity were
cursed to be slaves—one can see how conveniently and plausibly
such a view fitted the facts and desires found in the early naviga-
tors. Azurara, the chronicler of Prince Henry the Navigator's voyages,[9] tells us that it was natural to find blackamoors as the slaves
of lighter skinned men:

> these blacks were Moors (i.e. Mahomedans) like the others,
> though their slaves, in accordance with ancient custom which
> I believe to have been because of the curse which, after the

6. G. K. Hunter, loc. cit.
7. See Genesis 4 and 9. [Editor's note]
8. *The History of the World*, 1.vi.2 [1614; Raleigh (1552–1618) was a courtier, explorer,
   poet, and moralist].
9. Prince Henry the Navigator (1394–1460) helped sponsor many voyages of discovery
   from Europe to Africa, chiefly in search of a route to India. [Editor's note]

Deluge, Noah laid upon his son Cain [sic], cursing him in this
way: that his race should be subject to all the other races in the
world. And from his race these blacks are descended.[1]

The qualities of the 'Moors' who appear on the Elizabethan stage
are hardly at all affected by Elizabethan knowledge of real Moors
from real geographical locations, and, given the literary modes
available, this is hardly surprising. It is true that the first important
Moor-role—that of Muly Hamet in Peele's *The Battle of Alcazar* (*c.*
1589)—tells the story of a real man (with whom Queen Elizabeth
had a treaty) in a real historical situation. But the dramatic focus
that Peele manages to give to his Moorish character is largely depen-
dent on the devil and underworld associations he can suggest for
him—making him call up 'Fiends, Fairies, hags that fight in beds of
steel' and causing him to show more acquaintance with the geography of hell than with that of Africa. Aaron in *Titus Andronicus* is
liberated from even such slender ties as associate Muly Hamet with
geography. Aaron is in the play as the representative of a world of
generalized barbarism, which is Gothic in Tamora and Moorish in
Aaron, and unfocused in both. The purpose of the play is served by
a general opposition between Roman order and Barbarian disorder.
Shakespeare has the doubtful distinction of making explicit here
(perhaps for the first time in English literature) the projection of
black wickedness in terms of negro sexuality. The relationship
between Tamora and Aaron is meant, clearly enough, to shock our
normal sensibilities and their black baby is present as an emblem of
disorder. In this respect, as in most others, Eleazer in *Lust's Domin-
ion* (*c.* 1600)—the third pre-*Othello* stage-Moor—is copied from
Aaron. The location of this play (Spain) gives a historically plausible
excuse to present the devil in his favourite human form—'that of a
Negro or Moor', as Reginald Scott[2] tells us—but does not really use
the locale to establish any racial points.

These characters provide the dominant images that must have
been present in the minds of Shakespeare's original audience when
they entered the Globe to see a play called *The Moor of Venice*—an
expectation of pagan deviltry set against white Christian civilization—
excessive civilization perhaps in Venice, but civilization at least 'like
us'. * * * It is in such terms that the play opens. We hear from men
like us of a man not like us, of 'his Moorship', 'the Moor', 'the
thick-lips', 'and old black ram', 'a Barbary horse', 'the devil', of 'the
gross clasps of a lascivious Moor'. The sexual fear and disgust that
lies behind so much racial prejudice are exposed for our derisive

---

1. *Discovery and Conquest of Guinea* (Hakluyt Society, xcv [1896], 54).
2. Author (ca. 1538–1599) of *Discovery of Witchcraft* (1584), which reflected skeptically
   on much current belief about demonic forces. [Editor's note]

expectations to fasten upon them. And we are at this point bound to agree with these valuations, for no alternative view is revealed. There is, of course, a certain comic *brio* which helps to distance the whole situation, and neither Brabantio, nor Iago nor Roderigo can wholly command our identification. None the less we are drawn on to await the entry of a traditional Moor figure, the kind of person we came to the theatre expecting to find.

When the second scene begins, however, it is clear that Shakespeare is bent to ends other than the fulfilment of these expectations. The Iago/Roderigo relationship of I. i is repeated in the Iago/Othello relationship of the opening of I. ii; but Othello's response to the real-seeming circumstance with which Iago lards his discourse is very different from the hungrily self-absorbed questionings of Roderigo. Othello draws on an inward certainty about himself, a radiant clarity about his own well-founded moral position. This is no 'lascivious Moor', but a great Christian gentleman, against whom Iago's insinuations break like water against granite. Not only is Othello a Christian, moreover, he is the leader of Christendom in the last and highest sense in which Christendom existed as a viable entity, crusading against the 'black pagans'. He is to defend Cyprus against the Turk, the 'general enemy Ottoman' [1.3.49]. It was the fall of Cyprus which produced the alliance of Lepanto, and we should associate Othello with the emotion that Europe continued to feel— till well after the date of *Othello*—about that victory and about Don John of Austria.[3]

Shakespeare has presented to us a traditional view of what Moors are like, i.e. gross, disgusting, inferior, carrying the symbol of their damnation on their skin; and has caught our over-easy assent to such assumptions in the grip of a guilt which associates us and our assent with the white man representative of such views in the play—Iago. Othello acquires the glamour of an innocent man that *we* have wronged, and an admiration stronger than he could have achieved by virtue plainly represented. * * * Iago is a 'civilized' man; but where, for the 'inferior' Othello, appearance and reality, statement and truth are linked indissolubly, civilization for Iago consists largely of a capacity to manipulate appearances and probabilities:

> For when my outward action doth demonstrate
> The native act and figure of my heart
> In compliment extern, 'tis not long after
> But I will wear my heart upon my sleeve
> For daws to peck at: I am not what I am. [1.1.58–62]

3. See G. K. Hunter, loc. cit. [Don John of Austria (1545–1578) led the Venetian and Spanish forces that triumphed at Lepanto. See 153 above.]

Othello may be 'the devil' in appearance: but it is the 'fair' Iago who gives birth to the dark realities of sin and death in the play:

> It is engender'd. Hell and night
> Must bring this monstrous birth to the world's light
> [1.3.394–95]

The relationship between these two is developed in terms of appearance and reality. Othello controls the reality of action; Iago the 'appearance' of talk about action; Iago the Italian is isolated (even from his wife), envious, enigmatic (even to himself), self-centered; Othello the 'extravagant and wheeling stranger' is surrounded and protected by a network of duties, obligations, esteems, pious to his father-in-law, deferential to his superiors, kind to his subordinates, loving to his wife. To sum up, assuming that *soul* is reality and *body* is appearance, we may say that Iago is the white man with the black soul while Othello is the black man with the white soul. Long before Blake's little black boy had said

> I am black, but oh my soul is white.
> White as an angel is the English child,
> But I am black as if bereaved of light.

and before Kipling's Gunga Din:

> An' for all 'is dirty 'ide
> 'E was white, clear white inside . . .
> You're a better man than I am, Gunga Din![4]

Othello had represented the guilty awareness of Europe that the 'foreigner type' is only the type we do not know, whose foreignness vanishes when we have better acquaintance. * * *

Othello is then a play which manipulates our sympathies, supposing that we will have brought to the theatre a set of careless assumptions about 'Moors'. It assumes also that we will find it easy to abandon these as the play brings them into focus and identifies them with Iago, draws its elaborate distinction between the external appearance of devilishness and the inner reality.

Shakespeare's playcraft, however, would hardly have been able to superimpose these new valuations on his audience (unique as they were in this form) if it had not been for complicating factors which had begun to affect thought in his day.

The first counter-current I should mention is theological in origin and is found dispersed in several parts of the Bible. It was a fairly important doctrine of the Evangelists that faith could wash away

---

4. William Blake (1757–1827), poet and artist, included "The Little Black Boy" in his *Songs of Innocence* (1789). Rudyard Kipling (1865–1936), poet and novelist, wrote extensively about Anglo-India. [Editor's note]

the stains of sin, and the inheritance of misbelief, that the breach between chosen and non-chosen peoples could be closed by faith. The apostle Philip baptised the Ethiopian eunuch and thereupon, says Bede, the Ethiop changed his skin.[5] * * *

Augustine[6] asks who are meant by the Ethiopians; and answers that all nations are Ethiopians, black in their natural sinfulness; but they may become white in the knowledge of the Lord. *Fuistis enim aliquando tenebrae; nunc autem lux in Domino* (Ephesians 5. 8 ["For ye were sometimes darkness, but now *are ye* light in the Lord," King James Version]). As late as Bishop Joseph Hall, writing one of his *Occasional Meditations* (1630) 'on the sight of a blackamoor', we find the same use of *nigra sum sed speciosa* [I am black only in appearance]:

> This is our colour spiritually; yet the eye of our gracious God and Saviour, can see that beauty in us wherewith he is delighted. The true Moses marries a Blackamoor; Christ, his church. It is not for us to regard the skin, but the soul. If that be innocent, pure, holy, the blots of an outside cannot set us off from the love of him who hath said, *Behold, thou art fair, my Sister, my Spouse*: if that be foul and black, it is not in the power of an angelical brightness of our hide, to make us other than a loathsome eye-sore to the Almighty.

The relevance of this passage to Othello need not be stressed.

* * *

The sense that inferior and black-faced foreigners might in fact be figures from a more innocent world close to Christianity grew apace in the Renaissance as the voyagers gave their accounts, not of highly organized Mahomedan kingdoms, but of simple pagans, timid, naked as their mothers brought them forth, without laws and without arms (as Columbus first saw them and first described them) and perhaps having minds naturally prone to accept Christianity. The old ideals and dreams of travellers, the terrestial paradise, the fountain of youth, the kingdom of Prester John,[7] assumed a new immediacy. And so the old impulse to bring the Evangel to all nations acquired a new primitivist dynamic. * * * Alongside the view that such black pagans could only acquire Christian hope by enslavement grew an alternative vision of their innocence as bringing them near to God, by way

---

5. See 149 n. 2 above. Bede (672?–725) was a historian, theologian, and author of biblical commentaries. [Editor's note]
6. Saint Augustine (354–430), one of the most prominent of the early Church Fathers, is hugely influential for his autobiographical writing and ecclesiastical history, as well as for his biblical and theological commentaries. [Editor's note]
7. A mysterious king who, in a popular medieval legend, founded a perfect realm thought perhaps to exist somewhere in Africa or Asia. [Editor's note]

of nature. Nowhere was the opposition between these two views more dramatically presented than in the famous debate at Valladolid between Sepulveda and Las Casas.[8] Sepulveda asserted that the American Indians were 'slaves by nature', since their natural inferiority made it impossible for them to achieve the light of the gospel without enslavement.[9] Las Casas, on the other hand, dwelt on the innocence of the Indians, living *secundum naturam*, on their natural capacity for devotion, and on the appalling contrast between the mild and timid Indians and the inhumanity of their 'civilized' or 'Christian' exploiters. Of these two it was of course Las Casas who made the greatest impact in Europe. We should not forget that the Valladolid debate was decided in his favour; but it was not in Spain, but in France and England that primitivism grew most rapidly. * * *

The crown of all such Renaissance primitivism is Montaigne's *Essays*,[1] and especially that on the Cannibals, where the criticism of Spanish Christianity has become a *libertin* critique of modern European civility. Shakespeare, in *The Tempest*, seems to show a knowledge of this essay, and certainly *The Tempest* reveals a searching interest in the status of Western civilization parallel to Montaigne's, and a concern to understand the point of reconciliation between innocence and sophistication, ignorance and knowledge.

Of course, we must not assume that Shakespeare, because he had these concerns in *The Tempest*, must have had them also in *Othello*; but *The Tempest* at one end of his career, like *Titus Andronicus* at the other end, indicates that the polarities of thought on which *Othello* moves (if I am correct) were available to his mind.

I have spoken of 'polarities' in the plural because it is important to notice that Shakespeare does not present his *Othello* story in any simple primitivist terms. *Othello* is not adequately described as the exploitation of a noble savage by a corrupt European.[2] This is an element in the play, * * * but by giving too much importance to this it would be easy to underplay the extent to which Othello becomes what Iago and the society to which *we* belong assumes him to be.

---

8. Described most fully in English in L. Hanke, *Aristotle and the American Indians* (1959).
9. See Eric Williams, *Documents of West Indian History* (1963), item 155, discussing the view that a 'negro cannot become a Christian without being a slave'. Cf. the summary of Sepulveda's position in Hanke, op. cit., pp. 44 f. The same views persist today, though with interesting modifications in the vocabulary: 'He (the Negro) requires the constant control of white people to keep him in check. Without the presence of the white police force negroes would turn upon themselves and destroy each other. The white man is the only authority he knows.' (Quoted in E. T. Thompson, *Race Relations* [1939], p. 174.)
1. The *Essays* of Michel de Montaigne (1533–1592), much admired for their skeptical detachment and (as we would now say) cultural relativism, are frequently echoed in Shakespeare. [Editor's note]
2. But Iago's Spanish name (and his nautical imagery) may represent Shakespeare's awareness of this potentiality in his play at some level of his consciousness. The relevance of the figure of Sant' Iago Matamoros (Moor-slayer) has been suggested by G. N. Murphy, 'A Note on Iago's name', *Literature and Society*, ed. B. Slote (1964).

There is considerable strength in the anti-primitivist side of the great Renaissance debate (as that is represented in *Othello*) and this lies in the extent to which the whole social organism pictured is one we recognize as our own, and recognize as necessarily geared to reject 'extravagant and wheeling strangers'. I speak of the social organism here, not in terms of its official existence—its commands, duties, performances; for in these terms Othello's life is well meshed into the state machine:

> My services which I have done the Signiory
> Shall out-tongue his complaints. [1.2.18–19]

I speak rather of the unspoken assumptions and careless prejudices by which we all conduct most of our lives. And it is in these respects that Iago is the master of us all, the snapper-up of every psychological trifle, every unnoticed dropped handkerchief. It is by virtue of such a multitude of our tiny and unnoticed assents that Iago is able to force Othello into the actions he expects of him. Only the hermit can stand outside such social assumptions; but, by marrying, Othello has become part of society in this sense, the natural victim of the man-in-the-know, the man universally thought well of. And Iago's knowingness finds little or no resistance. We all believe the Iagos in our midst; they are, as our vocabulary interestingly insists, the 'realists'.

The dramatic function of Iago is to reduce the white 'reality' of Othello to the black 'appearance' of his face, indeed induce in him the belief that all reality is 'black', that Desdemona in particular, 'where I have garnered up my heart'

> . . . that was fresh
> As Dian's visage, is now begrimed and black
> As mine own face. [3.3.387–89] * * *

* * *

The dark reality originating in Iago's soul spreads across the play, blackening whatever it overcomes and making the deeds of Othello at last fit in with the prejudice that his face at first excited. Sometimes it is supposed that this proves the prejudice to have been justified. There is a powerful line of criticism on *Othello*, going back at least as far as A. W. Schlegel,[3] that paints the Moor as a savage at heart, one whose veneer of Christianity and civilization cracks as the play proceeds, to reveal and liberate his basic savagery: Othello turns out to be in fact what barbarians *have* to be.

---

3. August Wilhelm Schlegel, *Lectures on Dramatic Art* (1815), ii. 189.

This view, however comforting to our sense of society and our prejudices, does not find much support in the play itself. The fact that the darkness of 'Hell and night' spreads from Iago and then takes over Othello—this fact at least should prevent us from supposing that the blackness is inherent in Othello's barbarian nature. Othello himself, it is true, loses faith not only in Desdemona but in that fair quality of himself which Desdemona saw and worshipped: ('for she had eyes and chose me' [3.3.191]).

 * * * The tragedy becomes, as Helen Gardner has described it, a tragedy of the loss of faith.[4] And, such is the nature of Othello's heroic temperament, the loss of faith means the loss of all meaning and all value, all sense of light:

> I have no wife,
> O insupportable! O heavy hour!
> Methinks it should be now a huge eclipse
> Of sun and moon, and that the affrighted globe
> Should yawn at alteration. [5.2.99–103]

Universal darkness has buried all.

But the end of the play is not simply a collapse of civilization into barbarism, nor a destruction of meaning. Desdemona *was* true, faith *was* justified, the appearance was not the key to the truth. To complete the circle we must accept, finally and above all, that Othello was not the credulous and passionate savage that Iago has tried to make him, but that he was justified in his second, as in his first, self-defence:

> For nought I did in hate, but all in honour. [5.2.300]

The imposition of Iago's vulgar prejudices on Othello ('These Moors are changeable in their wills' [1.3.344], etc.) is so successful that it takes over not only Othello but almost all the critics. But Iago's suppression of Othello into the vulgar prejudice about him can only be sustained as the truth if we ignore the end of the play. The wonderful recovery here of the sense of ethical meaning in the world, even in the ashes of all that embodied meaning—this requires that we see the final speech of Othello as more than that of a repentant blackamoor 'cheering himself up', as Mr. Eliot phrased it.[5] It is in fact a marvellous *stretto* of all the themes that have sounded throughout the play. I shall only dwell on Othello's self-judgement and self-execution, repeating and reversing the judgement and execution on Desdemona and so, in a sense, cancelling them. Othello is the 'base

4. Helen Gardner, 'The Noble Moor', *Proceedings of the British Academy*, xli (1955).
5. T. S. Eliot, 'Shakespeare and the Stoicism of Seneca', reprinted in *Selected Essays* (1932), p. 130. [See above, p. 270.]

Indian' who threw away the white pearl Desdemona, but he is also the
state servant and Christian who, when the Infidel or 'black Pagan'
within him seemed to triumph,

> Took by the throat the circumcised dog
> And smote him—thus. [5.2.360–61]

With poetic justice, the Christian reality reasserts its superior position over the pagan appearance, not in terms that can be lived
through, but at least in terms that can be understood. We may
rejoice even as we sorrow, catharsis is achieved, for

> What may quiet us in a death so noble,[6]

as this in the Aleppo of the mind?

* * *

The domestic intensities of *King Lear* have been seen usefully
and interestingly (by Theodore Spencer, for example) in relation
to the intellectual history of the Renaissance.[7] The position of the
king obviously calls on one set of traditional assumptions, while
Edmund's doctrine of nature equally obviously draws on the views
of the *libertins*, of Montaigne and Machiavelli.[8] The pressure of
these larger formulations may be seen to add to the largeness of
scope in the play. *Othello*, on the other hand, is thought not to be a
play of this kind. 'The play itself is primarily concerned with the
effect of one human being on another',[9] says Spencer. It is true that
Iago operates in a less conceptualized situation than Edmund; but
the contrast between his world view and that of Othello is closely
related to the contrast between Edmund and Lear. On the one
side we have the chivalrous world of the Crusader, the effortless
superiority of the 'great man', the orotund public voice of the
leader, the magnetism of the famous lover. The values of the world
of late medieval and Renaissance magnificence seem compressed
in Othello—crusader, stoic, traveller, believer, orator, commander, lover—Chaucer's parfit knight, Spenser's Red Cross, the
Ruggiero of Ariosto.[1] In Iago we have the other face of the Renaissance (or Counter-Renaissance), rationalist, individual, empirical

---

6. Hunter quotes John Milton's *Samson Agonistes* (published 1671), line 1724. [Editor's
   note]
7. Theodore Spencer, *Shakespeare and the Nature of Man* (1943).
8. Niccolò Machiavelli (1469–1527), political theorist, historian, and sometime playwright, fascinated (and often repelled) English Renaissance audiences for his supposedly amoral pragmatism. [Editor's note]
9. Spencer, op. cit. (1961 ed.), p. 126.
1. Images of heroic chivalry in, respectively, *The Canterbury Tales* (late 14th century),
   The Faerie Queene (1590), and *Orlando Furioso* (1532). [Editor's note]

(or inductive), a master in the Machiavellian art of manipulating appearances, a Baconian or Hobbesian 'Realist'.[2]

In the conflict of Othello and Iago we have, as in that setting Edmund, Goneril and Regan against Lear and Gloucester, a collision of these two Renaissance views. Bradley points to a similarity between Lear and Othello, that they are both 'survivors of a heroic age living in a later and smaller world'. Both represent a golden age naïvety which was disappearing then (as now, and always). Lear's survival is across a temporal gap; his long life has carried him out of one age and stranded him in another. But Othello's travel is geographical rather than temporal, from the heroic simplicities of

> I fetch my life and being
> From men of royal siege [1.2.21]

into the supersubtle world of Venice, the most sophisticated and 'modern' city on earth, as it seemed to the Elizabethans.

Here, if anywhere, was the scene-setting for no merely domestic intrigue, but for an exercise in the quality of civilization, a contest between the capacities and ideals claimed by Christendom, and those that Christians were actually employing in that context where (as Marlowe says)

> . . . Indian Moors obey their Spanish lords.[3]

Othello's black skin makes the coexistence of his vulnerable romanticism and epic grandeur with the bleak or even pathological realism of Iago a believable fact. The lines that collide here started thousands of miles apart. But Shakespeare's choice of a black man for his Red Cross Knight, his Rinaldo,[4] has a further advantage. *Our* involvement in prejudice gives us a double focus on his reality. We admire him—I fear that one has to be trained as a literary critic to find him unadmirable—but we are aware of the difficulty of sustaining that vision of the golden world of poetry; and this is so because *we* feel the disproportion and the difficulty of his social life and of his marriage (as a social act). We are aware of the easy responses that Iago can command, not only of people on the stage but also in the audience. The perilous and temporary achievements of heroism are achieved most sharply in this play, because they have to be achieved in *our* minds, through *our* self-awareness.

---

2. Hunter brings the philosophers Sir Francis Bacon (1561–1626) and Thomas Hobbes (1588–1679) into the same orbit of unillusioned free inquiry as Machiavelli and Montaigne earlier. [Editor's note]
3. Marlowe, *Doctor Faustus*, 1. i. 122.
4. Protagonist of an early poem by Torquato Tasso (1544–1595), subsequently appearing in Tasso's *Jerusalem Delivered*, translated into English in 1660. [Editor's note]

STANLEY CAVELL

Epistemology and Tragedy:
A Reading of *Othello*†

* * *

We have known (say since G. Wilson Knight's "The Othello Music" [1930]) that Othello's language, call it his imagination, is at once his and the play's glory, and his shame; the source of his power and of his impotence; or we should have known (since Bradley's *Shakespearean Tragedy*) that Othello is the most romantic of Shakespeare's heroes [see 265 above], which may be a way of summarizing the same facts. And we ought to attend to the perception that Othello is the most Christian of the tragic heroes (expressed in Norman Rabkin's *Shakespeare and the Common Understanding* [1967]). Nor is there any longer any argument against our knowledge that Othello is black; and there can be no argument with the fact that he has just married, nor with the description, compared with the case of Shakespeare's other tragedies, that this one is not political but domestic.

We know more specifically, I take it, that Othello's blackness means something. But what specifically does it mean? Mean, I mean, to him—for otherwise it is not Othello's color that we are interested in but some generalized blackness, meaning perhaps "sooty" or "filthy," as elsewhere in the play. This difference may show in the way one takes Desdemona's early statement: "I saw Othello's visage in his mind" [1.3.250]. I think it is commonly felt that she means she overlooked his blackness in favor of his inner brilliance; and perhaps further felt that this is a piece of deception, at least of herself. But what the line more naturally says is that she saw his visage as he sees it, that she understands his blackness as he understands it, as the expression (or in his word, his manifestation) of his mind—which is not overlooking it. Then how does he understand it?

† From *Daedalus* 108.3 (Summer 1979): 35–41. © 1979 by the American Academy of Arts and Sciences. Reprinted by permission of MIT Press. The author's quotations from *Othello*—from *The Complete Works of William Shakespeare*, ed. G. B. Harrison (New York: Harcourt Brace, 1952)—have been retained, but bracketed references are to this Norton Critical Edition. Cavell's discussion of the play is situated in a tradition of philosophical reflection about skepticism, extending from Wittgenstein to Descartes, Montaigne, and beyond. For more information, see Cavell's revised version of the essay, "Othello and the Stake of the Other," in his *Disowning Knowledge in Six Plays of Shakespeare* (Cambridge, Eng.: Cambridge University Press, 1987), 125–42, as well as the introduction to the book, 1–37.

As the color of a romantic hero. For he, as he was and is, manifested by his parts, his title, and his "perfect soul" [1.2.31], is the
hero of the tales of romance he tells, some ones of which he wooed
and won Desdemona with, others of which he will die upon. It is
accordingly the color of one with enchanted powers and magical
protection, but above all it is the color of one of purity, of a perfect
soul. Desdemona, in entering his life, hence in entering his story of
his life, enters as a fit companion for such a hero; his perfection is
now opened toward hers. His absolute stake in his purity, and its
confirmation in hers, is shown in what he feels he has lost in losing
Desdemona's confirmation:

> . . . My name, that was as fresh
> As Dian's visage, is now begrimed and black
> As mine own face . . .
>
> [3.3.387–89]

Diana's is a name for the visage Desdemona saw to be in Othello's
mind. He loses its application to his own name, his charmed self,
when he no longer sees his visage in Desdemona's mind but in
Iago's, say in the world's capacity for rumor. To say he loses Desdemona's power to confirm his image of himself is to say that he
loses his old power of imagination. And this is to say that he loses
his grasp of his own nature; he no longer has the same voice in his
history. So then the question becomes: How has he come to displace Desdemona's imagination with Iago's? However terrible the
exchange, it must be less terrible than some other. Then we need
to ask not so much how Iago gained his power as how Desdemona
lost hers.

We know, one gathers, that Desdemona has lost her virginity,
the protection of Diana, by the time she appears to us. And surely
Othello knows this! But this change in her condition, while a big
enough fact to hatch millennia of plots, is not what Othello accuses
her of. (Though would that accusation have been much more unfair
than the unfaithfulness he does accuse her of?) I emphasize that I am
assuming that in Othello's mind the theme and condition of virginity
carry their full weight within a romantic universe. Here is Northrop
Frye, writing on the subject recently: "Deep within the stock convention of virgin-baiting is a vision of human integrity imprisoned in a
world it is in but not of, often forced by weakness into all kinds of
ruses and strategems, yet always managing to avoid the one fate
which really is worse than death, the annihilation of one's identity. . . . What is symbolized as a virgin is actually a human conviction, however expressed, that there is something at the core of one's
infinitely fragile being which is not only immortal but has discovered

the secret of invulnerability that eludes the tragic hero" (*The Secular Scripture* [1976], p. 86).

Now let us consolidate what we know in this sketch so far. We have to think in this play not merely about marriage but about the marriage of a romantic hero and of a Christian man, one whose imagination has to incorporate the idea of two becoming one in marriage and the idea that it is better to marry than to burn. It is a play, though it is thought of as domestic, in which not a marriage but an idea of marriage, or let us say an imagination of marriage, is worked out. "Why did I marry?" is the first question Othello asks himself, to express his first raid of suspicion (3.3.244). The question has never been from his mind. Iago's first question to him is "Are you fast married?' [1.2.11] and Othello's first set speech ends with something less than an answer: "But that I love the gentle Desdemona, / I would not my unhoused free condition / Put into circumscription and confine / For the sea's worth" [1.2.25–28]. Love is at most a necessary, not a sufficient, condition for marrying. And for some minds, a certain idea of love may compromise as much as validate the idea of marriage. It may be better, but it is not perfect to marry, as Saint Paul implies [see 155 above].

We have, further, to think in this play not merely generally of marriage but specifically of the wedding night. It is with this that the play opens. The central fact we know is that the whole beginning scene takes place while Othello and Desdemona are in their bridal bed. The simultaneity is marked: "Even now, now, very now, an old black ram / Is tupping your white ewe . . ." [1.1.85–86]. And the scene is one of treachery, alarms, of shouts, of armed men running through a sleeping city. The conjunction of the bridal chamber with a scene of emergency is again insisted on by Othello's reappearance from his bedroom to stop a brawl with his single presence; a reappearance repeated the first night in Cyprus. As though an appearance from his place of sex and dreams is what gives him the power to stop an armed fight with a word and a gesture. Or is this more than we know? Perhaps the conjunction is to imply that their "hour of love" [1.3.296–97], or their two hours, have each time been interrupted. There is reason to believe that the marriage has not been consummated, anyway reason to believe that Othello does not know whether it has. What is Iago's "Are you fast married?" asking? Whether a public, legal ceremony has taken place or whether a private act; or whether the public and the private have ratified one another? Othello answers by speaking of his nobility and his love. But apart from anything else this seems to assume that Iago's "you" was singular, not plural. And what does Othello mean in Cyprus by these apparently public words:

> . . . Come, my dear love,
> The purchase made, the fruits are to ensue—
> The profit's yet to come 'tween me and you.
>
> [2.3.8–10]

What is the purchase and what the fruits or profit? Othello has just had proclaimed a general celebration at once of the perdition of the Turkish fleet and of his nuptials [2.2]. If the fruits and profit is the resumption of their privacy, then the purchase was the successful discharge of his public office and his entry into Cyprus. But this success was not his doing; it was provided by a tempest. Is the purchase their (public) marriage? Then the fruits and profit is their conjugal love. Then he is saying that this is yet to come. It seems to me possible that the purchase, or price, was her virginity, and the fruits or profit their pleasure. There could hardly be greater emphasis on their having had just one shortened night together, isolated from this second night by a tempest (always in these matters symbolic, perhaps here of a memory, perhaps of an anticipation). Or is it, quite simply, that this is something he wishes to *say* publicly, whatever the truth between them? (How we imagine Desdemona's reaction to this would then become all important.)

I do not think that we must, or that we can, choose among these possibilities in Othello's mind. Rather, I think Othello cannot choose among them. My guiding hypothesis about the structure of the play is that the thing *denied our sight* throughout the opening scene— the thing, the scene, that Iago takes Othello back to again and again, retouching it for Othello's enchafed imagination—is what we are shown in the final scene, the scene of murder. This becomes our ocular proof of Othello's understanding of his two nights of married love. (It has been felt from Thomas Rymer [see 227 above] to [the modern British playwright and critic] G. B. Shaw that the play obeys the rhythm of farce, not of tragedy. One might say that in beginning with a sexual scene denied our sight, this play opens exactly as a normal comedy closes, as if it turned comedy inside out.) I will follow out this hypothesis here only to the extent of commenting on that final scene.

However one seeks to interpret the meaning of the great entering speech of the scene ("It is the cause, it is the cause, my soul. . . . Put out the light, and then put out the light" [5.2.1, 7]), I cannot take its mysteries, its privacies, its magniloquence, as separate from some massive denial to which these must be in service. Othello must mean that he is acting impersonally, but the words are those of a man in a trance, in a dream-state, fighting not to awaken; willing for anything but light. By "denial" here I do not initially mean something requiring psychoanalytical, or any other, theory. I mean merely to ask that we not, conventionally but insufferably, assume that we know this woman better than this man knows her—making Othello some kind of exotic, gorgeous, superstitious lunkhead; which is about what Iago thinks. However much Othello deserves each of these titles, however far he believes Iago's tidings, he cannot just believe them; somewhere he also *knows* them to be false. This is registered in the rapidity with which he is brought to the truth, with no further real evidence, with only a counter-story (about the handkerchief) that bursts over him, or from him, as the truth. Shall we say he recognizes the truth too late? The fact is, he recognizes it when he is ready to, as one alone can; in this case, when its burden is dead. I am not claiming that he is trying not to believe Iago, or wants not to believe what Iago has told him. (This might describe someone who, say, had a good opinion of Desdemona, not someone whose life is staked upon hers.) I am claiming, on the contrary, that we must understand Othello to be wanting to believe Iago, to be trying, against his knowledge, to believe him. Othello's eager insistence on Iago's honesty, his eager slaking of his thirst for knowledge with that poison, is not a sign of his stupidity in the presence of poison but of his devouring need of it. I do not quite say that he could not have accepted slander about Desdemona so quickly, to the quick, unless he already believed it; but rather that it is a thing he would rather believe than something yet more terrible to his mind; that the idea of Desdemona as an adulterous whore is more convenient to him than the idea of her as chaste. But what could be more terrible than Desdemona's faithlessness? Evidently her faithfulness. But how?

Note that in taking Othello's entering speech as part of a ritual of denial, in the context of taking the murder scene as a whole to be a dream-enactment of the invisible opening of the play, we have an answer implied to our original question about this play, concerning Othello's turning of Desdemona to stone. His image denies that he scarred her and shed her blood. It is a denial at once that he has taken her virginity and that she has died of him. The whole scene of murder is built on the concept of sexual intercourse or orgasm as a dying. There is a dangerously explicit quibble to this effect in the exchange,

> *Oth.*   Thou art on thy death bed.
> *Des.* Aye, but not yet to die.
>
>   [5.2.52–53]

The possible quibble only heightens the already heartbreaking poignance of the wish to die in her marriage bed after a long life.

Though Desdemona no more understands Othello's accusation of her than, in his darkness to himself, he does, she obediently shares his sense that this is their final night and that it is to be some dream-like recapitulation of their former two nights. This shows in her pre-monitions of death (the Willow Song, and the request that one of the wedding sheets be her shroud) and in her mysterious request to Emilia, ". . . tonight / Lay on my bed my wedding sheets" [4.2.106–07]; as if knowing, and faithful to, Othello's private dream of her, herself preparing the scene of her death as Othello, utilizing Iago's stage directions, imagines it must happen ("Do it not with poison, strangle her in her bed, even the bed she hath contaminated." "Good, good. The justice of it pleases. Very good" [4.1.201–03]; as if knowing that only with these sheets on their bed can his dream of her be con-tested. The dream is of contamination. The fact the dream works upon is the act of deflowering. Othello is reasonably literal about this, as reasonable as a man in a trance can be:

> . . . When I have plucked the rose,
> I cannot give it vital growth again,
> It must needs wither. I'll smell it on the tree.
> Ah, balmy breath, that dost almost persuade
> Justice to break her sword! One more, one more.
> Be thus when thou art dead, and I will kill thee,
> And love thee after. . . .
>
> [5.2.13–19]

(Necrophilia is an apt fate for a mind whose reason is suffocating in its sumptuous capacity for figuration, and which takes the dying into love literally to entail killing. "That death's unnatural that kills for loving" [5.2.42]; or that turns its object to live stone. It is apt as well that Desdemona sense death, or the figure of death, as the impending cause of death. And at the very end, facing himself, he will not recover from this. "I kissed thee ere I killed thee" [5.2.363]. And after too. And not just now when you died from me, but on our previous nights as well.)

The exhibition of wedding sheets in this romantic, superstitious, conventional environment can only refer to the practice of proving purity by staining. I mention in passing that this provides a satis-factory weight for the importance Othello attaches to his charmed (or farcical) handkerchief, the fact that it is spotted, spotted with strawberries.

Well, were the sheets stained or not? Was she a virgin or not? The answers seem as ambiguous as to our earlier question whether they are fast married. Is the final, fatal reenactment of their wed-ding night a clear denial of what really happened, so that we can just read off, by negation, what really happened? Or is it a straight reenactment, without negation, and the flower was still on the tree, as far as he knew? In that case, who was reluctant to see it plucked, he or she? On such issues, farce and tragedy are separated by the thickness of a membrane.

We of course have no answer to such questions. But what matters is that Othello has no answer; or rather he can give none, for any answer to the question, granted that I am right in taking the question to be his, is intolerable. The torture of logic in his mind we might represent as follows: Either I shed her blood and scarred her or I did not. If I did not then she was not a virgin and this is a stain upon me. If I did then she is no longer a virgin and this is a stain upon me. Either way I am contaminated. (I do not say that the sides of this dilemma are of equal significance for Othello.)

But this much logic anyone but a lunkhead might have mastered apart from actually marrying. (He himself may say as much when he asks himself, too late, why he married.) Then what quickens this logic for him? Call whatever it is Iago. What is Iago?

He is everything, we know, Othello is not. Critical and witty, for example, where Othello is commanding and eloquent; retentive where the other is lavish; concealed where the other is open; cynical where the other is romantic; conventional where the other is original; imagines flesh where the other imagines spirit; the imaginer and manager of the human guise; the bottom end of the world. And so on. A Christian has to call him devil. The single fact between Othello and Iago I focus on here is that Othello fails twice at the end to kill Iago, knowing he cannot kill him. This all but all-powerful chieftain is stopped at this nobody. It is the point of his impotence, and the meaning of it. Iago is everything Othello must deny, and which, denied, is not killed but works on, like poison, like furies.

In speaking of the point and meaning of Othello's impotence, I do not think of Othello as having been in an everyday sense impotent with Desdemona. I think of him, rather, as having been surprised by her, at what he has elicited from her; at, so to speak, a success rather than a failure. It is the dimension of her that shows itself in that difficult and dirty banter between her and Iago as they await Othello on Cyprus. Rather than imagine himself to have elicited that, or solicited it, Othello would imagine it elicited by anyone and everyone else. Surprised, let me say, to find that she is flesh and blood. It was the one thing he could not imagine for himself. For if she is flesh and blood then, since, they are one, so is he. But then although his potency of imagination can command the imagination of this child who is everything he is not, so that she sees his visage in his mind, she also sees that he is not identical with his mind, he is more than his imagination, black with desire, which she desires. Iago knows it, and Othello cannot bear what Iago knows, so he cannot outface the way in which he knows it, or knows anything. He cannot forgive her for existing, for being separate from him, outside, beyond command, commanding, her captain's captain.

It is an unstable frame of mind which compounds figurative with literal dying in love; and Othello unstably projects upon her, as he blames her:

> O perjured woman! Thou dost stone thy heart,
> And makest me call what I intend to do
> A murder, which I thought a sacrifice.
>
> [5.2.64–66]

As he is the one who gives out lies about her, so he is the one who will give her a stone heart for her stone body, as if in his words of stone which confound the figurative and the literal there is the confounding of the incantations of poetry and of magic. He makes of her the thing he feels (". . . my heart is turned to stone" [4.1.177–78]), but covers the ugliness of his thought with the beauty of his imagery—a debasement of himself and of his art of words. But what produces the idea of sacrifice? How did he manage the thought of her death as a sacrifice? To what was he to sacrifice her? To his image of himself and of her, to keep his image intact, uncontaminated; as if *this* were his protection from slander's image of him, say from a conventional view of his blackness. So he becomes conventional, sacrificing love to convention. But this was unstable; it could not be said. Yet better thought than the truth, which was that the central sacrifice of romance has already been made by them: her virginity, her intactness, her perfection, had been gladly foregone by her for him, for the sake of their union, for the seaming of it. It is the sacrifice he could not accept, for then he was not himself perfect. It must be displaced. The scar is the mark of finitude, of separateness; it must be borne whatever one's anatomical condition, or color. It is the sin or the sign of refusing imperfection that produces, or justifies, the visions and torments of devils that inhabit the region of this play.

If such a man as Othello is rendered impotent and murderous by aroused, or by having aroused, female sexuality; or let us say: if this man is horrified by human sexuality, in himself and in others; then no human being is free of this possibility. What I have wished to bring out is the nature of this possibility, or the possibility of this nature, the way human sexuality is the field in which the fantasy of finitude, of its acceptance and its repetitious overcoming, is worked out; the way human separateness is turned equally toward splendor and toward horror, mixing beauty and ugliness; turned toward before and after; toward flesh and blood. * * *

* * *

JAMES R. SIEMON

"Nay, That's Not Next": *Othello*, V.ii in Performance, 1760–1900[†]

Shakespeare's directing hand offers guidance to readers and performers, but individuals as well as eras have not merely ignored that
direction but have, on occasion, firmly rejected it. When taken as a
group, the evasions, embellishments, and outright contradictions of
Shakespeare's text that win acceptance in the late eighteenth- and
nineteenth-century performances of the final scene of *Othello* suggest a coherence of interpretation based on particular notions of
both tragedy and femininity. Understanding the strains that the
era put upon the scene makes us more aware of those notions, and,
at the same time, directs our attention to notable features of the
Shakespearean text itself.[1]

[†] From *Shakespeare Quarterly* 37.1 (1986): 38–51. © 1986 Folger Shakespeare Library.
Reprinted with the permission of Johns Hopkins University Press. The author's quota-
tions from *Othello* have been retained, but bracketed references are to this Norton
Critical Edition.

1. This essay is so heavily indebted to the influence of the late Bernard Beckerman that I
wish to record here my immense gratitude to him. The essay is primarily based upon
performance records in the Folger Shakespeare Library and the Harvard Theatre Collection, especially the annotated promptbooks, which number 58 items (in a field
defined by approximately 110 entries dating to 1900 in Charles H. Shattuck's *The
Shakespeare Promptbooks* [Urbana: Univ. of Illinois Press, 1965]), and which document
performances by leading actors in England and America. I am indebted to the Folger
Shakespeare Library and the Harvard Theatre Collection for assistance and for permission to cite manuscript sources, to the Graduate School of Boston University for
research funding and to Professor Lynda E. Boose, whose work on *Othello* has fur-
nished ideas and insights too numerous to mention. Professor Shattuck offered tren-
chant criticism at an important phase of writing.
   I refer throughout to the final scene of *Othello* as *Othello*, [5.2], though it was
variously labeled in the promptbooks and acting editions of the period under inves-
tigation. Quotations from the play itself, unless otherwise noted, are taken from the
Arden edition of *Othello*, ed. M. R. Ridley (1958; rpt. New York: Random House,
1967).
   Among invaluable critical sources for this study are: H. H. Furness's Variorum
Othello (1886; rpt. New York: American Scholar Publications, 1965) with its notes on
performance; Marvin Rosenberg's classic study, *The Masks of Othello* (Berkeley: Univ.
of California Press, 1961), and his "The 'Refinement' of *Othello* in the Eighteenth
Century British Theatre," *Studies in Philology*, 51 (1954), 75–94; Gino J. Matteo's
Shakespeare's "Othello": The Study and the Stage (Salzburg: Institut für Englische
Sprache und Literatur, 1974) treats the relation between criticism and performance. On
this relation, *see* also C. J. Carlisle, "The Nineteenth-Century Actors Versus the Closet
Critics," *Studies in Philology*, 51 (1954), 599–615. I have made abundant use of data and
insights from Matteo and from Arthur Colby Sprague's *Shakespeare and the Actors*
(Cambridge, Mass.: Harvard Univ. Press, 1948). Also very helpful is Carlisle's *Shakespeare from the Greenroom* (Chapel Hill: Univ. of North Carolina Press, 1969), which
has a section on *Othello*, [5.2] in performance. Students of *Othello* in performance
should see also William P. Halstead, *Shakespeare as Spoken: A Collation of 5000 Acting
Editions and Promptbooks of Shakespeare*, 11 (Ann Arbor: Univ. Microfilms International, 1977–80).

I

If, as William Winter maintains while looking back over nineteenth-century productions, performances of *Othello* can be classified according to their treatment of the final scene, it is not only because the scene demands crucial decisions about themes and characters.[2] The scene tests productions by its extremity, an emotional violence that elicited intensely negative reactions throughout the later eighteenth and the nineteenth centuries, from Dr. Johnson's plaint—"I am glad that I have ended my revisal of this dreadful scene. It is not to be endured" [see 245 above]—to the remarks of Halliwell as recorded in the Variorum edition:

> Without disputing the masterly power displayed in the composition of the present tragedy, there is something to my mind so revolting, both in the present scene and in the detestable character of Iago, which renders a study of the drama of *Othello* rather a painful duty than one of pleasure.

To which H. H. Furness adds:

> I do not shrink from saying that I wish this Tragedy had never been written. The pleasure, however keen or elevated, which the inexhaustible poetry of the preceding Acts can bestow, cannot possibly to my temperament, countervail, it does but increase, the unutterable agony of this closing scene.[3]

Surely it is not the amount of violence that makes this scene "not to be endured," "revolting," and a source of "unutterable agony." Two murders, one wounding, and a suicide hardly qualify the scene as exceptionally bloody for Shakespeare. Nor in the case of Dr. Johnson does the objection seemingly arise from a belief that domestic violence is unsuitable for tragedy. Johnson's own *Irene* demands the murder of a wife at her husband's instigation, a murder, moreover, that evidently was enacted on stage during part of the play's brief life.[4] The objections stem, I suspect, rather from the particular manner of the violence implied in the Shakespearean text—a matter of concern among the actors of the period as well. "This last scene," Fanny Kemble writes in 1884, "presents technical difficulties in its

---

2. William Winter, *Shakespeare on the Stage* (New York: Moffatt, 1911), p. 292.
3. Citation of Johnson's note from *Johnson on Shakespeare*, ed. Walter Raleigh (1908; rpt. London: Oxford Univ. Press, 1925), p. 200. Halliwell and Furness are cited in Furness's Variorum *Othello*, p. 300. See also Winter, p. 270.
4. See *The Poems of Samuel Johnson*, eds. David Nichol Smith and Edward L. McAdam (Oxford: Clarendon Press, 1974), pp. 274–75.

adequate representation which have never yet been even partially overcome."[5]

Viewed in the context of the critics' repugnance and the performer's scepticism, performance records from the later eighteenth and the nineteenth centuries—roughly the period bracketed by the remarks of Johnson and Furness—constitute a fascinating body of evidence, for in them one can see a culture trying to control a text that it desires to experience in the theatre but that it also strongly disapproves. Unlike *King Lear, Othello* was not rewritten for the English stage with a more acceptable ending; audiences demanded the final scene with its mixture of violence and eroticism despite the horrors it evoked in critics and the technical worries it created for performers.[6] As a result, the theatre became a place where limits were tested, technical matters becoming the loci of contests between desire and permissibility.

II

Decisions about the technical features of [5.2] are already important before a line of the scene has been spoken. As the text demands, Desdemona is always portrayed, when the scene opens, in bed asleep, her surroundings varying predictably enough with the particular period of the production. The surprising thing is the consistency with which the period keeps the bed approximately centered and as far upstage as possible, a position that Fanny Kemble found to create serious practical problems of visibility and audibility for Othello, whose first lines are most appropriately delivered while bending over Desdemona.[7] Not till the middle of the nineteenth century do performers like Fechter and Booth move the bed downstage and to one side, to a position, that is, from which Othello's facial expressions might be clearly observed as he kisses (and later kills) Desdemona and from which Desdemona's struggles might be easily concealed

5. Fanny Kemble, "Salvini's *Othello*," *Temple Bar*, 71 (1884), 368–78; 376.

6. A modified version was attempted for the French stage, but once having seen the final scene in its English form, French audiences demanded it be played that way—despite professed shock and outbreaks of fainting. See *Blackwood's Magazine*, 18 (1825), 299–300. The play offers a contrast to *King Lear*, which held the stage in Nahum Tate's adapted version during the same period. It should be emphasized that evidence of actors working upon reasonably accurate Shakespearean texts is abundant and early. Restoration playbooks seem to have been full Shakespearean texts (see Matteo, pp. 59–60). The Folger Library possesses a copy of a 1747 duodecimo (London: C. Hitch) thought to be marked in Garrick's hand, which collates Quarto and Folio versions. Extensive cutting, however, is the usual theatrical practice from early on, as remarks by an early eighteenth-century observer reveal; see *Original and Genuine Letters sent to the Tatler and Spectator*, ed. Charles Lille (London, 1725), I, 256–57.

7. Kemble, p. 378.

from the audience.[8] Perhaps the violence that takes place on that bed was made more tolerable, more "sacrificial" in the terminology of the period's commentators, through distance and symmetrical setting. "'Tradition' was right in placing Desdemona's couch at a remote part of the stage," observes Sir Theodore Martin, who condemned Fechter's relocation of the bed for "bringing it so far forward that every detail is thrust painfully on our senses."[9] Similarly complex interactions between the desire to see and the need to be protected from unmediated vision reveal themselves through other decisions about technical features and stage business.

Othello's entry in [5.2] also entails a significant technical decision as it becomes, in the early eighteenth century, an entrance not only "with light" (as in Quarto directions) but also with "a sword." The armed entry can be documented on the stage as early as 1761, and it persists in acting editions as well as in actors' promptbooks into the twentieth century.[1] An 1822 acting edition criticizes the armed entry as "incorrect and unnecessary," but includes it as "according to modern practice"; and, in fact, the evidence indicates that, during the late eighteenth and nineteenth centuries, the scene was felt to go better if—in spite of the decision for strangulation in [4.1] and the refusal to mar her perfect skin in [5.2] itself—Othello entered conspicuously carrying and sometimes even brandishing a sword. This initial entry with the sword leads, furthermore, to subsequent business in the middle of Othello's third line. The "yet" in "It is the cause. Yet I'll not shed her blood" is interpreted to suggest Othello in debate with himself, as if questions about using the knife were just being

8. See Booth's note in Furness's Variorum, p. 292. Booth's relocation of the bed was thought to be so serious that when in 1881 he and Henry Irving alternated in the roles of Othello and Iago, Irving had the bed moved back to center stage on the nights he played the Moor. Alan Hughes, *Henry Irving, Shakespearean* (Cambridge: Cambridge Univ. Press, 1981), p. 149.
9. "Shakespeare and His Latest Stage Interpreters," *Fraser's Magazine*, 64 (1861), 772–86; 783. Demands that the murder be treated as a sacrifice span the period; see Samuel Foote, *A Treatise on the Passions, So Far as They Regard the Stage* (London: 1747), pp. 33–34; and Winter, p. 296. Mrs. James calls Desdemona a "victim consecrated from the first," *Shakespeare's Heroines* (London: 1897), p. 182. James Boaden praises Mrs. Siddons's skill "in the performance of this gentle sacrifice," *Memoirs of the Life of John Philip Kemble* (London: 1825), p. 258. See also *The Theatrical Journal*, 6 June 1855, p. 184; and Bell's acting edition (London: 1777), p. 84; *Punch*, 14 December 1861, p. 241.
1. Acting editions with the armed entry include: Garland, 1765; Butters, 1787–89; Barker, ca. 1800; Oxberry, 1819; Charpentier, 1882. Among the promptbooks are John Palmer, 1766; anonymous, 1783 (Folger PR 1241 C95); Richard Power, 1803; John Howard Payne, ca. 1810. More modern instances of such entry can be found in Henry Jewett's promptbook of 1895–96 (Folger *Othello* promptbook 35) and Lewis Waller's promptbook of 1906 (Folger *Othello* promptbook Folio 1). Editions that do not claim to be "as performed" also include the armed entrance from early in the eighteenth century: see, for example, Lewis Theobald's 1733 edition. The lines about lust's blood in [5.1] that might suggest a wavering in Othello's resolve are, as far as I have been able to verify, never included in acting editions or promptbooks during the period.

resolved; and whether or not Othello flourished a naked weapon, it became tradition for him to lay down a sword during his initial speech. Even Edwin Booth, although he did not follow his father, Junius Brutus Booth, in entering with lamp and naked scimitar, felt compelled to half-draw and then relinquish a dagger while speaking his line.[2]

The implications of syntax are not the only factors which possibly led actors to favor such questionable embellishments. After all, an entry with light and sword in this scene would precisely repeat the entry of Iago on his own murderous errand in the previous scene. The visual point made by the similar entries of villain and hero would be strong, and the potential similarity between the two figures may have been further reinforced by the staging of Iago's earlier entry "in his shirt" [5.1.47], a nocturnal attire appropriate to Othello in [5.2]. Thus their kinship in murder could be emphasized, even though the period cuts Othello's appearance in [5.1], thereby deleting his lines about modeling himself after Iago.[3] But would not a suggestion of similarity between Othello and Iago run counter to the age's nearly universal insistence on Othello's nobility?[4] Perhaps not, if the impression of outward similarity were rapidly to give way to a representation of the internal differences that set them apart. And here Othello's candle has a possible part to play.

Since Desdemona is asleep when Othello enters, it would seem verisimilar by period standards that the stage be darkened, but if the scene were darkened, the full visual impact of the emotional agonies that differentiate Othello from Iago might be obscured by his Moorish makeup. Thus, there is a quite practical aspect to Othello's entry "with light," although entry with a candle (or, as in some cases, discovery with lamp) by no means solved the lighting problems of the scene as a whole. Even if performers did not universally follow the literalism of those eighteenth-century commentators who argued that a light must be extinguished during Othello's "put out the light" lines, the difficulty of lighting Othello's darkened face

2. See Folger *Othello* promptbooks 27, 17, 9, and Harvard Theatre Collection Ms. 219; on Booth's father, see Winter, p. 257. An observer in 1791 suggests that the second "yet" of the passage ("yet she must die") was "generally" accompanied by a threatening gesture toward Desdemona and complains that Kemble's choice to make this gesture with a dagger was inconsistent with the lines about not scarring Desdemona's skin (*The Theatrical Guardian*, 2 April 1791, p. 35).

3. Some very slight evidence suggests that Booth employed similarly striped cloaks for hero and villain in the two scenes. Compare the photograph of Booth as Iago in [5.1] in Winter (p. 270)—presumably the same sort of cloak referred to in Folger *Othello* promptbook 3 as Iago's "striped black and white cloak"—with the references to a trailing, striped cloak in Harvard Theatre Collection Ms. 219.

4. For this insistence, see Matteo, chap. 5, and Carlisle, *Shakespeare from the Greenroom*, p. 207.

remained.[5] With the advent of more sophisticated lighting in the nineteenth century, it became popular to add a light source to the scene in the form of a window. The light from such a window—a "Green Medium, or Calcium Light, to strike on Othello's face through Window C from R" in Kean's touring performances; simulated moonlight in Booth's performances of the 1880s; or lightning flashes according to the records of Salvini (1875), R. B. Mantell (1888) and Charles B. Hanford (1895)—provided this important illumination.[6] Technical solutions to problems of lighting achieved perhaps the most melodramatic embodiment with Mantell, who used the din of thunder and flash of lightning in counterpoint with music that played until Desdemona awakened:

THUNDER AND LIGHTNING It is the cause, it is the cause, my soul,
Let me not name it to you, you chaste stars:
It is the cause THUNDER AND LIGHTNING yet I'll not shed her blood
Nor scar that whiter skin of hers than snow,
And smooth, as monumental alabaster; THUNDER AND LIGHTNING
Yet she must die, else she'll betray more men.
Put out the light, and then put out the light?
THUNDER AND LIGHTNING[7]

Such sublime effects run counter to implications of the text, of course, for (even leaving aside the reference to "chaste stars") when Othello later laments Desdemona's death—

> O heavy hour!
> Methinks it should be now a huge eclipse
> Of sun and moon, and that the affrighted globe
> Should yawn at alteration.
>
> [5.2.100–103]

—the pathos arises from the fact that no world-altering tempest lends universal resonance to his action. The death of Desdemona is a smaller, more human matter, something to be hidden, as Othello

5. Samuel Foote, in comparing Garrick, Quin, and Barry as Othello, complains of the black makeup as hindering perceptions of the character (*Treatise*, p. 25). The failings of black makeup are discussed "as being destructive of the face, and preventing the possibility of the expression being noted" by Leman Thomas Rede in his consideration of Edmund Kean's innovative change to a brown preparation (*The Road to the Stage* [London: 1827], pp. 38–39); see also Carlisle, *Shakespeare from the Greenroom,* p. 190. See Theobald's remarks stressing the role of the candle on the darkened stage in *The Works of Shakespeare* (London: 1733), VII, 481.
6. Folger *Othello* promptbooks Tb 15 (Kean), 9 (Hanford), and 25 (Mantell). Salvini's standing by a window "with the lightning playing upon his face" in an 1875 performance is recorded in Joseph Knight's *Theatrical Notes* (London: 1893), pp. 23–24; see also Furness, p. 293. For Booth, see Harvard Theatre Collection Ms. 219. Forrest's use of moonlight and candle is described in Gabriel Harrison's *Edwin Forrest* (Brooklyn: 1889), pp. 92–93.
7. Folger *Othello* promptbook 25.

promptly hides it, and as the command to "let it be hid" (issued in the Shakespearean text, if not in the period's acting texts) would keep it. Might not some of the appeal of the simulated storm have arisen from the way such pyrotechnics counter the very domesticity potential in the scene's violence? A titanic, Byronic Othello sundering the universal order was perhaps more acceptable as a subject of high tragedy than the strangler of a defenseless wife.[8]

Yet defenseless she remains. Despite the inflation of Othello to sublime proportions, the agreement among performers concerning Desdemona's passivity is striking. A few productions in the mid-nineteenth century, most notably Charles Fechter's and Ira Aldridge's, have Desdemona attempt escape or resistance, it is true. While Fechter's performances apparently did not enact the full violence depicted by his stage directions, in Fechter's 1861 acting edition Desdemona "rushes to the door," and as Othello bars escape, "in mad fury, he whirls round his sword"; he "carries her to the bed on which he throws her; then stifles her cries with the pillow which he presses with both hands."[9] Aldridge, according to his Desdemona, Madge Kendal, "used to take Desdemona out of the bed by her hair and drag her around the stage before he smothered her"—a sequence "loudly hissed."[1] But such highly exciting action never really caught on in the theatre of the period, and, as we shall see, voiced objections have as much to do with notions of femininity as with standards of tragic decorum.

Rejecting Salvini's practice, according to which Desdemona rises from bed to confront Othello in her initial lines, Fanny Kemble berates Salvini for failure to follow stage tradition and the manifest "intention of Shakespeare . . . who makes Othello tell his wife that she is on her death-bed, and in reply to this furious command, 'Peace, be still,' receives the answer, 'I will. . . .'"[2] While leaving open the possibility that an actress "equal to the situation" might subsequently rise to throw herself in supplication at Othello's feet, Kemble asserts that as of 1884 no one had to her knowledge proven successful in such an active interpretation of Desdemona and she makes her own preference for a passive Desdemona clear:

8. In reviewing an 1837 *Othello*, Charles Rice firmly rejects the domestic potential in Desdemona: "in the domestic the character is not to be reckoned." *The London Theatre in the Eighteen-Thirties,* eds. Arthur Colby Sprague and Bertram Shuttleworth (London: Society for Theatre Research, 1950), p. 57.
9. *Charles Fechter's Acting Edition of "Othello"* (London: 1861), p. 104. Commentary in *The Athenaeum,* 2 November 1861, p. 587, approves Fechter's decision not to follow these directions to the letter; see also *Fraser's Magazine,* 64 (December 1861), 783. Contrast Booth's rejection of such lively antics as practiced by Salvini; see Carlisle, *Shakespeare from the Greenroom,* p. 207.
1. Cited in Herbert Marshall and Mildred Stock, *Ira Aldridge: The Negro Tragedian* (Carbondale: Southern Illinois Univ. Press, 1968), p. 312.
2. Kemble, p. 378.

> The terrified woman cowers down upon her pillow like a poor frightened child. Indeed the whole scene loses its most pitiful elements by allowing Desdemona to confront Othello standing, instead of uttering the piteous pleadings for mercy in the helpless prostration of her half recumbent position.[3]

In this preference, Kemble takes her place in a cultural tradition that spans the eighteenth and nineteenth centuries and is by no means limited to the theatre.

Three years before Dr. Johnson's 1765 edition of Shakespeare, Lord Kames's influential *Elements of Criticism* articulates the sentimentalist tradition into which the period's Desdemona will be made to fit.[4] Given the sentimentalist location of virtue in responsiveness, what could be a greater incitement to virtuous sentiment than the experience of innocent beauty in helpless distress? "Female beauty accordingly," Kames writes, "shows best in distress; being more apt to inspire love, than upon an ordinary occasion."[5] Would Desdemona be as appealing "in distress" if she made a show of physical resistance? The commentators of the period, both popular and learned, certainly insist on her passivity. So Hazlitt finds Desdemona's "whole character consists in having no will of her own."[6] Mrs. Jameson discovers that "gentleness gives the prevailing tone to the character—gentleness in its excess—gentleness verging on passiveness—gentleness, which not only cannot resent—but cannot resist." Furthermore, "in Desdemona we cannot but feel that the slightest manifestation of intellectual power or active will would have injured the dramatic effect."[7] Campbell's *Remarks on*

---

3. Kemble, p. 378. Compare the outraged response to Brooke's Desdemona having "struggled, in almost an erect position" as "out of character, even in the presence of an extreme so desperate," and citing Brabantio's lines about the never bold Desdemona as definitive. *The Athenaeum*, 10 September 1853, p. 1074. For an early, contrasting view, at odds with majority opinion, see Carlisle's account of actor-manager George Swan's notes on *Othello*, sent to David Garrick in 1773 and recommending, among other innovations, physical skirmishes between Othello and Desdemona (Carlisle, *Shakespeare from the Greenroom*, pp. 254–57). Booth suggests Desdemona come from the bed briefly but she "rests trembling against it" before "sinking to her knees" and "half reclining on the steps and dais of the bed"; her subsequent brief struggle with Othello should be hidden from the audience by Othello (Furness Variorum, p. 301).

4. The tradition is amply documented in Joseph W. Donohue, Jr., *Dramatic Character in the English Romantic Age* (Princeton: Princeton Univ. Press, 1970), pp. 50–52 and chap. 5.

5. *Elements of Criticism* (1762; rpt. New York: 1823), 1, 76. For an account of the relations between sexual passion and sensibility in the eighteenth century, see Jean H. Hagstrum, *Sex and Sensibility* (Chicago: Univ. of Chicago Press, 1980); on the nineteenth century, see Peter Gay, *Education of the Senses* (New York: Oxford Univ. Press, 1984). Steven Marcus claims that the "cult of sensibility was at its origins connected with sexuality, with sexual claims and influences," and relates the impulses of sensibility to the language of Victorian pornography (*The Other Victorians* [New York: Basic Books, 1964], esp. p. 208). On woman as victim during the period, see note [2, p. 305] below.

6. *Characters of Shakespeare's Plays* (London: 1817), p. 53. [See 255 above.]

7. *Shakespeare's Heroines*, pp. 175, 182.

the Life and Writings of Shakespeare (1838) gives the question its most explicit response:

> The terrors of the storm are also made striking to our imagination by the gentleness of the victim on which they fall,—Desdemona. Had one symptom of an angry spirit appeared in that lovely martyr, our sympathy with her would have been endangered; but Shakespeare knew better.[8]

And the tradition remains strong even in Bradley, for whom Desdemona

> is helplessly passive. She can do nothing whatever. She cannot retaliate even in speech; no, not even in silent feeling. And the chief reason of her helplessness only makes the sight of her suffering more exquisitely painful. She is helpless because her nature is infinitely sweet and her love absolute.[9]

This insistence on Desdemona as passive victim in the critic's meditation and the performer's representation, an insistence characteristic as well of the visual art derived from the play, which takes the juxtaposition of the armed Othello to the recumbent Desdemona as one of its most popular subjects, supports Nina Auerbach's thesis that the image of "prone womanhood" has a special attraction for the nineteenth century.[1] And the language evoked by the scene bolsters her argument that "Victorian womanhood is most delectable as a victim," as it mimics the language and strategies of pornography:

> It is an unalloyed delight . . . to see her sad, fearful, yet gentle as a bruised dove bend meekly to the implacable jealousy of the swart Othello, and receive her death, while kissing the hand which gives it.[2]

8. Cited in Matteo, p. 239.
9. A. C. Bradley, *Shakespearean Tragedy* (1905; rpt. London: Macmillan, 1915), p. 179. [See 262 above.] Compare Ellen Terry on the role: "My appearance was right—I was such a poor wraith of a thing. But it took strength to act this weakness and passiveness of Desdemona's. I soon found that like Cordelia, she has plenty of character." These remarks appear in the preface to the Booth edition of *Othello*, ed. William Winter (New York: 1881).
1. The Folger Library is rich in illustrations of the scene; for convenient viewing, see Delacroix's *Othello and Desdemona* (1847–49) in Peter Raby, *"Fair Ophelia": A Life of Harriet Smithson Berlioz* (Cambridge: Cambridge Univ. Press, 1982), p. 180; and Winifred H. Friedman, *Boydell's Shakespeare Gallery* (New York: Garland, 1976), pls. 194–96.
2. For an account of the importance of such images and of the cultural forces making the image of woman "most delectable as a victim" compelling for the period, see Auerbach's *Woman and the Demon* (Cambridge, Mass.: Harvard Univ. Press, 1982), esp. the chapter "The Myth of Womanhood: Victims." The cited passage is from *Tallis's Dramatic Magazine* (April 1851), 168. Compare Francis Gentleman who claims "pity never received a more powerful call than to see sleeping innocence at the brink of destruction" and describes audience reaction as "every soft sensation is put into a tremulative state, and the susceptible spectator must feel an exquisite share of painful pleasure, to see a determined murderer, who moves us more to compassion than detestation" (*The Dramatic Censor* [London: 1770], I, 147).

Furthermore, the related phenomenon of inflating Emilia's reactions to Othello's abuse of her lady into major, show-stopping expressions of grand outrage seems a particularly telling displacement of energy from the idealized feminine victim onto a domestic "virago" double.[3]

The cultural anxieties that might give rise to such commonly agreed upon decisions about the text (and commonly agreed upon images of woman) seem clear in H. N. Hudson's championing of Desdemona as an alternative to the emergent threat of "a new edition of woman"—the "mannish" woman.[4] Rhapsodic in his praise of Desdemona as unspeakably divine, Hudson defines her essence as submission, a quality all-the-more awe inspiring for its absence among contemporary women:

> Meek, uncomplaining, submissive even unto death where she owes allegiance, her character is not of the sort to take with a self-teaching, self-obeying generation; and I know not whether there be more of sacrilege in presuming to scrutinize her for myself or in holding her up for the scrutiny of others. The beauty of the woman is so hid in the obedience and affection of the wife, that it almost seems a profanation to praise it.
>
> (*Lectures on Shakespeare*, p. 336)

Hudson goes on to say that the "savans of the age" may sneer because she "does not approve herself a champion of women's rights" (p. 337), but Desdemona, in her reliance even unto death on the "awful prerogative of defenselessness" (p. 338) stands as a reproach to those "gone sick with a kind of atheistic philanthropy," and especially to those who champion a "heartless system of domestic equality and independence" that would reverse

> the doctrine and practice of our fathers, that married people 'must be complicated in affections and interest, that there be no distinction among them of mine and thine;' and that 'their goods should be as their children, not to be divided, but of one possession and provision.'
>
> (p. 340)

Whatever the psychological needs that might render feminine passivity attractive, Hudson's testimony reminds us of the social and economic dimension of that same appeal: Desdemona embodies allegiance to the spirit of the matrimonial property laws.

---

3. See James Boaden's *Memoirs of Mrs. Siddons* (London: 1893), p. 43; Matteo, pp. 181–82. The term "virago" for Emilia is Francis Gentleman's.
4. H. N. Hudson, *Lectures on Shakespeare* (New York: 1848), II, 339.

If critics and performers alike render Desdemona scarcely capable of her own defense, they also manage to reach a semblance of agreement concerning the manner of her death. In most eighteenth- and nineteenth-century productions, the Othello, who according to the Shakespearean text rolls his eyes and gnaws his lip in paroxysms of agitation, becomes too refined to strangle Desdemona with his bare hands. Descriptions from as early as 1725 indicate that a "stifling pillow" was the favored mode of murder, and using the pillow remains standard practice until the time of Charles Kemble and Macready, persisting, in fact, into the twentieth century.[5] A few mavericks—notably Italians like Salvini and Rossi—use bare hands. So, for example, Rossi kills Desdemona in an 1881 performance

> in full view of the audience . . . by strangling her with his hands after twisting her long hair about her neck, as he shook her violently and then dragged her about the bed and finally tossed her down upon the pillows. . . . Murmurs of dissatisfaction were audible in the house.[6]

Audiences may have demanded Desdemona's death, but they did not want to see it like this. So productions generally find means that at once reveal and conceal her dying agonies: either the pillow over her head or—another device running counter to implications of the text—closed curtains covering the bed.[7]

But the deed itself is prolonged in the text by being less than fully successful on the first attempt. Interestingly, although the second attack on Desdemona might seem to provide a promising opportunity for cutting, performances of the period keep both of Othello's acts of violence against her, and so are compelled, given the absence of Quarto or Folio stage directions, to find something to do on the lines:

> not yet quite dead?
> I that am cruel, am yet merciful,
> I would not have thee linger in thy pain.
> So, so.
>
> [87–90]

Until about 1770 Othello simply repeats his stifling actions on "So, so." In the 1770s, however, critics reiterate an argument that had

---

5. Folger *Othello* promptbooks Folio 2 and Folio 3; early reference to the "stifling pillow" occurs in *Original and Genuine Letters*, I, 257. Twentieth-century examples include Paul Robeson's *Othello* of 1930 and Arthur Lithgow's Antioch Area Theatre production of 1954.
6. Sprague, p. 212.
7. The curtains are closed by Othello *after* the deed [5.2.106] in Quarto and Folio texts.

been around since Rymer: stifled wives do not revive to speak again. And so, in spite of the text, in which Othello expressly tells Gratiano, "there lies your niece, / Whose breath these hands have newly stopp'd" [207–08], the dagger is chosen as the appropriate way to finish off Desdemona, a decision that meets with remarkable agreement for nearly a century thereafter. As the 1869 Booth/Hinton edition puts it, the stabbing, although not specified in original texts, is "according to the practice of the modern stage," and as far as I can tell, it is not until Salvini's performances of the 1880s that this collective agreement to circumvent the text is broken, Salvini putting his knees on Desdemona's breast on "So, so" in order to accelerate her end. Audience reaction to this violation of cultural unanimity was extremely negative.[8]

But would not the use of a dagger create potential problems of its own for a theatre concerned with verisimilitude? What about the resulting blood, for instance? Location of the bed far upstage could help solve such problems, and the advantages of death by dagger would seem attractive. Instead of an athletic struggle to enact a clumsy parody of a lover's embrace, the deed might become a less physical, more decorous procedure. Furthermore, use of the dagger facilitates the fixing of audience attention on Othello and his agonized sensibilities. So Booth is described in 1883:

> As he stabs her there is an expression of agonized loathing at his own deed & its necessity so vividly portrayed in his face, as he hangs his head & does not look at his own dagger nor at her, that it seems as if he could hardly do it![9]

Couple the use of the dagger with a pillow over Desdemona's face and the deed itself might need no further veiling. Thus decisions such as Booth's to enact the murder downstage or Macready's to hide the strangling behind curtains but allow the stabbing in full view of the audience might be understood as exploiting possibilities opened by new definitions of allowable liberty to be taken with the text,[1] yet the appeal of such new techniques in handling the murder deserves further consideration. Performers are encouraged to bring the murder up close to the audience, not merely because they have discovered technical means to get away with such proximity without offending audience sensibilities, but because, as the description

---

8. Sprague, p. 216.
9. Harvard Theatre Ms. 219. Compare Booth: "Hide your face in trembling hand while you stab and groan, 'so, so'; the steel is piercing your own heart" (Furness Variorum, p. 303).
1. For Macready, see Folger *Othello* promptbook 13.

of Booth's performance suggests, the age was prepared to appreciate the play, indeed to appreciate tragedy generally, primarily for
its glimpses into the sensibilities of the tragic hero and his own
self-destructive agonies. Manipulation of stage conditions—even
against apparent directives of the text—enables performers to
direct audience attention firmly toward Othello and his tragic self-
destruction, making him, in our eyewitness's account, the suffering
victim of necessity and his own noble nature. If, in the process, the
brutality of the murder is obscured, the loss is, one suspects, not
such as would trouble either Dr. Johnson or the predominant aesthetic of the period.

That aesthetic, as recently analyzed by Joseph Donohue, affects
both critical perceptions and actors' representations of tragedy in
three related ways. First of all, events in the overall plot are relegated to secondary status, becoming important only insofar as
they manage to reveal character.[2] Second, concentration is further focused on a particular central character's reactions at highly
charged moments.[3] Third, an emphasis on the need to feel sympathy for these central characters leads to reinterpretations of them.[4]
These assumptions—that character is the essence of drama and
that the momentary experiences of a particular character should
be the center of attention and sympathy—neatly match sentimentalist preoccupations.[5] Lord Kames, for example, writes with obvious
fascination about the "fluctuation of passion" that Othello mani-
fests in the opening soliloquy of [5.2]:

> love and jealousy represented, each exerting its whole force,
> but without any struggle; Othello was naturally inflexible: and
> the tenderest love could not divert him from a purpose he
> approved as right, not even for a moment: but every thing con-
> sistent with such a character is done to reconcile the two oppo-
> site passions; he is resolved to put her to death, but he will not
> shed her blood, nor so much as ruffle her skin.[6]

2. Donohue, p. 197. On the general nineteenth-century interest in character rather
than action in Shakespeare, see Robert W. Langbaum's chapter "Character versus
Action in Shakespeare" in *The Poetry of Experience* (New York: Random House,
1957); and Aron Y. Stavisky, *Shakespeare and the Victorians* (Norman: Univ. of Okla-
homa Press, 1969). Compare James Boaden's lament on the "rage of the English for
action" which "throws away a thousand delicate and essential touches of character"—
particularly by omitting the willow song scene from *Othello* (*Memoirs of Mrs. Siddons*,
p. 322).
3. Donohue, pp. 193, 212.
4. Donohue, p. 205.
5. Donohue, p. 280.
6. Kames, I, 129.

And later critics will share Kames's sympathetic fascination with characters caught in the throes of the passionate moment. Concerning the great Edmund Kean, much praised for his Shakespearean roles by Coleridge, Byron, and Leigh Hunt, John Keats finds chiefly worthy of praise the actor's ability to deliver "himself up to the instant feeling, without a shadow of a thought about anything else."[7] Hazlitt praises Shakespeare above all else for providing ample opportunities for the display of fluctuating emotions instead of forcing his characters to "hurry on to action":

> It was in raising passion to its height, from the lowest beginnings and in spite of all obstacles, in showing the conflict of the soul, the tug and war between love and hatred, rage, tenderness, jealousy, remorse, in laying open the strength and weakness of human nature, in uniting sublimity of thought with the anguish of the keenest woe, in putting in motion all the springs and impulses which make up this our mortal being, and at last blending them in that noble tide of deep and sustained passion, impetuous but majestic, 'that flows on to the Propontic and knows no ebb,' that the great excellence of Shakespeare lay.[8]

Such intense concentration on the emotional state of the central character lends itself quite understandably to sympathy for him as one, in the case of Othello, "perplexed in the extreme," and that sympathy constitutes the dominant response from the time of Johnson to that of Bradley.[9]

III

Between Desdemona's fatal stabbing and Othello's own death, eighteenth- and nineteenth-century performers found two particularly

---

7. *Poetical Works and Other Writings of John Keats,* ed. H. B. Forman (New York: Scribner's Sons, 1938–39), V, 232.
8. *Hazlitt on Theater,* eds. William Archer and Robert Lowe (New York: Hill and Wang, 1957), pp. 69–70.
9. See Matteo, pp. 181, 252 and Carlisle, *Shakespeare from the Greenroom,* p. 207. Compare the writer who rejoices "with a secret satisfaction" upon seeing his female wards "betrayed into tears" as the "distress of the play was heightened" (p. 241) and who goes on to characterize the "torments which the Moor suffers" as "so exquisitely drawn, as to render him as much an object of compassion, even in the barbarous action of murdering Desdemona, as the innocent person herself who falls under his hand" (*Guardian,* 37 [23 April 1713], 241–43). In Foote's *Treatise on the Passions,* the actor is admonished that "the Strugglings and Convulsions that torture and distract [Othello's] Mind, upon his resolving to murder her, cannot be too strongly painted, nor can the Act itself be accomplished with too much Grief and Tenderness" (pp. 33–35). Benjamin Victor praises the role of Othello for calling forth "all the various Passions of the Soul" and maintains that "In the distressful passages, at the heart breaking Anguish of his Jealousy, I have seen all the Men, susceptible of the tender Passions, in Tears" (*The History of the Theatres of London and Dublin* [London: 1761], II, 9–13).

interesting occasions for deviation from Shakespeare's text. First, Emilia is never granted her wish to be laid by Desdemona, although some productions provide a "couch" for her repose.[1] Thus the bloody corpses do not end up in a pile on the bed. Second, the lines reporting Brabantio's death from grief at Desdemona's betrayal of him are regularly omitted. One can imagine the relief accorded the sensibilities of the audience by these minor but strategic narrowings of focus in both plot and action.

The most intriguing variations on the scene, however, occur in the final moments surrounding Othello's death. Here the frequency of modification is striking, with virtually every promptbook recording changes in wording or action. Actors like Booth and Forrest, who published their own acting versions of the play, not only change the ending from one edition to the next, but also revise the acting editions further in production promptbooks.[2] Thus, agreement about anything in this portion of the play is remarkable, yet the promptbooks do agree on some things.

From the earliest surviving eighteenth-century promptbook (1766) until the 1870s, virtually all performers cut the moments that follow Othello's death; performances, with very few exceptions, cut the lines which give Lodovico and Gratiano's judgment on Othello's suicide: "O bloody period! / All that's spoke is marr'd" [362]. And, in fact, of the 52 promptbooks that I have examined for performances between 1766 and 1900 which relate theatrical practice for Othello's death, 23 end the play on some version of his suicide lines—"I took by the throat the circumcised dog, / And smote him thus"— adding sometimes an invented exclamation—"O Desdemona"—to his rather abrupt end. Perhaps the impulse at work here is the desire to ennoble Othello by letting his agony, rather than Venetian concerns with the aftermath, conclude the play, but one may wonder why from the 1770s until the 1870s, even in the promptbooks that do suggest action after his self-slaughter, Othello appears almost never to have been allowed to die upon a kiss (in 45 of the 52 promptbooks, marked for Othello's final moments, the lines about having kissed Desdemona before he killed her are missing, either through cutting or omission).

There are copious descriptions of stage Othellos in their death throes struggling to reach Desdemona: Macready dragging himself,

1. See, for example, Charles Kean's early promptbook, Folger *Othello* promptbook 11; Edmund Kean's 1831 promptbook, Folger *Othello* promptbook 17. Kemble's 1816 promptbook adds to the text the direction that Emilia "falls on the ground" (Folger *Othello* promptbook 19).
2. For instances of such revision, see Edwin Forrest's 1861 promptbook (Harvard Theatre Collection 13486.75.6), and Edwin Booth's preparation copy (Folger *Othello* promptbook 3).

supported by furniture, from the footlights toward the distant bed;
Kean falling backwards dead just before he can kiss his Desdemona; Phelps, Wallack, and Edwin Booth dying in similar attempts;
Gustavus Brooke pulling down the bed curtains over himself and
revealing in the process the unkissed Desdemona; Salvini stagger-
ing backward while keeping "his full front to the audience" and
dying just before he can reach the bed.[3] And when actors do finally
reach the bed for a kiss in the late nineteenth century, they are
condemned to slide or roll back off. So Edwin Forrest kisses Desdemona while "upon one knee" and then falls to the floor, and in an
1895 Henry Jewett promptbook, Othello "kisses Desdemona falls
from bed and rolls down steps onto stage."[4] Whatever the specific
details of execution, the audience is spared the effects of Othello's
"Falling upon Desdemona" as one 1802 acting edition printed in
Manchester by R. W. Dean suggests, or, even more graphically, "He
[falls across Desdemona and] dies," according to the Folger edition
used for one twentieth-century performance.[5] The end result in the
modified versions is the same: Desdemona's corpse is left in lovely,
lonely isolation. Leaving her chaste bed thus unviolated by Othello's own bleeding corpse would, obviously, rid the scene of some of
the more grossly physical elements in its mixture of eroticism and
violence, but no such clear justification suggests itself for the last
variation that the theatre of the period sometimes worked into the
scene in the text's despite.

In the 1766 promptbook, Iago is removed from the stage before
Othello's final apologia.[6] This change, while neither lessening the
violence and eroticism nor materially reducing running time, robs
the play of powerful theatrical possibilities. Edwin Booth's Iago, for
example, stood over Othello's corpse, pointing at the body while
"gazing up at the gallery with a malignant smile of satisfied hate."[7]
Why then do such major figures as Kean, Kemble, the elder Booth,
Phelps, Cooke, Young, Salvini, Forrest and others of less note move
Iago's exit up, and in the process abandon such rich opportunities?
Macready offers a clue when he dismisses Fechter's bizarre practice
of having Othello begin his suicide blow as a violent gesture apparently directed toward Iago. Macready professes himself uncon-
vinced that Othello's "lofty nature" could possibly "bestow a thought
upon that miserable thing, Iago, when his great mind had made

3. Sprague, p. 221. For Salvini, see Edward Tuckerman Mason, *The Othello of Tommasso
   Salvini* (New York: 1890), p. 107.
4. Gabriel Harrison, *Edwin Forrest*, p. 96; Folger *Othello* promptbook, Folio 1.
5. Folger *Othello* promptbook, Folio 4.
6. Folger *Othello* promptbook 27.
7. Sprague, p. 223.

itself up to die! To me it was in the worst taste of a small melodramatic theatre."[8]

Here are terms aptly fitted to a particular view of tragedy: a lofty nature, a great mind, that had made itself up—notice the absence of both body and other in Macready's phrasing—to self-destruction. In many of the period's stage versions, the role of Iago in the scene's second half, like that of Desdemona in its first half, has been reduced in order to keep attention where Dr. Johnson and his descendants probably would have preferred it—on the noble Moor and his own sad self-destruction.

To sum up. In the period's predominant mode of staging the final scene of *Othello,* audience gaze is first and last directed toward Othello. His face illuminated by candle, lamp, or simulated celestial light, he often enters in a threatening posture suggesting Iago's evil influence, and he virtually always is shown resisting an impulse to use his weapon on the sleeping Desdemona. The murder itself becomes the sacrifice of a largely passive victim by a protagonist whose own emotional conflicts are the center of attention. After smothering her with a pillow, or using bed curtains to block the view of his victim during the act, Othello's noble concern for her and the press of necessity force him to use a dagger to finish the deed. When the time comes for Othello's own final agony and death, audience attention is frequently directed away from Iago's important role in bringing about that death, its admiration for Othello's final gesture often uncompromised by the criticism of onlookers, and its vision unpoisoned by the sight of Othello topping the dead Desdemona in a potentially grotesque fulfillment of the promise to kill her and love her after.

If the performance records of this period may be said to cast a light backward to reveal anything about the Quarto and Folio texts themselves, they show, I believe, how much of the Shakespearean scene has to be adjusted, how many implicit and explicit directions have to be countermanded, before it will conform to the particular tragic mold favored by the majority of audiences, commentators, and performers of the eighteenth and nineteenth centuries. When change would come to the performance of Shakespeare on the twentieth-century stage, it would come gradually and piecemeal, as performers turned away from the traditional acting editions and the inherited business in response to increased demands for close study of relatively reliable Shakespearean texts. This performance "revolution" as it has been called is, of course, the product of many factors, but few would deny that one of its leading figures was one who, like Fanny Kemble, saw Salvini strangle his resistant Desdemona with

8. Sprague, p. 221.

bare hands—William Poel. And what Poel took away from his Salvini experiences was not Kemble's sense of having witnessed a violation of the manifest "intention" of Shakespeare but a belief that he
had been granted a revelation, showing how every effect in a great
performance ought to be tested by reference to authoritative texts.[9]
More than half a century after Poel and the Elizabeth revival movement, after having experienced the further innovations to be
wrought by those from Harley Granville-Barker to Peter Brook who
learned from Poel and his followers, we might have less interest (or
faith) in an imagined capacity to get back to the play as the playwright might have intended it, but the pressure to make the attempt
is a real factor in the theatre's eventual breaking with the traditional
emphases that this paper has traced.[1]

MICHAEL NEILL

Unproper Beds: Race, Adultery, and the Hideous in *Othello*[†]

> There is a glass of ink wherein you see
> How to make ready black-faced tragedy.
> George Chapman,
> *Bussy D'Ambois*, 4.2.89–90

I

The ending of *Othello* is perhaps the most shocking in Shakespearean tragedy. "I am glad that I have ended my revisal of this dreadful
scene," wrote Dr. Johnson; "it is not to be endured."[1] His disturbed
response is one that the play conspicuously courts: indeed Johnson

9. On Poel's reaction to Salvini's *Othello*, see Robert Speaight, *William Poel and the Eliz-*
    abethan Revival (Cambridge, Mass.: Harvard Univ. Press, 1954), p. 28. J. L. Styan
    emphasizes Poel's effect in *The Shakespeare Revolution* (Cambridge: Cambridge Univ.
    Press, 1977). Styan cites Tyrone Guthrie, who calls Poel "the founder of modern
    Shakespearean production," p. 64.
1. Styan traces Poel's lineage, p. 64ff. The various forces working to change Shakespear-
    ean production in the period following the 1890s are delineated in Cary M. Mazer's
    Shakespeare Refashioned (Ann Arbor: UMI Research Press, 1981).
†   From *Shakespeare Quarterly* 40.4 (1989): 383–412. © 1989 Folger Shakespeare Library.
    Reprinted with the permission of Johns Hopkins University Press. The author's quota-
    tions from *Othello* have been retained, but bracketed references are to this Norton
    Critical Edition. This excerpt omits some of Neill's footnotes, some fascinating visuals,
    and a sustained analysis of the play's action as "concentrating the audience's imagi-
    nation" on "the erotic act in the bedroom" (399). For this material, consult the origi-
    nal or the reprint in Neill's *Putting History to the Question: Power, Politics and Society*
    in English Renaissance Drama (New York: Columbia University Press, 2000),
    237–68.
1. Quoted in James R. Siemon, "'Nay, that's not next': *Othello*, V.ii in performance,
    1760–1900," *Shakespeare Quarterly*, 37 (1986), 38–51, esp. p. 39. [See 298 above.]

does no more than paraphrase the reaction of the scandalized Venetians, whose sense of the unendurable nature of what is before them
produces the most violently abrupted of all Shakespearean endings.
Though its catastrophe is marked by a conventional welter of stabbing and slaughter, *Othello* is conspicuously shorn of the funeral dig-
nities that usually serve to put a form of order upon such spectacles
of ruin: in the absence of any witness sympathetic enough to tell the
hero's story, the disgraced Othello has to speak what amounts to his
own funeral oration—and it is one whose lofty rhetoric is arrested
in mid-line by the "bloody period" of his own suicide [5.2.362]. "All
that's spoke is marred," observes Gratiano, but no memorializing
tributes ensue. Even Cassio's "he was great of heart" [366] may
amount to nothing more than a faint plea in mitigation for one whose
heart was swollen to bursting with intolerable emotion;[2] and in place
of the reassuring processional exeunt announced by the usual command to take up the tragic bodies, we get only Lodovico's curt order
to close up the scene of butchery: "The object poisons sight: / Let it
be hid" [369–70].[3] The tableau on the bed announces a kind of
plague, one that taints the sight as the deadly effluvia of pestilence
poison the nostrils.

The congruence between Dr. Johnson's desperately averted gaze
and Lodovico's fear of contamination is striking; but it is only
Johnson's agitated frankness that makes it seem exceptional. It
makes articulate the anxiety evident almost everywhere in the
play's history—a sense of scandal that informs the textual strategies
of editors and theatrical producers as much as it does the disturbed
reactions of audiences and critics. Contemplating the "unutterable
agony" of the conclusion, the Variorum editor, Furness, came to
wish that the tragedy had never been written;[4] and his choice of the
word "unutterable" is a telling one, for this ending, as its stern gestures of erasure demonstrate, has everything to do with what cannot be uttered and must not be seen.

The sensational effect of the scene upon its earliest audiences is
apparent from the imitations it spawned[5] and from the mesmerized

2. See Balz Engler, "Othello's Great Heart," *English Studies,* 68 (1987), 129–36. All
   Othello quotations are from the New Penguin edition, ed. Kenneth Muir (Harmondsworth: Penguin Books, 1968). All other Shakespeare quotations are from *The Riverside
   Shakespeare,* ed. G. Blakemore Evans (Boston: Houghton Mifflin, 1974).
3. The exceptional nature of this ending is also noted by Helen Gardner, "The Noble
   Moor," in Anne Ridler, ed., *Shakespeare Criticism 1935–1960* (Oxford: Oxford Univ.
   Press, 1963), pp. 348–70, esp. p. 366.
4. The Variorum *Othello,* ed. H. H. Furness (Philadelphia: J. B. Lippincott, 1886), p. 300;
   quoted in Siemon, p. 39. [See 298 above.]
5. Sensationalized bedchamber scenes that seem indebted to *Othello* include Lussurioso's
   murderous irruption into his father's bedchamber in *The Revenger's Tragedy* (c. 1606),
   Evadne's heavily eroticized murder of the king in *The Maid's Tragedy* (c. 1610), and the
   climatic bedroom scene that forms part of Ford's extensive reworking of *Othello* in
   Love's Sacrifice (c. 1632). Shakespeare himself appears to play on recollections of his

gaze of Henry Jackson, who left the first surviving account of *Othello* in performance. He saw *Othello* acted by the King's Men at Oxford in 1610 and wrote how

> the celebrated Desdemona, *slayn in our presence by her husband,* although she pleaded her case very effectively throughout, yet moved us more after she was dead, when, *lying in her bed,* she entreated the pity of the spectators by her very countenance.[6]

More than any other scene, it was this show of a wife murdered by her husband that gripped Jackson's imagination; but even more disturbing than the killing itself seems to have been the sight of the dead woman "lying in her bed."—a phrase that echoes Emilia's outrage: "My mistress here lies murdered in her bed" [5.2.189]. For Jackson, the *place* seems to matter almost as much as the fact of wife-murder—just as it did to the nineteenth-century Desdemona, Fanny Kemble, when she confessed to "feel[ing] horribly at the idea of being murdered *in my bed.*"[7]

The same anxious fascination is reflected in the first attempts to represent the play pictorially: it was the spectacle of the violated marriage bed that Nicholas Rowe selected to epitomize the tragedy in the engraving for his 1709 edition; and his choice was followed by the actors David Garrick and Sarah Siddons, wanting memorials of their own performances.[8] In the great period of Shakespeare illustration from the 1780s to the 1920s, the bedchamber scene was overwhelmingly preferred by publishers and artists, whose images combined to grant it the same representative significance as the graveyard in *Hamlet* or the monument in *Antony and Cleopatra*—as if announcing in this display of death-in-marriage a gestic account of the play's key meanings. * * * Both graveyard and monument, however, in their different ways help to clothe the tragic ending in traditional forms of rhetoric and ceremony that mitigate its terrors, shackling death within a frame of decorum. What makes the ending of *Othello* so unaccountably disturbing and so threatening to its spectators is precisely the brutal violation of decorum that is registered in

---

own coup de theatre in the bedroom scene of *Cymbeline* (c. 1609); and it is treated to a parodic reversal in Fletcher's *Monsieur Thomas* (c. 1615), where the humiliation of the comic protagonist is accomplished by means of "*A bed discovered with a* [female] *black More in it*" (5.5.2, s.d.), provoking his Emilia-like cry, "Rore againe, devil, rore againe" (1. 41).

6. Quoted in Julie Hankey, ed., *Othello,* Plays in Performance Series (Bristol: Bristol Classical Press, 1987), p. 18, italics added.

7. Quoted in Hankey, p. 315, italics added.

8. See Norman Sanders, ed., *Othello,* New Cambridge edition (Cambridge: Cambridge Univ. Press, 1984), p. 48.

the quasi-pornographic explicitness of the graphic tradition. The illustrators' voyeuristic manipulation of the parted curtains and their invariable focus upon the unconscious invitation of Desdemona's gracefully exposed body serve to foreground not merely the perverse eroticism of the scene but its aspect of forbidden disclosure.

Even more striking is the fact that these images were often designed to draw readers into texts whose bowdlerizing maneuvers aimed, as far as possible, to conceal everything that their frontispieces offer to reveal. While they could scarcely contrive to remove the scandalous property itself, late eighteenth- and nineteenth-century editors sought to restrict the curiosity that the final scene gratifies and to obscure its most threatening meanings by progressively excising from the text every explicit reference to the bed.[9]

Predictably enough, an even more anxious censorship operated in the theatre itself, where, however, its consequences were much more difficult to predict. In the most striking of many effacements, it became the practice for nineteenth-century Othellos to screen the murder from the audience by closing the curtains upon the bed. This move was ostensibly consistent with a general attempt at de-sensationalizing the tragedy, an attempt whose most obvious manifestation was the restrained "Oriental" Moor developed by Macready and others.[1] But the actual effect of the practice was apparently quite opposite, raising to a sometimes unbearable intensity the audience's scandalized fascination with the now-invisible scene. Years later Westland Marston could still recall the "thrilling" sensation as Macready thrust "his dark despairing face, through the curtains," its "contrast with the drapery" producing "a marvellous piece of colour";[2] and so shocking was this moment, according to John Forster, that in his presence a woman "hysterically fainted" at it.[3]

The reasons for so extreme a reaction can be glimpsed in the offended tone of the Melbourne *Argus* critic, attacking an 1855 production that had flouted this well-established convention: "[The] consummation," he indignantly insisted, "should take place behind the curtain and out of sight."[4] The revealing word "consummation,"

9. The process of cutting can be traced in Hankey.
1. For an account of the Orientalizing process that culminated in Beerbohm Tree's confident pronouncement that "Othello was an Oriental, not a negro: a stately Arab of the best caste," see Hankey, pp. 65–67, esp. p. 67.
2. Westland Marston, *Our Recent Actors*, quoted in Hankey, pp. 64, 317.
3. William Archer and Robert Lowe, eds., *Dramatic Essays by John Forster and George Henry Lewes,* quoted in Hankey, p. 64.
4. Quoted in Hankey, p. 317. This critic's reaction was echoed in the murmurs of dissatisfaction with which the audience greeted Rossi's 1881 London performance, when the Italian actor strangled his Desdemona in full view of the audience (see Siemon, p. 47). [See 307 above.]

when set beside the "hysterical" reaction to Macready's "marvellous piece of colour,"[5] suggests that the bed was so intensely identified with the anxieties about race and sex stirred up by the play that
it needed, as far as possible, to be removed from the public gaze. Yet
the effect of such erasure was only to give freer play to the fantasy
it was designed to check, so that the violent chiaroscuro of Macready's blackened face thrust between the virgin-white curtains
was experienced as a shocking sado-erotic climax. It was, of course,
a stage picture that significantly repeated an off-stage action twice
imagined in the first half of the play, when Othello, first in Venice
(1.2) and then in Cyprus (2.3), is unceremoniously roused from his
nuptial bed. The unconscious repetition must have had the effect
of underlining the perverse eroticism of the murder just at the point
where the parting of the bed-curtains and the display of Desdemona's corpse was about to grant final satisfaction to the audience's
terrible curiosity about the absent scene that dominates so much of
the play's action.

For all their ostentatious pudency, then, the Victorian attempts
at containing the danger of the play's ending reveal a reading unset-
tlingly consistent with the most sensational recent productions,
like Bernard Miles's 1971 Mermaid *Othello* or Ronald Eyre's at the
National in 1979, with their extraordinary emphasis on the significance and visibility of a bed.[6] It is a reading in which the stage
direction opening 5.2, *"Enter . . . Desdemona in her bed,"* announces
ocular proof of all that the audience have most desired and feared
to look upon, exposing to cruel light the obscure erotic fantasies
that the play both explores and disturbingly excites in its audience.
Forster's story of the woman who fainted at the sight of Macready's
"dark despairing face" records a moment when (despite more
than half a century of bleaching, "civilizing," and bowdlerizing) a
subterranean image erupted to confirm the deep fears of racial/
sexual otherness on which the play trades—fears that are made
quite embarrassingly explicit in the feverish self-betrayals of a

5. To some observers Macready's restrained, gentlemanly, and dignified Moor seemed
"almost English" (Hankey, p. 66); but the startling color contrast of this scene seems to
have acted as a disturbing reminder of Othello's blackness and therefore (to the Victorian mind) of his savage sexuality.
6. Both directors introduced the bed early, making it into the centerpiece of the brothel
scene; and Miles, whose production notoriously highlighted the sexual suggestiveness
of the murder with a naked Desdemona, emphasized the perverse excitements of the
earlier scene by leaving Iago and Roderigo at the end "to argue amongst the discarded
bedclothes and around the bed itself . . . [while Roderigo handled] the sheets in rapture." Eyre transposed this piece of stage business to his Othello at the beginning of the
scene: Donald Sinden was directed to pull the sheets from Desdemona's laundry basket,
throw them about the stage, and then at the line "This is a subtle whore" [4.2.21], press
the soiled linen to his face—"sniffing [at it] like a hound," according to one reviewer.
See Hankey, pp. 291, 281.

nineteenth-century Russian literary lady reacting to Ira Aldridge's performance of the part. In her account the play exhibits nothing less than the symbolic rape of the European "spirit" by the "savage, wild flesh" of black otherness:

> A full-blooded Negro, incarnating the profoundest creations of Shakespearean art, giving *flesh and blood* for the aesthetic judgment of educated European society. . . . How much nearer can one get to truth, to the very source of the highest aesthetic satisfaction? But *what is truth* . . . ? As the spirit is not the body, so the truth of art is not this profoundly raw flesh which we can take hold of, and call by name and, if you please, feel, pinch with our unbelieving, all-feeling hand . . . Not the Moscow Maly Theatre, but the African jungle should have been filled and resounded with . . . the cries of this black, powerful, howling flesh. But by the very fact that that flesh is so powerful—that it is genuinely black, so naturally *un-white* does it howl—that savage flesh did its fleshly work. It murdered and crushed the spirit . . . one's spirit cannot accept it—and in place of the highest enjoyment, this blatant flesh introduced into art, this *natural* black Othello, pardon me, causes only . . . revulsion.[7]

It is as if in Macready's coup the strange mixture of thrilled agitation, horror, and shame voiced here became focused with an unbearable intensity upon the occupation of the bed, where the transgression of racial boundaries was displayed as an offence punishable by death.

II

The racial fear and revulsion lurking beneath the ambiguous excitements of the theatrical and pictorial traditions is made crudely explicit in an early nineteenth-century caricature, apparently of Ira Aldridge's Othello, published as Number 9 in the series *Tregear's Black Jokes* * * *. The caricaturist sublimates his anxiety at the scene's sexual threat through the burlesque device of transforming Desdemona into an obese black woman, her snoring mouth grotesquely agape. The racialism paraded here for the amusement of early nineteenth-century Londoners is rarely so openly exhibited, but it has tainted even the most respectable *Othello* criticism until well into the present century. A sense of racial scandal is a consistent

---

7. N. S. Sokhanskaya ("N. Kokhanovskaya") in a letter to the Slavophile newspaper *Dyen* (1863), quoted in Herbert Marshall and Mildred Stock, *Ira Aldridge: The Negro Tragedian* (London: Rockliff, 1958), pp. 265–66. See also Siemon for English reactions to the scene "that [mimic] the language and strategies of pornography" [305 above].

thread in commentary on the play from Rymer's notorious effusions against the indecorum of a "Blackamoor" hero,[8] to Coleridge's assertion that Othello was never intended to be black and F. R. Leavis's triumphant demonstration that Othello was never intended for a hero.[9] It is as apparent in A. C. Bradley's nervously footnoted anxiety about how "the aversion of our blood" might respond to the sight of a black Othello[1] as it is in Charles Lamb's frank discovery of "something extremely revolting in the courtship and wedded caresses of Othello and Desdemona."[2] "To imagine is one thing," Bradley protests, "and to see is another," making painfully explicit his reaction against what Edward Snow describes as the play's insistence upon "bringing to consciousness things known in the flesh but 'too hideous to be shown.'"[3] For the neo-Freudian Snow, however, these forbidden things are the male psyche's repressed fears of female otherness, which the accident of Othello's race "merely forces him to live out with psychotic intensity."[4] It is clear, however, that for Bradley it was precisely Othello's blackness that made the play's sexual preoccupations so upsetting.

For Coleridge the idea of a black hero was unacceptable because blackness was equivalent to savagery and the notion of savage heroism an intolerable oxymoron. His application of critical skin-lightener began a tradition of sterile and seemingly endless debate about the exact degree and significance of Othello's racial difference, on which critics dissipated their energies until well into the present century—M. R. Ridley's * * * Arden edition (1958), with its ludicrous attempt to substitute "contour" for "colour" as the principle of discrimination, being only the most disgraceful recent example.[5] Since Coleridge, arguments about race in Othello have almost invariably been entangled, more or less explicitly, with arguments about culture in which gradations of color stand for gradations of "barbarity," "animality," and "primitive emotion." If the dominant nineteenth-century tradition sought to domesticate the play by removing the

8. Thomas Rymer, A Short View of Tragedy (1693), quoted in Brian Vickers, ed., Shakespeare: The Critical Heritage, 6 vols. (London and Boston: Routledge & Kegan Paul, 1974), Vol. 2, 27. [See 227 above.]
9. F. R. Leavis, "Diabolic Intellect and the Noble Hero," in The Common Pursuit (London: Chatto and Windus, 1952), pp. 136–59. For acute analyses of the racial assumptions underlying Leavis's approach, see Hankey, pp. 109–16, and Martin Orkin, "Othello and the 'plain face' of Racism," SQ, 38 (1987), 166–88, esp. pp. 183–86, now incorporated in his Shakespeare Against Apartheid (Craighall, South Africa: Ad. Donker, 1987). Both show how much Leavis's interpretation contributed to Olivier's version of the tragedy.
1. Shakespearean Tragedy (1904; rpt. New York: St. Martin's Press, 1985), p. 165 n. [See 269 n. 4 above.]
2. Quoted in Hankey, pp. 65–66. [See 247 above.]
3. "Sexual Anxiety and the Male Order of Things in Othello," English Literary Renaissance, 10 (1980), 384–412, esp. p. 387.
4. P. 400.
5. See M. R. Ridley, ed., Othello, Arden edition (London: Methuen, 1958), p. li.

embarrassment of savagery, the most common twentieth-century strategy has been to anthropologize it as the study of an assimilated savage who relapses into primitivism under stress. This was essentially Leavis's solution, and one can still hear it echoed in the New Cambridge editor's admiration for the weird mimicry of Laurence Olivier's "West African"/"West-Indian" Othello,[6] which he describes as a "virtuoso . . . portrait of a *primitive* man, at odds with the sophisticated society into which he has forced himself, *relapsing into barbarism* as a result of hideous misjudgement."[7]

At the other extreme stand revisionist readings like Martin Orkin's, which have sought to rehabilitate the tragedy by co-opting it to the anti-racist cause, insisting that "in its rejection of human pigmentation as a means of identifying worth, the play, as it always has done, continues to oppose racism."[8] Orkin's is an admirably motivated attempt to expose the racialist ideology underlying various critical and theatrical interpretations of the tragedy, but Shakespeare would surely have been puzzled to understand the claim that his play "opposes racism," cast as it is in a language peculiar to the politics of our own century.[9] It would no more have been possible for Shakespeare to "oppose racism" in 1604, one might argue, than for Marlowe to "oppose anti-semitism" in 1590: the argument simply could not be constituted in those terms. Julie Hankey, indeed, contemplating the pitfalls presented by Shakespeare's treatment of racial matters, concludes that his construction of racial difference is virtually beyond recovery, having become after four hundred years hopelessly obscured by a "patina of apparent topicality."[1] Hankey's position has at least the merit of historicist scruple but seems in the

6. The geographical referent of Olivier's mimicry significantly varies in different accounts of the production: Hankey, for example, refers to his "extraordinary transformation into a black African" (p. 111); Sanders praises "his careful imitation of West Indian gait and gesture" (p. 47); while Richard David speaks of "Olivier's . . . 'modern' negro, out of Harlem rather than Barbary" (*Shakespeare in the Theatre* [Cambridge: Cambridge Univ. Press, 1978], p. 46). The embarrassing conclusion must be that Olivier's much-praised fidelity to detail was simply fidelity to a generalized stereotype of "blackness."

7. Norman Sanders, p. 47, italics added. Sanders almost exactly paraphrases Laurence Lerner's account of the way in which "the primitive breaks out again in Othello," which Orkin uses to exemplify the way in which even liberal South African critics of the play find themselves reacting to it in terms of the paradigms of apartheid (pp. 184–85). Olivier himself declared that Othello "is a savage man," adding hurriedly, "not on account of his colour; I don't mean that" (Hankey, p. 109); but it is a little difficult to know quite what else he could have meant—especially in the light of reviewers' reactions to his mimicry of negritude, which concluded "that Othello's brutality was either of the jungle and essentially his own, or that, as one of Nature's innocents, he had taken the infection from a trivial and mean white society" (p. 111). Whatever the case, the choice is simply between noble and ignoble savagery. For a good account of the ideas behind the Olivier production and critical reactions to it, see Hankey, pp. 109–13.

8. P. 188.

9. The word "racism" itself dates from only 1936, and "racialism" from 1907 (*OED*).

1. P. 15.

end evasive, not unlike those liberal critiques that rob the play of its
danger by treating Othello's color simply as a convenient badge of
his estrangement from Venetian society[2]—in effect a distraction to
be cleared out of the way in order to expose the real core of the
drama, its tragedy of jealousy.[3] But the history that Hankey herself
traces is a testimony to the stubborn fact that *Othello* is a play full of
racial feeling—perhaps the first work in English to explore the roots
of such feeling; and it can hardly be accidental that it belongs to
the very period in English history in which something we can now
identify as a racialist ideology was beginning to evolve under the
pressures of nascent imperialism.[4] In this context it is all the more
curious, as Hankey notices, that Henry Jackson in 1610 seemed
utterly to ignore this aspect of the tragedy, presenting it simply as a
drama of wife-murder whose culprit is described in the most neutral
language as "her husband." We cannot now tell whether Jackson was
blind to the racial dimension of the action, or thought it of no interest or merely too obvious to require mention. But I want to argue that
his attention to the bed suggests a way round the dilemma posed by
this odd silence: to explain why the bed should have caught his eye is
to begin to understand theatrical strategies for thinking about racial
otherness that are specific to the work's own cultural context. If
Jackson elected to say nothing about these matters, it may have been
because there was for him no real way of voicing them, in that they
were still in some deep sense *unutterable*. But they were there on the
bed for all to see.

What is displayed on the bed is something, in Othello's own profoundly resonant phrase, "too hideous to be shown" [3.3.111]. The
wordplay here (unusually, in this drama of treacherously conflicting

2. Here I include my own essay "Changing Places in *Othello, Shakespeare Survey*, 37
   (1984), 115–31; I ought to have noticed more clearly the way in which racial identity is
   constructed as one of the most fiercely contested "places" in the play.
3. Honorable exceptions included Eldred Jones, *Othello's Countrymen: The African in
   English Renaissance Drama* (London: Oxford Univ. Press, 1965); G. K. Hunter's celebrated lecture on "Othello and Colour Prejudice," *Proceedings of the British Academy*,
   53 (1967), 139–57. [See 275 above.]; Doris Adler, "The Rhetoric of *Black and White in
   Othello*," *SQ*, 25 (1974), 248–57; G. M. Matthews, "*Othello* and the Dignity of Man," in
   Arnold Kettle, ed., *Shakespeare in a Changing World* (London: Lawrence & Wishart,
   1964), pp. 123–45; and Karen Newman, "'And wash the Ethiop white': femininity and
   the monstrous in *Othello*," in Jean E. Howard and Marion F. O'Connor, eds., *Shakespeare Reproduced: The Text in History and Ideology* (New York and London: Methuen,
   1987), pp. 141–62.
4. For more recent theoretical accounts of the evolution of a discourse of "Englishness" and
   "otherness" as an enabling adjunct of colonial conquest, see Stephen Greenblatt,
   Renaissance Self-Fashioning: From More to Shakespeare (Chicago and London: Univ. of
   Chicago Press, 1980), pp. 179–92; David Cairns and Shaun Richards, *Writing Ireland:
   Colonialism, Nationalism and Culture* (Manchester: Manchester Univ. Press, 1988),
   chap. 1, "What ish my Nation?" pp. 1–21; and Anne Laurence, "The Cradle to the
   Grave: English Observation of Irish Social Customs in the Seventeenth Century," *The
   Seventeenth Century*, 3 (1988), pp. 63–84.

meanings) amounts to a kind of desperate iteration: what is *hideous* is what should be kept *hidden,* out of sight.[5] "Hideous" in this sense is virtually an Anglo-Saxon equivalent for the Latinate "obscene"— referring to that which is profoundly improper, not merely indecent but tainted (in the original sense) or unclean; and that which should also, according to Shakespeare's own folk-etymology, be kept unseen, *off-stage,* hidden.[6] The play begins with Iago's evocation of just such an obscenity; it ends by seeking to return it to its proper darkness, closing the curtains that Iago first metaphorically plucked aside. In his frequently perceptive study of *Othello,* Edward Snow, observing that the play's "final gesture is on the side of repression," goes on to stress how necessarily that gesture is directed at the bed: "it is not just any object that is to be hidden but the 'tragic lodging' of the wedding-bed—the place of sexuality itself."[7] But Snow's own strategy expressly requires that he himself suppress the anxiety that attaches to the bed as the site of racial transgression—the anxiety on which depends so much of the play's continuing power to disturb.

III

One of the terrifying things about *Othello* is that its racial poisons seem so casually concocted, as if racism were just something that Iago, drawing in his improvisational way on a gallimaufry [heterogeneous mixture] of quite unsystematic prejudices and superstitions, made up as he went along. The characteristic pleasure he takes in his own felicitous invention only makes the effect more shocking. Iago lets horrible things loose and delights in watching them run; and the play seems to share that narcissistic fascination—or perhaps, better, Iago is the voice of its own fascinated self-regard. The play thinks abomination into being and then taunts the audience with the knowledge that it can never be *un*thought: "What you know, you know." It is a technique that works close to the unstable ground of consciousness itself; for it would be almost as difficult to say whether its racial anxieties are ones that the play discovers or implants in an audience as to say whether jealousy is something that Iago discovers or implants in Othello. Yet discovery, in the most literal theatrical sense, is what the last scene cruelly insists on. Like no other drama, *Othello* establishes an equivalency between psychological event (what happens "inside") and off-stage action (what happens

---

5. The wordplay, which may well reflect a folk-etymology, occurs elsewhere in Shakespeare: see, for example, *Twelfth Night,* 4.2.31 ("hideous darkness"), and *King John,* 5.4.22.
6. The proper derivation is from *caenum* = dirt; but the imagery of Carlisle's speech in *Richard II* clearly seems to imply the folk-etymology from *scaenum* = stage; "*show* so heinous, *black, obscene* a deed" (4.2.122); see also *Love's Labor's Lost,* 1.1.235–39.
7. P. 385.

"within"); thus it can flourish its disclosure of the horror on the bed like a psychoanalytic revelation.

The power of the offstage scene over the audience's prying imagination is immediately suggested by the irritable speculation of Thomas Rymer, the play's first systematic critic. Rymer spends several pages of his critique exposing what he regards as ludicrous inconsistencies between what the play tells the audience and what verisimilitude requires them to believe about the occupation of "the Matrimonial Bed." The time scheme, he insists, permits Othello and his bride to sleep together only once, on the first night in Cyprus, but "*once* will not do the Poets business: the *Audience* must suppose a great many bouts, to make the plot operate. They must deny their senses, to reconcile it to common sense."[8]

Rymer's method is taken to extraordinary extremes in a recent article by T. G. A. Nelson and Charles Haines, who set out to demonstrate, with a mass of circumstantial detail, that the marriage of Othello and Desdemona was never consummated at all. In this previously unsuspected embarrassment is to be found an explanation for the extreme suggestibility of the hero, and thus the hidden spring of the entire tragic action.[9] Their essay is remarkable not for the ingenuity of its finally unsustainable argument about the sequential "facts" of a plot whose time-scheme is so notoriously undependable, but for what it unconsciously reveals about the effect of *Othello* upon its audiences. Their entire procedure mirrors with disturbing fidelity the habit of obsessive speculation about concealed offstage action, into which the play entraps the viewer as it entraps its characters. Nelson and Haines become victims, like the hero himself, of the scopophile [= Peeping Tom] economy of this tragedy and prey to its voyeuristic excitements.

Recently, Norman Nathan has attempted a point-by-point rebuttal of Nelson and Haines, the ironic effect of which is to entrap him in the very speculation he wishes to cut short. "If a lack of consummation is so important to this play, why isn't the audience so informed?" he somewhat testily enquires.[1] An answer might be—to make them ask the question. *Othello* persistently goads its audience

---

8. Rymer [see 232 above].
9. T. G. A. Nelson and Charles Haines, "Othello's Unconsummated Marriage," *Essays in Criticism*, 33 (1983), 1–18. Their arguments were partially anticipated in a little-noticed article by Pierre Janton, "Othello's Weak Function," *Cahiers Élisabéthains*, 7 (1975), 43–50, and are paralleled in William Whallon, *Inconsistencies* (Cambridge: D. S. Brewer; Totowa, N.J.: Biblio, 1983). I regard my own willingness to take these arguments seriously ("Changing Places in *Othello*," p. 116, n. 1) as further evidence for the point I am making.
1. "Othello's Marriage Is Consummated," *Cahiers Élisabéthains*, 34 (1988), 79–82, esp. p. 81.

into speculation about what is happening behind the scenes. This preoccupation with offstage action is unique in Shakespeare. Elsewhere, whenever offstage action is of any importance, it is almost always carefully described, usually by an eyewitness whose account is not open to question, so that nothing of critical importance is left to the audience's imagination. But in *Othello* the real imaginative focus of the action is always the hidden marriage-bed, an inalienably private location, shielded, until the very last scene, from every gaze.[2] This disquietingly absent presence creates the margin within which Iago can operate as a uniquely deceitful version of the *nuntius*,[3] whose vivid imaginary descriptions taint the vision of the audience even as they colonize the minds of Brabantio and Othello:

> IAGO: Even now, now, very now, an old black ram
> Is tupping your white ewe . . . [1.1.85–86] * * *

* * *

It would be laboring the point to demonstrate in detail the centrality of the bed in the play's denouement. The pattern of alternating revelations and concealments in the final scene is enacted through and largely organized around the opening and closing of those bed-curtains which, like theatrical inverted commas, figure so conspicuously in representations of the final scene [1, 106, 122, 370]. In the murder on the bed, with its shocking literalization of Desdemona's conceit of wedding-sheets-as-shroud ("thou art on thy deathbed" [53]), the nuptial consummation that the play has kept as remorselessly in view as tormentingly out of sight achieves its perverse (adulterate) performance. It is on the bed, moreover, that Othello (in the quarto stage direction) throws himself, as though in a symbolic reassertion of the husband's place, when he first begins to glimpse the depths of Iago's treachery [203]. His place is symbolically usurped in Emilia's request to "lay me by my mistress' side" [243], and its loss is cruelly brought home in the despair of "Where should Othello go?" [277]. He can reclaim it finally only through a suicide that symmetrically repeats Desdemona's eroticized murder:

---

2. This aspect of the play is recognized by Stanley Cavell in *Disowning Knowledge In Six Plays of Shakespeare* (Cambridge: Cambridge Univ. Press, 1987): "My guiding hypothesis about the structure of the play is that the thing *denied our sight* throughout the opening scene—the thing, the scene, that Iago takes Othello back to again and again, retouching it for Othello's enchafed imagination—is what we are shown in the final scene, the scene of murder" (p. 132). [See 292 above.] See also James L. Calderwood, *The Properties of* Othello (Amherst: Univ. of Massachusetts Press, 1989), p. 125.
3. The conventional dramatic messenger who brings reliable information and news. [Editor's note]

> I kissed thee, ere I killed thee: no way but this,
> Killing myself, to die upon a kiss.
>
> [363–64]

The action of the play has rescued Othello and Desdemona from the calculated anonymity of Iago's pornographic fantasies, only for the ending to strip them of their identities once more: for most of the final scene, Othello is once again named only as "the Moor," and it is as if killing Desdemona had annihilated his sense of self to the point where he must repudiate even his own name ("That's he that was Othello: here I am" [1. 289]). Lodovico's speech reduces the corpses to the condition of a single nameless "object"—"the tragic loading of this bed" [368], "it"—something scarcely removed from the obscene impersonality of the image in which they were first displayed, "the beast with two backs" [1.1.113].[4] Like a man rubbing a dog's nose in its own excrement, Lodovico, as the voice of Venetian authority, forces Iago (and the audience with him) to look on what his fantasy has made ("This is thy work" [5.2.369]). But Iago's gaze is one that confirms the abolition of the lovers' humanity, and it thereby helps to license Lodovico's revulsion: "let it be hid." In that gesture of concealment, we may discern the official equivalent of Iago's retreat into obdurate silence: "Demand me nothing. What you know, you know: / From this time forth I never will speak word" [5.2.308–09]. Iago will no more utter his "cause" than Othello can nominate his; what they choose not to speak, we might say, Lodovico elects not to see.

IV

In so far as Lodovico voices the reaction of the audience, he articulates a scandal that is as much generic as it is social. It was precisely their sense of the play's ostentatious violation of the laws of kind that led Victorian producers to mutilate its ending. From the late eighteenth century it became usual to finish the play on the heroic note of Othello's suicide speech, tactfully removing the Venetians' choric expressions of outrage and dismay, as if recognizing how intolerably Lodovico's "Let it be hid" serves to focus attention on what it insists must not be attended to. By diverting the audience's gaze from this radical impropriety, the cut was meant to restore a semblance of tragic decorum to the catastrophe.[5] Other cuts sought to disguise as far as possible the erotic suggestiveness of the scene: in particular Othello's "To die upon a kiss" was almost invariably removed so as to ensure that at the curtain Desdemona's

---

4. The relation between names and identity in the play is sensitively analyzed by Calderwood, pp. 40–45, 50–52.
5. For a suggestive discussion of ideas of propriety and property in the play, see Calderwood, pp. 9–15.

body would remain in chaste isolation upon a bed "unviolated by Othello's own bleeding corpse."[6] In this way the significance of the bed might be restricted to the proper monumental symbolism so solemnly emphasized in Fechter's mid-century production, where it was made to appear "as portentous as a catafalque prepared for a great funeral pomp."[7]

Of course Shakespeare's ending does play on such iconic suggestions but much more ambiguously. When Othello's imagination transforms the sleeping Desdemona to "monumental alabaster" [5.2.5], his figure draws theatrical power from the resemblance between Elizabethan tester tombs and the beds of state on which they were modelled.[8] But his vain rhetorical effort to clothe the violence of murder in the stony proprieties of ritual is thoroughly subverted by other conventional meanings that reveal the bed as a site of forbidden mixture, a place of literary as well as social and racial adulteration.

If the first act of *Othello,* as Susan Snyder has shown, is structured as a miniature romantic comedy,[9] then the last act returns to comic convention in the form of cruel travesty. For the tragedy ends as it began with a bedding—the first clandestine and offstage, the second appallingly public; one callously interrupted, the other murderously consummated. A bedding, after all, is the desired end of every romantic plot; and Desdemona's "Will you come to bed, my lord" [5.2.24] sounds as a poignant echo of the erotic invitations which close up comedies like *A Midsummer Night's Dream:* "Lovers to bed" (5.1.364). But where comic decorum kept the bed itself offstage, consigning love's consummation to the illimitable end beyond the stage-ending, the bed in *Othello* is shamelessly displayed as the site of a blood-wedding which improperly appropriates the rites of comedy to a tragic conclusion.

The result, from the point of view of seventeenth-century orthodoxy, is a generic monster. Indeed, just such a sense of the monstrosity

6. Siemon, p. 50. [See 312 above.]
7. Henry Morley, *The Journal of a London Playgoer,* quoted in Hankey, p. 307. Fechter was the first to remove the bed from its traditional central position to the side of the stage, where he placed it with its back to the audience. If this was intended to diminish the threat of the scene, it apparently had the reverse effect, as Sir Theodore Martin complained, "bringing it so far forward that every detail is thrust painfully on our senses" (quoted in Siemon, p. 40). [See 300 above.]
8. The sense of this connection clearly persisted into the Restoration theatre: Rowe's illustration for *Antony and Cleopatra* (1709) shows the dead Cleopatra in her monument lying on what is evidently a bed, but in a posture recalling tomb-sculpture. It was not for nothing that the marriage-bed became a favorite model for so many Elizabethan and Jacobean dynastic tombs, where the figures of man and wife, frequently surrounded on the base of the tomb by their numerous offspring, signify the power of biological continuance, the authority of lineage. [*Elizabethan tester tombs:* the canopied beds of wealthy households, represented in funeral monuments.]
9. *The Comic Matrix of Shakespeare's Tragedies* (Princeton: Princeton Univ. Press, 1979), pp. 70–74. See also Cavell, p. 132. [See 292 above.]

of the play, its promiscuous yoking of the comic with the tragic, lay at
the heart of Rymer's objections to it. Jealousy and cuckoldry, after all,
like the misalliance of age and youth,[1] were themes proper to comedy;
and the triviality of the handkerchief plot epitomized for Rymer the
generic disproportion that must result from transposing them into a
tragic design. The words "monster" and "monstrous" punctuate his
attempts to catalogue the oxymoronic mixtures of this "Bloody Farce,"
a play he thought would have been better entitled "the *Tragedy of the
Handkerchief*."[2] Iago himself, as the inventor of this "burlesk" plot,
was the very spirit of the play's monstrosity: "The *Ordinary* of *Newgate* never had like Monster to pass under his examination."[3] Much
of the force of Rymer's invective, stems from the way in which he
was able to insinuate a direct connection between what he sensed as
the generic monstrosity of the tragedy and the social and moral
deformity he discovered in its action: the rhetorical energy that
charges his use of "monster" and "monstrous" derives from their
electric potency in the language of the play itself. It is clear, moreover, that for Rymer ideas of literary and biological kind were inseparable, so that the indecorum of the design was consequential upon
the impropriety of choosing a hero whose racially defined inferiority
must render him incapable of the lofty world of tragedy. "Never in
the World had any Pagan Poet his Brains turn'd at this Monstrous
rate," declared Rymer; and he went on to cite Iago's "Foul disproportion, thoughts unnatural" as a kind of motto for the play: "The Poet
here is certainly in the right, and by consequence the foundation of
the Play must be concluded to be Monstrous. . . ."[4]

Rymer's appropriation of Iago's language is scarcely coincidental.
Indeed it is possible to feel an uncanny resemblance between the
scornful excitement with which Rymer prosecutes the unsuspected
deformities of Shakespeare's design and Iago's bitter pleasure in
exposing the "civil monsters" lurking beneath the ordered surface
of the Venetian state. It is as if the same odd ventriloquy which
bespeaks the ensign's colonization of the hero's mind were at work

1. The misalliance of youth and age in the play is treated by Janet Stavropoulos, "Love
and Age in *Othello*," *Shakespeare Studies*, XIX (1987), 125–41.
2. Rymer [see 236 and 234 above]. Jonson seems to anticipate Rymer's mockery in the jealousy plot of *Volpone* (1606) when Corvino denounces his wife: "to seek and entertain a
parley / With a known knave, before a multitude! You were an actor with your handkerchief" (2.3.38–40). In a paper exploring the relations between *Othello* and the myth of
Hercules, "Othello *Furens*," delivered at the Folger Shakespeare Library on February 17, 1989, Robert S. Miola has suggested that the handkerchief is a version of the
robe of Nessus; such ludicrous shrinkages are characteristic of comic jealousy plots—
as, for example, in the transformation of Pinchwife's heroic sword to a penknife in
Wycherley's *The Country Wife*. Certain objects become grotesquely enlarged to the
jealous imagination or absurdly diminished in the eyes of the audience—it is on such
disproportion that the comedy of jealousy depends.
3. Rymer [see 233 above].
4. Rymer, quoted in Vickers, pp. 37, 42.

in the critic. It may be heard again in Coleridge's objection to the play's racial theme: "it would be something *monstrous* to conceive this beautiful Venetian girl falling in love with a veritable negro. It would argue a *disproportionateness,* a want of balance in Desdemona."[5] Even G. K. Hunter, in what remains one of the best essays on race in *Othello,* echoes this revealing language when he insists that "we feel the *disproportion* and the difficulty of Othello's social life and of his marriage (as a social act)."[6] For all Hunter's disconcerting honesty about the play's way of implicating the audience in the prejudice it explores, there is a disturbance here that the nervous parenthesis, "as a social act," seems half to acknowledge. The qualification admits, without satisfactorily neutralizing, his echo of Iago—for whom, after all, concepts of the social (or the "natural") serve exactly as useful devices for tagging sexual/racial transgression.

"Foul disproportion, thoughts unnatural" [3.3.235] is only Iago's way of describing the feelings of strangeness and wonder in which Othello discerns the seeds of Desdemona's passion for him: "She swore, in faith 'twas strange, 'twas passing strange, / 'Twas pitiful, 'twas wondrous pitiful" [1.3.159–60]. Like *Romeo and Juliet,* the play knows from the beginning that such a sense of miraculous otherness, though it may be intensified by the transgression of social boundaries, is part of the ground of all sexual desire; what Iago enables the play to discover is that this is also the cause of desire's frantic instability. That is why the fountain from which Othello's current runs can become the very source out of which his jealousy flows.[7] Much of the play's power to disturb comes from its remorseless insistence upon the intimacy of jealousy and desire, its demonstration that jealousy is itself an extreme and corrupted (adulterate) form of sexual excitement—an incestuously self-begotten monster of appetite, born only to feed upon itself, a creature of disproportionate desire whose very existence constitutes its own (natural) punishment. The more Othello is made to feel his marriage is a violation of natural boundaries, the more estranged he and Desdemona become; the more estranged they become, the more he desires her. Only murder, it seems, with its violent rapture of possession, can break such a spiral; but it does so at the cost of seeming to demonstrate the truth of all that Iago has implied about the natural consequences of transgressive desire.

---

5. T. M. Raysor, ed., *Shakespearean Criticism,* 2 vols. (London: J. M. Dent, 1960), Vol. I, 42, italics added. [See 258 above.]
6. "Othello and Colour Prejudice," p. 163, my italics. [See 288 above.]
7. For an account of the social basis of these contradictions, see Stallybrass ["Patriarchal Territories: The Body Enclosed" in Susan Snyder, ed., *"Othello": Critical Essays* (New York and London: Garland, 1998), pp. 251–74], pp. 265–67.

Iago's clinching demonstration of Desdemona's strangeness makes her a denizen of Lady Wouldbe's notorious metropolis of prostitution,[8] the city that Otway in *Venice Preserved* was to type "the whore of the Adriatic":[9] "In Venice they do let God see the pranks / They dare not show their husbands." It produces in Othello a terrible kind of arousal, which finds its expression in the pornographic emotional violence of the brothel scene—"I took you for that cunning whore of Venice / That married with Othello" [4.2.90–91]—where it is as if Othello were compelled to make real the fantasy that possessed him in the course of Iago's temptation: "I had been happy if the general camp, / Pioners and all, had tasted her sweet body" [3.3.344–45]. It is an arousal which his imagination can satisfy only in the complex fantasy of a revenge that will be at once an act of mimetic purgation (blood for blood, a blot for a blot), a symbolic reassertion of his sexual rights (the spotted sheets as a parodic sign of nuptial consummation), and an ocular demonstration of Desdemona's guilt (the blood-stain upon the white linen as the visible sign of hidden pollution): "Thy bed, lust-stained, shall with lust's blood be spotted" [5.1.36].[1] In this lurid metonymy for murder, Othello's mind locks onto the bed as the inevitable setting of the fatal end to which his whole being, as in some somnambulist nightmare, is now directed; and it is an ending that, through the long-deferred disclosure of the scene of sexual anxiety, can indeed seem to have been inscribed upon Othello's story from the very beginning.

In order fully to understand the potency of this theatrical image, it is necessary to see how it forms the nexus of a whole set of ideas about adultery upon which Othello's tragedy depends—culturally embedded notions of adulteration and pollution that are closely related to the ideas of disproportion and monstrosity exploited by Iago. The fact that they are linked by a web of association that operates at a largely subliminal level—or perhaps, more precisely, at the level of ideology—makes them especially difficult to disentangle and resistant to rational analysis,[2] and that is an essential

---

8. In Ben Jonson's *Volpone* (1606), Lady Wouldbe chats endlessly about (and embodies) the female promiscuity associated with the play's Venetian setting. [Editor's note]

9. For the opposite view of Venice, described by the traveler Thomas Coryat in *Coryat's Crudities* as "that most glorious, renowned and Virgin Citie of Venice," see Stallybrass, p. 265.

1. A curious sidelight is cast on nineteenth-century attempts to contain the scandal of the play's ending by the habit of having Othello finish off Desdemona with his dagger on "I would not have thee linger in thy pain"—a piece of stage business which must have heightened the sado-erotic suggestiveness of the scene (see Siemon, pp. 46–47). [308 above.]

2. Kenneth Burke beautifully observes the power of inarticulate suggestion in the play: ". . . there is whispering. There is something vaguely feared and hated. In itself it is hard to locate, being woven into the very nature of 'consciousness'; but by the artifice of Iago it is made local. The tinge of malice vaguely diffused through the texture of events and relationships can here be condensed into a single principle, a devil, giving the audience as it were flesh to sink their claw-thoughts in." [See 279 above.]

aspect of the play's way of entrapping the audience in its own obsessions. It is above all for "disproportion"—a word for the radical kinds of indecorum that the play at once celebrates and abhors—that the bed, not only in Iago's mind but in that of the audience he so mesmerizes, comes to stand.

V

Contemplating the final spectacle of the play, G. M. Matthews produces an unwitting paradox: "All that Iago's poison has achieved is an object that 'poisons sight': a bed on which a black man and a white girl, although they are dead, are embracing. Human dignity, the play says, is indivisible."[3] But if what the bed displays is indeed such an icon of humanist transcendence, then this ending is nearer to those of romantic comedy—or to that of *Romeo and Juliet*—than most people's experience of it would suggest: why should such an assertion of human dignity "poison sight"? Part of the answer lies in the fact that Matthews, in his desire for humane reassurance, has falsified the body count. To be fair, it is quite usual to imagine two bodies stretched out side by side under a canopy—and this is how it is commonly played. But if Emilia's "lay me by my mistress' side" [5.2.243] is (as it surely must be) a dramatized stage direction, there should be three.[4] The tableau of death will then recall a familiar tomb arrangement in which the figure of a man lies accompanied by two women, his first and second wives; and read in this fashion, the bed can look like a mocking reminder of the very suspicions that Iago voiced about Othello and Emilia early in the play—a memorialization of adultery. It would be absurd to suggest that this is how Lodovico or anyone else on the stage consciously sees it; but, for reasons that I hope to make clear, I think the covert suggestion of something adulterous in this alliance of corpses, combined with the powerful imagery of erotic death surrounding it, helps to account for the peculiar intensity of Lodovico's sense of scandal. The scandal is exacerbated by the fact that one of the bodies is black.

Jealousy can work as it does in this tragedy partly because of its complex entanglement with the sense that Iago so carefully nurtures in Othello of his own marriage as an adulterous transgression—an improper mixture from which Desdemona's unnatural counterfeiting naturally follows. "[I]t is the dark essence of Iago's whole enterprise," writes Stephen Greenblatt, ". . . to play upon Othello's buried perception of his own sexual relations with Desdemona as

---

3. "*Othello* and the Dignity of Man," p. 145.
4. Significantly, eighteenth- and nineteenth-century promptbooks reveal that Emilia's request was invariably denied.

adulterous."[5] Despite his teasing glance at the play's moral rhetoric
of color ("dark essence"), Greenblatt is really concerned only with
notions of specifically sexual transgression according to which "'An
adulterer is he who is too ardent a lover of his wife.'"[6] But this perception can be extended to another aspect of the relationship in
which the ideas of adultery and disproportionate desire are specifically linked to the question of race.

In the seventeenth century adultery was conceived (as the history of the two words reminds us) to be quite literally a kind of
adulteration—the pollution or corruption of the divinely ordained
bond of marriage, and thus in the profoundest sense a violation of
the natural order of things.[7] Its unnaturalness was traditionally
expressed in the monstrous qualities attributed to its illicit offspring, the anomalous creatures stigmatized as bastards.[8] A bastard, as the moral deformity of characters like Spurio, Edmund,
and Thersites [in Shakespeare's *Troilus and Cressida*], and the physical freakishness of Volpone's illegitimate offspring equally suggest,
is of his very nature a kind of monster—monstrous because he represents the offspring of an unnatural union, one that violates what
are proposed as among the most essential of all boundaries.[9]

It is Iago's special triumph to expose Othello's color as the apparent sign of just such monstrous impropriety. He can do this partly
by playing on the same fears of racial and religious otherness that
had led medieval theologians to define marriage with Jews,

---

5. P. 233.
6. Greenblatt, p. 248, quoting St. Jerome. Compare Tamyra's prevarication with her amorous husband (whom she is busy cuckolding with Bussy) in Chapman's *Bussy D'Ambois*:
   "your holy friar says / All couplings in the day that touch the bed / Adulterous are, even
   in the married" (3.1.91–93).
7. In addition to their usual technical sense, "adulterous" and "adulterate" came at about
   this time to carry the meaning "corrupted by base intermixture"; while by extension
   "adulterate" also came, like "bastard," to mean "spurious" and "counterfeit" (*OED*, adulterate, *ppl. a*, 2; adulterous, 3; bastard, *sb*. and *a*, 4. See also adulterate, *v*, 3; adulterine,
   3). Thus Ford's Penthea, who imagines her forced marriage to Bassanes as a species of
   adultery, finds her blood "seasoned by the forfeit / Of noble shame with *mixtures of pollution*" (*The Broken Heart*, 4.2.149–50, italics added).
8. So, by one of those strange linguistic contradictions that expose cultural double-think,
   an illegitimate son could be at once "spurious" and "unnatural" and a "natural son."
   When the bastard, Spurio, in a play that performs innumerable variations on the theme
   of the counterfeit and the natural, declares that "Adultery is my nature" (*The Revenger's
   Tragedy*, 1.3.177), he is simultaneously quibbling on the idea of himself as a "natural
   son" and elaborating a vicious paradox, according to which—by virtue of his adulterate
   birth (*natura*)—he is naturally unnatural, essentially counterfeit, and purely adulterous.
   A very similar series of quibbling associations underlies the counterfeiting Edmund's
   paean to the tutelary of bastards in *King Lear*. "Thou, Nature, art my goddess" (1.2.1 ff.).
9. When Ford's Hippolita curses her betrayer, Soranzo, for what she regards as his adulterous marriage to Annabella, she envisages adultery's monstrous offspring as consti-
   tuting its own punishment—"mayst thou live / To father bastards, may her womb bring
   forth / Monsters" (*'Tis Pity She's a Whore*, 4.1.99–101)—a curse that seems likely to be
   fulfilled when Soranzo discovers the existence of the "gallimaufry" (heterogeneous
   mixture) that is already "stuffed in [his bride's] corrupted bastard-bearing womb"
   (4.3.13–14).

Mahometans, or pagans as "interpretative adultery."¹ More generally, any mixture of racial "kinds" seems to have been popularly
thought of as in some sense adulterous—a prejudice that survives
in the use of such expressions as "bastard race" to denote the
"unnatural" offspring of miscegenation.² More specifically, Iago is
able to capitalize upon suggestions that cloud the exotic obscurity
of Othello's origins in the world of Plinian³ monsters, "the Anthropophagi, and men whose heads / Do grow beneath their shoulders"
[1.3.143–44]; even the green-eyed monster that he conjures from
beneath the general's "civil" veneer serves to mark Othello's resemblance to yet another Plinian race, the Horned Men (Gegetones or
Cornuti).⁴ In the Elizabethan popular imagination, of course, the
association of African races with the monsters supposed to
inhabit their continent made it easy for blackness to be imagined
as a symptom of the monstrous⁵—not least because the color itself
could be derived from an adulterous history. According to a widely
circulated explanation for the existence of black peoples (available
in both Leo Africanus and Hakluyt), blackness was originally vis-
ited upon the offspring of Noah's son Cham as a punishment for
adulterate disobedience of his father.⁶

---

1. *OED* adultery, 1b. It scarcely matters that Othello's contempt for the "circumcised dog"
   he killed in Aleppo shows that he sees himself as a Christian, since "Moor" was a vir-
   tual synonym for Muslim or pagan; and it is as a "pagan" that Brabantio identifies him
   [1.2.99].
2. In seventeenth-century English the word "bastard" was habitually applied to all products of generic mixture: thus mongrel dogs, mules, and leopards (supposedly half-lion
   and half-panther) were all, impartially, bastard creatures; and this is the sense that
   Perdita employs when she dismisses streaked gillyvors as "Nature's bastards" (*The
   Winter's Tale*, 4.4.83). In Jonson's *Volpone* the bastard nature of Volpone's "true . . .
   family" is redoubled by their having been "begot on . . . Gypsies, and Jews, and black-
   moors" (1.1.506–7). Jonson's location of this adulterate mingle-mangle in Venice may
   even suggest some general anxiety about the vulnerability of racial boundaries in a
   city so conspicuously on the European margin—one apparent also in *The Merchant
   of Venice*.
3. For Pliny, see 141–42 and 173 above. [Editor's note]
4. John Block Friedman, *The Monstrous Races in Medieval Art and Thought* (Cambridge
   Mass.: Harvard Univ. Press, 1981), pp. 16–17. Calderwood notes the resonance of Othello's
   lodging at the Sagittary—or Centaur [1.3.115]—stressing the monster's ancient significance as a symbol of lust, barbarism, and (through the Centaurs' assault on Lapith
   women) the violation of kind (Calderwood, *The Properties of* Othello, pp. 22–25, 36).
5. See Newman, "Femininity and the Monstrous in *Othello*," pp. 145–53; Elliot H. Tokson,
   The Popular Image of the Black Man in English Drama, 1550–1688 (Boston: G. K. Hall,
   1982), pp. 80–81; Friedman, pp. 101–2; and Calderwood, *The Properties of* Othello, p. 7.
6. Flouting his father's taboo upon copulation in the Ark, Cham, in the hope of producing
   an heir to all the dominions of the earth, "used company with his wife . . . for the which
   wicked and detestable fact, as an example for contempt of Almightie God, and disobedience of parents, God would a sonne should bee borne whose name was Chus, who
   not onely it selfe, but all his posteritie after him should bee so blacke and lothsome,
   that it might remaine a spectacle of disobedience to all the worlde. And of this blacke
   and cursed Chus came all these blacke Moores which are in Africa" (George Best,
   "Experiences and reasons of the Sphere . . . ," in Richard Hakluyt, *The Principal Navigations, Voyages, Traffiques & Discoveries of the English Nation*, 12 vols. (1598–1600;
   rpt. Glasgow: J. MacLehose, 1903–5), Vol. VII, 264.

In such a context the elopement of Othello and Desdemona, in defiance of her father's wishes, might resemble a repetition of the ancestral crime, confirmation of the adulterous history written upon the Moor's face.[7] Thus if he sees Desdemona as the fair page defaced by the adulterate slander of whoredom, Othello feels this defacement, at a deeper and more painful level, to be a taint contracted from him: "Her name that was as fresh / As Dian's visage is now begrimed and black / As mine own face" [3.3.387–89]. Tragedy, in Chapman's metaphor, is always "black-fac'd"; but Othello's dark countenance is like an inscription of his tragic destiny for more reasons than the traditional metaphoric associations of blackness with evil and death. Iago's genius is to articulate the loosely assorted prejudices and superstitions that make it so and to fashion from them the monster of racial animus and revulsion that devours everything of value in the play. Iago's trick is to make this piece of counterfeiting appear like a revelation, drawing into the light of day the hidden truths of his society. It is Iago who teaches Roderigo, Brabantio, and at last Othello himself to recognize in the union of Moor and Venetian an act of generic adulteration—something conceived, in Brabantio's words, "in spite of nature" [1.3.96]: "For nature so preposterously to err, / Being not deficient, blind, or lame of sense, / Sans witchcraft could not" [1.3.62–64]. Even more graphically, Iago locates their marriage in that zoo of adulterate couplings whose bastard issue (imaginatively at least) are the recurrent "monsters" of the play's imagery: "you'll have your daughter covered with a Barbary horse; you'll have your nephews neigh to you, you'll have coursers for cousins, and jennets for germans" [1.1.107–10]. Wickedly affecting to misunderstand Othello's anxiety about how Desdemona might betray her own faithful disposition ("And yet how nature erring from itself—"), Iago goes on to plant the same notion in his victim's mind:

> Ay, there's the point: as, to be bold with you,
> Not to affect many proposed matches
> Of her own clime, complexion, and degree,
> Whereto we see in all things *nature* tends,

---

7. The association of blackness with adultery is also encouraged by a well-known passage in Jeremiah, where the indelible blackness of the Moor's skin is analogized to the ingrained (but hidden) vices of the Jews: "Can the blacke More change his skin? or the leopard his spottes. . . . I have sene thine adulteries, & thy neyings, y filthines of thy whoredome" (Jeremiah, 13:23–27, Geneva version). In the context of *Othello,* the passage's rhetorical emphasis on discovery is suggestive, as is the Geneva version's marginal note. "Thy cloke of hypocrisie shal be pulled of and thy shame sene." A second marginal note observes that the prophet "compareth idolaters to horses inflamed after mares," a comparison that may be echoed in Iago's obscene vision of Othello as "a barbary horse" [1.1.10]. I am grateful to my colleague Dr. Kenneth Larsen for drawing this passage to my attention.

> Foh! One may smell in such a will most rank,
> Foul *disproportion, thoughts unnatural.*
>   [3.3.230–35, Neill's italics]

If at one moment Iago can make infidelity appear as the inevitable expression of Desdemona's Venetian nature, as the denizen of an unnatural city of prostituted adulterers, at another he can make it seem as though it were actually Desdemona's marriage that constituted the adulterous lapse, from which a liaison with one of her own kind would amount to the exercise of "her better judgement" [238]—a penitent reversion to her proper nature. The contradictions, as is always the way with an emotion like jealousy, are not self-canceling but mutually reinforcing.

In this way the relentless pressure of Iago's insinuation appears to reveal a particularly heinous assault on the natural order of things. Not only in its obvious challenge to patriarchal authority and in the subversion of gender roles implicit in its assertion of female desire,[8] but in its flagrant transgression of the alleged boundaries of kind itself, the love of Desdemona and Othello can be presented as a radical assault on the whole system of differences from which the Jacobean world was constructed.[9] The shocking iconic power of the bed in the play has everything to do with its being the site of that assault.

In early modern culture the marriage bed had a peculiar topographic and symbolic significance. It was a space at once more private and more public than for us. More private because (with the exception of the study or cabinet) it was virtually the *only* place of privacy available to the denizens of sixteenth- and early seventeenth-century households;[1] more public because as the domain of the most crucial of domestic offices—perpetuation of the lineage—it was the site of important public rituals of birth, wedding, and death. In the great houses of France, this double public/private function was even symbolized by the existence of two beds: an "official bed, majestic but unoccupied," located in the *chambre de parement,* and a private bed, screened from view in the more intimate domain of

8. See Newman, passim; and Greenblatt, pp. 239–54.
9. Whether or not one accepts Foucault's notion of the sixteenth century as the site of a major cultural shift in which a "pre-classical *episteme*" based on the recognition of similarity was replaced by a "classical *episteme*" based on the recognition of difference, it seems clear that the definition of racial "difference" or otherness was an important adjunct to the development of national consciousness in the period of early colonial expansion. See the work by Cairns and Richards, Laurence, and Greenblatt (cited above, n. [4, 322]).
1. See Danielle Régnier-Bohler, "Imagining the Self" in [Philippe Ariès and Georges Duby, gen. eds., *A History of Private Life*, trans. Arthur Goldhammer, 3. vols. (Cambridge, Mass., and London: Harvard Univ. Press [Belknap Press], 1987)], Vol. 2 (*Revelations of The Medieval World*), 311–93, esp. pp. 327–30.

the bedchamber proper.[2] Everywhere the same double role was acknowledged in the division of the bridal ritual between the public bringing to bed of bride and groom by a crowd of relatives and friends, and the private rite of consummation which ensued after the formal drawing of the bed curtains.[3] Part of the scandal of *Othello* arises from its structural reversal of this solemn division: the off-stage elopement in Act 1 turning the public section of the bridal into a furtive and private thing; the parted curtains of Act 5 exposing the private scene of the bed to a shockingly public gaze. The scene exposed, moreover, is one that confirms with exaggerated horror the always ambiguous nature of that "peninsula of privacy"; "the bed heightened private pleasure . . . . But the bed could also be a symbol of guilt, a shadowy place [or a place of subterfuge], a scene of crime; the truth of what went on here could never be revealed."[4] The principal cause of these anxieties, and hence of the fiercely defended privacy of the marriage bed, lay in the fact that it was a place of licensed sexual and social metamorphosis, where the boundaries of self and other, of family allegiance and of gender, were miraculously abolished as man and wife became "one flesh."[5] Because it was a space that permitted a highly specialized naturalization of what would otherwise constitute a wholly "unnatural" collapsing of differences, it must itself be protected by taboos of the most intense character. In the cruel system of paradoxy created by this play's ideas of race and adultery, Othello as both stranger and husband can be *both* the violator of these taboos and the seeming victim of their violation—adulterer and cuckold—as he is both black and "fair," Christian general and erring barbarian, insider and outsider, the author of a "monstrous act" and Desdemona's "kind lord."[6] As the most intimate site of these contradictions, it was inevitable that the bed should become the imaginative center of the play—the focus of Iago's corrupt fantasy, of Othello's tormented speculation, and always of the audience's intensely voyeuristic compulsions.

2. See Dominique Barthélemy and Philippe Contamine, "The Use of Private Space," in Ariès and Duby, Vol. 2, 395–505, esp. p. 500.
3. See Lawrence Stone, *The Family, Sex and Marriage in England 1500–1800* (New York: Harper and Row, 1977), p. 334; and Georges Duby and Philippe Braunstein, "The Emergence of the Individual," in Ariès and Duby, Vol. 2, 507–630, esp. p. 589.
4. Régnier-Bohler, p. 329.
5. The archaic spells that form part of the convention of epithalamia and wedding masques testify to a continuing sense (albeit overlaid with a show of sophisticated playfulness) of the marriage bed as a dangerously liminal space in the marital rite of passage.
6. Othello is made up of such paradoxical mixtures—at once the governing representative of rational order and the embodiment of ungovernable passion, cruel and merciful, general and "enfettered" subordinate, "honourable murderer"—he is an entire anomaly. See Newman, p. 153: "Othello is both hero and outsider because he embodies not only the norms of male power and privilege . . . but also the threatening power of the alien: Othello is a monster in the Renaissance sense of the word, a deformed creature like the hermaphrodites and other strange spectacles which so fascinated the early modern period."

At the beginning of the play, the monstrousness of Desdemona's passion is marked for Brabantio by its being fixed upon an object "naturally" unbearable to sight: "To fall in love with what she feared to look on! . . . Against all rules of nature" [1.3.98–101]. At the end she has become, for Lodovico, part of the "object [that] poisons sight." The bed now is the visible sign of *what has been improperly revealed* and must now be hidden from view again—the unnamed horror that Othello fatally glimpsed in the dark cave of Iago's imagination: "some monster in his thought / Too hideous to be shown" [3.3.110–11]; it is the token of everything that must not be seen and cannot be spoken ("Let me not name it to you, you chaste stars" [5.2.2], everything that the second nature of culture seeks to efface or disguise as "unnatural"—all that should be banished to outer (or consigned to inner) darkness; a figure for unlicensed desire itself. That banishment of what must not be contemplated is what is embodied in Lodovico's gesture of stern erasure. But, as Othello's quibble upon the Latin root of the word suggests, a *monster* is also what, by virtue of its very hideousness, demands to be *shown*. What makes the tragedy of *Othello* so shocking and painful is that it engages its audience in a conspiracy to lay naked the scene of forbidden desire, only to confirm that the penalty for such exposure is death and oblivion; in so doing, the play takes us into territory we recognize but would rather not see. It doesn't "oppose racism," but (much more disturbingly) illuminates the process by which such visceral superstitions were implanted in the very body of the culture that formed us. The object that "poisons sight" is nothing less than a mirror for the obscene desires and fears that *Othello* arouses in its audiences[7]—monsters that the play at once invents and naturalizes, declaring them unproper, even as it implies that they were always "naturally" there.

If the ending of this tragedy is unendurable, it is because it first tempts us with the redemptive vision of Desdemona's sacrificial self-abnegation and then insists, with all the power of its swelling rhetorical music, upon the hero's magnificence as he dismantles himself for death—only to capitulate to Iago's poisoned vision at the very moment when it has seemed poised to reaffirm the transcendent claims of their love—the claims of kind and kindness figured in the union between a black man and a white woman and the bed on which it was made.

---

7. For discussion of the "satisfaction" that the final scene grants an audience, see Calderwood, pp. 125–26.

MICHAEL D. BRISTOL

Charivari and the Comedy of Abjection in *Othello*†

If certain history plays can be read as rites of "uncrowning" then *Othello* might be read as a rite of "unmarrying." The specific organizing principle operative here is the social custom, common throughout early modern Europe, of charivari.[1] The abusive language, the noisy clamor under Brabantio's window, and the menace of violence in the opening scene of the play link the improvisations of Iago with the codes of a carnivalesque disturbance or charivari organized in protest over the marriage of the play's central characters. Charivari does not figure as an isolated episode here, however, nor has it been completed when the initial onstage commotion ends.[2] Despite the sympathy that Othello and Desdemona seem intended to arouse in the audience, the play as a whole is organized around the abjection and violent punishment of its central figures.

Charivari was a practice of noisy festive abuse in which a community enacted its specific objection to inappropriate marriages and more generally exercised a widespread surveillance of sexuality. As Natalie Davis has pointed out ("Reasons of Misrule"), this "community" actually consists of young men, typically the unmarried ones, who represent a social principle of male solidarity that is in some respects deeply hostile to precisely that form of institutionally sanctioned sexuality whose standards they are empowered to oversee.[3]

As a violent burlesque of marriage, charivari represents the heterosexual couple in grotesquely parodic form. The bride, frequently depicted by a man dressed as a woman, will typically be represented as hyperfeminine. The groom, against whom the larger share of social animosity is often directed, is invariably represented as a type of clown or bumpkin. In addition, the staging of a charivari requires a master of ceremonies, a popular festive ringleader whose task is the unmaking of a transgressive marriage (Neill). Even in its standard form, a full-blown charivari would be a disturbing spectacle to witness. The charivari that forms the comical substructure of *Othello* is even more powerfully troubling, because here the role of the clownish bridegroom is conflated with a derisory and abusive image of "The Moor."

---

† From *Renaissance Drama*, new series, 21 (1990): 3–21. © 1990 Northwestern University. Reprinted with permission of the University of Chicago Press. The author's quotations from *Othello* have been retained, but bracketed references are to this Norton Critical Edition.
1. See Neely, *Broken Nuptials*. On charivari, see Le Goff and Schmitt, Thompson, and Underdown 99–103.
2. Laroque; see also Nelson and Haines 5–7.
3. On the topic of "male solidarity" see Sedgwick.

The following analysis sketches out an interpretation of *Othello* as a carnivalesque text.[4] Carnival is operative as something considerably more than a novel decor for the *mise-en-scène* or an alternative thematics for interpretation. The play's structure is interpreted schematically as a carnivalesque derangement of marriage as a social institution and as an illustration of the contradictory role of heterosexual desire within that institution. The grotesque character of this popular festive scenario is heightened by its deployment of the stereotypical figure of an African, parodically represented by an actor in blackface. Heterosexual desire is staged here as an absurdly mutual attraction between a beautiful woman and a funny monster.

At the time of the play's earliest performances, the supplementary character of Othello's blackness would be apparent in the white actor's use of blackface to represent the conventionalized form of "The Moor." In the initial context of its reception, it seems unlikely that the play's appeal to invidious stereotypes would have troubled the conscience of anyone in the audience. Since what we now call racial prejudice did not fall outside prevailing social norms in Shakespeare's society, no one in the early audience would have felt sympathy for Othello simply on grounds that he was the victim of a racist society.[5] It is far more probable that "The Moor" would have been seen as comically monstrous. Under these conditions the aspects of charivari and of the comical abjection of the protagonists would have been clear to an audience for whom a racist sensibility was entirely normal (Newman).

At the end of the sixteenth century racism was not yet organized as a large-scale system of oppressive social and economic arrangements, but it certainly existed in the form of a distinctive and widely shared *affekt-complex*.[6] Racism in this early, prototypical, form entails a specific physical repugnance for the skin color and other typical features of black Africans. This sensibility was not yet generalized into an abstract or pseudoscientific doctrine of racial inferiority, and for this reason it would have been relatively difficult to conceive of a principled objection to this "commonsensical" attitude. The physical aversion of the English toward the racial other was rationalized through an elaborate mythology, supported in part by scriptural authority and reinforced by a body of popular narrative (Jordan, Tokson). Within this context, the image of the racial

4. Bakhtin, *Rabelais and His World* 145–96 and passim; see also his *Dialogic Imagination* 167–224 and Gaignebet.
5. Hunter, "Elizabethans and Foreigners" and "Othello and Colour Prejudice." [For the latter, see 275–88 above.] See also Jones and Orkin.
6. A shared ensemble of feelings typical of a community in a specific place and time. [Editor's note]

other is immediately available as a way of encoding deformity or the monstrous.

For Shakespeare and for his audience the sensibilities of racial difference are for all practical purposes abstract and virtually disembodied, since the mythology of African racial inferiority is not yet a fully implemented social practice within the social landscape of early modern Europe. Even at this early stage, however, it has already occurred to some people that the racial other is providentially foreordained for the role of the slave, an idea that is fully achieved in the eighteenth- and nineteenth-century institution of plantation slavery and in such successor institutions as segregation and apartheid. The large-scale forms of institutional racism that continue to be a chronic and intractable problem in modern societies are, of course, already latent within the abstract racial mythologies of the sixteenth century, since these mythologies enter into the construction of the social and sexual imagery both of the dominant and of the popular culture. In more recent contexts of reception the farcical and carnivalesque potentiality of the play is usually not allowed to manifest itself openly. To foreground the elements of charivari and comic abjection would disclose in threatening and unacceptable ways the text's ominous relationship to the historical formation of racism as a massive social fact in contemporary Europe, and in the successor cultures of North and South America as well as in parts of the African homeland itself. Against this background the text of *Othello* has to be construed as a highly significant document in the historical constitution both of racist sensibility and of racist political ideology.

As a seriocomic or carnivalesque masquerade, the play makes visible the normative horizons against which sexual partners must be selected and the latent social violence that marriage attempts to prevent, often unsuccessfully, from becoming manifest. To stage this action as the carnivalesque thrashing of the play's central characters is, of course, a risky choice for a director to make, since it can easily transform the complex equilibrium of the play from tragedy to *operabuffa*. Although the play is grouped with the tragedies in the First Folio and has always been viewed as properly belonging to this genre, commentators have recognized for a long time the precarious balance of this play at the very boundaries of farce.[7] *Othello* is a text that evidently lends itself very well to parody, burlesque, and caricature, and this is due in part to the racial otherness of its protagonist (Levine 14–20, Neill 391–93 [see 319–21 above]).

The relationship of marriage is established through forms of collective representation, ceremonial and public enactments that

---

7. Rymer 2: 27 [see 236 above]. See also Snyder 70–74.

articulate the private ethos of conjugal existence and mark out the communal responsibilities of the couple to implement and sustain socially approved "relations of reproduction." In the early modern period the ceremonial forms of marriage are accompanied (and opposed) by parodic doubling of the wedding feast in the forms of charivari.[8] This parodic doubling is organized by a carnivalesque wardrobe corresponding to a triad of dramatic agents—the clown (who represents the bridegroom), the transvestite (who represents the bride), and the "scourge of marriage," often assigned a suit of black (who represents the community of unattached males or "young men").[9] Iago of course is neither unattached nor young, but part of his success with his various dupes is his ability to present himself as "one of the boys." Iago's misogyny is expressed as the married man's *ressentiment* against marriage, against wives in general, and against his own wife in particular. But this *ressentiment* is only one form of the more diffuse and pervasive misogyny typically expressed in the charivari. And of course Iago's more sinister function is his ability to encourage a kind of complicity within the audience. In a performance he makes his perspective the perspective of the text and thus solicits from the audience a participatory endorsement of the action.

The three primary "characters" in charivari each has a normative function in the allocation of marriage partners and in the regulation of sexual behavior. These three figures parody the three persons of the wedding ceremony—bride, groom, and priest. The ensemble performs a travesty of the wedding ceremony itself. The ringleader or master of ceremonies may in some instances assist the partners in outwitting parental opposition, but this figure may also function as a nemesis of erotic desire itself and attempt to destroy the intended bond. In the actual practice of charivari, the married couple themselves are forced to submit to public ridicule and sometimes to violent punishment (Ingram, Muchembled). In its milder forms, a charivari allows the husband and wife to be represented by parodic doubles who are then symbolically thrashed by the ringleader and his followers.

This triad of social agents is common to many of Shakespeare's tragedies of erotic life, and it even appears in the comedies. Hamlet stages "The Murder of Gonzago" partly as a public rebuke to the unseemly marriage of Claudius and Gertrude (Davis, "Reasons of Misrule" 75). This is later escalated to a fantasy of the general abolition of the institution of monogamy, "I say we will have no moe marriage" (3.1.148). Hamlet's situation here expresses the powerful

8. See Alford; Belmont; Davis, "Charivari"; Grinberg; and Bristol.
9. For the importance of "youth groups" and of unmarried men see Davis, "The Reasons of Misrule."

ambivalence of the unattached male toward marriage as the institutional format in which heterosexual desire and its satisfaction are legitimated. His objection to the aberrant and offensive union of mother and uncle is predicated on the idealization of marriage and in this case on the specific marriage of mother and father. This idealization is, however, accompanied by the fantasy of a general dissolution of the institution of monogamy back into a dispensation of erotic promiscuity and the free circulation of sexual partners. A similar agenda, motivated by a similar ambivalence, is pursued by Don John in *Much Ado about Nothing,* and by Iachimo in *Cymbeline.*

The argument I hope to sketch out here requires that readers or viewers of *Othello* efface their response to the existence of Othello, Desdemona, and Iago as individual subjects endowed with personalities and with some mode of autonomous interiorized life. The reason for such selective or willful ignorance of some of the most compelling features of this text is to make the determinate theatrical surfaces visible. To the extent that the surface coding of this play is openly manifested, the analysis presented here will do violence to the existence of the characters in depth. I believe that the withdrawal of empathy and of identification from the play's main characters is difficult, not least because the experience of individual subjectivity as we have come to know it *is* objectively operative in the text. It has been suggested, in fact, that the pathos of individual subjectivity was actually invented by Shakespeare, or that this experience appears for the first time in the history of Western representation in that great sociocultural laboratory known as Elizabethan drama (Belsey, Brecht).

Whether this view is accurate or not, however, there is the more immediate difficulty that we desire, as readers and viewers, to reflect on and to identify with the complex pathos of individual subjectivity as it is represented in Shakespeare's oeuvre. This is especially so, perhaps, for professional readers and viewers, who are likely to have strong interests in the experience of the speaking/writing subject and in the problematic of autonomy and expressive unity. The constellation of interests and goal-values most characteristic of the institutional processing of literary texts has given rise to an extremely rich critical discourse on the question of the subject; it is precisely the power and the vitality of this discourse that makes the withdrawal of empathy from the characters so difficult. But when we acknowledge the characters not only as Othello, Desdemona, and Iago, but also as components in a carnivalesque "wardrobe" that is inscribed within this text, then this wardrobe assigns them the roles of clown, transvestite, and "scourge of marriage" in a charivari.

The clown is a type of public figure who embodies the "right to be other," as M. M. Bakhtin would have it (*Dialogic Imagination* 158–67), since the clown always and everywhere rejects the categories made available in routine institutional life. The clown is therefore both criminal and monster, although such alien and malevolent aspects are more often than not disguised. Etymologically "clown" is related to "colonus"—a farmer or settler, someone not from Rome but from the agricultural hinterland. As a rustic or hayseed the clown's relationship to social reality is best expressed through such contemporary idioms as "He's out of it!," "He doesn't know where it's at!," or simply "Mars!" In the drama of the early modern period a clown is often by convention a kind of country bumpkin, but he is also a kind of "professional outsider" of extremely flexible social provenance. Bakhtin has stressed the emancipatory capacity of the clown function, arguing that the clown mask embodies the "right to be other" or *refus d'identité*. However, there is a pathos of clowning as well, and the clown mask may represent everything that is socially and sexually maladroit, credulous, easily victimized. And just as there is a certain satisfaction in observing an assertive clown get the better of his superiors, so is there also satisfaction in seeing an inept clown abused and stripped of his dignity. This abuse or "thrashing" of the doltish outsider provides the audience with a comedy of abjection, a social genre in which the experience of exclusion and impotence can be displaced onto an even more helpless caste within society.

To think of Othello as a kind of blackface clown is perhaps distasteful, even though the role must have been written not for a black actor, but with the idea of black makeup or a false-face of some kind. Othello is a Moor, but only in quotation marks, and his blackness is not even skin deep but rather a transitory and superficial theatrical integument. Othello's Moorish origins are the mark of his exclusion; as a cultural stranger he is, of course, "out of it" in the most compelling and literal sense. As a foreigner he is unable to grasp and to make effective use of other Venetian codes of social and sexual conduct. He is thus a grotesque embodiment of the bridegroom—an exotic, monstrous, and funny substitute who transgresses the norms associated with the idea of a husband.

To link Othello to the theatrical function of a clown is not necessarily to be committed to an interpretation of his character as a fool. Othello's folly, like Othello's nobility and personal grandeur, is a specific interpretation of the character's motivation and of his competence to actualize those motives. The argument here, however, is that the role of Othello is already formatted in terms of the abject-clown function and that any interpretation of the character's "nature" therefore has to be achieved within that format. The eloquence of

Othello's language and the magnanimity of his character may in fact intensify the grotesque element. His poetic self-articulation is not so much the *expression* of a self-possessed subject but is instead a form of discursive indecorum that strains against the social meanings objectified in Othello's counter-festive *persona*. Stephen Greenblatt identifies the joke here as one of the "master plots of comedy," in which a beautiful young woman outwits an "old and outlandish" husband (234). Greenblatt reminds us here that Othello is functionally equivalent to the gull or butt of an abusive comic action, but he passes over the most salient feature of Othello's out-landishness, which is actualized in the blackface makeup essential to the depiction of this character. Greenblatt's discretion is no doubt a political judgment rather than an expression of a delicacy of taste. To present Othello in blackface, as opposed to presenting him just as a black man, would confront the audience with a comic spectacle of abjection rather than with the grand opera of misdirected pas-sion. Such a comedy of abjection has not found much welcome in the history of the play's reception.

The original audience of this play in Jacobean England may have had relatively little inhibition in its expression of invidious racial sentiments, and so might have seen the derisory implications of the situation more easily. During the nineteenth century, when institu-tional racism was naturalized by recourse to a "scientific" discourse on racial difference, the problem of Othello's outlandishness and the unsympathetic laughter it might evoke was "solved" by making him a Caucasoid Moor, instead of a "veritable Negro" (Newman 144). Without such a fine discrimination, a performance of *Othello* would have been not so much tragic as simply unbearable, part farce and part lynch-mob. In the present social climate, when racism, though still very widespread, has been officially anathematized, the possi-bility of a blackface Othello would still be an embarrassment and a scandal, though presumably for a different set of reasons. Either way, the element of burlesque inscribed in this text is clearly too destabilizing to escape repression.

If Othello can be recognized as an abject clown in a charivari, then the scenario of such a charivari would require a transvestite to play the part of the wife. In the context of popular culture in the early modern period, female disguise and female impersonation were common to charivari and to a variety of other festive obser-vances (Davis, "Women on Top"). This practice was, among other things, the expression of a widespread "fear" of women as both the embodiment of and the provocation to social transgression. Within the pervasive misogyny of the early modern period, women and their desires seemed to project the threat of a radical social undif-ferentiation (Woodbridge). The young men and boys who appeared in female dress at the time of Carnival seem to have been engaged in "putting women in their place" through an exaggerated pantomime of everything feminine. And yet this very practice required the emphatic foregrounding of the artifice required for any stable coding of gender difference. Was this festive transvestism legitimated by means of a general misrecognition of the social constitution of gender? Or did the participants understand at some level that the association of social badness with women was nothing more than a patriarchal social fiction that could only be sustained in and through continuous ritual affirmation?

Female impersonation is, of course, one of the distinctive and extremely salient features of Elizabethan and Jacobean dramaturgy, and yet surprisingly little is known of how this mode of representation actually worked (Rackin). The practice of using boy actors to play the parts of women derives from the more diffuse social practice of female impersonation in the popular festive milieu. Were the boy actors in Shakespeare's company engaging in a conventional form of ridicule of the feminine? Or were they engaged in a general parody of the artifice of gender coding itself? A transvestite presents the category of woman in quotation marks, and reveals that both "man" and "woman" are socially produced categories. In the drama of Shakespeare and his contemporaries, gender is at times an extremely mobile and shifting phenomenon without any solid anchor in sexual identity. To a considerable degree gender is a "flag of convenience" prompted by contingent social circumstances, and at times gender identity is negotiated with considerable grace and dexterity. The convention of the actor "boying" the woman's part is thus doubly parodic, a campy put-down of femininity and, at another level, a way to theorize the social misrecognition on which all gender allocations depend.

Desdemona's "femininity" is bracketed by the theatrical "boying" of his/her part. This renders her/his sexuality as a kind of sustained gestural equivocation, and this corresponds to the exaggerated and equivocal rhetorical aspect of Desdemona's self-presentation. As she puts it, "I saw Othello's visage in his mind" [1.3.250]; in other words, her initial attraction to him was not provoked by his physical appearance. The play thus stipulates that Desdemona herself accepts the social prohibition against miscegenation as the normative horizon within which she must act. On the face of it she cannot be physically attracted to Othello, and critics have usually celebrated this as the sign of her ability to transcend the limited horizons of her acculturation. These interpretations accept the premise of Othello as physically undesirable and therefore insinuate that Desdemona's faith is predicated on her blindness to the highly visible "monstrosity" of her "husband." In other words, her love is a misrecognition of her husband's manifestly undesirable qualities. Or is it a misrecognition of her own socially prohibited desire? Stanley Cavell interprets her lines as meaning that she saw his appearance in the way that he saw it, that she is able to enter into and to share Othello's self-acceptance and self-possession (129ff) [see 289 above]. In this view Desdemona is a kind of idealization of the social category of "wife," who can adopt the husband's own narrative fiction of self as her own imaginary object. Desdemona is thus both a fantasy of a sexually desirable woman and a fantasy of absolute sexual compliance. This figure of unconditional erotic submission is the obverse of the rebellious woman, or shrew, but, as the play shows us, this is also a socially prohibited *métier* for a woman. In fact, as Greenblatt has shown in his very influential essay, the idea that Desdemona might feel an ardent sexual desire for him makes Othello perceive Iago's insinuations of infidelity as plausible and even probable (237–52). The masculine imagination whose fantasy is projected in the figure of Desdemona cannot recognize itself as the object of another's desire.

Like all of Shakespeare's woman characters, Desdemona is an impossible sexual object, a female artifact created by a male imagination and objectified in a boy actor's body. This is, in its own way, just as artificial and as grotesque a theatrical manifestation as the blackface Othello who stands in for the category of the husband. What is distinctive about Desdemona is the way she embodies the category of an "ideal wife" in its full contradictoriness. She has been described as chaste or even as still a virgin and also as sexually aggressive, even though very little unambiguous textual support for either of these readings actually exists.[1] Her elopement, with a Moor no less, signals more unequivocally than a properly arranged marriage ever could that the biblical injunction to leave mother and father has been fulfilled. It is probably even harder to accept the idea of Desdemona as part of a comedy of abjection than it is to accept Othello in such a context. It is, however, only in such a theatrical context that the hyperbolic and exacerbated misrecognition on which marriage is founded can be theorized.

At the level of surface representation then, the play enacts a marriage between two complementary symbols of the erotic grotesque. This is a marriage between what is conventionally viewed as *ipso facto* hideous and repellent with what is most beautiful and desirable. The incongruity of this match is objectified in the theatrical hyper-embodiment of the primary categories of man and woman or

---

1. Arguments for a chaste or virginal Desdemona are found in Nelson and Haines as well as in Janton. The idea of a sexually aggressive Desdemona is to be found in Greenblatt 237ff. and in Booth.

husband and wife. It is not known to what extent Elizabethan and Jacobean theater practice deliberately foregrounded its own artifice. However, the symbolic practice of grotesque hyper-embodiment was well known in popular festive forms such as charivari. The theatrical coding of gender in the early modern period is still contaminated by the residue of these forms of social representation.

The marriage of grotesque opposites is no more a private affair or erotic dyad than a real marriage. Marriage in the early modern period, among many important social classes, was primarily a dynastic or economic alliance negotiated by a third party who represents the complex of social sanctions in which the heterosexual couple is inscribed.[2] The elopement of Desdemona and Othello, as well as their reliance on Cassio as a broker or clandestine go-between, already signals their intention deliberately to evade and thwart the will of family interests. To the extent that readers or viewers are conditioned by the normative horizons that interpret heterosexual love as mutual sexual initiative and the transcendence of all social obstacles, this elopement will be read as a romantic confirmation of the spiritual and disinterested character of their love (Luhmann). However, it can also be construed as a flagrant sexual and social blunder. Private heterosexual felicity of the kind sought by Othello and Desdemona attracts the evil eye of erotic nemesis.[3]

The figure of erotic nemesis and the necessary third party to this union is Othello's faithful lieutenant, Iago. It is Iago's task to show both his captain and his audience just how defenseless the heterosexual couple is against the resources of sexual surveillance. The romantic lovers, represented here through a series of grotesque distortions, do not enjoy an erotic autonomy, though such erotic autonomy is a misrecognition of the socially inscribed character of "private" sexuality. His abusive and derisory characterizations of the couple, together with his debasement of their sexuality, are a type of social commentary on the nature of erotic romance. The notion of mutual and autonomous self-selection of partners is impugned as a kind of mutual delusion that can only appear under the sign of monstrosity. In other words, the romantic couple can only "know" that their union is based on mutual love *and on nothing else* when they have "transcended" or violated the social codes and prohibitions that determine the allocation of sexual partners.

Iago is a Bakhtinian "agelast," that is, one who does not laugh. He is, of course, very witty, but his aim is always to provoke a degrading laughter at the follies of others rather than to enjoy the social experience of laughter *with* others. He is a de-mythologizer whose function

2. On the "triangular" character of erotic desire see Girard 1–52.
3. Dumouchel and Dupuy; see also Siebers.

is to reduce all expressivity to the minimalism of the *quid pro quo*.
The process represented here is the reduction of quality to quan-
tity, a radical undifferentiation of persons predicated on a strictly
mechanistic, universalized calculus of desire. Characters identified
with this persona appear throughout Shakespeare's oeuvre, usually
in the guise of a nemesis of hypocrisy and dissimulation. Hamlet's
"I know not 'seems'" (1.2.76) and Don John's "it must not be denied
but I am a plain-dealing villain" (*Much Ado about Nothing* 1.1.31) are
important variants of a social/cognitive process that proclaims itself
to be a critique of equivocation and the will to deception. It is ironic,
of course, that these claims of honesty and plain dealing are so often
made in the interests of malicious dissimulation. What appears to be
consistent, however, in all the variants of this character-type, is the
disavowal of erotic attachment and the contemptuous manipulation
of the erotic imagination.

The supposedly "unmotivated" malice enacted by this figure is
puzzling, I believe, only when read individualistically. Is Iago envious
of the pleasure Othello enjoys with Desdemona, or is he jealous of
Othello's supposed sexual enjoyment of Emilia? Of course, both of
these ideas are purely conjectural hypotheses that have no apparent
bearing on Iago's actions. In any case, Iago shows no sustained commitment to either of these ideas, as numerous commentators have
pointed out. Nevertheless, there is an important clue to understanding Iago as a social agent in these transitory ruminations. Iago seems
to understand that the complex of envy and jealousy is not an aberra-
tion within the socially distributed erotic economy, but is rather the
fundamental precondition of desire itself. Erotic desire is not
founded in a qualitative economy or in a rational market, but rather
in a mimetic and histrionic dispensation that Iago projects as the
envy-jealousy system (Agnew 6–7 et passim). In this system men are
the social agents, and women the objects of exchange. Iago's actions
are thus socially motivated by a diffuse and pervasive misogyny that
slides between fantasies of the complete abjection of all women and
fantasies of an exclusively masculine world.

Iago's success in achieving these fantasies is made manifest in the
unbearably hideous tableau of the play's final scene. If the play as a
whole is to be read as a ritual of unmarrying, then this ending is the
monstrous equivalent of a sexual consummation. What makes the
play unendurable would be the suspicion that this climax expresses
all too accurately an element present in the structure of every marriage. This is an exemplary action in which the ideal of companionate marriage as a socially sanctioned erotic union is dissolved back
into the chronic violence of the envy-jealousy system. Iago theorizes
erotic desire—and thus marriage—primarily by a technique of emp-
tying out Othello's character, so that nothing is left at the end except

the pathetic theatrical integument, the madly deluded and murderous blackface clown. Desdemona, the perfect wife, remains
perfectly submissive to the end. And Iago, with his theoretical or
pedagogical tasks completed, accepts in silence his allocation to
the function of sacrificial victim and is sent off to face unnamed
"brave punishments."

Finita la commedia. What does it mean to accept the *mise-en-
scène* of this play? And what does it mean to *know* that we wish it
could be otherwise? To the extent that we want to see a man and a
woman defying social conventions in order to fulfill mutual erotic
initiatives, the play will appear as a thwarted comedy, and our
response will be dominated by its pathos. But the play also shows us
what such mutual erotic initiatives look like from the outside, as a
comedy of abjection or charivari. The best commentators on this
play have recognized the degree to which it prompts a desire to prevent the impending debacle and the sense in which it is itself a kind
of atrical punishment of the observers.[4] This helpless and agonized refusal of the *mise-en-scène* should suggest something about
the corrosive effect on socially inscribed rituals of a radical or
"cruel" theatricality.

The idea of theatrical cruelty is linked to the radical aesthetics of
Antonin Artaud. However, the English term "cruelty" fails to capture an important inflection that runs through all of Artaud's discussion of theater. The concept is derived from words that mean
"raw" or "unprocessed." In French *"cruaute"* expresses with even
greater candor this relationship with *"le cru"* [the raw] and its opposition to *"le cuit"* [the cooked]. Cruelty here has the sense of something uncooked, or something prior to the process of a conventional
social transformation or adoption into the category of the meaning-
ful (Artaud 42 et passim). *Othello,* perhaps more than any other
Shakespeare play, raises fundamental questions about the institutional position and the aesthetic character of Shakespearean dramaturgy. Is Shakespeare raw—or is he cooked? Is it possible that
our present institutional protocol for interpreting his work is a way
of "cooking" the "raw" material to make it more palatable, more fit
for consumption?

The history of the reception of *Othello* is the history of attempts
to articulate ideologically correct, that is, palatable, interpretations. By screening off the comedy of abjection it is possible to
engage more affirmatively with the play's romantic *liebestod* [i.e.,
love-death]. Within these strategies, critics may find an abundance
of meanings for the tragic dimension of the play. In this orientation

---

4. In addition to Cavell and Greenblatt see, for example, Burke [see 271 above]; Neely,
"Women and Men in *Othello*"; Parker; Snow; and Stallybrass.

the semantic fullness of the text is suggested as a kind of aesthetic compensation for the cruelty of its final scenes. Rosalie Colie, for example, summarizes her interpretation with an account of the play's edifying power.

> In criticizing the artificiality he at the same time exploits in his play, Shakespeare manages in *Othello* to reassess and to reanimate the moral system and the psychological truths at the core of the literary love-tradition, to reveal its problematics and to reaffirm in a fresh and momentous context the beauty of its impossible ideals. (167)[5]

The fullness of the play, of course, is what makes it possible for viewers and readers to participate, however unwillingly, in the charivari, or ritual victimization of the imaginary heterosexual couple represented here. Such consensual participation is morally disquieting in the way it appears to solicit at least passive consent to violence against women and against outsiders, but at least we are not howling with unsympathetic laughter at their suffering and humiliation.

Colie's description of the play's semantic fullness is based in part on her concept of "un-metaphoring"—that is, the literalization of a metaphorical relationship or conventional figuration. This is a moderate version of the notion of theatrical cruelty or the unmaking of convention that does not radically threaten existing social norms. In other words, the fate of Desdemona and Othello is a cautionary fable about what happens if a system of conventional figurations of desire is taken literally. But the more powerful "un-metaphoring" of this play is related not to its fullness as a tragedy, but to its emptiness as a comedy of abjection. The violent interposing of the charivari here would make visible the *political* choice between aestheticized ritual affirmation and a genuine refusal of the sexual *mise-en-scène* in which this text is inscribed.

Othello occupies a problematic situation at the boundary between ritually sanctioned reality and theatrically consensual fiction. Does the play simply depict an inverted ritual of courtship and marriage, or does its performance before an audience that accepts its status as a fiction also invite complicity in a social ritual of comic abjection, humiliation, and victimization? What does it mean, to borrow a usage from the French, to "assist" at a performance of this text? At a time when large-scale social consequences of racist sensibilities had not yet become visible, it may well have been easy to accept the formal codes of charivari as the expression of legitimate social norms. In later contexts of reception it is not so easy to accept *Othello* in the

---

5. For other recuperative readings within quite different normative horizons see, for example, Newman; Barber and Wheeler 272–81; Heilman; Holland 197–216; and Kirsch 10–39.

form of a derisory ritual of racial and sexual persecution, because the social experience of racial difference has become such a massive scandal.

The history of both the interpretation and the performance of *Othello* has been characterized by a search for consoling and anaesthetic explanations that would make its depictions of humiliation and suffering more tolerable. On the other hand, some observers, like Horace Howard Furness, have been absolutely inconsolable and have even refused to countenance the play.[6] The need for consolation is of course prompted by the sympathy and even the admiration readers and spectators feel for the heterosexual couple who occupy the center of the drama. The argument I have tried to develop here is not intended to suggest that the characters do not deserve our sympathy. Nevertheless, *Othello* is a text of racial *and* sexual persecution. If the suffering represented in this drama is to be made intelligible for us, then it may no longer be possible to beautify the text. It may be more valuable to allow its structures of abjection and violence to become visible.

Works Cited

Agnew, Jean-Christophe. *Worlds Apart: The Market and the Theater in Anglo-American Thought, 1550–1750*. Cambridge: Cambridge UP, 1986.

Alford, Violet. "Rough Music or Charivari." *Folklore* 70 (1959): 505–18.

Artaud, Antonin. *The Theater and Its Double*. Trans. Mary Caroline Richards. New York: Grove, 1958.

Bakhtin, M. M. *The Dialogic Imagination*. Trans. Caryl Emerson and Michael Holquist. Austin: U of Texas P, 1981.

———. *Rabelais and His World*. Trans. Hélène Iswolsky. Cambridge: MIT P, 1968.

Barber, C. L., and Richard P. Wheeler. *The Whole Journey: Shakespeare's Power of Development*. Berkeley: U of California P, 1986.

Belmont, Nicole. "Fonction de la dérision et symbolisme du bruit dans le charivari." Le Goff and Schmitt 15–21.

Belsey, Catherine. *The Subject of Tragedy: Identity and Difference in Renaissance Drama*. London: Methuen, 1985.

Booth, Stephen. "The Best *Othello* I Ever Saw." *Shakespeare Quarterly* 40 (1989): 332–36.

Brecht, Bertolt. *The Messingkauf Dialogues*. Trans. John Willett. London: Methuen, 1965.

---

6. Furness found the play horrible, and wished Shakespeare had never written it (2: 149, 156). See also Cavell 98ff.

Bristol, Michael D. "Wedding Feast and Charivari." In his *Carnival and Theater: Plebian Culture and the Structure of Authority in Renaissance England*. New York: Methuen, 1985. 162–78.

Burke, Kenneth. "*Othello*: An Essay to Illustrate a Method." *Hudson Review* 4 (1951): 165–203.

Cavell, Stanley. *Disowning Knowledge in Six Plays of Shakespeare*. Cambridge: Cambridge UP, 1987.

Colie, Rosalie. *Shakespeare's Living Art*. Princeton: Princeton UP, 1974.

Davis, Natalie Zemon. "Charivari, honneur et communauté à Lyon et à Genève au XVIIᵉ siècle." Le Goff and Schmitt 207–20.

———. "The Reasons of Misrule: Youth Groups and Charivaris in Sixteenth-Century France." *Past and Present* 50 (1971): 49–75.

———. "Women on Top: Symbolic Sexual Inversion and Political Disorder in Early Modern Europe." *The Reversible World: Symbolic Inversion in Art and Society*. Ed. Barbara A. Babcock. Ithaca: Cornell UP, 1978. 147–90.

Dumouchel, Paul, and Jean-Pierre Dupuy. *L'Enfer des choses: René Girard et la logique de l'économie*. Paris: Seuil, 1979.

Furness, Horace Howard. *Letters*. Ed. Horace Howard Furness. 2 vols. Boston: Houghton, 1922.

Gaignebet, Claude, and Marie-Claude Florentin, eds. *Le Carnaval: Essais de Mythologie Populaire*. Paris: Pavot, 1974.

Girard, René. *Deceit, Desire, and the Novel: Self and Other in Literary Structure*. Trans. Yvonne Freccero. Baltimore: Johns Hopkins UP, 1965.

Greenblatt, Stephen. *Renaissance Self-Fashioning: From More to Shakespeare*. Chicago: U of Chicago P, 1980.

Grinberg, Martine. "Charivaris au Moyen Age et à la Renaissance. Condamnation des remariages ou rites d'inversion du temps?" Le Goff and Schmitt 141–47.

Heilman, Robert. *Magic in the Web: Action and Language in Othello*. Lexington: U of Kentucky P, 1956.

Holland, Norman. *The Shakespearean Imagination: A Critical Introduction*. Bloomington: U of Indiana P, 1964.

Hunter, G. K. "Elizabethans and Foreigners." *Shakespeare Survey* 17 (1964): 37–52.

———. "Othello and Colour Prejudice." *Proceedings of the British Academy* 53 (1967): 139–63.

Ingram, Martin. "Le charivari dans l'Angleterre du XVIᵉ et du XVIIᵉ siècle. Aperçu historique." Le Goff and Schmitt 251–64.

Janton, Pierre. "Othello's Weak Function." *Cahiers Elisabéthains* 34 (1988): 79–82.

Jones, Eldred D. *Othello's Countrymen: The African in English Renaissance Drama*. Oxford: Oxford UP, 1965.

Jordan, Winthrop D. *White over Black: American Attitudes toward the Negro, 1550–1812*. Chapel Hill: U of North Carolina P, 1968.

Kirsch, Arthur C. *Shakespeare and the Experience of Love*. Cambridge: Cambridge UP, 1981.

Laroque, François. "An Archaeology of the Dramatic Text: *Othello* and Popular Traditions." *Cahiers Elisabéthains* 32 (1987): 13–35.

Le Goff, Jacques, and Jean-Claude Schmitt, eds. *Le charivari: Actes de la table ronde organisée à Paris (25–27 avril 1977) par l'Ecole des Hautes Etudes en Sciences Sociales et le Centre National de la Recherche Scientifique*. Paris: Mouton, 1977.

Levine, Lawrence W. *Highbrow/Lowbrow: The Emergence of Cultural Hierarchy in America*. Cambridge: Harvard UP, 1988.

Luhmann, Niklas. *Love as Passion: The Codification of Intimacy*. Trans. Jeremy Gaines and Doris L. Jones. Cambridge: Harvard UP, 1986.

Muchembled, Robert. "Des conduites de bruit au spectacle des processions. Mutations mentales et déclin des fêtes populaires dans le Nord de la France (XV–XVI siècle)." Le Goff and Schmitt 229–36.

Neely, Carol Thomas. *Broken Nuptials in Shakespeare's Plays*. New Haven: Yale UP, 1985.

———. "Women and Men in *Othello*: 'What should such a fool / Do with so good a Woman?'" *The Woman's Part: Feminist Criticism of Shakespeare*. Ed. Carolyn Ruth Swift Lenz, Gayle Greene, and Carol Thomas Neely. Urbana: U of Illinois P, 1980. 211–39.

Neill, Michael. "Unproper Beds: Race, Adultery, and the Hideous in *Othello*." *Shakespeare Quarterly* 40 (1989): 383–412.

Nelson, T. G. A., and Charles Haines. "Othello's Unconsummated Marriage." *Essays in Criticism* 33 (1983): 1–18.

Newman, Karen. "'And wash the Ethiop white: Femininity and the Monstrous in *Othello*." *Shakespeare Reproduced: The Text in History and Ideology*. Ed. Jean E. Howard and Marion F. O'Connor. New York: Methuen, 1987. 143–62.

Orkin, Martin. "Othello and the 'Plain Face' of Racism." *Shakespeare Quarterly* 38 (1987): 166–88.

Parker, Patricia. "Shakespeare and Rhetoric: 'Dilation' and 'Delation' in *Othello*." *Shakespeare and the Question of Theory*. Ed. Patricia Parker and Geoffrey Hartman. London: Methuen, 1985. 54–74.

Rackin, Phyllis. "Androgyny, Mimesis, and the Marriage of the Boy Heroine on the English Renaissance Stage." *PMLA* 102 (1987): 29–41.

Rey-Flaud, Henri. *Le charivari: Les rituels fondamentaux de la sexualité*. Paris: Payot, 1985.

Rymer, Thomas. *A Short View of Tragedy. Shakespeare: The Critical Heritage.* Ed. Brian Vickers. 6 vols. London: Routledge, 1974–81. 2: 25–59.

Sedgwick, Eve Kosofsky. *Between Men: English Literature and Male Homosocial Desire.* New York: Columbia UP, 1985.

Shakespeare, William. *The Riverside Shakespeare.* Gnl. ed. G. Blakemore Evans. Boston: Houghton, 1974.

Siebers, Tobin. *The Mirror of Medusa.* Berkeley: U of California P, 1983.

Snow, Edward A. "Sexual Anxiety and the Male Order of Things in *Othello." English Literary Renaissance* 10 (1980): 384–412.

Snyder, Susan. *The Comic Matrix of Shakespeare's Tragedies.* Princeton: Princeton UP, 1979.

Stallybrass, Peter. "Patriarchal Territories: The Body Enclosed." *Rewriting the Renaissance: The Discourses of Sexual Difference in Early Modern Europe.* Ed. Margaret W. Ferguson, Maureen Quilligan, and Nancy J. Vickers. Chicago: U of Chicago P, 1986. 123–42.

Thompson, E. P. "Rough Music; Le Charivari Anglais." *Annales: Economies, sociétés, civilizations* 27 (1972): 285–312.

Tokson, Elliot H. *The Popular Image of the Black Man in English Drama, 1550–1688.* Boston: Hall, 1982.

Underdown, David. *Revel, Riot, and Rebellion: Popular Politics and Culture in England, 1603–1660.* Oxford: Clarendon, 1985.

Woodbridge, Linda. *Women and the English Renaissance: Literature and the Nature of Womankind, 1540–1620.* Urbana: U of Illinois P, 1984.

LOIS POTTER

[Five Modern Productions]†

[White Othellos]

By the end of the twentieth century the question of whether black actors should play black roles had become the question of whether any *except* black actors should play them. * * * The history of white actors in Othello after this date is littered with failures. * * *

---

† From *Shakespeare in Performance: "Othello"* (Manchester and New York: Manchester University Press, 2002), pp. 135, 147–50, 152–56, 185–96. Reprinted by permission of the publisher. The author's quotations from *Othello* have been retained, but bracketed references are to this Norton Critical Edition. Four of the productions discussed are available on video (see 388–89 below).

Olivier's [1964] performance * * * would soon become (on film and video) a source of embarrassment. * * * In 1981, Jonathan Miller's *Othello*, with * * * Anthony Hopkins as an Othello who made no attempt to seem black, brought the question of race-based casting into the open.

* * *

In 1961 at Stratford John Gielgud, at the peak of his career, played an Othello directed by Franco Zeffirelli. It should have been a triumph; instead, it was a first night of disasters. * * * Three years later Gielgud saw Laurence Olivier walk on to the stage of the National Theatre at the Old Vic, dressed like an African, barefoot, smiling with half-closed eyes, and radiating complete, self-contained self-satisfaction. 'Staggered', he suddenly remembered that in rehearsals Zeffirelli had tried unsuccessfully to convince him that 'this man is very vain' (Gielgud, 82–3).

[In his] entrance, which became famous, * * * Olivier, half in a dream, smelled a single red rose. * * * Edward Pechter has pointed out how this smelling of the rose not only prefigures 'I'll smell it on the tree' in Othello's final soliloquy but also establishes the sensuality of the character, often indicated elsewhere in the production by the sense of smell (Pechter, 143). This Othello did not bother to charm either his subordinates or the audience. He gave a powerful and not always sympathetic performance that, James Earl Jones thought, had 'all the paranoia, suspicions and defensiveness of a victim of racism' (Jones and Niven, 165–6). This * * * is not how Jones thought the part should be played, but it attests to Olivier's power of impersonation. As he explains in detail in his book *On Acting*, he changed his walk, worked to lower his voice, made himself up 'all over' by a special formula, and played a character who was authentically 'other' and very dangerous. * * *

[The] production was directed for film by Stuart Burge, and later put on to video. * * * [Both] offer a radically new reading. The most famous influence on John Dexter's interpretation was F. R. Leavis's 1937 essay * * * which argued that the traditional view of Othello's nobility and Iago's intellectuality was sentimental. * * *

A Leavisite concern for moral judgement, which characterized much literary criticism of this period, affected the playing of other characters as well as Othello. Derek Jacobi's Cassio, for example, is a complex figure. He takes a rather smug pleasure, in [1.2], when he asks Iago a question ('Ancient, what makes he here?': line 49) to which he already knows the answer. By the start of [2.1] he is already more vulnerable, as his lack of military experience makes him twitch every time a gun goes off. * * *

* * *

The excellent National Theatre publication compiled by Kenneth
Tynan gives a thorough account of what [the director John] Dexter and the actors worked out in the early stages of rehearsal,
though some of these ideas were intended for the actors' benefit
rather than the audience's and may have changed over time (Dexter's autobiography points out that Tynan did not actually record
what happened after the first reading: 18). It is unlikely, for
instance, that uninformed spectators would realize that Othello,
when he re-enters at [3.3.330], is supposed to have tried, and failed,
to make love to Desdemona (Tynan, 8), thus colouring the play's
crucial scene with a sense of sexual failure that carries through to
Act [4], with all its references to 'being a man'. * * *

* * *

Though at the time it seemed that Frank Finlay had been ordered
to sacrifice his Iago in the interest of a star performance by Olivier,
with hindsight it now seems that he belongs, like [Michael] MacLiam-
mór [Welles's Iago], to a new tradition of subdued, ordinary Iagos
who succeed because they are taken for granted by everyone else
rather than because they inspire any special trust, affection or admiration. * * * Dexter follows the nineteenth-century practice of having
Iago taken off the stage before the end, but not in order to give him
an impressive exit. The cue for his departure is 'The object poisons
sight; let it be hid', and, like an object, he is dragged away, whimper-
ing with pain.

There was thus no competition for the starring performance that
the audience wanted Olivier to give. At the same time, the effective-
ness of his impersonation created admiration rather than emotional
involvement. * * *

* * * [A]s a *tour de force* of mimicry, it is likely to be offensive.
* * * [O]nly the atmosphere of the early 1960s made such a performance possible. It was a time when Britain still believed itself to be
free of race prejudice and a white actor (Peter Sellers) could become
famous for his comic Indian accent. In April 1968, when Enoch
Powell made his famous 'Rivers of blood' speech urging a halt to
immigration to Britain, the extent and bitterness of racial conflict
within Britain became clear. This new consciousness about race
would change the way in which *Othello* could be played.

* * *

In mainstream British theatre, however, white actors continued
to play the title role. * * * [But a]s Ian McKellen suggested in
1986, [there was] a new embarrassment about racial impersonation:

'Every modern, white actor, taking on Othello, feels obliged to explain why he's not playing him black, which was surely Shakespeare's intention, when the unspoken reason is that to "black up" is as disgusting these days as a "nigger minstrel show".' McKellen went on to add that, precisely for this reason, he had no intention of ever playing the part himself (McKellen, *Acting*, 27). The rejection of impersonation, however, seems to have made Othello even harder for British actors. The directorial solution to the problem was to lower the play's emotional temperature and rely on the 'Chekhovian' realism of the Stratford style at its best. * * * [I]t is a style that works beautifully for everyone except Othello, who, reviewers frequently complain, seems to have wandered in from another play * * *.

The turning point in British attitudes to casting came suddenly in 1981, when Anthony Hopkins played Othello for Jonathan Miller in the BBC Shakespeare series. * * * Miller argued that the play was about jealousy, not race, and that casting a black actor would encourage audiences to 'equate the supposed simplicity of the black with the exorbitant jealousy of the character' (Fenwick, 18) * * * but what the director's critics really objected to was not his ideology but its practical result: a white actor was to play the most famous black character in drama, in a televised version likely to become the standard image of the play for a whole generation of school and university students. Miller was, and still is, accused of racism precisely because he did not make race an issue.

Miller explained very clearly what he wanted to do with *Othello*, and most reviewers made it equally clear that they did not agree with his choices. These were: believable 'ordinary' characters; low-key, naturalistic (sometimes barely audible) speech; a production set almost entirely indoors, with largely monochrome costumes which looked unquestionably seventeenth-century but without the gaudiness that suggests theatricality. * * *

* * *

Hopkins offers glimpses of qualities in Othello that would have fascinated others as well as Desdemona: his conjuring tricks over dinner at the beginning of [2.3] are a visual equivalent of the stories he once told Desdemona and her father; in poignant contrast, we later see the miserable and silent end of the dinner for Lodovico and Gratiano after Othello's public humiliation of Desdemona. Hopkins's naturalistic performance, by definition, is not grandiose or heroic. But it is not ordinary either; his incessant fiddling, little half-smiles and nervous nodding and murmuring while others speak to him suggest insecurity or absentmindedness, if not neurosis. By contrast, Bob Hoskins's cheerfully psychotic Iago is a man who needs no motive and who refuses to speak at the end because he has nothing to say * * *. The character laughs, or rather giggles, a lot. When Othello kills himself—quickly and efficiently—Iago responds as if this action were the ultimate practical joke. Miller let the story end with the sound of Iago's laughter ringing down the now-empty corridors.

If this conclusion was disturbing, the production's elimination of the exotic and the unusual was disturbing in other ways. It made the play a 'domestic tragedy' with no meaning beyond itself. * * * Miller's patterns are empty of moral significance; their 'curious perspectives' lead not to a true point of view but to a vanishing point. The production is still remembered less for its style than for the outcry over its casting, which brought what is now called identity politics into the public consciousness. It became clear that actors henceforth were going to have to *prove* their right to play Othello.

[*Sex and Soldiers*]

In 1989 Michael Billington wrote in *The Guardian*, 'Othello is currently the least revived of all Shakespeare's tragedies and the reasons are not far to seek: casting problems and racial guilt' (16 March 1989). During the next ten years all this was to change. Two major stage productions (by [Janet] Suzman and [Trevor] Nunn) became available on video, as did Oliver Parker's film * * *, *Othello* seemed to have become, as Edward Pechter put it, 'the Shakespearean tragedy of choice for the present generation'. Pechter saw this phenomenon as a consequence of the transformation of literary criticism 'by feminist, African American and postcolonialist studies' (Pechter, 2). These interests had been reflected, and even anticipated, by some theatre practitioners. * * * In the late twentieth century, however, critics were not only focusing on issues of race, class and gender but attempting to negotiate their competing demands for attention. Feminist approaches in particular tended to stress the parallels between the two different kinds of oppression from which Othello and Desdemona suffer. * * *

Feminism has strongly affected many late twentieth-century productions of the play, * * * not only in giving a strong role to Desdemona but also in making all three of the play's women victims of male abuse: Iago was clearly abusive toward Emilia, while the story of Bianca— * * * depicted by both directors—was given a horrific closure: rejected even by Emilia, her one possible ally, she was left at the end of [5.1] to be attacked, raped and—in the Suzman production—possibly killed by Iago-trained soldiers. * * * [T]he image of soldiers attacking the most socially powerless of the play's three women was indicative of something that has been part of many productions of the play: its hostile perspective on the military world.

* * *

In a pre-production talk during the run of his National Theatre *Othello* (1997), Sam Mendes distinguished what he saw as the two main production styles for the play: the 'operatic', with exotic costumes and long flowing robes, and (his own choice) the 'military' one. * * *

* * * Some early productions in modern dress had experimented with uniforms. * * * But it was John Barton's 'Victorian' production for the Royal Shakespeare Company in 1971 that had the greatest influence. As reviewers discovered, uniforms clarified the characters' rank and class, as well as the distinction between soldiers and civilians in the Venetian senate and the scene of Lodovico's arrival in Cyprus * * * [, which] also made it easier to see, as Ronald Bryden put it, 'why Othella should trust his senior NCO more than his new bride from home' and why characters were obsessed about their reputations: 'Where else, today, but in the Army could we accept a drunken fight spelling disgrace for Cassio or a man regarding his wife's infidelity as the ruin of his career?' (*Observer,* 12 September 1971). * * *

* * *

Though Trevor Nunn strongly emphasized the military setting of the play and the psychology of the men who choose a military career, his treatment of their world was relatively sympathetic, perhaps because his famous production (The Other Place, Stratford-upon-Avon, 1989), filmed for television in 1990, predated most of the negative publicity about the military. His is an almost loving recreation of a military camp. * * * The movement from Venice to Cyprus at the beginning of [2.1] is also a movement from the rather stuffy civilian world to the freer military one. Nunn establishes the basic decency of the army officers and men through their reactions to the news that Othello is about to arrive 'in full commission here for Cyprus' [2.1.29]. The soldiers react with consternation to the announcement that Othello is about to supersede Montano, obviously a popular officer; but Montano himself (Philip Scully), with his unhesitating and generous 'I am glad of it', immediately defuses the situation. * * *

Another memorable moment comes a few minutes later * * *. Still nervously waiting for news of Othello, the group falls into tense silence, broken only by the sound of somebody whistling. On video, Nunn has the camera imitate the spectator's gaze, panning across the group in search of the source of the whistling and eventually reaching the expressionless Emilia (Zoe Wanamaker), whose importance is thus established early. * * * Emilia likewise remains indifferent even when, a moment later, Desdemona's attempted cheerfulness breaks down; she begins to sob, and Cassio comforts her. There does not seem much danger that this quietly prim and embittered woman, who gives Iago the handkerchief as indifferently as she asks him to give it back, will take any trouble for the sake of this much younger woman, with whom she has so little in common.

* * *

* * * [But t]he delicately nuanced relationship between the two women reaches its turning point in [4.3]. In the previous scene, Othello has searched Desdemona's dressing table with a key taken from Emilia. Now, for Emilia's benefit, Desdemona unlocks a secret drawer in the same table, but, instead of the incriminating letters for which Othello had been looking, she takes out a little box of sweets that Cassio had given her in [3.3]; the two women, giggling like schoolgirls, share their illicit late-night feast. Emilia has resisted Desdemona's attempts at intimacy until now; but, at the end of the scene, when Desdemona says 'Good night', Emilia impulsively seizes and embraces her. It is this brief moment of friendship that explains why, contrary to all the indications she had given earlier, Emilia cannot let the death of Desdemona remain unexamined. While spectators of *Othello* are used to seeing Desdemona's dead hand feebly seized by another dying hand that has been groping for it, in Nunn's version that hand is Emilia's rather than Othello's, and the gesture is highlighted on the video by a close-up that emphasizes the 'wife for wife' pairing: 'the camera allows audiences to see the wedding ring each woman wears' (McGuire, 80).

* * * Two years after playing Iago, Ian McKellen starred in Richard Eyre's *Richard III* at the National Theatre (1991), a production which showed how an impoverished emotional and erotic life makes a society vulnerable to cheap substitutes like the fascist cult of ceremony and death. Though Nunn's society was warmer than Eyre's, McKellen's Iago can also be seen as perverting and exploiting the human need for love; Vaughan perceptively notices the number of times that the promptbook specifies that he is to 'cuddle' people (224). Yet the warmth is fake, as his costume shows: everything that can be buttoned is buttoned, in contrast with the relaxed look of the other characters' uniforms. * * *

* * * Willard White's relatively subdued manner [as Othello] is small-scale like the production: his 'fit' is rather muted, and, although he is able to speak such almost unspeakable lines as 'Blow me about in winds, roast me in sulphur, / Wash me in steep-down gulfs of liquid fire!' [5.2.285–86], he does so by making them a prayer rather than a scream of agony. On camera with McKellen he suffers from the contrast between his broad expansive face, which seems to have nothing to hide, and the mysterious folds and lines of McKellen's,

which invite the spectator to watch for the revelation of dark secrets in his not fully understood feelings.

* * *

The fact that the Oliver Parker film was released during 1994, a year dominated by the O. J. Simpson case, reinforced something already present in the film, the theme of wife-abuse. At the time of filming, the actor playing Othello, Laurence Fishburne, was best known to the general public for *What's Love Got to Do with It?*, the story of Ike Turner's abuse of his wife, the rock singer Tina Turner. This of course lent a special intensity to Othello's relationship with Desdemona, while Iago (Kenneth Branagh) was also played as a wife-abuser. * * * Isolated on Cyprus, both Desdemona and Emilia were natural victims.

Parker cut nearly fifty per cent of the text and provided plenty of visual excitement to accompany what remained. * * *

* * * But sometimes Parker's film language is, if anything, still more difficult to read than Welles's. The difficulties begin at the start: Desdemona is seen running though the streets of Venice, and anyone familiar with the story will realize that she is eloping; but a moment later she is seen in a gondola with a black man in a white mask, who is *not* Othello * * *. Unlike other films that try to show Othello's jealous fantasies, this one gives no indication that they *are* fantasies. Othello parts the curtains of his bed and sees Desdemona engaged in sex play with Cassio. He draws back, as if waking from a nightmare, but when he looks at the bed again the couple are still there. * * * In some of the dialogues the choice of close-up is puzzling: it may make sense to focus mainly on Othello's face during most of Iago's description of Cassio's dream, but it is hard to see why the camera shows mainly Iago's face during Othello's 'Now, forever farewell'. The final shot of the bed shows it loaded with the bodies of all four protagonists, leaving it uncertain whether Iago has died, or is about to die, like the others. * * *

These examples show not only the power of visual images but also the difficulty of interpreting them when they are not accompanied by words. One of the film's most puzzling, if memorable, visual effects is the plotting of Iago and Roderigo as they lie under a cart on which a (heterosexual) couple is having sex, an image that seems meant to raise questions about their relationship. At least one critic had no doubt that Iago was 'a gay man who loves Othello but cannot admit it and so destroys him and his wife' (Burt, 241). It is at any rate evident that Parker, like Welles, imagined Iago as impotent. * * *

Anna Patrick, an attractive and graceful woman with no touch of shrewishness (most of the lines suggesting this quality were cut) is a companion rather than servant to Desdemona and plays Emilia as very much in love with her 'wayward husband'; this is a marriage that she still hopes can be rescued. The two women are seen together more than in most other versions, as if to emphasize the parallelism in their stories. Cutting the text avoids the problem of why Emilia does not speak up earlier about the handkerchief, and one could imagine that she had forgotten all about it. At the end of [4.2], when Iago has comforted Desdemona, Emilia impulsively seizes his hand as if to thank him for being the man she always knew he was. The pay-off of this interpretation comes at the end. Othello names the handkerchief as the chief justification for his actions and, in the most exciting moment of the film, the camera rapidly cuts between the faces of Emilia (who realizes what this means) and Iago (who realizes, for the first time, what her knowledge means for him); Iago's lines to her are quiet but emphatic asides, prolonging the suspense as to whether she will indeed choose to 'be wise and get you home'. When she chooses instead to 'speak', Iago seizes her, uses her as a human shield on his way to the door, then stabs her and throws her body at his pursuers to slow them down. Although this western/gangster film cliché is an example of the film at its most obvious, the poignant and sympathetic treatment of Emilia shows what it is at its best.

Bibliography

Burt, Richard, 'The Love That Dare Not Speak Shakespeare's Name: New Shakesqueer Cinema', in L. Boose and R. Burt, eds., *Shakespeare the Movie: Popularizing the Plays on Film, TV, and Video*, London, 1997, pp. 240–8.

Dexter, John, *The Honourable Beast: A Posthumous Autobiography*, New York, 1993.

Fenwick, Henry, 'The Production', introduction to *The BBC TV Shakespeare: Othello*, London, 1981.

Gielgud, John, *Shakespeare: Hit or Miss* (with John Miller), London, 1991.

Jones, James Earl, and Penelope Niven, *James Earl Jones: Voices and Silences*, New York, 1993.

Leavis, F. R., 'Diabolic Intellect and the Noble Hero: or The Sentimentalist's Othello', *The Common Pursuit*, London, 1952; Harmondsworth, 1962, pp. 136–59.

McGuire, Philip C, 'Whose Work Is This? Loading the Bed in *Othello*', in Jay L. Halio and Hugh Richmond, eds, *Shakespearean Illuminations: Essays in Honor of Marvin Rosenberg*, Newark, Del., and London, 1998.

McKellen, Ian, *Acting Shakespeare* (reprint of souvenir programme of 31 August 1986).

Olivier, Laurence, *On Acting*, London, 1986.

Pechter, Edward, *'Othello' and Interpretive Traditions*, Iowa City, 1999.

Tynan, Kenneth, *Othello, by William Shakespeare: The National Theatre Production*, New York, 1967.

Bibliography

The material below is designed to help readers looking to find out more about the topics considered in this Norton Critical Edition. The fifteen lists—distinguishable but sometimes overlapping, frequently subdivided and supplemented with commentary—follow the sequence earlier in the book. The first four are linked with the "Textual Sources and Cultural Contexts" section. The next seven, keyed to the "Criticism" section, provide information about the critics up to and including Bradley, the texts from which their discussions are excerpted, and the critical contexts within which they produced their claims about *Othello*. The next three focus on how *Othello* has been represented on stage, in movies and videos, and in mostly recent spinoffs and offshoots. The final section lists books currently available whose purposes overlap in some respect with this one.

I. TEXTUAL SOURCES

According to Geoffrey Bullough's authoritative study, Cinthio's *Moor of Venice* is the only absolutely certain textual source for *Othello*. The tale, which Shakespeare seems to have had open beside him (or firmly in his mind) as he worked on the play, is available in various modern English versions, as detailed in the first list below. William Carew Hazlitt reprints a 1795 translation; Furness, the Taylor version printed in this Norton Critical Edition; both include the Italian original. Ross and Dean provide excerpts from Cinthio in their own translations. Bullough translates the whole tale along with excerpts from the narrator's introduction (239–52). Honigmann reprints Bullough's translation and provides a long list of verbal parallels between the narrative and Shakespeare's play. Neill includes a specially commissioned translation by Bruno Ferraro.

Once beyond Cinthio, we enter into speculative territory, encountering material that (in Bullough's terminology) Shakespeare "possibly" or "probably" or "almost certainly" used in writing his play. Lewis Lewkenor's 1599 translation of Gaspar Contarini's *Commonwealth and Government of Venice* belongs in the last category. When Brabantio proposes to raise "some special officers of night" (1.1.179), he alludes to a Venetian practice that Lewkenor highlights in just these terms. The echo led Edmond Malone, in his 1790 edition of the play, to "have no doubt" that Shakespeare read the book "before he wrote this play" (1.236), and most later editors have agreed. But whether Shakespeare read Contarini or not, Venice occupied a substantial and resonant place in his imagination, and in the imaginations of many of his contemporaries; and the items in the second list below are meant to suggest what this place looked like.

On the one hand, Venice projected an image in which English audiences could flatteringly see themselves: a politically independent and cosmopolitan commercial and maritime power, rich in artistic achievement, that represented "the ideal of civilized European liberty" (Hadfield, *Literature*, 232) and stood as the bulwark of Christian order against infidel incursions. This view, hinted at by Brabantio's dismissal of robbery ("This is Venice: / My house is not a grange" [1.1.102–03]), is reinforced by the "relative ease" with which the Duke and the senate "sort out prejudice and other political problems" in Brabantio's case against Othello in 1.3 (Hadfield, *Amazons*, 42). This view of Venice, though, is only part of the story. As Richard Strier remarks, the "military situation" puts the "impartiality" of Venetian due process "under interesting pressure" (200). Iago's remark that "the state . . . Cannot with safety cast" Othello (1.1.144–46) suggests that the senate's decision may be driven by fear and self-interest as much as by disinterested statesmanship. Moreover, in what was probably the most widespread of the "Myths of Venice" circulating in England at the time (Rosand; see also Klein et al., Marrapodi et al., and McPherson), Venice was seen as the home of avarice, decadence, sexual profligacy and Catholicism—everything G. K. Hunter sums up as "Italian vice." As a result, Venice registers as both a dream and a nightmare, at once a desirable home and a place you fear to visit, an "unstable mixture of admiration and loathing" (Jones, 101)—like the protagonist of the play.

Both sides are on display in Figure 15. Taken from *Coryat's Crudities*, a travel narrative published in 1611, it represents one of Venice's "nobler Cortezans," who is "here inserted," the author tells us, "according to her Venetian habites, with my owne neare vnto her, made in that forme as we saluted each other." The publication date means that *Coryat's Crudities* cannot have been a source for *Othello*, but the book suggests the kind of baggage about Venice that Shakespeare's audiences carried with them into the play. Coryat sojourned in Venice for "more than six weeks, a third of his total trip abroad" (Schutte, vii–viii), and of the 133 pages describing the city, 11 are devoted to the courtesans, "famoused ouer all Christendome" (261–74). Coryat is regularly defensive about his contact with the courtesans. That his visits took in so "many particulars," including the

Figure 15. Signor Tomaso Odcombiano meets Margarita Emiliana, "bella cortesana di Venetia." Engraving in *Coryat's Crudities* (London, 1611). Used by permission of the Folger Shakespeare Library. Shelfmark STC 5808 copy 1.

interiors of their living and working quarters, should not, he insists, "cast an aspersion of wantonnesse vpon me." But why, as Kim Hall shrewdly asks, "does Coryate include this image if he thinks readers might find it unseemly?" (245). The official answer is that Coryat is a

good Protestant and, like Milton in *Areopagitica*, he does not believe
in a cloistered virtue: "a vertuous man will be the more confirmed
and setled in vertue by the obseruation of some vices." But as always,
when it comes to Renaissance English responses to Venice, that's
only part of the story. In the transformative delight of his "neare
vnto" Margareta Emiliana, "seem[ing] to enter into the Paradise of
Venus," Thomas Coryat of Odcombe metamorphoses (as the caption
indicates) into "Il Signior Tomaso Odcambiano." The rube from a
Somerset village has acquired the right stuff to cope as an equal with
the most sophisticated intimacies Venice has to offer.

The third list below includes items related to John Leo Africanus's
History and Description of Africa, discussed briefly above (149–50),
which was translated by John Pory and published in 1600. The book's
claim to have served as a source for *Othello* rests on its resemblances
to some of the details in the protagonist's speech to the senate in 1.3
and, more importantly, on the striking similarities generally between
Othello's and John Leo's adventurous lives. According to Pory, Al-
Hassan Ibn-Mohammed Al-Wezaz Al-Fasi, born a Muslim, left his
native Granada in the face of the Spanish Reconquista at the end of
the fifteenth century and emigrated to Fez in Morocco, where he
achieved prominence as a scholar and diplomat. In 1518, he was
captured on the Mediterranean by Spanish pirates and presented as
a gift to Pope Leo X, from whom, converting to Catholicism a year
or so later, he took his baptismal name (Giovanni Leone). He wrote
his Africa book in Rome during the 1520s and eventually returned
to north Africa, where he reconverted to Islam and lived out his
days in circumstances of which nothing is known.

This synopsis should explain why so many commentators believe
that Shakespeare must have known John Leo's book, or at least
dipped into its early pages. The case can probably never be proved,
and claims that John Leo was a model for Othello seem too literal-
minded. It is rather that deep structural analogies exist between
John Leo and the protagonist of the play. Each is a "wheeling
stranger / Of here and everywhere" (1.1.133–34), moving back and
forth between Europe and Africa, Islam and Christianity, negotiating religious and cultural differences as they go. As much a supplement to *Othello* as a source for it, John Leo's *History* is a fascinating
object of interest in its own right and worth all the attention it is
getting in recent and current work.

In the list below, Hadfield, Hall's edition, Kamps and Singh, and
Mancall include excerpts from John Leo's *History*; the whole book is
available in the reprint edited by Brown. For commentaries, readers
might start with the engaging and richly informative evocations in
Davis and Maalouf. Since John Leo's life has always been a fictional—

constructed or made—phenomenon, the transition between a historian's and a novelist's account is not abrupt.

Bullough, Geoffrey. "Othello." In Narrative and Dramatic Sources of
Shakespeare. Vol. 7, Major Tragedies. London and New York:
Routledge and Columbia University Press, 1975, 193–265.

Dean, Leonard F. A Casebook on "Othello." New York: Thomas
Crowell, 1961, 255–64.

Furness, Horace Howard, ed. A New Variorum Edition of "Othello."
7th ed. Philadelphia: Lippincott, 1886, 376–89.

Hazlitt, William Carew, ed. Shakespeare's Library: A Collection of
the Plays, Romances, Novels, Poems, and Histories Employed by
Shakespeare in the Composition of His Works. London, 1844. Rpt.
New York: AMS, 1965, 2.282–308.

Honigmann, E. A. J., ed. Othello. Walton-on-Thames, Eng.: Nelson, 1997, 369–87.

Neill, Michael, ed. Othello, the Moor of Venice. Oxford: Oxford
University Press, 2006, 434–44.

Ross, Lawrence J., ed. The Tragedy of Othello, The Moor of Venice.
Indianapolis and New York: Bobbs-Merrill, 1974, 263–75.

Contarini, Gasparo. The Commonwealth and Gouernment of Venice, written by the Cardinall Gasper Contareno, and translated out
of Italian into English, by Lewes Lewkenor, Esquire. With sundry
other collections, annexed by the translator for the more cleere and
exact satisfaction of the reader. With a short chronicle in the end,
of the liues and raignes of the Venetian dukes, from the very begin-
ninges of their citie. London, 1599. Rpt. New York: Da Capo,
1969.

Coryat, Thomas. Coryats Crudities, Hastily gobbled vp in five Moneths
trauells in France, Sauoy, Italy, Rhetia comonly called the Grisons
country, Heluetia alias Switzerland, some parts of high Germany,
and the Netherlands; Newly digested in the hungry aire of ODCOMBE
in the County of Somerset, & now dispersed to the nourishment
of the trauelling Members of this Kingdome. London, 1611. Rpt.
London: Scolar Press, 1978

Hadfield, Andrew. Literature, Travel, and Colonial Writing in the
English Renaissance, 1545–1625. Oxford: Clarendon, 1998.

———, ed. Amazons, Savages, and Machiavels: Travel and Colonial
Writing in English, 1550–1630: An Anthology. Oxford and New
York: Oxford University Press, 2001.

Hall, Kim F., ed. William Shakespeare: "Othello, the Moor of Venice":
Texts and Contexts. Boston and New York: Bedford/St. Martin's,
2007.

Holderness, Graham. *Shakesperare and Venice*. Farnham, Surrey, Eng., and Burlington, Vt.: Ashgate, 2010.

Hunter, G. K. "English Folly and Italian Vice: The Moral Landscape of John Marston." In Hunter, *Dramatic Identities and Cultural Tradition: Studies in Shakespeare and His Contemporaries*. Liverpool: Liverpool University Press, 1978, 110–32.

Jones, Ann Rosalind. "Italians and Others: Venice and the Irish in *Coryat's Crudities* and *The White Devil*." *Renaissance Drama* 18 (1987): 101–19.

Klein, Holger, and Michele Marrapodi, eds. *Shakespeare and Italy*. Lewiston, N.Y.: Edwin Mellen Press, 1999.

Malone, Edmond. *The Plays and Poems of William Shakespeare*. 10 vols. London, 1790. Rpt. New York: AMS Press, 1966.

Marrapodi, Michele, A. J. Hoenselaars, Marcello Cappuzzo, and L. Falzon Santucci, eds. *Shakespeare's Italy: Functions of Italian Locations in Renaissance Drama*. Manchester, Eng.: Manchester University Press, 1993.

McPherson, David C. *Shakespeare, Jonson, and the Myth of Venice*. Newark: University of Delaware Press, 1990.

Rosand, David. *Myths of Venice: The Figuration of a State*. Chapel Hill: University of North Carolina Press, 2001.

Schutte, William M. Introduction. In Thomas Coryat, *Coryat's Crudities*, v–xvi.

Strier, Richard. "Shakespeare and Legal Systems: The Better the Worse (But Not Vice Versa)." In Bradin Cormack, Martha C. Nussbaum, and Richard Strier, eds. *Shakespeare and the Law: A Conversation Among Disciplines and Professions*. Chicago: University of Chicago Press, 174–200.

Tosi, Laura, and Shaul Bassi, eds. *Visions of Venice in Shakespeare*. Farnham, Surrey, Eng., and Burlington, Vt.: Ashgate, 2011.

Andrea, Bernadette. "Assimilation or Dissimulation?: Leo Africanus's 'Geographical Historie of Africa' and the Parable of Amphibia." *A Review of International English Literature* 32:3 (July 2001): 7–29

Bartels, Emily C. "Cultural Traffic: *The History and Description of Africa* and the Unmooring of the Moor." In Bartels, *Speaking of the Moor: From "Alcazar" to "Othello."* Philadelphia: University of Pennsylvania Press, 2008, 138–54.

Brown, Robert, ed. *The History and Description of Africa and of the Notable Things Therein Contained, written by Al-Hassan Ibn-Mohammed Al-Wezaz Al-Fasi, a Moor, Baptised as Giovannie Leone, But better Known as Leo Africanus. Done into English in the year 1600, by John Pory*. London, 1600. Rpt. London: Hakluyt Society, 1896.

Burton, Jonathan. "'A Most Wily Bird': Leo Africanus, *Othello* and the Trafficking in Difference." In Ania Loomba and Martin Orkin, eds. *Post-Colonial Shakespeares*. London and New York: Routledge, 1998, 43–63.

———. "'Bondslaves and Pagans Shall Our Statesmen Be': *Othello*, Leo Africanus, and Muslim Ambassadors to Europe." In Burton, *Traffic and Turning: Islam and English Drama, 1579–1624*. Newark: University of Delaware Press, 2005, 233–46.

Davis, Natalie Zemon. *Trickster Travels: In Search of Leo Africanus, A Sixteenth-Century Muslim Between Worlds*. London: Faber, 2006.

Hadfield, Andrew, ed. *Amazons, Savages, and Machiavels: Travel and Colonial Writing in English, 1550–1630: An Anthology*. Oxford and New York: Oxford University Press, 2001, 139–51.

Hall, Kim F. *Things of Darkness: Economies of Race and Gender in Early Modern England*. Ithaca and London: Cornell University Press, 1995, 28–40.

———, ed. *William Shakespeare: "Othello, the Moor of Venice": Texts and Contexts*. Boston and New York: Bedford/St. Martin's, 2007, 258–61.

Hennessey, Oliver. "Talking with the Dead: Leo Africanus, Esoteric Yeats, and Early Modern Imperialism." *English Literary History* 71 (2004): 1019–38.

Johnson, Rosalind. "African Presence in Shakespearean Drama: Parallels Between Othello and the Historical Leo Africanus." In Ivan Van Sertima, ed. *African Presence in Early Europe*. New Brunswick and Oxford: Transaction, 1985, 276–87.

Kamps, Ivo, and Jyotsna G. Singh, eds. *Travel Knowledge: European "Discoveries" in the Early Modern Period*. New York and Houndmills, Basingstoke, Hampshire, Eng.: Palgrave Macmillan, 2001, 249–57.

Maalouf, Amin. *Léon, l'Africain*. 1986. Translated by Peter Sluglett as *Leo Africanus*. New York: Norton, 1989.

Mancall, Peter C., ed. *Travel Narratives from the Age of Discovery: An Anthology*. Oxford and New York: Oxford University Press, 2006.

Whitney, Lois. "Did Shakespeare Know Leo Africanus?" *PMLA* 37 (1922): 470–83.

Zhiri, Oumelbanine. "Leo Africanus's Description of Africa." In Kamps and Singh, *Travel Knowledge*, 285–66.

2. TRAVEL

The items below relate to the discussion of travel and romance at the beginning of "Othello in Its Own Time." They range temporally from the Middle Ages to current times, and in approach from historical to theoretical and pedagogical. The broad range is appropriate to the subject. Like the titles of Hakluyt and Purchas's collections, travel writing is inclusive rather than exclusive, interested more in exploring and accumlating exotic materials than in organizing or resisting them.

Attar, Karina F., and Lynn Shutters, eds. *Teaching Medieval and Early Modern Cross-Cultural Encounters*. Houndmills, Basing-stoke, Hampshire, Eng., and New York: Palgrave Macmillan, 2014.

Bosman, Anston. "Shakespeare and Globalization." In Margreta De Grazia and Stanley Wells, eds. *The New Cambridge Companion to Shakespeare*. Cambridge, Eng.: Cambridge University Press, 2010, 285–302.

Cavallo, Jo Ann. "Encountering Saracens in Italian Chivalric Epic and Folk Performance Traditions." In Attar and Shutters, eds. *Teaching*, 159–78.

Hadfield, Andrew. *Literature, Travel, and Colonial Writing in the English Renaissance, 1545–1625*. Oxford: Clarendon, 1998.

———, ed. *Amazons, Savages, and Machiavels: Travel and Colonial Writing in English, 1550–1630: An Anthology*. Oxford and New York: Oxford University Press, 2001.

Hakluyt, Richard. *The Principall Navigations, Voiages, and Discoveries of the English Nation: Made by Sea or Over Land to the Most Remote and Farthest Distant Quarters of the Earth at Any Time within the Compasse of These 1500 Years: Divided into Three Several Parts According to the Positions of the Regions Whereunto They Were Directed; the First Containing the Personall Travels of the English unto Indœa, Syria, Arabia . . . the Second, Comprehending the Worthy Discoveries of the English Towards the North and Northeast by Sea, as of Lapland . . . the Third and Last, Including the English Valiant Attempts in Searching Almost all the Corners of the Vaste and New World of America . . . Whereunto is Added the Last Most Renowned English Navigation Round About the Whole Globe of the Earth*. London, 1589.

Higgins, Iain Macleod. *Writing East: The "Travels" of Sir John Mandeville*. Philadelphia: University of Pennsylvania Press, 1997.

Kamps, Ivo, and Jyotsna G. Singh, eds. "Travelers into the Levant." In Kamps and Syngh, *Travel Knowledge: European "Discoveries" in the Early Modern Period*. New York and Houndmills, Basing-stoke, Hampshire, Eng.: Palgrave Macmillan, 2001, 21–124.

Loomba, Ania. "Outsiders in Shakespeare's England." In Margreta de Grazia and Stanley Wells, eds. *The Cambridge Companion to Shakespeare*. Cambridge, Eng.: Cambridge University Press, 2001, 147–66.

Mancall, Peter C., ed. *Travel Narratives from the Age of Discovery: An Anthology*. Oxford and New York: Oxford University Press, 2006.

Pentland, Elizabeth. "Teaching English Travel Writing from 1500 to the Present." In Attar and Shutters, *Teaching*, 71–85.

Purchas, Samuel. *Hakluytus Posthumus or Purchas his pilgrimes. Contayning a history of the world, in sea voyages & lande-travells, by Englishmen & others. Wherein Gods wonders in nature & providence, the actes, arts, varieties, & vanities of men, with a world of the worlds rarities, are by a world of eywitnesse-authors, related to the world. Some left written by M. Hakluyt at his death. More since added. His also perused & perfected. All examined, abreviated with discourse. Adorned with pictures and expressed in mapps. In fower parts. Each containing five bookes.* London, 1625

Schleck, Julia. "Stranger than Fiction: Early Modern Travel Narratives and the Anti-Racist Classroom." In Attar and Shutters, *Teaching*, 87–101.

Sebek, Barbara. "Different Shakespeares: A Course on Engendering Global Consciousness in Early Modern England." In Attar and Shutters, *Teaching*, 103–19.

Sherman, William. "Stirrings and Searchings, 1500–1720." In Peter Hulme and Tim Youngs, eds. *Cambridge Companion to Travel Writing.* Cambridge, Eng.: Cambridge University Press, 2002, 17–36.

Singh, Jyotsna. Introduction: The Global Renaissance. In Singh, ed. *A Companion to the Global Renaissance.* London: Blackwell, 2009, 1–28.

3. CONTEXTUAL SOURCES—RACE

For reasons sketched out earlier (144–47) and developed in greater detail in items listed below by Bartels, Neill ("Mulattos"), and Floyd-Wilson ("Retrospective"), the relevance of race to *Othello* is by no means self-evident, especially in attempts to recover the play's original impact. But as Ben Okri says, if *Othello* "did not begin as a play about race, then its history has made it one" (72), and it is bound to figure centrally in any current approach to the play.

The following lists provide a sample of the vast outpouring of recent and current thinking about the topic. The first tends to concentrate on *Othello*; the second extends to Shakespeare more generally and to the early modern period.

Adelman, Janet. "Iago's Alter Ego: Race as Projection in *Othello*." *Representations* 48 (1997): 125–44.

Bartels, Emily C. "Making More of the Moor: Aaron, Othello, and Renaissance Refashionings of Race." *Shakespeare Quarterly* 41 (1990): 433–54.

Callaghan, Dympna. "'Othello Was a White Man': Properties of Race on Shakespeare's Stage." In Terence Hawkes, ed. *Alternative*

Shakespeares: Volume 2. London and New York: Routledge, 1996, 192–215.

Cowhig, Ruth. "The Importance of Othello's Race." *Journal of Commonwealth Literature* 12 (1977): 153–61.

de Reuck, Jenny. "Blackface and Madonna: Race and Gender as Conditions of Reception in Recovering *Othello*." In R. S. White, Charles Edelman, and Christopher Wortham, eds. *Shakespeare: Readers, Audiences, Players*. Nedlands: University of Western Australia Press, 1998, 220–32.

Erickson, Peter. "Images of White Identity in *Othello*." In Philip C. Kolin, ed. *"Othello": New Critical Essays*. New York and London: Routledge, 2002, 133–45.

———. "Race Words in *Othello*." In Ruben Espinosa and David Ruite, eds. *Shakespeare and Immigration*. Burlington, Vt., and Farnham, Surrey, Eng.: Ashgate, 2014, 159–76.

Kaul, Mythili. "Background: Black or Tawny? Stage Representations of Othello from 1604 to the Present." In Kaul, ed. *"Othello": New Essays by Black Writers*. Washington, D.C.: Howard University Press, 1997, 1–19.

Little, Jr., Arthur L. "Witnessing Whiteness." In Little, *Shakespeare Jungle Fever: National-Imperial Re-Visions of Race, Rape, and Sacrifice*. Stanford: Stanford University Press, 2001, 68–101.

Neill, Michael. "'Mulattos', 'Blacks,' and 'Indian Moors': *Othello* and Early Modern Constructions of Human Difference." *Shakespeare Quarterly* 49 (1998): 361–74.

———. "*Othello* and Race." In Peter Erickson and Maurice Hunt, eds. *Approaches to Teaching Shakespeare's "Othello."* New York: Modern Language Association of America, 2005, 37–52.

Okri, Ben. "Leaping out of Shakespeare's Terror." In Okri, *A Way of Being Free*. London: Phoenix House, 1989, 71–87.

Suzman, Janet. "South Africa in *Othello*." In Jonathan Bate, Jill L. Levenson, and Dieter Mehl, eds. *Shakespeare and the Twentieth Century: The Selected Proceedings of the International Shakespeare Association World Congress, Los Angeles, 1996*. Newark: University of Delaware Press; London: Associated University Presses, 1998, 23–40.

Vaughan, Virginia Mason. "Race Mattered: *Othello* in Late Eighteenth-Century England." *Shakespeare Survey 51*. Cambridge, Eng.: Cambridge University Press, 1998, 57–66.

———. "Shakespeare's Moor of Venice." In Vaughan, *Performing Blackness on English Stages, 1500–1800*. Cambridge, Eng.: Cambridge University Press, 2005, 93–106.

Alexander, Catherine M. S., and Stanley Wells, eds. *Shakespeare and Race*. Cambridge, Eng.: Cambridge University Press, 2000.

Barthelemy, Anthony Gerard. *Black Face, Maligned Race: The Representation of Blacks in English Drama from Shakespeare to Southerne*. Baton Rouge and London: Louisiana State University Press, 1987.

Burton, Jonathan, and Ania Loomba, eds. *Race in Early Modern England: A Documentary Companion*. Houndmills, Basingstoke, Hampshire, Eng., and New York: Palgrave Macmillan, 2007.

Chapman, Matthieu A. "The Appearance of Blacks on the Early Modern Stage: *Love's Labour's Lost*'s African Connections to Court." *Early Theatre* 17:2 (2014): 77–94.

Chedgzoy, Ruth. "Blackness Yields to Beauty: Desirability and Difference in Early Modern Culture." In Gordon McMullan, ed. *Renaissance Configurations: Voices, Bodies, Spaces, 1580–1690*. Houndmills, Basingstoke, Hampshire, Eng.: Palgrave Macmillan; New York: St. Martin's Press, 1998, 108–28.

Dadabhoy, Ambereen. "The Moor of America: Approaching the Crisis of Race and Religion in the Renaissance and the Twenty-First Century." In Karina F. Attar and Lynn Shutters, eds. *Teaching Medieval and Early Modern Cross-Cultural Encounters*. Houndmills, Basingstoke, Hampshire, Eng., and New York: Palgrave Macmillan, 2014, 123–40.

Erickson, Peter, and Clark Hulse, eds. *Early Modern Visual Culture: Representation, Race, and Empire in Renaissance England*. Philadelphia: University of Pennsylvania Press, 2000.

Floyd-Wilson, Mary. *English Ethnicity and Race in Early Modern Drama*. Cambridge, Eng.: Cambridge University Press, 2003.

———. "Moors, Race, and the Study of English Renaissance Literature: A Brief Retrospective." *Literature Compass* 3:5 (June 2006): 1044–52.

Hall, Kim F. "'These Bastard Signs of Fair': Literary Whiteness in Shakespeare's Sonnets." In Ania Loomba and Martin Orkin, eds. *Post-Colonial Shakespeares*. London: Routledge, 1998, 64–83.

———. *Things of Darkness: Economies of Race and Gender in Early Modern England*. Ithaca: Cornell University Press, 1995.

Hendricks, Margo, ed. "Forum: Race and the Study of Shakespeare." *Shakespeare Studies* 26. Cranbury, N.J., London, and Mississauga, Ontario: Associated University Presses, 1998, 19–79.

———, and Patricia Parker, eds. *Women, "Race," and Writing in the Early Modern Period*. London and New York: Routledge, 1994.

Iyengar, Sujata. *Shades of Difference: Mythologies of Skin Color in Early Modern England*. Philadelphia: University of Pennsylvania Press, 2005.

Loomba, Ania, "'Delicious traffick': Alterity and Exchange on Early Modern Stages." *Shakespeare Survey* 52. Cambridge, Eng.: Cambridge University Press, 1999, 201–14.

———. *Shakespeare and Race*. Oxford Shakespeare Topics. Oxford: Oxford University Press, 2001.

Orkin, Martin. *Shakespeare Against Apartheid*. Craighall, South Africa: Ad Donker, 1987.

People of Color in European Art History. <medievalpoc.tumblr.com>

Tokson, Elliot H. *The Popular Image of the Black Man in English Drama, 1550–1688*. Boston: Hall, 1982.

Vaughan, Alden, and Virginia Mason Vaughan. "Before Othello: Elizabethan Representations of Sub-Saharan Africans." *The Virginia and Mary Quarterly* 54 (1997): 19–44.

4. THE DOMESTIC SPHERE

The items listed below provide more information and ideas about the topics discussed in the second part of "*Othello* in Its Own Time": wives and daughters, domesticity, patriarchal authority and the shape (or shapelessness) of sexual desire. Like race, these topics have become central to recent approaches to *Othello* (and other artifacts of early modern culture); but unlike race, they exhibit clear continuities to long-sustained traditions of theatrical production and critical thought. The self-conscious endeavor of opening the stage to nonaristocratic interests and tastes— "remaking British tragedy," in Geoffrey Cox's phrase—goes back to Shakespeare's time (as see the many Renaissance plays and premodern commentaries in the second list below). From this angle, the innovative emphasis on the domestic sphere in current work—on "history from below" or "herstory"—extends an ongoing conversation.

The first of the three following lists concentrates on social history. The second emphasizes connections between social history and literary/theatrical expression in the Renaissance, sometimes focusing on *Othello*. The third reflects the current interest in Desdemona and the other women in *Othello*, though by including Jameson, Clarke, Faucit, and Terry, I am again suggesting continuity with earlier interests.

Amussen, Susan. "Gender, Family and the Social Order, 1560–1725." In Anthony Fletcher and John Stevenson, eds. *Order and Disorder in Early Modern England*. Cambridge, Eng., and New York: Cambridge University Press, 1985, 196–217.

Davies, Kathleen M. "Continuity and Change in Literary Advice on Marriage." In Outhwaite, *Marriage and Society*, 58–80.

———. "The Sacred Condition of Equality—How Original Were Puritan Doctrines of Marriage?" *Social History* 2 (1977): 563–79.

Ezell, Margaret J. M. *The Patriarch's Wife: Literary Evidence and the History of the Family*. Chapel Hill: University of North Carolina Press, 1987.

Goody, Jack. *The Development of the Family and Marriage in Europe*. Cambridge, Eng.: Cambridge University Press, 1983.

Haller, Mandeville, and William Haller. "The Puritan Art of Love." *Huntington Library Quarterly* 5 (1942): 235–72.

Hill, Christopher. "The Spiritualization of the Household." In *Society and Puritanism in Pre-Revolutionary England*. New York: Schocken, 1964, 443–81.

Huebert, Ronald. *Privacy in the Age of Shakespeare*. Toronto: University of Toronto Press, 2016.

Hull, Suzanne W. *Chaste, Silent and Obedient: English Books for Women 1475–1640*. San Marino, Calif.: Huntington Library, 1982.

Orlin, Lena Cowen. *Elizabethan Households: An Anthology*. Washington, D.C.: Folger Shakespeare Library, 1995.

———. *Locating Privacy in Tudor London*. Oxford: Oxford University Press, 2007.

———. *Private Matters and Public Culture in Post-Reformation England*. Ithaca: Cornell University Press, 1994.

Outhwaite, R. B., ed. *Marriage and Society: Studies in the Social History of Marriage*. New York: St. Martins, 1981.

Ozment, Stephen. *When Fathers Ruled: Family Life in Reformation Europe*. Cambridge, Mass.: Harvard University Press, 1983.

Powell, Chilton Lathan. *English Domestic Relations, 1487–1653: A Study of Matrimony and Family Life in Theory and Practice*. New York: Columbia University Press, 1917.

Schücking, Levin L. *The Puritan Family: A Social Study from the Literary Sources*. 1929. Trans. Brian Battershaw. New York: Schocken, 1969.

Stone, Lawrence. *The Family, Sex and Marriage in England, 1500–1800*. 1977. Abridged ed. Harmondsworth, Middlesex, Eng.: Penguin, 1979.

Underdown, David. "The Taming of the Scold—the Enforcement of Patriarchal Authority in Early Modern England." In Outhwaite, *Marriage and Society*, 116–36.

Wright, Louis B. *Middle-Class Culture in Elizabethan England*. Chapel Hill: University of North Carolina Press, 1935.

Ziegler, Georgiana. "'My Lady's Chamber': Female Space, Female Chastity in Shakespeare." *Textual Practice* 4 (1990): 73–90.

Adams, Henry Hitch. *English Domestic Or Homiletic Tragedy, 1575–1642: Being an Account of the Development of the Tragedy of the Common Man Showing its Great Dependence on Religious Morality, Illustrated with Striking Examples of the Interposition of*

Providence For the Amendment of Men's Manners. 1943. Rpt. New York: Blom, 1965.

Belsey, Catherine. *Shakespeare and the Loss of Eden: The Construction of Family Values in Early Modern Culture*. London: Macmillan, 1999.

Benson, Sean. *Shakespeare, "Othello" and Domestic Tragedy*. London and New York: Continuum, 2012.

Callaghan, Dympna, "Looking Well to Linens: Women and Cultural Production in *Othello* and Shakespeare's England." In Jean E. Howard and Scott Cutler Shershow, eds. *Marxist Shakespeares*. London and New York: Routledge, 2000, 53–81.

Cannon, Charles Dale, ed. *A Warning for Fair Women*. The Hague: Mouton, 1975.

Cawley, A. C. *English Domestic Drama: "A Yorkshire Tragedy."* Leeds: Leeds University Press, 1966.

Clark, Andrew. *Domestic Drama: A Survey of the Origins, Antecedents, and Nature of the Domestic Play in England, 1500–1640*. 2 vols. Salzburg Studies in English Literature. Jacobean Drama Studies 49. Salzburg: Institut für Englische Sprache und Literatur, Universität Salzburg, 1975.

Comensoli, Viviana. *"Household Business": Domestic Plays of Early Modern England*. Toronto: University of Toronto Press, 1996.

Cox, Jeffrey N. "Romantic Tragic Drama and its Eighteenth-Century Precursors: Remaking British Tragedy." In Rebecca Bushnell, ed. *A Companion to Tragedy*. Malden, Mass.: Blackwell, 2005, 411–34.

Dubrow, Heather. *A Happier Eden: the Politics of Marriage in the Stuart Epithalamium*. Ithaca: Cornell University Press, 1990.

———. *Shakespeare and Domestic Loss: Forms of Deprivation, Mourning, and Recuperation*. Cambridge Studies in Renaissance Literature and Culture 32. Cambridge, Eng.: Cambridge University Press, 1999.

Hall, Kim F. "Marriage and the Household." In Hall, ed. *William Shakespeare, "Othello," the Moor of Venice: Texts and Contexts*. Boston and New York: Bedford/St. Martin's, 2007, 262–90.

Henderson, Diana E. "The Theater and Domestic Culture." In John D. Cox and David Scott Kastan, eds. *A New History of Early English Drama*. New York: Columbia University Press, 1997, 173–94.

Jordan, Constance. *Renaissance Feminism: Literary Texts and Political Models*. Ithaca: Cornell University Press, 1990, 289–97.

Lieblein, Leanore. "The Context of Murder in English Domestic Plays, 1590–1610." *Studies in English Literature* 23 (1983): 181–96.

Morgan, Arthur Eustace. *English Domestic Drama*. Folcraft, Penn.: Folcraft Press, 1912.

Pechter, Edward. "*Patient Grissil* and the Trials of Marriage." *Elizabethan Theatre 14*. Toronto: Meany, 1996, 83–108.

Sturgess, Keith, ed. *Three Elizabethan Domestic Tragedies: "Arden of Faversham," "A Yorkshire Tragedy," "A Woman Killed With Kindness."* Harmondsworth, Middlesex, Eng.: Penguin, 1969.

Symonds, John Addington. "Domestic Drama." In *Shakspere's Predecessors in the English Drama*. London: Smith, Elder, 1884, 412–84.

Vaughan, Virginia Mason. "Marital Discourse: Husbands and Wives." In Vaughan, *"Othello": A Contextual History*. Cambridge, Eng.: Cambridge University Press, 1994, 71–89.

Wilkins, George. *The Miseries of Enforced Marriage*. 1607. Ed. Glenn H. Blayney. Oxford: Malone Society Reprints, 1964.

Adamson, W. D. "Unpinned or Undone? Desdemona's Critics and the Problem of Sexual Innocence." *Shakespeare Studies* 13 (1980): 169–86.

Bovilsky, Lara. "Desdemona's Blackness." In Bovilsky, *Barbarous Play: Race on the English Renaissance Stage*. Minneapolis: University of Minnesota Press, 2008, 37–65.

Clarke, Mary Cowden. *The Girlhood of Shakespeare's Heroines*. New York: Putnam, 1851.

Deats, Sara Munson. "'Truly, an obedient lady': Desdemona, Emilia, and the Doctrine of Obedience in *Othello*." In Philip C. Kolin, ed. *"Othello": New Critical Essays*. New York and London: Routledge, 233–54.

Faucit, Helena. *On Some of Shakespeare's Female Characters*. Edinburgh: Blackwoods, 1885. Rpt. New York: AMS Press, 1970.

Grennan, Eamon. "The Women's Voices in *Othello*: Speech, Song, Silence," *Shakespeare Quarterly* 38 (1987): 275–92.

Jameson, Anna B. *Characteristics of Women—Moral, Poetical, and Historical*. 1832. Rpt. *Shakespeare's Heroines*. London: George Bell & Sons, 1905.

Pechter, Edward. "Why Should We Call Her Whore? Bianca in *Othello*." In Jonathan Bate, Jill L. Levenson, and Dieter Mehl, eds. *Shakespeare and the Twentieth Century: The Selected Proceedings of the International Shakespeare Association World Congress, Los Angeles, 1996*. Newark: University of Delaware Press; London: Associated University Presses, 1998, 364–77.

Ronk, Martha. "Desdemona's Self-Presentation." *English Literary Renaissance* 35 (2005): 52–72.

Rutter, Carol Chillington. "Unpinning Desdemona (Again) or 'Who would be toll'd with Wenches in a shew?'" *Shakespeare Bulletin* 28 (2010): 111–32.

Terry, Ellen. *Four Lectures on Shakespeare*. Ed. Christopher St. John. London: Martin Hopkinson Ltd., 1932.

Vanita, Ruth. "'Proper' Men and 'Fallen' Women: The Unprotected-ness of Wives in *Othello*." *Studies in English Literature* 34 (1994): 341–56.

Walen, Denise A. "Unpinning Desdemona." *Shakespeare Quarterly* 58 (2007): 487–508.

5. RYMER

A lawyer, critic, and occasional poet and playwright, Rymer achieved some eminence during his lifetime (he was chosen to be the royal archivist at the end of his career), but is known today almost exclusively for his 1693 attack on *Othello*, excerpted in this edition. The text is taken from the unique early quarto edition, A *Short View of Tragedy, Its Original, Excellency and Corruption. With Some Reflections on Shakespeare and Other Practitioners for the Stage* (London, 1693). A facsimile edition was published by the Scolar Press in 1970. The authoritative modern edition is available in *The Critical Works of Thomas Rymer*, edited with an introduction and notes by Curt A. Zimansky (New Haven: Yale University Press, 1956).

6. GILDON

Gildon was a prolific editor, essayist, critic, and occasionally poet and dramatist. The first two passages are taken from the first edition of his *Miscellaneous Letters and Essays on Several Subjects: Philosophical, Moral, Historical, Critical, Amorous, &c. in Prose and Verse* (London, 1694). The full title for his response to Rymer is "Some Reflections on Mr. Rymer's *Short View of Tragedy* and an Attempt at a Vindication of Shakespeare, in an Essay Directed to John Dryden Esq." The third excerpt is from the extensive *Remarks on the Plays of Shakespeare* in Gildon's edition of *The Works of Mr. William Shakespear*, vol. 7, claimed as an appendage in 1710 to Nicholas Rowe's 1709 edition of Shakespeare's plays. Though the claim was spurious, the *Remarks* are by "a very long way the most extended account of the plays to have appeared by that date," an "inaugurating moment" in the history of Shakespeare criticism (Holland, 1.xxvii). No modern edition of Gildon exists, but a facsimile edition of the *Miscellaneous Letters* in conjunction with Dennis's *Impartial Critick* is available with a preface by Arthur Freeman (New York and London: Garland, 1973); and Pickering and Chatto issued a facsimile of vol. 7 of the Rowe edition (London, 1999), from which Holland's introduction is quoted just above.

7. JOHNSON

Journalist, literary critic and biographer, lexicographer, poet, playwright, fiction writer, moralist, conversationalist, Johnson was so smart and influential that in the days of the period-course curriculum, "The Age of Johnson" was commonly offered by English Departments throughout North America. The excerpts from the Preface to his edition of Shakespeare—a foundational document in the history of Shakespeare criticism that manages to be entertaining and shrewdly intelligent at the same time—are taken from *The Plays of Shakespeare. Accurately Printed from the Text of Samuel Johnson, George Steevens, and Isaac Reed. With the Preface of Dr. Johnson, and a Copious Glossary* (Edinburgh, 1832). Johnson's notes to *Othello* are quoted from vol. 19 of the 21-vol. edition of *The Plays of William Shakespeare, with the Corrections and Illustrations of Various Commentators, to Which Are Added Notes by Samuel Johnson and George Steevens* (London, 1813). The authoritative modern edition of these texts may be found in vols. 7 and 8 of the Yale edition of *The Works of Samuel Johnson, Johnson on Shakespeare*, edited by Arthur Sherbo with an introduction by Bertrand H. Bronson (New Haven and London: Yale University Press, 1968). Bronson's subsequent *Selections from Johnson on Shakespeare*, edited with Jean M. O'Meara (New Haven and London: Yale University Press, 1986), reprints some of Johnson's extensive quotations from earlier editors not included in the 1968 edition.

8. LAMB

Lamb's occasional essays, written under the pseudonym Elia, were very popular throughout the nineteenth century and still make enjoyable reading. The *Tales from Shakespeare*, written with his sister Mary and published in 1807, significantly shaped the ideas and images by which Victorian children (and adults) came to appreciate Shakespeare. Lamb was on friendly terms with many of the poets and critics of his time, including Coleridge, Wordsworth, Hazlitt, Leigh Hunt, and Robert Southey, among whom existed a regular traffic of ideas and sentiments. Lamb's claim for Shakespeare's superiority as a literary rather than theatrical experience was frequently echoed (both about *Othello* and Shakespeare in general) by subsequent critics, including Coleridge and Bradley in excerpts above.

The Lamb passage printed here was originally published in 1811 in the *Reflector* under "Theatralia No. 1. On Garrick, and Acting, and the Plays of Shakespeare, Considered with Reference to Their Fitness for Stage Representation." The text is taken from Lamb's *Complete Works in Prose and Verse: From the Original Editions, with the Cancelled Passages Restored, and Many Pieces Now First Collected*, edited and prefaced by R. H. Shepherd, two vols. (New York: Hoventon, 1874), 1:253–65. The authoritative modern edition may be found in *The Works of Charles and Mary Lamb*, edited by Edward Verrall Lucas, seven vols. (London: Methuen, 1903–05), 1:97–111.

9. HAZLITT

In his remarkably productive career, Hazlitt produced journalism, theatrical reviews, paintings, a biography of Napoleon, essays and books of literary criticism and history, moral philosophy, psychological and epistemological theory, and what would now be called cultural and political critique. His specific observations about Shakespeare have long been appreciated for their acute intelligence, but his refusal to compartmentalize (for Hazlitt, the imagination was not a specialized poetic faculty but the motor of all human behavior) has tended until recently to obscure the systematic coherence and power of his Shakespearean commentary.

The first excerpt included in this edition combines the two reviews Hazlitt published a couple of weeks apart in the *Examiner*. Discussion specific to Kean's performance is generally deleted, following the pattern Hazlitt suggested when assimilating this material into the *Othello* chapter of his *Characters of Shakespear's Plays* (1817). The second excerpt above is taken from this chapter up to the point where Hazlitt turns to the Iago material that occupies him for the rest of his discussion. The text is from an 1869 publication edited with minor revisions by William Carew Hazlitt (the author's grandson) as reissued in 1901.

Howe's authoritative *Complete Hazlitt* includes *The Characters* in volume 4 and the *Examiner* reviews in volume 5, as Hazlitt reprinted them in 1818 in *A View of the English Stage*—that is, without the note about "the rankness and gross impropriety of the personal connection" between Othello and Desdemona. Howe published the note separately in volume 20, along with some discussion of the debate that it generated, and it is included in Jackson's edition, which is based on the original reviews. Howe's edition has been usefully supplemented (though not superseded) by Wu's *Selected Hazlitt*, which includes *The Characters* in volume 1 and *A View of the English Stage* (no mention of the note) in volume 3. White's anthology presents a generous sampling of Hazlitt's Shakespeare commentary.

Hazlitt, William. "On Mr. Kean's Iago." *Examiner* (July 24, 1814), 478–79.

———. "On Mr. Kean's Iago (Concluded)." *Examiner* (August 7, 1814), 505–07.

———. *The Characters of Shakespear's Plays.* Ed. William Carew Hazlitt. Bohn's Standard Library. London: Bell, 1901.

_____. A *View of the English Stage, or A Series of Dramatic Criticism.* Ed. W. Spencer Jackson. Bohn's Standard Library. London: Bell, 1906.

Howe, P. P., ed. *The Complete Works of William Hazlitt.* 21 vols. London: Dent, 1930–34.

White, R. S., ed. *Hazlitt's Criticism of Shakespeare: A Selection.* Studies in British Literature 18. Lewiston, Queenston, and Lampeter, Eng.: Edwin Mellen, 1996.

Wu, Duncan, ed. *Selected Writings of William Hazlitt.* 9 vols. London: Pickering, 1998.

10. COLERIDGE

Coleridge was a polymath of titanic intellectual energy. Though his philosophical, theological, and political writings no longer excite general interest, his innovative poetry arguably remains a presence (the conversation poems opened doors for Wordsworth into territory we continue to explore), and his criticism still a vital force. His central ideas—the distinction between poetic and scientific language, the imagination as reconciler of opposites, the organic unity of poetic texts—served generations of critics until very recently and retain substantial authority. Most important, in working out his ideas about the special unity of poetic language, he developed the interpretive strategies of "practical criticism" (he invented the phrase), which sustain the study of literature even now in high school and college classrooms.

Shakespeare was always Coleridge's primary exhibit of literary value, though given the scattered and occasional nature of his Shakespearean commentary, it is hard to represent anything like the full and coherent scope of his thought. Only a small portion of Coleridge's Shakespearean commentary was published by the author; the rest derives from lecture notes transcribed by his auditors or written by Coleridge himself in manuscripts, from transcripts of his conversation (*Table Talk*), and from material edited (and sometimes augmented if not constructed) after Coleridge's death by his son-in-law and nephew, Henry Nelson Coleridge, and published as Coleridge's *Literary Remains*. All the passages included here are quoted from Ashe's edition except for the first Desdemona passage, which is quoted (including the final translation of the Latin phrase) from p. 111 of the 1989 *Selection* Foakes produced from his authoritative *Lectures on Literature 1808–1819*. Four of the excerpts are not based on Coleridge's 1819 lecture notes: the first Iago passage is taken from Coleridge's *Lear* lecture given a week after the *Othello*; the third Othello passage is from *Table Talk* for December 29, 1822; the first Desdemona passage is taken from notes for an 1813 lecture comparing *Othello* and *The Winter's Tale*; the second Desdemona passage is taken from *Table Talk* for September 27, 1830. The last three sentences of the first Othello passage and the whole of the last passage were published (by Ashe and more recent editors) in conjunction with the 1819 lecture, but derive from *The Literary Remains*. Foakes does not include these passages, and earlier modern editions by Raysor and Hawkes acknowledge doubts about their authenticity. They are included here partly because, as Hawkes says of one of them, "it represents the spirit of Coleridge's own analysis, and makes a good point which is tacitly in the body of the original manuscript" (176); in addition, the passages were accepted as authentic for a century after Coleridge's death and continue to be represented as part of the Coleridgean legacy even now and even among scholars who may know better.

Ashe, T., ed. *Lectures and Notes on Shakspere and Other English Poets by Samuel Taylor Coleridge*. 1883. Rpt. London: George Bell and Sons, 1897.

Foakes, R. A., ed. *Coleridge's Criticism of Shakespeare: A Selection*. London: Athlone, 1989.

————, ed. *Samuel Taylor Coleridge: Lectures on Literature 1808–1819*, 2 parts. *The Collected Works of Samuel Taylor Coleridge*, vol. 5. London and Princeton: Routledge and Princeton University Press, 1987.

Hawkes, Terence, ed. *Coleridge's Writings on Shakespeare*. New York: G. P. Putnam's Sons, 1959.

Raysor, Thomas Middleton, ed. *Coleridge: Shakespearean Criticism*. 2nd ed. 2 vols. London: Dent, 1960.

II. BRADLEY

The son of an Evangelical minister, Bradley was educated at Oxford University, where he encountered some of the leading figures of Victorian intellectual life. He taught philosophy at Oxford, moved into literature at the universities of Liverpool and Glasgow, and finally returned to Oxford as Professor of Poetry from 1901 to 1906. First published in 1904, *Shakespearean Tragedy* is technically a twentieth-century production, but as Bradley acknowledges in the preface, the book is "based on a selection from materials used in teaching" dating from his early career, and it resonates with ideas and critical assumptions derived from nineteenth-century thought. Despite its adherence to apparently old-fashioned ideas— a tendency to focus on the protagonist's inner life independently of the action, much derided in early twentieth-century modernist reactions to Victorianism; an idealist commitment to transcendence strongly repudiated by currently dominant materialist and historicist criticism—the book has sustained an enormous popularity through to our time.

Readers interested in finding out more about Bradley's life and work might start with Cooke and then branch out to the relatively sympathetic account in Hunter and the relatively unsympathetic one in Hawkes. Bradley develops the methodological and theoretical assumptions behind the discussions in *Shakespearean Tragedy* in the essays collected in his *Oxford Lectures on Poetry* (1909; rpt. Bloomington: Indiana University Press, 1961)—of which the three listed below are the most immediately relevant.

Bradley, A. C. "Hegel's Theory of Tragedy." In Bradley, *Oxford Lectures*, 69–95.
———. "Poetry for Poetry's Sake." In Bradley, *Oxford Lectures*, 3–34.
———. "Shakespeare's Theatre and Audience." In Bradley, *Oxford Lectures*, 361–93.
Cooke, Katharine. *A. C. Bradley and His Influence in Twentieth-Century Shakespearean Criticism*. Oxford: Clarendon, 1972.
Hawkes, Terence. "A Sea Shell." In Hawkes, *That Shakespeherian Rag: Essays on a Critical Process*. London and New York: Methuen, 1986, 27–50.
Hunter, G. K. "A. C. Bradley's *Shakespearean Tragedy*." In Hunter, *Dramatic Identities and Cultural Tradition: Studies in Shakespeare and His Contemporaries*. Liverpool: Liverpool University Press, 1978, 270–85.

12. PERFORMANCE (*OTHELLO* ON STAGE)

The list below identifies some commentaries about the rich and ongoing history of *Othello* on stage. The material is weighted toward earlier performance ("Movies and Videos" following gives prominence to more-recent productions). The discussions in modern scholarly editions are good places to start (Sanders, Honigmann, McMillin, and Neill). Johnson-Haddad's pedagogical approach deserves special emphasis; she describes ways in which the mixing and matching of different performances enables students and teachers to appreciate the diversity of *Othello*'s theatrical possibility. Rosenberg's and Hankey's studies work to a similar purpose; both go through the play scene by scene, discussing various productions in chronological order. Hankey tends less than Rosenberg to treat the performers and their roles in isolation from other production features, and her second edition includes more-recent performances, though at the cost of dropping information and interpretation about earlier work.

Carlisle, Carol Jones. "Actors' Criticisms of *Othello*." In *Shakespeare from the Greenroom: Actors' Criticisms of Four Major Tragedies*. Chapel Hill: University of North Carolina Press, 1969, 172–263.

Hankey, Julie, ed. *Othello*. Plays in Performance Series. Bristol: Bristol Classical Press, 1987.

———. *Othello*. 2nd ed. Shakespeare in Production. Cambridge, Eng.: Cambridge University Press, 2005.

Honigmann, E. A. J. "The Play in the Theatre." In Honigmann, ed. *Othello*. Walton-on-Thames, Eng.: Nelson, 1997, 90–102.

Johnson-Haddad, Miranda. "Teaching *Othello* through Performance Choices." In Peter Erickson and Maurice Hunt, eds. *Approaches to Teaching Shakespeare's "Othello."* New York: Modern Language Association of America, 2005, 156–61.

Jones, James Earl. *Othello*. Actors on Shakespeare Series. London: Faber, 2003.

———, and Penelope Niven. *James Earl Jones: Voices and Silences*. New York: Scribner, 1993.

Matteo, Gino J. *Shakespeare's "Othello": The Study and the Stage, 1604–1904*. Salzburg Studies in English Literature. Poetic Drama Series 11. Salzburg: Institut für Englische Sprache und Literatur, Universität Salzburg, 1974.

McMillin, Scott. "Criticism and Productions of *Othello* since 1984." In Sanders, ed. *Othello*. 2nd ed. Cambridge, Eng.: Cambridge University Press, 2003, 52–61.

Neill, Michael. "The Play in Performance." In Neill, ed. *Othello, the Moor of Venice*. Oxford: Oxford University Press, 2006, 36–113.

O'Connor, John, and Katharine Goodland. *A Directory of Shakespeare in Performance, 1970–2005*. Vol. 1: Great Britain. Houndmills, Basingstoke, Hampshire, Eng., and New York: Palgrave Macmillan, 2007.

Odell, George C. D. *Shakespeare from Betterton to Irving*. 2 vols. New York: Scribner, 1920.

Rosenberg, Marvin. *The Masks of "Othello": The Search for the Identity of Othello, Iago, and Desdemona by Three Centuries of Actors and Critics*. Berkeley, Los Angeles, and London: University of California Press, 1961.

Sanders, Norman. "Stage History." In Sanders, ed. *Othello*. Cambridge, Eng.: Cambridge University Press, 1984, 38–51.

Spencer, Hazelton. *Shakespeare Improved: The Restoration Versions in Quarto and on the Stage*. Cambridge, Mass.: Harvard University Press, 1927.

Sprague, Arthur Colby. "Edmund Kean as Othello" and "Edwin Booth as Iago." In Sprague, *Shakespearian Players and Performances*. Cambridge, Mass.: Harvard University Press, 1953, 71–86 and 121–35.

———. "*Othello.*" In Sprague, *Shakespeare and the Actors: The Stage Business in His Plays (1660–1905)*. Cambridge, Mass.: Harvard University Press, 1948, 185–223.

Stanislavski, Constantin. *Stanislavski Produces "Othello."* Trans. Helen Nowak. New York: Theatre Arts Books, 1963.

13. PERFORMANCE (MOVIES AND VIDEOS)

The movies made performances of *Othello* available to a much broader audience than could afford or had access to or were comfortable with going to see plays. Digital technology has allowed still more of us to watch performances on TVs or computers. By the 1990s, cinematic and video versions of *Othello* had proliferated amazingly (see the Rothwell/Melzer and Holderness/McCullough filmographies in the first list below). The process seems to be accelerating; the webpage for the *Othello* volume in Cambridge's relaunched Shakespeare on Screen series, cited in the third list below (Hatchuel and Vienne-Guerrin), includes a link to a free pdf download, "*Othello* on Screen: A Comprehensive Film Bibliography," extending to 63 pages.

There are significant differences between watching a big screen at the cineplex or a little one, and further differences between the little screen at home or in the classroom (or a bar). The differences are even more significant between watching movies or videos, on the one hand, and watching live theater, on the other; "live" is one main basis for the distinction, and the extent to which audiences seem to control or be controlled in what they see is another. (The National Theatre Live productions, in which live performances are piped into movie theaters in supposedly real time, confuses this distinction in interesting ways—hence the half-hearted applause from some moviegoers at the end of the show.)

Shakespeareans frequently advance the advantages of theatrical experience, especially for its less coercive directions of the spectators' gaze; but as Russell Jackson points out, this claim "fails to acknowledge that a film—like a theatre performance—is not complete until interpreted by the audience" (5). Besides, in terms of the mixing-and-matching context I've been promoting here, the preference might be reversed. Videos especially allow us to move pretty much at will back and forth between different productions, identifying a variety of performative possibilities, then choosing among them, then trying to understand the bases for our choices.

The first list below itemizes works about Shakespeare onscreen generally. The second identifies six *Othello* performances from the last 50 years currently available as DVDs, each with its own Internet Movie Database URL. Though not a comprehensive list, these *Othello*s have attracted some of the most extensive response (the Potter excerpt above discusses four of them). The identifying names in bold for each—sometimes the director, sometimes the lead actor, depending on recognizability—link with the critical discussions in the third list, wherever the titles of these discussions fail to make the connection apparent.

Coursen, H. R. *Teaching Shakespeare with Film and Television: A Guide*. Westport, Conn.: Greenwood Press, 1997.

Holderness, Graham. *Visual Shakespeare: Essays in Film and Television*. Hatfield, Hertfordshire, Eng.: University of Hertfordshire Press, 2002.

———, and Christopher McCullough. "Shakespeare on the Screen: A Selective Filmography." In Anthony Davies and Stanley Wells, eds. *Shakespeare and the Moving Image: The Plays on Film and Television*. Cambridge, Eng.: Cambridge University Press, 1994, 18–49.

Jackson, Russell. *Theatres on Film: How the Cinema Imagines the Stage*. Manchester and New York: Manchester University Press, 2013.

Rothwell, Kenneth S., and Annabelle Henkin Melzer. *Shakespeare on Screen: An International Filmography and Videography*. New York: Neal-Schuman, 1990, 208–27.

Starks, Lisa S., and Courtney Lehmann, eds. "Part IV: Film in the Alternative Classroom: Shakespeare and Radical Pedagogy." In Starks and Lehmann, eds. *The Reel Shakespeare: Alternative Cinema and Theory*. Madison and Teaneck, N.J.: Fairleigh Dickinson University Press; London: Associated University Presses, 2002, 189–228.

Orson **Welles** directs himself and Mícháel MacLiammóir in a movie released in 1952. <www.imdb.com/title/tt0045251>

Stuart Burge directs a film version of John Dexter's 1964 London production, featuring Laurence **Olivier** and Frank Finlay, 1965. <www.imdb.com/title/tt0059555>

Jonathan **Miller** directs Anthony Hopkins and Bob Hoskins in a version made for the BBC, 1981. <www.imdb.com/title/tt0082861>

Janet **Suzman** directs John Kani and Richard Haddon Haines in a 1989 movie version of the production staged in Johannesburg in 1987. <www.imdb.com/title/tt0378503>

Trevor **Nunn** directs Willard White and Ian McKellen in a 1990 made-for-TV version of his 1989 Royal Shakespeare Company production. <www.imdb.com/title/tt0357995>

Oliver Parker directs Laurence **Fishburne** and Kenneth Branagh in a movie released in 1995. <www.imdb.com/title/tt0114057>

Boose, Lynda E. "Grossly Gaping Viewers and Jonathan Miller's *Othello*." In Boose and Richard Burt, eds. *Shakespeare, the Movie: Popularizing the Plays on Film, TV, and Video*. London and New York: Routledge, 1997, 186–97.

Brode, Douglas. "The Green-eyed Monster: *Othello, the Moor of Venice*." In Brode, *Shakespeare in the Movies: From the Silent Era to "Shakespeare in Love*." New York: Oxford University Press, 2000, 151–74. **Welles, Olivier, and Fishburne**

Buchanan, Judith. "Virgin and Ape, Venetian and Infidel: Labelings of Otherness in Oliver Parker's *Othello*." In Mark Thornton Burnett and Ramona Wray, eds. *Shakespeare, Film and Fin de Siècle*. New York: St. Martin's, 2000, 179–202. **Fishburne**

Buchman, Lorne Michael. "Naming Time in *Othello*." In Buchman, *Still in Movement: Shakespeare on Screen*. Oxford: Oxford University Press, 1991, 126–44. **Welles**

Buhler, Stephen M. "Three Versions of *Othello*." In *Shakespeare in the Cinema: Ocular Proof*. Albany: State University of New York Press, 2001, 11–32. **Fishburne**

Bulman, J. C., and H. R. Coursen, eds. *Shakespeare on Television: An Anthology of Essays and Reviews*. Hanover, N.H., and London: University Press of New England, 1988, 57–59 and 277–79. **Miller**

Burnett, Mark Thornton. "Racial Identities, Global Economies." In Burnett, *Filming Shakespeare in the Global Marketplace*. Houndmills, Basingstoke, Hampshire, Eng., and New York: Palgrave, 2007, 66–86. **Fishburne**

Cartmell, Deborah. "Screening *Othello* and *The Tempest*." In Cartmell, *Interpreting Shakespeare on Screen*. Houndmills, Basingstoke, Hampshire, Eng., and New York: Palgrave, 2000, 67–93. **Welles**

Coursen, H. R. "Editing for Film: The 1995 *Othello*." In Coursen, *Teaching Shakespeare*. Cited in list above, 122–36. **Fishburne**

———. "More Iago Than Moor." In Coursen, *Shakespeare in Space: Recent Shakespeare Productions on Screen*. Studies in Shakespeare 14. New York: Peter Lang, 2002. **Fishburne**

Davies, Anthony. "Filming *Othello*." In Davies and Stanley Wells, eds. *Shakespeare and the Moving Image: The Plays on Film and Television*. Cambridge, Eng.: Cambridge University Press, 1994, 196–210. **Welles and Olivier**

————. "Orson Welles's *Othello*." In Davies, *Filming Shakespeare's Plays: The Adaptations of Laurence Olivier, Orson Welles, Peter Brook and Akira Kurosawa*. Cambridge, Eng.: Cambridge University Press, 1988, 100–18.

————. "The Shakespeare Films of Laurence Olivier." In Russell Jackson, ed, *Cambridge Companion to Shakespeare on Film*. 2nd ed. Cambridge, Eng., and New York: Cambridge University Press, 2010, 167–86.

Donaldson, Peter S. "Mirrors and M/Others: The Welles *Othello*." In Donaldson, ed. *Shakespearean Films/Shakespearean Directors*. Boston: Unwin Hyman, 1990, 97–107.

Dorval, Patricia. "Shakespeare on Screen: Threshold Aesthetics in Oliver Parker's *Othello*." *Early Modern Literary Studies* 6:1 (May 2000): 1.1–15. **Fishburne** <extra.shu.ac.uk/emls/06-1/dorvothe .htm>

Hatchuel, Sarah, and Nathalie Vienne-Guerrin, eds. *Shakespeare on Screen: "Othello."* Cambridge, Eng.: Cambridge University Press, 2015. <www.cambridge.org/us/academic/subjects/literature /renaissance-and-early-modern-literature/shakespeare-screen -othello>

Hodgdon, Barbara. "Kiss Me Deadly; or, The Des/Demonized Spectacle." In Virginia Mason Vaughan and Kent Cartwright, eds. *"Othello": New Perspectives*. Rutherford, Madison, and Teaneck, N.J.: Fairleigh Dickinson University Press; London and Toronto: Associated University Presses, 1991, 214–55. **Welles**

————. "Race-ing *Othello*, Re-Engendering White-out." In Hodgdon, *The Shakespeare Trade: Performances and Appropriations*. Philadelphia: University of Pennsylvania Press, 1998, 39–73. **Olivier, Suzman, Nunn, and Fishburne**

Holland, Peter. "Rethinking Blackness: The Case of Olivier's *Othello*." In Hatchuel and Vienne-Guerrin, *Shakespeare on Screen*, 43–58.

Howlett, Kathy M. "The Voyeuristic Pleasures of Perversion: Orson Welles's *Othello*." In Howlett, *Framing Shakespeare on Film: How the Frame Reveals Meaning*. Athens: Ohio University Press, 2000, 52–91.

Iyengar, Sujata. "White Faces, Blackface: The Production of 'Race' in *Othello*." In Philip C. Kolin, ed. *"Othello": New Critical Essays*. New York and London: Routledge, 2002, 103–31. **Olivier and Nunn**.

Jacobs, Alfred. "Orson Welles's *Othello*: Shakespeare Meets Film Noir." In Jonathan Bate, Jill L. Levenson, and Dieter Mehl, eds. *Shakespeare and the Twentieth Century: The Selected Proceedings of the International Shakespeare Association World Congress, Los Angeles, 1996*. Newark: University of Delaware Press; London: Associated University Presses, 1998, 113–24.

Jones, Nicholas. "A Bogus Hero: Welles's Othello and the Construction of Race." *Shakespeare Bulletin* 23 (2005): 9–28.

Jorgens, Jack J. "Orson Welles's *Othello*." In Jorgens, *Shakespeare on Film*. Bloomington and London: Indiana University Press, 1977, 175–90.

———. "Stuart Burge and John Dexter's *Othello*." In Jorgens, *Shakespeare on Film*, 191–217.

Kauffmann, Stanley. "Shrinking Shakespeare." *New Republic* 214 (February 12, 1996): 30–31. **Fishburne**

Lefait, Sébastien. "*Othello* Retold: Orson Welles's *Filming Othello*." In Hatchuel and Vienne-Guerrin, *Shakespeare on Screen*, 59–75.

MacLiammóir, Micháel. *Put Money in Thy Purse: The Filming of Orson Welles' "Othello."* London: Eyre Methuen, 1976.

Mason, Pamela. "Orson Welles and Filmed Shakespeare." In Russell Jackson, ed. *The Cambridge Companion to Shakespeare on Film*. Cambridge, Eng.: Cambridge University Press, 2000, 183–98.

McGuire, Philip C. "Whose Work Is This? Loading the Bed in *Othello*." In Jay L. Halio and Hugh Richmond, eds. *Shakespearean Illuminations: Essays in Honor of Marvin Rosenberg*. Newark: University of Delaware Press; London: Associated University Presses, 1998, 70–92. **Olivier**

Miller, Jonathan. *Subsequent Performances*. London: Faber, 1986.

Newstok, Scott L. "Touch of Shakespeare: Welles Unmoors Othello." *Shakespeare Bulletin* 23 (2005): 29–86.

Rafferty, Terence. "Fidelity and Infidelity." *New Yorker* (December 18, 1995): 124–27. **Fishburne**

Rothwell, Kenneth. *A History of Shakespeare on Screen: A Century of Film and Television*. 2nd ed. Cambridge, Eng.: Cambridge University Press, 2004. **Welles, Olivier, and Fishburne**

Seeff, Adele. "*Othello* at the Market Theatre." *Shakespeare Bulletin* 27 (2009): 377–98. **Suzman**

Smallwood, Robert. "On *Othello*, Directed by Trevor Nunn at the Other Place, Stratford-upon-Avon." *Shakespeare Quarterly* 41 (1990): 110–14.

Suzman, Janet. "South Africa in *Othello*." In Jonathan Bate, Jill L. Levenson, and Dieter Mehl, eds. *Shakespeare and the Twentieth Century: The Selected Proceedings of the International Shakespeare Association World Congress, Los Angeles, 1996*. Newark: University of Delaware Press; London: Associated University Presses, 1998, 23–40.

Tatspause, Patricia. "The Tragedies of Love on Film." In Russell Jackson, ed. *The Cambridge Companion to Shakespeare on Film*. Cambridge, Eng.: Cambridge University Press, 2000, 135–59. **Welles, Olivier, and Fishburne**

Taylor, Neil. "National and Racial Stereotypes in Shakespeare's Films." In Russell Jackson, ed. *The Cambridge Companion to Shakespeare on Film*. Cambridge, Eng.: Cambridge University Press, 2000, 267–79. **Welles, Olivier, and Fishburne**

Thompson, Ayanna. "Two Actors on Shakespeare, Race, and Performance: A Conversation between Harry J. Lennix and Laurence Fishburne." *Shakespeare Bulletin* 27 (2009): 399–414.

Tynan, Kenneth. "The Actor: Tynan Interviews Olivier." *Tulane Drama Review* 11 (1966): 71–101.

———, ed. *"Othello": The National Theatre Production*. New York: Stein and Day, 1967. **Olivier**

Vaughan, Virginia Mason. "Orson Welles and the Patriarchal Eye." In Vaughan, *"Othello": A Contextual History*. Cambridge, Eng.: Cambridge University Press, 1995, 199–216.

———. Vaughan, Virginia Mason. "*Othello* for the 1990s: Trevor Nunn's 1989 Royal Shakespeare Company Production." In Vaughan, *"Othello": A Contextual History*. Cambridge, Eng.: Cambridge University Press, 1995, 217–32.

Willis, Susan. *The BBC Shakespeare Plays: Making the Televised Canon*. Chapel Hill and London: University of North Carolina Press, 1991. **Miller**

Wine, Martin L. *"Othello": Text and Performance*. London: Macmillan, 1984. **Olivier and Miller**

14. OFFSHOOTS OR SPINOFFS

About ten years after *Othello* was first produced, the playwright John Webster, represented as the creepy street urchin lurking around the theater in the film *Shakespeare in Love*, wrote *The Duchess of Malfi*, in which the protagonist, strangled apparently to death, revives, only to be strangled again. Webster's play is filled with echoes of *Othello*, and the similarity to Desdemona's fate can hardly be a coincidence. The Duchess's double death is one of the earliest examples of an *Othello* offshoot or spinoff: Material from Shakespeare's play is developed and absorbed into a new imaginative construct that nonetheless derives power from its proximity to the Shakespearean original. This process occurs repeatedly from Webster's time up to our own, when it seems to be proliferating.

How much do audiences need to know that they are hearing echoes of a Shakespearean original—or should they know anything at all? Without endorsing ignorance, we should concede that knowledge—too much, the wrong kind, or inappropriately applied— can sometimes have undesirable consequences. An audience watching *The Duchess of Malfi* with *Othello* on the brain might have difficulty engaging Webster's very different kind of dramatic power.

The problem is clearer with more-recent productions, such as those in the first list below. In Geoffrey Sax's 2001 made-for-the-BBC movie, when John Othello becomes the first black commissioner of the London Metropolitan Police, his friend and fellow officer, Ben Jago, furious at being bypassed for the job, goads John into murdering his (of course white) girlfriend, Dessie. Countless details resonate with Shakespeare's play, but anyone focused intensely on the movie's echoes and transformations may be too detached or distracted to engage the thrilling representations of race and sex and power played out in the film's stylishly contemporary London setting.

Or consider Tim Blake Nelson's movie *O*, released the same year, in which Odin, a black high school basketball star called O, is driven to murder his girlfriend, Desi, by his teammate, Hugo ("white girls are snakes, bro"), who is himself motivated by jealousy (Hugo's father, the team coach, pays more attention to O than to his own son). The protagonist's age and the setting, somewhere in the American South, make O's links to *Othello* more tenuous than those in Sax's movie, and there is evidence to suggest that O tries to sever the connection altogether. Sax's title will suggest a Shakespearean original even to anyone who has never encountered *Othello*; but by changing the film's name to *O* (*Othello* was its working title prior to release), Nelson (or the producers or distributors or some other amorphously anonymous Hollywood agency) produced an audience for most of whom no Shakespearean connection existed at all. At the same time, who would deny that O's impact derives significantly from the power of a Shakespearean original?

The connections between *O* and *Othello* are not identical to those between Sax's film and Shakespeare's play, and the *Duchess-Othello* connections are yet another matter. But they have a lot in common, and "Offshoots or Spinoffs" in the title above is meant to suggest an overriding differentiation into which these three examples (and any others we can think up) might be absorbed. Offshoots stay connected to the branch from which they spring, while spinoffs have lost or abandoned contact with their originating body and thus escaped its gravitational pull. This distinction is not original to me; pretty much everyone who ventures into this area works out of some form of the same distinction. To take examples from the second list below: "*Performances*" vs. "*Appropriations*" (Hodgdon, *The Shakespeare Trade*); "'complete', straightforward versions" vs. "free adaptations" (Holderness and McCullough, 18 [see 388 above]); "adaptations" vs. "appropriations," and "use" vs. "abuse" (McKinnon, "Problem of Naming"); "adaptation" vs. "appropriation" (Sanders); "Returning to Shakespeare" vs. "Leaving Him?" (Thompson).

However necessary, these distinctions fail to establish clarity for individual cases. The most nose-thumbing pastiche (Marowitz's

An Othello, for example, cited in the first list below) can be seen as staying with Shakespeare, and every production, no matter how faithful to Globe practices or Shakespearean intentions, can be seen as leaving him. Maybe "can be seen" is the salient consideration here—suggesting an interpretive rather than a textual category. If all texts can be construed as both offshoots and spinoffs, then why should we emphasize one construction rather than another? Peter Erickson, for instance, arguing in favor of "re-visions" rather than "adaptations" (yet another version of the same distinction), claims that "for a culture to keep growing, it also needs change and new directions" ("Late"). Erickson's position collides with Raymond Williams's argument about "human cultural activity," cited in this book's introduction (xiv above), that the old is potentially a rich source for the new, and that the way back might *be* a way forward. Shifting perspective from textual objects to interpretive actions does not, then, lead to a decisive conclusion, but at least it makes clear that something more is at stake than merely finding the right words to establish categories of textual difference.

The first list below, just a tiny fraction of what might be included, offers a representative sampling of almost exclusively modern or current works. The one exception is *Oroonoko*, Aphra Behn's 1688 prose romance about an African royal slave with sexual charisma who murders his wife, is tortured, and commits suicide in a bloody climax. Highly popular in its own day, *Oroonoko* inspired Thomas Southerne's dramatic adaptation (1695), through which it had a strong impact on the antislavery debates throughout the eighteenth century. Largely absent from view for two centuries, it was rediscovered only recently, when racial concerns coincided with feminist interests (Behn was effectively the first professional woman writer), and in this sense is not altogether an exception to the emphasis on modern and current works in the first list below.

Salman Rushdie's prominence in this list derives from the way his books, beginning with *The Satanic Verses*, in which Saladin Chamcha literally enacts Othello's metaphor in 3.3.82 by turning into a goat, keep coming back obsessively to *Othello*. Salih's and Phillips's novels are undeservedly less well-known than Rushdie's. *Season of Migration to the North* plays with ironic intelligence against the sentimentalized charisma with which some later versions of Shakespeare's protagonist have been endowed. "I am no Othello," says the murderously seductive Mustafa Sa'eed at the book's center. "Othello was a lie" (95). Against this romanticized mendacity, the breathtaking evocations of Sudanese village life may offer some kind of compensatory truth. *The Nature of Blood* is a quiet and reflective book, juxtaposing Jewish and African diasporic narratives from current to Renaissance times. Unemphatic, almost laconic in its refusal to reflect on its disparate material, Phillips's book is nonetheless as affecting as the more flamboyant and dramatic fictions in Rushdie and Salih.

The Vogel, Sears, and MacDonald plays testify to the power of *Othello*'s women to excite and reinforce interest, especially during the 1990s, when all three were first produced. *Desdemona*, Toni Morrison's joint venture with Peter Sellars and Rokia Traoré produced in London and Berkeley in 2011, suggests that this interest has not diminished over time. The Vogel piece, despite its title, gives special prominence to Bianca, who not only shares social space with Desdemona and Emilia but decisively shapes the action. Sears's play is noteworthy for centering the action on an invented black woman, Billie, whom the (never-seen-on-stage) Desdemona character displaces in the Othello character's affections. In the context of these women-centered plays, Murray Carlin's *Not Now, Sweet Desdemona* is the odd man out. Focusing on a Caribbean outsider rehearsing *Othello* with a privileged South African woman with whom he is having an affair, *Not Now, Sweet Desdemona* puts the Othello character, for all his sense of besieged masculinity, into the driver's seat. In its gender relations and political ambitions, Carlin's play evokes the utopian aspirations of the 1960s—a period rapidly coming to seem as remote as the high Victorian age.

The second list below includes some general reflection about off-shoots and spinoffs, but most of the items focus on particular examples. When these coincide with material in the first list, and where the coincidence isn't evident, I have identified the link in bold.

Behn, Aphra. *Oroonoko*. Ed. Joanna Lipking. New York and London: Norton, 1997.

Dove, Rita. *Sonata Mulattica: A Life in Five Movements and a Short Play*. New York and London: Norton, 2009.

Carlin, Murray. *Not Now, Sweet Desdemona: A Duologue for Black and White Within the Realm of Shakespeare's "Othello."* Nairobi, Lusaka, and Addis Ababa: Oxford University Press, 1969.

Fischlin, Daniel, and Mark Fortier, eds. *Adaptations of Shakespeare: A Critical Anthology of Plays from the Seventeenth Century to the Present*. New York and London: Routledge, 2000.

Knowles, Ric, ed. *The Shakespeare's Mine: Adapting Shakespeare in Anglophone Canada*. Toronto: Playwrights Press, 2009.

Lester, Julius. *Othello: A [young adult] Novel*. New York and London: Scholastic, 1995.

MacDonald, Ann-Marie. *Good-night Desdemona (Good-morning Juliet)*. Toronto: Coach House Press, 1990.

Marowitz, Charles. *An Othello*. 1972. In Marowitz, *Open Space Plays: Selected by Charles Marowitz*. Harmondsworth: Penguin, 1974, 253–310.

McGoohan, Patrick [director], and Richie Havens [Othello]. *Catch My Soul* [rock opera]. 1974. <www.imdb.com/title/tt0071289>

Mitchell, Ken, and Humphrey and the Dumptrucks. *Cruel Tears* [a "country opera"]. Vancouver: Talon Books, 1977. Rpt. in Knowles, *Shakespeare's Mine*.

Morrison, Toni. *Desdemona*. Lyrics by Rokia Traoré. Foreword by Peter Sellars. London: Oberon, 2012.

Nelson, Tim Blake [director]. *O*. 2001. <www.imdb.com/title/tt0184791>

Phillips, Caryl. *The Nature of Blood*. New York: Knopf, 1997.

Rushdie, Salman. *Fury*. New York: Random House, 2001.

———. *The Moor's Last Sigh*. New York: Random House, 1995.

———. *The Satanic Verses*. New York: Viking, 1988.

Salih, Tayeb. *Season of Migration to the North*. 1969. Trans. Denys Johnson-Davies. Rpt. Oxford: Heinemann, 1991.

Sax, Geoffrey. *Othello*. 2001. <www.imdb.com/title/tt0275577>

Sears, Djanet. *Harlem Duet*. Scirocco Drama Series. Toronto: Shillingford, 1997. Rpt. in Fischlin, *Adaptations of Shakespeare*, and in Knowles, *Shakespeare's Mine*.

Vogel, Paula. *Desdemona: A Play about a Handkerchief*. New York: Dramatists Play Service, 1994. Rpt. In Fischlin, *Adaptations of Shakespeare*.

Wesker, Arnold. 1987. *Lady Othello: A Love Story*. In Wesker, *Lady Othello and Other Plays*. Harmondsworth: Penguin, 1990, 189–258.

Burnett, Mark Thornton. "Racial Identities, Global Economies." In Burnett, *Filming Shakespeare in the Global Marketplace*. Houndmills, Basingstoke, Hampshire, Eng., and New York: Palgrave Macmillan, 2007, 66–86. **Nelson**

Carney, Jo Eldridge. "'Being Born a Girl': Toni Morrison's *Desdemona*." *Borrowers and Lenders: The Journal of Shakespeare and Appropriation* 9 (2014). <borrowers.uga.edu/1217/show>

Cartelli, Thomas. "Enslaving the Moor: *Othello*, *Oroonoko*, and the Recuperation of Intractability." In Cartelli, *Repositioning Shakespeare: National Formations, Postcolonial Appropriations*. London and New York: Routledge, 1999, 123–46.

———. "'Like Othello': Tayeb Salih's *Season of Migration* and Postcolonial Self-Fashioning." In Cartelli, *Repositioning Shakespeare: National Formations, Postcolonial Appropriations*. London and New York: Routledge, 1999, 147–68.

Cohn, Ruby. *Modern Shakespearean Offshoots*. Princeton: Princeton University Press, 1976.

Daileader, Celia R. *Racism, Misogyny, and the "Othello" Myth: Interracial Couples from Shakespeare to Spike Lee*. Cambridge, Eng.: Cambridge University Press, 2005.

Denselow, Robin. "*Desdemona*." *Guardian* (July 20, 2012). <www
.theguardian.com/stage/2012/jul/20/desdemona-review>
Morrison

Erickson, Peter. *Citing Shakespeare: The Reinterpretation of Race
in Contemporary Literature and Art.* Houndmills, Basingstoke,
Hampshire, Eng., and New York: Palgrave Macmillan, 2007. **Phillips and Sears**

———. " 'Late' has no meaning here: Imagining a Second Chance
in Toni Morrison's *Desdemona*." *Borrowers and Lenders: The Journal of Shakespeare and Appropriation* 8:1 (Spring/Summer 2013).
<borrowers.uga.edu/710/show>

———. " 'Othello's Back': *Othello* as Mock Tragedy in Rita Dove's
Sonata Mulattica." *Journal of Narrative Theory* 41:3 (Fall 2011):
362–77.

Ferguson, Margaret. "Transmuting Othello: Aphra Behn's *Oroonoko*." In Marianne Novy, ed. *Cross-Cultural Performances: Differences in Women's Revisions of Shakespeare.* Urbana: University
of Illinois Press, 1993, 15–49.

Ghazoul, Ferial J. "The Arabization of *Othello*." *Comparative Literature* 50 (1998): 1–31.

Hodgdon, Barbara. "Kiss Me Deadly; or, The Des/Demonized
Spectacle." In Virginia Mason Vaughan and Kent Cartwright,
eds. *"Othello": New Perspectives.* Rutherford, Madison, and Teaneck,
N.J.: Fairleigh Dickinson University Press; London: Associated
University Presses, 1991, 214–55. **Marowitz**

———. "Race-ing *Othello*, Re-Engendering White-out, II." In Richard Burt and Lynda E. Boose, eds. *Shakespeare the Movie II:
Popularizing the Plays on Film, TV, Video, and DVD.* New York
and London: Routledge, 2003, 89–104. **Nelson and Sax**

Hopkins, Lisa. "*Othello.* Adapted for television by Andrew Davies."
Early Modern Literary Studies 8:1 (2002): 11.1–4. **Sax** <extra.shu
.ac.uk/emls/08-1/othelrev.htm>

Howard, Jean E. "Objects and the Displaced Subject: Shakespeare's
Othello and Salih's *Season of Migration to the North*." *Shakespearean International Yearbook 11.* Burlington, Vt., and Farnham, Surrey, Eng.: Ashgate, 2011, 217–33.

Howard, Tony. "Shakespeare's Cinematic Offshoots." In Russell
Jackson, ed. *The Cambridge Companion to Shakespeare on
Film.* Cambridge, Eng.: Cambridge University Press, 2000,
293–313.

Huang, Alexa, and Elizabeth Rivlin, eds. *Shakespeare and the Ethics
of Appropriation.* New York and Houndmills, Basingstoke, Hampshire, Eng.: Palgrave Macmillan, 2014.

Knowles, Ric. "*Othello* in Three Times." In Knowles, *Shakespeare
and Canada: Essays on Production, Translation, and Adaptation.*

Bruxelles and New York: P.I.E.-Peter Lang, 2004, 137–64. **Mac-Donald, Mitchell, and Sears**

Leggatt, Alexander. "Teen Shakespeare: *10 Things I Hate about You* and *O*." In Paul Nelson and June Schlueter, eds. *Acts of Criticism: Performance Matters in Shakespeare and His Contemporaries.* Cranbury, N.J.: Associated University Presses, 2006, 245–58.

Loomba, Ania. "'Local-Manufacture Made-in-India Othello Fellows': Issues of Race, Hybridity and Location in Post-Colonial Shakespeares." In Loomba and Martin Orkin, eds. *Post-Colonial Shakespeares.* London and New York: Routledge, 1998, 143–63. **Rushdie, *Moor's Last Sigh***

Ludot-Vlasa, Ronan. "Intertextuality in Tim Blake Nelson's *O*." In Sarah Hatchuel and Nathalie Vienne-Guerrin, eds. *Shakespeare on Screen: "Othello."* Cambridge, Eng.: Cambridge University Press, 2015, 92–106.

Maguire, Laurie. *"Othello": Language and Writing.* London: Bloomsbury, 2014, 108–22. **Nelson and Sax**

McKinnon, James. "'Playing the Race Bard': How Shakespeare and *Harlem Duet* Sold (at) the 2006 Stratford Shakespeare Festival." In Daniel Fischlin, ed. *OuterSperes: Shakespeare, Intermedia, and the Limits of Adaptation.* Toronto: University of Toronto Press, 2014, 290–318.

———. "'The Problem of Naming': Distinguishing Different Kinds of Adaptation." In McKinnon, *The Dramaturgy of Appropriation: How Canadian Playwrights Use and Abuse Shakespeare and Chekhov.* PhD thesis. Toronto: University of Toronto, 2010, 33–42. <https://tspace.library.utoronto.ca/bitstream/1807/33818/6/McKinnon_James_S_201011_PhD_thesis.pdf>

———. "An Other *Othello*: Djanet Sears's Appropriation of Shakespeare in *Harlem Duet*." In McKinnon, *The Dramaturgy*, 115–70.

Mitchell, Elvis. "The Moor Shoots Hoops." *New York Times* (August 31, 2001). **Nelson** <www.nytimes.com/2001/08/31/movies/film-review-the-moor-shoots-hoops.html>

Neill, Michael. "The Look of Othello." *Shakespeare Survey 62.* Cambridge, Eng.: Cambridge University Press, 2009, 104–22. **Marowitz**

Owens, W. R., and Lizabeth Goodman, eds. *Shakespeare, Aphra Behn and the Canon.* London and New York: Routledge, 1996.

Rippy, Marguerite Hailey. "All Our *Othello*s: Black Monsters and White Masks on the American Screen." In Courtney Lehmann and Lisa S. Starks, eds. *Spectacular Shakespeare: Critical Theory and Popular Cinema.* Madison, Rutherford, and Teaneck, N.J.: Fairleigh Dickinson University Press, 2001, 25–46.

Sanders, Julie. *Adaptation and Appropriation.* New York and London: Routledge, 2006.

Singh, Jyotsna. "Othello's Identity, Postcolonial Theory, and Con-temporary African Rewritings of Othello." In Margo Hendricks and Patricia Parker, eds. Women, "Race," and Writing in the Early Modern Period. New York and London: Routledge, 1993, 287–99. **Carlin and Salih**

Smith, Peter. "'Institutionally Racist': Sax's Othello and Tethered Presentism." In Sarah Hatchuel and Nathalie Vienne-Guerrin, eds. Shakespeare on Screen: "Othello." Cambridge, Eng.: Cambridge University Press, 2015, 76–91.

Taylor, Neil. "National and Racial Stereotypes in Shakespeare's Films." In Russell Jackson, ed. The Cambridge Companion to Shakespeare on Film. Cambridge, Eng.: Cambridge University Press, 2000, 267–79. **Nelson**

Thompson, Ayanna. "The Blackfaced Bard: Returning to Shake-speare or Leaving Him?" Shakespeare Bulletin 27 (2009): 437–56.

———. "Conclusion: Passing Race and Passing Shakespeare in Peter Sellars's Othello." In Thompson, Passing Strange: Shakespeare, Race, and Contemporary America. Oxford and New York: Oxford University Press, 2011, 169–81.

———. "Desdemona: Toni Morrison's Response to Othello." In Dympna Callaghan, ed. A Feminist Companion to Shakespeare. 2nd ed. Oxford and Malden, Mass.: Wiley-Blackwell, 2016, 494–507.

15. BIBLIOGRAPHIES, COLLECTIONS OF CRITICISM, STUDY GUIDES

The following books share one or another of the basic aims of this Norton Critical Edition—representing Othello's original context and response history in a format designed chiefly for students and teachers. Currently available editions of the play aren't included here, but many of the most reliable are listed on pages 3–5 above.

Barthelemy, Anthony, ed. Critical Essays on Shakespeare's "Othello." New York: Hall, 1994.

Bradshaw, Graham. The Connell Guide to Shakespeare's "Othello." London: Connell Guides, 2012.

Dean, Leonard F., ed. A Casebook on "Othello." New York: Crowell, 1961.

Erickson, Peter, and Maurice Hunt, eds. Approaches to Teaching Shakespeare's "Othello." New York: Modern Language Associa-tion of America, 2005.

Hadfield, Andrew. A Routledge Literary Sourcebook on William Shakespeare's "Othello." New York and London: Routledge, 2003.

Hall, Joan Lord. *"Othello": A Guide to the Play*. Greenwood Guides to Shakespeare. Westport, Conn., and London: Greenwood Press, 1999.

Hall, Kim F., ed. *William Shakespeare, "Othello, the Moor of Venice": Texts and Contexts*. Boston and New York: Bedford/St. Martin's, 2007.

Kolin, Philip C. *"Othello": New Critical Essays*. New York and London: Routledge, 2002.

Maguire, Laurie. *"Othello": Language and Writing*. London: Bloomsbury, 2014.

Mason, Pamela. *Shakespeare: "Othello."* Cambridge Student Guide. Cambridge, Eng.: Cambridge University Press, 2002.

Mikesell, Margaret Lael, and Virginia Mason Vaughan, eds. *"Othello": An Annotated Bibliography*. New York: Garland, 1990.

Nostbakken, Faith. *Understanding "Othello": A Student Casebook to Issues, Sources, and Historical Documents*. Westport, Conn., and London: Greenwood Press, 2000.

O'Brien, Peggy, et al. *Shakespeare Set Free: Teaching "Twelfth Night" and "Othello."* New York: Washington Square Press, 2006.

Potter, Nicholas. *"Othello": Character Studies*. London: Bloomsbury Academic, 2008.

———, ed. *William Shakespeare: "Othello": Essays, Articles, Reviews*. Columbia Critical Guides. New York: Columbia University Press, 2000.

Orlin, Lena Cowen, ed. *"Othello": William Shakespeare*. New Casebooks. Houndmills, Basingstoke, Hampshire, Eng., and New York: Palgrave Macmillan, 2004.

———, ed. *"Othello": The State of Play*. London: Bloomsbury, 2014.

Scott, Mark W., ed. *"Othello."* In *Shakespearean Criticism: Excerpts from the Criticism of William Shakespeare's Plays and Poetry, from the First Published Appraisals to Current Evaluations*. Vol. 4. Detroit: Gale, 1987, 362–608.

Smith, Emma. *William Shakespeare, "Othello."* Writers and Their Work. Horndon, Devon, Eng.: Northcote House, 2005.

Smith, John Hazel. *Shakespeare's "Othello": A Bibliography*. New York: AMS, 1988.

Vaughan, Virginia Mason, and Kent Cartwright, eds. *"Othello": New Perspectives*. Rutherford, N.J.: Fairleigh Dickinson University Press; London: Associated University Presses, 1991.

Wain, John, ed. *Shakespeare's "Othello": A Casebook*. Rev. ed. Houndmills, Basingstoke, Hampshire, Eng., and London: Palgrave Macmillan, 1994.